THE LOEB CLASSICAL LIBRARY

FOUNDED BY JAMES LOEB, LL.D.

EDITED BY
G. P. GOOLD, PH.D.

FORMER EDITORS

† T. E. PAGE, C.H., LITT.D. † E. CAPPS, PH.D., LL.D.
† W. H. D. ROUSE, LITT.D. † L. A. POST, L.H.D.
E. H. WARMINGTON, M.A., F.R.HIST.SOC.

DIODORUS OF SICILY

II

DIODORUS OF SICILY

IN TWELVE VOLUMES

II

BOOKS II (*continued*) 35–IV, 58

WITH AN ENGLISH TRANSLATION BY

C. H. OLDFATHER

PROFESSOR OF ANCIENT HISTORY AND LANGUAGES,
THE UNIVERSITY OF NEBRASKA

CAMBRIDGE, MASSACHUSETTS
HARVARD UNIVERSITY PRESS
LONDON
WILLIAM HEINEMANN LTD
MCMLXXIX

American ISBN 0-674-99334-9
British ISBN 0 434 99303 4

First printed 1935
Reprinted 1953, 1961, 1967, 1979

Printed in Great Britain

CONTENTS

	PAGE
INTRODUCTION TO BOOKS II, 35–IV, 58	vii
BOOK II (*continued*)	1
BOOK III	85
BOOK IV, 1–58	335
A PARTIAL INDEX OF PROPER NAMES	535

MAPS—

1. ASIA . . . . *At end*
2. AEGYPTUS–ETHIOPIA . . . . . . ,,

INTRODUCTION

Books II, 35–IV, 58

Book II, 35–42 is devoted to a brief description of India which was ultimately derived from Megasthenes. Although Diodorus does not mention this author, his use of him is established by the similarity between his account of India and the *Indica* of Arrian and the description of that land by Strabo, both of whom avowedly drew their material from that writer. Megasthenes was in the service of Seleucus Nicator and in connection with embassies to the court of king Sandracottus (Chandragupta) at Patna was in India for some time between 302 and 291 B.C. In his *Indica* in four Books he was not guilty of the romances of Ctesias, but it is plain that he was imposed upon by interpreters and guides, as was Herodotus on his visit to Egypt. It cannot be known whether Diodorus used Megasthenes directly or through a medium; his failure to mention his name a single time is a little surprising, if he used him directly.[1] The Scythians, the Amazons of Asia Minor, and the Hyperboreans are then briefly discussed, and Chapters 48–54 are devoted to Syria, Palestine, and Arabia. It is thought that this last section may go

[1] On Megasthenes see now B. C. J. Timmer, *Megasthenes en de Indische Maatschappij*, Amsterdam, 1930.

INTRODUCTION

back to the Stoic philosopher, Poseidonius of Apameia, especially because of its explanation of the varied colouring of birds and different kinds of animals as being due to the "helpful influence and strength of the sun." The Book closes with a description of a fabulous people living in a political Utopia on an island "in the ocean to the south," the account purporting to be the adventure of a certain Iambulus, which may indeed be the name of the author of the original tale.

The Third Book opens with an account of the Ethiopians on the upper Nile, then describes the working of the gold mines on the border between Egypt and Ethiopia, and includes a long discussion of the Red Sea and the peoples dwelling about it, with some mention of the tribes along the shores of the Indian Ocean and the Persian Gulf. Much of this material was drawn from the geographer Agatharchides of Cnidus, whose work, *On the Red Sea*, is preserved to us in the excerpts of Photius. This work of Agatharchides, composed in the latter part of the second century B.C., embraced five Books and is on the whole a sober and fairly trustworthy discussion of that region; much of it was certainly based upon the stories and accounts of travellers in these parts and on personal observation. With chapter 49 Diodorus turns to Libya and embarks upon the myths of the Libyans about the Gorgons and Amazons, this subject serving to lead him over into Greek mythology, which is the theme of the entire Fourth Book.

Since, as Diodorus tells us, Ephorus, and Callisthenes and Theopompus, contemporaries of Ephorus, had not included the myths in their histories,

INTRODUCTION

Diodorus opens the Fourth Book with a defence of his exposition of Greek mythology. The gods were once kings and heroes who have been deified because of the great benefits which they conferred upon mankind; they have been the object of veneration by men of old and we " should not fail to cherish and maintain for the gods the pious devotion which has been handed down to us from our fathers " (ch. 8. 5); if their deeds appear superhuman it is because they are measured by the weakness of the men of Diodorus' day. Much of this material was drawn directly from Dionysius of Mitylene who lived in Alexandria in the second century B.C. and composed, doubtless with the aid of the library in that city and certainly with considerable indulgence in the romantic, his *Kyklos*, a kind of encyclopaedia of mythology, which included accounts of the Argonauts, Dionysus, the Amazons, events connected with the Trojan War, and all this he described with such devotion and assiduity that he was given the nickname Skytobrachion (" of the leathern arm "). It is generally held that for his account of Heracles Diodorus took generously from a *Praise of Heracles* by Matris of Thebes,[1] who is otherwise unknown and composed his encomium with vigorous rhetorical flourishes, taking care to mention every maiden ravished by Heracles and her child, in order to establish Heraclean ancestry for the numerous families in the Greek world which raised such a claim. But here and there, when he touched the western Mediterranean, Diodorus used Timaeus of Tauromenium, who, an exile in Athens for the best

[1] Cp. E. Holzer, *Matris, ein Beitrag zur Quellenkritik Diodors*, Program Tübingen, 1881.

INTRODUCTION

fifty years of his life, completed, not long before his death about 250 B.C. and almost altogether from literary sources, a history of Sicily and the western Mediterranean in thirty-eight Books. Any attempt to continue further the quest for the sources of Diodorus in this section of his work must run into the sands.

THE LIBRARY OF HISTORY
OF
DIODORUS OF SICILY

BOOK II

ΔΙΟΔΩΡΟΥ

ΤΟΥ ΣΙΚΕΛΙΩΤΟΥ

ΒΙΒΛΙΟΘΗΚΗΣ ΙΣΤΟΡΙΚΗΣ

ΒΙΒΛΟΣ ΔΕΥΤΕΡΑ

35. Ἡ τοίνυν Ἰνδικὴ τετράπλευρος οὖσα τῷ σχήματι, τὴν μὲν πρὸς ἀνατολὰς νεύουσαν πλευρὰν καὶ τὴν πρὸς[1] μεσημβρίαν ἡ μεγάλη περιέχει θάλαττα, τὴν δὲ πρὸς τὰς ἄρκτους τὸ Ἡμωδὸν ὄρος διείργει τῆς Σκυθίας, ἣν κατοικοῦσι τῶν Σκυθῶν οἱ προσαγορευόμενοι Σάκαι· τὴν δὲ τετάρτην[2] πρὸς δύσιν ἐστραμμένην διείληφεν ὁ Ἰνδὸς προσαγορευόμενος ποταμός, μέγιστος ὢν 2 τῶν πάντων μετὰ τὸν Νεῖλον. τὸ δὲ μέγεθος τῆς ὅλης Ἰνδικῆς φασιν ὑπάρχειν ἀπὸ μὲν ἀνατολῶν πρὸς δύσιν δισμυρίων ὀκτακισχιλίων σταδίων, ἀπὸ δὲ τῶν ἄρκτων πρὸς μεσημβρίαν τρισμυρίων δισχιλίων. τηλικαύτη δ' οὖσα τὸ μέγεθος δοκεῖ τοῦ κόσμου μάλιστα περιέχειν τὸν τῶν θερινῶν τροπῶν κύκλον, καὶ πολλαχῇ μὲν ἐπ' ἄκρας τῆς Ἰνδικῆς ἰδεῖν ἔστιν ἀσκίους ὄντας τοὺς γνώμονας, νυκτὸς δὲ τὰς ἄρκτους

[1] τὴν πρὸς Bekker: πρὸς D, τὴν πρὸς τὴν Vulgate.
[2] τὴν after τετάρτην omitted by D, Bekker, Vogel.

---

[1] The Indian Ocean.

THE LIBRARY OF HISTORY
OF
DIODORUS OF SICILY

BOOK II

35. Now India is four-sided in shape and the side which faces east and that which faces south are embraced by the Great Sea,[1] while that which faces north is separated by the Emodus range of mountains from that part of Scythia which is inhabited by the Scythians known as the Sacae; and the fourth side, which is turned towards the west, is marked off by the river known as the Indus, which is the largest of all streams after the Nile. As for its magnitude, India as a whole, they say, extends from east to west twenty-eight thousand stades, and from north to south thirty-two thousand. And because it is of such magnitude, it is believed to take in a greater extent of the sun's course in summer[2] than any other part of the world, and in many places at the Cape of India the gnomons of sundials may be seen which do not cast a shadow, while at night the Bears are

[2] Lit. "of the summer turnings" of the sun, *i.e.*, the course which the sun seems to traverse in the heavens from the solstice on June 22 to the equinox in September, corresponding to the part of the earth lying between the Tropic of Cancer and the equator.

ἀθεωρήτους· ἐν δὲ τοῖς ἐσχάτοις οὐδ' αὐτὸν τὸν ἀρκτοῦρον φαίνεσθαι· καθ' ὃν δὴ τόπον[1] φασὶ καὶ τὰς σκιὰς κεκλίσθαι πρὸς μεσημβρίαν.

3 Ἡ δ' οὖν Ἰνδικὴ πολλὰ μὲν ὄρη καὶ μεγάλα ἔχει δένδρεσι παντοδαποῖς καρπίμοις πλήθοντα, πολλὰ δὲ πεδία καὶ μεγάλα καρποφόρα, τῷ μὲν κάλλει διάφορα, ποταμῶν δὲ πλήθεσι διαρρεόμενα. τὰ πολλὰ δὲ τῆς χώρας ἀρδεύεται, καὶ διὰ τοῦτο διττοὺς ἔχει τοὺς κατ' ἔτος καρπούς· ζώων τε παντοδαπῶν γέμει διαφόρων τοῖς μεγέθεσι καὶ ταῖς ἀλκαῖς, τῶν μὲν χερσαίων, τῶν 4 δὲ καὶ πτηνῶν. καὶ πλείστους δὲ καὶ μεγίστους ἐλέφαντας ἐκτρέφει, χορηγοῦσα τὰς τροφὰς ἀφθόνους, δι' ἃς ταῖς ῥώμαις τὰ θηρία ταῦτα πολὺ προέχει τῶν κατὰ τὴν Λιβύην γεννωμένων· διὸ καὶ πολλῶν θηρευομένων ὑπὸ τῶν Ἰνδῶν καὶ πρὸς τοὺς πολεμικοὺς ἀγῶνας κατασκευαζομένων μεγάλας συμβαίνει ῥοπὰς γίνεσθαι πρὸς τὴν νίκην.

36. Ὁμοίως δὲ καὶ τοὺς ἀνθρώπους ἡ πολυκαρπία τρέφουσα τοῖς τε ἀναστήμασι τῶν σωμάτων καὶ τοῖς ὄγκοις ὑπερφέροντας κατασκευάζει· εἶναι δ' αὐτοὺς συμβαίνει καὶ πρὸς τὰς τέχνας ἐπιστήμονας, ὡς ἂν ἀέρα μὲν ἕλκοντας καθαρόν, ὕδωρ δὲ λεπτομερέστατον 2 πίνοντας. ἡ δὲ γῆ πάμφορος οὖσα τοῖς ἡμέροις καρποῖς ἔχει καὶ φλέβας καταγείους πολλῶν καὶ παντοδαπῶν μετάλλων· γίνεται γὰρ ἐν αὐτῇ πολὺς μὲν ἄργυρος καὶ χρυσός, οὐκ ὀλίγος δὲ χαλκὸς καὶ σίδηρος, ἔτι δὲ καττίτερος καὶ τἆλλα τὰ πρὸς κόσμον τε καὶ χρείαν καὶ πολεμικὴν

[1] τόπον Hertlein: τρόπον.

BOOK II. 35. 2–36. 2

not visible; in the most southerly parts not even Arcturus can be seen, and indeed in that region, they say, the shadows fall towards the south.[1]

Now India has many lofty mountains that abound in fruit trees of every variety, and many large and fertile plains, which are remarkable for their beauty and are supplied with water by a multitude of rivers. The larger part of the country is well watered and for this reason yields two crops each year; and it abounds in all kinds of animals, remarkable for their great size and strength, land animals as well as birds. It also breeds elephants both in the greatest numbers and of the largest size, providing them with sustenance in abundance, and it is because of this food that the elephants of this land are much more powerful than those produced in Libya; consequently large numbers of them are made captive by the Indians and trained for warfare, and it is found that they play a great part in turning the scale to victory.

36. The same is true of the inhabitants also, the abundant supply of food making them of unusual height and bulk of body; and another result is that they are also skilled in the arts, since they breathe a pure air and drink water of the finest quality. And the earth, in addition to producing every fruit which admits of cultivation, also contains rich underground veins of every kind of ore; for there are found in it much silver and gold, not a little copper and iron, and tin also and whatever else is suitable

---

[1] Cp. Strabo, 2. 5. 37: "In all the regions that lie between the tropic and the equator the shadows fall in both directions, that is, towards the north and towards the south . . . and the inhabitants are called Amphiscians" (*i.e.*, "throwing shadows both ways"; tr. of Jones in *L.C.L.*).

3 παρασκευὴν ἀνήκοντα. χωρὶς δὲ τῶν δημητριακῶν καρπῶν φύεται κατὰ τὴν Ἰνδικὴν πολλὴ μὲν κέγχρος, ἀρδευομένη τῇ τῶν ποταμίων ναμάτων δαψιλείᾳ, πολὺ δ' ὄσπριον καὶ διάφορον, ἔτι δ' ὄρυζα καὶ ὁ προσαγορευόμενος βόσπορος, καὶ μετὰ ταῦτ' ἄλλα πολλὰ τῶν πρὸς διατροφὴν χρησίμων· καὶ τούτων τὰ πολλὰ ὑπάρχει αὐτοφυῆ. οὐκ ὀλίγους δὲ καὶ ἄλλους ἐδωδίμους καρποὺς φέρει δυναμένους τρέφειν ζῷα, περὶ ὧν μακρὸν ἂν εἴη γράφειν.

4 Διὸ καί φασι μηδέποτε τὴν Ἰνδικὴν ἐπισχεῖν λιμὸν ἢ καθόλου σπάνιν τῶν πρὸς τροφὴν ἥμερον ἀνηκόντων. διττῶν γὰρ ὄμβρων ἐν αὐτῇ γινομένων καθ' ἕκαστον ἔτος, τοῦ μὲν χειμερινοῦ, καθὰ παρὰ τοῖς ἄλλοις, ὁ σπόρος τῶν πυρίνων γίνεται καρπῶν, τοῦ δ' ἑτέρου κατὰ τὴν θερινὴν τροπὴν[1] σπείρεσθαι συμβαίνει τὴν ὄρυζαν καὶ τὸν βόσπορον, ἔτι δὲ σήσαμον καὶ κέγχρον· κατὰ δὲ τὸ πλεῖστον ἀμφοτέροις τοῖς καρποῖς οἱ κατὰ τὴν Ἰνδικὴν ἐπιτυγχάνουσι, πάντων δέ, τελεσφορουμένων θατέρου τῶν καρπῶν, οὐκ

5 ἀποτυγχάνουσιν. οἵ τε αὐτοματίζοντες καρποὶ καὶ αἱ κατὰ τοὺς ἑλώδεις τόπους φυόμεναι ῥίζαι διάφοροι ταῖς γλυκύτησιν οὖσαι πολλὴν παρέχονται τοῖς ἀνθρώποις δαψίλειαν· πάντα γὰρ σχεδὸν τὰ κατὰ τὴν χώραν πεδία γλυκεῖαν ἔχει τὴν ἀπὸ τῶν ποταμῶν ἰκμάδα καὶ τὴν ἀπὸ τῶν ὄμβρων τῶν ἐν τῷ θέρει[2] κατ' ἐνιαυτὸν κυκλικῇ τινι περιόδῳ παραδόξως εἰωθότων γίνεσθαι,

---

[1] καθ' ἣν after τροπὴν deleted by Vogel.
[2] γινομένων after θέρει deleted by Reiske.

for adornment, necessity, and the trappings of war. In addition to the grain of Demeter[1] there grows throughout India much millet, which is irrigated by the abundance of running water supplied by the rivers, pulse in large quantities and of superior quality, rice also and the plant called *bosporos*,[2] and in addition to these many more plants which are useful for food; and most of these are native to the country. It also yields not a few other edible fruits, that are able to sustain animal life, but to write about them would be a long task.

This is the reason, they say, why a famine has never visited India[3] or, in general, any scarcity of what is suitable for gentle fare. For since there are two rainy seasons in the country each year, during the winter rains the sowing is made of the wheat crops as among other peoples, while in the second, which comes at the summer solstice, it is the general practice to plant the rice and *bosporos*, as well as sesame and millet; and in most years the Indians are successful in both crops, and they never lose everything, since the fruit of one or the other sowing comes to maturity. The fruits also which flourish wild and the roots which grow in the marshy places, by reason of their remarkable sweetness, provide the people with a great abundance of food. For practically all the plains of India enjoy the sweet moisture from the rivers and from the rains which come with astonishing regularity, in a kind of fixed

[1] Wheat.
[2] A kind of millet; called *bosmoron* in Strabo, 15. 1. 13.
[3] This statement may be true in the sense of a general and protracted famine; but the Buddhist records often refer to scarcity of food because of drought or floods; cp. *The Cambridge History of India*, I. p. 203.

δαψιλείᾳ[1] χλιαρῶν πιπτόντων ὑδάτων ἐκ τοῦ περιέχοντος ἀέρος, καὶ τὰς ἐν τοῖς ἕλεσι ῥίζας ἕψοντος τοῦ καύματος, καὶ μάλιστα τῶν μεγάλων 6 καλάμων. συμβάλλονται δὲ παρὰ τοῖς Ἰνδοῖς καὶ τὰ νόμιμα πρὸς τὸ μηδέποτε ἔνδειαν τροφῆς παρ' αὐτοῖς εἶναι· παρὰ μὲν γὰρ τοῖς ἄλλοις ἀνθρώποις οἱ πολέμιοι καταφθείροντες τὴν χώραν ἀγεώργητον κατασκευάζουσι, παρὰ δὲ τούτοις τῶν γεωργῶν ἱερῶν καὶ ἀσύλων ἐωμένων, οἱ πλησίον τῶν παρατάξεων γεωργοῦντες ἀνε- 7 παίσθητοι τῶν κινδύνων εἰσίν. ἀμφότεροι γὰρ οἱ πολεμοῦντες ἀλλήλους μὲν ἀποκτείνουσιν ἐν ταῖς μάχαις, τοὺς δὲ περὶ τὴν γεωργίαν ὄντας ἐῶσιν ἀβλαβεῖς, ὡς κοινοὺς ὄντας ἁπάντων εὐεργέτας, τάς τε χώρας τῶν ἀντιπολεμούντων οὔτ' ἐμπυρίζουσιν οὔτε δενδροτομοῦσιν.

37. Ἔχει δὲ καὶ ποταμοὺς ἡ χώρα τῶν Ἰνδῶν πολλοὺς καὶ μεγάλους πλωτούς, οἳ τὰς πηγὰς ἔχοντες ἐν τοῖς ὄρεσι τοῖς πρὸς τὰς ἄρκτους κεκλιμένοις φέρονται διὰ τῆς πεδιάδος, ὧν οὐκ ὀλίγοι συμμίσγοντες ἀλλήλοις ἐμβάλλουσιν εἰς 2 ποταμὸν τὸν ὀνομαζόμενον Γάγγην. οὗτος δὲ τὸ πλάτος γινόμενος σταδίων τριάκοντα φέρεται μὲν ἀπὸ τῆς ἄρκτου πρὸς μεσημβρίαν, ἐξερεύγεται δ' εἰς τὸν ὠκεανόν, ἀπολαμβάνων εἰς τὸ πρὸς ἕω μέρος τὸ ἔθνος τὸ τῶν Γανδαριδῶν, 3 πλείστους ἔχον καὶ μεγίστους ἐλέφαντας. διὸ καὶ τῆς χώρας ταύτης οὐδεὶς πώποτε βασιλεὺς ἔπηλυς ἐκράτησε, πάντων τῶν ἀλλοεθνῶν φοβου-

---

[1] δαψιλείᾳ Oldfather: δαψίλεια D, δαψίλειαν A B, Bekker, Dindorf, Vogel, δαψίλειαν . . . ἀέρος omitted H.

BOOK II. 36. 5–37. 3

cycle, every year in the summer, since warm showers fall in abundance from the enveloping atmosphere and the heat ripens[1] the roots in the marshes, especially those of the tall reeds. Furthermore, the customs of the Indians contribute towards there never being any lack of food among them; for whereas in the case of all the rest of mankind their enemies ravage the land and cause it to remain uncultivated, yet among the Indians the workers of the soil are let alone as sacred and inviolable, and such of them as labour near the battle-lines have no feeling of the dangers. For although both parties to the war kill one another in their hostilities, yet they leave uninjured those who are engaged in tilling the soil, considering that they are the common benefactors of all, nor do they burn the lands of their opponents or cut down their orchards.

37. The land of the Indians has also many large navigable rivers which have their sources in the mountains lying to the north and then flow through the level country; and not a few of these unite and empty into the river known as the Ganges. This river, which is thirty stades in width, flows from north to south and empties into the ocean, forming the boundary towards the east of the tribe of the Gandaridae, which possesses the greatest number of elephants and the largest in size. Consequently no foreign king has ever subdued this country, all alien

---

[1] Literally, "boils" or "heats." Strabo (15. 1. 20) says that what other peoples call the "ripening" of fruits is called by the Indians the "heating."

μένων τό τε πλῆθος καὶ τὴν ἀλκὴν τῶν θηρίων. καὶ γὰρ Ἀλέξανδρος ὁ Μακεδὼν ἁπάσης τῆς Ἀσίας κρατήσας μόνους τοὺς Γανδαρίδας οὐκ ἐπολέμησε· καταντήσας γὰρ ἐπὶ τὸν Γάγγην ποταμὸν μετὰ πάσης τῆς δυνάμεως, καὶ τοὺς ἄλλους Ἰνδοὺς καταπολεμήσας, ὡς ἐπύθετο τοὺς Γανδαρίδας ἔχειν τετρακισχιλίους ἐλέφαντας πολεμικῶς κεκοσμημένους, ἀπέγνω τὴν ἐπ' αὐτοὺς στρατείαν.

4 Ὁ δὲ παραπλήσιος τῷ Γάγγῃ ποταμός, προσαγορευόμενος δὲ Ἰνδός, ἄρχεται μὲν ὁμοίως ἀπὸ τῶν ἄρκτων, ἐμβάλλων δὲ εἰς τὸν ὠκεανὸν ἀφορίζει τὴν Ἰνδικήν· πολλὴν δὲ διεξιὼν πεδιάδα χώραν δέχεται ποταμοὺς οὐκ ὀλίγους πλωτούς, ἐπιφανεστάτους δ' Ὕπανιν καὶ Ὑδά-
5 σπην καὶ Ἀκεσῖνον. χωρὶς δὲ τούτων ἄλλο πλῆθος ποταμῶν παντοδαπῶν διαρρεῖ καὶ ποιεῖ κατάφυτον[1] πολλοῖς κηπεύμασι καὶ καρποῖς παντοδαποῖς τὴν χώραν. τοῦ δὲ κατὰ τοὺς ποταμοὺς πλήθους καὶ τῆς τῶν ὑδάτων ὑπερβολῆς αἰτίαν φέρουσιν οἱ παρ' αὐτοῖς φιλόσοφοι καὶ
6 φυσικοὶ τοιαύτην· τῆς Ἰνδικῆς φασι τὰς περικειμένας χώρας, τήν τε Σκυθῶν καὶ Βακτριανῶν, ἔτι δὲ καὶ τῶν Ἀριανῶν, ὑψηλοτέρας εἶναι τῆς Ἰνδικῆς, ὥστ' εὐλόγως εἰς τὴν ὑποκειμένην χώραν πανταχόθεν συρρεούσας τὰς λιβάδας ἐκ τοῦ κατ' ὀλίγον ποιεῖν τοὺς τόπους καθύγρους καὶ γεννᾶν

[1] κατάφυτον Dindorf: κατάρρυτον.

[1] A fuller account of this incident is given in Book 17. 93. But Alexander did not reach the river system of the Ganges, the error being due to a confusion of the Ganges with the

BOOK II. 37. 3-6

nations being fearful of both the multitude and the strength of the beasts. In fact even Alexander of Macedon, although he had subdued all Asia, refrained from making war upon the Gandaridae alone of all peoples; for when he had arrived at the Ganges river with his entire army, after his conquest of the rest of the Indians, upon learning that the Gandaridae had four thousand elephants equipped for war he gave up his campaign against them.[1]

The river which is nearly the equal of the Ganges and is called the Indus rises like the Ganges in the north, but as it empties into the ocean forms a boundary of India; and in its course through an expanse of level plain it receives not a few navigable rivers, the most notable being the Hypanis,[2] Hydaspes, and Acesinus. And in addition to these three rivers a vast number of others of every description traverse the country and bring it about that the land is planted in many gardens and crops of every description. Now for the multitude of rivers and the exceptional supply of water the philosophers and students of nature among them advance the following cause: The countries which surround India, they say, such as Scythia, Bactria, and Ariana, are higher than India, and so it is reasonable to assume that the waters which come together from every side into the country lying below them, gradually cause the regions to become soaked and to generate a multitude of

---

Sutlej, a tributary of the Indus; cp. W. W. Tarn, "Alexander and the Ganges," *Journal of Hellenic Studies*, 43 (1923), 93 ff.

[2] In Book 17. 93. 1 and Arrian, 5. 24. 8, this river is called the Hyphasis, which is the name preferred by most modern writers. Strabo (15. 1. 27, 32), however, calls it the Hypanis, and Quintus Curtius (9. 1. 35), Hypasis.

7 ποταμῶν πλῆθος. ἴδιον δέ τι συμβαίνει περί τινα τῶν κατὰ τὴν Ἰνδικὴν ποταμῶν τὸν ὀνομαζόμενον Σίλλαν, ῥέοντα δ' ἔκ τινος ὁμωνύμου κρήνης· ἐπὶ γὰρ τούτου μόνου τῶν ἁπάντων ποταμῶν οὐδὲν τῶν ἐμβαλλομένων εἰς αὐτὸν ἐπιπλεῖ, πάντα δ' εἰς τὸν βυθὸν καταδύεται παραδόξως.

38. Τὴν δ' ὅλην Ἰνδικὴν οὖσαν ὑπερμεγέθη λέγεται κατοικεῖν ἔθνη πολλὰ καὶ παντοδαπά, καὶ τούτων μηδὲν ἔχειν τὴν ἐξ ἀρχῆς γένεσιν ἔπηλυν, ἀλλὰ πάντα δοκεῖν ὑπάρχειν αὐτόχθονα, πρὸς δὲ τούτοις μήτε ξενικὴν ἀποικίαν προσδέχεσθαι πώποτε
2 μήτ' εἰς ἄλλο ἔθνος[1] ἀπεσταλκέναι. μυθολογοῦσι δὲ τοὺς ἀρχαιοτάτους ἀνθρώπους τροφαῖς μὲν κεχρῆσθαι τοῖς αὐτομάτως φυομένοις ἐκ τῆς γῆς καρποῖς, ἐσθῆσι δὲ ταῖς δοραῖς τῶν ἐγχωρίων ζῴων, καθάπερ καὶ παρ' Ἕλλησιν. ὁμοίως δὲ καὶ τῶν τεχνῶν τὰς εὑρέσεις καὶ τῶν ἄλλων τῶν πρὸς βίον χρησίμων ἐκ τοῦ κατ' ὀλίγον γενέσθαι, τῆς χρείας αὐτῆς ὑφηγουμένης εὐφυεῖ ζῴῳ καὶ συνεργοὺς ἔχοντι πρὸς ἅπαντα χεῖρας καὶ λόγον καὶ ψυχῆς ἀγχίνοιαν.
3 Μυθολογοῦσι δὲ παρὰ τοῖς Ἰνδοῖς οἱ λογιώτατοι, περὶ οὗ[2] καθῆκον ἂν εἴη συντόμως διελθεῖν. φασὶ γὰρ ἐν τοῖς ἀρχαιοτάτοις χρόνοις, παρ' αὐτοῖς ἔτι τῶν ἀνθρώπων κωμηδὸν οἰκούντων, παραγενέσθαι τὸν Διόνυσον ἐκ τῶν πρὸς ἑσπέραν τόπων ἔχοντα δύναμιν ἀξιόλογον· ἐπελθεῖν δὲ τὴν Ἰνδικὴν ἅπασαν, μηδεμιᾶς οὔσης

---

[1] ἄλλο ἔθνος MSS., Bekker: ἀλλοεθνεῖς emendation of Dindorf and adopted by Vogel (cp. ch. 39. 4).
[2] οὗ Vogel: ὧν F, Bekker, Dindorf.

---

[1] The same words appear in Book 1. 8. 9.

rivers. And a peculiar thing happens in the case of one of the rivers of India, known as the Silla, which flows from a spring of the same name; for it is the only river in the world possessing the characteristic that nothing cast into it floats, but that everything, strange to say, sinks to the bottom.

38. Now India as a whole, being of a vast extent, is inhabited, as we are told, by many peoples of every description, and not one of them had its first origin in a foreign land, but all of them are thought to be autochthonous; it never receives any colony from abroad nor has it ever sent one to any other people. According to their myths the earliest human beings used for food the fruits of the earth which grew wild, and for clothing the skins of the native animals, as was done by the Greeks. Similarly too the discovery of the several arts and of all other things which are useful for life was made gradually, necessity itself showing the way to a creature which was well endowed by nature and had, as its assistants for every purpose, hands and speech and sagacity of mind.[1]

The most learned men among the Indians recount a myth which it may be appropriate to set forth in brief form. This, then, is what they say: In the earliest times, when the inhabitants of their land were still dwelling in scattered clan-villages,[2] Dionysus came to them from the regions to the west of them with a notable army; and he traversed all India, since there was as yet no notable city which would

[2] It was the teaching of Aristotle that the State (or city) rises out of the Household through the intermediate institution of the Village. So the Indians, in this case, were in the second stage of this evolution; Dionysus, as is stated below, combines the villages into cities and thus makes the good life possible.

4 ἀξιολόγου πόλεως[1] δυναμένης ἀντιτάξασθαι. ἐπιγενομένων δὲ καυμάτων μεγάλων, καὶ τῶν τοῦ Διονύσου στρατιωτῶν λοιμικῇ νόσῳ διαφθειρομένων, συνέσει διαφέροντα τὸν ἡγεμόνα τοῦτον ἀπαγαγεῖν τὸ στρατόπεδον ἐκ τῶν πεδινῶν τόπων εἰς τὴν ὀρεινήν· ἐν ταύτῃ[2] δὲ πνεόντων ψυχρῶν ἀνέμων καὶ τῶν ναματιαίων ὑδάτων καθαρῶν ῥεόντων πρὸς αὐταῖς ταῖς πηγαῖς, ἀπαλλαγῆναι τῆς νόσου τὸ στρατόπεδον. ὀνομάζεσθαι δὲ τῆς ὀρεινῆς τὸν τόπον τοῦτον Μηρόν, καθ' ὃν ὁ Διόνυσος ἐξέτρεψε τὰς δυνάμεις ἐκ τῆς νόσου· ἀφ' οὗ δὴ καὶ τοὺς Ἕλληνας περὶ τοῦ θεοῦ τούτου παραδεδωκέναι τοῖς μεταγενεστέροις τεθράφθαι τὸν Διόνυσον ἐν μηρῷ.

5 Μετὰ δὲ ταῦτα τῆς παραθέσεως τῶν καρπῶν ἐπιμεληθέντα μεταδιδόναι τοῖς Ἰνδοῖς, καὶ τὴν εὕρεσιν τοῦ οἴνου καὶ τῶν ἄλλων τῶν εἰς τὸν βίον χρησίμων παραδοῦναι. πρὸς δὲ τούτοις πόλεών τε ἀξιολόγων γενηθῆναι κτίστην, μεταγαγόντα τὰς κώμας εἰς τοὺς εὐθέτους τόπους, τιμᾶν τε καταδεῖξαι τὸ θεῖον καὶ νόμους εἰσηγήσασθαι καὶ δικαστήρια, καθόλου δὲ πολλῶν καὶ καλῶν ἔργων εἰσηγητὴν γενόμενον θεὸν νομισθῆναι καὶ
6 τυχεῖν ἀθανάτων τιμῶν. ἱστοροῦσι δ' αὐτὸν καὶ γυναικῶν πλῆθος μετὰ τοῦ στρατοπέδου περιάγεσθαι, καὶ κατὰ τὰς ἐν τοῖς πολέμοις παρατάξεις τυμπάνοις καὶ κυμβάλοις κεχρῆσθαι, μήπω σάλπιγγος εὑρημένης. βασιλεύσαντα δὲ πάσης τῆς Ἰνδι-

[1] τῆς after πόλεως omitted C D, Dindorf, Vogel, retained by Bekker.
[2] ἐν ταύτῃ Dindorf, Vogel: ἐνταῦθα C F, Bekker.

BOOK II. 38. 3–6

have been able to oppose him. But when an oppressive heat came and the soldiers of Dionysus were being consumed by a pestilential sickness, this leader, who was conspicuous for his wisdom, led his army out of the plains into the hill-country; here, where cool breezes blew and the spring waters flowed pure at their very sources, the army got rid of its sickness. The name of this region of the hill-country, where Dionysus relieved his forces of the sickness, is Meros; and it is because of this fact that the Greeks have handed down to posterity in their account of this god the story that Dionysus was nourished in a thigh (*meros*).[1]

After this he took in hand the storing of the fruits and shared this knowledge with the Indians, and he communicated to them the discovery of wine and of all the other things useful for life. Furthermore, he became the founder of notable cities by gathering the villages together in well-situated regions, and he both taught them to honour the deity and introduced laws and courts; and, in brief, since he had been the introducer of many good works he was regarded as a god and received immortal honours. They also recount that he carried along with his army a great number of women, and that when he joined battle in his wars he used the sounds of drums and cymbals, since the trumpet had not yet been discovered. And after he had reigned over all

---

[1] When Zeus, at the request of Semelê, appeared to her with his thunderbolts, the sight was too much for her mortal eyes and her child by Zeus, Dionysus, was born untimely. Zeus covered the babe in his thigh until it came to maturity. There is no agreement among modern writers on the location of Meros.

κῆς ἔτη δύο πρὸς τοῖς πεντήκοντα γήρᾳ τελευτῆσαι. διαδεξαμένους δὲ τοὺς υἱοὺς αὐτοῦ τὴν ἡγεμονίαν ἀεὶ τοῖς ἀφ᾽ ἑαυτῶν ἀπολιπεῖν τὴν ἀρχήν· τὸ δὲ τελευταῖον πολλαῖς γενεαῖς ὕστερον καταλυθείσης τῆς ἡγεμονίας δημοκρατηθῆναι τὰς πόλεις.

39. Περὶ μὲν οὖν τοῦ Διονύσου καὶ τῶν ἀπογόνων αὐτοῦ τοιαῦτα μυθολογοῦσιν οἱ τὴν ὀρεινὴν τῆς Ἰνδικῆς κατοικοῦντες. τόν τε Ἡρακλέα φασὶ παρ᾽ αὐτοῖς γεγενῆσθαι, καὶ παραπλησίως τοῖς Ἕλλησι τό τε ῥόπαλον καὶ τὴν λεοντῆν αὐτῷ 2 προσάπτουσι. τῇ δὲ τοῦ σώματος ῥώμῃ καὶ ἀλκῇ πολλῷ τῶν ἄλλων ἀνθρώπων διενεγκεῖν, καὶ καθαρὰν ποιῆσαι τῶν θηρίων γῆν τε καὶ θάλατταν. γήμαντα δὲ πλείους γυναῖκας υἱοὺς μὲν πολλούς, θυγατέρα δὲ μίαν γεννῆσαι, καὶ τούτων ἐνηλίκων γενομένων πᾶσαν τὴν Ἰνδικὴν διελόμενον εἰς ἴσας τοῖς τέκνοις μερίδας, ἅπαντας τοὺς υἱοὺς ἀποδεῖξαι βασιλέας, μίαν δὲ θυγατέρα θρέψαντα καὶ ταύτην 3 βασίλισσαν ἀποδεῖξαι. κτίστην τε πόλεων οὐκ ὀλίγων γενέσθαι, καὶ τούτων τὴν ἐπιφανεστάτην καὶ μεγίστην προσαγορεῦσαι Παλίβοθρα. κατασκευάσαι δ᾽ ἐν αὐτῇ καὶ βασίλεια πολυτελῆ καὶ πλῆθος οἰκητόρων καθιδρῦσαι· τήν τε πόλιν ὀχυρῶσαι τάφροις ἀξιολόγοις ποταμίοις ὕδασι 4 πληρουμέναις.[1] καὶ τὸν μὲν Ἡρακλέα τὴν ἐξ ἀνθρώπων μετάστασιν ποιησάμενον ἀθανάτου τυχεῖν τιμῆς, τοὺς δ᾽ ἀπογόνους αὐτοῦ βασιλεύσαντας ἐπὶ πολλὰς γενεὰς καὶ πράξεις ἀξιολόγους μεταχειρισαμένους μήτε στρατείαν ὑπερ-

---

[1] πληρουμέναις Rhodomann: πληρουμένοις C F, πληρουμένην οἷς D.

BOOK II. 38. 6–39. 4

India for fifty-two years he died of old age. His sons, who succeeded to the sovereignty, passed the rule on successively to their descendants; but finally, many generations later, their sovereignty was dissolved and the cities received a democratic form of government.

39. As for Dionysus, then, and his descendants, such is the myth as it is related by the inhabitants of the hill-country of India. And with regard to Heracles they say that he was born among them and they assign to him, in common with the Greeks, both the club and the lion's skin. Moreover, as their account tells us, he was far superior to all other men in strength of body and in courage, and cleared both land and sea of their wild beasts. And marrying several wives, he begot many sons, but only one daughter; and when his sons attained to manhood, dividing all India into as many parts as he had male children, he appointed all his sons kings, and rearing his single daughter he appointed her also a queen.[1] Likewise, he became the founder of not a few cities, the most renowned and largest of which he called Palibothra. In this city he also constructed a costly palace and settled a multitude of inhabitants, and he fortified it with remarkable ditches which were filled with water from the river. And when Heracles passed from among men he received immortal honour, but his descendants, though they held the kingship during many generations and accomplished notable deeds, made no campaign beyond their own frontiers and despatched

---

[1] Arrian, *Indica*, 8 f., gives a much fuller account of this daughter, whose name was Pandaea.

DIODORUS OF SICILY

ὅριον ποιήσασθαι μήτε ἀποικίαν εἰς ἄλλο ἔθνος[1] ἀποστεῖλαι. ὕστερον δὲ πολλοῖς ἔτεσι τὰς πλείστας μὲν τῶν πόλεων δημοκρατηθῆναι, τινῶν δ' ἐθνῶν τὰς βασιλείας διαμεῖναι μέχρι τῆς 'Αλεξάνδρου διαβάσεως.

5 Νομίμων δ' ὄντων παρὰ τοῖς Ἰνδοῖς ἐνίων ἐξηλλαγμένων θαυμασιώτατον ἄν τις ἡγήσαιτο τὸ καταδειχθὲν ὑπὸ τῶν ἀρχαίων παρ' αὐτοῖς φιλοσόφων· νενομοθέτηται γὰρ παρ' αὐτοῖς δοῦλον μὲν μηδένα εἶναι τὸ παράπαν, ἐλευθέρους δ' ὑπάρχοντας τὴν ἰσότητα τιμᾶν ἐν πᾶσι. τοὺς γὰρ μαθόντας μήθ' ὑπερέχειν μήθ' ὑποπίπτειν ἄλλοις κράτιστον ἕξειν βίον πρὸς ἁπάσας τὰς περιστάσεις· εὔηθες[2] γὰρ εἶναι νόμους μὲν ἐπ' ἴσης τιθέναι πᾶσι, τὰς δ' συνουσίας[3] ἀνωμάλους κατασκευάζειν.

40. Τὸ δὲ πᾶν πλῆθος τῶν Ἰνδῶν εἰς ἑπτὰ μέρη διῄρηται, ὧν ἐστι τὸ μὲν πρῶτον σύστημα φιλοσόφων, πλήθει μὲν τῶν ἄλλων μερῶν λειπόμενον, τῇ δ' ἐπιφανείᾳ πάντων πρωτεῦον. ἀλειτούργητοι γὰρ ὄντες οἱ φιλόσοφοι πάσης ὑπουργίας οὔθ' ἑτέρων κυριεύουσιν οὔθ' ὑφ' ἑτέρων δεσπόζονται.

2 παραλαμβάνονται δ' ὑπὸ μὲν τῶν ἰδιωτῶν εἴς τε τὰς ἐν τῷ βίῳ θυσίας καὶ εἰς τὰς τῶν τετελευτηκότων ἐπιμελείας, ὡς θεοῖς γεγονότες προσφιλέστατοι καὶ περὶ τῶν ἐν ᾅδου μάλιστ' ἐμπείρως ἔχοντες, ταύτης τε τῆς ὑπουργίας δῶρά τε καὶ τιμὰς

[1] ἄλλο ἔθνος C F, Dindorf, Bekker: ἀλλοεθνεῖς remaining MSS., Vogel.
[2] εὔηθες Rhodomann: εὐήθεις.
[3] So Capps: οὐσίας MSS., Vogel, ἐξουσίας Dindorf, Bekker.

no colony to any other people. But many years later most of the cities had received a democratic form of government, although among certain tribes the kingship endured until the time when Alexander crossed over into Asia. 334 B.C.

As for the customs of the Indians which are peculiar to them, a man may consider one which was drawn up by their ancient wise men to be the most worthy of admiration; for the law has ordained that under no circumstances shall anyone among them be a slave, but that all shall be free and respect the principle of equality in all persons. For those, they think, who have learned neither to domineer over others nor to subject themselves to others will enjoy a manner of life best suited to all circumstances; since it is silly to make laws on the basis of equality for all persons, and yet to establish inequalities in social intercourse.

40. The whole multitude of the Indians is divided into seven castes,[1] the first of which is formed of the order of the philosophers, which in number is smaller than the rest of the castes, but in dignity ranks first. For being exempt from any service to the state the philosophers are neither the masters nor the servants of the others. But they are called upon by the private citizens both to offer the sacrifices which are required in their lifetime and to perform the rites for the dead, as having proved themselves to be most dear to the gods and as being especially experienced in the matters that relate to the underworld, and for this service they receive both notable

[1] Cp. the account of the castes in Strabo, 15. 1. 39 ff., and in Arrian, *Indica*, 11 ff., and the article "Caste" in the *Encyclopaedia Britannica*.

DIODORUS OF SICILY

λαμβάνουσιν ἀξιολόγους· τῷ δὲ κοινῷ τῶν Ἰνδῶν μεγάλας παρέχονται χρείας παραλαμβανόμενοι μὲν κατὰ τὸ νέον ἔτος ἐπὶ τὴν μεγάλην σύνοδον, προλέγοντες δὲ τοῖς πλήθεσι περὶ αὐχμῶν καὶ ἐπομβρίας, ἔτι δ' ἀνέμων εὐπνοίας καὶ νόσων καὶ τῶν ἄλλων τῶν δυναμένων τοὺς ἀκούοντας ὠφελῆσαι.
3 τὰ μέλλοντα γὰρ προακούσαντες οἵ τε πολλοὶ καὶ ὁ βασιλεὺς ἐκπληροῦσιν ἀεὶ τὸ μέλλον ἐκλείπειν καὶ προκατασκευάζουσιν ἀεί τι τῶν χρησίμων. ὁ δ' ἀποτυχὼν τῶν φιλοσόφων ἐν ταῖς προρρήσεσιν ἄλλην μὲν οὐδεμίαν ἀναδέχεται τιμωρίαν ἢ βλασφημίαν, ἄφωνος δὲ διατελεῖ τὸν λοιπὸν βίον.

4 Δεύτερον δ' ἐστὶ μέρος τὸ τῶν γεωργῶν, οἳ τῷ πλήθει τῶν ἄλλων πολὺ προέχειν δοκοῦσιν. οὗτοι δὲ πολέμων καὶ τῆς ἄλλης λειτουργίας ἀφειμένοι περὶ τὰς γεωργίας ἀσχολοῦνται· καὶ οὐδεὶς ἂν πολέμιος περιτυχὼν γεωργῷ κατὰ τὴν χώραν ἀδικήσειεν ἄν,[1] ἀλλ' ὡς κοινοὺς εὐεργέτας ἡγούμενοι
5 πάσης ἀδικίας ἀπέχονται. διόπερ ἀδιάφθορος ἡ χώρα διαμένουσα καὶ καρποῖς βρίθουσα πολλὴν ἀπόλαυσιν παρέχεται τῶν ἐπιτηδείων τοῖς ἀνθρώποις. βιοῦσι δ' ἐπὶ τῆς χώρας μετὰ τέκνων καὶ γυναικῶν οἱ γεωργοί, καὶ τῆς εἰς τὴν πόλιν καταβάσεως παντελῶς ἀφεστήκασι· τῆς δὲ χώρας μισθοὺς τελοῦσι τῷ βασιλεῖ διὰ τὸ πᾶσαν τὴν Ἰνδικὴν βασιλικὴν εἶναι, ἰδιώτῃ δὲ μηδενὶ γῆν

---

[1] ἂν D, Dindorf, Vogel: omitted by Vulgate, Bekker.

BOOK II. 40. 2–5

gifts and honours. Moreover, they furnish great services to the whole body of the Indians, since they are invited at the beginning of the year to the Great Synod and foretell to the multitude droughts and rains, as well as the favourable blowing of winds, and epidemics, and whatever else can be of aid to their auditors. For both the common folk and the king, by learning in advance what is going to take place, store up from time to time that of which there will be a shortage and prepare beforehand from time to time anything that will be needed. And the philosopher who has erred[1] in his predictions is subjected to no other punishment than obloquy and keeps silence for the remainder of his life.

The second caste is that of the farmers, who, it would appear, are far more numerous than the rest. These, being exempt from war duties and every other service to the state, devote their entire time to labour in the fields; and no enemy, coming upon a farmer in the country, would think of doing him injury, but they look upon the farmers as common benefactors and therefore refrain from every injury to them.[2] Consequently the land, remaining as it does unravaged and being laden with fruits, provides the inhabitants with a great supply of provisions. And the farmers spend their lives upon the land with their children and wives and refrain entirely from coming down into the city. For the land they pay rent to the king, since all India is royal land and no man of private station is permitted

---

[1] Strabo (*loc. cit.*) says he must have erred "three times."
[2] Cp. chap. 36. 6 f.

ἐξεῖναι κεκτῆσθαι· χωρὶς δὲ τῆς μισθώσεως τετάρτην εἰς τὸ βασιλικὸν τελοῦσι.

6 Τρίτον δ' ἐστὶ φῦλον τὸ τῶν βουκόλων καὶ
ποιμένων καὶ καθόλου πάντων τῶν νομέων, οἳ
πόλιν μὲν ἢ κώμην οὐκ οἰκοῦσι, σκηνίτῃ δὲ βίῳ
χρῶνται, οἱ δ' αὐτοὶ καὶ κυνηγοῦντες καθαρὰν
ποιοῦσι τὴν χώραν ὀρνέων τε καὶ θηρίων. εἰς
ταῦτα δ' ἀσκοῦντες καὶ φιλοτεχνοῦντες[1] ἐξημεροῦσι
τὴν Ἰνδικήν, πλήθουσαν πολλῶν καὶ παντοδαπῶν
θηρίων τε καὶ ὀρνέων τῶν κατεσθιόντων τὰ σπέρματα τῶν γεωργῶν.

41. Τέταρτον δ' ἐστὶ μέρος τὸ τῶν τεχνιτῶν· καὶ
τούτων οἱ μέν εἰσιν ὁπλοποιοί, οἱ δὲ τοῖς γεωργοῖς
ἤ τισιν ἄλλοις τὰ χρήσιμα πρὸς ὑπηρεσίαν κατασκευάζουσιν. οὗτοι δ' οὐ μόνον ἀτελεῖς εἰσιν, ἀλλὰ
καὶ σιτομετρίαν ἐκ τοῦ βασιλικοῦ λαμβάνουσι.

2 Πέμπτον δὲ τὸ[2] στρατιωτικόν, εἰς τοὺς πολέμους
εὐθετοῦν, τῷ μὲν πλήθει δεύτερον, ἀνέσει δὲ καὶ
παιδιᾷ πλείστῃ χρώμενον ἐν ταῖς εἰρήναις. τρέφεται
δ' ἐκ τοῦ βασιλικοῦ πᾶν τὸ πλῆθος τῶν στρατιωτῶν
καὶ τῶν πολεμιστῶν ἵππων τε καὶ ἐλεφάντων.

3 Ἕκτον δ' ἐστὶ τὸ τῶν ἐφόρων· οὗτοι δὲ πολυ-
πραγμονοῦντες πάντα καὶ ἐφορῶντες τὰ κατὰ τὴν
Ἰνδικὴν ἀπαγγέλλουσι τοῖς βασιλεῦσιν, ἐὰν δ' ἡ
πόλις αὐτῶν ἀβασίλευτος ᾖ, τοῖς ἄρχουσιν.

4 Ἕβδομον δ' ἐστὶ μέρος τὸ βουλεῦον μὲν καὶ
συνεδρεῦον τοῖς ὑπὲρ τῶν κοινῶν βουλευομένοις,
πλήθει μὲν ἐλάχιστον, εὐγενείᾳ δὲ καὶ φρονήσει

[1] φιλοτεχνοῦντες B D, Vogel: φιλοπονοῦντες F, Dindorf, Bekker, φιλοσοφοῦντες A C.
[2] τὸ added by Hertlein.

[1] i.e. of the produce.

to possess any ground; and apart from the rental they pay a fourth part[1] into the royal treasury.

The third division is that of the neatherds and shepherds, and, in general, of all the herdsmen who do not dwell in a city or village but spend their lives in tents; and these men are also hunters and rid the country of both birds and wild beasts. And since they are practised in this calling and follow it with zest they are bringing India under cultivation, although it still abounds in many wild beasts and birds of every kind, which eat up the seeds sown by the farmers.

41. The fourth caste is that of the artisans; of these some are armourers and some fabricate for the farmers or certain others the things useful for the services they perform. And they are not only exempt from paying taxes but they even receive rations from the royal treasury.

The fifth caste is that of the military, which is at hand in case of war; they are second in point of number and indulge to the fullest in relaxation and pastimes in the periods of peace. And the maintenance of the whole multitude of the soldiers and of the horses and elephants for use in war is met out of the royal treasury.

The sixth caste is that of the inspectors. These men inquire into and inspect everything that is going on throughout India, and report back to the kings or, in case the state to which they are attached has no king, to the magistrates.

The seventh caste is that of the deliberators and councillors, whose concern is with the decisions which affect the common welfare. In point of number this group is the smallest, but in nobility of birth and

μάλιστα θαυμαζόμενον· ἐκ τούτων γὰρ οἵ τε σύμβουλοι τοῖς βασιλεῦσίν εἰσιν οἵ τε διοικηταὶ τῶν κοινῶν καὶ οἱ δικασταὶ τῶν ἀμφισβητουμένων, καὶ καθόλου τοὺς ἡγεμόνας καὶ τοὺς ἄρχοντας ἐκ τούτων ἔχουσι.

5 Τὰ μὲν οὖν μέρη τῆς διῃρημένης πολιτείας παρ' Ἰνδοῖς σχεδὸν ταῦτ' ἔστιν· οὐκ ἔξεστι δὲ γαμεῖν ἐξ ἄλλου γένους ἢ προαιρέσεις ἢ τέχνας μεταχειρίζεσθαι, οἷον στρατιώτην ὄντα γεωργεῖν ἢ τεχνίτην ὄντα φιλοσοφεῖν.

42. Ἔχει δ' ἡ τῶν Ἰνδῶν χώρα πλείστους καὶ μεγίστους ἐλέφαντας, ἀλκῇ τε καὶ μεγέθει πολὺ διαφέροντας. ὀχεύεται δὲ τοῦτο τὸ ζῷον οὐχ ὥσπερ τινές φασιν, ἐξηλλαγμένως, ἀλλ' ὁμοίως ἵπποις καὶ τοῖς ἄλλοις τετράποσι ζῴοις· κυοῦσι δὲ τοὺς μὲν ἐλαχίστους μῆνας ἑκκαίδεκα, τοὺς δὲ
2 πλείστους ὀκτωκαίδεκα. τίκτουσι δὲ καθάπερ ἵπποι κατὰ τὸ πλεῖστον ἕν, καὶ τρέφουσι τὸ γεννηθὲν αἱ[1] μητέρες ἐπ' ἔτη ἕξ. ζῶσι δ' οἱ πλεῖστοι καθάπερ ὁ μακροβιώτατος ἄνθρωπος, οἱ δὲ μάλιστα γηράσαντες ἔτη διακόσια.

3 Εἰσὶ δὲ παρ' Ἰνδοῖς καὶ ἐπὶ τοὺς ξένους ἄρχοντες τεταγμένοι καὶ φροντίζοντες ὅπως μηδεὶς ξένος ἀδικῆται· τοῖς δ' ἀρρωστοῦσι τῶν ξένων ἰατροὺς εἰσάγουσι καὶ τὴν ἄλλην ἐπιμέλειαν ποιοῦνται, καὶ τελευτήσαντας θάπτουσιν, ἔτι δὲ τὰ καταλειφθέντα
4 χρήματα τοῖς προσήκουσιν ἀποδιδόασιν. οἵ τε δικασταὶ τὰς κρίσεις παρ' αὐτοῖς ἀκριβῶς διαγινώσκουσι, καὶ πικρῶς τοῖς ἁμαρτάνουσι προσφέρονται.

---

[1] αἱ added by Reiske.

wisdom the most worthy of admiration; for from their body are drawn the advisers for the kings and the administrators of the affairs of state and the judges of disputes, and, speaking generally, they take their leaders and magistrates from among these men.

Such in general terms are the groups into which the body politic of the Indians is divided. Furthermore, no one is allowed to marry a person of another caste or to follow another calling or trade, as, for instance, that one who is a soldier should become a farmer, or an artisan should become a philosopher.

42. The country of the Indians also possesses a vast number of enormous elephants, which far surpass all others both in strength and in size. Nor does this animal cover the female in a peculiar manner, as some say, but in the same way as horses and all other four-footed beasts; and their period of gestation is in some cases sixteen months at the least and in other cases eighteen months at the most. They bring forth, like horses, but one young for the most part, and the females suckle their young for six years. The span of life for most of them is about that of men who attain the greatest age, though some which have reached the highest age have lived two hundred years.

There are among the Indians also magistrates appointed for foreigners who take care that no foreigner shall be wronged; moreover, should any foreigner fall sick they bring him a physician and care for him in every other way, and if he dies they bury him and even turn over such property as he has left to his relatives. Again, their judges examine accurately matters of dispute and proceed rigorously against such as are guilty of wrongdoing.

DIODORUS OF SICILY

Περὶ μὲν οὖν τῆς Ἰνδικῆς καὶ τῶν κατ' αὐτὴν ἀρχαιολογουμένων ἀρκεσθησόμεθα τοῖς ῥηθεῖσιν.

43. Περὶ δὲ τῶν Σκυθῶν τῶν οἰκούντων τὴν ὅμορον χώραν ἐν μέρει διέξιμεν. οὗτοι γὰρ τὸ μὲν ἐξ ἀρχῆς ὀλίγην ἐνέμοντο χώραν, ὕστερον δὲ κατ' ὀλίγον αὐξηθέντες διὰ τὰς ἀλκὰς καὶ τὴν ἀνδρείαν πολλὴν μὲν κατεκτήσαντο χώραν, τὸ δ' ἔθνος εἰς 2 μεγάλην ἡγεμονίαν καὶ δόξαν προήγαγον. τὸ μὲν οὖν πρῶτον παρὰ τὸν Ἀράξην ποταμὸν ὀλίγοι κατῴκουν παντελῶς καὶ διὰ τὴν ἀδοξίαν καταφρονούμενοι· ἕνα δὲ τῶν ἀρχαίων ἔχοντες βασιλέα φιλοπόλεμον καὶ διαφέροντα στρατηγίᾳ προσεκτήσαντο χώραν, τῆς μὲν ὀρεινῆς ἕως πρὸς τὸν Καύκασον, τῆς δὲ πεδινῆς τὰ παρὰ τὸν ὠκεανὸν καὶ τὴν Μαιῶτιν λίμνην καὶ τὴν ἄλλην χώραν ἕως Τανάιδος ποταμοῦ.

3 Ὕστερον δὲ μυθολογοῦσι Σκύθαι παρ' αὐτοῖς γενέσθαι γηγενῆ παρθένον· ταύτην δ' ἔχειν τὰ μὲν ἄνω μέρη τοῦ σώματος μέχρι τῆς ζώνης γυναικεῖα, τὰ δὲ κατώτερα ἐχίδνης. ταύτῃ δὲ Δία μιγέντα γεννῆσαι παῖδα Σκύθην ὄνομα. τοῦτον δὲ γενόμενον ἐπιφανέστατον τῶν πρὸ αὐτοῦ τοὺς λαοὺς ἀφ' ἑαυτοῦ Σκύθας προσαγορεῦσαι. τῶν δὲ ἀπογόνων τούτου τοῦ βασιλέως ἀδελφοὺς δύο γενέσθαι διαφόρους ἀρετῇ, καὶ τὸν μὲν Πάλον, τὸν 4 δὲ Νάπην ὠνομάσθαι. τούτων δ' ἐπιφανεῖς πράξεις κατεργασαμένων καὶ διελομένων τὴν βασιλείαν, ἀφ' ἑκατέρου τοὺς λαοὺς τοὺς μὲν Πάλους, τοὺς

---

[1] The Aras.
[2] The Sea of Azof.

BOOK II. 42. 4–43. 4

As for India, then, and its antiquities we shall be satisfied with what has been said.

43. But now, in turn, we shall discuss the Scythians who inhabit the country bordering upon India. This people originally possessed little territory, but later, as they gradually increased in power, they seized much territory by reason of their deeds of might and their bravery and advanced their nation to great leadership and renown. At first, then, they dwelt on the Araxes [1] river, altogether few in number and despised because of their lack of renown; but since one of their early kings was warlike and of unusual skill as a general they acquired territory, in the mountains as far as the Caucasus, and in the steppes along the ocean and Lake Maeotis [2] and the rest of that country as far as the Tanaïs [3] river.

At a later time, as the Scythians recount the myth, there was born among them a maiden sprung from the earth; the upper parts of her body as far as her waist were those of a woman, but the lower parts were those of a snake. With her Zeus lay and begat a son whose name was Scythes. This son became more famous than any who had preceded him and called the folk Scythians after his own name. Now among the descendants of this king there were two brothers who were distinguished for their valour, the one named Palus and the other Napes.[4] And since these two performed renowned deeds and divided the kingship between them, some of the people were called Pali after one of them and some Napae

[3] The Don.
[4] A similar story is in Herodotus (4. 8 ff.), where, however, the father is Heracles and the sons are Agathyrsus, Gelonus, and Scythes.

δὲ Νάπας προσαγορευθῆναι. μετὰ δέ τινας χρόνους τοὺς ἀπογόνους τούτων τῶν βασιλέων ἀνδρείᾳ καὶ στρατηγίᾳ διενεγκόντας πολλὴν μὲν πέραν τοῦ Ταναΐδος ποταμοῦ χώραν καταστρέψασθαι μέχρι τῆς Θρᾴκης, ἐπὶ δὲ θάτερα μέρη στρατεύσαντας διατεῖναι τῇ δυνάμει[1] μέχρι τοῦ κατ' Αἴγυπτον Νείλου. 5 πολλὰ δὲ καὶ μεγάλα τῶν ἀνὰ μέσον τούτων ἐθνῶν καταδουλωσαμένους προβιβάσαι τὴν ἡγεμονίαν τῶν Σκυθῶν τῇ μὲν ἐπὶ τὸν πρὸς ἀνατολὰς ὠκεανόν, τῇ δ' ἐπὶ τὴν Κασπίαν θάλατταν καὶ Μαιῶτιν λίμνην· ηὐξήθη γὰρ ἐπὶ πολὺ τοῦτο τὸ ἔθνος καὶ βασιλεῖς ἔσχεν ἀξιολόγους, ἀφ' ὧν τοὺς μὲν Σάκας προσαγορευθῆναι, τοὺς δὲ Μασσαγέτας, τινὰς δ' Ἀριμασποὺς, καὶ τούτοις ὁμοίως ἄλλους 6 πλείονας. ὑπὸ δὲ τούτων τῶν βασιλέων πολλὰ μὲν καὶ τῶν ἄλλων τῶν καταπολεμηθέντων ἐθνῶν μετῳκίσθαι, δύο δὲ μεγίστας ἀποικίας γενέσθαι, τὴν μὲν ἐκ τῶν Ἀσσυρίων μετασταθεῖσαν εἰς τὴν μεταξὺ χώραν τῆς τε Παφλαγονίας καὶ τοῦ Πόντου, τὴν δ' ἐκ τῆς Μηδίας παρὰ τὸν Τάναϊν καθιδρυθεῖσαν, ἧς τοὺς λαοὺς Σαυρομάτας ὀνομασθῆναι. 7 τούτους δ' ὕστερον πολλοῖς ἔτεσιν αὐξηθέντας πορθῆσαι πολλὴν τῆς Σκυθίας, καὶ τοὺς καταπολεμηθέντας ἄρδην ἀναιροῦντας ἔρημον ποιῆσαι τὸ πλεῖστον μέρος τῆς χώρας.

44. Μετὰ δὲ ταῦτα ἀναρχίας γενομένης κατὰ τὴν Σκυθίαν, ἐβασίλευσαν γυναῖκες ἀλκῇ διαφέ-

[1] τῇ δυνάμει II, Dindorf, Vogel (cp. 1. 4. 3): τὴν δύναμιν A B D, Bekker.

[1] Probably the south side of the Black Sea is meant; cp. chap. 46. 2.

BOOK II. 43. 4-44. 1

after the other. But some time later the descendants of these kings, because of their unusual valour and skill as generals, subdued much of the territory beyond the Tanaïs river as far as Thrace, and advancing with their armies to the other side [1] they extended their power as far as the Nile in Egypt.[2] And after enslaving many great peoples which lay between the Thracians and the Egyptians they advanced the empire of the Scythians on the one side as far as the ocean to the east, and on the other side to the Caspian Sea and Lake Maeotis; for this people increased to great strength and had notable kings, one of whom gave his name to the Sacae, another to the Massagetae, another to the Arimaspi, and several other tribes received their names in like manner. It was by these kings that many of the conquered peoples were removed to other homes, and two of these became very great colonies: the one was composed of Assyrians [3] and was removed to the land between Paphlagonia and Pontus, and the other was drawn from Media and planted along the Tanaïs, its people receiving the name Sauromatae. Many years later this people became powerful and ravaged a large part of Scythia, and destroying utterly all whom they subdued they turned most of the land into a desert.

44. After these events there came in Scythia a period of revolutions, in which the sovereigns were women endowed with exceptional valour. For

[2] In this incursion, which occurred between 630 and 625 B.C., the Scythians overran Palestine, but according to Herodotus (1. 105) were turned back from Egypt by Psammetichus. A vivid picture of these foes from the north is preserved in *Jeremiah*, 4-5 *passim*.

[3] These are the "White Syrians" of Strabo (12. 3. 9).

ρουσαι. ἐν τούτοις γὰρ τοῖς ἔθνεσιν αἱ γυναῖκες γυμνάζονται πρὸς πόλεμον παραπλησίως τοῖς ἀνδράσι καὶ ταῖς ἀνδρείαις οὐδὲν λείπονται τῶν ἀνδρῶν. διὸ καὶ γυναικῶν ἐπιφανῶν πολλαὶ καὶ μεγάλαι πράξεις ἐπετελέσθησαν οὐ μόνον κατὰ τὴν Σκυθίαν, ἀλλὰ καὶ κατὰ τὴν ὅμορον ταύτης 2 χώραν. Κύρου μὲν γὰρ τοῦ Περσῶν βασιλέως πλεῖστον ἰσχύσαντος τῶν καθ' αὑτὸν καὶ στρατεύσαντος ἀξιολόγοις δυνάμεσιν εἰς τὴν Σκυθίαν, ἡ βασίλισσα τῶν Σκυθῶν τό τε στρατόπεδον τῶν Περσῶν κατέκοψε καὶ τὸν Κῦρον αἰχμάλωτον γενόμενον ἀνεσταύρωσε· τό τε συσταθὲν ἔθνος τῶν Ἀμαζόνων τοσοῦτον ἀνδρείᾳ διήνεγκεν ὥστε μὴ μόνον πολλὴν χώραν ὅμορον καταδραμεῖν, ἀλλὰ καὶ πολλὴν τῆς Εὐρώπης καὶ τῆς Ἀσίας 3 καταστρέψασθαι. ἡμεῖς δ' ἐπειδὴ περὶ τῶν Ἀμαζονίδων ἐμνήσθημεν, οὐκ ἀνοίκειον εἶναι νομίζομεν διελθεῖν περὶ αὐτῶν, εἰ καὶ διὰ τὴν παραδοξολογίαν μύθοις ὅμοια φανήσεται τὰ ῥηθέντα.

45. Παρὰ τὸν Θερμώδοντα τοίνυν ποταμὸν ἔθνους κρατοῦντος[1] γυναικοκρατουμένου, καὶ τῶν γυναικῶν ὁμοίως τοῖς ἀνδράσι τὰς πολεμικὰς χρείας μεταχειριζομένων, φασὶ μίαν ἐξ αὐτῶν βασιλικὴν ἐξουσίαν ἔχουσαν ἀλκῇ καὶ ῥώμῃ διενεγκεῖν· συστησαμένην δὲ γυναικῶν στρατόπεδον γυμνάσαι τε τοῦτο καί τινας τῶν ὁμόρων καταπολεμῆσαι. 2 αὐξομένης δὲ τῆς περὶ αὐτὴν ἀρετῆς τε καὶ δόξης

[1] κρατοῦντος MSS: κατοικοῦντος Rhodomann, Dindorf, Vogel.

BOOK II. 44. 1–45. 2

among these peoples the women train for war just as do the men and in acts of manly valour are in no wise inferior to the men. Consequently distinguished women have been the authors of many great deeds, not in Scythia alone, but also in the territory bordering upon it. For instance, when Cyrus the king of the Persians, the mightiest ruler of his day, made a campaign with a vast army into Scythia, the queen of the Scythians not only cut the army of the Persians to pieces but she even took Cyrus prisoner and crucified him [1]; and the nation of the Amazons, after it was once organized, was so distinguished for its manly prowess that it not only overran much of the neighbouring territory but even subdued a large part of Europe and Asia. But for our part, since we have mentioned the Amazons, we feel that it is not foreign to our purpose to discuss them, even though what we shall say will be so marvellous that it will resemble a tale from mythology.

45. Now in the country along the Thermodon river,[2] as the account goes, the sovereignty was in the hands of a people among whom the women held the supreme power, and its women performed the services of war just as did the men. Of these women one, who possessed the royal authority, was remarkable for her prowess in war and her bodily strength, and gathering together an army of women she drilled it in the use of arms and subdued in war some of the neighbouring peoples. And since her valour and fame increased, she made war upon

[1] There are many different accounts of the death of Cyrus, but they all agree that he met his end fighting on the far eastern border of his empire.

[2] In Pontus (cp. Strabo, 12. 3. 14–15).

συνεχῶς ἐπὶ τὰ πλησιόχωρα τῶν ἐθνῶν στρατεύειν, καὶ τῆς τύχης εὐροούσης φρονήματος ἐμπίμπλασθαι, καὶ θυγατέρα μὲν Ἄρεος αὐτὴν προσαγορεῦσαι, τοῖς δ' ἀνδράσι προσνεῖμαι τὰς ταλασιουργίας καὶ τὰς τῶν γυναικῶν κατ' οἴκους ἐργασίας. νόμους τε καταδεῖξαι, δι' ὧν τὰς μὲν γυναῖκας ἐπὶ τοὺς πολεμικοὺς ἀγῶνας προάγειν, τοῖς δ' 3 ἀνδράσι ταπείνωσιν καὶ δουλείαν περιάπτειν. τῶν δὲ γεννωμένων τοὺς μὲν ἄρρενας ἐπήρουν τά τε σκέλη καὶ τοὺς βραχίονας, ἀχρήστους κατασκευάζοντες πρὸς τὰς πολεμικὰς χρείας, τῶν δὲ θηλυτερῶν τὸν δεξιὸν μαστὸν ἐπέκαον, ἵνα μὴ κατὰ τὰς ἀκμὰς[1] τῶν σωμάτων ἐπαιρόμενος ἐνοχλῇ· ἀφ' ἧς αἰτίας συμβῆναι τὸ ἔθνος τῶν Ἀμαζόνων ταύτης 4 τυχεῖν τῆς προσηγορίας. καθόλου δὲ διαφέρουσαν αὐτὴν συνέσει καὶ στρατηγίᾳ πόλιν μὲν κτίσαι μεγάλην παρὰ τὰς ἐκβολὰς τοῦ Θερμώδοντος ποταμοῦ, τοὔνομα Θεμίσκυραν, καὶ βασίλεια κατασκευάσαι περιβόητα, κατὰ δὲ τὰς στρατείας ἐπιμελομένην πολὺ τῆς εὐταξίας τὸ μὲν πρῶτον καταπολεμῆσαι πάντας τοὺς ὁμόρους μέχρι τοῦ Ταναΐδος 5 ποταμοῦ. καὶ ταύτην μέν φασι ταύτας τὰς πράξεις ἐπιτελεσαμένην καὶ κατά τινα μάχην λαμπρῶς ἀγωνισαμένην ἡρωικῶς τελευτῆσαι τὸν βίον.

46. Διαδεξαμένην δὲ τὴν ταύτης θυγατέρα τὴν βασιλείαν ζηλῶσαι μὲν τὴν ἀρετὴν τῆς μητρός, ὑπερβαλέσθαι δὲ ταῖς κατὰ μέρος πράξεσι. τὰς

[1] ἀκμὰς Dindorf: μάχας.

BOOK II. 45. 2–46. 1

people after people of neighbouring lands, and as the tide of her fortune continued favourable, she was so filled with pride that she gave herself the appellation of Daughter of Ares; but to the men she assigned the spinning of wool and such other domestic duties as belong to women. Laws also were established by her, by virtue of which she led forth the women to the contests of war, but upon the men she fastened humiliation and slavery. And as for their children, they mutilated both the legs and the arms of the males, incapacitating them in this way for the demands of war, and in the case of the females they seared the right breast that it might not project when their bodies matured and be in the way; and it is for this reason that the nation of the Amazons received the appellation it bears.[1] In general, this queen was remarkable for her intelligence and ability as a general, and she founded a great city named Themiscyra at the mouth of the Thermodon river and built there a famous palace; furthermore, in her campaigns she devoted much attention to military discipline and at the outset subdued all her neighbours as far as the Tanaïs river. And this queen, they say, accomplished the deeds which have been mentioned, and fighting brilliantly in a certain battle she ended her life heroically.

46. The daughter of this queen, the account continues, on succeeding to the throne emulated the excellence of her mother, and even surpassed her in

[1] Amazon is commonly derived from ἀ and μαζός, a form of μαστός ("breast"), and so means "without a breast," because the right breast was got rid of, that it might not hinder the use of the bow. For a slightly different account, cp. Book 3. 53.

μὲν γὰρ παρθένους ἀπὸ τῆς πρώτης ἡλικίας ἔν τε ταῖς θήραις γυμνάζειν καὶ καθ' ἡμέραν ἀσκεῖν τὰ πρὸς πόλεμον ἀνήκοντα, καταδεῖξαι δὲ καὶ θυσίας μεγαλοπρεπεῖς Ἄρει τε καὶ Ἀρτέμιδι τῇ προσα-
2 γορευομένῃ Ταυροπόλῳ· στρατεύσασαν δ' εἰς τὴν πέραν τοῦ Τανάιδος ποταμοῦ χώραν καταπολεμῆσαι πάντα τὰ ἔθνη τὰ συνεχῆ μέχρι τῆς Θρᾴκης· ἀνακάμψασαν δὲ μετὰ πολλῶν λαφύρων εἰς τὴν οἰκείαν ναοὺς μεγαλοπρεπεῖς κατασκευάσαι τῶν προειρημένων θεῶν, καὶ τῶν ὑποτεταγμένων ἐπιεικῶς ἄρχουσαν ἀποδοχῆς τυγχάνειν τῆς μεγίστης. στρατεῦσαι δὲ καὶ ἐπὶ θάτερα μέρη, καὶ πολλὴν τῆς Ἀσίας κατακτήσασθαι, καὶ διατεῖναι τῇ δυνάμει μέχρι τῆς Συρίας.
3 Μετὰ δὲ τὴν ταύτης τελευτὴν ἀεὶ τὰς προσηκούσας τῷ γένει διαδεχομένας τὴν βασιλείαν ἄρξαι μὲν ἐπιφανῶς, αὐξῆσαι δὲ τὸ ἔθνος τῶν Ἀμαζονίδων δυνάμει τε καὶ δόξῃ. μετὰ δὲ ταῦτα πολλαῖς γενεαῖς ὕστερον, διαβεβοημένης κατὰ πᾶσαν τὴν οἰκουμένην τῆς περὶ αὐτὰς ἀρετῆς, Ἡρακλέα φασὶ τὸν ἐξ Ἀλκμήνης καὶ Διὸς ἆθλον λαβεῖν παρ' Εὐρυσθέως τὸν Ἱππολύτης
4 τῆς Ἀμαζόνος ζωστῆρα. διόπερ στρατεῦσαι μὲν αὐτόν, παρατάξει δὲ μεγάλῃ νικήσαντα τό τε στρατόπεδον τῶν Ἀμαζόνων κατακόψαι καὶ τὴν Ἱππολύτην μετὰ τοῦ ζωστῆρος ζωγρήσαντα τὸ ἔθνος τοῦτο τελέως συντρῖψαι. διόπερ τοὺς περιοικοῦντας βαρβάρους τῆς μὲν ἀσθενείας αὐτῶν καταφρονήσαντας,

some particular deeds. For instance, she exercised in the chase the maidens from their earliest girlhood and drilled them daily in the arts of war, and she also established magnificent festivals both to Ares and to the Artemis who is called Tauropolus.[1] Then she campaigned against the territory lying beyond the Tanaïs and subdued all the peoples one after another as far as Thrace; and returning to her native land with much booty she built magnificent shrines to the deities mentioned above, and by reason of her kindly rule over her subjects received from them the greatest approbation. She also campaigned on the other side [2] and subdued a large part of Asia and extended her power as far as Syria.

After the death of this queen, as their account continues, women of her family, succeeding to the queenship from time to time, ruled with distinction and advanced the nation of the Amazons in both power and fame. And many generations after these events, when the excellence of these women had been noised abroad through the whole inhabited world, they say that Heracles, the son of Alcmenê and Zeus, was assigned by Eurystheus the Labour of securing the girdle of Hippolytê the Amazon.[3] Consequently he embarked on this campaign, and coming off victorious in a great battle he not only cut to pieces the army of Amazons but also, after taking captive Hippolytê together with her girdle, completely crushed this nation. Consequently the neighbouring barbarians, despising the weakness of

---

[1] The Taurian Artemis, so well known from the *Iphigeneia among the Taurians* of Euripides.

[2] *i.e.* south of the Black Sea.

[3] The story is given in detail in Book 4. 16.

τῶν δὲ καθ' ἑαυτοὺς μνησικακήσαντας, πολεμῆσαι συνεχῶς τὸ ἔθνος ἐπὶ τοσοῦτον ὥστε μηδ' ὄνομα τοῦ γένους τῶν Ἀμαζονίδων ἀπολιπεῖν. μετὰ γὰρ τὴν Ἡρακλέους στρατείαν ὀλίγοις ὕστερον ἔτεσι κατὰ τὸν Τρωικὸν πόλεμόν φασι Πενθεσίλειαν τὴν βασιλεύουσαν τῶν ὑπολελειμμένων Ἀμαζονίδων, Ἄρεος μὲν οὖσαν θυγατέρα, φόνον δ' ἐμφύλιον ἐπιτελεσαμένην, φυγεῖν ἐκ τῆς πατρίδος διὰ τὸ μύσος. συμμαχήσασαν δὲ τοῖς Τρωσὶ μετὰ τὴν Ἕκτορος τελευτὴν πολλοὺς ἀνελεῖν τῶν Ἑλλήνων, ἀριστεύσασαν δ' αὐτὴν ἐν τῇ παρατάξει καταστρέψαι τὸν βίον ἡρωικῶς ὑπ' Ἀχιλλέως ἀναιρεθεῖσαν. τῶν μὲν οὖν Ἀμαζονίδων ἐσχάτην ταύτην λέγουσιν ἀνδρείᾳ διενεγκεῖν, καὶ τὸ λοιπὸν ἀεὶ τὸ ἔθνος ταπεινούμενον ἀσθενῆσαι παντελῶς· διὸ καὶ κατὰ τοὺς νεωτέρους καιρούς, ἐπειδάν τινες περὶ τῆς αὐτῶν ἀνδρείας διεξίωσι, μύθους ἡγοῦνται πεπλασμένους τὰς περὶ τῶν Ἀμαζονίδων ἀρχαιολογίας.

47. Ἡμεῖς δ' ἐπεὶ τὰ πρὸς ἄρκτους κεκλιμένα μέρη τῆς Ἀσίας ἠξιώσαμεν ἀναγραφῆς, οὐκ ἀνοίκειον εἶναι νομίζομεν τὰ περὶ τῶν Ὑπερβορέων μυθολογούμενα διελθεῖν. τῶν γὰρ τὰς παλαιὰς μυθολογίας ἀναγεγραφότων Ἑκαταῖος καί τινες ἕτεροί φασιν ἐν τοῖς ἀντιπέρας τῆς Κελτικῆς τόποις κατὰ τὸν ὠκεανὸν εἶναι νῆσον οὐκ ἐλάττω

---

[1] Quintus Smyrnaeus (1. 24 f.) says that she killed her sister Hippolytê on a hunt, while hurling her spear at a stag.

[2] There seems good reason (see R. Hennig, " Die Anfänge des kulturellen und Handelsverkehr in der Mittelmeerwelt," *Historische Zeitschrift*, 139 (1928), 1–33) to see in this people who live " beyond the north wind," as their name signifies,

this people and remembering against them their past injuries, waged continuous wars against the nation to such a degree that they left in existence not even the name of the race of the Amazons. For a few years after the campaign of Heracles against them, they say, during the time of the Trojan War, Penthesileia, the queen of the surviving Amazons, who was a daughter of Ares and had slain one of her kindred, fled from her native land because of the sacrilege.[1] And fighting as an ally of the Trojans after the death of Hector she slew many of the Greeks, and after gaining distinction in the struggle she ended her life heroically at the hands of Achilles. Now they say that Penthesileia was the last of the Amazons to win distinction for bravery and that for the future the race diminished more and more and then lost all its strength; consequently in later times, whenever any writers recount their prowess, men consider the ancient stories about the Amazons to be fictitious tales.

47. Now for our part, since we have seen fit to make mention of the regions of Asia which lie to the north, we feel that it will not be foreign to our purpose to discuss the legendary accounts of the Hyperboreans.[2] Of those who have written about the ancient myths, Hecataeus and certain others say that in the regions beyond the land of the Celts [3] there lies in the ocean an island no smaller

an early acquaintance of the Greeks, through the medium of the Celts, with Britain and its inhabitants. In this chapter Apollo would be the Celtic sun-god Borvon, and the "sacred precinct" of Apollo would be the famous Stone Age remains of Stonehenge.

[3] *i.e.* Gaul.

τῆς Σικελίας. ταύτην ὑπάρχειν μὲν κατὰ τὰς ἄρκτους, κατοικεῖσθαι δὲ ὑπὸ τῶν ὀνομαζομένων Ὑπερβορέων ἀπὸ τοῦ πορρωτέρω κεῖσθαι τῆς βορείου πνοῆς· οὖσαν δ' αὐτὴν εὔγειόν τε καὶ πάμφορον, ἔτι δ' εὐκρασίᾳ διαφέρουσαν, διττοὺς
2 κατ' ἔτος ἐκφέρειν καρπούς. μυθολογοῦσι δ' ἐν αὐτῇ τὴν Λητὼ γεγονέναι· διὸ καὶ τὸν Ἀπόλλω μάλιστα τῶν ἄλλων θεῶν παρ' αὐτοῖς τιμᾶσθαι· εἶναι δ' αὐτοὺς ὥσπερ ἱερεῖς τινας Ἀπόλλωνος διὰ τὸ τὸν θεὸν τοῦτον καθ' ἡμέραν ὑπ' αὐτῶν ὑμνεῖσθαι μετ' ᾠδῆς συνεχῶς καὶ τιμᾶσθαι διαφερόντως. ὑπάρχειν δὲ καὶ κατὰ τὴν νῆσον τέμενός τε Ἀπόλλωνος μεγαλοπρεπὲς καὶ ναὸν ἀξιόλογον ἀναθήμασι πολλοῖς κεκοσμημένον, σφαι-
3 ροειδῆ τῷ σχήματι. καὶ πόλιν μὲν ὑπάρχειν ἱερὰν τοῦ θεοῦ τούτου, τῶν δὲ κατοικούντων αὐτὴν τοὺς πλείστους εἶναι κιθαριστάς, καὶ συνεχῶς ἐν τῷ ναῷ κιθαρίζοντας ὕμνους λέγειν τῷ θεῷ μετ' ᾠδῆς, ἀποσεμνύνοντας αὐτοῦ τὰς πράξεις.
4 Ἔχειν δὲ τοὺς Ὑπερβορέους ἰδίαν τινὰ διάλεκτον, καὶ πρὸς τοὺς Ἕλληνας οἰκειότατα διακεῖσθαι, καὶ μάλιστα πρὸς τοὺς Ἀθηναίους καὶ Δηλίους, ἐκ παλαιῶν χρόνων παρειληφότας τὴν εὔνοιαν ταύτην. καὶ τῶν Ἑλλήνων τινὰς μυθολογοῦσι παραβαλεῖν εἰς Ὑπερβορέους, καὶ ἀναθήματα πολυτελῆ καταλιπεῖν γράμμασιν Ἑλληνικοῖς ἐπι-
5 γεγραμμένα. ὡσαύτως δὲ καὶ ἐκ τῶν Ὑπερβορέων

---

[1] The mother by Zeus of Apollo and Artemis.
[2] The island of Delos was from the earliest period of the Greek civilization a centre of the worship of Apollo.

BOOK II. 47. 1-5

than Sicily. This island, the account continues, is situated in the north and is inhabited by the Hyperboreans, who are called by that name because their home is beyond the point whence the north wind (Boreas) blows; and the island is both fertile and productive of every crop, and since it has an unusually temperate climate it produces two harvests each year. Moreover, the following legend is told concerning it: Leto[1] was born on this island, and for that reason Apollo is honoured among them above all other gods; and the inhabitants are looked upon as priests of Apollo, after a manner, since daily they praise this god continuously in song and honour him exceedingly. And there is also on the island both a magnificent sacred precinct of Apollo and a notable temple which is adorned with many votive offerings and is spherical in shape. Furthermore, a city is there which is sacred to this god, and the majority of its inhabitants are players on the cithara; and these continually play on this instrument in the temple and sing hymns of praise to the god, glorifying his deeds.

The Hyperboreans also have a language, we are informed, which is peculiar to them, and are most friendly disposed towards the Greeks, and especially towards the Athenians and the Delians,[2] who have inherited this good-will from most ancient times. The myth also relates that certain Greeks visited the Hyperboreans and left behind them there costly votive offerings bearing inscriptions in Greek letters. And in the same way Abaris,[3] a Hyperborean, came

[3] Abaris is apparently a purely mythical figure, who in some authors sailed on his arrow, as on a witch's broomstick, through the air over rivers and seas.

DIODORUS OF SICILY

Ἄβαριν εἰς τὴν Ἑλλάδα καταντήσαντα τὸ παλαιὸν ἀνασῶσαι τὴν πρὸς Δηλίους εὔνοιάν τε καὶ συγγένειαν. φασὶ δὲ καὶ τὴν σελήνην ἐκ ταύτης τῆς νήσου φαίνεσθαι παντελῶς ὀλίγον ἀπέχουσαν τῆς γῆς καί τινας ἐξοχὰς γεώδεις ἔχουσαν ἐν
6 αὐτῇ φανεράς. λέγεται δὲ καὶ τὸν θεὸν δι' ἐτῶν ἐννεακαίδεκα καταντᾶν εἰς τὴν νῆσον, ἐν οἷς αἱ τῶν ἄστρων ἀποκαταστάσεις ἐπὶ τέλος ἄγονται· καὶ διὰ τοῦτο τὸν ἐννεακαιδεκαετῆ χρόνον ὑπὸ τῶν Ἑλλήνων Μέτωνος ἐνιαυτὸν ὀνομάζεσθαι. κατὰ δὲ τὴν ἐπιφάνειαν ταύτην τὸν θεὸν κιθαρίζειν τε καὶ χορεύειν συνεχῶς τὰς νύκτας ἀπὸ ἰσημερίας ἐαρινῆς ἕως πλειάδος ἀνατολῆς ἐπὶ τοῖς ἰδίοις εὐημερήμασι τερπόμενον. βασιλεύειν δὲ τῆς πόλεως ταύτης καὶ τοῦ τεμένους ἐπάρχειν τοὺς ὀνομαζομένους Βορεάδας, ἀπογόνους ὄντας Βορέου, καὶ κατὰ γένος ἀεὶ διαδέχεσθαι τὰς ἀρχάς.

48. Τούτων δ' ἡμῖν διευκρινημένων μεταβιβάσομεν τὸν λόγον ἐπὶ τὰ ἕτερα μέρη τῆς Ἀσίας τὰ μὴ τετευχότα τῆς ἀναγραφῆς, καὶ μάλιστα τὰ κατὰ τὴν Ἀραβίαν. αὕτη γὰρ κεῖται μὲν μεταξὺ Συρίας καὶ τῆς Αἰγύπτου, πολλοῖς δὲ καὶ παντοδαποῖς ἔθνεσι διείληπται. τὰ μὲν οὖν πρὸς τὴν ἕω μέρη κατοικοῦσιν Ἄραβες οὓς ὀνομάζουσι Ναβαταίους, νεμόμενοι χώραν τὴν μὲν ἔρημον, τὴν δὲ
2 ἄνυδρον, ὀλίγην δὲ καρποφόρον. ἔχουσι δὲ βίον λῃστρικόν, καὶ πολλὴν τῆς ὁμόρου χώρας κατατρέ-

---

[1] The "Metonic Cycle" is described in Book 12. 36. The cycle of Meton, which was introduced in Athens in 432 B.C., was designed to reconcile the lunar and the solar year, the latter being reckoned at $365\frac{5}{19}$ days. That this nineteen-year cycle

BOOK II. 47. 5-48. 2

to Greece in ancient times and renewed the goodwill and kinship of his people to the Delians. They say also that the moon, as viewed from this island, appears to be but a little distance from the earth and to have upon it prominences, like those of the earth, which are visible to the eye. The account is also given that the god visits the island every nineteen years, the period in which the return of the stars to the same place in the heavens is accomplished; and for this reason the nineteen-year period is called by the Greeks the " year of Meton."[1] At the time of this appearance of the god he both plays on the cithara and dances continuously the night through from the vernal equinox until the rising of the Pleiades, expressing in this manner his delight in his successes. And the kings of this city and the supervisors of the sacred precinct are called Boreadae, since they are descendants of Boreas, and the succession to these positions is always kept in their family.

48. But now that we have examined these matters we shall turn our account to the other parts of Asia which have not yet been described, and more especially to Arabia. This land is situated between Syria and Egypt, and is divided among many peoples of diverse characteristics. Now the eastern parts are inhabited by Arabs, who bear the name of Nabataeans and range over a country which is partly desert and partly waterless, though a small section of it is fruitful. And they lead a life of brigandage, and overrunning a large part of the neighbouring terri-

was actually inaugurated at this time has been maintained, most recently, by W. B. Dinsmoor, *The Archons of Athens in the Hellenistic Age* (1931), pp. 320-1 and *passim*.

χοντες ληστεύουσιν, ὄντες δύσμαχοι κατὰ τοὺς πολέμους. κατὰ γὰρ τὴν ἄνυδρον χώραν λεγομένην κατεσκευακότες εὔκαιρα φρέατα, καὶ ταῦτα πεποιηκότες τοῖς ἄλλοις ἔθνεσιν[1] ἄγνωστα, συμφεύγουσιν εἰς τὴν χώραν ταύτην ἀκινδύνως.

3 αὐτοὶ μὲν γὰρ εἰδότες τὰ κατακεκρυμμένα τῶν ὑδάτων, καὶ ταῦτ' ἀνοίγοντες, χρῶνται δαψιλέσι ποτοῖς· οἱ δὲ τούτους ἐπιδιώκοντες ἀλλοεθνεῖς σπανίζοντες τῆς ὑδρείας διὰ τὴν ἄγνοιαν τῶν φρεάτων, οἱ μὲν ἀπόλλυνται διὰ τὴν σπάνιν τῶν ὑδάτων, οἱ δὲ πολλὰ κακοπαθήσαντες μόγις εἰς τὴν

4 οἰκείαν σώζονται. διόπερ οἱ ταύτην τὴν χώραν κατοικοῦντες Ἄραβες, ὄντες δυσκαταπολέμητοι, διατελοῦσιν ἀδούλωτοι, πρὸς δὲ τούτοις ἔπηλυν μὲν ἡγεμόνα τὸ παράπαν οὐ προσδέχονται, διατελοῦσι δὲ τὴν ἐλευθερίαν διαφυλάττοντες ἀσάλευτον.

5 διόπερ οὔτ' Ἀσσύριοι τὸ παλαιὸν οὔθ' οἱ Μήδων καὶ Περσῶν, ἔτι δὲ Μακεδόνων βασιλεῖς ἠδυνήθησαν αὐτοὺς καταδουλώσασθαι, πολλὰς μὲν καὶ μεγάλας δυνάμεις ἐπ' αὐτοὺς ἀγαγόντες, οὐδέποτε δὲ τὰς ἐπιβολὰς συντελέσαντες.

6 Ἔστι δ' ἐν τῇ χώρᾳ τῶν Ναβαταίων καὶ πέτρα καθ' ὑπερβολὴν ὀχυρά, μίαν ἀνάβασιν ἔχουσα, δι' ἧς κατ' ὀλίγους ἀναβαίνοντες ἀποτίθενται τὰς ἀποσκευάς. λίμνη τε μεγάλη φέρουσα πολλὴν

[1] ἄλλοις ἔθνεσιν MSS.: ἀλλοεθνέσιν Dindorf, Vogel.

[1] A fuller description of this custom is given in Book 19. 94 in connection with the expedition of Antigonus against the Nabataeans.
[2] Cp. chap. 1. 5.
[3] The city of Petra (rock); cp. Book 19. 97 and Strabo, 16. 21.

BOOK II. 48. 2-6

tory they pillage it, being difficult to overcome in war. For in the waterless region, as it is called, they have dug wells at convenient intervals and have kept the knowledge of them hidden from the peoples of all other nations, and so they retreat in a body into this region out of danger.[1] For since they themselves know about the places of hidden water and open them up, they have for their use drinking water in abundance; but such other peoples as pursue them, being in want of a watering-place by reason of their ignorance of the wells, in some cases perish because of the lack of water and in other cases regain their native land in safety only with difficulty and after suffering many ills. Consequently the Arabs who inhabit this country, being difficult to overcome in war, remain always unenslaved; furthermore, they never at any time accept a man of another country as their over-lord and continue to maintain their liberty unimpaired. Consequently neither the Assyrians of old, nor the kings of the Medes and Persians, nor yet those of the Macedonians have been able to enslave them, and although they led many great forces against them, they never brought their attempts to a successful conclusion.[2]

There is also in the land of the Nabataeans a rock,[3] which is exceedingly strong since it has but one approach, and using this ascent they mount it a few at a time and thus store their possessions in safety. And a large lake [4] is also there which pro-

[4] The Dead Sea; cp. Strabo 16. 42 f. The remainder of this chapter appears in the same words in Book 19. 98, which has been the basis of many changes in the text of the present passage.

ἄσφαλτον, ἐξ ἧς λαμβάνουσιν οὐκ ὀλίγας προσό-
7 δους. αὕτη δ' ἔχει τὸ μὲν μῆκος σταδίων ὡς
πεντακοσίων, τὸ δὲ πλάτος ὡς ἑξήκοντα, τὸ δ'
ὕδωρ δυσῶδες καὶ διάπικρον, ὥστε μὴ δύνασθαι
μήτ' ἰχθῦν τρέφειν μήτ' ἄλλο τῶν καθ' ὕδατος
εἰωθότων ζῴων εἶναι. ἐμβαλλόντων δ' εἰς αὐτὴν
ποταμῶν μεγάλων τῇ γλυκύτητι διαφόρων, τούτων
μὲν περιγίνεται κατὰ τὴν δυσωδίαν, ἐξ αὐτῆς
δὲ μέσης κατ' ἐνιαυτὸν ἐκφυσᾷ ἀσφάλτου μέγεθος
ποτὲ μὲν μεῖζον ἢ τρίπλεθρον, ἔστι δ' ὅτε δυοῖν
πλέθρων· ἐφ' ᾧ[1] δὴ συνήθως οἱ περιοικοῦν-
τες βάρβαροι τὸ μὲν μεῖζον καλοῦσι ταῦρον, τὸ δ'
8 ἔλαττον μόσχον ἐπονομάζουσιν. ἐπιπλεούσης δὲ τῆς
ἀσφάλτου πελαγίας ὁ τύπος[2] φαίνεται τοῖς[3] ἐξ
ἀποστήματος θεωροῦσιν οἱονεὶ νῆσος. τὴν δ' ἔκπτω-
σιν τῆς ἀσφάλτου συμβαίνει φανερὰν γίνεσθαι τοῖς
ἀνθρώποις πρὸ ἡμερῶν εἴκοσι·[4] κύκλῳ γὰρ τῆς
λίμνης ἐπὶ πολλοὺς σταδίους ὀσμὴ προσπίπτει μετὰ
πνεύματος, καὶ πᾶς ὁ περὶ τὸν τόπον ἄργυρός τε
καὶ χρυσὸς καὶ χαλκὸς ἀποβάλλει τὴν ἰδιότητα τοῦ
χρώματος. ἀλλ' αὕτη μὲν ἀποκαθίσταται πάλιν,
ἐπειδὰν ἀναφυσηθῆναι[5] συμβῇ πᾶσαν τὴν ἄσφαλ-
τον· ὁ δὲ πλησίον τόπος ἔμπυρος ὢν καὶ δυσώδης
ποιεῖ τὰ σώματα τῶν ἀνθρώπων ἐπίνοσα καὶ παντε-
9 λῶς ὀλιγοχρόνια. ἀγαθὴ δ' ἐστὶ φοινικόφυτος ὅσην
αὐτῆς συμβαίνει ποταμοῖς διειλῆφθαι χρησίμοις
ἢ πηγαῖς δυναμέναις ἀρδεύειν. γίνεται δὲ περὶ

---

[1] ᾧ Wesseling: ὦν.
[2] τύπος Schäfer: τόπος.
[3] μὲν after τοῖς deleted by Dindorf.
[4] δύο after εἴκοσι deleted by Dindorf.
[5] ἀναφυσηθῆναι Dindorf: ἀναφυσῆσαι.

duces asphalt in abundance, and from it they derive not a little revenue. It has a length of about five hundred stades and a width of about sixty, and its water is so ill-smelling and so very bitter that it cannot support fish or any of the other animals which commonly live in water. And although great rivers of remarkable sweetness empty into it, the lake gets the better of them by reason of its evil smell, and from its centre it spouts forth once a year a great mass of asphalt,[1] which sometimes extends for more than three plethra, and sometimes for only two; and when this occurs the barbarians who live about the lake usually call the larger flow a " bull " and to the smaller one they give the name " calf." Since the asphalt floats on the surface of the lake, to those who view it from a distance it takes the appearance of an island. And the fact is that the emission of the asphalt is made known to the natives twenty days before it takes place; for to a distance of many stades around the lake the odour, borne on the wind, assails them, and every piece of silver and gold and brass in the locality loses its characteristic lustre. But this returns again as soon as all the asphalt has been spouted forth; and the region round about, by reason of its being exposed to fire and to the evil odours, renders the bodies of the inhabitants susceptible to disease and makes the people very short-lived. Yet the land is good for the growing of palms, wherever it happens to be traversed by rivers with usable water or to be supplied with springs which can irrigate it. And

[1] Asphalt even now occasionally floats ashore from the Dead Sea.

τοὺς τόπους τούτους[1] ἐν αὐλῶνί τινι καὶ τὸ καλούμενον βάλσαμον, ἐξ οὗ πρόσοδον ἁδρὰν[2] λαμβάνουσιν, οὐδαμοῦ μὲν τῆς ἄλλης οἰκουμένης εὑρισκομένου τοῦ φυτοῦ τούτου, τῆς δ' ἐξ αὐτοῦ χρείας εἰς φάρμακα τοῖς ἰατροῖς καθ' ὑπερβολὴν εὐθετούσης.

49. Ἡ δ' ἐχομένη τῆς ἀνύδρου καὶ ἐρήμου χώρας Ἀραβία τοσοῦτο διαφέρει ταύτης ὥστε διὰ τὸ πλῆθος τῶν ἐν αὐτῇ φυομένων καρπῶν τε καὶ τῶν ἄλλων ἀγαθῶν Εὐδαίμονα Ἀραβίαν προσαγορευθῆναι. 2 κάλαμον μὲν γὰρ καὶ σχοῖνον καὶ τὴν ἄλλην ὕλην τὴν ἀρωματίζουσαν πολλὴν φέρει καὶ καθόλου παντοδαπὰς φύλλων εὐωδίας, καὶ τῶν ἀποσταζόντων δακρύων ὀσμαῖς ποικίλαις διείληπται· τήν τε γὰρ σμύρναν καὶ τὸν προσφιλέστατον τοῖς θεοῖς εἴς τε τὴν οἰκουμένην ἅπασαν διαπόμπιμον λιβανωτὸν αἱ ταύτης[3] ἐσχατιαὶ φέρουσι. 3 τοῦ δὲ κόστου καὶ κασίας, ἔτι δὲ κιναμώμου καὶ τῶν ἄλλων τῶν τοιούτων χόρτοι καὶ θάμνοι βαθεῖαι τοσαῦται πεφύκασιν ὥστε τὰ παρὰ τοῖς ἄλλοις σπανίως ἐπὶ βωμοὺς θεῶν τιθέμενα παρ' ἐκείνοις καὶ κλιβάνων ὑπάρχειν ἐκκαύματα, καὶ τὰ παρὰ τοῖς ἄλλοις μικρῷ δείγματι ὑπάρχοντα

---

[1] τούτους omitted by C D F, Vogel; but cp. 19. 98. 4.
[2] ἁδρὰν Vogel, from 19. 98. 4: μικρὰν D, Bekker, who adds οὐ, λαμπρὰν Π, Dindorf.
[3] αἱ ταύτης Reiske: ἀπ' αὐτῆς αἱ ταύτης.

---

[1] The Jordan valley at Jericho.
[2] Strabo (16. 2. 41) briefly describes how the resin, perhaps the Biblical "balm of Gilead," was extracted from this tree.

BOOK II. 48. 9-49. 3

there is also found in these regions in a certain valley [1] the balsam tree, as it is called, from which they receive a substantial revenue, since this tree is found nowhere else in the inhabited world and the use of it for medicinal purposes is most highly valued by physicians.[2]

49.[3] That part of Arabia which borders upon the waterless and desert country is so different from it that, because both of the multitude of fruits which grow therein and of its other good things, it has been called Arabia Felix. For the reed [4] and the rush [5] and every other growth that has a spicy scent are produced in great abundance, as is also, speaking generally, every kind of fragrant substance which is derived from leaves, and the land is distinguished in its several parts by the varied odours of the gums which drip from them; for myrrh and that frankincense which is most dear to the gods and is exported throughout the entire inhabited world are produced in the farthest parts of this land. And *kostos* [6] and *cassia* [7] and cinnamon and all other plants of this nature [8] grow there in fields and thickets of such depth that what all other peoples sparingly place upon the altars of the gods is actually used by them as fuel under their pots, and what is found among all other peoples in small speci-

[3] Chaps. 49–53 are commonly attributed to Posidonius (cp. Jacoby, *FGR HiST.*, No. 87, F 114).
[4] The " sweet reed " (sweet-flag) of Theophrastus, *Enquiry into Plants*, 9. 7. 1, 3 (Vol. 2, pp. 247 f. in *L.C.L.* tr. by Hort).
[5] Ginger-grass; cp. *ibid.*
[6] *Saussurea Lappa*; cp. *ibid.*
[7] *Cinnamomum iners, idem,* 9. 5. 3 (Vol. 2, pp. 243 f. in *L.C.L.*).
[8] *i.e.* aromatic plants.

παρ' ἐκείνοις στιβάδας οἰκετικὰς ἐπὶ τῶν οἰκιῶν παρέχεσθαι. τό τε καλούμενον κινάμωμον διάφορον χρείαν παρεχόμενον καὶ ῥητίνη καὶ τερέβινθος ἄπλατος εὐώδης φύεται περὶ τοὺς τόπους. 4 ἐν δὲ τοῖς ὄρεσιν οὐ μόνον ἐλάτη καὶ πεύκη φύεται δαψιλής, ἀλλὰ καὶ κέδρος καὶ ἄρκευθος ἄπλατος καὶ τὸ καλούμενον βόρατον. πολλαὶ δὲ καὶ ἄλλαι φύσεις εὐώδεις καρποφοροῦσαι τὰς ἀπορροίας καὶ προσπνεύσεις ἔχουσι τοῖς ἐγγίσασι προσηνεστάτας. καὶ γὰρ αὐτὸ τὸ τῆς γῆς ἔχει τι φυσικὸν ἔνατμον καὶ θυμιάμασιν ἡδέσιν ἐοικός. 5 διὸ καὶ κατά τινας τόπους τῆς Ἀραβίας ὀρυττομένης τῆς γῆς εὑρίσκονται φλέβες εὐώδεις, ὧν μεταλλευομένων ἐξαίσιοι τὸ μέγεθος λατομίαι γίνονται· ἐκ δὲ τούτων τὰς οἰκίας συλλέγοντες κατασκευάζουσιν· αἷς ὅταν ἐκ τοῦ περιέχοντος προσπέσωσι ψεκάδες, τὸ διατηκόμενον[1] ὑπὸ[2] τῆς ἰκμάδος συρρεῖ εἰς τὰς ἁρμογὰς τῶν λίθων, καὶ πηγνύμενον συμφυεῖς ἀπεργάζεται τοίχους.

50. Μεταλλεύεται δὲ κατὰ τὴν Ἀραβίαν καὶ ὁ προσαγορευόμενος ἄπυρος χρυσός, οὐχ ὥσπερ παρὰ τοῖς ἄλλοις ἐκ ψηγμάτων καθεψόμενος, ἀλλ' εὐθὺς ὀρυττόμενος εὑρίσκεται τὸ[3] μέγεθος καρύοις κασταναϊκοῖς παραπλήσιος, τὴν δὲ χρόαν οὕτω φλογώδης ὥστε τοὺς ἐντιμοτάτους λίθους ὑπὸ τῶν τεχνιτῶν ἐνδεθέντας ποιεῖν τὰ κάλλιστα

[1] τὸ διατηκόμενον Wesseling: τὸ omitted A D, διὰ τὸ τηκόμενον C F.
[2] ὑπὸ Dindorf: ἀπό.
[3] μὲν after τὸ added by Jacoby.

[1] Turpentine tree; cp. Theophrastus, *ibid.* 3. 15. 3–4 and *passim.*

mens there supplies material for the mattresses of the servants in their homes. Moreover, the cinnamon, as it is called, which is exceptionally useful, and resin of the pine, and the terebinth,[1] are produced in these regions in great abundance and of sweet odour. And in the mountains grow not only silver fir and pine in abundance, but also cedar and the Phoenician cedar [2] in abundance and *boraton*,[3] as it is called. There are also many other kinds of fruit-bearing plants of sweet odour, which yield sap and fragrances most pleasing to such as approach them. Indeed the very earth itself is by its nature full of a vapour which is like sweet incense. Consequently, in certain regions of Arabia, when the earth is dug up, there are discovered veins of sweet odour, in the working of which quarries of extraordinary magnitude are formed; and from these they gather stones and build their houses. And as for their houses, whenever rain drops from the enveloping atmosphere, that part [4] which is melted down by the moisture flows into the joints of the stones and hardening there makes the walls solid throughout.

50. There is also mined in Arabia the gold called "fireless,"[5] which is not smelted from ores, as is done among all other peoples, but is dug out directly from the earth; it is found in nuggets about the size of chestnuts, and is so fiery-red in colour that when it is used by artisans as a setting for the most precious gems it makes the fairest of adornments.

---

[2] These two cedars are distinguished in Theophrastus, *ibid.* 3. 12. 3–4 (Vol. 2, pp. 235 f. in *L.C.L.*).

[3] Juniper.

[4] Presumably, the clay of the roof.

[5] *i.e.* unsmelted.

DIODORUS OF SICILY

2 τῶν κοσμημάτων. θρεμμάτων τε παντοδαπῶν τοσοῦτο κατ' αὐτὴν ὑπάρχει πλῆθος ὥστε ἔθνη πολλὰ νομάδα βίον ᾑρημένα δύνασθαι καλῶς διατρέφεσθαι, σίτου μὲν μὴ προσδεόμενα, τῇ δ' ἀπὸ τούτων δαψιλείᾳ χορηγούμενα. θηρίων τε πλῆθος ἀλκίμων ἡ προσορίζουσα τῇ Συρίᾳ τρέφει· καὶ γὰρ λέοντας καὶ παρδάλεις ἐν αὐτῇ πολλῷ πλείονας καὶ μείζους καὶ ταῖς ἀλκαῖς διαφόρους πεφυκέναι ἤπερ ἐν τῇ Λιβύῃ συμβέβηκε· πρὸς δὲ τούτοις οἱ καλούμενοι Βαβυλώνιοι τίγρεις.

3 φέρει δὲ καὶ ζῷα διφυῆ καὶ μεμιγμένα ταῖς ἰδέαις, ὧν αἱ μὲν ὀνομαζόμεναι στρουθοκάμηλοι περιειλήφασι τοῖς τύποις μίγματα πτηνῶν[1] καὶ καμήλων ἀκολούθως τῇ προσηγορίᾳ. τὸ μὲν γὰρ μέγεθος ἔχουσι νεογενεῖ καμήλῳ παραπλήσιον, τὰς δὲ κεφαλὰς πεφρικυίας[2] θριξὶ λεπταῖς, τοὺς δ' ὀφθαλμοὺς μεγάλους καὶ κατὰ τὴν χρόαν μέλανας, ἀπαραλλάκτους κατὰ τὸν τύπον καὶ τὸ 4 χρῶμα τοῖς τῶν καμήλων. μακροτράχηλον δ' ὑπάρχον ῥύγχος ἔχει βραχὺ παντελῶς καὶ εἰς ὀξὺ συνηγμένον. ἐπτέρωται δὲ ταρσοῖς μαλακῶς[3] τετριχωμένοις, καὶ δυσὶ σκέλεσι στηριζόμενον καὶ ποσὶ διχήλοις χερσαῖον ἅμα φαίνεται καὶ πτηνόν.
5 διὰ δὲ τὸ βάρος οὐ δυνάμενον ἐξᾶραι καὶ πέτεσθαι κατὰ τῆς γῆς ὠκέως ἀκροβατεῖ, καὶ διωκόμενον ὑπὸ τῶν ἱππέων τοῖς ποσὶ τοὺς ὑποπίπτοντας λίθους οὕτως εὐτόνως ἀποσφενδονᾷ πρὸς τοὺς διώκοντας ὥστε πολλάκις καρτεραῖς πληγαῖς

[1] πτηνῶν Rhodomann, Dindorf, Bekker: χηνῶν MSS., Vogel.
[2] πεφρικυίας Cobet: πεφυκυίας.

There is also in the land such a multitude of herds that many tribes which have chosen a nomad life are able to fare right well, experiencing no want of grain but being provided for in abundance by their herds. That part of the country which borders upon Syria breeds a multitude of fierce wild beasts; for the lions and leopards there are far more numerous and larger and superior in ferocity as compared with those of Libya, and in addition to these there are the Babylonian tigers, as they are called. And it produces animals which are of double form and mingled in their natures, to which belong the struthocameli, which, as their name implies, embrace in their form the compound of a bird [1] and of a camel. For in size they are like a newly-born camel, but their heads bristle with fine hair, and their eyes are large and black, indistinguishable in general appearance and colour from those of the camel. It is also long-necked and has a beak which is very short and contracted to a sharp point. And since it has wings with feathers which are covered with a fine hair, and is supported upon two legs and on feet with cloven hoofs, it has the appearance of a land animal as well as of a bird. But being unable by reason of its weight to raise itself in the air and to fly, it swiftly skims over the land, and when pursued by hunters on horseback with its feet it hurls stones as from a sling upon its pursuers, and with such force

---

[1] The MSS. write "of a goose." Oppian, *Cynegetica*, 3. 483, says that the animal was of the nature of a camel and of an "ostrich" (*strouthos*).

---

[3] μαλακῶς suggested by Vogel, adopted by Jacoby: μαλακοῖς.

αὑτοὺς περιπίπτειν. ἐπειδὰν δὲ περικατάληπτον
6 ᾖ, τὴν κεφαλὴν εἴς τινα θάμνον ἢ τοιαύτην
σκέπην ἀποκρύπτεται, οὐχ, ὡς οἴονταί τινες,
ἀφροσύνῃ καὶ νωθρότητι ψυχῆς διὰ τὸ μὴ βλέπειν
ἑτέρους μηδ' αὐτὸ βλέπεσθαι διαλαμβάνον ὑφ'
ἑτέρων, ἀλλὰ διὰ τὸ τοῦ σώματος ἔχειν τοῦτο τὸ
μέρος ἀσθενέστατον σκέπην αὑτῷ[1] πρὸς σωτηρίαν
7 περιποιεῖ· ἀγαθὴ γὰρ ἡ φύσις διδάσκαλος ἅπασι
τοῖς ζῴοις πρὸς διατήρησιν οὐ μόνον ἑαυτῶν,
ἀλλὰ καὶ τῶν γεννωμένων, διὰ τῆς συγγενοῦς
φιλοζωΐας τὰς διαδοχὰς εἰς ἀΐδιον ἄγουσα διαμονῆς
κύκλον.

51. Αἱ δὲ καλούμεναι καμηλοπαρδάλεις τὴν[2]
μίξιν ἀμφοτέρων ἔχουσι τῶν ἐν τῇ προσηγορίᾳ
περιειλημμένων ζῴων. τῷ μὲν γὰρ μεγέθει μικρό-
τεραι τῶν καμήλων εἰσὶ καὶ βραχυτραχηλότεραι,[3]
τὴν δὲ κεφαλὴν καὶ τὴν τῶν ὀμμάτων διάθεσιν
παρδάλει παρεμφερεῖς[4] διατετύπωνται· τὸ δὲ
κατὰ τὴν ῥάχιν κύρτωμα παρεμφερὲς ἔχουσαι
καμήλῳ, τῷ χρώματι καὶ τῇ τριχώσει παρδάλεσιν
ἐοίκασιν· ὁμοίως δὲ καὶ τὴν οὐρὰν μακρὰν ἔχουσαι
2 τὴν τοῦ θηρίου φύσιν ἀποτυποῦνται. γίνονται δὲ
καὶ τραγέλαφοι καὶ βούβαλοι καὶ ἄλλα πλείω γένη
δίμορφα ζῴων καὶ τὴν σύνθεσιν ἐκ τῶν πλεῖστον
τὴν φύσιν κεχωρισμένων ἔχοντα, περὶ ὧν τὰ κατὰ

[1] αὑτῷ Jacoby : αὐτῷ.
[2] μὲν after τὴν deleted by Dindorf.
[3] μακροτραχηλότεραι has been suggested.
[4] παρεμφερεῖς Hertlein : προσεμφερῆ D, προσεμφερεῖ A B, παρεμφερεῖ C.

BOOK II. 50. 5-51. 2

that they often receive severe wounds. And whenever it is overtaken and surrounded, it hides its head in a bush or some such shelter, not, as some men suppose, because of its folly and stupidity of spirit, as if it thought that since it could not see the others it could not itself be seen by others either, but because its head is the weakest part of its body it seeks a shelter for it in order to save its life; for Nature is an excellent instructor of all animals for the preservation not only of their own lives but also of their offspring, since by planting in them an innate love of life she leads successive generations into an eternal cycle of continued existence.

51. The camelopards,[1] as they are called, represent the mixing of the two animals which are included in the name given to it. For in size they are smaller than the camel and have shorter necks,[2] but in the head and the arrangement of the eyes they are formed very much like a leopard; and although they have a hump on the back like the camel, yet with respect to colour and hair they are like leopards; likewise in the possession of a long tail they imitate the nature of this wild beast. There are also bred *tragelaphoi* (goat-stags) and *bubali*[3] and many other varieties of animals which are of double form and combine in one body the natures of creatures most widely different, about all of which it would

[1] "Camel-leopards," or giraffes.
[2] "Longer necks" has been suggested. Agatharchides (*ap.* Photius 455. 4) had said that their necks were so long that they could get their food from the "tops of trees." Giraffes had been exhibited in Alexandria in the third century B.C., and one was brought to Rome by Julius Caesar in 46 B.C. (Dio 43. 23).
[3] Apparently a kind of antelope.

3 μέρος μακρὸν ἂν εἴη γράφειν. δοκεῖ γὰρ ἡ συνεγγίζουσα χώρα τῇ μεσημβρίᾳ τὴν ἀφ' ἡλίου δύναμιν ζωτικωτάτην οὖσαν πολλὴν ἐμπνεῖσθαι, καὶ διὰ τοῦτο πολλῶν καὶ ποικίλων, ἔτι δὲ καλῶν ζῴων
4 φύσεις γεννᾶν· διὰ δὲ τὰς αὐτὰς αἰτίας κατὰ μὲν τὴν Αἴγυπτον τούς τε κροκοδείλους φύεσθαι καὶ τοὺς ποταμίους ἵππους, κατὰ δὲ τὴν Αἰθιοπίαν καὶ τὴν τῆς Λιβύης ἔρημον ἐλεφάντων τε πλῆθος καὶ παντοδαπῶν ὄφεών τε καὶ τῶν ἄλλων θηρίων καὶ δρακόντων ἐξηλλαγμένων τοῖς τε μεγέθεσι καὶ ταῖς ἀλκαῖς, ὁμοίως δὲ καὶ τοὺς περὶ τὴν Ἰνδικὴν ἐλέφαντας, ὑπερβάλλοντας τοῖς τε ὄγκοις καὶ πλήθεσιν, ἔτι δὲ ταῖς ἀλκαῖς.

52. Οὐ μόνον δ' ἐν ταύταις ταῖς χώραις ζῷα γεννᾶται ταῖς ἰδέαις ἐξηλλαγμένα διὰ τὴν ἀφ' ἡλίου συνεργίαν καὶ δύναμιν, ἀλλὰ καὶ λίθων παντοίων ἐκφύσεις διάφοροι ταῖς χρόαις καὶ ταῖς λαμπρότησι
2 διαφανεῖς. τοὺς γὰρ κρυστάλλους λίθους ἔχειν τὴν σύστασιν ἐξ ὕδατος καθαροῦ παγέντος οὐχ ὑπὸ ψύχους, ἀλλ' ὑπὸ θείου πυρὸς δυνάμεως, δι' ἣν ἀσήπτους μὲν αὐτοὺς διαμένειν, βαφῆναι δὲ πολυ-
3 μόρφως ἀναθυμιάσει πνεύματος. σμαράγδους γὰρ καὶ τὰ καλούμενα βηρύλλια κατὰ τὰς ἐν τοῖς χαλκουργείοις μεταλλείας γινόμενα διὰ τὴν ἀπὸ τῶν θείων βαφὴν καὶ σύνδεσιν συγχρώζεσθαι, τοὺς δὲ χρυσολίθους ὑπὸ καπνώδους ἀναθυμιάσεως ἡλίου θερμότητι φυομένους λέγουσι τυγχάνειν
4 τούτου τοῦ χρώματος. διὸ καὶ τοὺς ὀνομαζομένους ψευδοχρύσους κατασκευάζεσθαι διὰ τοῦ θνητοῦ καὶ ὑπ' ἀνθρώπων γεγονότος πυρὸς βαπτο-

---

[1] Perhaps emeralds.

BOOK II. 51. 2–52. 4

be a long task to write in detail. For it would seem that the land which lies to the south breathes in a great deal of the sun's strength, which is the greatest source of life, and that, for that reason, it generates breeds of beautiful animals in great number and of varied colour; and that for the same reason there are produced in Egypt both the crocodiles and the river-horses, in Ethiopia and in the desert of Libya a multitude of elephants and of reptiles of every variety and of all other wild beasts and of serpents, which differ from one another in size and ferocity, and likewise in India the elephants of exceptional bulk and number and ferocity.

52. In these countries are generated not only animals which differ from one another in form because of the helpful influence and strength of the sun, but also outcroppings of every kind of precious stone which are unusual in colour and resplendent in brilliancy. For the rock-crystals, so we are informed, are composed of pure water which has been hardened, not by the action of cold, but by the influence of a divine fire, and for this reason they are never subject to corruption and take on many hues when they are breathed upon. For instance *smaragdi*[1] and *beryllia*,[2] as they are called, which are found in the shafts of the copper mines, receive their colour by having been dipped and bound together in a bath of sulphur, and the chrysoliths,[3] they say, which are produced by a smoky exhalation due to the heat of the sun, thereby get the colour they have. For this reason what is called "false gold," we are told, is fabricated by mortal fire, made

[2] A diminutive of the word beryl.
[3] "Gold-stones," perhaps the topaz.

μένων τῶν κρυστάλλων. τὰς δὲ τῶν ἀνθράκων φύσεις φωτὸς δύναμιν ἐμπιληθεῖσαν τῇ πήξει φασὶν[1] ἀποτελεῖν τῷ μᾶλλον καὶ ἧττον τὰς ἐν αὑτοῖς διαφοράς. παραπλησίως δὲ καὶ τὰς τῶν ὀρνέων μορφὰς ἐπιχρώζεσθαι, τὰς μὲν ὁλοπορφύρους φαινομένας, τὰς δὲ κατὰ μέρος παντοίαις χρόαις διειλημμένας· τὰ μὲν γὰρ φλόγινα, τὰ δὲ κροκώδη, τινὰ δὲ σμαραγδίζοντα, πολλὰ δὲ χρυσοειδῆ φαίνεσθαι κατὰ τὰς πρὸς τὸ φῶς ἐγκλίσεις αὐτῶν, καὶ καθόλου πολυειδεῖς καὶ δυσερμηνεύτους ἀποτελεῖσθαι χρόας· ὅπερ καὶ ἐπὶ τῆς κατ' οὐρανὸν ἴριδος ὁρᾶσθαι γινόμενον ὑπὸ τοῦ περὶ τὸν ἥλιον 6 φωτός. ἐκ δὲ τούτων τοὺς φυσιολόγους συλλογιζομένους ἀποφαίνεσθαι διότι καὶ τὴν ἄνωθεν τῆς τῶν προειρημένων ἐκφύσεως ποικιλίαν ἔβαψεν ἡ συγγενὴς θερμασία, συνεργήσαντος ἡλίου τοῦ 7 ζωοποιοῦντος τὰς ἑκάστων μορφάς. καθόλου δὲ καὶ τῆς περὶ τὰ ἄνθη διαφορᾶς τῆς χρόας καὶ τῆς τῆς γῆς ποικιλίας τοῦτον ὑπάρχειν αἴτιον καὶ δημιουργόν· οὗ τὴν φυσικὴν ἐνέργειαν τὰς θνητὰς τέχνας μιμησαμένας βάπτειν ἕκαστα καὶ ποικίλλειν, 8 μαθητρίας γενομένας τῆς φύσεως. τὰ μὲν γὰρ χρώματα τὸ φῶς ἀπεργάζεσθαι, τὰς δὲ ὀσμὰς τῶν καρπῶν καὶ τὰς ἰδιότητας τῶν χυλῶν, ἔτι δὲ τὰ μεγέθη τῶν ζῴων καὶ τὰς ἑκάστου διαθέσεις, πρὸς δὲ τούτοις τὰς τῆς γῆς ἰδιότητας, γεννᾶν τὴν

[1] φασὶν Rhodomann: φύσιν.

---

[1] Such as carbuncles, rubies, and garnets.

BOOK II. 52. 4–8

by man, by dipping the rock crystals into it. And as for the natural qualities of the dark-red stones,[1] it is the influence of the light, as it is compressed to a greater or less degree in them when they are hardening, which, they say, accounts for their differences. In like manner, it is reported, the different kinds of birds get their colouring, some kinds appearing to the eye as pure red, other kinds marked with colours of every variety one after the other; for some birds are flaming red in appearance, others saffron yellow, some emerald green, and many of the colour of gold when they turn towards the light, and, in brief, hues are produced in great variety and difficult to describe; and this same thing can be seen taking place in the case of the rainbow in the heavens by reason of the light of the sun. And it is from these facts that the students of nature draw their arguments when they affirm that the variety of colouring that is put forth by the things which we have mentioned above was caused by the heat coincident with their creation which dyed them, the sun, which is the source of life, assisting in the production of each several kind. And it is generally true, they continue, that of the differences in the hues of the flowers and of the varied colours of the earth the sun is the cause and creator; and the arts of mortal men, imitating the working of the sun in the physical world, impart colouring and varied hues to every object, having been instructed in this by nature. For the colours, they continue, are produced by the light, and likewise the odours of the fruits and the distinctive quality of their juices, the different sizes of the animals and their several forms, and the peculiarities which the earth shows, all are

περὶ τὸν ἥλιον θερμασίαν, εἰς πολυτραφῆ χώραν καὶ γόνιμον ὕδωρ ἐνθάλπουσαν καὶ δημιουργὸν
9 γινομένην τῆς ἑκάστου φύσεως. διόπερ οὔτε ἡ Παρία λύγδος οὔτ' ἄλλη θαυμαζομένη πέτρα τοῖς Ἀραβίοις λίθοις ἐξισωθῆναι δύναται, ὧν λαμπροτάτη μὲν ἡ λευκότης, βαρύτατος δὲ ὁ σταθμός, ἡ δὲ λειότης ὑπερβολὴν ἑτέροις οὐκ ἀπολείπουσα. αἰτία δὲ τῆς χώρας τῆς κατὰ μέρος ἰδιότητος, καθάπερ προεῖπον, ἡ περὶ τὸν ἥλιον δύναμις, θερμασίᾳ μὲν πήξασα, ξηρότητι δὲ πιλήσασα, φέγγει δὲ λαμπρύνασα.

53. Διὸ καὶ τὸ τῶν ὀρνέων γένος πλείστης θερμασίας κεκοινωνηκὸς ἐγένετο διὰ μὲν τὴν κουφότητα πτηνόν, διὰ δὲ τὴν ἀφ' ἡλίου συνεργίαν ποικίλον, καὶ μάλιστα κατὰ τὰς προσκειμένας[1] ἡλίῳ
2 χώρας. ἡ μὲν γὰρ Βαβυλωνία ταώνων ἐκτρέφει πλῆθος παντοίαις χρόαις ἐπηνθισμένων, αἱ δὲ τῆς Συρίας ἐσχατιαὶ ψιττακοὺς καὶ πορφυρίωνας καὶ μελεαγρίδας καὶ ἄλλας ζῴων ἰδίας φύσεις τοῖς
3 χρώμασι καὶ ποικίλας συγκρίσεις. ὁ δ' αὐτὸς λόγος καὶ κατὰ τὰς ἄλλας χώρας τῆς γῆς τὰς κατὰ τὴν ὁμοίαν κρᾶσιν κειμένας, λέγω δ' Ἰνδικὴν καὶ τὴν Ἐρυθρὰν θάλατταν, ἔτι δὲ Αἰθιοπίαν καὶ
4 τινα μέρη τῆς Λιβύης. ἀλλὰ τῆς μὲν πρὸς ἀνατολὰς κεκλιμένης πιοτέρας οὔσης εὐγενέστερα καὶ μείζονα φύεται ζῷα· τῆς δ' ἄλλης ἀεὶ κατὰ τὸν τῆς ἀρετῆς λόγον ἕκαστα ταῖς διαθέσεσι γεννᾶται.
5 Ὁμοίως δὲ καὶ τῶν δένδρων οἱ φοίνικες κατὰ μὲν

[1] προσκειμένας Jacoby: προκειμένας.

generated by the heat of the sun which imparts its warmth to a fertile land and to water endowed with the generative power and thus becomes the creator of each separate thing as it is. Consequently, neither the white marble of Paros nor any other stone which men admire can be compared with the precious stones of Arabia, since their whiteness is most brilliant, their weight the heaviest, and their smoothness leaves no room for other stones to surpass them. And the cause of the peculiar nature of the several parts of the country is, as I have said, the influence of the sun, which has hardened it by its heat, compressed it by its dryness, and made it resplendent by its light.

53. Hence it is that the race of birds also, having received the most warmth, became flying creatures because of their lightness,[1] and of varied colour because of the influence of the sun, this being especially true in the lands which lie close to the sun. Babylonia, for instance, produces a multitude of peacocks which have blossomed out with colours of every kind, and the farthest parts of Syria produce parrots and purple coots and guinea-fowls and other kinds of animals of distinctive colouring and of every combination of hues. And the same reasoning applies also to all the other countries of the earth which lie in a similar climate, such as India and the Red Sea and Ethiopia and certain parts of Libya. But the eastern part, being more fertile, breeds nobler and larger animals; and as for the rest of Libya, each animal is produced in form and characteristics corresponding to the quality of the soil.

Likewise as regards trees, the palms of Libya bear

[1] Cp. Book 1. 7. 5.

τὴν Λιβύην αὐχμηροὺς καὶ μικροὺς ἐκφέρουσι καρπούς, τῆς δὲ Συρίας κατὰ μὲν τὴν Κοίλην οἱ καρυωτοὶ προσαγορευόμενοι γεννῶνται, διάφοροι κατά τε τὴν γλυκύτητα καὶ τὸ μέγεθος, ἔτι δὲ
6 τοὺς χυμούς. τούτων δὲ πολλῷ μείζους κατὰ τὴν Ἀραβίαν καὶ τὴν Βαβυλωνίαν ὁρᾶν ἔστι γινομένους, κατὰ μὲν τὸ μέγεθος ἓξ δακτύλων ὄντας, τῇ δὲ χρόα τοὺς μὲν μηλίνους, τοὺς δὲ φοινικοῦς, ἐνίους δὲ πορφυρίζοντας· ὥσθ' ὑπ' αὐτῶν ἅμα καὶ τὴν ὄψιν τέρπεσθαι καὶ τὴν γεῦσιν ψυχαγωγεῖσθαι. τὰ δὲ στελέχη τῶν φοινίκων τὸ μὲν μῆκος ἀέριον ἔχει, τὴν δὲ περιφέρειαν ψιλὴν πανταχόθεν
7 μέχρι τῆς κορυφῆς. ἀκρόκομα δ' ὄντα διαφόρους ἔχει τὰς ἀπὸ τῆς κόμης διαθέσεις· τὰ μὲν γὰρ πάντῃ τοὺς ῥάδικας ἔχει περικεχυμένους, καὶ κατὰ μέσον ἔκ τινος περιρραγέντος φλοιοῦ βοτρυώδη καρπὸν ἀνίησι, τὰ δὲ ἐφ' ἓν μέρος ἔχοντα κεκλιμένας τὰς ἐπὶ τῆς κορυφῆς κόμας σχηματισμὸν ἀποτελεῖ λαμπάδος ἀπαιθυσσομένης, ἔνια δ' ἐπ' ἀμφότερα τὰ μέρη περικλώμενα καὶ διπλῇ τῇ καταθέσει τῶν κλάδων ἀμφίχαιτα γινόμενα γραφικὴν ἀποτελεῖ τὴν πρόσοψιν.

54. Τῆς δ' ὅλης Ἀραβίας τὴν μὲν ἐπὶ μεσημβρίαν νεύουσαν Εὐδαίμονα προσαγορεύουσι, τὴν δ' ἐνδοτέρω κειμένην νέμεται πλῆθος Ἀράβων νομάδων καὶ σκηνίτην βίον ᾑρημένων. οὗτοι δὲ θρεμματοτροφοῦντες ἀγέλας μεγάλας βοσκημάτων ἐναυλίζονται
2 πεδίοις ἀμετρήτοις. ἡ δ' ἀνὰ μέσον ταύτης τε καὶ τῆς Εὐδαίμονος Ἀραβίας ἔρημος καὶ ἄνυδρός ἐστι, καθάπερ προείρηται· τὰ δὲ πρὸς δυσμὰς μέρη

---

[1] *i.e.* at the side. The lamp of Diodorus' period had its

dry and small fruit, but in Coele-Syria dates called *caryoti* are produced which excel as to both sweetness and size and also as to their juices. But dates much larger than these can be seen growing in Arabia and Babylonia, six fingers in size and in colour either yellow like the quince, or dark red, or in some cases tending to purple, so that at the same time they both delight the eye and gratify the taste. The trunk of the palm stretches high in the air and its surface is smooth all over as far as its crown. But though they all have a tuft of foliage at the top, yet the arrangement of the foliage varies; for in some cases the fronds spread out in a complete circle and from the centre the trunk sends up, as if from out its broken bark, the fruit in a cluster like grapes, in other cases the foliage at the crown droops down on only one side so that it produces the appearance of a lamp from which the flame flares out,[1] and occasionally they have their fronds bent down on both sides and by this double arrangement of the branches show a crown of foliage all about the trunk, thus presenting a picturesque appearance.

54. That part of Arabia as a whole which lies to the south is called Felix, but the interior part is ranged over by a multitude of Arabians who are nomads and have chosen a tent life. These raise great flocks of animals and make their camps in plains of immeasurable extent. The region which lies between this part and Arabia Felix is desert and waterless, as has been stated[2]; and the parts of Arabia which lie to

nozzle on the side opposite the handle, and so the comparison is apt.

[2] Cp. chap. 48.

κεκλιμένα τῆς Ἀραβίας διείληπται πεδίοις ἀμμώδεσιν ἀερίοις τὸ μέγεθος, δι' ὧν οἱ τὰς ὁδοιπορίας ποιούμενοι καθάπερ οἱ ἐν τοῖς πελάγεσι πρὸς τὰς ἀπὸ τῶν ἄρκτων σημασίας τὴν διέξοδον 3 ποιοῦνται. τὸ δ' ὑπολειπόμενον μέρος τῆς Ἀραβίας τὸ πρὸς τὴν Συρίαν κεκλιμένον πλήθει γεωργῶν καὶ παντοδαπῶν ἐμπόρων, οἳ διὰ τὰς τῶν φορτίων εὐκαίρους ἀντιδόσεις τὰ παρ' ἀμφοτέροις σπανίζοντα πρὸς δαψίλειαν τῶν χρησίμων 4 διορθοῦνται. ἡ δὲ παρὰ τὸν ὠκεανὸν Ἀραβία κεῖται μὲν ὑπεράνω τῆς Εὐδαίμονος, ποταμοῖς δὲ πολλοῖς καὶ μεγάλοις διειλημμένη πολλοὺς ποιεῖ τόπους λιμνάζοντας καὶ μεγάλων ἑλῶν 5 περιμέτρους. τοῖς δ' ἐκ τῶν ποταμῶν ἐπακτοῖς ὕδασι καὶ τοῖς ἐκ τῶν θερινῶν ὄμβρων γινομένοις ἀρδεύοντες πολλὴν χώραν, καὶ διπλοῦς καρποὺς λαμβάνουσι. τρέφει δὲ ὁ τόπος οὗτος ἐλεφάντων ἀγέλας καὶ ἄλλα ζῷα κητώδη χερσαῖα[1] καὶ δίμορφα, ταῖς ἰδέαις ἐξηλλαγμένα· πρὸς δὲ τούτοις θρεμμάτων παντοδαπῶν πληθύει, καὶ μάλιστα βοῶν καὶ προβάτων τῶν τὰς μεγάλας καὶ παχείας ἐχόντων οὐράς.

6 Πλεῖστα δὲ καὶ διαφορώτατα γένη καμήλων τρέφει, τῶν τε ψιλῶν καὶ δασέων καὶ διπλοῦν ἀνατετακότων τὸ κατὰ τὴν ῥάχιν κύρτωμα καὶ διὰ τοῦτο διτύλων ὀνομαζομένων, ὧν αἱ μὲν γάλα παρεχόμεναι καὶ κρεοφαγούμεναι πολλὴν παρέχονται τοῖς ἐγχωρίοις δαψίλειαν, αἱ δὲ πρὸς νωτοφορίαν ἠσκημέναι πυρῶν μὲν ἀνὰ δέκα μεδίμνους νωτοφοροῦσιν, ἀνθρώπους δὲ κατακει-

[1] θηρία after χερσαῖα omitted by E.

BOOK II. 54. 2-6

the west are broken by sandy deserts spacious as the air in magnitude, through which those who journey must, even as voyagers upon the seas, direct their course by indications obtained from the Bears. The remaining part of Arabia, which lies towards Syria, contains a multitude of farmers and merchants of every kind, who by a seasonable exchange of merchandise make good the lack of certain wares in both countries by supplying useful things which they possess in abundance. That Arabia which lies along the ocean is situated above Arabia Felix, and since it is traversed by many great rivers, many regions in it are converted into stagnant pools and into vast stretches of great swamps. And with the water which is brought into them from the rivers and that which comes with the summer rains they irrigate a large part of the country and get two crops yearly. This region also breeds herds of elephants and other monstrous land animals, and animals of double shape which have developed peculiar forms; and in addition to these it abounds in domestic animals of every kind, especially in cattle and in the sheep with large and fat tails.

This land also breeds camels in very great numbers and of most different kinds, both the hairless and the shaggy, and those which have two humps, one behind the other, along their spines and hence are called *dituloi*.[1] Some of these provide milk and are eaten for meat, and so provide the inhabitants with a great abundance of this food, and others, which are trained to carry burdens on their backs, can carry some ten *medimni*[2] of wheat and bear up five

---

[1] "Double-humped" or "double-knobbed."
[2] About 14½ bushels, or 900 pounds.

μένους ἐπὶ κλίνης πέντε βαστάζουσιν· αἱ δὲ ἀνάκωλοι καὶ λαγαραὶ ταῖς συστάσεσι δρομάδες εἰσί, καὶ διατείνουσι πλεῖστον ὁδοῦ μῆκος, καὶ μάλιστα πρὸς τὰς διὰ τῆς ἀνύδρου καὶ ἐρήμου 7 συντελουμένας ὁδοιπορίας. αἱ δ' αὐταὶ καὶ κατὰ τοὺς πολέμους εἰς τὰς μάχας ἔχουσαι τοξότας ἄγονται δύο ἀντικαθημένους ἀλλήλοις ἀντινώτους· τούτων δὲ ὁ μὲν τοὺς κατὰ πρόσωπον ἀπαντῶντας, ὁ δὲ τοὺς ἐπιδιώκοντας ἀμύνεται.

Περὶ μὲν οὖν τῆς Ἀραβίας καὶ τῶν ἐν αὐτῇ φυομένων εἰ καὶ πεπλεονάκαμεν, ἀλλ' οὖν πολλὰ τοῖς φιλαναγνωστοῦσι πρὸς φιληκοΐαν ἀπηγγέλκαμεν.

55. Περὶ δὲ τῆς κατὰ τὸν ὠκεανὸν εὑρεθείσης νήσου κατὰ τὴν μεσημβρίαν καὶ τῶν κατ' αὐτὴν παραδοξολογουμένων πειρασόμεθα συντόμως διελθεῖν, προεκθέμενοι τὰς αἰτίας τῆς εὑρέσεως ἀκριβῶς. 2 Ἰαμβοῦλος ἦν ἐκ παίδων παιδείαν ἐζηλωκώς, μετὰ δὲ τὴν τοῦ πατρὸς τελευτὴν ὄντος ἐμπόρου καὶ αὐτὸς ἔδωκεν ἑαυτὸν ἐπὶ τὴν ἐμπορίαν· ἀναβαίνων δὲ[1] τῆς Ἀραβίας ἐπὶ τὴν ἀρωματοφόρον ὑπό τινων λῃστῶν συνελήφθη μετὰ τῶν συνοδοιπόρων. τὸ μὲν οὖν πρῶτον μετά τινος τῶν συνεαλωκότων ἀπεδείχθη νομεύς, ὕστερον δ' ὑπό τινων Αἰθιόπων μετὰ τοῦ συνόντος λῃστευθεὶς ἀπήχθη πρὸς τὴν 3 παραθαλάττιον τῆς Αἰθιοπίας. οὗτοι δὲ συνηρπά-

[1] διὰ after δὲ deleted by Kallenberg.

---

[1] Perhaps Ceylon, if the unknown writer of the following account of a fabulous people and a political Utopia localized it in any known spot.

BOOK II. 54. 6–55. 3

men lying outstretched upon a couch. Others which have short legs and are slender in build are dromedaries and can go at full stretch a day's journey of a very great distance, especially in the trips which they make through the waterless and desert region. And also in their wars the same animals carry into battle two bowmen who ride back to back to each other, one of them keeping off enemies who come on them from in front, the other those who pursue in the rear.

With regard, then, to Arabia and the products of that land, even if we have written at too great length, we have at any rate reported many things to delight lovers of reading.

55. But with regard to the island [1] which has been discovered in the ocean to the south and the marvellous tales told concerning it, we shall now endeavour to give a brief account, after we have first set forth accurately the causes which led to its discovery. There was a certain Iambulus [2] who from his boyhood up had been devoted to the pursuit of education, and after the death of his father, who had been a merchant, he also gave himself to that calling; and while journeying inland to the spice-bearing region of Arabia [3] he and his companions on the trip were taken captive by some robbers. Now at first he and one of his fellow-captives were appointed to be herdsmen, but later he and his companion were made captive by certain Ethiopians and led off to the coast of Ethiopia. They were kid-

[2] Perhaps the author of the following account, which is known only from this passage.

[3] The "spice-bearing country" was usually placed in Somaliland, but according to Strabo (1. 2. 32) it is in Arabia, where Diodorus also apparently places it.

γησαν εἰς καθαρμὸν τῆς χώρας, ὄντες ἀλλοεθνεῖς. νόμιμον γὰρ ἦν τοῖς τῇδε κατοικοῦσιν Αἰθίοψι παραδεδομένον ἐκ παλαιῶν χρόνων, χρησμοῖς θεῶν κεκυρωμένον, διὰ γενεῶν μὲν εἴκοσι, ἐτῶν δ' ἑξακοσίων, τῆς γενεᾶς ἀριθμουμένης τριακονταετοῦς· τοῦ δὲ καθαρμοῦ γινομένου δυσὶν ἀνθρώποις ἦν αὐτοῖς πλοιάριον κατεσκευασμένον τῷ μεγέθει σύμμετρον, τούς τ' ἐν τῇ θαλάττῃ χειμῶνας ἀναφέρειν ἰσχῦον καὶ ῥᾳδίως ὑπὸ δυοῖν ἀνθρώπων ὑπηρετεῖσθαι δυνάμενον· εἰς δὲ τοῦτο τροφὴν δυσὶν ἀνθρώποις ἱκανὴν εἰς ἓξ μῆνας ἐνθέμενοι, καὶ τοὺς ἄνδρας ἐμβιβάσαντες, προσέταττον ἀνάγεσθαι κατὰ τὸν χρησμόν. πλεῖν δὲ διεκελεύοντο πρὸς τὴν 4 μεσημβρίαν· ἥξειν γὰρ αὐτοὺς εἰς νῆσον εὐδαίμονα καὶ ἐπιεικεῖς ἀνθρώπους, παρ' οἷς μακαρίως ζήσεσθαι. ὁμοίως δὲ καὶ τὸ ἑαυτῶν ἔθνος ἔφασαν, ἐὰν μὲν οἱ πεμφθέντες εἰς τὴν νῆσον διασωθῶσιν, ἑξακοσίων ἐτῶν εἰρήνης καὶ βίου κατὰ πᾶν εὐδαίμονος ἀπολαύσειν· εἰ δὲ καταπλαγέντες τὸ μῆκος τοῦ πελάγους εἰς τοὐπίσω ποιήσονται τὸν πλοῦν, ὡς ἀσεβεῖς καὶ λυμεῶνας ὅλου τοῦ ἔθνους 5 τιμωρίαις περιπεσεῖσθαι ταῖς μεγίσταις. τοὺς μὲν οὖν Αἰθίοπάς φασι μεγάλην πανήγυριν ἀγαγεῖν παρὰ τὴν θάλατταν, καὶ θυσίας μεγαλοπρεπεῖς ἐπιτελέσαντας καταστέψαι τοὺς σκεψομένους καὶ καθαρμὸν ποιησομένους τοῦ ἔθνους ἐξαποστεῖλαι. 6 τούτους δὲ πλεύσαντας πέλαγος μέγα καὶ χειμασθέντας ἐν μησὶ τέτταρσι προσενεχθῆναι τῇ προση-

BOOK II. 55. 3–6

napped in order that, being of an alien people, they might effect the purification of the land. For among the Ethiopians who lived in that place there was a custom, which had been handed down from ancient times, and had been ratified by oracles of the gods, over a period of twenty generations or six hundred years, the generation being reckoned at thirty years; and at the time when the purification by means of the two men was to take place, a boat had been built for them sufficient in size and strong enough to withstand the storms at sea, one which could easily be manned by two men; and then loading it with food enough to maintain two men for six months and putting them on board they commanded them to set out to sea as the oracle had ordered. Furthermore, they commanded them to steer towards the south; for, they were told, they would come to a happy island and to men of honourable character, and among them they would lead a blessed existence. And in like manner, they stated, their own people, in case the men whom they sent forth should arrive safely at the island, would enjoy peace and a happy life in every respect throughout six hundred years; but if, dismayed at the extent of the sea, they should turn back on their course they would, as impious men and destroyers of the entire nation, suffer the severest penalties. Accordingly, the Ethiopians, they say, held a great festal assembly by the sea, and after offering costly sacrifices they crowned with flowers the men who were to seek out the island and effect the purification of the nation and then sent them forth. And these men, after having sailed over a vast sea and been tossed about four months by storms, were carried to the island

μανθείσῃ νήσῳ, στρογγύλῃ μὲν ὑπαρχούσῃ τῷ σχήματι, τὴν δὲ περίμετρον ἐχούσῃ σταδίων ὡς πεντακισχιλίων.

56. Ἤδη δ' αὐτῶν ἐγγιζόντων τῇ νήσῳ τῶν ἐγχωρίων τινὰς ἀπαντήσαντας καταγαγεῖν τὸ σκάφος· τοὺς δὲ κατὰ τὴν νῆσον συνδραμόντας θαυμάζειν μὲν τὸν τῶν ξένων κατάπλουν, προσενεχθῆναι δὲ αὐτοῖς ἐπιεικῶς καὶ μεταδιδόναι τῶν παρ' αὐτοῖς 2 χρησίμων. εἶναι δὲ τοὺς τὴν νῆσον οἰκοῦντας ταῖς τε τῶν σωμάτων ἰδιότησι καὶ ταῖς ἀγωγαῖς πολὺ διαλλάττοντας τῶν κατὰ τὴν ἡμετέραν οἰκουμένην· πάντας μὲν γὰρ παραπλησίους εἶναι τοῖς ἀναπλάσμασι τῶν σωμάτων, καὶ κατὰ τὸ μέγεθος ὑπεράγειν τοὺς τέτταρας πήχεις, τὰ δὲ ὀστᾶ τοῦ σώματος ἔχειν ἐπὶ ποσὸν καμπτόμενα καὶ πάλιν ἀποκαθιστάμενα παραπλησίως τοῖς 3 νευρώδεσι τόποις. εἶναι δὲ τοῖς σώμασιν ἁπαλοὺς μὲν καθ' ὑπερβολήν, εὐτονωτέρους δὲ πολὺ τῶν παρ' ἡμῖν· δραξαμένων γὰρ αὐτῶν ταῖς χερσὶν ὁδηποτοῦν μηδένα δύνασθαι τὸ τοῖς δακτύλοις περιληφθὲν ἐκτρέψαι. τρίχας δ' ἁπλῶς μηδαμῇ τοῦ σώματος ἔχειν πλὴν ἐν τῇ κεφαλῇ καὶ ὀφρύσι καὶ βλεφάροις, ἔτι δὲ καὶ πώγωνι, τὰ δὲ ἄλλα μέρη τοῦ σώματος οὕτω λεῖα ὥστε μηδὲ τὸν ἐλάχιστον 4 χνοῦν ἐν τῷ σώματι φαίνεσθαι. εἶναι δὲ καὶ τῷ κάλλει διαπρεπεῖς καὶ ταῖς ἄλλαις περιγραφαῖς τοῦ σώματος εὐρύθμους. καὶ τὰ μὲν τῆς ἀκοῆς τρήματα πολὺ τῶν παρ' ἡμῖν ἔχειν εὐρυχωρέστερα, καὶ καθάπερ ἐπιγλωττίδας αὐτοῖς ἐκπεφυκέναι. 5 ἴδιον δέ τι καὶ περὶ τὴν γλῶτταν αὐτοὺς ἔχειν, τὸ μὲν φυσικῶς αὐτοῖς συγγεγενημένον, τὸ δ' ἐξ ἐπινοίας φιλοτεχνούμενον· δίπτυχον μὲν γὰρ αὐτοὺς

BOOK II. 55. 6–56. 5

about which they had been informed beforehand; it was round in shape and had a circumference of about five thousand stades.

56. But when they were now drawing near to the island, the account proceeds, some of the natives met them and drew their boat to land; and the inhabitants of the island, thronging together, were astonished at the arrival of the strangers, but they treated them honourably and shared with them the necessities of life which their country afforded. The dwellers upon this island differ greatly both in the characteristics of their bodies and in their manners from the men in our part of the inhabited world; for they are all nearly alike in the shape of their bodies and are over four cubits in height, but the bones of the body have the ability to bend to a certain extent and then straighten out again, like the sinewy parts. They are also exceedingly tender in respect to their bodies and yet more vigorous than is the case among us; for when they have seized any object in their hands no man can extract it from the grasp of their fingers. There is absolutely no hair on any part of their bodies except on the head, eyebrows and eyelids, and on the chin, but the other parts of the body are so smooth that not even the least down can be seen on them. They are also remarkably beautiful and well-proportioned in the outline of the body. The openings of their ears are much more spacious than ours and growths have developed that serve as valves, so to speak, to close them. And they have a peculiarity in regard to the tongue, partly the work of nature and congenital with them and partly intentionally brought about by artifice; among them, namely, the tongue

ἔχειν τὴν γλῶτταν ἐπὶ ποσόν, τὰ δ' ἐνδοτέρω προσδιαιρεῖν,[1] ὥστε διπλῆν αὐτὴν γίνεσθα ιμέχρι
6 τῆς ῥίζης. διὸ καὶ ποικιλωτάτους αὐτοὺς εἶναι[2] ταῖς φωναῖς οὐ μόνον πᾶσαν ἀνθρωπίνην καὶ διηρθρωμένην διάλεκτον μιμουμένους, ἀλλὰ καὶ τὰς τῶν ὀρνέων πολυφωνίας, καὶ καθόλου πᾶσαν ἤχου ἰδιότητα προΐεσθαι· τὸ δὲ πάντων παραδοξότατον, ἅμα πρὸς δύο τῶν ἐντυγχανόντων λαλεῖν ἐντελῶς, ἀποκρινομένους τε καὶ ταῖς ὑποκειμέναις περιστάσεσιν οἰκείως ὁμιλοῦντας· τῇ μὲν γὰρ ἑτέρᾳ πτυχὶ πρὸς τὸν ἕνα, τῇ δ' ἄλλῃ πάλιν ὁμοίως πρὸς τὸν ἕτερον διαλέγεσθαι.

7 Εὐκρατότατον δ' εἶναι τὸν ἀέρα παρ' αὐτοῖς, ὡς ἂν κατὰ τὸν ἰσημερινὸν οἰκοῦντας, καὶ μήθ' ὑπὸ καύματος μήθ' ὑπὸ ψύχους ἐνοχλουμένους. καὶ τὰς ὀπώρας δὲ παρ' αὐτοῖς παρ' ὅλον τὸν ἐνιαυτὸν ἀκμάζειν, ὥσπερ καὶ ὁ ποιητής φησιν

ὄχνη ἐπ' ὄχνῃ γηράσκει, μῆλον δ' ἐπὶ μήλῳ,
αὐτὰρ ἐπὶ σταφυλῇ σταφυλή, σῦκον δ' ἐπὶ σύκῳ.

εἶναι δὲ διὰ παντὸς παρ' αὐτοῖς τὴν ἡμέραν ἴσην τῇ νυκτί, καὶ κατὰ τὸ μέσον τῆς ἡμέρας μὴ γίνεσθαι παρ' αὐτοῖς σκιὰν μηδενὸς διὰ τὸ κατὰ κορυφὴν εἶναι τὸν ἥλιον.

57. Βιοῦν δ' αὐτοὺς κατὰ συγγενείας καὶ συστήματα, συνηγμένων τῶν οἰκείων οὐ πλειόνων ἢ τετρακοσίων· τούτους δ' ἐν τοῖς λειμῶσι διαζῆν, πολλὰ τῆς χώρας ἐχούσης πρὸς διατροφήν· διὰ γὰρ τὴν

---

[1] προσδιαιρεῖν Schäfer: πρὸς διαίρεσιν.
[2] καὶ after εἶναι deleted by Dindorf.

is double for a certain distance, but they divide the inner portions still further, with the result that it becomes a double tongue as far as its base. Consequently they are very versatile as to the sounds they can utter, since they imitate not only every articulate language used by man but also the varied chatterings of the birds, and, in general, they can reproduce any peculiarity of sound. And the most remarkable thing of all is that at one and the same time they can converse perfectly with two persons who fall in with them, both answering questions and discoursing pertinently on the circumstances of the moment; for with one division of the tongue they can converse with the one person, and likewise with the other talk with the second.

Their climate is most temperate, we are told, considering that they live at the equator, and they suffer neither from heat nor from cold. Moreover, the fruits in their island ripen throughout the entire year, even as the poet writes,[1]

> Here pear on pear grows old, and apple close
> On apple, yea, and clustered grapes on grapes,
> And fig on fig.

And with them the day is always the same length as the night, and at midday no shadow is cast of any object because the sun is in the zenith.

57. These islanders, they go on to say, live in groups which are based on kinship and on political organizations, no more than four hundred kinsmen being gathered together in this way; and the members spend their time in the meadows, the land supplying them with many things for sustenance;

[1] *Odyssey*, 7. 120-21, describing the land of the Phaeacians.

ἀρετὴν τῆς νήσου καὶ τὴν εὐκρασίαν τοῦ ἀέρος γεννᾶσθαι τροφὰς αὐτομάτους πλείους τῶν ἱκανῶν.
2 φύεσθαι γὰρ παρ' αὐτοῖς κάλαμον πολύν, φέροντα καρπὸν δαψιλῆ, παρεμφερῆ τοῖς λευκοῖς ὀρόβοις. τοῦτον οὖν συναγαγόντες βρέχουσιν ἐν ὕδατι θερμῷ, μέχρι ἂν τὸ μέγεθος σχῶσιν ὡς ᾠοῦ περιστερᾶς· ἔπειτα συνθλάσαντες καὶ τρίψαντες ἐμπείρως ταῖς χερσὶ διαπλάττουσιν ἄρτους, οὓς ὀπτήσαντες σιτοῦνται διαφόρους ὄντας τῇ γλυ-
3 κύτητι. εἶναι δὲ καὶ πηγὰς ὑδάτων δαψιλεῖς, τὰς μὲν θερμῶν εἰς λουτρὰ καὶ κόπων ἀφαίρεσιν εὐθέτους, τὰς δὲ ψυχρῶν τῇ γλυκύτητι διαφόρους καὶ πρὸς ὑγίειαν συνεργεῖν δυναμένας. ὑπάρχειν δὲ παρ' αὐτοῖς καὶ παιδείας πάσης ἐπιμέλειαν, μάλιστα
4 δὲ ἀστρολογίας· γράμμασί τε αὐτοὺς χρῆσθαι κατὰ μὲν τὴν δύναμιν τῶν σημαινόντων εἴκοσι καὶ ὀκτὼ τὸν ἀριθμόν, κατὰ δὲ τοὺς χαρακτῆρας ἑπτά, ὧν ἕκαστον τετραχῶς μετασχηματίζεσθαι. γράφουσι δὲ τοὺς στίχους οὐκ εἰς τὸ πλάγιον ἐκτείνοντες, ὥσπερ ἡμεῖς, ἀλλ' ἄνωθεν κάτω καταγράφοντες εἰς ὀρθόν.[1] πολυχρονίους δ' εἶναι τοὺς ἀνθρώπους καθ' ὑπερβολήν, ὡς ἂν ἄχρι πεντήκοντα καὶ ἑκατὸν ἐτῶν ζῶντας καὶ γινομένους
5 ἀνόσους κατὰ τὸ πλεῖστον. τὸν δὲ πηρωθέντα ἢ καθόλου τι ἐλάττωμα ἔχοντα ἐν τῷ σώματι μεθιστάνειν ἑαυτὸν ἐκ τοῦ ζῆν ἀναγκάζουσι κατά τινα νόμον ἀπότομον. νόμιμον δ' αὐτοῖς ἐστι ζῆν ἄχρι ἐτῶν ὡρισμένων, καὶ τὸν χρόνον τοῦτον

---

[1] ὀρθὸν transposed by Wesseling: after ἀπότομον in second sentence below.

for by reason of the fertility of the island and the mildness of the climate, food-stuffs are produced of themselves in greater quantity than is sufficient for their needs. For instance, a reed grows there in abundance, and bears a fruit in great plenty that is very similar to the white vetch.[1] Now when they have gathered this they steep it in warm water until it has become about the size of a pigeon's egg; then after they have crushed it and rubbed[2] it skilfully with their hands, they mould it into loaves, which are baked and eaten, and they are of surprising sweetness. There are also in the island, they say, abundant springs of water, the warm springs serving well for bathing and the relief of fatigue, the cold excelling in sweetness and possessing the power to contribute to good health. Moreover, the inhabitants give attention to every branch of learning and especially to astrology; and they use letters which, according to the value of the sounds they represent, are twenty-eight in number, but the characters are only seven, each one of which can be formed in four different ways. Nor do they write their lines horizontally, as we do, but from the top to the bottom perpendicularly. And the inhabitants, they tell us, are extremely long-lived, living even to the age of one hundred and fifty years, and experiencing for the most part no illness. Anyone also among them who has become crippled or suffers, in general, from any physical infirmity is forced by them, in accordance with an inexorable law, to remove himself from life. And there is also a law among them that they should live only for a stipulated number of

---

[1] Possibly a reference to rice.
[2] In order to remove the husk.

ἐκπληρώσαντας ἑκουσίως μεταλλάττειν ἐξηλλαγμένῳ θανάτῳ· φύεσθαι γὰρ παρ' αὐτοῖς ἰδιοφυῆ[1] βοτάνην, ἐφ' ἧς ὅταν τις κοιμηθῇ, λεληθότως καὶ προσηνῶς εἰς ὕπνον κατενεχθεὶς ἀποθνῄσκει.

58. Γυναῖκας δὲ μὴ γαμεῖν, ἀλλὰ κοινὰς ἔχειν, καὶ τοὺς γεννηθέντας παῖδας ὡς κοινοὺς τρέφοντας ἐπ' ἴσης ἀγαπᾶν· νηπίων δ' ὄντων αὐτῶν πολλάκις τὰς τρεφούσας διαλλάττειν τὰ βρέφη, ὅπως μηδ' αἱ μητέρες ἐπιγινώσκωσι τοὺς ἰδίους. διόπερ μηδεμιᾶς παρ' αὐτοῖς γινομένης φιλοτιμίας ἀστασιάστους καὶ τὴν ὁμόνοιαν περὶ πλείστου ποιουμένους διατελεῖν.

2 Εἶναι δὲ παρ' αὐτοῖς καὶ ζῷα, μικρὰ μὲν τοῖς μεγέθεσι, παράδοξα δὲ τῇ φύσει τοῦ σώματος καὶ τῇ δυνάμει τοῦ αἵματος· εἶναι γὰρ αὐτὰ τῷ σχήματι στρογγύλα καὶ παρεμφερέστατα ταῖς χελώναις, τὴν δ' ἐπιφάνειαν δυσὶ γραμμαῖς μηλίναις κεχιασμένα, ἐφ' ἑκάστης δὲ ἄκρας ἔχειν 3 ὀφθαλμὸν καὶ στόμα· διὸ καὶ τέτταρσιν ὄμμασι βλέποντα καὶ τοῖς ἴσοις στόμασι χρώμενα εἰς ἕνα φάρυγα συνάγειν τὰ σιτία, καὶ διὰ τούτου καταπινομένης τῆς τροφῆς εἰς μίαν κοιλίαν συρρεῖν ἅπαντα· ὁμοίως δὲ τὰ σπλάγχνα καὶ τἄλλα τὰ ἐντὸς πάντα ἔχειν μοναχά. πόδας δὲ ὑποκεῖσθαι κύκλῳ τῆς περιφερείας πολλούς, δι' ὧν δύνασθαι πορεύεσθαι 4 πρὸς ὃ ἂν μέρος βούληται. τὸ δ' αἷμα τούτου τοῦ ζῴου θαυμάσιον ἔχειν δύναμιν· πᾶν γὰρ τὸ διατμηθὲν ἔμπνουν σῶμα κολλᾶν παραχρῆμα, κἂν

[1] ἰδιοφυῆ Dindorf: διφυῆ.

---

[1] Plato's famous theory recurs here.

years, and that at the completion of this period they should make away with themselves of their own accord, by a strange manner of death; for there grows among them a plant of a peculiar nature, and whenever a man lies down upon it, imperceptibly and gently he falls asleep and dies.

58. They do not marry, we are told, but possess their children in common, and maintaining the children who are born as if they belonged to all, they love them equally [1]; and while the children are infants those who suckle the babes [2] often change them around in order that not even the mothers may know their own offspring. Consequently, since there is no rivalry among them, they never experience civil disorders and they never cease placing the highest value upon internal harmony.

There are also animals among them, we are told, which are small in size but the object of wonder by reason of the nature of their bodies and the potency of their blood; for they are round in form and very similar to tortoises, but they are marked on the surface by two diagonal yellow stripes, at each end of which they have an eye and a mouth; consequently, though seeing with four eyes and using as many mouths, yet it gathers its food into one gullet, and down this its nourishment is swallowed and all flows together into one stomach; and in like manner its other organs and all its inner parts are single. It also has beneath it all around its body many feet, by means of which it can move in whatever direction it pleases. And the blood of this animal, they say, has a marvellous potency; for it immediately glues on to its place any living member that has been

[2] *i.e.* the wet-nurses of the community.

ἀποκοπεῖσα χεὶρ ἢ ὅμοιον εἰπεῖν τύχῃ, δι' αὐτοῦ κολλᾶσθαι προσφάτου τῆς τομῆς οὔσης, καὶ τἄλλα δὲ μέρη τοῦ σώματος, ὅσα μὴ κυρίοις τόποις
5 καὶ συνέχουσι τὸ ζῆν κατέχεται. ἕκαστον δὲ τῶν συστημάτων τρέφειν ὄρνεον εὐμέγεθες ἰδιάζον τῇ φύσει, καὶ διὰ τούτου πειράζεται τὰ νήπια τῶν βρεφῶν ποίας τινὰς ἔχει τὰς τῆς ψυχῆς διαθέσεις· ἀναλαμβάνουσι γὰρ αὐτὰ ἐπὶ τὰ ζῷα, καὶ τούτων πετομένων τὰ μὲν τὴν διὰ τοῦ ἀέρος φορὰν ὑπομένοντα τρέφουσι, τὰ δὲ περιναύτια γινόμενα καὶ θάμβους πληρούμενα ῥίπτουσιν, ὡς οὔτε πολυχρόνια καθεστῶτα οὔτε τοῖς ἄλλοις τοῖς τῆς ψυχῆς λήμασιν ἀξιόλογα.
6 Ἑκάστου δὲ συστήματος ὁ πρεσβύτερος ἀεὶ τὴν ἡγεμονίαν ἔχει, καθάπερ τις βασιλεύς, καὶ τούτῳ πάντες πείθονται· ὅταν δ' ὁ πρῶτος τελέσας τὰ ἑκατὸν καὶ πεντήκοντα ἔτη κατὰ τὸν νόμον ἀπαλλάξῃ ἑαυτὸν τοῦ ζῆν, ὁ μετὰ τοῦτον πρεσβύ-
7 τατος διαδέχεται τὴν ἡγεμονίαν. ἡ δὲ περὶ τὴν νῆσον θάλαττα, ῥοώδης οὖσα καὶ μεγάλας ἀμπώτεις καὶ πλημύρας ποιουμένη, γλυκεῖα τὴν γεῦσιν καθέστηκε. τῶν δὲ παρ' ἡμῖν ἄστρων τὰς ἄρκτους καὶ πολλὰ[1] καθόλου μὴ φαίνεσθαι. ἑπτὰ δ' ἦσαν αὗται νῆσοι παραπλήσιαι μὲν τοῖς μεγέθεσι, σύμμετρον δ' ἀλλήλων διεστηκυῖαι, πᾶσαι δὲ τοῖς αὐτοῖς ἔθεσι καὶ νόμοις χρώμεναι.

59. Πάντες δ' οἱ κατοικοῦντες ἐν αὐταῖς, καίπερ δαψιλεῖς ἔχοντες πάντων χορηγίας αὐτοφυεῖς, ὅμως οὐκ ἀνέδην χρῶνται ταῖς ἀπολαύσεσιν, ἀλλὰ τὴν

[1] πολλὰ E, Wesseling : πολλὰ τὸ C, πολλὰ τῶν καθ' ἡμᾶς all other MSS.

severed; even if a hand or the like should happen to have been cut off, by the use of this blood it is glued on again, provided that the cut is fresh, and the same thing is true of such other parts of the body as are not connected with the regions which are vital and sustain the person's life. Each group of the inhabitants also keeps a bird of great size and of a nature peculiar to itself, by means of which a test is made of the infant children to learn what their spiritual disposition is; for they place them upon the birds, and such of them as are able to endure the flight through the air as the birds take wing they rear, but such as become nauseated and filled with consternation they cast out, as not likely either to live many years and being, besides, of no account because of their dispositions.

In each group the oldest man regularly exercises the leadership, just as if he were a kind of king, and is obeyed by all the members; and when the first such ruler makes an end of his life in accordance with the law upon the completion of his one hundred and fiftieth year, the next oldest succeeds to the leadership. The sea about the island has strong currents and is subject to great flooding and ebbing of the tides and is sweet in taste. And as for the stars of our heavens, the Bears and many more, we are informed, are not visible at all. The number of these islands was seven, and they are very much the same in size and at about equal distances from one another, and all follow the same customs and laws.

59. Although all the inhabitants enjoy an abundant provision of everything from what grows of itself in these islands, yet they do not indulge in the enjoyment of this abundance without restraint, but they

λιτότητα διώκουσι καὶ τὴν ἀρκοῦσαν τροφὴν προσφέρονται· κρέα δὲ καὶ τἆλλα πάντα ὀπτὰ καὶ ἐξ ὕδατος ἑφθὰ σκευάζουσι· τῶν δ' ἄλλων τῶν τοῖς μαγείροις πεφιλοτεχνημένων χυμῶν καὶ τῆς κατὰ τὰς ἀρτύσεις ποικιλίας ἀνεπινόητοι παντελῶς εἰσι.

2 σέβονται δὲ θεοὺς τὸ περιέχον πάντα καὶ ἥλιον καὶ καθόλου πάντα τὰ οὐράνια. ἰχθύων δὲ παντοδαπῶν πλῆθος ἁλιεύοντες ποικίλως καὶ τῶν πτηνῶν οὐκ

3 ὀλίγα θηρεύουσι. γίνεται δὲ παρ' αὐτοῖς ἀκροδρύων τε πλῆθος αὐτομάτων, καὶ ἐλαῖαι φύονται καὶ ἄμπελοι, ἐξ ὧν ἔλαιόν τε ποιοῦσι δαψιλὲς καὶ οἶνον. ὄφεις τε τοῖς μεγέθεσι διαφέροντας, οὐδὲν δὲ ἀδικοῦντας τοὺς ἀνθρώπους, ἐδώδιμον ἔχειν τὴν

4 σάρκα καὶ γλυκύτητι διαφέρουσαν. ἐσθῆτας δὲ αὐτοὺς κατασκευάζειν ἔκ τινων καλάμων ἐχόντων ἐν τῷ μέσῳ χνοῦν λαμπρὸν καὶ μαλακόν, ὃν συνάγοντας καὶ τοῖς θαλαττίοις ὀστρέοις συγκεκομμένοις[1] μίσγοντας θαυμαστὰ κατασκευάζειν ἱμάτια πορφυρᾶ. ζῴων δὲ παρηλλαγμένας φύσεις καὶ διὰ τὸ παράδοξον ἀπιστουμένας.

5 Πάντα δὲ παρ' αὐτοῖς ὡρισμένην ἔχειν[2] τάξιν τὰ κατὰ τὴν δίαιταν, οὐχ ἅμα πάντων τὰς τροφὰς καὶ τὰς αὐτὰς λαμβανόντων· διατετάχθαι δ' ἐπί τινας ὡρισμένας ἡμέρας ποτὲ μὲν ἰχθύων βρῶσιν, ποτὲ δὲ ὀρνέων, ἔστι δ' ὅτε χερσαίων, ἐνίοτε δὲ ἐλαίων

6 καὶ τῶν λιτοτάτων προσοψημάτων. ἐναλλὰξ δὲ αὐτοὺς τοὺς μὲν ἀλλήλοις διακονεῖν, τοὺς δὲ

---

[1] συγκεκομμένοις Reiske: συγκεκολλημένοις.
[2] ἔχειν Reiske: ἔχει.

BOOK II. 59. 1-6

practise simplicity and take for their food only what suffices for their needs. Meat and whatever else is roasted or boiled in water are prepared by them, but of all the other dishes ingeniously concocted by professional cooks, such as sauces and the various kinds of seasonings, they have no notion whatsoever. And they worship as gods that which encompasses all things [1] and the sun, and, in general, all the heavenly bodies. Fishes of every kind in great numbers are caught by them by sundry devices and not a few birds. There is also found among them an abundance of fruit trees growing wild, and olive trees and vines grow there, from which they make both olive oil and wine in abundance. Snakes also, we are told, which are of immense size and yet do no harm to the inhabitants, have a meat which is edible and exceedingly sweet. And their clothing they make themselves from a certain reed which contains in the centre a downy substance [2] that is bright to the eye and soft, which they gather and mingle with crushed sea-shells and thus make remarkable garments of a purple hue. As for the animals of the islands, their natures are peculiar and so amazing as to defy credence.

All the details of their diet, we are told, follow a prescribed arrangement, since they do not all take their food at the same time nor is it always the same; but it has been ordained that on certain fixed days they shall eat at one time fish, at another time fowl, sometimes the flesh of land animals, and sometimes olives and the most simple side-dishes. They also take turns in ministering to the needs of one

---

[1] *i.e.* the atmosphere or aether.
[2] Probably cotton is meant.

ἁλιεύειν, τοὺς δὲ περὶ τὰς τέχνας εἶναι, ἄλλους δὲ περὶ ἄλλα τῶν χρησίμων ἀσχολεῖσθαι, τοὺς δ' ἐκ περιόδου κυκλικῆς λειτουργεῖν, πλὴν τῶν 7 ἤδη γεγηρακότων. ἔν τε ταῖς ἑορταῖς καὶ ταῖς εὐωχίαις[1] λέγεσθαί τε καὶ ᾄδεσθαι παρ' αὐτοῖς εἰς τοὺς θεοὺς ὕμνους καὶ ἐγκώμια, μάλιστα δὲ εἰς τὸν ἥλιον, ἀφ'[2] οὗ τάς τε νήσους καὶ ἑαυτοὺς προσαγορεύουσι.

8 Θάπτουσι δὲ τοὺς τελευτήσαντας ὅταν ἄμπωτις γένηται καταχωννύντες εἰς τὴν ἄμμον, ὥστε κατὰ τὴν πλημυρίδα τὸν τόπον ἐπιχώννυσθαι. τοὺς δὲ καλάμους, ἐξ ὧν ὁ καρπὸς τῆς τροφῆς γίνεται, φασὶ σπιθαμιαίους[3] ὄντας τὸ πάχος κατὰ τὰς τῆς σελήνης ἀναπληρώσεις ἀναπληροῦσθαι, καὶ πάλιν κατὰ τὰς ἐλαττώσεις ἀνὰ λόγον ταπεινοῦσθαι. 9 τὸ δὲ τῶν θερμῶν πηγῶν ὕδωρ γλυκὺ καὶ ὑγιεινὸν ὄν[4] διαφυλάττει τὴν θερμασίαν, καὶ οὐδέποτε ψύχεται, ἐὰν μὴ ψυχρὸν ὕδωρ ἢ οἶνος συμμίσγηται.

60. Ἑπτὰ δ' ἔτη μείναντας παρ' αὐτοῖς τοὺς περὶ τὸν Ἰαμβοῦλον ἐκβληθῆναι ἄκοντας, ὡς κακούργους καὶ πονηροῖς ἐθισμοῖς συντεθραμμένους. πάλιν οὖν τὸ πλοιάριον κατασκευάσαντας συναναγκασθῆναι τὸν χωρισμὸν ποιήσασθαι, καὶ τροφὴν ἐνθεμένους πλεῦσαι πλέον ἢ τέτταρας μῆνας· ἐκπεσεῖν δὲ κατὰ τὴν Ἰνδικὴν εἰς ἄμμους καὶ 2 τεναγώδεις τόπους· καὶ τὸν μὲν ἕτερον αὐτῶν ὑπὸ τοῦ κλύδωνος διαφθαρῆναι, τὸν δὲ Ἰαμβοῦλον πρός τινα κώμην προσενεχθέντα ὑπὸ τῶν ἐγχωρίων

[1] εὐωχίαις Wesseling; εὐχαῖς MSS., Bekker.
[2] ἀφ' added by Kallenberg.
[3] σπιθαμιαίους Reiske : στεφανιαίους MSS., Bekker.
[4] ὄν added by Dindorf.

another, some of them fishing, others working at the crafts, others occupying themselves in other useful tasks, and still others, with the exception of those who have come to old age, performing the services of the group in a definite cycle. And at the festivals and feasts which are held among them, there are both pronounced and sung in honour of the gods hymns and spoken laudations, and especially in honour of the sun, after whom they name both the islands and themselves.[1]

They inter their dead at the time when the tide is at the ebb, burying them in the sand along the beach, the result being that at flood-tide the place has fresh sand heaped upon it. The reeds, they say, from which the fruit for their nourishment is derived, being a span in thickness increase at the times of full-moon and again decrease proportionately as it wanes. And the water of the warm springs, being sweet and health-giving, maintains its heat and never becomes cold, save when it is mixed with cold water or wine.

60. After remaining among this people for seven years, the account continues, Iambulus and his companion were ejected against their will, as being malefactors and as having been educated to evil habits. Consequently, after they had again fitted out their little boat they were compelled to take their leave, and when they had stored up provisions in it they continued their voyage for more than four months. Then they were shipwrecked upon a sandy and marshy region of India; and his companion lost his life in the surf, but Iambulus, having found his way to a certain village, was then brought by the

[1] *i.e.* "The Islands and Children of the Sun."

ἀναχθῆναι πρὸς τὸν βασιλέα εἰς πόλιν Παλίβοθρα, πολλῶν ἡμερῶν ὁδὸν ἀπέχουσαν τῆς θαλάττης. 3 ὄντος δὲ φιλέλληνος τοῦ βασιλέως καὶ παιδείας ἀντεχομένου, μεγάλης αὐτὸν ἀποδοχῆς καταξιῶσαι· τὸ δὲ τελευταῖον μετά τινος ἀσφαλείας τὸ μὲν πρῶτον εἰς τὴν Περσίδα διελθεῖν, ὕστερον δὲ εἰς τὴν Ἑλλάδα διασωθῆναι.

Ὁ δὲ Ἰαμβοῦλος[1] ταῦτά τε ἀναγραφῆς ἠξίωσε καὶ περὶ τῶν κατὰ τὴν Ἰνδικὴν οὐκ ὀλίγα συνετάξατο τῶν ἀγνοουμένων παρὰ τοῖς ἄλλοις. ἡμεῖς δὲ τὴν ἐν ἀρχῇ τῆς βίβλου γεγενημένην ἐπαγγελίαν τετελεκότες αὐτοῦ περιγράψομεν τήνδε τὴν βίβλον.

[1] οὗτος after Ἰαμβοῦλος omitted E, all editors.

natives into the presence of the king at Palibothra, a city which was distant a journey of many days from the sea. And since the king was friendly to the Greeks and devoted to learning he considered Iambulus worthy of cordial welcome; and at length, upon receiving a permission of safe-conduct, he passed over first of all into Persia and later arrived safe in Greece.

Now Iambulus felt that these matters deserved to be written down, and he added to his account not a few facts about India, facts of which all other men were ignorant at that time. But for our part, since we have fulfilled the promise made at the beginning of this Book, we shall bring it to a conclusion at this point.

BOOK III

Τάδε ἔνεστιν ἐν τῇ τρίτῃ τῶν
Διοδώρου βίβλων

Περὶ Αἰθιόπων τῶν ὑπὲρ τῆς Λιβύης καὶ τῶν παρ' αὐτοῖς ἀρχαιολογουμένων.

Περὶ τῶν χρυσείων μετάλλων τῶν ἐν ταῖς ἐσχατιαῖς τῆς Αἰγύπτου καὶ τῆς κατασκευῆς τοῦ χρυσοῦ.

Περὶ τῶν κατοικούντων ἐθνῶν τὴν παράλιον τὴν παρὰ τὸν Ἀραβικὸν κόλπον καὶ καθόλου πᾶσαν τὴν παρὰ τὸν ὠκεανὸν μέχρι τῆς Ἰνδικῆς. ἐν δὲ τούτοις δηλοῦται τὰ κατὰ μέρος ἔθνη τίσι νομίμοις χρῆται καὶ παρὰ τίνας αἰτίας πολλὰ παρ' αὐτοῖς ἱστορεῖται παντελῶς ἐξηλλαγμένα καὶ διὰ τὸ παράδοξον ἀπιστούμενα.

Περὶ τῶν κατὰ τὴν Λιβύην ἀρχαιολογουμένων καὶ περὶ Γοργόνων καὶ Ἀμαζονίδων καὶ Ἄμμωνος καὶ Ἄτλαντος ἱστορουμένων.

Περὶ τῶν κατὰ τὴν Νῦσαν μυθολογουμένων, ἐν οἷς ἐστι καὶ περὶ Τιτάνων καὶ Διονύσου καὶ μητρὸς θεῶν.

CONTENTS OF THE THIRD BOOK OF DIODORUS

On the Ethiopians who dwell beyond Libya and their antiquities (chaps. 1–11).

On the gold mines on the farthest borders of Egypt and the working of the gold (chaps. 12–14).

On the peoples who dwell upon the coast of the Arabian Gulf and, speaking generally, upon all the coast of the ocean as far as India. In this connection there is a discussion of the customs which each people follows and of the reasons why history records many things in connection with them which are entirely unique and are not believed because they are contrary to what one expects (chaps. 15–48).

On the antiquities of Libya and the history of the Gorgons and Amazons, and of Ammon and Atlas (chaps. 49–61).

On the myths related about Nysa, in connection with which there is also an account of the Titans and Dionysus and the Mother of the Gods (chaps. 62–74).

ΒΙΒΛΟΣ ΤΡΙΤΗ

1. Τῶν πρὸ ταύτης βίβλων δυοῖν οὐσῶν ἡ μὲν πρώτη περιέχει τὰς κατὰ τὴν Αἴγυπτον πράξεις τῶν ἀρχαίων βασιλέων καὶ τὰ μυθολογούμενα περὶ τῶν παρ' Αἰγυπτίοις θεῶν, πρὸς δὲ τούτοις περὶ τοῦ Νείλου καὶ τῶν ἐν αὐτῇ φυομένων καρπῶν τε καὶ παντοδαπῶν ζῴων, περί τε τῆς τοποθεσίας τῆς[1] Αἰγύπτου καὶ τῶν νομίμων τῶν παρὰ τοῖς ἐγχωρίοις καὶ τῶν δικαστηρίων, ἡ δὲ δευτέρα τὰς κατὰ τὴν Ἀσίαν[2] ἐν τοῖς ἀρχαίοις συντελεσθείσας πράξεις ὑπὸ τῶν Ἀσσυρίων, ἐν αἷς ἐστιν ἥ τε Σεμιράμιδος γένεσις καὶ αὔξησις, καθ' ἣν ἔκτισε μὲν Βαβυλῶνα καὶ πολλὰς ἄλλας πόλεις, ἐστράτευσε δὲ ἐπὶ τὴν Ἰνδικὴν μεγάλαις δυνάμεσιν· ἑξῆς δὲ περὶ τῶν Χαλδαίων καὶ τῆς παρ' αὐτοῖς τῶν ἄστρων παρατηρήσεως, καὶ περὶ τῆς Ἀραβίας καὶ τῶν ἐν αὐτῇ παραδόξων, περί τε τῆς Σκυθῶν βασιλείας, καὶ περὶ Ἀμαζόνων, καὶ τὸ τελευταῖον περὶ τῶν Ὑπερβορέων. ἐν δὲ ταύτῃ τὰ συνεχῆ τοῖς προϊστορημένοις προστιθέντες διέξιμεν περὶ Αἰθιόπων καὶ τῶν Λιβύων καὶ τῶν ὀνομαζομένων Ἀτλαντίων.[3]

2. Αἰθίοπας τοίνυν ἱστοροῦσι πρώτους ἀνθρώπων ἁπάντων γεγονέναι, καὶ τὰς ἀποδείξεις τούτων ἐμφανεῖς εἶναί φασιν. ὅτι μὲν γὰρ οὐκ ἐπήλυδες

---

[1] οὔσης after τῆς deleted by Reiske.
[2] καὶ τὰς after Ἀσίαν deleted by Dindorf.

BOOK III

1. OF the two preceding Books the First embraces the deeds in Egypt of the early kings and the accounts, as found in their myths, of the gods of the Egyptians; there is also a discussion of the Nile and of the products of the land, and also of its animals, which are of every kind, and a description of the topography of Egypt, of the customs prevailing among its inhabitants, and of its courts of law. The Second Book embraces the deeds performed by the Assyrians in Asia in early times, connected with which are both the birth and the rise to power of Semiramis, in the course of which she founded Babylon and many other cities and made a campaign against India with great forces; and after this is an account of the Chaldaeans and of their practice of observing the stars, of Arabia and the marvels of that land, of the kingdom of the Scythians, of the Amazons, and finally of the Hyperboreans. In this present Book we shall add the matters which are connected with what I have already narrated, and shall describe the Ethiopians and the Libyans and the people known as the Atlantians.

2. Now the Ethiopians, as historians relate, were the first of all men and the proofs of this statement, they say, are manifest. For that they did not come into their land as immigrants from abroad but were

---

[3] ’Ατλαντίων Dindorf: ’Ατλαντίδων.

DIODORUS OF SICILY

ἐλθόντες, ἀλλ' ἐγγενεῖς ὄντες τῆς χώρας δικαίως αὐτόχθονες ὀνομάζονται, σχεδὸν παρὰ πᾶσι συμφωνεῖσθαι·[1] ὅτι δὲ τοὺς ὑπὸ τὴν μεσημβρίαν οἰκοῦντας πιθανόν ἐστι πρώτους ὑπὸ τῆς γῆς ἐζωογονῆσθαι, προφανὲς ὑπάρχειν ἅπασι· τῆς γὰρ περὶ τὸν ἥλιον θερμασίας ἀναξηραινούσης τὴν γῆν ὑγρὰν οὖσαν ἔτι[2] κατὰ τὴν τῶν ὅλων γένεσιν καὶ ζωογονούσης, εἰκὸς εἶναι τὸν ἐγγυτάτω τόπον ὄντα τοῦ ἡλίου πρῶτον ἐνεγκεῖν φύσεις ἐμψύχους.

2 φασὶ δὲ παρ' αὐτοῖς πρώτοις καταδειχθῆναι θεοὺς τιμᾶν καὶ θυσίας ἐπιτελεῖν καὶ πομπὰς καὶ πανηγύρεις καὶ τἆλλα δι' ὧν ἄνθρωποι τὸ θεῖον τιμῶσι· διὸ καὶ τὴν παρ' αὐτοῖς εὐσέβειαν διαβεβοῆσθαι παρὰ πᾶσιν ἀνθρώποις, καὶ δοκεῖν τὰς παρ' Αἰθίοψι θυσίας μάλιστ' εἶναι τῷ δαιμονίῳ κεχαρισμένας.

3 μάρτυρα δὲ τούτων παρέχονται τὸν πρεσβύτατον σχεδὸν καὶ μάλιστα τῶν ποιητῶν θαυμαζόμενον παρ' Ἕλλησι· τοῦτον γὰρ κατὰ τὴν Ἰλιάδα παρεισάγειν τόν τε Δία καὶ τοὺς ἄλλους μετ' αὐτοῦ θεοὺς ἀποδημοῦντας εἰς Αἰθιοπίαν πρός τε τὰς θυσίας τὰς ἀπονεμομένας αὐτοῖς κατ' ἔτος καὶ εὐωχίαν κοινὴν παρὰ τοῖς Αἰθίοψι,

Ζεὺς γὰρ ἐς Ὠκεανὸν μετ' ἀμύμονας Αἰθιοπῆας χθιζὸς ἔβη μετὰ δαῖτα, θεοὶ δ' ἅμα πάντες ἕποντο.

4 λέγουσι δὲ καὶ τῆς εἰς τὸ θεῖον εὐσεβείας φανερῶς αὐτοὺς κομίζεσθαι τὰς χάριτας, μηδέποτε δεσπο-

---

[1] συμφωνεῖσθαι Wesseling: συμφωνεῖται.
[2] δὲ after ἔτι deleted by Vogel.

---

[1] *i.e.* "sprung from the soil itself."

natives of it and so justly bear the name of "autochthones"[1] is, they maintain, conceded by practically all men; furthermore, that those who dwell beneath the noon-day sun were, in all likelihood, the first to be generated by the earth, is clear to all; since, inasmuch as it was the warmth of the sun which, at the generation of the universe, dried up the earth when it was still wet and impregnated it with life,[2] it is reasonable to suppose that the region which was nearest the sun was the first to bring forth living creatures. And they say that they were the first to be taught to honour the gods and to hold sacrifices and processions and festivals and the other rites by which men honour the deity; and that in consequence their piety has been published abroad among all men, and it is generally held that the sacrifices practised among the Ethiopians are those which are the most pleasing to heaven. As witness to this they call upon the poet who is perhaps the oldest and certainly the most venerated among the Greeks; for in the *Iliad*[3] he represents both Zeus and the rest of the gods with him as absent on a visit to Ethiopia to share in the sacrifices and the banquet which were given annually by the Ethiopians for all the gods together:

> For Zeus had yesterday to Ocean's bounds
> Set forth to feast with Ethiop's faultless men,
> And he was followed there by all the gods.

And they state that, by reason of their piety towards the deity, they manifestly enjoy the favour of the gods, inasmuch as they have never experienced the

[2] Cp. Book 1. 7. 4.   [3] Book 1. 423–4.

τείας ἐπήλυδος πεῖραν λαβόντας· ἐξ αἰῶνος γὰρ ἐν ἐλευθερίᾳ μεμενηκέναι καὶ τῇ πρὸς ἀλλήλους ὁμονοίᾳ, πολλῶν μὲν καὶ δυνατῶν ἐστρατευκότων ἐπ' αὐτούς, μηδενὸς δὲ τῆς ἐπιβολῆς καθικομένου.

3. Καμβύσην μὲν γὰρ μεγάλῃ δυνάμει στρατεύσαντα τήν τε στρατιὰν ἀποβαλεῖν ἅπασαν καὶ αὐτὸν τοῖς ὅλοις κινδυνεῦσαι· Σεμίραμιν δέ, τῷ μεγέθει τῶν ἐπιβολῶν καὶ πράξεων διωνομασμένην, ἐπὶ βραχὺ τῆς Αἰθιοπίας προελθοῦσαν ἀπογνῶναι τὴν ἐπὶ τὸ σύμπαν ἔθνος στρατείαν· τούς τε περὶ Ἡρακλέα καὶ Διόνυσον ἐπιόντας ἅπασαν τὴν οἰκουμένην μόνους τοὺς Αἰθίοπας τοὺς ὑπὲρ Αἰγύπτου μὴ καταπολεμῆσαι διά τε τὴν εὐσέβειαν τῶν ἀνδρῶν καὶ τὸ δυσκράτητον τῆς ἐπιβολῆς.

Φασὶ δὲ καὶ τοὺς Αἰγυπτίους ἑαυτῶν ἀποίκους ὑπάρχειν, Ὀσίριδος ἡγησαμένου τῆς ἀποικίας. 2 καθόλου γὰρ τὴν νῦν οὖσαν Αἴγυπτον λέγουσιν οὐ χώραν, ἀλλὰ θάλατταν γεγονέναι κατὰ τὴν ἐξ ἀρχῆς τοῦ κόσμου σύστασιν· ὕστερον μέντοι τοῦ Νείλου κατὰ τὰς ἀναβάσεις τὴν ἐκ τῆς Αἰθιοπίας ἰλὺν καταφέροντος ἐκ τοῦ κατ' ὀλίγον προσχωσθῆναι. ὅτι δ' ἐστὶν αὐτῶν ἡ χώρα πᾶσα ποταμόχωστος ἐναργεστάτην ἔχειν ἀπόδειξιν τὴν 3 γινομένην κατὰ τὰς ἐκβολὰς τοῦ Νείλου· καθ' ἕκαστον γὰρ ἔτος ἀεὶ νέας ἰλύος ἀθροιζομένης πρὸς τὰ στόματα τοῦ ποταμοῦ καθορᾶται τὸ μὲν πέλαγος ἐξωθούμενον τοῖς προσχώμασιν, ἡ δὲ χώρα τὴν αὔξησιν λαμβάνουσα. τὰ δὲ πλεῖστα τῶν νομίμων τοῖς Αἰγυπτίοις ὑπάρχειν Αἰθιοπικά, τηρουμένης

---

[1] An account of his campaign is in Herodotus 3. 25.

rule of an invader from abroad; for from all time they have enjoyed a state of freedom and of peace one with another, and although many and powerful rulers have made war upon them, not one of these has succeeded in his undertaking.

3. Cambyses,[1] for instance, they say, who made war upon them with a great force, both lost all his army and was himself exposed to the greatest peril; Semiramis also, who through the magnitude of her undertakings and achievements has become renowned, after advancing a short distance into Ethiopia gave up her campaign against the whole nation; and Heracles and Dionysus, although they visited all the inhabited earth, failed to subdue the Ethiopians alone who dwell above Egypt, both because of the piety of these men and because of the insurmountable difficulties involved in the attempt.

They say also that the Egyptians are colonists sent out by the Ethiopians, Osiris having been the leader of the colony. For, speaking generally, what is now Egypt, they maintain, was not land but sea when in the beginning the universe was being formed; afterwards, however, as the Nile during the times of its inundation carried down the mud from Ethiopia, land was gradually built up from the deposit. Also the statement that all the land of the Egyptians is alluvial silt deposited by the river receives the clearest proof, in their opinion, from what takes place at the outlets of the Nile; for as each year new mud is continually gathered together at the mouths of the river, the sea is observed being thrust back by the deposited silt and the land receiving the increase. And the larger part of the customs of the Egyptians are, they hold, Ethiopian, the

τῆς παλαιᾶς συνηθείας παρὰ τοῖς ἀποικισθεῖσι. 4 τό τε γὰρ τοὺς βασιλεῖς θεοὺς νομίζειν καὶ τὸ περὶ τὰς ταφὰς μάλιστα σπουδάζειν καὶ πολλὰ τοιαῦθ' ἕτερα πράττειν Αἰθιόπων ὑπάρχειν ἐπιτηδεύματα, τάς τε τῶν ἀγαλμάτων ἰδέας καὶ τοὺς τῶν γραμ- 5 μάτων τύπους Αἰθιοπικοὺς ὑπάρχειν· διττῶν[1] γὰρ Αἰγυπτίοις ὄντων γραμμάτων, τὰ μὲν δημώδη προσαγορευόμενα πάντας μανθάνειν, τὰ δ' ἱερὰ καλούμενα παρὰ μὲν τοῖς Αἰγυπτίοις μόνους γινώσκειν τοὺς ἱερεῖς παρὰ τῶν πατέρων ἐν ἀπορρήτοις μανθάνοντας, παρὰ δὲ τοῖς Αἰθίοψιν 6 ἅπαντας τούτοις χρῆσθαι τοῖς τύποις. τά τε συστήματα τῶν ἱερέων παραπλησίαν ἔχειν τάξιν παρ' ἀμφοτέροις τοῖς ἔθνεσι· καθαρεύειν γὰρ ἅπαντας τοὺς περὶ τὴν τῶν θεῶν θεραπείαν ὄντας, ὁμοίως ἐξυρημένους καὶ τὰς στολὰς τὰς αὐτὰς ἔχοντας καὶ τὸν τοῦ σκήπτρου τύπον ἀροτροειδῆ καθεστῶτα, ὃν ἔχοντας τοὺς βασιλεῖς χρῆσθαι πίλοις μακροῖς ἐπὶ τοῦ πέρατος ὀμφαλὸν ἔχουσι καὶ περιεσπειραμένοις ὄφεσιν, οὓς καλοῦσιν ἀσπίδας· τοῦτο δὲ τὸ παράσημον ἔοικε συνεμφαίνειν ὅτι τοὺς ἐπιθέσθαι τολμήσοντας τῷ βασιλεῖ συμβή- 7 σεται θανατηφόροις περιπεσεῖν δήγμασι. πολλὰ δὲ καὶ ἄλλα λέγουσι περὶ τῆς αὐτῶν ἀρχαιότητος καὶ τῆς τῶν Αἰγυπτίων ἀποικίας, περὶ ὧν οὐδὲν κατεπείγει γράφειν.

4. Περὶ δὲ τῶν Αἰθιοπικῶν γραμμάτων τῶν παρ' Αἰγυπτίοις καλουμένων ἱερογλυφικῶν ῥητέον, ἵνα

[1] διττῶν Stroth : ἰδίων.

---

[1] Cp. Book 1. 81. 1 and note.
[2] Now commonly called the "hieratic."

colonists still preserving their ancient manners. For instance, the belief that their kings are gods, the very special attention which they pay to their burials, and many other matters of a similar nature are Ethiopian practices, while the shapes of their statues and the forms of their letters are Ethiopian; for of the two kinds of writing [1] which the Egyptians have, that which is known as " popular " (demotic) is learned by everyone, while that which is called " sacred " [2] is understood only by the priests of the Egyptians, who learn it from their fathers as one of the things which are not divulged, but among the Ethiopians everyone uses these forms of letters. Furthermore, the orders of the priests, they maintain, have much the same position among both peoples; for all are clean [3] who are engaged in the service of the gods, keeping themselves shaven, like the Ethiopian priests, and having the same dress and form of staff, which is shaped like a plough and is carried by their kings, who wear high felt hats which end in a knob at the top and are circled by the serpents which they call asps; and this symbol appears to carry the thought that it will be the lot of those who shall dare to attack the king to encounter death-carrying stings.[4] Many other things are also told by them concerning their own antiquity and the colony which they sent out that became the Egyptians, but about this there is no special need of our writing anything.

4. We must now speak about the Ethiopian writing which is called hieroglyphic among the Egyptians,

[3] *i.e.* they observe certain rites and practices of purification.
[4] The snake was the sacred uraeus, the symbol of the Northern Kingdom.

μηδὲν παραλίπωμεν τῶν ἀρχαιολογουμένων. συμβέβηκε τοίνυν τοὺς μὲν τύπους ὑπάρχειν αὐτῶν ὁμοίους ζῴοις παντοδαποῖς καὶ ἀκρωτηρίοις ἀνθρώπων, ἔτι δ' ὀργάνοις, καὶ μάλιστα τεκτονικοῖς· οὐ γὰρ ἐκ τῆς τῶν συλλαβῶν συνθέσεως ἡ γραμματικὴ παρ' αὐτοῖς τὸν ὑποκείμενον λόγον ἀποδίδωσιν, ἀλλ' ἐξ ἐμφάσεως τῶν μεταγραφομένων καὶ
2 μεταφορᾶς μνήμῃ συνηθλημένης. γράφουσι γὰρ ἱέρακα καὶ κροκόδειλον, ἔτι δ' ὄφιν καὶ τῶν[1] ἐκ τοῦ σώματος τῶν ἀνθρώπων ὀφθαλμὸν καὶ χεῖρα καὶ πρόσωπον καὶ ἕτερα τοιαῦτα. ὁ μὲν οὖν ἱέραξ αὐτοῖς σημαίνει πάντα τὰ ὀξέως γινόμενα, διὰ τὸ τὸ ζῷον τοῦτο τῶν πτηνῶν σχεδὸν ὑπάρχειν ὀξύτατον. μεταφέρεταί τε ὁ λόγος ταῖς οἰκείαις μεταφοραῖς εἰς πάντα τὰ ὀξέα καὶ τὰ τούτοις
3 οἰκεῖα παραπλησίως τοῖς εἰρημένοις. ὁ δὲ κροκόδειλος σημαντικός ἐστι πάσης κακίας, ὁ δὲ ὀφθαλμὸς δίκης τηρητὴς καὶ παντὸς τοῦ σώματος φύλαξ. τῶν δ' ἀκρωτηρίων ἡ μὲν δεξιὰ τοὺς δακτύλους ἐκτεταμένους ἔχουσα σημαίνει βίου πορισμόν, ἡ δ' εὐώνυμος συνηγμένη τήρησιν καὶ
4 φυλακὴν χρημάτων. ὁ δ' αὐτὸς λόγος καὶ ἐπὶ τῶν ἄλλων τύπων τῶν ἐκ τοῦ σώματος καὶ τῶν ὀργανικῶν καὶ τῶν ἄλλων ἁπάντων· ταῖς γὰρ ἐν ἑκάστοις ἐνούσαις ἐμφάσεσι συνακολουθοῦντες, καὶ μελέτῃ πολυχρονίῳ καὶ μνήμῃ γυμνάζοντες τὰς ψυχάς, ἑκτικῶς ἕκαστα τῶν γεγραμμένων ἀναγινώσκουσι.

5. Τῶν δὲ παρ' Αἰθίοψι νομίμων οὐκ ὀλίγα δοκεῖ

[1] τῶν Hertlein: τόν.

in order that we may omit nothing in our discussion of their antiquities. Now it is found that the forms of their letters take the shape of animals of every kind, and of the members of the human body, and of implements and especially carpenters' tools; for their writing does not express the intended concept by means of syllables joined one to another, but by means of the significance of the objects which have been copied and by its figurative meaning which has been impressed upon the memory by practice. For instance, they draw the picture of a hawk, a crocodile, a snake, and of the members of the human body—an eye, a hand, a face, and the like. Now the hawk signifies to them everything which happens swiftly, since this animal is practically the swiftest of winged creatures. And the concept portrayed is then transferred, by the appropriate metaphorical transfer, to all swift things and to everything to which swiftness is appropriate, very much as if they had been named. And the crocodile is a symbol of all that is evil, and the eye is the warder of justice and the guardian of the entire body. And as for the members of the body, the right hand with fingers extended signifies a procuring of livelihood, and the left with the fingers closed, a keeping and guarding of property. The same way of reasoning applies also to the remaining characters, which represent parts of the body and implements and all other things; for by paying close attention to the significance which is inherent in each object and by training their minds through drill and exercise of the memory over a long period, they read from habit everything which has been written.

5. As for the customs of the Ethiopians, not a few

πολὺ τῶν παρὰ τοῖς ἄλλοις διαφέρειν, καὶ μάλιστα τὰ περὶ τὴν αἵρεσιν τῶν βασιλέων. οἱ μὲν γὰρ ἱερεῖς ἐξ αὑτῶν τοὺς ἀρίστους προκρίνουσιν, ἐκ δὲ τῶν καταλεχθέντων, ὃν ἂν ὁ θεὸς κωμάζων κατά τινα συνήθειαν περιφερόμενος λάβῃ, τοῦτον τὸ πλῆθος αἱρεῖται βασιλέα· εὐθὺς δὲ καὶ προσκυνεῖ καὶ τιμᾷ καθάπερ θεόν, ὡς ὑπὸ τῆς τοῦ δαιμονίου 2 προνοίας ἐγκεχειρισμένης αὐτῷ τῆς ἀρχῆς. ὁ δ' αἱρεθεὶς διαίτῃ τε χρῆται τῇ τεταγμένῃ κατὰ τοὺς νόμους καὶ τἆλλα πράττει κατὰ τὸ πάτριον ἔθος, οὔτ' εὐεργεσίαν οὔτε τιμωρίαν ἀπονέμων οὐδενὶ παρὰ τὸ δεδογμένον ἐξ ἀρχῆς παρ' αὐτοῖς νόμιμον· ἔθος δ' αὐτοῖς ἐστι μηδένα τῶν ὑποτεταγμένων θανάτῳ περιβάλλειν, μηδ' ἂν καταδικασθεὶς ἐπὶ θανάτῳ τις φανῇ τιμωρίας ἄξιος, ἀλλὰ πέμπειν τῶν ὑπηρετῶν τινα σημεῖον ἔχοντα θανάτου πρὸς τὸν παρανενομηκότα· οὗτος δ' ἰδὼν τὸ σύσσημον, καὶ παραχρῆμα εἰς τὴν ἰδίαν οἰκίαν ἀπελθών, ἑαυτὸν ἐκ τοῦ ζῆν μεθίστησι. φεύγειν δ' ἐκ[1] τῆς ἰδίας χώρας εἰς τὴν ὅμορον καὶ τῇ μεταστάσει τῆς πατρίδος λύειν τὴν τιμωρίαν, καθάπερ παρὰ τοῖς 3 Ἕλλησιν, οὐδαμῶς συγκεχώρηται. διὸ καί φασί τινα, τοῦ θανατηφόρου σημείου πρὸς αὐτὸν ἀποσταλέντος ὑπὸ τοῦ βασιλέως, ἐπιβαλέσθαι μὲν ἐκ τῆς Αἰθιοπίας φεύγειν, αἰσθομένης δὲ τῆς μητρὸς καὶ τῇ ζώνῃ τὸν τράχηλον αὐτοῦ σφιγγούσης, ταύτῃ μηδὲ καθ' ἕνα τρόπον τολμῆσαι προσενεγκεῖν τὰς

---

[1] δ' ἐκ Vogel: δὲ MSS., Bekker, Dindorf.

of them are thought to differ greatly from those of the rest of mankind, this being especially true of those which concern the selection of their kings. The priests, for instance, first choose out the noblest men from their own number, and whichever one from this group the god may select, as he is borne about in a procession in accordance with a certain practice of theirs, him the multitude take for their king; and straightway it both worships and honours him like a god, believing that the sovereignty has been entrusted to him by Divine Providence. And the king who has been thus chosen both follows a regimen which has been fixed in accordance with the laws and performs all his other deeds in accordance with the ancestral custom, according neither favour nor punishment to anyone contrary to the usage which has been approved among them from the beginning. It is also a custom of theirs that the king shall put no one of his subjects to death, not even if a man shall have been condemned to death and is considered deserving of punishment, but that he shall send to the transgressor one of his attendants bearing a token of death; and the guilty person, on seeing the warning, immediately retires to his home and removes himself from life. Moreover, for a man to flee from his own into a neighbouring country and thus by moving away from his native land to pay the penalty of his transgression, as is the custom among the Greeks, is permissible under no circumstances. Consequently, they say, when a man to whom the token of death had been sent by the king once undertook to flee from Ethiopia, and his mother, on learning of this, bound his neck about with her girdle, he dared not so much as raise his

χεῖρας, αὐτὸν δ' ἀγχόμενον καρτερῆσαι μέχρι τῆς τελευτῆς, ἵνα μὴ τοῖς συγγενέσιν ὀνείδη καταλίπῃ μείζω.

6. Πάντων δ' ἐστὶ παραδοξότατον τὸ γινόμενον περὶ τὴν τελευτὴν τῶν βασιλέων. κατὰ γὰρ τὴν Μερόην οἱ περὶ τὰς τῶν θεῶν θεραπείας τε καὶ τιμὰς διατρίβοντες ἱερεῖς, μεγίστην καὶ κυριωτάτην τάξιν ἔχοντες, ἐπειδὰν ἐπὶ νοῦν αὐτοῖς ἔλθῃ, πέμπουσιν ἄγγελον πρὸς τὸν βασιλέα, κελεύοντες 2 ἀποθνῄσκειν. τοὺς γὰρ θεοὺς αὐτοῖς ταῦτα κεχρηματικέναι, καὶ δεῖν τὸ πρόσταγμα τῶν ἀθανάτων ὑπὸ θνητῆς φύσεως μηδαμῶς παροραθῆναι. καὶ ἑτέρους δ' ἐπιφθέγγονται λόγους, οἵους ἂν[1] ἁπλῇ διανοίᾳ προσδέξαιτο φύσις ἀρχαία μὲν καὶ δυσεξαλείπτῳ συνηθείᾳ συντεθραμμένη, λόγον δ' οὐκ ἔχουσα τὸν ἐναντιωσόμενον τοῖς οὐκ ἀναγκαίως 3 προσταττομένοις. κατὰ μὲν οὖν τοὺς ἐπάνω χρόνους ὑπήκουον οἱ βασιλεῖς τοῖς ἱερεῦσιν, οὐχ ὅπλοις οὐδὲ βίᾳ κρατηθέντες, ἀλλ' ὑπ' αὐτῆς τῆς δεισιδαιμονίας τοὺς λογισμοὺς κατισχυόμενοι· κατὰ δὲ τὸν δεύτερον Πτολεμαῖον ὁ βασιλεὺς τῶν Αἰθιόπων Ἐργαμένης, μετεσχηκὼς Ἑλληνικῆς ἀγωγῆς καὶ φιλοσοφήσας, πρῶτος ἐθάρρησε κατα- 4 φρονῆσαι τοῦ προστάγματος. λαβὼν γὰρ φρόνημα τῆς βασιλείας ἄξιον παρῆλθε μετὰ τῶν[2] στρατιωτῶν εἰς τὸ ἄβατον, οὗ συνέβαινεν εἶναι τὸν χρυσοῦν ναὸν τῶν Αἰθιόπων, καὶ τοὺς μὲν ἱερεῖς

[1] ἂν added by Dindorf.
[2] τῶν omitted by D, Vogel.

[1] The Greeks considered strangling a shameful death, but it would have been a "greater disgrace" for an Ethiopian to flee from his country.

BOOK III. 5. 3-6. 4

hands against her in any way but submitted to be strangled until he died, that he might not leave a greater disgrace [1] to his kinsmen.

6. Of all their customs the most astonishing is that which obtains in connection with the death of their kings.[2] For the priests at Meroë who spend their time in the worship of the gods and the rites which do them honour, being the greatest and most powerful order, whenever the idea comes to them, dispatch a messenger to the king with orders that he die. For the gods, they add, have revealed this to them, and it must be that the command of the immortals should in no wise be disregarded by one of mortal frame. And this order they accompany with other arguments, such as are accepted by a simple-minded nature, which has been bred in a custom that is both ancient and difficult to eradicate and which knows no argument that can be set in opposition to commands enforced by no compulsion. Now in former times the kings would obey the priests, having been overcome, not by arms nor by force, but because their reasoning powers had been put under a constraint by their very superstition; but during the reign of the second Ptolemy the king of the Ethiopians, Ergamenes, who had had a Greek education and had studied philosophy, was the first to have the courage to disdain the command. For assuming a spirit which became the position of a king he entered with his soldiers into the unapproachable place where stood, as it turned out, the golden shrine of the Ethiopians, put the priests to the sword, and after

285-246 B.C.

---

[2] Some of the following account is found in Strabo (17. 2. 1-3, especially § 3, tr. by Jones, in the *L.C.L.*).

ἀπέσφαξε, τὸ δὲ ἔθος τοῦτο καταλύσας διωρθώσατο πρὸς τὴν ἑαυτοῦ προαίρεσιν.

7. Τὸ δὲ περὶ τοὺς φίλους τοῦ βασιλέως νόμιμον, καίπερ ὂν παράδοξον, διαμένειν ἔφασαν ἕως τῶν καθ' ἡμᾶς χρόνων. ἔθος γὰρ ὑπάρχειν λέγουσι τοῖς Αἰθίοψιν, ἐπὰν ὁ βασιλεὺς μέρος τι τοῦ σώματος πηρωθῇ δι' ἡνδηποτοῦν αἰτίαν, ἅπαντας τοὺς συνήθεις συναποβάλλειν τοῦτο κατὰ προαίρεσιν· αἰσχρὸν γὰρ ὑπολαμβάνειν τοῦ βασιλέως πεπηρωμένου τὸ σκέλος ἀρτίποδας εἶναι τοὺς φίλους, καὶ μὴ πάντας ἐν ταῖς ἐξόδοις συνέπεσθαι 2 χωλοὺς ὁμοίως· ἄτοπον γὰρ εἶναι τὸ συμπενθεῖν μὲν καὶ[1] συλλυπεῖσθαι καὶ τῶν ἄλλων ὁμοίως ἀγαθῶν ἁπάντων τε καὶ κακῶν κοινωνεῖν τὴν βεβαίαν φιλίαν, τῆς δ' εἰς τὸ σῶμα λύπης ἄμοιρον γίνεσθαι. φασὶ δὲ σύνηθες εἶναι καὶ τὸ συντελευτᾶν ἑκουσίως τοὺς ἑταίρους τοῖς βασιλεῦσι, καὶ τοῦτον εἶναι τὸν θάνατον ἔνδοξον καὶ φιλίας ἀληθινῆς 3 μάρτυρα. διόπερ μὴ ῥᾳδίως ἐπιβουλὴν γίνεσθαι παρὰ τοῖς Αἰθίοψι κατὰ τοῦ βασιλέως, ὡς ἂν τῶν φίλων ἁπάντων[2] ἐπ' ἴσης προνοουμένων τῆς τ' ἐκείνου καὶ τῆς ἰδίας ἀσφαλείας. ταῦτα μὲν οὖν τὰ νόμιμα παρὰ τοῖς Αἰθίοψίν ἐστι τοῖς τὴν μητρόπολιν αὐτῶν οἰκοῦσι καὶ νεμομένοις τήν τε νῆσον τὴν Μερόην καὶ τὴν χώραν τὴν πλησίον Αἰγύπτου.

8. Ἔστι δὲ καὶ ἄλλα γένη τῶν Αἰθιόπων παμπληθῆ, τὰ μὲν ἐξ ἀμφοτέρων τῶν μερῶν τὴν παραποτάμιον τοῦ Νείλου κατοικοῦντα καὶ τὰς ἐν τῷ

[1] τὸ after καὶ deleted by Dindorf.
[2] So Eichstädt: κατὰ τῶν φίλων ὡς ἂν τοῦ βασιλέως καὶ τῶν φίλων ἁπάντων.

abolishing this custom thereafter ordered affairs after his own will.

7. As for the custom touching the friends of the king, strange as it is, it persists, they said, down to our own time. For the Ethiopians have the custom, they say, that if their king has been maimed in some part of his body through any cause whatever, all his companions suffer the same loss of their own choice; because they consider that it would be a disgraceful thing if, when the king had been maimed in his leg, his friends should be sound of limb, and if in their goings forth from the palace they should not all follow the king limping as he did; for it would be strange that steadfast friendship should share sorrow and grief and bear equally all other things both good and evil, but should have no part in the suffering of the body. They say also that it is customary for the comrades of the kings even to die with them of their own accord and that such a death is an honourable one and a proof of true friendship. And it is for this reason, they add, that a conspiracy against the king is not easily raised among the Ethiopians, all his friends being equally concerned both for his safety and their own. These, then, are the customs which prevail among the Ethiopians who dwell in their capital[1] and those who inhabit both the island of Meroë and the land adjoining Egypt.

8. But there are also a great many other tribes of the Ethiopians, some of them dwelling in the land lying on both banks of the Nile and on the islands in

[1] Napata.

DIODORUS OF SICILY

ποταμῷ νήσους, τὰ δὲ τὴν ὅμορον τῆς Ἀραβίας νεμόμενα, τὰ δ' ἐν τοῖς μεσογείοις τῆς Λιβύης
2 καθιδρυμένα. οἱ πλεῖστοι δὲ τούτων καὶ μάλισθ' οἱ παρὰ τὸν ποταμὸν οἰκοῦντες ταῖς μὲν χρόαις εἰσὶ μέλανες, ταῖς δὲ ἰδέαις σιμοί, τοῖς δὲ τριχώμασιν οὖλοι. καὶ ταῖς μὲν ψυχαῖς παντελῶς ὑπάρχουσιν ἄγριοι καὶ τὸ θηριῶδες ἐμφαίνοντες, οὐχ οὕτω δὲ τοῖς θυμοῖς ὡς τοῖς ἐπιτηδεύμασιν· αὐχμηροὶ γὰρ ὄντες τοῖς ὅλοις σώμασι τοὺς μὲν ὄνυχας ἐπὶ πολὺ παρηγμένους ἔχουσι τοῖς θηρίοις παραπλησίως, τῆς δὲ πρὸς ἀλλήλους φιλανθρωπίας
3 πλεῖστον ὅσον ἀφεστήκασι· καὶ τὴν μὲν φωνὴν ὀξεῖαν προβάλλοντες, τῶν δὲ παρὰ τοῖς ἄλλοις ἐπιτηδευομένων εἰς βίον ἥμερον οὐδ' ὁτιοῦν ἔχοντες, μεγάλην ποιοῦσι πρὸς τὰ καθ' ἡμᾶς ἔθη τὴν διαφοράν.

4 Καθοπλίζονται δ' αὐτῶν οἱ μὲν ἀσπίσιν ὠμοβοΐναις καὶ μικροῖς δόρασιν, οἱ δὲ ἀκοντίοις ἀναγκύλοις, ἐνίοτε δὲ ξυλίνοις τόξοις τετραπήχεσιν, οἷς τοξεύουσι μὲν τῷ ποδὶ προσβαίνοντες, ἀναλωθέντων δὲ τῶν οἰστῶν σκυτάλαις ξυλίναις διαγωνίζονται. καθοπλίζουσι δὲ καὶ τὰς γυναῖκας, ὁρίζοντες αὐταῖς τεταγμένην ἡλικίαν, ὧν ταῖς πλείσταις νόμιμόν ἐστι χαλκοῦν κρίκον φέρειν ἐν τῷ χείλει
5 τοῦ στόματος. ἐσθῆτι δέ τινες μὲν αὐτῶν ἁπλῶς οὐ χρῶνται, γυμνῆτα βίον ἔχοντες δι' αἰῶνος καὶ πρὸς μόνα τὰ καύματα ποριζόμενοι βοήθειαν αὐτουργὸν ἐκ τοῦ παραπεσόντος· τινὲς δὲ τῶν προβάτων τὰς οὐρὰς ἀποκόπτοντες ἐκ τῶν ὄπισθεν καλύπτουσι διὰ τούτων τὰ ἰσχία, καθάπερ αἰδῶ

the river, others inhabiting the neighbouring country of Arabia,[1] and still others residing in the interior of Libya. The majority of them, and especially those who dwell along the river, are black in colour and have flat noses and woolly hair. As for their spirit they are entirely savage and display the nature of a wild beast, not so much, however, in their temper as in their ways of living; for they are squalid all over their bodies, they keep their nails very long like the wild beasts, and are as far removed as possible from human kindness to one another; and speaking as they do with a shrill voice and cultivating none of the practices of civilized life as these are found among the rest of mankind, they present a striking contrast when considered in the light of our own customs.

As for their arms, some of them use shields of raw ox-hide and short spears, others javelins without a slinging-thong and sometimes bows of wood, four cubits in length, with which they shoot by putting their foot against them, and after their arrows are exhausted they finish the fight with wooden clubs. They also arm their women, setting an age limit for their service, and most of these observe the custom of wearing a bronze ring in the lip. As for clothing, certain of them wear none whatsoever, going naked all their life long and making for themselves of whatever comes to hand a rude protection from the heat alone; others, cutting off the tails and the ends of the hides of their sheep, cover their loins with them, putting the tail before them to screen, after a

[1] The land between the Nile and the Red Sea; cp. Vol. I, p. 217 and note.

DIODORUS OF SICILY

ταύτην προβαλλόμενοι· ἔνιοι δὲ χρῶνται ταῖς δοραῖς τῶν κτηνῶν, εἰσὶ δ' οἳ περιζώμασι μέχρι μέσου[1] τὸ σῶμα καλύπτουσιν, ἐκ τῶν τριχῶν πλέκοντες, ὡς ἂν τῶν παρ' αὐτοῖς προβάτων ὄντων μὴ φερόντων ἔρια διὰ τὴν ἰδιότητα τῆς χώρας.
6 τροφῇ δὲ χρῶνται τινὲς μὲν λαμβάνοντες τὸν γεννώμενον ἐν τοῖς ὕδασι καρπόν, ὃς αὐτοφυὴς ἀνατέλλει περί τε τὰς λίμνας καὶ τοὺς ἑλώδεις τόπους, τινὲς δὲ τῆς ἁπαλωτάτης ὕλης τοὺς ἀκρεμόνας περικλῶντες, οἷς καὶ τὰ σώματα σκιάζοντες περὶ τὰς μεσημβρίας καταψύχουσιν, ἔνιοι δὲ σπείροντες σήσαμον καὶ λωτόν, εἰσὶ δ' οἳ ταῖς ῥίζαις τῶν καλάμων ταῖς ἁπαλωτάταις διατρεφόμενοι. οὐκ ὀλίγοι δ' αὐτῶν καὶ ταῖς τοξείαις ἐνηθληκότες τῶν πτηνῶν εὐστόχως πολλὰ τοξεύουσι, δι' ὧν τὴν τῆς φύσεως ἔνδειαν ἀναπληροῦσιν· οἱ πλεῖστοι δὲ τοῖς ἀπὸ τῶν βοσκημάτων κρέασι καὶ γάλακτι καὶ τυρῷ τὸν πάντα βίον διαζῶσι.

9. Περὶ δὲ θεῶν οἱ μὲν ἀνώτερον Μερόης οἰκοῦντες ἐννοίας ἔχουσι διττάς. ὑπολαμβάνουσι γὰρ τοὺς μὲν αὐτῶν αἰώνιον ἔχειν καὶ ἄφθαρτον τὴν φύσιν, οἷον ἥλιον καὶ σελήνην καὶ τὸν σύμπαντα κόσμον, τοὺς δὲ νομίζουσι θνητῆς φύσεως κεκοινωνηκέναι καὶ δι' ἀρετὴν καὶ κοινὴν εἰς ἀνθρώπους εὐεργεσίαν
2 τετευχέναι τιμῶν ἀθανάτων· τήν τε γὰρ Ἶσιν καὶ τὸν Πᾶνα, πρὸς δὲ τούτοις Ἡρακλέα καὶ Δία

[1] μέσου Dindorf: μέσον.

---

[1] The obscure description of this custom may be clarified by a statement of Strabo (17. 2. 3) who apparently is greatly condensing the same source which Diodorus has used in this passage. Strabo writes of the Ethiopians: " . . . and some go naked, or wear around their loins small sheep-skins or

BOOK III. 8. 5–9. 2

manner, the shameful part[1]; and some make use of the skins of their domestic animals, while there are those who cover their bodies as far as the waist with shirts, which they weave of hair, since their sheep do not produce wool by reason of the peculiar nature of the land. For food some gather the fruits which are generated in their waters and which grow wild in both the lakes and marshy places, certain of them pluck off the foliage of a very tender kind of tree, with which they also cover their bodies in the midday and cool them in this way, some sow sesame and lotus,[2] and there are those who are nourished by the most tender roots of the reeds. Not a few of them are also well trained in the use of the bow and bring down with good aim many birds, with which they satisfy their physical needs; but the greater number live for their entire life on the meat and milk and cheese of their herds.

9. With regard to the gods, the Ethiopians who dwell above Meroë entertain two opinions: they believe that some of them, such as the sun and the moon and the universe as a whole, have a nature which is eternal and imperishable, but others of them, they think, share a mortal nature and have come to receive immortal honours because of their virtue and the benefactions which they have bestowed upon all mankind; for instance, they revere Isis and Pan, and also Heracles and Zeus, considering that

---

girdles of well-woven hair" (tr. of Jones in the *L.C.L.*). When this statement is combined with that of Diodorus, it would appear that when the tail of the sheep was cut off a portion of the hide was left attached to it and that this hide was put about the loins in such a way that the tail hung down in front.

[2] Cp. Book 1. 34. 6.

σέβονται, μάλιστα νομίζοντες ὑπὸ τούτων εὐηργετῆσθαι τὸ τῶν ἀνθρώπων γένος. ὀλίγοι δὲ τῶν Αἰθιόπων καθόλου θεοὺς οὐ νομίζουσιν εἶναι· διὸ καὶ τὸν ἥλιον ὡς πολεμιώτατον ὄντα κατὰ τὰς ἀνατολὰς βλασφημήσαντες φεύγουσι πρὸς τοὺς ἑλώδεις τῶν τόπων.

3 Παρηλλαγμένοις δ' ἔθεσι χρῶνται καὶ περὶ τοὺς παρ' αὐτοῖς τελευτῶντας· οἱ μὲν γὰρ εἰς τὸν ποταμὸν βάλλοντες ἀφιᾶσιν, ἀρίστην ἡγούμενοι ταφὴν ταύτην, οἱ δὲ περιχέαντες ὕελον ἐν ταῖς οἰκίαις φυλάττοντες νομίζουσι δεῖν μήτε τῶν τελευτώντων ἀγνοεῖσθαι τὰς ὄψεις τοῖς συγγενέσι μήτ' ἐπιλανθάνεσθαι τοὺς προσήκοντας τῷ γένει τῶν προσῳκειωμένων, ἔνιοι δ' εἰς ὀστρακίνας σοροὺς ἐμβάλλοντες κατορύττουσι κύκλῳ τῶν ἱερῶν, καὶ τὸν ἐπὶ τούτοις γινόμενον ὅρκον μέγιστον ἡγοῦνται.

4 Τὰς δὲ βασιλείας ἐγχειρίζουσιν οἱ μὲν τοῖς εὐπρεπεστάτοις, τύχης ἡγούμενοι δῶρα ἀμφότερα, τήν τε μοναρχίαν καὶ τὴν εὐπρέπειαν, οἱ δὲ τοῖς ἐπιμελεστάτοις κτηνοτρόφοις παραδιδόασι τὴν ἀρχήν, ὡς μόνους ἄριστα τῶν ὑποτεταγμένων φροντιοῦντας, ἔνιοι δὲ τοῖς πλουσιωτάτοις τοῦτο τὸ τίμιον ἀπονέμουσιν, ἡγούμενοι μόνους αὐτοὺς ἐπικουρεῖν τοῖς ὄχλοις δύνασθαι διὰ τὴν ἑτοιμότητα τῆς εὐπορίας, εἰσὶ δ' οἳ τοὺς ἀνδρείᾳ διαφέροντας αἱροῦνται βασιλεῖς, κρίνοντες τοὺς ἐν πολέμῳ πλεῖστον δυναμένους ἀξίους εἶναι μόνους τυγχάνειν τῶν πρωτείων.

BOOK III. 9. 2-4

these deities in particular have been benefactors of the race of men. But a few of the Ethiopians do not believe in the existence of any gods at all[1]; consequently at the rising of the sun they utter imprecations against it as being most hostile to them, and flee to the marshes of those parts.

Different also from those of other peoples are the customs they observe with respect to their dead; for some dispose of them by casting them into the river, thinking this to be the best burial; others, after pouring glass about the bodies,[2] keep them in their houses, since they feel that the countenances of the dead should not be unknown to their kinsmen and that those who are united by ties of blood should not forget their near relations; and some put them in coffins made of baked clay and bury them in the ground in a ring about their temples, and they consider that the oath taken by them is the strongest possible.

The kingship some of them bestow upon the most comely, believing both supreme power and comeliness to be gifts of fortune, while others entrust the rule to the most careful keepers of cattle, as being the only men who would give the best thought to their subjects; some assign this honour to the wealthiest, since they feel that these alone can come to the aid of the masses because they have the means ready at hand; and there are those who choose for their kings men of unusual valour, judging that the most efficient in war are alone worthy to receive the meed of honour.

[1] Strabo (17. 2. 3, tr. by Jones in the *L.C.L.*) says that these Ethiopians lived near the torrid zone.
[2] Cp. Book 2. 15 for a fuller account of this custom.

10. Τῆς δὲ παρὰ τὸν Νεῖλον χώρας τῆς ἐν τῇ Λιβύῃ κειμένης ἐστί τι μέρος τῷ κάλλει διαφέρον· τροφάς τε γὰρ φέρει δαψιλεῖς καὶ ποικίλας, καὶ πρὸς τὰς τῶν καυμάτων ὑπερβολὰς ἔχει βοηθείας εὐθέτους τὰς ἐν τοῖς ἕλεσι καταφυγάς· διὸ καὶ περιμάχητος οὗτος ὁ τόπος γίνεται τοῖς τε Λίβυσι καὶ τοῖς Αἰθίοψι, καὶ πρὸς ἀλλήλους ὑπὲρ αὐτοῦ 2 πολεμοῦντες διατελοῦσι. φοιτᾷ δ' εἰς αὐτὸν καὶ πλῆθος ἐλεφάντων ἐκ τῆς ἄνω χώρας, ὥς μὲν ἔνιοι λέγουσι, διὰ τὴν δαψίλειαν καὶ τὴν ἡδονὴν τῆς νομῆς· ἕλη γὰρ θαυμαστὰ παρεκτείνεται τοῖς χείλεσι τοῦ ποταμοῦ, πολλῆς καὶ παντοίας ἐν 3 αὐτοῖς φυομένης τροφῆς. διόπερ ὅταν γεύσωνται τοῦ θρύου καὶ τοῦ καλάμου, διὰ τὴν γλυκύτητα τῆς τροφῆς μένει καὶ τὴν τῶν ἀνθρώπων δίαιταν καταφθείρει· δι' ἣν αἰτίαν καταναγκάζονται φεύγειν[1] τούτους τοὺς τόπους, ὄντες νομάδες καὶ σκηνῖται, τὸ σύνολον τῷ συμφέροντι τὰς πατρίδας 4 ὁρίζοντες. αἱ δ' ἀγέλαι τῶν εἰρημένων θηρίων τὴν μεσόγειον χώραν ἐκλείπουσι διὰ σπάνιν τροφῆς, ἅτε συντόμως τῶν φυομένων ἐν τῇ γῇ πάντων αὐαινομένων· διὰ γὰρ τὴν τοῦ καύματος ὑπερβολὴν καὶ τὴν λειψυδρίαν τῶν πηγαίων καὶ ποταμίων ὑδάτων σκληρὰς καὶ σπανίους συμβαίνει γίνεσθαι τὰς τροφάς.

5 Ὡς δέ τινές φασιν, ὄφεις θαυμαστοὶ γίνονται τό τε μέγεθος καὶ τὸ πλῆθος κατὰ τὴν θηριώδη καλουμένην χώραν· οὗτοι δὲ περὶ τὰς συστάσεις τῶν ὑδάτων ἐπιτίθενται τοῖς ἐλέφασι, καὶ τραπέντες εἰς ἀλκὴν περιπλέκονται ταῖς σπείραις εἰς τὰ

[1] εἰς after φεύγειν deleted by Vogel.

10. In that part of the country which lies along the Nile in Libya [1] there is a section which is remarkable for its beauty; for it bears food in great abundance and of every variety and provides convenient places of retreat in its marshes where one finds protection against the excessive heat; consequently this region is a bone of contention between the Libyans and the Ethiopians, who wage unceasing warfare with each other for its possession. It is also a gathering-place for a multitude of elephants from the country lying above it because, as some say, the pasturage is abundant and sweet; for marvellous marshes stretch along the banks of the river and in them grows food in great plenty and of every kind. Consequently, whenever they taste of the rush and the reed, they remain there because of the sweetness of the food and destroy the means of subsistence of the human beings; and because of this the inhabitants are compelled to flee from these regions, and to live as nomads and dwellers in tents—in a word, to fix the bounds of their country by their advantage. The herds of the wild beasts which we have mentioned leave the interior of the country because of the lack of food, since every growing thing in the ground quickly dries up; for as a result of the excessive heat and the lack of water from springs and rivers it comes to pass that the plants for food are rough and scanty.

There are also, as some say, in the country of the wild beasts, as it is called, serpents which are marvellous for their size and multitude; these attack the elephants at the water-holes, pit their strength against them, and winding themselves in coils about

[1] *i.e.* on the west bank.

σκέλη, καὶ πέρας ἕως τούτου συνέχουσι βιαζόμενοι καὶ σφίγγοντες τοῖς δεσμοῖς ἕως ἂν ἀφρίσαντα τὰ θηρία πέσῃ διὰ τὸ βάρος. ἔπειτ' ἀθροιζόμενοι τὸ πεσὸν σαρκοφαγοῦσι, ῥᾳδίως ἐπικρατοῦντες διὰ 6 τὴν δυσκινησίαν τοῦ ζῴου. ἀπολειπομένου δ' ἀπορήματος, διὰ τίν' αἰτίαν οὐ συνέπονται τοῖς ἐλέφασιν εἰς τὴν προειρημένην παραποταμίαν διώκοντες τὰς συνήθεις τροφάς, φασὶ[1] τοὺς τηλικούτους ὄφεις τὴν μὲν ἐπίπεδον τῆς χώρας φεύγειν, περὶ δὲ τὴν ὑπώρειαν ἐν ταῖς φάραγξι ταῖς εἰς[2] τὸ μῆκος ἀνηκούσαις καὶ τοῖς σπηλαίοις τοῖς τὸ βάθος ἔχουσι συνεχῶς ἐναυλίζεσθαι· διόπερ τοὺς συμφέροντας καὶ συνήθεις τόπους μηδαμῶς ἐκλείπειν, αὐτοδιδάκτου πρὸς τὰ τοιαῦτα τῆς φύσεως οὔσης ἅπασι τοῖς ζῴοις.

Περὶ μὲν οὖν Αἰθιόπων καὶ τῆς χώρας αὐτῶν τοσαῦτα λέγομεν.

11. Περὶ δὲ τῶν συγγραφέων ἡμῖν διοριστέον, ὅτι πολλοὶ συγγεγράφασι περί τε τῆς Αἰγύπτου καὶ τῆς Αἰθιοπίας, ὧν οἱ μὲν ψευδεῖ φήμῃ πεπιστευκότες, οἱ δὲ παρ' ἑαυτῶν πολλὰ τῆς ψυχαγωγίας 2 ἕνεκα πεπλακότες, δικαίως ἂν ἀπιστοῖντο. Ἀγαθαρχίδης[1] μὲν γὰρ ὁ Κνίδιος ἐν τῇ δευτέρᾳ βίβλῳ τῶν περὶ τὴν Ἀσίαν, καὶ ὁ τὰς γεωγραφίας συνταξάμενος Ἀρτεμίδωρος ὁ Ἐφέσιος κατὰ τὴν ὀγδόην βίβλον, καί τινες ἕτεροι τῶν ἐν Αἰγύπτῳ κατοικούντων, ἱστορηκότες τὰ πλεῖστα τῶν προει-

[1] δὲ after φασὶ deleted by Reiske.
[2] εἰς added by Wesseling, Vogel; omitted by Bekker, Dindorf.

[1] An historian and geographer of the second century B.C.

BOOK III. 10. 5–11. 2

their legs continue squeezing them tighter and tighter in their bands until at last the beasts, covered with foam, fall to the ground from their weight. Thereupon the serpents gather and devour the flesh of the fallen elephant, overcoming the beast with ease because it moves only with difficulty. But since it still remains a puzzle why, in pursuit of their accustomed food, they do not follow the elephants into the region along the river, which I have mentioned, they say that the serpents of such great size avoid the level part of the country and continually make their homes at the foot of mountains in ravines which are suitable to their length and in deep caves; consequently they never leave the regions which are suitable to them and to which they are accustomed, Nature herself being the instructor of all the animals in such matters.

As for the Ethiopians, then, and their land, this is as much as we have to say.

11. Concerning the historians, we must distinguish among them, to the effect that many have composed works on both Egypt and Ethiopia, of whom some have given credence to false report and others have invented many tales out of their own minds for the delectation of their readers, and so may justly be distrusted. For example, Agatharchides of Cnidus [1] in the second Book of his work on Asia, and the compiler of geographies, Artemidorus of Ephesus,[2] in his eighth Book, and certain others whose homes were in Egypt, have recounted most of what I have set forth above and are, on the whole,

---

[2] His work in eleven books on the lands and peoples about the Mediterranean Sea was composed around 100 B.C.

3 ρημένων ἐν πᾶσι σχεδὸν ἐπιτυγχάνουσι. καὶ γὰρ ἡμεῖς καθ' ὃν καιρὸν παρεβάλομεν εἰς Αἴγυπτον, πολλοῖς μὲν τῶν ἱερέων ἐνετύχομεν, οὐκ ὀλίγοις δὲ καὶ πρεσβευταῖς ἀπὸ τῆς Αἰθιοπίας παροῦσιν εἰς λόγους ἀφικόμεθα· παρ' ὧν ἀκριβῶς ἕκαστα πυθόμενοι, καὶ τοὺς λόγους τῶν ἱστορικῶν ἐξελέγξαντες, τοῖς μάλιστα συμφωνοῦσιν ἀκόλουθον τὴν ἀναγραφὴν πεποιήμεθα.

4 Περὶ μὲν οὖν Αἰθιόπων τῶν πρὸς τῇ δύσει κατοικούντων ἀρκεσθησόμεθα τοῖς ῥηθεῖσι, περὶ δὲ τῶν κατὰ τὴν μεσημβρίαν καὶ τὴν Ἐρυθρὰν θάλατταν κειμένων ἐν μέρει διέξιμεν. δοκεῖ δ' ἡμῖν ἁρμόττειν προδιελθεῖν περὶ τῆς τοῦ χρυσοῦ κατασκευῆς τῆς ἐν τούτοις τοῖς τόποις γινομένης.

12. Περὶ γὰρ τὰς ἐσχατιὰς τῆς Αἰγύπτου καὶ τῆς ὁμορούσης Ἀραβίας τε καὶ Αἰθιοπίας τόπος ἐστὶν ἔχων μέταλλα πολλὰ καὶ μεγάλα χρυσοῦ, συναγομένου πολλοῦ πολλῇ κακοπαθείᾳ τε καὶ δαπάνῃ. τῆς γὰρ γῆς μελαίνης οὔσης τῇ φύσει καὶ διαφυὰς καὶ φλέβας ἐχούσης μαρμάρου τῇ λευκότητι διαφερούσας καὶ πάσας τὰς περιλαμπομένας φύσεις ὑπερβαλλούσας τῇ λαμπρότητι, οἱ προσεδρεύοντες τοῖς μεταλλικοῖς ἔργοις τῷ πλήθει τῶν ἐργαζο-
2 μένων κατασκευάζουσι τὸν χρυσόν. οἱ γὰρ βασιλεῖς τῆς Αἰγύπτου τοὺς ἐπὶ κακουργίᾳ καταδικασθέντας καὶ τοὺς κατὰ πόλεμον αἰχμαλωτισθέντας, ἔτι δὲ τοὺς ἀδίκοις διαβολαῖς περιπεσόντας καὶ διὰ θυμὸν εἰς φυλακὰς παραδεδομένους, ποτὲ μὲν αὐτούς, ποτὲ δὲ καὶ μετὰ πάσης συγγενείας, ἀθροίσαντες παραδιδόασι πρὸς τὴν τοῦ χρυσοῦ

---

[1] The Persian Gulf.

BOOK III. 11. 2–12. 2

accurate in all they have written. Since, to bear witness ourselves, during the time of our visit to Egypt, we associated with many of its priests and conversed with not a few ambassadors from Ethiopia as well who were then in Egypt; and after inquiring carefully of them about each matter and testing the stories of the historians, we have composed our account so as to accord with the opinions on which they most fully agree.

Now as for the Ethiopians who dwell in the west, we shall be satisfied with what has been said, and we shall discuss in turn the peoples who live to the south and about the Red Sea.[1] However, we feel that it is appropriate first to tell of the working of the gold as it is carried on in these regions.

12. At the extremity of Egypt and in the contiguous territory of both Arabia and Ethiopia there lies a region which contains many large gold mines, where the gold is secured in great quantities with much suffering and at great expense.[2] For the earth is naturally black and contains seams and veins of a marble[3] which is unusually white and in brilliancy surpasses everything else which shines brightly by its nature, and here the overseers of the labour in the mines recover the gold with the aid of a multitude of workers. For the kings of Egypt gather together and condemn to the mining of the gold such as have been found guilty of some crime and captives of war, as well as those who have been accused unjustly and thrown into prison because of their anger, and not only such persons but occasionally all their relatives as well, by this means not only

[2] Cp. the account of the mines in Spain (Book 5. 35 ff.).
[3] *i.e.* a quartz-rock; cp. below, § 5.

DIODORUS OF SICILY

μεταλλείαν, ἅμα μὲν τιμωρίαν λαμβάνοντες παρὰ τῶν καταγνωσθέντων, ἅμα δὲ διὰ τῶν ἐργαζομένων 3 μεγάλας προσόδους λαμβάνοντες. οἱ δὲ παραδοθέντες, πολλοὶ μὲν τὸ πλῆθος ὄντες, πάντες δὲ πέδαις δεδεμένοι, προσκαρτεροῦσι τοῖς ἔργοις συνεχῶς καὶ μεθ' ἡμέραν καὶ δι' ὅλης τῆς νυκτός, ἀνάπαυσιν μὲν οὐδεμίαν λαμβάνοντες, δρασμοῦ δὲ παντὸς φιλοτίμως εἰργόμενοι· φυλακαὶ γὰρ ἐκ στρατιωτῶν βαρβάρων καὶ ταῖς διαλέκτοις διαφόροις[1] χρωμένων ἐφεστήκασιν, ὥστε μηδένα δύνασθαι δι' ὁμιλίας ἢ φιλανθρώπου τινὸς ἐντεύξεως 4 φθεῖραί τινα τῶν ἐπιστατούντων. τῆς δὲ τὸν χρυσὸν ἐχούσης γῆς τὴν μὲν σκληροτάτην πυρὶ πολλῷ καύσαντες καὶ ποιήσαντες χαύνην προσάγουσι τὴν διὰ τῶν χειρῶν κατεργασίαν· τὴν δὲ ἀνειμένην πέτραν καὶ μετρίῳ πόνῳ δυναμένην ὑπείκειν λατομικῷ σιδήρῳ καταπονοῦσι μυριάδες 5 ἀκληρούντων ἀνθρώπων. καὶ τῆς μὲν ὅλης πραγματείας ὁ τὸν λίθον διακρίνων τεχνίτης καθηγεῖται καὶ τοῖς ἐργαζομένοις ὑποδείκνυσι· τῶν δὲ πρὸς τὴν ἀτυχίαν ταύτην ἀποδειχθέντων οἱ μὲν σώματος ῥώμῃ διαφέροντες τυπίσι σιδηραῖς τὴν μαρμαρίζουσαν πέτραν κόπτουσιν, οὐ τέχνην τοῖς ἔργοις, ἀλλὰ βίαν προσάγοντες, ὑπονόμους δὲ διακόπτοντες, οὐκ ἐπ' εὐθείας, ἀλλ' ὡς ἂν ἡ 6 διάφυσις ᾖ τῆς ἀποστιλβούσης πέτρας. οὗτοι μὲν οὖν διὰ τὰς ἐν ταῖς διώρυξι καμπὰς καὶ σκολιότητας ἐν σκότει διατρίβοντες λύχνους ἐπὶ τῶν μετώπων πεπηγμένους[2] περιφέρουσι· πολ-

---

[1] διαφόροις Dindorf: διαφόρως.
[2] So Capps, πεπραγματευμένους all editors, πεφραγμένους

BOOK III. 12. 2-6

inflicting punishment upon those found guilty but also securing at the same time great revenues from their labours. And those who have been condemned in this way—and they are a great multitude and are all bound in chains—work at their task unceasingly both by day and throughout the entire night, enjoying no respite and being carefully cut off from any means of escape; since guards of foreign soldiers who speak a language different from theirs stand watch over them, so that not a man, either by conversation or by some contact of a friendly nature, is able to corrupt one of his keepers. The gold-bearing earth [1] which is hardest they first burn with a hot fire, and when they have crumbled it in this way they continue the working of it by hand; and the soft rock which can yield to moderate effort is crushed with a sledge by myriads of unfortunate wretches. And the entire operations are in charge of a skilled worker who distinguishes the stone [2] and points it out to the labourers; and of those who are assigned to this unfortunate task the physically strongest break the quartz-rock [3] with iron hammers, applying no skill to the task, but only force, and cutting tunnels through the stone, not in a straight line but wherever the seam of gleaming rock may lead. Now these men, working in darkness as they do because of the bending and winding of the passages, carry lamps bound on their foreheads; and since

[1] Here and below "earth" must be the equivalent of the "marble" mentioned before.
[2] *i.e.* picks out that which is gold-bearing.
[3] Literally, "the rock which contains the marble."

CE; cp. Agatharchides 25 (Müller): οὗτοι μὲν οὖν λύχνους προσδεδεμένους τοῖς μετώποις ἔχοντες λατομοῦσιν.

λαχῶς δὲ πρὸς τὰς τῆς πέτρας ἰδιότητας μετασχηματίζοντες τὰ σώματα καταβάλλουσιν εἰς ἔδαφος τὰ λατομούμενα θραύματα· καὶ τοῦτο ἀδιαλείπτως ἐνεργοῦσι πρὸς ἐπιστάτου βαρύτητα καὶ πληγάς.

13. Οἱ δὲ ἄνηβοι παῖδες εἰσδυόμενοι διὰ τῶν ὑπονόμων εἰς τὰ κεκοιλωμένα τῆς πέτρας ἀναβάλλουσιν ἐπιπόνως τὴν ῥιπτουμένην κατὰ μικρὸν πέτραν καὶ πρὸς τὸν ἐκτὸς τοῦ στομίου τόπον εἰς ὕπαιθρον ἀποκομίζουσιν. οἱ δ' ὑπὲρ ἔτη τριάκοντα παρὰ τούτων λαμβάνοντες ὡρισμένον μέτρον τοῦ λατομήματος ἐν ὅλμοις λιθίνοις τύπτουσι σιδηροῖς ὑπέροις, ἄχρι ἂν ὀρόβου τὸ μέγεθος κατεργάσωνται. 2 παρὰ δὲ τούτων τὸν ὀροβίτην λίθον αἱ γυναῖκες καὶ οἱ πρεσβύτεροι τῶν ἀνδρῶν ἐκδέχονται, καὶ μύλων ἐξῆς πλειόνων ὄντων ἐπὶ τούτους ἐπιβάλλουσι, καὶ παραστάντες ἀνὰ τρεῖς ἢ δύο πρὸς τὴν κώπην ἀλήθουσιν, ἕως ἂν εἰς σεμιδάλεως τρόπον τὸ δοθὲν μέτρον κατεργάσωνται. προσούσης δ' ἅπασιν ἀθεραπευσίας σώματος καὶ τῆς τὴν αἰδῶ περιστελλούσης ἐσθῆτος μὴ προσούσης, οὐκ ἔστιν ὃς ἰδὼν οὐκ ἂν ἐλεήσειε τοὺς ἀκληροῦντας διὰ τὴν ὑπερβολὴν 3 τῆς ταλαιπωρίας. οὐ γὰρ τυγχάνει συγγνώμης οὐδ' ἀνέσεως ἁπλῶς οὐκ ἄρρωστος, οὐ πεπηρωμένος, οὐ γεγηρακώς, οὐ γυναικὸς ἀσθένεια, πάντες δὲ πληγαῖς ἀναγκάζονται προσκαρτερεῖν τοῖς ἔργοις, μέχρι ἂν κακουχούμενοι τελευτήσωσιν ἐν ταῖς ἀνάγκαις. διόπερ οἱ δυστυχεῖς φοβερώ-

---

[1] i.e. as the gold-bearing stratum turns in one direction and another.
[2] Agatharchides 26 (ed. Müller), whom Diodorus is following here, say these workers were " under " thirty.

much of the time they change the position of their bodies to follow the particular character[1] of the stone they throw the blocks, as they cut them out, on the ground; and at this task they labour without ceasing beneath the sternness and blows of an overseer.

13. The boys there who have not yet come to maturity, entering through the tunnels into the galleries formed by the removal of the rock, laboriously gather up the rock as it is cast down piece by piece and carry it out into the open to the place outside the entrance. Then those who are above[2] thirty years of age take this quarried stone from them and with iron pestles pound a specified amount of it in stone mortars, until they have worked it down to the size of a vetch. Thereupon the women and older men receive from them the rock of this size and cast it into mills of which a number stand there in a row, and taking their places in groups of two or three at the spoke or handle of each mill they grind it until they have worked down the amount given them to the consistency of the finest flour. And since no opportunity is afforded any of them to care for his body and they have no garment to cover their shame, no man can look upon the unfortunate wretches without feeling pity for them because of the exceeding hardships they suffer. For no leniency or respite of any kind is given to any man who is sick, or maimed, or aged, or in the case of a woman for her weakness,[3] but all without exception are compelled by blows to persevere in their labours, until through ill-treatment they die in the midst of their tortures. Consequently the poor unfortunates be-

[3] Or "illness."

τερον ἀεὶ τὸ μέλλον τοῦ παρόντος ἡγοῦνται διὰ τὴν ὑπερβολὴν τῆς τιμωρίας, ποθεινότερον δὲ τοῦ ζῆν τὸν θάνατον προσδέχονται.

14. Τὸ δὲ τελευταῖον οἱ τεχνῖται παραλαβόντες τὸν ἀληλεσμένον λίθον πρὸς τὴν ὅλην ἄγουσι συντέλειαν· ἐπὶ γὰρ πλατείας σανίδος μικρὸν ἐγκεκλιμένης τρίβουσι τὴν κατειργασμένην μάρμαρον ὕδωρ ἐπιχέοντες· εἶτα τὸ μὲν γεῶδες αὐτῆς ἐκτηκόμενον διὰ τῶν ὑγρῶν καταρρεῖ κατὰ τὴν τῆς σανίδος ἔγκλισιν, τὸ δὲ χρυσίον[1] ἔχον ἐπὶ 2 τοῦ ξύλου παραμένει διὰ τὸ βάρος. πολλάκις δὲ τοῦτο ποιοῦντες, τὸ μὲν πρῶτον ταῖς χερσὶν ἐλαφρῶς τρίβουσι, μετὰ δὲ ταῦτα σπόγγοις ἀραιοῖς κούφως ἐπιθλίβοντες τὸ χαῦνον καὶ γεῶδες διὰ τούτων ἀναλαμβάνουσι, μέχρι ἂν ὅτου καθαρὸν 3 γένηται τὸ ψῆγμα τοῦ χρυσοῦ. τὸ δὲ τελευταῖον ἄλλοι τεχνῖται παραλαμβάνοντες μέτρῳ καὶ σταθμῷ τὸ συνηγμένον εἰς κεραμεοῦς χύτρους ἐμβάλλουσι· μίξαντες δὲ κατὰ τὸ πλῆθος ἀνάλογον μολίβδου βῶλον καὶ χόνδρους ἁλῶν, ἔτι δὲ βραχὺ καττιτέρου, καὶ κρίθινον πίτυρον προσεμβάλλουσιν· ἁρμοστὸν δ' ἐπίθημα ποιήσαντες καὶ πηλῷ φιλοπόνως περιχρίσαντες ὀπτῶσιν ἐν καμίνῳ πέντε ἡμέρας καὶ 4 νύκτας ἴσας ἀδιαλείπτως· ἔπειτα ἐάσαντες ψυχθῆναι τῶν μὲν ἄλλων οὐδὲν εὑρίσκουσιν ἐν τοῖς ἀγγείοις, τὸν δὲ χρυσὸν καθαρὸν λαμβάνουσιν ὀλίγης ἀπουσίας γεγενημένης. ἡ μὲν οὖν ἐργασία τοῦ χρυσοῦ περὶ τὰς ἐσχατιὰς τῆς Αἰγύπτου γινομένη μετὰ τοσούτων καὶ τηλικούτων πόνων 5 συντελεῖται· αὐτὴ γὰρ ἡ φύσις, οἶμαι, ποιεῖ

[1] Vogel suggests χρυσόν.

lieve, because their punishment is so excessively severe, that the future will always be more terrible than the present and therefore look forward to death as more to be desired than life.

14. In the last steps the skilled workmen receive the stone which has been ground to powder and take it off for its complete and final working; for they rub the marble [1] which has been worked down upon a broad board which is slightly inclined, pouring water over it all the while; whereupon the earthy matter in it, melted away by the action of the water, runs down the inclined board, while that which contains the gold remains on the wood because of its weight. And repeating this a number of times, they first of all rub it gently with their hands, and then lightly pressing it with sponges of loose texture they remove in this way whatever is porous and earthy, until there remains only the pure gold-dust. Then at last other skilled workmen take what has been recovered and put it by fixed measure and weight into earthen jars, mixing with it a lump of lead proportionate to the mass, lumps of salt and a little tin, and adding thereto barley bran; thereupon they put on it a close-fitting lid, and smearing it over carefully with mud they bake it in a kiln for five successive days and as many nights; and at the end of this period, when they have let the jars cool off, of the other matter they find no remains in the jars, but the gold they recover in pure form, there being but little waste. This working of the gold, as it is carried on at the farthermost borders of Egypt, is effected through all the extensive labours here described; for Nature herself, in my opinion, makes

[1] Cp. p. 115, n. 3.

πρόδηλον ὡς ὁ[1] χρυσὸς γένεσιν μὲν ἐπίπονον ἔχει, φυλακὴν δὲ χαλεπήν, σπουδὴν δὲ μεγίστην, χρῆσιν δὲ ἀνὰ μέσον ἡδονῆς τε καὶ λύπης.

Ἡ μὲν οὖν τῶν μετάλλων τούτων εὕρεσις ἀρχαία παντελῶς ἐστιν, ὡς ἂν ὑπὸ τῶν παλαιῶν 6 βασιλέων καταδειχθεῖσα. περὶ δὲ τῶν ἐθνῶν[2] τῶν κατοικούντων τήν τε παράλιον τοῦ Ἀραβίου κόλπου καὶ Τρωγοδυτικήν, ἔτι δ' Αἰθιοπίαν τὴν πρὸς μεσημβρίαν καὶ νότον, πειρασόμεθα διεξιέναι.

15. Περὶ πρώτων δὲ τῶν Ἰχθυοφάγων ἐροῦμεν τῶν κατοικούντων τὴν παράλιον τὴν ἀπὸ Καρμανίας καὶ Γεδρωσίας ἕως τῶν ἐσχάτων τοῦ μυχοῦ τοῦ κατὰ τὸν Ἀράβιον κόλπον ἱδρυμένου, ὃς εἰς τὴν μεσόγειον ἀνήκων ἄπιστον διάστημα δυσὶν ἠπείροις περικλείεται πρὸς τὸν ἔκπλουν, τῇ μὲν ὑπὸ τῆς Εὐδαίμονος Ἀραβίας, τῇ δ' ὑπὸ τῆς Τρωγοδυτικῆς. 2 τούτων δὲ τῶν βαρβάρων τινὲς μὲν γυμνοὶ τὸ παράπαν βιοῦντες κοινὰς ἔχουσι τὰς γυναῖκας καὶ τὰ τέκνα παραπλησίως ταῖς τῶν θρεμμάτων ἀγέλαις, ἡδονῆς δὲ καὶ πόνου τὴν φυσικὴν μόνον ἀντίληψιν ποιούμενοι τῶν αἰσχρῶν καὶ καλῶν οὐδεμίαν 3 λαμβάνουσιν ἔννοιαν. τὰς δὲ οἰκήσεις ἔχουσιν οὐκ ἄπωθεν τῆς θαλάττης παρὰ τὰς ῥαχίας, καθ' ἃς εἰσιν οὐ μόνον βαθεῖαι κοιλάδες, ἀλλὰ καὶ φάραγγες ἀνώμαλοι καὶ στενοὶ παντελῶς αὐλῶνες σκολιαῖς ἐκτροπαῖς ὑπὸ τῆς φύσεως διειλημμένοι. τούτων δὲ τῇ χρείᾳ τῶν ἐγχωρίων πεφυκότων ἁρμοζόντως, τὰς ἐκτροπὰς καὶ[3] διεξόδους συγκεχώκασι λίθοις

[1] ὁ Reiske: ὁ μέν.
[2] τούτων after ἐθνῶν deleted by Dindorf.
[3] For καὶ Capps suggests κατὰ τάς, "at their outlets."

BOOK III. 14. 5–15. 3

it clear that whereas the production of gold is laborious, the guarding of it is difficult, the zest for it very great, and that its use is half-way between pleasure and pain.

Now the discovery of these mines is very ancient, having been made by the early kings. But we shall undertake to discuss the peoples which inhabit the coast of the Arabian Gulf[1] and that of the Trogodytes and the part of Ethiopia that faces the noon-day sun and the south wind.

15. The first people we shall mention are the Ichthyophagi[2] who inhabit the coast which extends from Carmania and Gedrosia[3] to the farthest limits of the arm of the sea which is found at the Arabian Gulf, which extends inland an unbelievable distance and is enclosed at its mouth by two continents, on the one side by Arabia Felix and on the other by the land of the Trogodytes. As for these barbarians, certain of them go about entirely naked and have the women and children in common like their flocks and herds, and since they recognize only the physical perception of pleasure and pain they take no thought of things which are disgraceful and those which are honourable. They have their dwellings not far from the sea along the rocky shores, where there are not only deep valleys but also jagged ravines and very narrow channels which Nature has divided by means of winding side-branches. These branches being by their nature suited to their need, the natives close up the passages and[4] outlets with heaps of great

---

[1] The Red Sea. [2] Fish-eaters.
[3] Approximately modern south-eastern Persia and Baluchistan.
[4] Or "at their outlets"; cp. critical note.

μεγάλοις, δι' ὧν ὥσπερ δικτύων τὴν θήραν τῶν
4 ἰχθύων ποιοῦνται. ὅταν γὰρ ἡ πλημυρὶς τῆς
θαλάττης ἐπὶ τὴν χέρσον φέρηται λάβρως, ὃ ποιεῖ
δὶς τῆς ἡμέρας περὶ τρίτην καὶ ἐνάτην μάλιστά πως
ὥραν, ἡ μὲν θάλαττα πᾶσαν τὴν ῥαχίαν ἐπικλύζουσα
καλύπτει, καὶ λάβρῳ καὶ πολλῷ κύματι συναποκο-
μίζει πρὸς τὴν χέρσον ἄπιστον πλῆθος παντοίων
ἰχθύων, οἳ τὸ μὲν πρῶτον ἐν τῇ παραλίῳ μένουσι,
νομῆς χάριν πλανώμενοι περὶ τὰς ὑποδύσεις καὶ τὰ
κοιλώματα· ἐπὰν δ' ὁ τῆς ἀμπώτεως ἔλθῃ χρόνος,
τὸ μὲν ὑγρὸν ἐκ τοῦ κατ' ὀλίγον διὰ τῶν κεχωσμένων
λίθων καὶ φαράγγων ἀπορρεῖ, οἱ δ' ἰχθῦς ἐν τοῖς
5 κοιλώμασι καταλείπονται. κατὰ δὲ τοῦτον τὸν
καιρὸν τὸ πλῆθος τῶν ἐγχωρίων μετὰ τέκνων καὶ
γυναικῶν εἰς τὰς ῥαχίας ἀθροίζεται καθάπερ ἀφ'
ἑνὸς κελεύσματος. σχιζομένων δὲ τῶν βαρβάρων
εἰς τὰ κατὰ μέρος συστήματα, πρὸς τοὺς ἰδίους
ἕκαστοι τόπους μετὰ βοῆς ἐξαισίου φέρονται,
καθάπερ αἰφνιδίου τινὸς κυνηγίας ἐμπεπτωκυίας.
6 εἶθ' αἱ μὲν γυναῖκες μετὰ τῶν παίδων τοὺς ἐλάτ-
τονας τῶν ἰχθύων καὶ πλησίον ὄντας τῆς χέρσου
συλλαμβάνουσαι ῥίπτουσιν ἐπὶ τὴν γῆν, οἱ δὲ τοῖς
σώμασιν ἀκμάζοντες προσφέρουσι τὰς χεῖρας τοῖς
διὰ τὸ μέγεθος δυσκαταγωνίστοις· ἐκπίπτουσι γὰρ
ἐκ τοῦ πελάγους ὑπερμεγέθεις οὐ μόνον σκορπίοι
καὶ μύραιναι καὶ κύνες, ἀλλὰ καὶ φῶκαι καὶ πολλὰ
τοιαῦτα ξένα καὶ ταῖς ὄψεσι καὶ ταῖς προσηγορίαις.
7 ταῦτα δὲ τὰ θηρία καταμάχονται τεχνικῆς μὲν
ὅπλων κατασκευῆς οὐδὲν ἔχοντες, κέρασι δὲ αἰγῶν

stones, and by means of these, as if with nets, they carry on the catching of the fish. For whenever the flood-tide of the sea sweeps violently over the land, which happens twice daily and usually about the third and ninth hour, the sea covers in its flood all the rocky shore and together with the huge and violent billow carries to the land an incredible multitude of fish of every kind, which at first remain along the coast, wandering in search of food among the sheltered spots and hollow places; but whenever the time of ebb comes, the water flows off little by little through the heaps of rocks and ravines, but the fish are left behind in the hollow places. At this moment the multitude of the natives with their children and women gather, as if at a single word of command, at the rocky shores. And the barbarians, dividing into several companies, rush in bands each to its respective place with a hideous shouting, as if they had come unexpectedly upon some prey. Thereupon the women and children, seizing the smaller fish which are near the shore, throw them on the land, and the men of bodily vigour lay hands upon the fish which are hard to overcome because of their size; for there are driven out of the deep creatures of enormous size, not only sea-scorpions[1] and sea-eels and dog-fish, but also seals[2] and many other kinds which are strange both in appearance and in name. These animals they subdue without the assistance of any skilful device of weapons but by piercing them through with sharp goathorns and by

[1] Perhaps the *scorpaena scrofa*, which is described in Athenaeus 320 D, where Gulick (in the *L.C.L.*) suggests "sculpin" as an "inexact but convenient" equivalent.
[2] Perhaps the *phoca monachus* of *Odyssey* 4. 404.

ὀξέσι κατακεντοῦντες καὶ ταῖς ἀπορρῶξι πέτραις ἐπιτέμνοντες· πάντα γὰρ ἡ χρεία διδάσκει τὴν φύσιν, οἰκείως τοῖς ὑποκειμένοις καιροῖς ἁρμοζομένην πρὸς τὴν ἐκ τῆς ἐλπίδος εὐχρηστίαν.

16. Ἐπειδὰν δ' ἀθροίσωσιν ἰχθύων παντοδαπῶν πλῆθος, μεταφέρουσι τοὺς ληφθέντας καὶ πάντας ὀπτῶσιν ἐπὶ τῶν πετρῶν τῶν ἐγκεκλιμένων πρὸς μεσημβρίαν. διαπύρων δ' οὐσῶν διὰ τὴν τοῦ καύματος ὑπερβολήν, βραχὺν ἐάσαντες χρόνον στρέφουσι, κἄπειτα τῆς οὐρᾶς λαμβανόμενοι σείουσι 2 τὸν ὅλον ὄγκον. καὶ αἱ μὲν σάρκες θρυπτόμεναι διὰ τὴν θερμασίαν ἀποπίπτουσιν, αἱ δ' ἄκανθαι ῥιπτούμεναι πρὸς ἕνα τόπον μέγαν σωρὸν ἀποτελοῦσιν, ἀθροιζόμεναι χρείας ἕνεκεν περὶ ἧς μικρὸν ὕστερον ἐροῦμεν. μετὰ δὲ ταῦτα τὰς μὲν σάρκας ἐπί τινος λεωπετρίας κατατιθέμενοι πατοῦσιν ἐπιμελῶς ἐφ' ἱκανὸν χρόνον καὶ καταμίσγουσι τὸν τοῦ παλιού- 3 ρου καρπόν· τούτου γὰρ συναναχρωσθέντος τὸ πᾶν γίνεται χρῆμα[1] κολλῶδες· καὶ δοκεῖ τοῦτο καθάπερ ἡδύσματος παρ' αὐτοῖς ἔχειν τάξιν. τὸ δὲ τελευταῖον τὸ καλῶς πατηθὲν εἰς πλινθίδας παραμήκεις τυποῦντες τιθέασιν εἰς τὸν ἥλιον· ἃς συμμέτρως ξηρανθείσας καθίσαντες κατευωχοῦνται, οὐ μὴν πρὸς μέτρον ἢ σταθμὸν ἐσθίοντες, ἀλλὰ πρὸς τὴν ἰδίαν ἑκάστου[2] βούλησιν, τὴν φυσικὴν 4 ὄρεξιν ἔχοντες τῆς ἀπολαύσεως περιγραφήν· ἀνεκλείπτοις[3] γὰρ καὶ διὰ παντὸς ἑτοίμοις χρῶνται ταμιεύμασιν, ὡς ἂν τοῦ Ποσειδῶνος τὸ τῆς Δήμητρος ἔργον μετειληφότος.

[1] χρῆμα Reiske: χρῶμα MSS, Bekker, Dindorf.
[2] ἑκάστου MSS, Bekker, Vogel: ἕκαστος Hertlein, Dindorf.
[3] ἀνεκλείπτοις Dindorf: ἀνεκλείπτως.

gashing them with the jagged rocks; for necessity teaches Nature everything, as Nature, in her own fashion, by seizing upon the opportunities which lie at hand adapts herself to their hoped-for utilization.

16. Whenever they have collected a multitude of all kinds of fish they carry off their catch and bake the whole of it upon the rocks which are inclined towards the south. And since these stones are red-hot because of the very great heat, they leave the fish there for only a short time and then turn them over, and then, picking them up bodily by the tail, they shake them. And the meat, which has become tender by reason of the warmth, falls away, but the backbones are cast into a single spot and form a great heap, being collected for a certain use of which we shall speak a little later. Then placing the meat upon a smooth stone they carefully tread upon it for a sufficient length of time and mix with it the fruit of the Christ's thorn[1]; for when this has been thoroughly worked into the meat the whole of it becomes a glutinous mass, and it would appear that this takes the place among them of a relish. Finally, when this has been well trodden, they mould it into little oblong bricks and place them in the sun; and after these have become thoroughly dry they sit down and feast upon them, eating not according to any measure or weight but according to every man's own wish, inasmuch as they make their physical desire the bounds of their indulgence. For they have at all times stores which are unfailing and ready for use, as though Poseidon had assumed the task of Demeter.

[1] A shrub of the buckthorn family.

Ἐνίοτε δὲ τηλικοῦτον ἐκ τοῦ πελάγους εἰς τὴν χέρσον κυλινδεῖται κῦμα καὶ τὰς ῥαχίας ἐφ' ἡμέρας πολλὰς κατακλύζει λάβρον,[1] ὥστε μηδένα δύνασθαι τοῖς τόποις προσεγγίζειν. διόπερ κατὰ τούτους τοὺς καιροὺς σπανίζοντες τροφῆς τὸ μὲν πρῶτον τοὺς κόγχους συλλέγουσι, τηλικούτους τὸ μέγεθος ὧν εὑρίσκονταί τινες τετραμναῖοι· τὰ μὲν γὰρ κύτη συντρίβουσι λίθους εὐμεγέθεις ἐμβάλλοντες, τὴν δ' ἐντὸς σάρκα κατεσθίουσιν ὠμήν, τῆς γεύσεως οὔσης παρεμφεροῦς τοῖς ὀστρέοις. ἐπὰν δὲ διὰ τὴν συνέχειαν τῶν πνευμάτων ἐπὶ πλείονα χρόνον πλήθειν συμβαίνῃ τὸν ὠκεανόν, καὶ τὴν εἰωθυῖαν θήραν τῶν ἰχθύων ἐκκλείσῃ τὸ τῆς περιστάσεως ἀδύνατον, ἐπὶ τοὺς κόγχους, ὡς εἴρηται, τρέπονται. εἰ δὲ ἡ ἐκ τῶν κόγχων τροφὴ σπανίζει, καταφεύγουσιν ἐπὶ τὸν τῶν ἀκανθῶν σωρόν· ἐκ τούτου γὰρ ἐκλέγοντες τὰς ἐγχύλους καὶ προσφάτους τῶν ἀκανθῶν διαιροῦσι κατ' ἄρθρον, καὶ τὰς μὲν αὐτόθεν τοῖς ὀδοῦσι κατεργάζονται, τὰς δὲ σκληρὰς λίθοις θραύοντες καὶ προϋπεργαζόμενοι κατεσθίουσι, παραπλησίαν διάθεσιν ἔχοντες τοῖς φωλεύουσι τῶν θηρίων.

17. Τῆς μὲν οὖν ξηρᾶς τροφῆς τὸν εἰρημένον τρόπον εὐποροῦσι, τῆς δ' ὑγρᾶς παράδοξον ἔχουσι καὶ παντελῶς ἀπιστουμένην τὴν χρῆσιν. ταῖς μὲν γὰρ θήραις προσκαρτεροῦσιν ἐφ' ἡμέρας τέτταρας, εὐωχούμενοι πανδημεὶ μεθ' ἱλαρότητος καὶ ταῖς ἀνάρθροις ᾠδαῖς ἀλλήλους ψυχαγωγοῦντες· πρὸς δὲ τούτοις ἐπιμίσγονται τότε ταῖς γυναιξὶν αἷς ἂν τύχωσι παιδοποιΐας ἕνεκα, πάσης ἀσχολίας

[1] For λάβρον Vogel suggests λάβρως (ch. 15. 4).

BOOK III. 16. 4–17. 1

But at times a tidal wave of such size rolls in from the sea upon the land, a violent wave that for many days submerges the rocky shores, that no one can approach those regions. Consequently, being short of food at such times, they at first gather the mussels, which are of so great a size that some of them are found that weigh four minas[1]; that is, they break their shells by throwing huge stones at them and then eat the meat raw, its taste resembling somewhat that of oysters. And whenever it comes to pass that the ocean is high for a considerable period because of the continued winds, and the impossibility of coping with that state of affairs prevents them from making their usual catch of fish, they turn, as has been said, to the mussels. But if the food from the mussels fails them, they have recourse to the heap of backbones; that is, they select from this heap such backbones as are succulent and fresh and take them apart joint by joint, and then they grind some at once with their teeth, though the hard ones they first crush with rocks and thus prepare them before they eat them, their level of life being much the same as that of the wild beasts which make their homes in dens.

17. Now as for dry[2] food they get an abundance of it in the manner described, but their use of wet food is astonishing and quite incredible. For they devote themselves assiduously for four days to the sea-food they have caught, the whole tribe feasting upon it merrily while entertaining one another with inarticulate songs; and furthermore, they lie at this time with any women they happen to meet in order to beget children, being relieved of every concern

[1] About five pounds. [2] *i.e.* "solid."

ἀπολελυμένοι διὰ τὴν εὐκοπίαν καὶ τὴν ἑτοιμότητα τῆς τροφῆς. τῇ δὲ πέμπτῃ πρὸς τὴν ὑπώρειαν ἐπείγονται πανδημεὶ ποτοῦ χάριν, ἔνθα συρρύσεις ὑδάτων γλυκέων εἰσί, πρὸς αἷς οἱ νομάδες τὰς ἀγέλας τῶν θρεμμάτων ποτίζουσιν. ἡ δὲ ὁδοιπορία τούτων παραπλήσιος γίνεται ταῖς ἀγέλαις τῶν βοῶν, πάντων φωνὴν ἀφιέντων οὐκ ἔναρθρον, ἀλλ' ἦχον μόνον ἀποτελοῦσαν. τῶν δὲ τέκνων τὰ μὲν νήπια παντελῶς αἱ μητέρες ἐν ταῖς ἀγκάλαις φέρουσι, τὰ δὲ κεχωρισμένα τοῦ γάλακτος οἱ πατέρες, τὰ δ' ὑπὲρ πενταετῆ χρόνον ὄντα προάγει μετὰ τῶν γονέων σὺν παιδιᾷ, πεπληρωμένα χαρᾶς, ὡς ἂν πρὸς τὴν ἡδίστην ἀπόλαυσιν ὁρμώμενα. ἡ γὰρ φύσις αὐτῶν ἀδιάστροφος οὖσα τὴν ἀναπλήρωσιν τῆς ἐνδείας ἡγεῖται μέγιστον ἀγαθόν, οὐδὲν τῶν ἐπεισάκτων ἡδέων ἐπιζητοῦσα. ὅταν δὲ ταῖς τῶν νομάδων ποτίστραις ἐγγίσωσι καὶ τοῦ ποτοῦ πληρωθῶσι[1] τὰς κοιλίας, ἐπανέρχονται, μόγις βαδίζοντες διὰ τὸ βάρος. κἀκείνην μὲν τὴν ἡμέραν οὐδενὸς γεύονται, κεῖται δ' ἕκαστος ὑπεργέμων καὶ δύσπνους καὶ τὸ σύνολον παρεμφερὴς τῷ μεθύοντι. τῇ δ' ἑξῆς ἐπὶ τὴν ἀπὸ τῶν ἰχθύων πάλιν τροφὴν ἀνακάμπτουσι· καὶ τοῦτον τὸν τρόπον ἡ δίαιτα κυκλεῖται παρ' αὐτοῖς πάντα τὸν τοῦ ζῆν χρόνον.

Οἱ μὲν οὖν τὴν παράλιον τὴν ἐντὸς τῶν στενῶν κατοικοῦντες οὕτω βιοῦσι, νόσοις μὲν διὰ τὴν ἁπλότητα τῆς τροφῆς σπανίως περιπίπτοντες, ὀλιγοχρονιώτεροι δὲ πολὺ τῶν παρ' ἡμῖν ὄντες.

18. Τοῖς δὲ τὴν ἐκτὸς τοῦ κόλπου παράλιον νεμομέ-

[1] Dindorf suggests πληρώσωσι.

because their food is easily secured and ready at hand. But on the fifth day the whole tribe hurries off in search of drink to the foothills of the mountains, where there are springs of sweet water at which the pastoral folk water their flocks and herds. And their journey thither is like that of herds of cattle, all of them uttering a cry which produces, not articulate speech, but merely a confused roaring. As for their children, the women carry the babies continually in their arms, but the fathers do this after they have been separated from their milk, while those above five years of age lead the way accompanied by their parents, playing as they go and full of joy, as though they were setting out for pleasure of the sweetest kind. For the nature of this people, being as yet unperverted, considers the satisfying of their need to be the greatest possible good, desiring in addition none of the imported pleasures. And so soon as they arrive at the watering-places of the pastoral folk and have their bellies filled with the water, they return, scarcely able to move because of the weight of it. On that day they taste no food, but everyone lies gorged and scarcely able to breathe, quite like a drunken man. The next day, however, they turn again to the eating of the fish; and their way of living follows a cycle after this fashion throughout their lives.

Now the inhabitants of the coast inside the Straits lead the kind of life which has been described, and by reason of the simplicity of their food they rarely are subject to attacks of disease, although they are far shorter-lived than the inhabitants of our part of the world.

18. But as for the inhabitants of the coast outside

DIODORUS OF SICILY

νοις πολλῷ τούτων παραδοξότερον εἶναι τὸν βίον συμβέβηκεν, ὡς ἂν ἄδιψον ἐχόντων καὶ ἀπαθῆ τὴν φύσιν. ἀπὸ γὰρ τῶν οἰκουμένων τόπων εἰς τὴν ἔρημον ὑπὸ τῆς τύχης ἐκτετοπισμένοι τῆς μὲν ἀπὸ τῶν ἰχθύων ἄγρας εὐποροῦσιν, ὑγρὰν δὲ τροφὴν 2 οὐκ ἐπιζητοῦσι. προσφερόμενοι γὰρ τὸν ἰχθῦν ἔγχυλον, μικρὰν ἔχοντα τῶν ὠμῶν τὴν παραλλαγήν, οὐχ οἷον ὑγρὰν τροφὴν ἐπιζητοῦσιν, ἀλλ' οὐδ' ἔννοιαν ἔχουσι ποτοῦ. στέργουσι δὲ τὴν ἐξ ἀρχῆς δίαιταν ὑπὸ τῆς τύχης αὐτοῖς προσκληρωθεῖσαν, εὐδαιμονίαν ἡγούμενοι τὴν ἐκ τῆς ἐνδείας αὐτοῦ τοῦ λυποῦντος ὑπεξαίρεσιν.

3 Τὸ δὲ πάντων παραδοξότατον, ἀπαθείᾳ τοσοῦτον ὑπερβάλλουσι πάντας ὥστε μὴ ῥᾳδίως πιστευθῆναι τὸν λόγον. καίτοι γε πολλοὶ τῶν ἀπ' Αἰγύπτου πλεόντων διὰ τῆς Ἐρυθρᾶς θαλάττης ἔμποροι μέχρι τοῦ νῦν, πολλάκις προσπεπλευκότες πρὸς τὴν τῶν Ἰχθυοφάγων χώραν, ἐξηγοῦνται σύμφωνα τοῖς ὑφ' ἡμῶν εἰρημένοις περὶ τῶν ἀπαθῶν 4 ἀνθρώπων. καὶ ὁ τρίτος δὲ Πτολεμαῖος, ὁ φιλοτιμηθεὶς περὶ τὴν θήραν τῶν ἐλεφάντων τῶν περὶ τὴν χώραν ταύτην ὄντων, ἐξέπεμψεν ἕνα τῶν φίλων, ὄνομα Σιμμίαν, κατασκεψόμενον τὴν χώραν· οὗτος δὲ μετὰ τῆς ἁρμοττούσης χορηγίας ἀποσταλεὶς ἀκριβῶς, ὥς φησιν Ἀγαθαρχίδης ὁ Κνίδιος ἱστοριογράφος, ἐξήτασε τὰ κατὰ τὴν παραλίαν ἔθνη. φησὶν οὖν τὸ τῶν ἀπαθῶν Αἰθιόπων

---

[1] The Epicurean doctrine. Cp. Lucretius 2. 20–1: *ergo corpoream ad naturam pauca videmus esse opus omnino, quae demant cumque dolorem.* ("Therefore we see that few things altogether are necessary for the bodily nature, only such in each case as take pain away"; tr. of Rouse.)

BOOK III. 18. 1–4

the gulf, we find that their life is far more astonishing than that of the people just described, it being as though their nature never suffers from thirst and is insensible to pain. For although they have been banished by fortune from the inhabited regions into the desert, they fare quite well from their catch of the fish, but wet food they do not require. For since they eat the fish while it is yet juicy and not far removed from the raw state, they are so far from requiring wet food that they have not even a notion of drinking. And they are content with that food which was originally allotted to them by fortune, considering that the mere elimination of that pain which arises from want (of food) is happiness.[1]

But the most surprising thing of all is, that in lack of sensibility they surpass all men, and to such a degree that what is recounted of them is scarcely credible. And yet many merchants of Egypt, who sail, as is their practice, through the Red Sea down to this day and have often sailed as far as the land of the Ichthyophagi, agree in their accounts with what we have said about the human beings who are insensible to pain. The third Ptolemy[2] also, who was passionately fond of hunting the elephants which are found in that region, sent one of his friends named Simmias to spy out the land; and he, setting out with suitable supplies, made, as the historian Agatharchides of Cnidus asserts, a thorough investigation of the nations lying along the coast. Now he[3] says that the nation of the "insensible" Ethiopians[4]

---

[2] Ptolemy Euergetes I, who reigned 246–221 B.C.

[3] *i.e.* Agatharchides, who is the chief source of Diodorus in this section of his work; cp. Agatharchides, 41 (Müller).

[4] The Ethiopians of the east; cp. Book 2. 22. 2 and note.

DIODORUS OF SICILY

ἔθνος τὸ σύνολον ποτῷ μὴ χρῆσθαι, μηδὲ τὴν φύσιν αὐτῶν ἐπιζητεῖν διὰ τὰς προειρημένας αἰτίας. καθόλου δ' ἀποφαίνεται μήτ' εἰς σύλλογον ἔρχεσθαι πρὸς τοὺς ἀλλοεθνεῖς, μήτε τὸ ξένον τῆς ὄψεως τῶν προσπλεόντων κινεῖν τοὺς ἐγχωρίους, ἀλλ' ἐμβλέποντας ἀτενῶς ἀπαθεῖς ἔχειν καὶ ἀκινήτους τὰς αἰσθήσεις, ὡς ἂν[1] μηδενὸς παρόντος. οὔτε γὰρ ξίφος σπασαμένου τινὸς καὶ καταφέροντος ὑπεξέφυγον, οὔθ' ὕβριν οὐδὲ[2] πληγὰς ὑπομένοντες ἠρεθίζοντο, τό τε πλῆθος οὐ συνηγανάκτει τοῖς πάσχουσιν, ἀλλ' ἐνίοτε τέκνων ἢ γυναικῶν σφαττομένων ἐν ὀφθαλμοῖς ἀπαθεῖς ταῖς διαθέσεσιν ἔμενον, οὐδεμίαν ἔμφασιν ὀργῆς ἢ πάλιν ἐλέου διδόντες. καθόλου δὲ τοῖς ἐκπληκτικωτάτοις δεινοῖς περιπίπτοντες ἠρεμαῖοι διέμενον, βλέποντες μὲν ἀτενῶς εἰς τὰ συντελούμενα, ταῖς δὲ κεφαλαῖς παρ' ἕκαστα διανεύοντες. διὸ καί φασιν αὐτοὺς διαλέκτῳ μὲν μὴ χρῆσθαι, μιμητικῇ δὲ δηλώσει διὰ τῶν χειρῶν διασημαίνειν ἕκαστα τῶν πρὸς τὴν χρείαν ἀνηκόντων. καὶ τὸ πάντων θαυμασιώτατον, φῶκαι τοῖς γένεσι τούτοις συνδιατρίβουσαι θήραν ποιοῦνται τῶν ἰχθύων καθ' αὑτὰς παραπλησίως ἀνθρώποις. ὁμοίως δὲ καὶ περὶ τὰς κοίτας καὶ τὴν τῶν γεννηθέντων ἀσφάλειαν μεγίστῃ πίστει τὰ γένη χρῆσθαι ταῦτα πρὸς ἄλληλα· χωρὶς γὰρ ἀδικήματος ἀλλοφύλοις ζῴοις ἡ συναναστροφὴ γίνεται μετ' εἰρήνης καὶ πάσης εὐλαβείας. Οὗτος μὲν οὖν ὁ βίος, καίπερ ὢν παράδοξος, ἐκ παλαιῶν χρόνων τετήρηται τοῖς γένεσι τούτοις, εἴτε ἐθισμῷ

---

[1] ἂν deleted by Vogel.
[2] οὐδὲ Dindorf: οὔτε.

makes no use whatsoever of drink and that their nature does not require it for the reasons given above. And as a general thing, he relates, they have no intercourse with other nations nor does the foreign appearance of people who approach their shores have any effect upon the natives, but looking at them intently they show no emotion and their expressions remain unaltered, as if there were no one present. Indeed when a man drew his sword and brandished it at them they did not turn to flight, nor, if they were subjected to insult or even to blows, would they show irritation, and the majority were not moved to anger in sympathy with the victims of such treatment; on the contrary, when at times children or women were butchered before their eyes they remained " insensible " in their attitudes, displaying no sign of anger or, on the other hand, of pity. In short, they remained unmoved in the face of the most appalling horrors, looking steadfastly at what was taking place and nodding their heads at each incident. Consequently, they say, they speak no language, but by movements of the hands which describe each object they point out everything they need. And the most marvellous fact of all is that seals live with these tribes and catch the fish for themselves in a manner similar to that employed by the human beings. Likewise with respect to their lairs and the safety of their offspring these two kinds of beings place the greatest faith in one another; for the association with animals of a different species continues without any wrongdoing and with peace and complete observance of propriety. Now this manner of life, strange as it is, has been observed by these tribes from very early times, whether it

διὰ τὸν χρόνον εἴτε ἀναγκαίᾳ χρείᾳ διὰ τὸ κατεπεῖγον ἡρμοσμένος.

19. Οἰκήσεσι δὲ τὰ ἔθνη οὐχ ὁμοίαις χρῆται, πρὸς δὲ τὰς τῆς περιστάσεως ἰδιότητας διηλλαγμέναις ἐμβιοῦσι. τινὲς μὲν γὰρ ἐν σπηλαίοις κατοικοῦσι κεκλιμένοις μάλιστα πρὸς τὰς ἄρκτους, ἐν οἷς καταψύχουσιν ἑαυτοὺς διά τε τὸ βάθος τῆς σκιᾶς καὶ διὰ τὰς περιπνεούσας αὔρας· τὰ μὲν γὰρ πρὸς μεσημβρίαν νεύοντα, τοῖς ἴπνοις παραπλησίαν ἔχοντα τὴν θερμασίαν, ἀπρόσιτα τοῖς ἀνθρώποις 2 ἐστὶ διὰ τὴν τοῦ καύματος ὑπερβολήν. οἱ δὲ τῶν πρὸς ἄρκτον νευόντων σπηλαίων σπανίζοντες ἀθροίζουσι τὰς πλευρὰς τῶν ἐκ τοῦ πελάγους ἐκπιπτόντων κητῶν· τῆς δὲ τούτων δαψιλείας πολλῆς οὔσης, καταπλέξαντες ἐξ ἑκατέρου μέρους κυρτὰς καὶ[1] πρὸς ἀλλήλας νενευκυίας, τῷ προσφάτῳ φύκει ταύτας διαπλέκουσι. σκεπαζομένης οὖν τῆς καμάρας, ἐν ταύτῃ τὸ βαρύτατον τοῦ καύματος ἀναπαύονται, τῆς κατὰ φύσιν χρείας αὐτοδίδακτον τέχνην ὑφηγουμένης.

3 Τρίτος δὲ τρόπος ἐστὶ τοῖς Ἰχθυοφάγοις τῆς σκηνώσεως τοιοῦτος. ἐλαῖαι[2] φύονται πάνυ πολλαὶ περὶ τοὺς τόπους τούτους, τὰ μὲν περὶ τὴν ῥίζαν ἔχουσαι προσκλυζόμενα τῇ θαλάττῃ, πυκναὶ δὲ τοῖς φυλλώμασι, τὸν δὲ καρπὸν ὅμοιον ἔχουσαι τῷ

[1] κυρτὰς καὶ ABD, Wesseling, Eichstädt; κύρτας FGMN, Dindorf, Bekker, Vogel.
[2] ἐλαῖαι Casaubon, cp. Agatharchides, 43; Capps suggests ἐλαῖαί τινες for ἐλάται of the MSS.

[1] Diodorus evidently refers to the interweaving of the rib-ends at the top, like the poles of the tepee or wigwam of the American Indian.

BOOK III. 18. 7–19. 3

has been fashioned by habit over the long space of time or by a need imposed by necessity because of stress of circumstances.

19. As for their dwelling-places, those used by these tribes are not all similar, but they inhabit homes modified to suit the peculiar nature of their surroundings. For instance, certain of them make their home in caves which open preferably towards the north and in which they cool themselves, thanks to the deep shade and also to the breezes which blow about them; since those which face the south, having as they do a temperature like that of an oven, cannot be approached by human beings because of the excessive heat. But others who can find no caves facing the north collect the ribs of the whales which are cast up by the sea; and then, since there is a great abundance of these ribs, they interweave them[1] from either side, the curve outwards and leaning towards each other, and then weave fresh seaweed through them.[2] Accordingly, when this vaulted structure is covered over, in it they gain relief from the heat when it is most intense, the necessity imposed by Nature suggesting to them a skill in which they were self-taught.

A third method by which the Ichthyophagi find a dwelling for themselves is as follows. Olive trees[3] grow about these regions in very great numbers and their roots are washed by the sea, but they bear thick foliage and a fruit which resembles the sweet

---

[2] Strabo (15. 2. 2) also says that their dwellings were made of whale ribs; cp. his account (15. 2. 11–13) of the "spouting whales" of the Persian Gulf (tr. by Jones in the *L.C.L.*).

[3] Or "olive trees of a kind"; see critical note. Since the fruit is quite different the emendation seems justified.

4 καστανα(ϊ)κῷ[1] καρύῳ. ταύτας ἀλλήλαις συμπλέκοντες καὶ συνεχῆ σκιὰν ποιοῦντες ἰδιαζούσαις σκηναῖς ἐμβιοῦσιν· ἅμα γὰρ ἐν γῇ καὶ θαλάττῃ διατρίβοντες ἐπιτερπῶς διεξάγουσι, τὸν μὲν ἥλιον φεύγοντες τῇ διὰ τῶν ἀκρεμόνων σκιᾷ, τὸ δὲ φυσικὸν περὶ τοὺς τόπους καῦμα τῇ συνεχεῖ τοῦ κύματος προσκλύσει διορθούμενοι, ταῖς δὲ περιπνοαῖς τῶν εὐκαίρων ἀνέμων εἰς ῥᾳστώνην ἄγοντες τὰ σώματα.

Ῥητέον δ' ἡμῖν καὶ περὶ τοῦ τετάρτου μέρους τῆς
5 σκηνώσεως. ἐκ γὰρ τοῦ παντὸς αἰῶνος σεσώρευται τοῦ μνίου φόρτος ἄπλατος, ὄρει παρεμφερής· οὗτος ὑπὸ τῆς συνεχοῦς τοῦ κύματος πληγῆς πεπιλημένος τὴν φύσιν ἔχει στερέμνιον καὶ συμπεπλεγμένην ἄμμῳ. ἐν τούτοις οὖν τοῖς ἀναστήμασιν ὑπονόμους ἀνδρομήκεις ὀρύττοντες, τὸν μὲν κατὰ κορυφὴν τόπον ἐῶσι στέγην, κάτωθεν δ' αὐλῶνας παραμήκεις καὶ πρὸς ἀλλήλους συντετρημένους κατασκευάζουσιν. ἐν δὲ τούτοις ἀναψύχοντες ἑαυτοὺς ἀλύπους κατασκευάζουσι, καὶ κατὰ τὰς ἐπικλύσεις τῶν κυμάτων ἐκπηδῶντες περὶ τὴν θήραν τῶν ἰχθύων ἀσχολοῦνται· ὅταν δὲ ἄμπωτις γένηται, κατευωχησόμενοι[2] τὰ ληφθέντα συμφεύγουσι πάλιν εἰς τοὺς προειρημένους αὐλῶνας.
6 τοὺς δὲ τελευτήσαντας θάπτουσι κατὰ μὲν τὸν τῆς ἀμπώτεως καιρὸν ἐῶντες ἐρριμμένους, ὅταν δ' ἡ πλημυρὶς ἐπέλθῃ, ῥίπτουσιν εἰς τὴν θάλατταν τὰ σώματα. διὸ καὶ τὴν ἰδίαν ταφὴν τροφὴν τῶν

---

[1] κασταναϊκῷ Eichstädt : κασταίνῳ.
[2] So Eichstädt : κατευωχησάμενοι.

BOOK III. 19. 3-6

chestnut. These trees they interlace, forming in this way a continuous shade, and live in tents of this peculiar kind; for passing their days as they do on land and in the water at the same time, they lead a pleasurable life, since they avoid the sun by means of the shade cast by the branches and offset the natural heat of the regions with the continual washing of the waves against them, giving their bodies comfort and ease by the pleasant breezes which blow about them.

We must speak also about the fourth kind of habitation. From time immemorial there has been heaped up a quantity of seaweed of tremendous proportions, resembling a mountain, and this has been so compacted by the unceasing pounding of the waves that it has become hard and intermingled with sand. Accordingly, the natives dig in these heaps tunnels of the height of a man, leaving the upper portion for a roof, and in the lower part they construct passage-ways connected with each other by borings.[1] As they cool themselves in these tunnels they free themselves from all troubles, and leaping forth from them at the times when the waves pour over the shore they busy themselves with the catching of the fish; then, when the ebb-tide sets in, they flee back together into these same passage-ways to feast upon their catch. Their dead, moreover, they "bury" by leaving the bodies just as they are cast out [2] at the ebb of the tide, and then when the flood-tide sets in they cast the bodies into the sea. Consequently, by making their own interment a

[1] This custom and the following about the disposal of the dead is recounted by Strabo (16. 4. 14) in connection with the "Turtle-eaters."

[2] *i.e.* without formal burial.

ἰχθύων ποιούμενοι κυκλούμενον ἰδιοτρόπως τὸν βίον ἔχουσι παρ' ὅλον τὸν αἰῶνα.

20. Ἓν δὲ γένος τῶν Ἰχθυοφάγων τοιαύτας ἔχει τὰς οἰκήσεις ὥστε πολλὴν ἀπορίαν παρέχεσθαι τοῖς τὰ τοιαῦτα φιλοτιμουμένοις ζητεῖν· ἐν γὰρ ἀποκρήμνοις φάραγξι καθίδρυνταί τινες, εἰς ἃς ἐξ ἀρχῆς ἦν ἀδύνατον παραβάλλειν τοὺς ἀνθρώπους, ἄνωθεν μὲν ἐπεχούσης πέτρας ὑψηλῆς καὶ πανταχόθεν ἀποτόμου, ἐκ πλαγίων δὲ κρημνῶν ἀπροσίτων ὑφαιρουμένων τὰς παρόδους, τὴν δὲ λοιπὴν πλευρὰν τοῦ πελάγους ὁρίζοντος, ὃ πεζῇ μὲν διελθεῖν ἀδύνατον, σχεδίαις δὲ οὐ χρῶνται τὸ παράπαν, πλοίων τε τῶν παρ' ἡμῖν ὑπάρχουσιν ἀνεννόητοι.
2 τοιαύτης δὲ ἀπορίας περὶ αὐτοὺς οὔσης, ὑπολείπεται λέγειν αὐτόχθονας αὐτοὺς ὑπάρχειν, ἀρχὴν μὲν τοῦ πρώτου γένους μηδεμίαν ἐσχηκότας, ἀεὶ δ' ἐξ αἰῶνος γεγονότας, καθάπερ ἔνιοι τῶν φυσιολόγων περὶ πάντων τῶν φυσιολογουμένων ἀπεφήναντο.
3 ἀλλὰ γὰρ περὶ μὲν τῶν τοιούτων ἀνεφίκτου τῆς ἐπινοίας ἡμῖν οὔσης οὐδὲν κωλύει τοὺς τὰ πλεῖστα ἀποφηναμένους ἐλάχιστα γινώσκειν, ὡς ἂν τῆς ἐν τοῖς λόγοις πιθανότητος τὴν μὲν ἀκοὴν πειθούσης, τὴν δ' ἀλήθειαν οὐδαμῶς εὑρισκούσης.

21. Ῥητέον δ' ἡμῖν καὶ περὶ τῶν καλουμένων Χελωνοφάγων, ὃν τρόπον ἔχουσι τὴν ὅλην διάθεσιν τοῦ βίου. νῆσοι γάρ εἰσι κατὰ τὸν ὠκεανὸν πλησίον τῆς γῆς κείμεναι, πολλαὶ μὲν τὸ πλῆθος, μικραὶ δὲ τοῖς μεγέθεσι καὶ ταπειναί, καρπὸν δὲ οὔθ' ἥμερον οὔτ' ἄγριον ἔχουσαι. ἐν ταύταις διὰ τὴν πυκνότητα κῦμα μὲν οὐ γίνεται, τοῦ κλύδωνος

---

[1] Cp. Book 1. 6. 2.

nutriment of the fish, they have a life which follows in singular fashion a continuous cycle throughout all eternity.

20. One tribe of the Ichthyophagi has dwellings so peculiar that they constitute a great puzzle to men who take a pride in investigating such matters; for certain of them make their homes among precipitous crags which these men could not possibly have approached at the outset, since from above there overhangs a lofty rock, sheer at every point, while on the sides unapproachable cliffs shut off entrance, and on the remaining face the sea hems them in, which cannot be passed through on foot, and they do not use rafts at all, while of boats such as we have they have no notion. Such being the puzzle concerning them, the only solution left to us is that they are autochthonous, and that they experienced no beginning of the race they originally sprang from, but existed always from the beginning of time, as certain natural philosophers have declared to be true of all the phenomena of nature.[1] But since the knowledge of such matters is unattainable by us, nothing prevents those who have the most to say about them from knowing the least, inasmuch as, while plausibility may persuade the hearing, it by no means discovers the truth.

21. We must speak also about the Chelonophagi,[2] as they are called, and the nature of their entire manner of life. There are islands in the ocean, which lie near the land, many in number, but small in size and low-lying, and bearing no food either cultivated or wild. Because these islands are so near to one another no waves occur among them,

[2] Turtle-eaters; cp. Strabo 16. 4. 14 ff.

θραυομένου περὶ τὰς ἄκρας τῶν νήσων, χελωνῶν δὲ θαλαττίων πλῆθος ἐνδιατρίβει περὶ τοὺς τόπους τούτους, πανταχόθεν καταφεῦγον πρὸς τὴν ἐκ τῆς γαλήνης σκέπην. αὗται δὲ τὰς μὲν νύκτας ἐν βυθῷ διατρίβουσιν ἀσχολούμεναι περὶ τὴν νομήν, τὰς δ' ἡμέρας εἰς τὴν ἀνὰ μέσον τῶν νήσων θάλατταν φοιτῶσαι κοιμῶνται μετέωροι τοῖς κύτεσι πρὸς τὸν ἥλιον, παρεμφερῆ τὴν πρόσοψιν ποιοῦσαι ταῖς κατεστραμμέναις ἀκάτοις· ἐξαίσιοι γὰρ τοῖς μεγέθεσιν ὑπάρχουσι καὶ τῶν ἐλαχίστων ἁλιάδων οὐκ ἐλάττους. οἱ δὲ τὰς νήσους κατοικοῦντες βάρβαροι κατὰ τοῦτον τὸν καιρὸν ἠρέμα προσνήχονται ταῖς χελώναις· πρὸς ἑκάτερον δὲ μέρος πλησιάσαντες, οἱ μὲν πιέζουσιν, οἱ δ' ἐξαίρουσιν, ἕως ἂν[1] ὕπτιον γένηται τὸ ζῷον. ἔπειθ' οἱ μὲν ἐξ ἑκατέρου μέρους οἰακίζουσι τὸν ὅλον ὄγκον, ἵνα μὴ στραφὲν τὸ ζῷον καὶ νηξάμενον τῷ τῆς φύσεως βοηθήματι φύγῃ κατὰ βάθους, εἷς δ' ἔχων μέρμιθα μακρὰν καὶ δήσας τῆς οὐρᾶς νήχεται πρὸς τὴν γῆν καὶ προσέλκεται μετάγων τὸ ζῷον ἐπὶ τὴν χέρσον, συμπαρακομιζομένων τῶν ἐξ ἀρχῆς τὴν ἐπίθεσιν πεποιημένων. ὅταν δ' εἰς τὴν νῆσον ἐκκομίσωσι, τὰ μὲν ἐντὸς πάντα βραχὺν χρόνον ἐν ἡλίῳ παροπτήσαντες κατευωχοῦνται, τοῖς δὲ κύτεσιν οὖσι σκαφοειδέσι χρῶνται πρός τε τὸν εἰς τὴν ἤπειρον διάπλουν, ὃν ποιοῦνται τῆς ὑδρείας ἕνεκεν, καὶ πρὸς τὰς σκηνώσεις, τιθέντες πρηνεῖς ἐφ' ὑψηλῶν τόπων, ὥστε δοκεῖν τούτοις τὴν φύσιν δεδωρῆσθαι μιᾷ χάριτι πολλὰς χρείας·

[1] ἂν added by Dindorf.

since the surf breaks upon the outermost islands, and so a great multitude of sea-turtles tarry in these regions, resorting thither from all directions to gain the protection offered by the calm. These animals spend the nights in deep water busied with their search for food, but during the days they resort to the sea which lies between the islands and sleep on the surface with their upper shells towards the sun, giving to the eye an appearance like that of overturned boats; for they are of extraordinary magnitude and not smaller than the smallest fishing skiffs. And the barbarians who inhabit the islands seize the occasion and swim quietly out to the turtles; and when they have come near the turtle on both sides, those on the one side push down upon it while those on the other side lift it up, until the animal is turned over on its back. Then the men, taking hold on both sides, steer the entire bulk of the creature, to prevent it from turning over and making its escape into the deep water by swimming with the means with which Nature has endowed it, and one man with a long rope, fastening it to its tail, swims towards the land, and drawing the turtle along after him he hauls it to the land, those who had first attacked it assisting him in bringing it in. And when they have got the turtles upon the shore of their island, all the inside meat they bake slightly for a short time in the sun and then feast upon it, but the upper shells, which are shaped like a boat, they use both for sailing over to the mainland, as they do in order to get water, and for their dwellings, by setting them right side up upon elevations, so that it would appear that Nature, by a single act of favour, had bestowed upon these peoples the

τὴν γὰρ αὐτὴν αὐτοῖς εἶναι τροφήν, ἀγγεῖον, οἰκίαν, ναῦν.

6 Οὐ μακρὰν δὲ τούτων διεστῶτες νέμονται τὴν παράλιον βάρβαροι βίον ἀνώμαλον ἔχοντες. διατρέφονται γὰρ ἀπὸ τῶν ἐκπιπτόντων εἰς τὴν χέρσον κητῶν, ποτὲ μὲν δαψίλειαν τροφῆς ἔχοντες διὰ τὰ μεγέθη τῶν εὑρισκομένων θηρίων, ποτὲ δὲ διαλειμμάτων γινομένων κακῶς ἀπαλλάττουσιν ὑπὸ τῆς ἐνδείας· καθ' ὃν δὴ χρόνον ἀναγκάζονται κατεργάζεσθαι διὰ τὴν σπάνιν τῶν ἀρχαίων ὀστῶν χόνδρους καὶ τὰς ἄκρας τῶν πλευρῶν ἐκφύσεις.

Τῶν μὲν οὖν Ἰχθυοφάγων τὰ γένη τοσαῦτ' ἐστὶ καὶ τοιούτοις χρῶνται βίοις, ὡς ἐν κεφαλαίοις εἰπεῖν.

22. Ἡ δὲ κατὰ τὴν Βαβυλωνίαν παράλιος συνάπτει μὲν ἡμέρῳ καὶ καταφύτῳ χώρᾳ, τοσοῦτο δέ ἐστι πλῆθος τῶν ἰχθύων τοῖς ἐγχωρίοις ὥστε τοὺς ἀναλίσκοντας μὴ δύνασθαι ῥᾳδίως περιγενέσθαι

2 τῆς δαψιλείας. παρὰ γὰρ τοὺς αἰγιαλοὺς ἱστᾶσι καλάμους πυκνοὺς καὶ πρὸς ἀλλήλους διαπεπλεγμένους, ὥστε τὴν πρόσοψιν εἶναι δικτύῳ παρὰ θάλατταν ἑστηκότι. κατὰ δὲ πᾶν τὸ[1] ἔργον ὑπάρχουσι πυκναὶ θύραι, τῇ μὲν πλοκῇ ταρσώδεις, τὰς στροφὰς[2] δ' ἔχουσαι πρὸς τὰς εἰς ἑκάτερα τὰ μέρη κινήσεις εὐλύτους. ταύτας ὁ κλύδων φερό-

[1] τό added by Dindorf.
[2] στροφή is not known elsewhere in the sense of "hinge" and probably στροφεῖς (i.e. στροφέας) without the article, the reading of C E, is what Diodorus actually wrote.

---

[1] In using the term "Babylonia" Diodorus must be thinking of the satrapy of that name, which included the

BOOK III. 21. 5–22. 2

satisfaction of many needs; for the same gift constitutes for them food, vessel, house and ship.

Not far distant from these people the coast is inhabited by barbarians who lead an irregular life. For they depend for their food upon the whales which are cast up on the land, at times enjoying an abundance of food because of the great size of the beasts which they discover, but at times, when interruptions of the supply occur, they suffer greatly from the shortage; and when the latter is the case they are forced by the scarcity of food to gnaw the cartilages of old bones and the parts which grow from the ends of the ribs.

As for the Ichthyophagi, then this is the number of their tribes and such, speaking summarily, are the ways in which they live.

22. But the coast of Babylonia[1] borders on a land which is civilized and well planted and there is such a multitude of fish for the natives that the men who catch them are unable readily to keep ahead of the abundance of them. For along the beaches they set reeds close to one another and interwoven, so that their appearance is like that of a net which has been set up along the edge of the sea. And throughout the entire construction there are doors which are fixed close together and resemble basket-work [2] in the way they are woven, but are furnished with hinges that easily yield to movements of the water in either direction. These doors are opened by the

north coast of the Persian Gulf and presumably extended down the west coast of the Gulf as far as "the uninhabited portion of Arabia" (cp. Book 18. 6. and below ch. 23. 1).

[2] *i.e.* they are closely woven, so as to offer resistance to the water.

μενος μὲν εἰς τὴν γῆν κατὰ τὸν τῆς πλημυρίδος καιρὸν ἀνοίγει, παλισσυτῶν δὲ κατὰ τὴν ἄμπωτιν
3 ἀποκλείει. διόπερ συμβαίνει καθ' ἑκάστην ἡμέραν πλημυρούσης μὲν τῆς θαλάττης ἐκ βυθοῦ τοὺς ἰχθῦς συνεκφερομένους διὰ τῶν θυρῶν παρεισπίπτειν, ἀναχωρούσης δὲ μὴ δύνασθαι τοῖς ὑγροῖς συνδιαρρεῖν διὰ τῆς τῶν καλάμων πλοκῆς. διὸ καὶ παρὰ τὸν ὠκεανὸν ἐνίοτε σωροὺς ἰχθύων σπαιρόντων ὁρᾶν ἔστι γινομένους, οὓς ἀναλεγόμενοι συνεχῶς οἱ πρὸς τούτοις τεταγμένοι δαψιλεῖς
4 ἀπολαύσεις ἔχουσι καὶ μεγάλας προσόδους. ἔνιοι δὲ τῶν περὶ τοὺς τόπους διατριβόντων, πεδιάδος τε καὶ ταπεινῆς τῆς χώρας ὑπαρχούσης, τάφρους ὀρύττουσιν ἀπὸ θαλάττης εὐρείας ἐπὶ πολλοὺς σταδίους μέχρι ἰδίων ἐπαύλεων, ῥαβδωτὰς δὲ θύρας ἐπ' ἄκρας αὐτὰς ἐπιστήσαντες ἀναβαινούσης μὲν τῆς πλημυρίδος ἀνοίγουσιν, εἰς δὲ τοὐναντίον μεταπιπτούσης κλείουσιν. εἶτα τῆς μὲν θαλάττης διὰ τῶν τῆς θύρας ἀραιωμάτων ἀπορρεούσης, τῶν δ' ἰχθύων ἀποληφθέντων ἐν ταῖς τάφροις, ταμιεύονται καὶ λαμβάνουσιν ὅσους ἂν προαιρῶνται καὶ καθ' ὃν ἂν χρόνον βούλωνται.

23. Διεληλυθότες δὲ περὶ τῶν παροικούντων τὴν ἀπὸ τῆς Βαβυλωνίας παράλιον ἕως Ἀραβίου κόλπου, περὶ τῶν ἑξῆς τούτοις ἐθνῶν διέξιμεν. κατὰ γὰρ τὴν Αἰθιοπίαν τὴν ὑπὲρ Αἰγύπτου παρὰ τὸν Ἄσαν καλούμενον ποταμὸν παροικεῖ τὸ τῶν Ῥιζοφάγων ἔθνος. ἐκ γὰρ τῶν πλησιοχώρων

waves as they roll towards the shore at the time of flood-tide, and are closed at ebb-tide as they surge back. Consequently it comes about that every day, when the sea is at flood-tide, the fish are carried in from the deep water with the tide and pass inside through the doors, but when the sea recedes they are unable to pass with the water through the interwoven reeds. As a result it is possible at times to see beside the ocean heaps being formed of gasping fish, which are being picked up unceasingly by those who have been appointed to this work, who have from their catch subsistence in abundance as well as large revenues. And some of the inhabitants of these parts, because the country is both like a plain and low-lying, dig wide ditches leading from the sea over a distance of many stades to their private estates, and setting wicker gates at their openings they open these when the flood-tide is coming inland and close them when the tide changes to the opposite direction. Then, inasmuch as the sea pours out through the interstices of the gate but the fish are held back in the ditches, they have a controlled store of fish and can take of them as many as they choose and at whatever time they please.

23. Now that we have discussed the peoples who dwell on the coast from Babylonia to the Arabian Gulf,[1] we shall describe the nations who live next to them. For in the Ethiopia which lies above Egypt there dwells beside the river Asa [2] the nation of the Rhizophagi.[3] For the barbarians here dig

[1] The Red Sea.
[2] Called Astabara by Agatharchides (*On the Red Sea*, 50) and Astaboras by Strabo (16. 4. 8).
[3] Root-eaters.

DIODORUS OF SICILY

ἑλῶν[1] τὰς ῥίζας τῶν καλάμων ὀρύττοντες οἱ
βάρβαροι πλύνουσι φιλοτίμως· ποιήσαντες δὲ
καθαρὰς κόπτουσι λίθοις, μέχρι ἂν γένηται τὸ
ἔργον λεῖον καὶ κολλῶδες· ἔπειτα περιπλάσαντες
χειροπληθιαίους ὄγκους ἐν ἡλίῳ παροπτῶσι, καὶ
ταύτῃ χρώμενοι τροφῇ πάντα τὸν βίον διατελοῦσιν.
2 ἀνεκλείπτους δ' ἔχοντες τὰς τῆς τροφῆς ταύτης
δαψιλείας, καὶ πρὸς ἀλλήλους ἀεὶ εἰρήνην ἄγοντες,
ὑπὸ πλήθους λεόντων πολεμοῦνται· ἐμπύρου γὰρ
τοῦ πέριξ ἀέρος ὄντος ἐκ τῆς ἐρήμου πρὸς αὐτοὺς
φοιτῶσι λέοντες σκιᾶς ἕνεκεν, οἱ δὲ καὶ θήρας τῶν
ἐλαττόνων θηρίων. διόπερ τοὺς ἐκ τῶν τελμάτων
ἐξιόντας τῶν Αἰθιόπων ὑπὸ τούτων τῶν θηρίων
ἀναλίσκεσθαι συμβαίνει· ἀδυνατοῦσι γὰρ ὑφίστα-
σθαι τὰς ἀλκὰς τῶν λεόντων, ὡς ἂν μηδεμίαν
βοήθειαν ὅπλων ἔχοντες, καὶ πέρας ἄρδην ἂν
αὐτῶν διεφθάρη τὸ γένος, εἰ μὴ ἡ[2] φύσις τι αὐτοῖς
3 αὐτόματον ἐποίησε βοήθημα. ὑπὸ γὰρ τὴν ἀνα-
τολὴν τοῦ κυνὸς παραδόξως[3] γινομένης νηνεμίας
περὶ τοὺς τόπους τοσοῦτο πλῆθος ἀθροίζεται
κωνώπων, ὑπερέχον δυνάμει τοὺς γνωριζομένους,
ὥστε τοὺς μὲν ἀνθρώπους καταφυγόντας εἰς τὰς
ἑλώδεις λίμνας μηδὲν πάσχειν, τοὺς δὲ λέοντας
πάντας φεύγειν ἐκ τῶν τόπων, ἅμα μὲν ὑπὸ τοῦ
δηγμοῦ κακουχουμένους, ἅμα δὲ τὸν ἀπὸ τῆς
φωνῆς ἦχον καταπεπληγμένους.

24. Ἑπόμενοι[4] δὲ τούτοις εἰσὶν οἵ τε Ὑλοφάγοι

---

[1] ἑλῶν added by Rhodomann but by no other editors; yet cp. Agatharchides (50): ἐκ τοῦ παρήκοντος ἕλους τὰς ῥίζας τῶν καλάμων ὀρύττει; Strabo 16. 4. 9; Book 2. 36. 5.

[2] ἡ added by Dindorf.

[3] μηδεμιᾶς after παραδόξως deleted by Vogel, but retained by Bekker, Dindorf, who read μυίας (AB) for νηνεμίας.

BOOK III. 23. 1–24. 1

up the roots of the reeds which grow in the neighbouring marshes and then thoroughly wash them; and after they have made them clean they crush them with stones until the stuff is without lumps and glutinous; and then, moulding it into balls as large as can be held in the hand, they bake it in the sun and on this as their food they live all their life long. Enjoying as they do the unfailing abundance of this food and living ever at peace with one another, they are nevertheless preyed upon by a multitude of lions; for since the air about them is fiery hot, lions come out of the desert to them in search of shade and in some cases in pursuit of the smaller animals. Consequently it comes to pass that when the Ethiopians come out of the marshy lands they are eaten by these beasts; for they are unable to withstand the might of the lions, since they have no help in the form of weapons, and indeed in the end the race of them would have been utterly destroyed had not Nature provided them with an aid which acts entirely of itself. For at the time of the rising of the dog-star,[1] whenever a calm unexpectedly comes on, there swarms to these regions such a multitude of mosquitoes, surpassing in vigour those that are known to us, that while the human beings find refuge in the marshy pools and suffer no hurt, all the lions flee from those regions, since they not only suffer from their stings but are at the same time terrified by the sound of their humming.

24. Next to these people are the Hylophagi [2]

[1] Sirius.   [2] Wood-eaters.

---

[4] ἑπόμενοι Bekker: ἐχόμενοι.

DIODORUS OF SICILY

καὶ οἱ Σπερματοφάγοι καλούμενοι. τούτων δ' οἱ μὲν ὑπὸ τὴν θερείαν τὸν πίπτοντα καρπὸν ἀπὸ τῶν δένδρων ὄντα πολὺν ἀθροίζοντες ἀπόνως διατρέφονται, κατὰ δὲ τὸν ἄλλον καιρὸν τῆς βοτάνης τῆς ἐν ταῖς σκιαζομέναις συναγκείαις[1] φυομένης προσφέρονται τὴν προσηνεστάτην· στερεὰ γὰρ οὖσα τὴν φύσιν, καὶ καυλὸν ἔχουσα παραπλήσιον ταῖς λεγομέναις[2] βουνιάσιν, ἐκπληροῖ τὴν τῆς ἀναγκαίας
2 τροφῆς ἔνδειαν. οἱ δὲ Ὑλοφάγοι μετὰ τέκνων καὶ γυναικῶν ἐπὶ τὰς νομὰς ἐξιόντες ἀναβαίνουσιν ἐπὶ τὰ δένδρα καὶ τοὺς ἁπαλοὺς τῶν ἀκρεμόνων προσφέρονται. τοιαύτην δ' ἐκ τῆς συνεχοῦς μελέτης τὴν ἐπ' ἄκρους τοὺς κλάδους ἀναδρομὴν ποιοῦνται πάντες ὥστε ἄπιστον εἶναι τὸ γινόμενον· καὶ γὰρ μεταπηδῶσιν ἀφ' ἑτέρου ἐφ' ἕτερον δένδρον ὁμοίως τοῖς ὀρνέοις, καὶ τὰς ἀναβάσεις ἐπὶ τῶν λεπτοτάτων κλάδων ποιοῦνται χωρὶς κινδύνων.
3 ἰσχνότητι γὰρ σώματος καὶ κουφότητι διαφέροντες, ἐπειδὰν τοῖς ποσὶ σφάλλωνται, ταῖς χερσὶν ἀντιλαμβάνονται· κἂν τύχωσι πεσόντες ἀφ' ὕψους, οὐδὲν πάσχουσι διὰ τὴν κουφότητα· καὶ πάντα δὲ κλάδον ἔγχυλον τοῖς ὀδοῦσι κατεργαζόμενοι πέττου-
4 σιν εὐκόπως ταῖς κοιλίαις. οὗτοι δ' ἀεὶ βιοῦσι γυμνοὶ μὲν ἐσθῆτος, κοιναῖς δὲ χρώμενοι γυναιξὶν ἀκολούθως καὶ τοὺς γεννηθέντας παῖδας κοινοὺς ἡγοῦνται. διαπολεμοῦσι δὲ πρὸς ἀλλήλους περὶ τῶν τόπων ῥάβδοις ὡπλισμένοι, καὶ ταύταις ἀμυνόμενοι τοὺς ἐναντίους διασπῶσι τοὺς χειρωθέντας. τελευτῶσι δ' αὐτῶν οἱ πλεῖστοι λιμῷ καταπονηθέντες, ὅταν

---

[1] σχιζομένης καὶ after συναγκείαις deleted by Reiske.
[2] λεγομέναις Vogel: γινομέναις.

BOOK III. 24. 1-4

and the Spermatophagi,[1] as they are called. The latter gather the fruit as it falls in great abundance from the trees in the summer season and so find their nourishment without labour, but during the rest of the year they subsist upon the most tender part of the plant which grows in the shady glens; for this plant, being naturally stiff and having a stem like the bounias,[2] as we call it, supplies the lack of the necessary food. The Hylophagi, however, setting out with children and wives in search of food, climb the trees and subsist off the tender branches. And this climbing of theirs even to the topmost branches they perform so well as a result of their continued practice that a man can scarcely believe what they do; indeed they leap from one tree to another like birds and make their way up the weakest branches without experiencing dangers. For being in body unusually slender and light, whenever their feet slip they catch hold instead with their hands, and if they happen to fall from a height they suffer no hurt by reason of their light weight; and every juicy branch they chew so thoroughly with their teeth that their stomachs easily digest them. These men go naked all their life, and since they consort with their women in common they likewise look upon their offspring as the common children of all. They fight with one another for the possession of certain places, arming themselves with clubs, with which they also keep off enemies, and they dismember whomsoever they have overcome. Most of them die from becoming exhausted by hunger, when cataracts form upon

---

[1] Seed-eaters, called by Strabo (16. 4. 9) Spermophagi.
[2] "French turnip," *Brassica Napus*.

τῶν ὀμμάτων ἀπογλαυκωθέντων τὸ σῶμα στερηθῇ τῆς ἀναγκαίας ἐκ ταύτης τῆς αἰσθήσεως χρείας.

25. Τὴν δὲ ἑξῆς χώραν τῶν Αἰθιόπων ἐπέχουσιν οἱ καλούμενοι Κυνηγοί, σύμμετροι μὲν κατὰ τὸ πλῆθος, βίον δ' οἰκεῖον ἔχοντες τῇ προσηγορίᾳ. θηριώδους γὰρ οὔσης τῆς χώρας καὶ παντελῶς λυπρᾶς, ἔτι δὲ ὑδάτων ῥύσεις ναματιαίων ἐχούσης ὀλίγας, καθεύδουσι μὲν ἐπὶ τῶν δένδρων διὰ τὸν ἀπὸ τῶν θηρίων φόβον, ὑπὸ δὲ τὴν ἑωθινὴν πρὸς τὰς συρρύσεις τῶν ὑδάτων μεθ' ὅπλων φοιτῶντες ἑαυτοὺς ἀποκρύβουσιν εἰς τὴν ὕλην καὶ σκοπεύου- 2 σιν ἐπὶ τῶν δένδρων. κατὰ δὲ τὸν τοῦ καύματος καιρόν, ἐρχομένων βοῶν τε ἀγρίων καὶ παρδάλεων καὶ τῶν ἄλλων θηρίων πλήθους πρὸς τὸ ποτόν, ταῦτα μὲν διὰ τὴν ὑπερβολὴν τοῦ τε καύματος καὶ δίψους λάβρως προσφέρεται τὸ ὑγρόν, μέχρι ἂν ἐμπλησθῇ, οἱ δ' Αἰθίοπες, γενομένων αὐτῶν βαρέων καὶ δυσκινήτων, καταπηδῶντες ἀπὸ τῶν δένδρων καὶ χρώμενοι ξύλοις πεπυρακτωμένοις καὶ λίθοις, ἔτι δὲ τοξεύμασι, ῥᾳδίως καταπονοῦσι. 3 κατὰ δὲ συστήματα ταύταις χρώμενοι ταῖς κυνηγίαις σαρκοφαγοῦσι τὰ ληφθέντα, καὶ σπανίως μὲν ὑπὸ τῶν ἀλκιμωτάτων ζῴων αὐτοὶ διαφθείρονται, τὰ δὲ πολλὰ δόλῳ τὴν ἐκ βίας ὑπεροχὴν 4 χειροῦνται. ἐὰν δέ ποτε τῶν κυνηγουμένων ζῴων σπανίζωσι, τὰς δορὰς τῶν πρότερον εἰλημμένων βρέξαντες ἐπιτιθέασιν ἐπὶ πῦρ ἁπαλόν· σποδίσαντες δὲ τὰς τρίχας τὰ δέρματα διαιροῦσι, καὶ κατεσθίοντες βεβιασμένως ἀναπληροῦσι τὴν ἔνδειαν. τοὺς δὲ ἀνήβους παῖδας γυμνάζουσιν ἐπὶ σκοπὸν

---

[1] Hunters.

their eyes and the body is deprived of the necessary use of this organ of sense.

25. The next part of the country of the Ethiopians is occupied by the Cynegi,[1] as they are called, who are moderate in number and lead a life in keeping with their name. For since their country is infested by wild beasts and is utterly worthless,[2] and has few streams of spring water, they sleep in the trees from fear of the wild beasts, but early in the morning, repairing with their weapons to the pools of water, they secrete themselves in the woods and keep watch from their positions in the trees. And at the time when the heat becomes intense, wild oxen and leopards and a multitude of every other kind of beast come to drink, and because of the excessive heat and their great thirst they greedily quaff the water until they are gorged, whereupon the Ethiopians, the animals having become sluggish and scarcely able to move, leap down from the trees, and by the use of clubs hardened in the fire and of stones and arrows easily kill them. They hunt in this way in companies and feed upon the flesh of their prey, and although now and then they are themselves slain by the strongest animals, yet for the most part they master by their cunning the superior strength of the beasts. And if at any time they find a lack of animals in their hunt they soak the skins of some which they had taken at former times and then hold them over a low fire; and when they have singed off the hair they divide the hides among themselves, and on such fare as has been forced upon them they satisfy their want. Their boys they train in shooting at a mark and give

[2] *i.e.* not suitable for agriculture.

βάλλειν, καὶ μόνοις διδόασι τροφὴν τοῖς ἐπιτυχοῦσι. διὸ καὶ θαυμαστοὶ ταῖς εὐστοχίαις ἄνδρες γίνονται, κάλλιστα διδασκόμενοι ταῖς τοῦ λιμοῦ πληγαῖς.

26. Ταύτης δὲ τῆς χώρας εἰς τὰ πρὸς δυσμὰς μέρη πολὺ διεστηκότες Αἰθίοπες ὑπάρχουσιν Ἐλεφαντομάχοι κυνηγοί. νεμόμενοι γὰρ δρυμώδεις καὶ πυκνοὺς τοῖς δένδρεσι τόπους παρατηροῦσι τῶν ἐλεφάντων τὰς εἰσόδους καὶ τὰς ἐκτροπάς, σκοπὰς ἀπὸ τῶν ὑψηλοτάτων δένδρων ποιούμενοι· καὶ ταῖς μὲν ἀγέλαις αὐτῶν οὐκ ἐπιτίθενται διὰ τὸ μηδεμίαν ἐλπίδα ἔχειν κατορθώσεως, τοῖς δὲ καθ' ἕνα πορευομένοις ἐπιβάλλουσι τὰς 2 χεῖρας, παραδόξοις ἐγχειροῦντες τολμήμασιν. ὅταν γὰρ τὸ ζῷον διεξιὸν[1] γένηται κατὰ τὸ δένδρον ἐν ᾧ συμβαίνει τὸν σκοπεύοντα κεκρύφθαι, ἅμα τῷ παραλλάττειν τὸν τόπον ταῖς μὲν χερσὶν ἐδράξατο τῆς οὐρᾶς, τοῖς δὲ ποσὶν ἀντέβη πρὸς τὸν ἀριστερὸν μηρόν· ἔχων δ' ἐκ τῶν ὤμων ἐξηρτημένον πέλεκυν, κοῦφον μὲν πρὸς τὴν ἀπὸ τῆς μιᾶς χειρὸς πληγήν, ὀξὺν δὲ καθ' ὑπερβολήν, τοῦτον λαβόμενος ἐν τῇ δεξιᾷ χειρὶ νευροκοπεῖ τὴν δεξιὰν ἰγνύν, πυκνὰς καταφέρων πληγὰς καὶ διὰ τῆς ἀριστερᾶς χειρὸς οἰακίζων τὸ ἴδιον σῶμα. παράδοξον δὲ ὀξύτητα τοῖς ἔργοις προσφέρουσιν, ὡς ἂν ἄθλου τῆς ἰδίας ψυχῆς ἑκάστῳ[2] προκειμένου· ἢ γὰρ χειρώσασθαι τὸ ζῷον ἢ τελευτᾶν αὐτὸν λείπεται, τῆς περιστάσεως οὐκ ἐπιδεχομένης ἕτερον 3 ἀποτέλεσμα. τὸ δὲ νευροκοπηθὲν ζῷον ποτὲ μὲν διὰ τὴν δυσκινησίαν ἀδυνατοῦν στρέφεσθαι καὶ συνεγκλινόμενον ἐπὶ τὸν πεπονθότα τόπον πίπτει

---

[1] διεξιὸν Dindorf: δεξιόν.
[2] ἑκάστῳ Reiske: ἑκάστου.

food only to those who hit it. Consequently, when they come to manhood, they are marvellously skilled in marksmanship, being most excellently instructed by the pangs of hunger.

26. Far distant from this country towards the parts to the west are Ethiopians known as Elephant-fighters, hunters also. For dwelling as they do in regions covered with thickets and with trees growing close together, they carefully observe the places where the elephants enter and their favourite resorts, watching them from the tallest trees; and when they are in herds they do not set upon them, since they would have no hope of success, but they lay hands on them as they go about singly, attacking them in an astonishingly daring manner. For as the beast in its wandering comes near the tree in which the watcher happens to be hidden, the moment it is passing the spot he seizes its tail with his hands and plants his feet against its left flank; he has hanging from his shoulders an axe, light enough so that a blow may be struck with one hand and yet exceedingly sharp, and seizing this in his right hand he hamstrings the elephant's right leg, raining blows upon it and maintaining the position of his own body with his left hand. And they bring an astonishing swiftness to bear upon the task, since there is a contest between the two of them for their very lives; for all that is left to the hunter is either to get the better of the animal or to die himself, the situation not admitting another conclusion. As for the beast which has been hamstrung, sometimes being unable to turn about because it is hard for it to move and sinking down on the place where it has been hurt, it falls to the ground and causes the death of the Ethiopian

DIODORUS OF SICILY

καὶ τὸν Αἰθίοπα συναπόλλυσι, ποτὲ δὲ πρὸς πέτραν ἢ δένδρον ἀποθλίψαν τὸν ἄνθρωπον τῷ βάρει πιέζει 4 μέχρι ἂν ἀποκτείνῃ. ἔνιοι δὲ τῶν ἐλεφάντων περιαλγεῖς γινόμενοι τοῦ μὲν ἀμύνεσθαι τὸν ἐπιβουλεύσαντα μακρὰν ἀφεστήκασι, τὴν δὲ φυγὴν διὰ τοῦ πεδίου ποιοῦνται, μέχρις ἂν οὗ συνεχῶς ὁ[1] προσβεβηκὼς τύπτων εἰς τὸν αὐτὸν τόπον τῷ πελέκει διακόψας τὰ νεῦρα ποιήσῃ πάρετον τὸ ζῷον. ὅταν δὲ τὸ ζῷον πέσῃ, συντρέχουσι κατὰ συστήματα, καὶ ζῶντος ἔτι τέμνοντες τὰς σάρκας ἐκ τῶν ὄπισθεν μερῶν εὐωχοῦνται.

27. Ἔνιοι δὲ τῶν πλησίον κατοικούντων χωρὶς κινδύνων θηρεύουσι τοὺς ἐλέφαντας τέχνῃ τῆς βίας περιγινόμενοι. εἴωθε γὰρ τοῦτο τὸ ζῷον, ἐπειδὰν ἀπὸ τῆς νομῆς πληρωθῇ, πρὸς ὕπνον καταφέρεσθαι, διαφορὰν ἐχούσης τῆς περὶ αὐτὸ 2 διαθέσεως πρὸς τὰ λοιπὰ τῶν τετραπόδων· οὐ γὰρ δύναται τοῖς γόνασι πρὸς τὴν γῆν συγκαθιέναι τὸν ὅλον ὄγκον, ἀλλὰ πρὸς δένδρον ἀνακλιθὲν ποιεῖται τὴν διὰ τῶν ὕπνων ἀνάπαυσιν. διόπερ τὸ δένδρον διὰ τὴν γινομένην πρὸς αὐτὸ πλεονάκις πρόσκλισιν τοῦ ζῴου τετριμμένον τέ ἐστι καὶ ῥύπου πλῆρες, πρὸς δὲ τούτοις ὁ περὶ αὐτὸ τόπος ἴχνη τε ἔχει καὶ σημεῖα πολλά, δι᾿ ὧν οἱ τὰ τοιαῦτα ἐρευνῶντες Αἰθίοπες γνωρίζουσι τὰς τῶν ἐλεφάντων κοίτας. 3 ὅταν οὖν ἐπιτύχωσι τοιούτῳ δένδρῳ, πρίζουσιν αὐτὸ παρὰ τὴν γῆν, μέχρι ἂν ὀλίγην ἔτι τὴν ῥοπὴν ἔχῃ πρὸς τὴν πτῶσιν· εἶθ᾿ οὗτοι μὲν τὰ σημεῖα τῆς ἰδίας παρουσίας ἀφανίσαντες ταχέως ἀπαλλάτ-

[1] ὁ after προσβεβηκὼς MSS, corrected by Ursinus and adopted by Dindorf, Bekker; Vogel reads προβεβηκὼς (D) ὁ.

along with its own, and sometimes squeezing the man against a rock or tree it crushes him with its weight until it has killed him. In some cases, however, the elephant in the extremity of its suffering is far from thinking of turning on its attacker, but flees across the plain until the man who has set his feet upon it, striking on the same place with his axe, has severed the tendons and paralysed the beast. And as soon as the beast has fallen they run together in companies, and cutting the flesh off the hind-quarters of the elephant while it is still alive they hold a feast.

27. But some of the natives who dwell near by hunt the elephants without exposing themselves to dangers, overcoming their strength by cunning. For it is the habit of this animal, whenever it has had its fill of grazing, to lie down to sleep, the manner in which it does this being different from that of all other four-footed animals; for it cannot bring its whole bulk to the ground by bending its knees, but leans against a tree and thus gets the rest which comes from sleep. Consequently the tree, by reason of the frequent leaning against it by the animal, becomes both rubbed and covered with mud, and the place about it, furthermore, shows both tracks and many signs, whereby the Ethiopians who search for such traces discover where the elephants take their rest. Accordingly, when they come upon such a tree, they saw it near the ground until it requires only a little push to make it fall; thereupon, after removing the traces of their own presence, they quickly depart in antici-

τονται, φθάνοντες τὴν ἔφοδον τοῦ ζῴου, ὁ δ' ἐλέφας πρὸς τὴν ἑσπέραν ἐμπλησθεὶς τῆς τροφῆς ἐπὶ τὴν συνήθη καταντᾷ κοίτην. κατακλιθεὶς δὲ ἀθρόῳ[1] τῷ βάρει παραχρῆμα μετὰ τῆς τοῦ δένδρου φορᾶς ἐπὶ τὴν γῆν καταφέρεται, πεσὼν δ' ὕπτιος μένει τὴν νύκτα κείμενος διὰ τὸ τὴν τοῦ σώματος φύσιν
4 ἀδημιούργητον εἶναι πρὸς ἀνάστασιν. οἱ δὲ πρίσαντες τὸ δένδρον Αἰθίοπες ἅμ' ἡμέρᾳ καταντῶσι, καὶ χωρὶς κινδύνων ἀποκτείναντες τὸ ζῷον σκηνοποιοῦνται περὶ τὸν τόπον καὶ παραμένουσι μέχρι ἂν τὸ πεπτωκὸς ἀναλώσωσι.

28. Τούτων δὲ τῶν γενῶν τὰ μὲν πρὸς ἑσπέραν μέρη κατοικοῦσιν Αἰθίοπες οἱ προσαγορευόμενοι Σιμοί, τὰ δὲ πρὸς μεσημβρίαν κεκλιμένα νέμεται τὸ
2 τῶν Στρουθοφάγων[2] γένος. ἔστι γὰρ παρ' αὐτοῖς ὀρνέου τι γένος μεμιγμένην ἔχον τὴν φύσιν τῷ χερσαίῳ ζῴῳ, δι' ἣν τῆς συνθέτου τέτυχε προσηγορίας. τοῦτο δὲ μεγέθει μὲν οὐ λείπεται τῆς μεγίστης ἐλάφου, τὸν δὲ αὐχένα μακρὸν ἔχον καὶ περιφερεῖς τὰς πλευρὰς καὶ πτερωτὰς ὑπὸ τῆς φύσεως δεδημιούργηται. καὶ κεφάλιον μὲν ἀσθενὲς ἔχει καὶ μικρόν,[3] μηροῖς δὲ καὶ κώλοις ὑπάρχει
3 καρτερώτατον, διχήλου τῆς βάσεως οὔσης. τοῦτο

---

[1] ἀθρόῳ Dindorf: ἀθρόως.
[2] Bekker suggests Στρουθοκαμηλοφάγων.
[3] μικρὸν Rhodomann: μακρόν.

---

[1] Strabo (16. 4. 10) in a similar account of the hunting of elephants says this is because " its legs have a continuous and unbending bone "; cp. a similar account of how the Germans capture the elk of the Hercynian forest in Caesar, *Gallic War*, 6. 27 (tr. by Edwards in the *L.C.L.*). J. E. Tennent, *The Natural History of Ceylon*, pp. 100–106, gives examples of the prevalence of the idea, both in antiquity and the Middle

BOOK III. 27. 3–28. 3

pation of the approach of the animal, and towards evening the elephant, filled with food, comes to his accustomed haunt. But as soon as he leans against the tree with his entire weight he at once rolls to the ground along with the tree, and after his fall he remains there lying on his back the night through, since the nature of his body is not fashioned for rising.[1] Then the Ethiopians who have sawn the tree gather at dawn, and when they have slain the beast without danger to themselves they pitch their tents at the place and remain there until they have consumed the fallen animal.

28. The parts west of these tribes are inhabited by Ethiopians who are called Simi,[2] but those towards the south are held by the tribe of the Struthophagi.[3] For there is found among them a kind of bird having a nature which is mingled with that of the land animal, and this explains the compound name it bears.[4] This animal is not inferior in size to the largest deer and has been fashioned by Nature with a long neck and a round body, which is covered with feathers. Its head is weak and small, but it has powerful thighs and legs and its foot is cloven. It is unable to fly in the air

---

Ages, that the legs of the elephant had no joints. The facts lying back of the account in our author are that elephants, after wallowing in pools, rub their sides against trees and that they do often sleep leaning against rocks or trees.

[2] Flat-nosed.

[3] Bird-eaters; but see the following note.

[4] Probably a double compound stood above, such as "Struthocamelophagi" (cp. the critical note). The struthocameli (from *strouthos*, "sparrow," and *kamelos*, *i.e.* the "bird like a camel," or the "ostrich") are described in Book 2. 50. 3.

πέτεσθαι μὲν μετέωρον οὐ δύναται διὰ τὸ βάρος, τρέχει δὲ πάντων ὠκύτατον, μικρὸν ἄκροις τοῖς ποσὶ τῆς γῆς ἐπιψαῦον· μάλιστα δ' ὅταν κατ' ἀνέμου πνοὰς ἐξαίρῃ τὰς πτέρυγας, ὑπεξάγει καθαπερεί τις ναῦς ἱστιοδρομοῦσα· τοὺς δὲ διώκοντας ἀμύνεται διὰ τῶν ποδῶν ἀποσφενδονῶν[1]
4 παραδόξως λίθους χειροπληθιαίους. ὅταν δ' ἐν νηνεμίᾳ διώκηται, ταχὺ συνιζουσῶν[2] τῶν πτερύγων ἀδυνατεῖ χρήσασθαι τοῖς τῆς φύσεως προτερήμασι, καὶ ῥᾳδίως καταλαμβανόμενον ἁλίσκεται.
5 τούτων δὲ τῶν ζῴων ἀμυθήτων ὄντων τῷ πλήθει κατὰ τὴν χώραν, οἱ βάρβαροι παντοδαπὰς μηχανὰς ἐπινοοῦσι κατ' αὐτῶν τῆς θήρας· ῥᾳδίως δὲ πολλῶν ἁλισκομένων ταῖς μὲν σαρξὶ χρῶνται πρὸς διατροφήν, ταῖς δὲ δοραῖς πρὸς ἐσθῆτα καὶ στρωμνήν.
6 ὑπὸ δὲ τῶν Σιμῶν ὀνομαζομένων Αἰθιόπων πολεμούμενοι διακινδυνεύουσι πρὸς τοὺς ἐπιτιθεμένους, ὅπλοις ἀμυντηρίοις χρώμενοι τοῖς τῶν ὀρύγων κέρασι· ταῦτα δὲ μεγάλα καὶ τμητικὰ καθεστῶτα μεγάλην παρέχεται χρείαν, δαψιλείας οὔσης κατὰ τὴν χώραν διὰ τὸ πλῆθος τῶν ἐχόντων αὐτὰ ζῴων.

29. Βραχὺ δὲ τούτων ἀπέχοντες Ἀκριδοφάγοι κατοικοῦσι τὰ συνορίζοντα πρὸς τὴν ἔρημον, ἄνθρωποι μικρότεροι μὲν τῶν ἄλλων, ἰσχνοὶ δὲ τοῖς ὄγκοις, μέλανες δὲ καθ' ὑπερβολήν. κατὰ γὰρ τὴν ἐαρινὴν ὥραν παρ' αὐτοῖς ζέφυροι καὶ λίβες παμμεγέθεις ἐκριπτοῦσιν ἐκ τῆς ἐρήμου πλῆθος ἀκρίδων ἀμύθητον, τοῖς τε μεγέθεσι διαλλάττον καὶ τῇ χρόᾳ τοῦ πτερώματος εἰδεχθὲς καὶ ῥυπαρόν.

[1] So Wesseling: ἀποσφενδονῶσα.

BOOK III. 28. 3–29. 1

because of its weight, but it runs more swiftly than any other animal, barely touching the earth with the tips of its feet; and especially when it raises its wings adown the blasts of the wind it makes off like a ship under full sail; and it defends itself against its pursuers by means of its feet, hurling, as if from a sling, in an astonishing manner, stones as large as can be held in the hand. But when it is pursued at a time of calm, its wings quickly collapse, it is unable to make use of the advantages given it by Nature, and being easily overtaken it is made captive. And since these animals abound in the land in multitude beyond telling, the barbarians devise every manner of scheme whereby to take them; moreover, since they are easily caught in large numbers, their meat is used for food and their skins for clothing and bedding. But being constantly warred upon by the Ethiopians known as "Simi," they are in daily peril from their attackers, and they use as defensive weapons the horns of gazelles; these horns, being large and sharp, are of great service and are found in abundance throughout the land by reason of the multitude of the animals which carry them.

29. A short distance from this tribe on the edge of the desert dwell the Acridophagi,[1] men who are smaller than the rest, lean of body, and exceeding dark. For among them in the spring season strong west and south-west winds drive out of the desert a multitude beyond telling of locusts, of great and unusual size and with wings of an ugly, dirty colour.

---

[1] Locust-eaters.

[2] συνιζουσῶν Rhodomann: συνιδρουσῶν MSS and all editors.

2 ἐκ τούτου δαψιλεῖς τροφὰς ἔχουσιν ἅπαντα τὸν βίον, ἰδιοτρόπως αὐτῶν ποιούμενοι τὴν θήραν. παρὰ γὰρ τὴν χώραν αὐτῶν ἐπὶ πολλοὺς σταδίους παρήκει χαράδρα βάθος ἔχουσα καὶ πλάτος ἀξιόλογον· ταύτην πληροῦσιν ἀγρίας ὕλης, οὔσης ἀφθόνου κατὰ τὴν χώραν· ἔπειθ' ὅταν τῶν προειρημένων ἀνέμων πνεόντων προσφέρηται τὰ νέφη τῶν ἀκρίδων, καταδιελόμενοι πάντα τὸν τῆς χαράδρας 3 τόπον πυροῦσι τὸν ἐν αὐτῇ χόρτον. ἐγειρομένου δὲ καπνοῦ πολλοῦ καὶ δριμέος, αἱ μὲν ἀκρίδες ὑπερπετόμεναι τὴν χαράδραν, καὶ διὰ τὴν τοῦ καπνοῦ δριμύτητα πνιγόμεναι, καταπίπτουσιν ἐπὶ τὴν γῆν ὀλίγον διαπετασθεῖσαι τόπον, τῆς δὲ τούτων ἀπωλείας ἐπὶ πλείονας ἡμέρας γινομένης μεγάλοι διανίστανται σωροί· καὶ τῆς χώρας ἐχούσης ἁλμυρίδα πολλήν, πάντες προσφέρουσι ταύτην ἀθρόοις τοῖς σωροῖς, καὶ διατήξαντες οἰκείως ποιοῦσι τήν τε γεῦσιν πρόσφορον καὶ τὸν 4 ἀποθησαυρισμὸν ἄσηπτον καὶ [1] πολυχρόνιον. ἡ μὲν οὖν διατροφὴ τούτοις παραχρῆμα καὶ τὸν ὕστερον χρόνον ἀπὸ τούτων τῶν ζῴων ὑπάρχει· οὔτε γὰρ κτηνοτροφοῦσιν οὔτε θαλάττης ἐγγὺς οἰκοῦσιν οὔτε ἄλλης ἐπικουρίας οὐδεμιᾶς τυγχάνουσι· τοῖς δὲ σώμασιν ὄντες κοῦφοι καὶ τοῖς ποσὶν ὀξύτατοι βραχύβιοι παντελῶς εἰσιν, ὡς ἂν τῶν πολυχρονιωτάτων παρ' αὐτοῖς οὐχ ὑπερβαλλόντων ἔτη τετταράκοντα.

5 Τὸ δὲ τοῦ βίου τέλος οὐ μόνον παράδοξον ἔχουσιν, ἀλλὰ καὶ πάντων ἀκληρότατον. ὅταν γὰρ πλησιάζῃ τὸ γῆρας, ἐμφύονται τοῖς σώμασι

[1] ἄσηπτον καὶ omitted by D, Vogel; retained by Bekker, Dindorf.

BOOK III. 29. 2–5

From these locusts they have food in abundance all their life long, catching them in a manner peculiar to themselves. For along the border of their land over many stades there extends a ravine of considerable depth and width; this they fill with wood from the forests, which is found in plenty in their land; and then, when the winds blow which we have mentioned and the clouds of the locusts approach, they divide among themselves the whole extent of the ravine and set fire to the brush in it. And since a great volume of pungent smoke rises, the locusts, as they fly over the ravine, are choked by the pungency of the smoke and fall to the ground after they have flown through it only a short space, and as the destruction of them continues over several days, great heaps of them are raised up; moreover, since the land contains a great amount of brine, all the people bring this to the heaps, after they have been gathered together, soak them to an appropriate degree with the brine and thus both give the locusts a palatable taste and make their storage free from rot and lasting for a long time.[1] Accordingly, the food of this people, at the moment and thereafter, consists of these animals; for they possess no herds nor do they live near the sea nor do they have at hand any other resources; and light in body and very swift of foot as they are, they are also altogether short-lived, the oldest among them not exceeding forty years of age.

As for the manner in which they end their lives, not only is it astounding but extremely pitiful. For when old age draws near there breed in their

[1] A much shorter account of the same custom is in Strabo (16. 4. 12).

πτερωτοὶ φθεῖρες οὐ μόνον διάφοροι τοῖς εἴδεσιν, ἀλλὰ καὶ ταῖς ἰδέαις ἄγριοι καὶ παντελῶς εἰδεχθεῖς.
6 ἀρξάμενον δὲ τὸ κακὸν ἀπὸ τῆς γαστρὸς καὶ τοῦ θώρακος ἐπινέμεται πάντα τὸν ὄγκον ἐν ὀλίγῳ χρόνῳ. ὁ δὲ πάσχων τὸ μὲν πρῶτον ὡς ὑπὸ ψώρας τινὸς ἐρεθιζόμενος μετρίως ὀδαξᾶσθαι φιλοτιμεῖται, μεμιγμένην ἔχοντος τοῦ πάθους ἀλγηδόσι τὴν χαράν· μετὰ δὲ ταῦτα ἀεὶ μᾶλλον τῶν ἐγγενομένων θηρίων εἰς τὴν ἐπιφάνειαν ἐκπιπτόντων συνεκχεῖται πλῆθος ἰχῶρος λεπτοῦ, τὴν δριμύτητα παντελῶς ἔχοντος ἀνυπομόνητον.
7 διόπερ ὁ συνεχόμενος τῷ πάθει βιαιότερον ἀμύττει τοῖς ὄνυξι, στεναγμοὺς μεγάλους προϊέμενος. κατὰ δὲ τὰς τῶν χειρῶν ἐξελκώσεις τοσοῦτο πλῆθος ἐκπίπτει τῶν ἑρπετῶν ὥστε μηδὲν ἀνύειν τοὺς ἀπολέγοντας, ὡς ἂν ἄλλων ἐπ' ἄλλοις ἐκφαινομένων καθάπερ ἔκ τινος ἀγγείου πολλαχῶς κατατετρημένου. οὗτοι μὲν οὖν εἰς τοιαύτην διάλυσιν τοῦ σώματος καταστρέφουσι τὸν βίον δυστυχῶς, εἴτε διὰ τὴν ἰδιότητα τῆς τροφῆς εἴτε διὰ τὸν ἀέρα τοιαύτης τυγχάνοντες περιπετείας.

30. Τῷ δὲ ἔθνει τούτῳ χώρα παρήκει κατὰ τὸ μέγεθος πολλὴ καὶ κατὰ τὰς τῆς νομῆς ποικιλίας ἀγαθή· ἔρημος δ' ἐστὶ καὶ παντελῶς ἄβατος, οὐκ ἀπ' ἀρχῆς σπανίζουσα τοῦ γένους τῶν ἀνθρώπων, ἀλλ' ἐν τοῖς ὕστερον χρόνοις ἔκ τινος ἐπομβρίας ἀκαίρου πλῆθος φαλαγγίων καὶ σκορπίων ἐξενέγ-
2 κασα. τοσοῦτο γὰρ ἱστοροῦσιν ἐπιπολάσαι τῶν

bodies winged lice, which not only have an unusual form but are also savage and altogether loathsome in aspect. The affliction begins on the belly and the breast and in a short time spreads over the whole body. And the person so affected is at first irritated by a kind of itching and insists on scratching himself a bit, the disease at this point offering a satisfaction combined with pain; but after this stage the animals, which have been continuously engendered more and more in the body, break out to the surface and there is a heavy discharge of a thin humour, the sting of which is quite unbearable. Consequently the man who is in the grip of the disease lacerates himself with his nails the more violently, groaning and moaning deeply. And as his hands tear at his body, such a multitude of the vermin pours forth that those who try to pick them off accomplish nothing, since they issue forth one after another, as from a kind of vessel that is pierced throughout with holes. And so these wretches end their lives in a dissolution of the body after this manner, a miserable fate, meeting with such a sudden reversal of fortune either by reason of the peculiar character of their food or because of the climate.

30. Along the borders of this people there stretches a country great in size and rich in its varied pasturage; but it is without inhabitants and altogether impossible for man to enter; not that it has from the first never known the race of men, but in later times, as a result of an unseasonable abundance of rain, it brought forth a multitude of venomous spiders and scorpions. For, as historians relate,[1] so great a multitude of these

[1] Cp. Strabo 16. 4. 12; Aelian, *History of Animals*, 17. 40; Pliny 8. 29.

DIODORUS OF SICILY

εἰρημένων θηρίων πλῆθος ὥστε τοὺς κατοικοῦντας ἀνθρώπους τὸ μὲν πρῶτον πανδημεὶ κτείνειν[1] τὸ τῇ φύσει πολέμιον, ἀπεριγενήτου δὲ τοῦ πλήθους[2] ὄντος καὶ τῶν δηγμάτων ὀξεῖς τοῖς πληγεῖσι τοὺς θανάτους ἐπιφερόντων, ἀπογνόντας τὴν πάτριον γῆν τε καὶ δίαιταν φυγεῖν ἐκ τῶν τόπων. οὐ χρὴ δὲ θαυμάζειν οὐδὲ ἀπιστεῖν τοῖς λεγομένοις, πολλὰ τούτων παραδοξότερα κατὰ πᾶσαν τὴν οἰκουμένην γεγονότα διὰ τῆς ἀληθοῦς ἱστορίας 3 παρειληφότας. περὶ γὰρ τὴν Ἰταλίαν μυῶν πλῆθος ἀρουραίων ἐγγεννηθὲν τοῖς πεδίοις ἐξέβαλέ τινας ἐκ τῆς πατρίου χώρας, κατὰ δὲ τὴν Μηδίαν ἐπιπολάσαντες ἀμύθητοι στρουθοὶ καὶ τὰ σπέρματα τῶν ἀνθρώπων ἀφανίζοντες ἠνάγκασαν εἰς ἑτερογενεῖς τόπους μεταστῆναι, τοὺς δὲ καλουμένους Αὐταριάτας βάτραχοι τὴν ἀρχέγονον σύστασιν ἐν τοῖς νέφεσι λαμβάνοντες καὶ πίπτοντες ἀντὶ τῆς συνήθους ψεκάδος ἐβιάσαντο τὰς πατρίδας καταλιπεῖν καὶ καταφυγεῖν εἰς τοῦτον τὸν τόπον ἐν ᾧ 4 νῦν καθίδρυνται. καὶ μὴν τίς οὐχ ἱστόρησεν Ἡρακλεῖ τῶν ὑπὲρ τῆς ἀθανασίας ἄθλων συντελεσθέντων ἕνα καταριθμούμενον καθ' ὃν ἐξήλασεν ἐκ τῆς Στυμφαλίδος λίμνης τὸ πλῆθος τῶν ἐπιπολασάντων ὀρνίθων ἐν αὐτῇ; ἀνάστατοι δὲ κατὰ τὴν Λιβύην πόλεις τινὲς ἐγένοντο πλήθους λεόντων ἐπελθόντος ἐκ τῆς ἐρήμου.

Ταῦτα μὲν οὖν ἡμῖν εἰρήσθω πρὸς τοὺς ἀπί-

[1] πᾶν M, omitted F, πάντα other MSS, after κτείνειν deleted by Vogel.
[2] πλήθους Hertlein: πάθους.

BOOK III. 30. 2-4

animals came to abound that, although at the outset the human beings dwelling there united in killing the natural enemy, yet, because the multitude of them was not to be overcome and their bites brought swift death to their victims, they renounced both their ancestral land and mode of life and fled from these regions. Nor is there any occasion to be surprised at this statement or to distrust it, since we have learned through trustworthy history of many things more astonishing than this which have taken place throughout all the inhabited world. In Italy, for instance, such a multitude of field-mice was generated in the plains that they drove certain people out of their native country; in Media birds, which came to abound beyond telling and made away with the seeds sown by the inhabitants, compelled them to remove into regions held by another people; and in the case of the Autariatae,[1] as they are called, frogs were originally generated in the clouds, and when they fell upon the people in place of the customary rain, they forced them to leave their native homes and to flee for safety to the place where they now dwell. And who indeed has not read in history, in connection with the Labours which Heracles performed in order to win his immortality, the account of the one Labour in the course of which he drove out of the Stymphalian Lake the multitude of birds which had come to abound in it? Moreover, in Libya certain cities have become depopulated because a multitude of lions came out of the desert against them.

Let these instances, then, suffice in reply to those

[1] A people of Illyria; Justin (15. 2) also says that they were driven out in this way.

DIODORUS OF SICILY

στως διὰ τὸ παράδοξον πρὸς τὰς ἱστορίας διακειμένους· πάλιν δ' ἐπὶ τὰ συνεχῆ τοῖς προειρημένοις μεταβησόμεθα.

31. Τὰς δ' ἐσχατιὰς τῶν πρὸς μεσημβρίαν μερῶν κατοικοῦσιν ἄνδρες ὑπὸ μὲν τῶν Ἑλλήνων καλούμενοι Κυναμολγοί, κατὰ δὲ τὴν τῶν πλησιοχώρων βαρβάρων διάλεκτον Ἄγριοι. οὗτοι δὲ πώγωνας μὲν φέρουσι παμμεγέθεις, κυνῶν δὲ τρέφουσιν ἀγρίων ἀγέλας πρὸς τὴν τοῦ βίου χρείαν εὐθέτους.
2 ἀπὸ γὰρ τῶν πρώτων τροπῶν τῶν θερινῶν μέχρι μέσου χειμῶνος Ἰνδικοὶ βόες ἀμύθητοι τὸ πλῆθος ἐπιφοιτῶσιν αὐτῶν τὴν χώραν, ἀδήλου τῆς αἰτίας οὔσης· οὐδεὶς γὰρ οἶδεν εἴθ' ὑπὸ ζῴων πολλῶν καὶ σαρκοφάγων πολεμούμενοι φεύγουσιν, εἴτε δι' ἔνδειαν τροφῆς ἐκλείποντες τοὺς οἰκείους τόπους εἴτε δι' ἄλλην περιπέτειαν, ἣν ἡ μὲν πάντα τὰ παράδοξα γεννῶσα φύσις κατασκευάζει, τὸ δὲ τῶν
3 ἀνθρώπων γένος ἀδυνατεῖ τῷ νῷ συνιδεῖν. οὐ μὴν ἀλλὰ τοῦ πλήθους οὐ κατισχύοντες δι' ἑαυτῶν περιγενέσθαι τοὺς κύνας ἐπαφιᾶσι, καὶ μετὰ τούτων ποιούμενοι τὴν θήραν πολλὰ πάνυ τῶν ζῴων χειροῦνται· τῶν δὲ ληφθέντων ἃ μὲν πρόσφατα κατεσθίουσιν, ἃ δὲ εἰς ἅλας συντιθέντες ἀποθησαυρίζουσι. πολλὰ δὲ καὶ τῶν ἄλλων ζῴων διὰ τῆς τῶν κυνῶν ἀλκῆς θηρεύοντες ἀπὸ κρεοφαγίας τὸν βίον ἔχουσι.

4 Τὰ μὲν οὖν τελευταῖα γένη τῶν πρὸς μεσημβρίαν οἰκούντων ἐν μορφαῖς ἀνθρώπων τὸν βίον

---

[1] Milkers of bitches. [2] Savages.
[3] Strabo (16. 4. 10) also says that the dogs hunt the cattle; but Agatharchides (60) and Aelian (*History of Animals*, 16. 31)

BOOK III. 30. 4–31. 4

who adopt a sceptical attitude towards histories because they recount what is astonishing; and now we shall in turn pass on to what follows the subjects we have been treating.

31. The borders of the parts to the south are inhabited by men whom the Greeks call "Cynamolgi,"[1] but who are known in the language of the barbarians who live near them as Agrii.[2] They wear great beards and maintain packs of savage dogs which serve to meet the needs of their life. For from the time of the beginning of the summer solstice until mid-winter, Indian cattle, in a multitude beyond telling, resort to their country, the reason for this being uncertain; for no man knows whether they are in flight because they are being attacked by a great number of carnivorous beasts, or because they are leaving their own regions by reason of a lack of food, or because of some other reversal of fortune which Nature, that engenders all astonishing things, devises, but which the mind of the race of men cannot comprehend. However, since they have not the strength of themselves to get the better of the multitude of the cattle, they let the dogs loose on them, and hunting them by means of the dogs they overcome a very great number of the animals; and as for the beasts which they have taken, some of them they eat while fresh and some they pack down with salt and store up. Many also of the other animals they hunt, thanks to the courage of their dogs, and so maintain themselves by the eating of flesh.[3]

Now the most distant tribes of those peoples who live to the south have indeed the forms of men but

add that this people drink the milk of bitches when they have no meat.

DIODORUS OF SICILY

ἔχει θηριώδη· λείπεται δὲ διελθεῖν ὑπὲρ δύο ἐθνῶν, τῶν τε Αἰθιόπων καὶ τῶν Τρωγοδυτῶν. ἀλλὰ περὶ μὲν Αἰθιόπων ἀναγεγράφαμεν ἐν ἄλλοις, περὶ δὲ τῶν Τρωγοδυτῶν νῦν ἐροῦμεν.

32. Οἱ τοίνυν Τρωγοδύται προσαγορεύονται μὲν ὑπὸ τῶν Ἑλλήνων Νομάδες, βίον δ' ἔχοντες ἀπὸ θρεμμάτων νομαδικὸν κατὰ συστήματα τυραννοῦνται, καὶ μετὰ τῶν τέκνων τὰς γυναῖκας ἔχουσι κοινὰς πλὴν μιᾶς τῆς τοῦ τυράννου· τὸν δὲ ταύτῃ πλησιάσαντα πρόστιμον ὁ δυνάστης πράττεται 2 τεταγμένον ἀριθμὸν προβάτων. κατὰ δὲ τὸν τῶν ἐτησίων καιρὸν γινομένων παρ' αὐτοῖς ὄμβρων μεγάλων, ἀφ' αἵματος καὶ γάλακτος διατρέφονται, μίσγοντες ταῦτα καὶ βραχὺν χρόνον ἑψήσαντες. μετὰ δὲ ταῦτα διὰ τὴν τῶν καυμάτων ὑπερβολὴν τῆς νομῆς ξηραινομένης καταφεύγουσιν εἰς τοὺς ἑλώδεις τόπους, καὶ περὶ τῆς τῆς χώρας νομῆς πρὸς 3 ἀλλήλους διαμάχονται. τῶν δὲ βοσκημάτων τὰ πρεσβύτερα καὶ νοσεῖν ἀρχόμενα καταναλίσκοντες ἀπὸ τούτων τὸν ἅπαντα χρόνον διατρέφονται. διόπερ τὴν τῶν γονέων προσηγορίαν ἀνθρώπων μὲν οὐδενὶ προσάπτουσι, ταύρῳ δὲ καὶ βοΐ καὶ πάλιν κριῷ καὶ προβάτῳ· τούτων δὲ τοὺς μὲν πατέρας, τὰς δὲ μητέρας καλοῦσι διὰ τὸ πορίζεσθαι τὰς ἐφημέρους τροφὰς ἀεὶ παρὰ τούτων, ἀλλὰ μὴ παρὰ τῶν γεγεννηκότων. ποτῷ δ' οἱ μὲν ἰδιῶται συγχρῶνται παλιούρων βρέγματι, τοῖς δὲ δυνάσταις ἀπό τινος ἄνθους κατασκευάζεται πόμα παραπλήσιον τῷ χειρίστῳ παρ' ἡμῖν γλεύκει. ταῖς δὲ

---

[1] Much of what follows is in Strabo (16. 4. 17). The spelling of Trogodytes, without the λ, is supported by D, the oldest

BOOK III. 31. 4–32. 3

their life is that of the beasts; however, it remains for us to discuss two peoples, the Ethiopians and the Trogodytes. But about the Ethiopians we have written in other connections, and so we shall now speak of the Trogodytes.

32. The Trogodytes,[1] we may state, are called Nomads by the Greeks, and living as they do a nomadic life off their flocks, each group of them has its tyrant, and their women, like their children, they hold in common, with the single exception of the wife of the tyrant; but if any man goes in to this woman the ruler exacts of him a fine of a specified number of sheep. At the time of the etesian winds, when there are heavy rains in their country, they live off blood and milk which they mix together and seethe for a short while. But after this season the pasturage is withered by the excessive heat, and they retreat into the marshy places and fight with each other for the pasturage of the land. They eat the older animals of their flocks and such as are growing sick and maintain themselves on them at all times. Consequently they give the name of parents to no human being, but rather to a bull and a cow, and also to a ram and a sheep; these they call their fathers or their mothers, by reason of the fact that they ever secure their daily food from them, and not from those who had begotten them. And as a drink the common people make use of juice from the plant Christ's-thorn, but for the rulers there is prepared from a certain flower a beverage like the vilest of our sweet new wines. Following after their

MS., and Vogel (I. lxxii) regrets that he did not adopt it. On further grounds for this spelling cp. Kallenberg, *Textkritik u. Sprachgebrauch Diodors*, I. 1.

DIODORUS OF SICILY

ἀγέλαις τῶν θρεμμάτων ἐπακολουθοῦντες ἄλλην ἐξ ἄλλης χώραν ἐπιπορεύονται, φεύγοντες τὸ
4 τοῖς αὐτοῖς τόποις ἐνδιατρίβειν. καὶ γυμνοὶ μέν εἰσι πάντες τὰ σώματα πλὴν τῶν ἰσχίων, ἃ δέρμασι σκεπάζουσι· τὰ δ' αἰδοῖα πάντες οἱ Τρωγοδύται παραπλησίως τοῖς Αἰγυπτίοις περιτέμνονται πλὴν τῶν ἀπὸ τοῦ συμπτώματος ὀνομαζομένων κολοβῶν· οὗτοι γὰρ μόνοι τὴν ἐντὸς τῶν στενῶν νεμόμενοι χώραν ἐκ νηπίου ξυροῖς ἀποτέμνονται πᾶν τὸ τοῖς ἄλλοις μέρος περιτομῆς τυγχάνον.

33. Ὁπλισμὸν δ' ἔχουσι τῶν Τρωγοδυτῶν οἱ μὲν ὀνομαζόμενοι Μεγάβαροι κυκλοτερεῖς ὠμοβοΐνας ἀσπίδας καὶ ῥόπαλον τύλους ἔχον περισιδήρους, οἱ δὲ ἄλλοι τόξα καὶ λόγχας. ταφαὶ δὲ
2 παντελῶς ἐξηλλαγμέναι[1] ἐπιχωριάζουσι· τοῖς γὰρ τῶν παλιούρων λύγοις δήσαντες τῶν τετελευτηκότων τὰ σώματα προσάπτουσι τὸν αὐχένα τοῖς σκέλεσι, θέντες δὲ τὸν νεκρὸν ἐπί τινος ἀναστήματος βάλλουσι λίθοις χειροπληθέσι γελῶντες, μέχρι ἂν ὅτου τοῖς λίθοις περιχώσαντες ἀποκρύψωσι τὰ σώματα· τὸ δὲ τελευταῖον αἰγὸς κέρας ἐπιθέντες ἀπολύονται, συμπάθειαν οὐδεμίαν λαμβάνοντες.
3 πολεμοῦσι δὲ πρὸς ἀλλήλους οὐχ ὁμοίως τοῖς Ἕλλησιν ὑπὲρ γῆς[2] ἤ τινων ἄλλων ἐγκλημάτων, ἀλλ' ὑπὲρ τῆς ἐπιγινομένης ἀεὶ νομῆς. ἐν δὲ ταῖς φιλονεικίαις τὸ μὲν πρῶτον ἀλλήλους τοῖς λίθοις βάλλουσι, μέχρι ἄν τινες τρωθῶσι, καὶ τὸ λοιπὸν ἐπὶ τὸν τῶν τόξων ἀγῶνα καταντῶσι. πολλοὶ δὲ ἐν ἀκαρεῖ χρόνῳ τελευτῶσιν, ὡς ἂν εὐ-

---
[1] So Wesseling: ταφαῖς . . ἐξηλλαγμέναις.
[2] γῆς Dindorf: ὀργῆς.

herds and flocks they move about from one land to another, avoiding any stay in the same regions. And they are all naked as to their bodies except for the loins, which they cover with skins; moreover, all the Trogodytes are circumcised like the Egyptians with the exception of those who, because of what they have experienced, are called "colobi"[1]; for these alone of all who live inside the Straits[2] have in infancy all that part cut completely off with the razor which among other peoples merely suffers circumcision.

33. As for the arms of the Trogodytes, those who bear the name of Megabari have round shields covered with raw ox-hide and a club with iron knobs, but the rest of them have bows and arrows and lances. Again, the burials practised by them differ entirely from all others; for after binding the bodies of the dead with withes of Christ's-thorn they tie the neck to the legs, and then placing the corpse upon a mound they cast at it stones as large as can be held in the hand, making merry the while, until they have built up a heap of stones and have hidden the bodies from sight; and finally they set up a goat's horn on the heap and separate, having shown no fellow-feeling for the dead. And they fight with one another, not, as the Greeks do, for the possession of land or because of some alleged misdeeds, but for the pasturage as it comes up at one time and another. In their quarrels they at first hurl stones at each other, until some are wounded, and the rest of the time they resort to the struggle with bows and arrows. And it is but a moment before many are

[1] The word means "mutilated" (persons whose sexual organs have been removed).
[2] At the entrance into the Red Sea.

στόχως μὲν βαλλόντων διὰ τὴν ἐν τούτοις ἄθλησιν,
τὸν δὲ σκοπὸν ἐχόντων γυμνὸν τῶν σκεπαστηρίων
4 ὅπλων. διαλύουσι δὲ τὴν μάχην τῶν γυναικῶν
αἱ πρεσβύτεραι, προβαλλόμεναι[1] μὲν εἰς τὸ μέσον,
ἐντροπῆς δὲ τυγχάνουσαι· νόμιμον γάρ ἐστιν
αὐτοῖς ταύτας κατὰ μηδένα τῶν τρόπων τύπτειν,
ὅθεν ἅμα τῷ φανῆναι παύονται τοῦ τοξεύειν.
5 οἱ δὲ διὰ τὸ γῆρας οὐ δυνάμενοι ταῖς ποίμναις
ἀκολουθεῖν βοὸς οὐρᾷ τὸν αὐχένα περισφίγξαντες
ἑαυτῶν ἀπολύονται τοῦ ζῆν προθύμως· τοῦ δὲ τὸν
θάνατον ἀναβαλλομένου τὴν ἐξουσίαν ὁ βουλόμενος ἔχει τὸν δεσμὸν ὡς ἐπ' εὐνοίᾳ περιθεῖναι καὶ
6 μετὰ νουθετήσεως στερῆσαι τοῦ ζῆν. ὁμοίως δὲ
νόμιμον αὐτοῖς ἐστι τοὺς πηρωθέντας ἢ νόσοις
δυσιάτοις συνεχομένους ἐξάγειν ἐκ τοῦ ζῆν·
μέγιστον γὰρ τῶν κακῶν ἡγοῦνται τὸ φιλοψυχεῖν
τὸν μηδὲν ἄξιον τοῦ ζῆν πράττειν δυνάμενον. διὸ
καὶ πάντας[2] ἰδεῖν ἔστι τοὺς Τρωγοδύτας ἀρτίους
μὲν τοῖς σώμασιν, ἰσχύοντας δ' ἔτι ταῖς ἡλικίαις,
ὡς ἂν μηδενὸς ὑπερβάλλοντος τὰ ἑξήκοντα ἔτη.

7 Καὶ περὶ μὲν τῶν Τρωγοδυτῶν ἱκανῶς εἰρήκαμεν·
εἰ δέ τις τῶν ἀναγινωσκόντων διὰ τὸν ξενισμὸν καὶ
τὸ παράδοξον τῶν ἀναγεγραμμένων βίων ἀπιστήσει
ταῖς ἱστορίαις, θεὶς πρὸ τῆς διανοίας παρ' ἄλληλα
τόν τε περὶ τὴν Σκυθίαν ἀέρα καὶ τὸν περὶ τὴν
Τρωγοδυτικήν, καὶ τὰς ἑκατέρων διαφορὰς ἰδών,
οὐκ ἀπιστήσει τοῖς ἱστορημένοις.

34. Τοσαύτη γὰρ παραλλαγὴ τῶν παρ' ἡμῖν
ἀέρων πρὸς τοὺς ἱστορημένους ὥστε τὴν κατὰ

[1] So the MSS. and Bekker; Dindorf and Vogel read προ-
αλλόμεναι ("leaping in front of").
[2] μὲν after πάντας deleted by Dindorf.

dead, since they are accurate shooters by reason of their practice in archery and the object at which they are aiming is bare of protective armour. The fighting is terminated by the older women, who rush into the fray and offer themselves as a protection to the fighters, and are the object of respect; for it is a custom with these people that they shall in no wise strike one of these women, and so at their appearance they cease shooting. Those who can no longer accompany the flocks by reason of old age bind the tail of an ox about their own necks and so put an end to their lives of their own free will; and if a man postpones his death, anyone who wishes has the authority to fasten the noose about his neck, as an act of good-will, and, after admonishing the man, to take his life. Likewise it is a custom of theirs to remove from life those who have become maimed or are in the grip of incurable diseases; for they consider it to be the greatest disgrace for a man to cling to life when he is unable to accomplish anything worth living for. Consequently, a man can see every Trogodyte sound in body and of vigorous age, since no one of them lives beyond sixty years.

But we have said enough about the Trogodytes; and if anyone of our readers shall distrust our histories because of what is strange and astonishing in the different manners of life which we have described, when he has considered and compared the climate of Scythia and that of the Trogodyte country and has observed the differences between them, he will not distrust what has been here related.

34. So great, for instance, is the contrast between our climate and the climates which we have described that the difference, when considered in detail,

2 μέρος διαφοράν ἄπιστον εἶναι. ὅπου μὲν γὰρ διὰ τὴν ὑπερβολὴν τοῦ ψύχους πήγνυνται μὲν οἱ μέγιστοι ποταμοί, στέγοντος τοῦ κρυστάλλου διαβάσεις στρατοπέδων καὶ ἁμαξῶν καταγόμων ἐφόδους, πήγνυται δὲ ὁ οἶνος καὶ τὰ λοιπὰ τῶν χυμῶν ὥστε μαχαίραις ἀποτέμνεσθαι, καὶ τὰ τούτων θαυμασιώτερα, τὰ μὲν ἀκρωτήρια τῶν ἀνθρώπων τῆς ἐσθῆτος παρατριβούσης περιρρεῖ, τὰ δὲ ὄμματα ἀμαυροῦται, τὸ δὲ πῦρ ἀλεωρὰν οὐ ποιεῖ, καὶ χαλκοῖ μὲν ἀνδριάντες ῥήγνυνται, κατὰ δέ τινας καιροὺς διὰ τὴν πυκνότητα τῶν νεφῶν οὔτε ἀστραπὴν οὔτε βροντὴν γίνεσθαι περὶ τοὺς τόπους φασί· πολλὰ δὲ καὶ ἄλλα τούτων παραδοξότερα συντελεῖται, τοῖς μὲν ἀγνοοῦσιν ἄπιστα,
3 τοῖς δὲ πεῖραν εἰληφόσιν ἀνυπομόνητα. περὶ δὲ τὰς ἐσχατιὰς τῆς Αἰγύπτου καὶ Τρωγοδυτικῆς διὰ τὴν ὑπερβολὴν τῆς ἀφ' ἡλίου θερμασίας κατὰ τὸν τῆς μεσημβρίας καιρὸν οὐδὲ συνορᾶν ἀλλήλους οἱ παρεστῶτες δύνανται διὰ τὴν παχύτητα τῆς περὶ τὸν ἀέρα πυκνώσεως, χωρὶς δὲ ὑποδέσεως πάντες ἀδυνατοῦσι βαδίζειν, ὡς ἂν τοῖς ἀνυποδήτοις παρα-
4 χρῆμα φλυκτίδων γινομένων. κατὰ δὲ τὸ ποτόν, ἐὰν μὴ τὴν ἔνδειαν ἑτοίμως ἀφαιρῆται, ταχέως τελευτῶσιν, ὡς ἂν τῆς θερμασίας τὴν τῶν ὑγρῶν ἐν τῷ σώματι φύσιν ὀξέως ἀναλισκούσης. πρὸς δὲ τούτοις, ὅταν τις εἰς χαλκοῦν ἀγγεῖον ἐμβαλών τῶν ἐδωδίμων ὁδηποτοῦν μεθ' ὕδατος εἰς τὸν ἥλιον θῇ,
5 ταχέως ἕψεται χωρὶς πυρὸς καὶ ξύλων. ἀλλ' ὅμως οἱ κατοικοῦντες ἀμφοτέρας τὰς εἰρημένας χώρας οὐχ οἷον φεύγειν βούλονται τὴν ὑπερβολὴν τῶν συμβαινόντων αὐτοῖς κακῶν, ἀλλὰ καὶ τοὐναντίον ἑκουσίως προΐενται[1] τὸ ζῆν ἕνεκα τοῦ μὴ βιασθῆναι

BOOK III. 34. 1-5

surpasses belief. For example, there are countries where, because of the excessive cold, the greatest rivers are frozen over, the ice sustaining the crossing of armies and the passage of heavily laden wagons, the wine and all other juices freeze so that they must be cut with knives, yea, what is more wonderful still, the extremities of human beings fall off when rubbed by the clothing, their eyes are blinded, fire furnishes no protection, even bronze statues are cracked open, and at certain seasons, they say, the clouds are so thick that in those regions there is neither lightning nor thunder; and many other things, more astonishing than these, come to pass, which are unbelievable to such as are ignorant of them, but cannot be endured by any who have actually experienced them. But on the farthermost bounds of Egypt and the Trogodyte country, because of the excessive heat from the sun at midday, men who are standing side by side are unable even to see one another by reason of the thickness of the air as it is condensed, and no one can walk about without foot-gear, since blisters appear at once on any who go barefoot. And as for drink, unless it is ready to hand to satisfy the need of it, they speedily perish, since the heat swiftly exhausts the natural moistures in the body. Moreover, whenever any man puts any food into a bronze vessel along with water and sets it in the sun, it quickly boils without fire or wood. Nevertheless, the inhabitants of both the lands which we have mentioned,[1] far from desiring to escape from the excessive evils which befall them, actually, on the contrary, give up their lives of their own accord simply to avoid being com-

[1] *i.e.* Scythia and the Trogodyte land.

[1] προίενται Dindorf: προσιέναι BDG, ποιέναι other MSS.

6 διαίτης ἑτέρας καὶ βίου πειραθῆναι. οὕτως αὐτοφυὲς ἔχει τι φίλτρον πᾶσα συνήθης χώρα, καὶ περιγίνεται τῆς ἐκ τῶν ἀέρων κακοπαθείας ὁ 7 χρόνος ὁ τὴν ἐκ νηπίου παραλαβὼν ἡλικίαν. τὰς δὲ τηλικαύτας ἐπ' ἀμφότερα διαφορὰς οὐ πολὺ διορίζει τόπου διάστημα. ἀπὸ γὰρ τῆς Μαιώτιδος λίμνης, ᾗ προσοικοῦσί τινες τῶν Σκυθῶν ἐν πάγει καὶ ψύχεσιν ὑπερβάλλουσι καθιδρυμένοι, πολλοὶ τῶν πλοϊζομένων οὐριοδρομούσαις ναυσὶ φορτίσιν εἰς μὲν Ῥόδον δεκαταῖοι καταπεπλεύκασιν, ἐξ ἧς εἰς Ἀλεξάνδρειαν τεταρταῖοι καταντῶσιν, ἐκ δὲ ταύτης κατὰ τὸν Νεῖλον πλέοντες πολλοὶ δεκαταῖοι κατηντήκασιν εἰς Αἰθιοπίαν, ὥστε ἀπὸ τῶν κατεψυγμένων μερῶν τῆς οἰκουμένης ἐπὶ τὰ θερμότατα μέρη μὴ πλέον εἴκοσι καὶ τεττάρων ἡμερῶν εἶναι τὸν πλοῦν τοῖς κατὰ τὸ συνεχὲς κομιζομένοις. 8 διόπερ τῆς διαφορᾶς τῆς τῶν ἀέρων ἐν ὀλίγῳ διαστήματι μεγάλης οὔσης οὐδὲν παράδοξον καὶ τὴν δίαιταν καὶ τοὺς βίους, ἔτι δὲ τὰ σώματα πολὺ διαλλάττειν τῶν παρ' ἡμῖν.

35. Ἐπεὶ δὲ τῶν ἐθνῶν καὶ βίων τὰ κεφάλαια τῶν δοκούντων εἶναι παραδόξων διεληλύθαμεν, περὶ τῶν[1] θηρίων τῶν κατὰ τὰς ὑποκειμένας χώρας 2 ἐν μέρει διέξιμεν. ἔστι γὰρ ζῷον ὃ καλεῖται μὲν ἀπὸ τοῦ συμβεβηκότος ῥινόκερως, ἀλκῇ δὲ καὶ βίᾳ παραπλήσιον ὂν[2] ἐλέφαντι, τῷ δὲ ὕψει ταπεινότερον, τὴν μὲν δορὰν ἰσχυροτάτην ἔχει, τὴν δὲ χρόαν πυξοειδῆ. ἐπὶ δ' ἄκρων τῶν μυκτήρων

[1] ὄντων after τῶν deleted by Eichstädt.
[2] ὂν added by Dindorf.

[1] i.e. as to severe cold and severe heat.

pelled to make trial of a different fare and manner of life. Thus it is that every country to which a man has grown accustomed holds a kind of spell of its own over him, and the length of time which he has spent there from infancy overcomes the hardship which he suffers from its climate. And yet countries so different in both ways [1] are separated by no great interval of space. For from Lake Maeotis,[2] near which certain Scythians dwell, living in the midst of frost and excessive cold, many sailors of merchant vessels, running before a favourable wind, have made Rhodes in ten days, from which they have reached Alexandria in four, and from that city many men, sailing by way of the Nile,[3] have reached Ethiopia in ten, so that from the cold parts of the inhabited world to its warmest parts the sailing time is not more than twenty-four days, if the journey is made without a break. Consequently, the difference in climates in a slight interval being so great, it is nothing surprising that both the fare and the manners of life as well as the bodies of the inhabitants should be very different from such as prevail among us.

35. And now that we have discussed the principal facts concerning the nations and the manners of life which men consider astonishing, we shall speak in turn of the wild animals of the countries which we are considering. There is an animal, for instance, which is called, from its characteristic, rhinoceros [4]; in courage and strength it is similar to the elephant but not so high, and it has the toughest hide known and a colour like box-wood.[5] At the tip of its nostrils

[2] The Sea of Azof.
[3] *i.e.* instead of by the Red Sea.
[4] Nose-horn.   [5] *i.e.* pale yellow.

φέρει κέρας τῷ τύπῳ σιμόν, τῇ δὲ στερεό-
3 τητι σιδήρῳ παρεμφερές. τοῦτο περὶ τῆς
νομῆς ἀεὶ διαφερόμενον ἐλέφαντι τὸ μὲν κέρας
πρός τινα τῶν πετρῶν θήγει, συμπεσὸν δ' εἰς
μάχην τῷ προειρημένῳ θηρίῳ καὶ ὑποδῦνον ὑπὸ
τὴν κοιλίαν ἀναρρήττει τῷ κέρατι καθάπερ ξίφει
τὴν σάρκα. τῷ δὲ τοιούτῳ τρόπῳ τῆς μάχης
χρώμενον ἔξαιμα ποιεῖ τὰ θηρία καὶ πολλὰ διαφθείρει. ὅταν δὲ ὁ ἐλέφας φθάσας τὴν ὑπὸ τὴν
κοιλίαν ὑπόδυσιν τῇ προβοσκίδι προκαταλάβηται
τὸν ῥινόκερων, περιγίνεται ῥᾳδίως τύπτων τοῖς
ὀδοῦσι καὶ τῇ βίᾳ πλέον ἰσχύων.

4 Αἱ δὲ σφίγγες γίνονται μὲν περί τε τὴν Τρωγοδυτικὴν καὶ τὴν Αἰθιοπίαν, ταῖς δὲ μορφαῖς
ὑπάρχουσιν οὐκ ἀνόμοιοι ταῖς γραφομέναις, μόνον
δὲ ταῖς δασύτησι διαλλάττουσι, τὰς δὲ ψυχὰς
ἡμέρους ἔχουσαι καὶ πανούργους ἐπὶ πλέον καὶ
διδασκαλίαν μεθοδικὴν ἐπιδέχονται.

5 Οἱ δ' ὀνομαζόμενοι κυνοκέφαλοι τοῖς μὲν σώμασιν
ἀνθρώποις δυσειδέσι παρεμφερεῖς εἰσι, ταῖς δὲ
φωναῖς μυγμοὺς ἀνθρωπίνους προΐενται. ἀγριώ-
τατα δὲ ταῦτα τὰ ζῷα καὶ παντελῶς ἀτιθάσευτα
καθεστῶτα τὴν ἀπὸ τῶν ὀφρύων πρόσοψιν αὐστη-
ροτέραν ἔχει. ταῖς δὲ θηλείαις ἰδιώτατον συμβαίνει
τὸ τὴν μήτραν ἐκτὸς τοῦ σώματος φέρειν πάντα
τὸν χρόνον.

6 Ὁ δὲ λεγόμενος κῆπος ὠνόμασται μὲν ἀπὸ τῆς

---

[1] *i.e.* bent backwards. Diodorus uses a term familiar to the Greeks but not used of a back-pointing horn.

BOOK III. 35. 2-6

it carries a horn which may be described as snub[1] and in hardness is like iron. Since it is ever contesting with the elephant about pasturage it sharpens its horn on stones, and when it opens the fight with this animal it slips under his belly and rips open the flesh with its horn as with a sword. By adopting this kind of fighting it drains the blood of the beasts and kills many of them. But if the elephant has avoided the attempt of the rhinoceros to get under his belly and has seized it beforehand with his trunk, he easily overcomes it by goring it with his tusks and making use of his superior strength.

There are also sphinxes[2] in both the Trogodyte country and Ethiopia, and in shape they are not unlike those depicted in art save that they are more shaggy of hair, and since they have dispositions that are gentle and rather inclined towards cunning they yield also to systematic training.

The animals which bear the name cynocephali[3] are in body like misshapen men, and they make a sound like the whimpering of human beings. These animals are very wild and quite untamable, and their eyebrows give them a rather surly expression. A most peculiar characteristic of the female is that it carries the womb on the outside of its body during its entire existence.

The animal called the cepus[4] has received its

[2] The large baboon (*Papio sphinx*).
[3] Dog-heads, the sacred dog-faced baboon (*Papio hamadryas*).
[4] A long-tailed monkey. The more common form of the word was "cebus," but the explanation of the name shows that Diodorus used the spelling of the text (*kepos*, "garden," was used metaphorically in the sense of "pleasure" or "grace").

περὶ τὸν ὄγκον ὅλον ὡραίας καὶ προσηνοῦς ἡλικίας, τὸ δὲ πρόσωπον ἔχων ὅμοιον λέοντι τὸ λοιπὸν σῶμα φέρει πάνθηρι παραπλήσιον, πλὴν τοῦ μεγέθους, ὃ παρισοῦται δορκάδι.

7 Πάντων δὲ τῶν εἰρημένων ζῴων ὁ σαρκοφάγος ταῦρος ἀγριώτατός ἐστι καὶ παντελῶς δυσκαταμάχητος. τῷ μὲν γὰρ ὄγκῳ τοῦτο μεῖζόν ἐστι τῶν ἡμέρων ταύρων, ὀξύτητι δὲ ποδῶν οὐ λειπόμενον ἵππου, τῷ στόματι δὲ διεστηκὸς ἄχρι τῶν ὤτων.[1] τὸ δὲ χρῶμα πυρρὸν ἔχει καθ' ὑπερβολήν, καὶ τὰ μὲν ὄμματα γλαυκότερα λέοντος καὶ τὰς νύκτας ἀστράπτοντα, τὰ δὲ κέρατα φύσεως ἰδιοτρόπου κοινωνοῦντα· τὸν μὲν γὰρ ἄλλον χρόνον αὐτὰ κινεῖ παραπλησίως τοῖς ὠσί, κατὰ δὲ τὰς μάχας ἵστησιν ἀραρότως. τὴν δὲ τῆς τριχὸς ἐπαγωγὴν
8 ἔχει τοῖς ἄλλοις ζῴοις ἐναντίαν. ἔστι δὲ τὸ θηρίον ἀλκῇ τε καὶ δυνάμει διάφορον, ὡς ἂν ἐπιτιθέμενον τοῖς ἀλκιμωτάτοις τῶν ζῴων καὶ τὴν τροφὴν ἔχον ἐκ τῆς τῶν χειρωθέντων σαρκοφαγίας. διαφθείρει δὲ καὶ τὰς ποίμνας τῶν ἐγχωρίων, καὶ καταπληκτικῶς ἀγωνίζεται πρὸς ὅλα συστή-
9 ματα τῶν ποιμένων καὶ κυνῶν ἀγέλας. λέγεται δὲ καὶ τὸ δέρμα ἄτρωτον ἔχειν· πολλῶν γοῦν ἐπιβεβλημένων λαβεῖν ὑποχείριον μηδένα κατισχυκέναι. τὸ δ' εἰς ὄρυγμα πεσὸν ἢ δι' ἄλλης ἀπάτης χειρωθὲν ὑπὸ τοῦ θυμοῦ γίνεται περιπνιγές, καὶ τῆς ἐλευθερίας οὐδαμῶς ἀλλάττεται τὴν ἐν τῷ τιθασεύεσθαι φιλανθρωπίαν. διόπερ εἰκότως οἱ Τρωγοδύται τοῦτο τὸ θηρίον κράτιστον κρίνουσιν, ὡς ἂν τῆς φύσεως αὐτῷ δεδωρημένης ἀλκὴν

[1] ὤτων (Agatharchides 76) Dindorf: ὀμμάτων MSS., Bekker.

name from the beautiful and pleasing grace which characterizes its entire body, and it has a head like that of a lion, but the rest of its body is like that of a panther, save in respect to its size, in which it resembles a gazelle.

But of all the animals named the carnivorous bull is the wildest and altogether the hardest to overcome. For in bulk he is larger than the domestic bulls, in swiftness of foot he is not inferior to a horse, and his mouth opens clear back to the ears. His colour is a fiery red, his eyes are more piercing than those of a lion and shine at night, and his horns enjoy a distinctive property; for at all other times he moves them like his ears, but when fighting he holds them rigid. The direction of growth of his hair is contrary to that of all other animals. He is, again, a remarkable beast in both boldness and strength, since he attacks the boldest animals and finds his food in devouring the flesh of his victims. He also destroys the flocks of the inhabitants and engages in terrible combats with whole bands of the shepherds and packs of dogs. Rumour has it that their skin cannot be pierced; at any rate, though many men have tried to capture them, no man has ever brought one under subjection. If he has fallen into a pit or been captured by some other ruse he becomes choked with rage, and in no case does he ever exchange his freedom for the care which men would accord to him in domestication. It is with reason, therefore, that the Trogodytes hold this wild beast to be the strongest of all, since Nature has endowed it with the

μὲν λέοντος, ἵππου δὲ τάχος, ῥώμην δὲ ταύρου, τῆς δὲ πάντων κρατίστης σιδήρου φύσεως οὐχ ἡττώμενον.

10 Ὁ δὲ λεγόμενος παρ' Αἰθίοψι κροκόττας μεμιγμένην μὲν ἔχει φύσιν κυνὸς καὶ λύκου, τὴν δ' ἀγριότητα φοβερωτέραν ἀμφοτέρων, τοῖς δὲ ὀδοῦσι πάντων ὑπεράγει. πᾶν γὰρ ὀστῶν μέγεθος συντρίβει ῥᾳδίως, καὶ τὸ καταποθὲν διὰ τῆς κοιλίας πέττει παραδόξως. τοῦτο δὲ τὸ ζῷον τῶν ψευδῶς παραδοξολογούντων ἱστοροῦντες ἔνιοι μιμεῖσθαι τὴν τῶν ἀνθρώπων διάλεκτον ἡμᾶς μὲν οὐ πείθουσιν.

36. Ὄφεων δὲ γένη παντοδαπὰ καὶ τοῖς μεγέθεσιν ἄπιστα θεωρεῖσθαί φασιν οἱ τὴν πλησίον τῆς ἐρήμου καὶ θηριώδους κατοικοῦντες. ἑκατὸν γὰρ πηχῶν τὸ μῆκος ἑορακέναι τινὲς ἀποφαινόμενοι δικαίως ἂν οὐχ ὑφ' ἡμῶν μόνον, ἀλλὰ καὶ ὑπὸ τῶν ἄλλων ἁπάντων ψευδολογεῖν ὑποληφθείησαν· προστιθέασι γὰρ τῷ διαπιστουμένῳ πολλῷ παραδοξότερα, λέγοντες ὅτι τῆς χώρας οὔσης πεδιάδος, ὅταν τὰ μέγιστα τῶν θηρίων περισπειραθῇ, ποιεῖ ταῖς ἐγκυκλωθείσαις ἐπ' ἀλλήλαις σπείραις ἀναστήματα πόρρωθεν φαινόμενα λόφῳ παραπλήσια.
2 τῷ μὲν οὖν μεγέθει τῶν ῥηθέντων θηρίων οὐκ ἄν τις ῥᾳδίως συγκατάθοιτο· περὶ δὲ τῶν μεγίστων θηρίων[1] τῶν εἰς ὄψιν ἐληλυθότων καὶ κομισθέντων ἔν τισιν ἀγγείοις εὐθέτοις εἰς τὴν Ἀλεξάνδρειαν ποιησόμεθα τὴν ἀναγραφήν, προστιθέντες καὶ τῆς[2] θήρας τὴν κατὰ μέρος οἰκονομίαν.

[1] θηρίων ὄφεων MSS.: ὄφεων deleted by Vogel, θηρίων deleted by Eichstädt, Dindorf, Bekker.
[2] κατὰ μέρος after τῆς deleted by Dindorf.

[1] Probably a kind of hyena.

prowess of a lion, the speed of a horse, and the might of a bull, and since it is not subdued by the native strength of iron which is the greatest known.

The animal which the Ethiopians call the crocottas [1] has a nature which is a mixture of that of a dog and that of a wolf, but in ferocity it is more to be feared than either of them, and with respect to its teeth it surpasses all animals; for every bone, no matter how huge in size, it easily crushes, and whatever it has gulped down its stomach digests in an astonishing manner. And among those who recount marvellous lies about this beast there are some who relate that it imitates the speech of men, but for our part they do not win our credence.

36. As for snakes, those peoples which dwell near the country which is desert and infested by beasts say that there is every kind of them, of a magnitude surpassing belief. For when certain writers state that they have seen some one hundred cubits long, it may justly be assumed, not only by us but by everybody else, that they are telling a falsehood; indeed they add to this tale, which is utterly distrusted, things far more astonishing, when they say that, since the country is flat like a plain, whenever the largest of these beasts coil themselves up, they make, by the coils which have been wound in circles and rest one upon another, elevations which seen from a distance resemble a hill. Now a man may not readily agree as to the magnitude of the beasts of which we have just spoken; but we shall describe the largest beasts which have actually been seen and were brought to Alexandria in certain well-made receptacles, and shall add a detailed description of the manner in which they were captured.

3 Ὁ γὰρ δεύτερος Πτολεμαῖος, περί τε τὴν τῶν ἐλεφάντων κυνηγίαν φιλοτιμηθεὶς καὶ τοῖς τὰς παραδόξους θήρας τῶν ἀλκιμωτάτων ζῴων ποιουμένοις μεγάλας ἀπονέμων δωρεάς, πολλὰ δὲ χρήματα δαπανήσας εἰς ταύτην τὴν ἐπιθυμίαν, ἐλέφαντάς τε συχνοὺς πολεμιστὰς περιεποιήσατο καὶ τῶν ἄλλων ζῴων ἀθεωρήτους καὶ παραδόξους φύσεις ἐποίησεν εἰς γνῶσιν ἐλθεῖν τοῖς Ἕλλησι.

4 διὸ καί τινες τῶν κυνηγῶν, ὁρῶντες τὴν τοῦ βασιλέως μεγαλοψυχίαν ἐν ταῖς δωρεαῖς, συστραφέντες εἰς ἱκανὸν πλῆθος ἔκριναν παραβαλέσθαι ταῖς ψυχαῖς, καὶ τῶν μεγάλων ὄφεων ἕνα θηρεύσαντες ἀνακομίσαι ζῶντα εἰς τὴν Ἀλεξάνδρειαν

5 πρὸς τὸν Πτολεμαῖον. μεγάλης δ' οὔσης καὶ παραδόξου τῆς ἐπιβολῆς, ἡ τύχη συνεργήσασα ταῖς ἐπινοίαις αὐτῶν καὶ τὸ τέλος οἰκεῖον περιεποίησε τῆς πράξεως. σκοπεύσαντες γὰρ ἕνα τῶν ὄφεων τριάκοντα πηχῶν διατρίβοντα περὶ τὰς συστάσεις τῶν ὑδάτων, τὸν μὲν ἄλλον χρόνον ἀκίνητον τοῦ σώματος τὸ κύκλωμα τηροῦντα, κατὰ δὲ τὰς ἐπιφανείας τῶν διὰ τὴν δίψαν ζῴων φοιτώντων ἐπὶ τὸν τόπον ἄφνω διανιστάμενον, καὶ τῷ μὲν στόματι διαρπάζοντα, τῷ δὲ σπειράματι καταπλέκοντα τὸν ὄγκον τῶν φανέντων ζῴων, ὥστε μηδενὶ τρόπῳ δύνασθαι τὸ παραπεσὸν ἐκφυγεῖν—, προμήκους οὖν ὄντος τοῦ ζῴου καὶ νωθροῦ τὴν φύσιν ἐλπίσαντες βρόχοις καὶ σειραῖς κυριεύσειν, τὸ μὲν πρῶτον παρῆσαν ἐπ' αὐτὸ τεθαρρηκότες, ἔχοντες ἐξηρτυμένα πάντα τὰ πρὸς τὴν χρείαν,

---

[1] Ptolemy Philadelphus, 285–246 B.C. Ptolemy's interest in wild animals has long been known from this passage and

BOOK III. 36. 3-5

The second Ptolemy,[1] who was passionately fond of the hunting of elephants and gave great rewards to those who succeeded in capturing against odds the most valiant of these beasts, expending on this hobby great sums of money, not only collected great herds of war-elephants, but also brought to the knowledge of the Greeks other kinds of animals which had never before been seen and were objects of amazement. Consequently certain of the hunters, observing the princely generosity of the king in the matter of the rewards he gave, rounding up a considerable number decided to hazard their lives and to capture one of the huge snakes and bring it alive to Ptolemy at Alexandria. Great and astonishing as was the undertaking, fortune aided their designs and crowned their attempt with the success which it deserved. For they spied one of the snakes, thirty cubits long, as it loitered near the pools in which the water collects; here it maintained for most of the time its coiled body motionless, but at the appearance of an animal which came down to the spot to quench its thirst it would suddenly uncoil itself, seize the animal in its jaws, and so entwine in its coil the body of the creature which had come into view that it could in no wise escape its doom. And so, since the beast was long and slender and sluggish in nature, hoping that they could master it with nooses and ropes, they approached it with confidence the first time, having ready to hand everything which

Theocritus 2. 67-8. That he was as deeply interested in introducing new breeds of domesticated animals into Egypt is attested by a papyrus (*P. Cairo Zenon* I. 59,075), written in 257 B.C., in which an Ammonite chief from east of the Jordan river says that he is sending the king a gift of horses, dogs, asses and several specimens of cross-breeding with the wild ass.

6 ὡς δ' ἐπλησίαζον, ἀεὶ μᾶλλον ἐξεπλήττοντο τῷ δέει, θεωροῦντες ὄμμα πυρωπὸν καὶ λιχμωμένην πάντῃ τὴν γλῶτταν, ἔτι δὲ τῇ τραχύτητι τῶν φολίδων ἐν τῇ διὰ τῆς ὕλης πορείᾳ καὶ παρατρίψει ψόφον ἐξαίσιον κατασκευάζοντα, τὸ μέγεθός τε τῶν ὀδόντων ὑπερφυὲς καὶ στόματος ἀγρίαν πρόσοψιν 7 καὶ κυκλώματος ἀνάστημα παράδοξον. διόπερ τῷ φόβῳ τὰ χρώματα τῶν προσώπων ἀποβεβληκότες δειλῶς ἐπέβαλον τοὺς βρόχους ἀπὸ τῆς οὐρᾶς· τὸ δὲ θηρίον ἅμα τῷ προσάψασθαι τοῦ σώματος τὸν κάλων ἐπεστράφη μετὰ πολλοῦ φυσήματος καταπληκτικῶς, καὶ τὸν μὲν πρῶτον ἁρπάζει τῷ στόματι μετεωρισθὲν ὑπὲρ τῆς κεφαλῆς, καὶ τὰς σάρκας ἔτι ζῶντος κατεσιτεῖτο, τὸν δὲ δεύτερον φεύγοντα τῇ σπείρᾳ πόρρωθεν ἐπεσπάσατο, καὶ περιειληθὲν ἔσφιγγε τὴν κοιλίαν τῷ δεσμῷ· οἱ δὲ λοιποὶ πάντες ἐκπλαγέντες διὰ τῆς φυγῆς τὴν σωτηρίαν ἐπορίσαντο.

37. Οὐ μὴν ἀπέγνωσαν τὴν θήραν, ὑπερβαλλούσης τῆς ἀπὸ τοῦ βασιλέως χάριτος καὶ δωρεᾶς τοὺς ἀπὸ τῆς πείρας ἐγνωσμένους κινδύνους, φιλοτεχνίᾳ δὲ καὶ δόλῳ τὸ τῇ βίᾳ δυσκαταγώνιστον ἐχειρώσαντο, τοιάνδε τινὰ μηχανὴν πορισάμενοι. κατεσκεύασαν ἀπὸ σχοίνου πυκνῆς περιφερὲς πλόκανον, τῷ μὲν τύπῳ τοῖς κύρτοις ἐμφερές, τῷ δὲ μεγέθει καὶ τῇ διαλήψει τῆς χώρας δυνάμενον 2 δέξασθαι τὸν ὄγκον τοῦ θηρίου. κατοπτεύσαντες οὖν τὸν φωλεὸν αὐτοῦ καὶ τὴν ὥραν τῆς τε ἐπὶ τὴν νομὴν ἐξόδου καὶ πάλιν τῆς ἐπανόδου, ὡς

they might need; but as they drew near it they constantly grew more and more terrified as they gazed upon its fiery eye and its tongue darting out in every direction, caught the hideous sound made by the roughness of its scales as it made its way through the trees and brushed against them, and noted the extraordinary size of its teeth, the savage appearance of its mouth, and the astonishing height of its heap of coils. Consequently, after they had driven the colour from their cheeks through fear, with cowardly trembling they cast the nooses about its tail; but the beast, the moment the rope touched its body, whirled about with so mighty a hissing as to frighten them out of their wits, and raising itself into the air above the head of the foremost man it seized him in its mouth and ate his flesh while he still lived, and the second it caught from a distance with a coil as he fled, drew him to itself, and winding itself about him began squeezing his belly with its tightening bond; and as for all the rest, stricken with terror they sought their safety in flight.

37. Nevertheless, the hunters did not give up their attempt to capture the beast, the favour expected of the king and his reward outweighing the dangers which they had come to know full well as the result of their experiment, and by ingenuity and craft they did subdue that which was by force well-nigh invincible, devising a kind of contrivance like the following:—They fashioned a circular thing woven of reeds closely set together, in general shape resembling a fisherman's creel and in size and capacity capable of holding the bulk of the beast. Then, when they had reconnoitred its hole and observed the time when it went forth to feed and

τάχισθ' ὥρμησεν ἐπὶ τὴν ἄγραν τὴν συνήθη τῶν ἑτερογενῶν ζῴων, τὸ μὲν προϋπάρχον τοῦ φωλεοῦ στόμα λίθοις εὐμεγέθεσι καὶ γῇ συνῳκοδόμησαν, τὸν δὲ πλησίον τῆς λόχμης τόπον ὑπόνομον ποιήσαντες καὶ τὸ πλόκανον εἰς αὐτὸν ἐνθέντες ἐναντίον ἐποίησαν τὸ στόμιον, ὥστε ἐξ ἑτοίμου τῷ θηρίῳ
3 τὴν εἴσοδον ὑπάρχειν. κατὰ δὲ τὴν ἐπάνοδον τοῦ ζῴου παρεσκευασμένοι τοξότας καὶ σφενδονήτας, ἔτι δὲ ἱππεῖς πολλούς, πρὸς δὲ τούτοις σαλπικτὰς καὶ τὴν ἄλλην ἅπασαν χορηγίαν, ἅμα[1] τῷ προσπελάζειν τὸ μὲν θηρίον μετεωρότερον τῶν ἱππέων ἐξῆρε τὸν αὐχένα, οἱ δ' ἐπὶ τὴν θήραν ἠθροισμένοι προσεγγίσαι μὲν οὐκ ἐτόλμων, νενουθετημένοι ταῖς προγεγενημέναις συμφοραῖς, πόρρωθεν δὲ πολλαῖς χερσὶν ἐφ' ἕνα καὶ μέγαν σκοπὸν βάλλοντες ἐτύγχανον, καὶ τῇ τε τῶν ἱππέων ἐπιφανείᾳ καὶ πλήθει κυνῶν ἀλκίμων, ἔτι δὲ τῷ διὰ τῶν σαλπίγγων ἤχῳ, κατέπληττον τὸ ζῷον. διόπερ ὑποχωροῦντος αὐτοῦ[2] πρὸς τὴν οἰκείαν λόχμην τοσοῦτον ἐπεδίωκον
4 ὥστε μὴ παροξύνειν ἐπὶ πλέον. ὡς δὲ τῆς ἐνῳκοδομημένης φάραγγος ἤγγισεν, ἀθρόως ψόφον μὲν πολὺν διὰ τῶν ὅπλων ἐποίησαν, ταραχὴν δὲ καὶ φόβον διὰ τῆς τῶν ὄχλων ἐπιφανείας καὶ σαλπίγγων. τὸ δὲ θηρίον τὴν μὲν εἴσοδον οὐχ ηὕρισκε, τὴν δὲ τῶν κυνηγῶν ὁρμὴν καταπληττόμενον κατέφυγεν εἰς τὸ πλησίον κατεσκευασμένον στόμιον.
5 πιμπλαμένου δὲ τοῦ πλοκάνου τῇ διαλύσει τῆς σπείρας, ἔφθασαν τῶν κυνηγῶν τινες προσιπτάμενοι, καὶ πρὸ τοῦ στραφῆναι τὸν ὄφιν ἐπὶ τὴν

---

[1] δὲ after ἅμα deleted by Reiske.
[2] αὐτοῦ deleted by Dindorf, retained by Bekker, Vogel.

returned again, so soon as it had set out to prey upon the other animals, as was its custom, they stopped the opening of its old hole with large stones and earth, and digging an underground cavity near its lair they set the woven net in it and placed the mouth of the net opposite the opening, so that it was in this way all ready for the beast to enter. Against the return of the animal they had made ready archers and slingers and many horsemen, as well as trumpeters and all the other apparatus needed, and as the beast drew near it raised its neck in air higher than the horsemen. Now the company of men who had assembled for the hunt did not dare to draw near it, being warned by the mishaps which had befallen them on the former occasion, but shooting at it from afar, and with many hands aiming at a single target, and a large one at that, they kept hitting it, and when the horsemen appeared and the multitude of bold fighting-dogs, and then again when the trumpets blared, they got the animal terrified. Consequently, when it retreated to its accustomed lair, they closed in upon it, but only so far as not to arouse it still more. And when it came near the opening which had been stopped up, the whole throng, acting together, raised a mighty din with their arms and thus increased its confusion and fear because of the crowds which put in their appearance and of the trumpets. But the beast could not find the opening and so, terrified at the advance of the hunters, fled for refuge into the mouth of the net which had been prepared near by. And when the woven net began to be filled up as the snake uncoiled itself, some of the hunters anticipated its movements by leaping forward, and before the snake

ἔξοδον κατελάβοντο δεσμοῖς τὸ στόμιον πρόμηκες ὂν καὶ πεφιλοτεχνημένον πρὸς ταύτην τὴν ὀξύτητα· ἐξελκύσαντες δὲ τὸ πλόκανον καὶ φάλαγγας
6 ὑποθέντες μετέωρον[1] ἐξῆραν. τὸ δὲ θηρίον ἀπειλημμένον ἐν ἀπεστενωμένῳ τόπῳ παρὰ φύσιν συριγμὸν ἐξαίσιον ἠφίει καὶ τοῖς ὀδοῦσι τὴν περιέχουσαν σχοῖνον κατέσπα, πάντῃ δὲ διασειόμενον προσδοκίαν ἐποίησε τοῖς φέρουσιν ὡς ἐκπηδῆσον ἐκ τοῦ περιέχοντος αὐτὸ φιλοτεχνήματος. διὸ καὶ καταπλαγέντες ἔθεσαν ἐπὶ τὴν γῆν τὸν ὄφιν, καὶ τοὺς περὶ τὴν οὐρὰν τόπους κατακεντοῦντες ἀντιπεριέσπων τοῦ θηρίου τὸν ἀπὸ τῶν ὀδόντων σπαραγμὸν ἐπὶ τὴν αἴσθησιν τῶν ἀλγούντων μερῶν.
7 Ἀπενέγκαντες δ' εἰς τὴν Ἀλεξάνδρειαν ἐδωρήσαντο τῷ βασιλεῖ, παράδοξον θέαμα καὶ τοῖς ἀκούσασιν ἀπιστούμενον. τῇ δ' ἐνδείᾳ τῆς τροφῆς καταπονήσαντες τὴν ἀλκὴν τοῦ θηρίου τιθασὸν ἐκ τοῦ κατ' ὀλίγον ἐποίησαν, ὥστε θαυμαστὴν
8 αὐτοῦ γενέσθαι τὴν ἐξημέρωσιν. ὁ δὲ Πτολεμαῖος τοῖς μὲν κυνηγοῖς τὰς ἀξίας ἀπένειμε δωρεάς, τὸν δ' ὄφιν ἔτρεφε τετιθασευμένον καὶ τοῖς εἰς τὴν βασιλείαν παραβάλλουσι ξένοις μέγιστον παρεχό-
9 μενον καὶ παραδοξότατον θέαμα. διόπερ τηλικούτου μεγέθους ὄφεως εἰς ὄψιν κοινὴν κατηντηκότος οὐκ ἄξιον ἀπιστεῖν τοῖς Αἰθίοψιν οὐδὲ μῦθον ὑπολαμβάνειν τὸ θρυλούμενον ὑπ' αὐτῶν. ἀποφαίνονται γὰρ ὁρᾶσθαι κατὰ τὴν χώραν αὐτῶν ὄφεις τηλικούτους τὸ μέγεθος ὥστε μὴ

---

[1] So Dindorf: μετεωρότερον.

could turn about to face the entrance they closed and fastened with ropes the mouth, which was long and had been shrewdly devised with such swiftness of operation in mind; then they hauled out the woven net and putting rollers under it drew it up into the air. But the beast, enclosed as it was in a straitened place, kept sending forth an unnatural and terrible hissing and tried to pull down with its teeth the reeds which enveloped it, and by twisting itself in every direction created the expectation in the minds of the men who were carrying it that it would leap out of the contrivance which enveloped it. Consequently, in terror, they set the snake down on the ground, and by jabbing it about the tail they diverted the attention of the beast from its work of tearing with its teeth to its sensation of pain in the parts which hurt.

When they had brought the snake to Alexandria they presented it to the king, an astonishing sight which those cannot credit who have merely heard the tale. And by depriving the beast of its food they wore down its spirit and little by little tamed it, so that the domestication of it became a thing of wonder. As for Ptolemy, he distributed among the hunters the merited rewards, and kept and fed the snake, which had now been tamed and afforded the greatest and most astonishing sight for the strangers who visited his kingdom. Consequently, in view of the fact that a snake of so great a size has been exposed to the public gaze, it is not fair to doubt the word of the Ethiopians or to assume that the report which they circulated far and wide was a mere fiction. For they state that there are to be seen in their country snakes so great in size that they not only eat both

DIODORUS OF SICILY

μόνον βοῦς τε καὶ ταύρους καὶ τῶν ἄλλων ζῴων τὰ τηλικαῦτα τοῖς ὄγκοις ἀναλίσκειν, ἀλλὰ καὶ τοῖς ἐλέφασιν εἰς ἀλκὴν συνίστασθαι, καὶ διὰ μὲν τῆς σπείρας ἐμπλεκομένους τοῖς σκέλεσιν ἐμποδίζειν τὴν κατὰ φύσιν κίνησιν, τὸν δ' αὐχένα μετεωρίσαντας ὑπὲρ[1] τὴν προβοσκίδα τὴν κεφαλὴν ἐναντίαν ποιεῖν τοῖς τῶν ἐλεφάντων ὄμμασι, διὰ δὲ τοῦ πυρωποῦ τῶν ὀφθαλμῶν ἀστραπῇ παραπλησίας[2] τὰς λαμπηδόνας προβάλλοντας ἀποτυφλοῦν τὴν ὅρασιν, καὶ σφήλαντας ἐπὶ τὴν γῆν σαρκοφαγεῖν τὰ χειρωθέντα τῶν ζῴων.

38. Διευκρινηκότες δ' ἀρκούντως τὰ περὶ τὴν Αἰθιοπίαν καὶ Τρωγοδυτικὴν καὶ τὴν ταύταις συναπτούσαν μέχρι τῆς διὰ καῦμα ἀοικήτου, πρὸς δὲ ταύταις περὶ τῆς παραλίας τῆς παρὰ τὴν Ἐρυθρὰν θάλατταν καὶ τὸ Ἀτλαντικὸν πέλαγος τὸ πρὸς μεσημβρίαν κεκλιμένον, περὶ τοῦ καταλελειμμένου μέρους, λέγω δὲ τοῦ Ἀραβίου κόλπου, ποιησόμεθα τὴν ἀναγραφήν, τὰ μὲν ἐκ τῶν ἐν Ἀλεξανδρείᾳ βασιλικῶν ὑπομνημάτων ἐξειληφότες, τὰ δὲ παρὰ τῶν αὐτοπτῶν πεπυσμένοι. 2 τοῦτο γὰρ τὸ μέρος τῆς οἰκουμένης καὶ τὸ περὶ τὰς Βρεττανικὰς νήσους καὶ τὴν ἄρκτον ἥκιστα πέπτωκεν ὑπὸ τὴν κοινὴν ἀνθρώπων ἐπίγνωσιν. ἀλλὰ περὶ μὲν τῶν πρὸς ἄρκτον κεκλιμένων μερῶν τῆς οἰκουμένης τῶν συναπτόντων τῇ διὰ ψῦχος ἀοικήτῳ διέξιμεν, ὅταν τὰς Γαΐου Καίσαρος

[1] ὑπὲρ Reiske: ὑπό.
[2] So Dindorf: παραπλησίως.

---

[1] The Persian Gulf and contiguous shores must be meant.

BOOK III. 37. 9–38. 2

oxen and bulls and other animals of equal bulk, but even join issue in battle with the elephants, and by intertwining their coil about the elephants' legs they prevent the natural movement of them and by rearing their necks above their trunks they put their heads directly opposite the eyes of the elephants, and sending forth, by reason of the fiery nature of their eyes, brilliant flashes like lightning, they first blind their sight and then throw them to the ground and devour the flesh of their conquered foes.

38. But now that we have examined with sufficient care Ethiopia and the Trogodyte country and the territory adjoining them, as far as the region which is uninhabited because of excessive heat, and, beside these, the coast of the Red Sea [1] and the Atlantic deep [2] which stretches towards the south, we shall give an account of the part which still remains—and I refer to the Arabian Gulf [3]—drawing in part upon the royal records preserved in Alexandria, and in part upon what we have learned from men who have seen it with their own eyes. For this section of the inhabited world and that about the British Isles and the far north have by no means come to be included in the common knowledge of men. But as for the parts of the inhabited world which lie to the far north and border on the area which is uninhabited because of the cold, we shall discuss them when we record the

[2] Apparently Diodorus uses the term "Atlantic," although it is derived from the word "Atlas," and regularly designated the western ocean, in the sense employed by the geographer Eratosthenes, who, about 200 B.C., applied it to the entire expanse of water which surrounded the "inhabited world" (cp. H. Berger, *Geschichte der wissenschaftlichen Erdkunde der Griechen*², pp. 323, 377, 396).

[3] The Red Sea.

3 πράξεις ἀναγράφωμεν· οὗτος γὰρ τὴν Ῥωμαίων ἡγεμονίαν εἰς ἐκεῖνα τὰ μέρη πορρωτάτω προβιβάσας πάντα τὸν πρότερον ἀγνοούμενον τόπον
4 ἐποίησε πεσεῖν εἰς σύνταξιν ἱστορίας· ὁ δὲ προσαγορευόμενος Ἀράβιος κόλπος ἀνεστόμωται μὲν εἰς τὸν κατὰ μεσημβρίαν κείμενον ὠκεανόν, τῷ μήκει δ' ἐπὶ πολλοὺς πάνυ παρήκων σταδίους τὸν μυχὸν ἔχει περιοριζόμενον ταῖς ἐσχατιαῖς τῆς Ἀραβίας καὶ Τρωγοδυτικῆς. εὖρος δὲ κατὰ μὲν τὸ στόμα καὶ τὸν μυχὸν ὑπάρχει περὶ ἑκκαίδεκα σταδίους, ἀπὸ δὲ Πανόρμου λιμένος πρὸς τὴν ἀντιπέρας ἤπειρον μακρᾶς νεὼς διωγμὸν ἡμερήσιον. τὸ δὲ μέγιστόν ἐστι διάστημα κατὰ τὸ Τύρκαιον ὄρος καὶ Μακαρίαν νῆσον πελαγίαν, ὡς ἂν τῶν ἠπείρων οὐχ ὁρωμένων ἀπ' ἀλλήλων.
5 ἀπὸ δὲ τούτου τὸ πλάτος ἀεὶ μᾶλλον συγκλείεται καὶ τὴν συναγωγὴν ἔχει μέχρι τοῦ στόματος. ὁ δὲ παράπλους αὐτοῦ κατὰ πολλοὺς τόπους ἔχει νήσους μακράς, στενοὺς μὲν διαδρόμους ἐχούσας, ῥοῦν δὲ πολὺν καὶ σφοδρόν. ἡ μὲν οὖν κεφαλαιώδης τοῦ κόλπου τούτου θέσις ὑπάρχει τοιαύτη. ἡμεῖς δ' ἀπὸ τῶν ἐσχάτων[1] τοῦ μυχοῦ τόπων ἀρξάμενοι τὸν ἐφ' ἑκάτερα τὰ μέρη παράπλουν τῶν ἠπείρων καὶ τὰς ἀξιολογωτάτας κατ' αὐτὰς ἰδιότητας διέξιμεν· πρῶτον δὲ ληψόμεθα τὸ δεξιὸν μέρος, οὗ τὴν παραλίαν τῶν Τρωγοδυτῶν ἔθνη νέμεται μέχρι τῆς ἐρήμου.

[1] τούτου after ἐσχάτων deleted by Dindorf.

[1] Cp. Book 1. 4. 7.
[2] The Indian Ocean.

BOOK III. 38. 2-5

deeds of Gaius Caesar; for he it was who extended the Roman Empire the farthest into those parts and brought it about that all the area which had formerly been unknown came to be included in a narrative of history [1]; but the Arabian Gulf, as it is called, opens into the ocean which lies to the south,[2] and its innermost recess, which stretches over a distance of very many stades in length, is enclosed by the farthermost borders of Arabia and the Trogodyte country. Its width at the mouth and at the innermost recess is about sixteen [3] stades, but from the harbour of Panormus to the opposite mainland is a day's run for a warship. And its greatest width is at the Tyrcaeus [4] mountain and Macaria, an island out at sea, the mainlands there being out of sight of each other. But from this point the width steadily decreases more and more and continually tapers as far as the entrance. And as a man sails along the coast he comes in many places upon long islands with narrow passages between them, where the current runs full and strong. Such, then, is the setting, in general terms, of this gulf. But for our part, we shall make our beginning with the farthest regions of the innermost recess and then sail along its two sides past the mainlands, in connection with which we shall describe what is peculiar to them and most deserving of discussion; and first of all we shall take the right side,[5] the coast of which is inhabited by tribes of the Trogodytes as far inland as the desert.

[3] Strabo (16. 4. 4) and others say the straits at Deirê are sixty stades wide (about seven miles), which is much nearer the present width than the "sixteen" of Diodorus.

[4] Panormus and this mountain are otherwise unknown.

[5] *i.e.* the western or Egyptian side.

DIODORUS OF SICILY

39. Ἀπὸ πόλεως τοίνυν Ἀρσινόης κομιζομένοις παρὰ τὴν δεξιὰν ἤπειρον ἐκπίπτει κατὰ πολλοὺς τόπους ἐκ πέτρας εἰς θάλατταν ὕδατα πολλά, πικρᾶς ἁλμυρίδος ἔχοντα γεῦσιν. παραδραμόντι δὲ τὰς πηγὰς ταύτας[1] ὑπέρκειται μεγάλου πεδίου μιλτώδη χρόαν ἔχον ὄρος καὶ τὴν ὅρασιν τῶν ἐπὶ πλέον ἀτενιζόντων εἰς αὐτὸ λυμαινόμενον. ὑπὸ δὲ τὰς ἐσχατιὰς τῆς ὑπωρείας κεῖται λιμὴν σκολιὸν ἔχων τὸν εἴσπλουν, ἐπώνυμος
2 Ἀφροδίτης. ὑπέρκεινται δὲ τούτου νῆσοι τρεῖς, ὧν δύο μὲν πλήρεις εἰσὶν ἐλαιῶν καὶ σύσκιοι, μία δὲ λειπομένη τῷ πλήθει τῶν προειρημένων δένδρων, πλῆθος δ' ἔχουσα τῶν ὀνομαζομένων
3 μελεαγρίδων. μετὰ δὲ ταῦτα κόλπος ἐστὶν εὐμεγέθης ὁ καλούμενος Ἀκάθαρτος, καὶ πρὸς αὐτῷ βαθεῖα καθ' ὑπερβολὴν χερρόνησος, ἧς κατὰ τὸν αὐχένα στενὸν ὄντα διακομίζουσι τὰ σκάφη πρὸς τὴν ἀντιπέρας θάλατταν.
4 παρακομισθέντι δὲ τοὺς τόπους τούτους κεῖται νῆσος πελαγία μὲν τῷ διαστήματι, τὸ δὲ μῆκος εἰς ὀγδοήκοντα σταδίους παρεκτείνουσα, καλουμένη δὲ Ὀφιώδης, ᾗ τὸ μὲν παλαιὸν ὑπῆρχε πλήρης παντοδαπῶν καὶ φοβερῶν ἑρπετῶν, ἀφ' ὧν καὶ ταύτης ἔτυχε τῆς προσηγορίας, ἐν δὲ τοῖς μεταγενεστέροις χρόνοις ὑπὸ τῶν κατὰ τὴν Ἀλεξάνδρειαν βασιλέων οὕτως ἐξημερώθη φιλοτίμως ὥστε μηδὲν ἔτι κατ' αὐτὴν ὁρᾶσθαι τῶν προϋπαρξάντων ζῴων.

[1] ταύτας Eichstädt: αὐτάς.

BOOK III. 39. 1 4

39. In the course of the journey,[1] then, from the city of Arsinoê along the right mainland, in many places numerous streams, which have a bitter salty taste, drop from the cliffs into the sea. And after a man has passed these waters, above a great plain there towers a mountain whose colour is like ruddle and blinds the sight of any who gaze steadfastly upon it for some time. Moreover, at the edge of the skirts of the mountain there lies a harbour, known as Aphroditê's Harbour, which has a winding entrance. Above [2] this harbour are situated three islands, two of which abound in olive trees and are thickly shaded, while one falls short of the other two in respect of the number of these trees but contains a multitude of the birds called *meleagrides*.[3] Next there is a very large gulf which is called Acathartus,[4] and by it is an exceedingly long peninsula, over the narrow neck of which men transport their ships to the opposite sea. And as a man coasts along these regions he comes to an island which lies at a distance out in the open sea and stretches for a length of eighty stades; the name of it is Ophiodes [5] and it was formerly full of fearful serpents of every variety, which was in fact the reason why it received this name, but in later times the kings at Alexandria have laboured so diligently on the reclaiming of it that not one of the animals which were formerly there is any longer to be seen on the island.

[1] Strabo (16. 4. 5 ff.) follows much the same order in his description of the Gulf.

[2] Strabo (16. 4. 5) says these islands lie " off," Agatharchides (81), that they lie " in " the harbour.

[3] Guinea-fowls.

[4] *i.e.* " Foul."

[5] *i.e.* " Snaky."

5 Οὐ παραλειπτέον δ' ἡμῖν οὐδὲ τὴν αἰτίαν τῆς περὶ τὴν ἡμέρωσιν φιλοτιμίας. εὑρίσκεται γὰρ ἐν τῇ νήσῳ ταύτῃ τὸ καλούμενον τοπάζιον, ὅπερ ἐστὶ λίθος διαφαινόμενος ἐπιτερπής, ὑάλῳ παρεμφερὴς καὶ θαυμαστὴν ἔγχρυσον πρόσοψιν παρεχό-
6 μενος. διόπερ ἀνεπίβατος τοῖς ἄλλοις τηρεῖται, θανατουμένου παντὸς τοῦ προσπλεύσαντος ὑπὸ τῶν καθεσταμένων ἐπ' αὐτῆς[1] φυλάκων. οὗτοι δὲ τὸν ἀριθμὸν ὄντες ὀλίγοι βίον ἔχουσιν ἀτυχῆ. ἵνα μὲν γὰρ μηδεὶς λίθος διακλαπῇ, πλοῖον οὐκ ἀπολείπεται τὸ παράπαν ἐν τῇ νήσῳ· οἱ δὲ παραπλέοντες αὐτὴν διὰ τὸν ἀπὸ τοῦ βασιλέως φόβον πόρρωθεν παραθέουσι· τροφαὶ δὲ αἱ μὲν παρακομιζόμεναι ταχέως ἐκλείπουσιν, ἕτεραι δ' ἐγχώριοι
7 τὸ σύνολον οὐχ ὑπάρχουσι. διόπερ ὅταν τῶν σιτίων ὀλίγα καταλείπηται, κάθηνται πάντες οἱ κατὰ τὴν κώμην προσδεχόμενοι τὸν τῶν κομιζόντων τὰς τροφὰς κατάπλουν· ὧν βραδυνόντων εἰς τὰς
8 ἐσχάτας ἐλπίδας συστέλλονται. ὁ δὲ προειρημένος λίθος φυόμενος ἐν ταῖς πέτραις τὴν μὲν ἡμέραν διὰ τὸ πνῖγος οὐχ ὁρᾶται, κρατούμενος ὑπὸ τοῦ περὶ τὸν ἥλιον φέγγους, τῆς δὲ νυκτὸς ἐπιγινομένης ἐν σκότει διαλάμπει καὶ πόρρωθεν
9 δῆλός ἐστιν ἐν ᾧ ποτ' ἂν ᾖ τόπῳ. οἱ δὲ νησοφύλακες κλήρῳ διῃρημένοι τοὺς τόπους ἐφεδρεύουσι, καὶ τῷ φανέντι λίθῳ περιτιθέασι σημείου χάριν ἄγγος τηλικοῦτον ἡλίκον ἂν ᾖ τὸ μέγεθος τοῦ στίλβοντος λίθου· τῆς δ' ἡμέρας περιιόντες περιτέμνουσι τὸν σημειωθέντα τόπον τῆς πέτρας, καὶ παραδιδόασι τοῖς διὰ τῆς τέχνης δυναμένοις ἐκλεαίνειν τὸ παραδοθὲν οἰκείως.

[1] ἐπ' αὐτῆς Hertlein: ὑπ' αὐτῶν.

BOOK III. 39. 5-9

However, we should not pass over the reason why the kings showed diligence in the reclamation of this island. For there is found on it the topaz, as it is called, which is a pleasing transparent stone, similar to glass, and of a marvellous golden hue. Consequently no unauthorized person may set foot upon the island and it is closely guarded, every man who has approached it being put to death by the guards who are stationed there. And the latter are few in number and lead a miserable existence. For in order to prevent any stone being stolen, not a single boat is left on the island; furthermore, any who sail by pass along it at a distance because of their fear of the king; and the provisions which are brought to it are quickly exhausted and there are absolutely no other provisions in the land. Consequently, whenever only a little food is left, all the inhabitants of the village sit down and await the arrival of the ship of those who are bringing the provisions, and when these are delayed they are reduced to their last hopes. And the stone we have mentioned, being found in the rocks, is not discernible during the day because of the stifling heat, since it is overcome by the brilliance of the sun, but when night falls it shines in the dark and is visible from afar, in whatever place it may be. The guards on the island divide these places by lot among themselves and stand watch over them, and when the stone shines they put around it, to mark the place, a vessel corresponding in size to the chunk of stone which gives out the light; and when day comes and they go their rounds they cut out the area which has been so marked and turn it over to men who are able by reason of their craftsmanship to polish it properly.

DIODORUS OF SICILY

40. Παραπλεύσαντι δὲ τούτους τοὺς τόπους πολλὰ μὲν Ἰχθυοφάγων ἔθνη κατοικεῖ τὴν παράλιον, πολλοὶ δὲ νομάδες Τρωγοδύται. πρὸς δὲ τούτοις ὄρη παντοῖα ταῖς ἰδιότησιν ὑπάρχει μέχρι λιμένος τοῦ προσαγορευθέντος σωτηρίας, ὃς ἔτυχε τῆς ὀνομασίας ταύτης ἀπὸ τῶν πρώτων πλευσάντων
2 Ἑλλήνων καὶ διασωθέντων. ἀπὸ δὲ τούτων τῶν μερῶν ἄρχεται συναγωγὴν λαμβάνειν ὁ κόλπος καὶ τὴν ἐπιστροφὴν ἐπὶ τὰ κατὰ τὴν Ἀραβίαν μέρη ποιεῖσθαι. καὶ τὴν φύσιν δὲ τῆς χώρας καὶ θαλάττης ἀλλοίαν εἶναι συμβέβηκε διὰ τὴν ἰδιότητα
3 τῶν τόπων· ἥ τε γὰρ ἤπειρος ταπεινὴ καθορᾶται, μηδαμόθεν ἀναστήματος ὑπερκειμένου, ἥ τε θάλαττα τεναγώδης οὖσα τὸ βάθος οὐ πλέον εὑρίσκεται τριῶν ὀργυιῶν, καὶ τῇ χρόᾳ παντελῶς ὑπάρχει χλωρά. τοῦτο δ' αὐτῇ φασι συμβαίνειν οὐ διὰ τὸ τὴν τῶν ὑγρῶν φύσιν εἶναι τοιαύτην, ἀλλὰ διὰ τὸ πλῆθος τοῦ διαφαινομένου καθ' ὕδατος μνίου
4 καὶ φύκους. ταῖς μὲν οὖν ἐπικώποις τῶν νεῶν εὔθετός ἐστιν ὁ τόπος, κλύδωνα μὲν οὐκ ἐκ πολλοῦ κυλίων διαστήματος, θήραν δ' ἰχθύων ἄπλατον παρεχόμενος· αἱ δὲ τοὺς ἐλέφαντας διάγουσαι, διὰ τὰ βάρη βαθύπλοι καθεστῶσαι καὶ ταῖς κατασκευαῖς ἐμβριθεῖς, μεγάλους καὶ δεινοὺς ἐπιφέρουσι κινδύνους τοῖς ἐν αὐταῖς πλέουσι.
5 διάρσει γὰρ ἱστίων θέουσαι καὶ διὰ τὴν τῶν πνευμάτων βίαν πολλάκις νυκτὸς ὠθούμεναι, ὁτὲ μὲν πέτραις προσπεσοῦσαι ναυαγοῦσι, ποτὲ δ' εἰς τεναγώδεις ἰσθμοὺς ἐμπίπτουσιν· οἱ δὲ ναῦται παρακαταβῆναι μὲν ἀδυνατοῦσι διὰ τὸ πλέον

---

[1] *i.e.* "Safety."

BOOK III. 40. 1-5

40. After sailing past these regions one finds that the coast is inhabited by many nations of Ichthyophagi and many nomadic Trogodytes. Then there appear mountains of all manner of peculiarities until one comes to the Harbour of Soteria,[1] as it is called, which gained this name from the first Greek sailors who found safety there. From this region onwards the gulf begins to become contracted and to curve toward Arabia. And here it is found that the nature of the country and of the sea has altered by reason of the peculiar characteristic of the region; for the mainland appears to be low as seen from the sea, no elevation rising above it, and the sea, which runs to shoals, is found to have a depth of no more than three fathoms, while in colour it is altogether green. The reason for this is, they say, not because the water is naturally of that colour, but because of the mass of seaweed and tangle which shows from under water. For ships, then, which are equipped with oars the place is suitable enough, since it rolls along no wave from a great distance and affords, furthermore, fishing in the greatest abundance; but the ships which carry the elephants,[2] being of deep draft because of their weight and heavy by reason of their equipment, bring upon their crews great and terrible dangers. For running as they do under full sail and often times being driven during the night before the force of the winds, sometimes they will strike against rocks and be wrecked or sometimes run aground on slightly submerged spits. The sailors are unable to go over the sides of the ship because the water is

[2] A little south of this region, according to Strabo (16. 4. 7), lay the city of Ptolemaïs, founded under Ptolemy Philadelphus near the hunting-grounds for elephants.

εἶναι τὸ βάθος ἀνδρομήκους, διὰ δὲ τῶν κοντῶν
τῷ σκάφει βοηθοῦντες ὅταν μηδὲν ἀνύωσιν,
ἐκβάλλουσιν ἅπαντα πλὴν τῆς τροφῆς· οὐδ' οὕτω
δὲ τῆς ἀποστροφῆς[1] τυγχάνοντες εἰς μεγάλην
ἀπορίαν ἐμπίπτουσι διὰ τὸ μήτε νῆσον μήτ'
ἄκραν ἠπείρου μήτε ναῦν ἑτέραν πλησίον ὑπάρ-
χουσαν ὁρᾶσθαι· ἄξενοι γὰρ παντελῶς οἱ τόποι
καὶ σπανίους ἔχοντες τοὺς ναυσὶ διακομιζομένους.
6 χωρὶς δὲ τούτων τῶν κακῶν ὁ κλύδων ἐν ἀκαρεῖ
χρόνῳ τῷ κύτει τῆς νεὼς τοσοῦτο πλῆθος ἄμμου
προσβάλλει καὶ συσσωρεύει παραδόξως ὥστε τὸν
κύκλῳ τόπον περιχώννυσθαι καὶ τὸ σκάφος
ὥσπερ ἐπίτηδες ἐνδεσμεύεσθαι τῇ χέρσῳ.
7 Οἱ δὲ τούτῳ τῷ συμπτώματι περιπεσόντες τὸ μὲν
πρῶτον μετρίως ὀδύρονται πρὸς κωφὴν ἐρημίαν,
οὐ παντελῶς ἀπεγνωκότες εἰς τέλος[2] τὴν σωτηρίαν·
πολλάκις γὰρ τοῖς τοιούτοις ἐπιφανεὶς ὁ τῆς
πλημυρίδος κλύδων ἐξῆρεν εἰς ὕψος, καὶ τοὺς
ἐσχάτως κινδυνεύοντας ὡσπερεὶ θεὸς ἐπιφανεὶς
διεφύλαξεν· ὅταν δὲ ἀπὸ μὲν τῶν θεῶν ἡ προειρη-
μένη μὴ παρακολουθήσῃ βοήθεια, τὰ δὲ τῆς
τροφῆς λίπῃ, τοὺς μὲν ἀσθενεστέρους οἱ κατισχύοντες ἐκβάλλουσιν εἰς θάλατταν, ὅπως τοῖς
ὀλίγοις τὰ λειπόμενα τῶν ἀναγκαίων πλείονας
ἡμέρας ἀντέχῃ, πέρας δὲ πάσας τὰς ἐλπίδας
ἐξαλείψαντες ἀπόλλυνται πολὺ χεῖρον τῶν προαπο-
θανόντων· οἱ μὲν γὰρ ἐν ἀκαρεῖ χρόνῳ τὸ πνεῦμα

[1] So Wesseling, Vogel, τροφῆς MSS., Bekker, σωτηρίας Dindorf, ἀναστροφῆς Bezzel, *Coniecturae Diodoreae*, 10 f.
[2] εἰς τέλος deleted by Dindorf, Vogel, retained by Bekker.

[1] The reference is to the " epiphany " of a god in tragedy, effected by the use of a " machine " which suddenly hoisted

deeper than a man's height, and when in their efforts to rescue their vessel by means of their punting-poles they accomplish nothing, they jettison everything except their provisions; but if even by this course they do not succeed in effecting an escape, they fall into great perplexity by reason of the fact that they can make out neither an island nor a promontory nor another ship near at hand;—for the region is altogether inhospitable and only at rare intervals do men cross it in ships. And to add to these evils the waves within a moment's time cast up such a mass of sand against the body of the ship and heap it up in so incredible a fashion that it soon piles up a mound round about the place and binds the vessel, as if of set purpose, to the solid land.

Now the men who have suffered this mishap, at the outset bewail their lot with moderation in the face of a deaf wilderness, having as yet not entirely abandoned hope of ultimate salvation; for oftentimes the swell of the flood-tide has intervened for men in such a plight and raised the ship aloft, and suddenly appearing, as might a *deus ex machina*, has brought succour to men in the extremity of peril.[1] But when such god-sent aid has not been vouchsafed to them and their food fails, then the strong cast the weaker into the sea in order that for the few left the remaining necessities of life may last a greater number of days. But finally, when they have blotted out of their minds all their hopes, these perish by a more miserable fate than those who had died before; for whereas the latter in a moment's time returned to Nature

him into view, that he might offer to the problems of the tragedy a solution which was beyond the power of mortals to foresee or bring to pass.

τῇ δούσῃ φύσει πάλιν ἀπέδωκαν, οἱ δ' εἰς πολλὰς ταλαιπωρίας καταμερίσαντες τὸν θάνατον πολυχρονίους τὰς συμφορὰς ἔχοντες τῆς τοῦ βίου
8 καταστροφῆς τυγχάνουσι. τὰ δὲ σκάφη ταῦτα τῶν ἐπιβατῶν οἰκτρῶς στερηθέντα, καθάπερ τινὰ κενοτάφια, διαμένει πολὺν χρόνον πανταχόθεν περιχωννύμενα, τοὺς δ' ἱστοὺς καὶ τὰς κεραίας μετεώρους ἔχοντα πόρρωθεν τοὺς ὁρῶντας εἰς οἶκτον καὶ συμπάθειαν ἄγει τῶν ἀπολωλότων. πρόσταγμα γάρ ἐστι βασιλέως ἐᾶν τὰ τοιαῦτα συμπτώματα τοῖς πλέουσι διασημαίνειν τοὺς τὸν
9 ὄλεθρον περιποιοῦντας τόπους. παρὰ δὲ τοῖς πλησίον κατοικοῦσιν Ἰχθυοφάγοις παραδέδοται λόγος, ἐκ προγόνων ἔχων φυλαττομένην τὴν φήμην, ὅτι μεγάλης τινὸς γενομένης ἀμπώτεως ἐγεώθη τοῦ κόλπου πᾶς ὁ τόπος ὁ τὴν χλωρὰν ἔχων τοῦ τύπου[1] πρόσοψιν, μεταπεσούσης τῆς θαλάττης εἰς τἀναντία μέρη, καὶ φανείσης τῆς ἐπὶ τῷ βυθῷ χέρσου πάλιν ἐπελθοῦσαν ἐξαίσιον πλήμην ἀποκαταστῆσαι τὸν πόρον εἰς τὴν προϋπάρχουσαν τάξιν.

41. Ἀπὸ δὲ τούτων τῶν τόπων τὸν μὲν ἀπὸ Πτολεμαΐδος παράπλουν ἕως τῶν Ταύρων ἀκρωτηρίων προειρήκαμεν, ὅτε Πτολεμαίου τὴν τῶν ἐλεφάντων θήραν ἀπηγγείλαμεν· ἀπὸ δὲ τῶν Ταύρων ἐπιστρέφει μὲν ἡ παράλιος πρὸς τὰς ἀνατολάς, κατὰ δὲ τὴν θερινὴν τροπὴν αἱ σκιαὶ πίπτουσι πρὸς μεσημβρίαν ἐναντίως ταῖς παρ'

---

[1] τύπου Eichstädt: τόπου.

[1] The older commentators saw in this story a memory of the miraculous passage of the Israelites through the Red Sea.

BOOK III. 40. 7–41. 1

the spirit which she had given them, these parcelled out their death into many separate hardships before they finally, suffering long-protracted tortures, were granted the end of life. As for the ships which have been stripped of their crews in this pitiable fashion, there they remain for many years, like a group of cenotaphs, embedded on every side in a heap of sand, their masts and yard-arms still standing aloft, and they move those who behold them from afar to pity and sympathy for the men who have perished. For it is the king's command to leave in place such evidences of disasters that they may give notice to sailors of the region which works their destruction. And among the Ichthyophagi who dwell near by has been handed down a tale which has preserved the account received from their forefathers, that once, when there was a great receding of the sea, the entire area of the gulf which has what may be roughly described as the green appearance became land, and that, after the sea had receded to the opposite parts and the solid ground in the depths of it had emerged to view, a mighty flood came back upon it again and returned the body of water to its former place.[1]

41. The voyage along the coast, as one leaves these regions, from Ptolemaïs as far as the Promontories of the Tauri we have already mentioned, when we told of Ptolemy's hunting of the elephants [2]; and from the Tauri the coast swings to the east, and at the time of the summer solstice the shadows fall to the south, opposite to what is true with us, at about the second

---

[2] Cp. chap. 18, where, however, there is no mention of either Ptolemaïs or the Promontories of the Tauri.

2 ἡμῖν ἄχρι πρὸς ὥραν δευτέραν. ἔχει δὲ καὶ ποταμοὺς ἡ χώρα, ῥέοντας ἐκ τῶν ὀρῶν τῶν προσαγορευομένων Ψεβαίων. διείληπται δὲ καὶ πεδίοις μεγάλοις φέρουσι μαλάχης καὶ καρδάμου καὶ φοίνικος ἄπιστα μεγέθη· ἐκφέρει δὲ καὶ καρποὺς παντοίους, τὴν μὲν γεῦσιν ἔχοντας 3 νωθράν, ἀγνοουμένους δὲ παρ' ἡμῖν. ἡ δὲ πρὸς τὴν μεσόγειον ἀνατείνουσα πλήρης ἐστὶν ἐλεφάντων καὶ ταύρων ἀγρίων καὶ λεόντων καὶ πολλῶν ἄλλων παντοδαπῶν θηρίων ἀλκίμων. ὁ δὲ πόρος νήσοις διείληπται καρπὸν μὲν οὐδένα φερούσαις ἥμερον, ἐκτρεφούσαις δ' ὀρνέων ἴδια γένη καὶ ταῖς 4 προσόψεσι θαυμαστά. ἡ δ' ἑξῆς θάλαττα βαθεῖα παντελῶς ἐστι, καὶ κήτη φέρει παντοδαπὰ παράδοξα τοῖς μεγέθεσιν, οὐ μέντοι λυποῦντα τοὺς ἀνθρώπους, ἐὰν μή τις ἀκουσίως αὐτῶν ταῖς λοφιαῖς περιπέσῃ· οὐ δύνανται γὰρ διώκειν τοὺς πλέοντας, ὡς ἂν κατὰ τὴν ἐκ[1] τῆς θαλάττης ἄρσιν ἀμαυρουμένων αὐτοῖς τῶν ὀμμάτων ὑπὸ τοῦ κατὰ τὸν ἥλιον φέγγους. ταῦτα μὲν οὖν τὰ μέρη τῆς Τρωγοδυτικῆς ἔσχατα γνωρίζεται, περιγραφόμενα ταῖς ἄκραις ἃς ὀνομάζουσι Ψεβαίας.

42. Τὸ δ' ἄλλο μέρος τῆς ἀντιπέρας παραλίου τὸ προσκεκλιμένον Ἀραβίᾳ πάλιν ἀναλαβόντες ἀπὸ τοῦ μυχοῦ διέξιμεν. οὗτος γὰρ ὀνομάζεται Ποσείδειον, ἱδρυσαμένου Ποσειδῶνι πελαγίῳ βωμὸν Ἀρίστωνος τοῦ πεμφθέντος ὑπὸ Πτολεμαίου πρὸς κατασκοπὴν τῆς ἕως ὠκεανοῦ παρηκούσης

[1] ἐκ added by Wesseling.

BOOK III. 41. 1–42. 1

hour of the day.[1] The country also has rivers, which flow from the Psebaean mountains, as they are called. Moreover, it is checkered by great plains as well, which bear mallows, cress, and palms, all of unbelievable size; and it also brings forth fruits of every description, which have an insipid taste and are unknown among us. That part which stretches towards the interior is full of elephants and wild bulls and lions and many other powerful wild beasts of every description. The passage by sea is broken up by islands which, though they bear no cultivated fruit, support varieties of birds which are peculiar to them and marvellous to look upon. After this place the sea is quite deep and produces all kinds of sea-monsters of astonishing size, which, however, offer no harm to men unless one by accident falls upon their back-fins; for they are unable to pursue the sailors, since when they rise from the sea their eyes are blinded by the brilliance of the sun. These, then, are the farthest known parts of the Trogodyte country, and are circumscribed by the ranges which go by the name of Psebaean.

42. But we shall now take up the other side, namely, the opposite shore which forms the coast of Arabia, and shall describe it, beginning with the innermost recess. This bears the name Poseideion,[2] since an altar was erected here to Poseidon Pelagius[3] by that Ariston who was dispatched by Ptolemy to investigate the coast of Arabia as far as the ocean.

[1] The direction of the shadow to the south at about 7 a.m. on June 21st shows that the place was south of the tropic of Cancer.

[2] The Roman Posidium, the present Ras-Mohammed, at the southern tip of the Peninsula of Sinai (cp. Strabo 16. 4. 18).

[3] *i.e.* " of the sea."

DIODORUS OF SICILY

2 Ἀραβίας. ἑξῆς δὲ τοῦ μυχοῦ τόπος ἐστὶ παραθαλάττιος ὁ τιμώμενος ὑπὸ τῶν ἐγχωρίων διαφερόντως διὰ τὴν εὐχρηστίαν τὴν ἐξ αὐτοῦ. οὗτος δ᾿ ὀνομάζεται μὲν Φοινικών, ἔχει δὲ πλῆθος τούτου τοῦ φυτοῦ πολύκαρπον καθ᾿ ὑπερβολὴν καὶ πρὸς
3 ἀπόλαυσιν καὶ τρυφὴν[1] διαφέρον. πᾶσα δ᾿ ἡ σύνεγγυς χώρα σπανίζει ναματιαίων ὑδάτων καὶ διὰ τὴν πρὸς μεσημβρίαν ἔγκλισιν ἔμπυρος ὑπάρχει· διὸ καὶ τὸν κατάφυτον τόπον, ἐν ἀπανθρωποτάτοις ὄντα μέρεσι καὶ χορηγοῦντα τὰς τροφάς, εἰκότως οἱ βάρβαροι καθιερώκασι. καὶ γὰρ ὕδατος οὐκ ὀλίγαι πηγαὶ καὶ λιβάδες ἐκπίπτουσιν ἐν αὐτῷ, ψυχρότητι χιόνος οὐδὲν λειπόμεναι· αὗται δ᾿ ἐφ᾿ ἑκάτερα τὰ μέρη τὰ κατὰ τὴν[2] γῆν χλοερὰ ποιοῦσι καὶ παντελῶς
4 ἐπιτερπῆ. ἔστι δὲ καὶ βωμὸς ἐκ στερεοῦ λίθου παλαιὸς τοῖς χρόνοις, ἐπιγραφὴν ἔχων ἀρχαίοις γράμμασιν ἀγνώστοις. ἐπιμέλονται δὲ τοῦ τεμένους ἀνὴρ καὶ γυνή, διὰ βίου τὴν ἱερωσύνην ἔχοντες. μακρόβιοι δ᾿ εἰσὶν οἱ τῇδε κατοικοῦντες, καὶ τὰς κοίτας ἐπὶ τῶν δένδρων ἔχουσι διὰ τὸν ἀπὸ τῶν θηρίων φόβον.

5 Παραπλεύσαντι δὲ τὸν Φοινικῶνα[3] πρὸς ἀκρωτηρίῳ τῆς ἠπείρου νῆσός ἐστιν ἀπὸ τῶν ἐναυλιζομένων ἐν αὐτῇ ζῴων Φωκῶν νῆσος ὀνομαζομένη· τοσοῦτο γὰρ πλῆθος τῶν θηρίων τούτων ἐνδιατρίβει τοῖς τόποις ὥστε θαυμάζειν τοὺς ἰδόντας. τὸ δὲ προκείμενον ἀκρωτήριον τῆς νήσου κεῖται κατὰ τὴν καλουμένην Πέτραν καὶ τὴν Παλαιστίνην·[4]

[1] διατροφὴν Π. [2] τὴν omitted by D, Vogel.
[3] So Dindorf: Φοινικοῦντα.
[4] τῆς Ἀραβίας after Παλαιστίνην deleted by Vogel, placed after Πέτραν by Salmasius, Bekker, Dindorf.

BOOK III. 42. 1-5

Directly after the innermost recess is a region along the sea which is especially honoured by the natives because of the advantage which accrues from it to them. It is called the Palm-grove and contains a multitude of trees of this [1] kind which are exceedingly fruitful and contribute in an unusual degree to enjoyment and luxury. But all the country round about is lacking in springs of water and is fiery hot because it slopes to the south; accordingly, it was a natural thing that the barbarians made sacred the place which was full of trees and, lying as it did in the midst of a region utterly desolate, supplied their food. And indeed not a few springs and streams of water gush forth there, which do not yield to snow in coldness; and these make the land on both sides of them green and altogether pleasing. Moreover, an altar is there built of hard stone and very old in years, bearing an inscription in ancient letters of an unknown tongue. The oversight of the sacred precinct is in the care of a man and a woman who hold the sacred office for life. The inhabitants of the place are long-lived and have their beds in the trees because of their fear of the wild beasts.

After sailing past the Palm-grove one comes to an island off a promontory of the mainland which bears the name Island of Phocae [2] from the animals which make their home there; for so great a multitude of these beasts spend their time in these regions as to astonish those who behold them. And the promontory which stretches out in front of the island lies over against Petra, as it is called, and Palestine; for to

[1] *i.e.* date-palms.
[2] Seals.

εἰς γὰρ ταύτην τόν τε λίβανον καὶ τἄλλα φορτία τὰ πρὸς εὐωδίαν ἀνήκοντα κατάγουσιν, ὡς λόγος, ἐκ τῆς ἄνω λεγομένης Ἀραβίας οἵ τε Γερραῖοι καὶ Μιναῖοι.[1]

43. Τὴν δ' ἑξῆς παραθαλάττιον τὸ μὲν παλαιὸν ἐνέμοντο Μαρανῖται, μετὰ δὲ ταῦτα Γαρινδανεῖς, ὄντες πλησιόχωροι. τὴν δὲ χώραν κατέσχον τοιῷδέ τινι τρόπῳ· ἐν τῷ πρόσθεν λεχθέντι Φοινικῶνι συντελουμένης πανηγύρεως πενταετηρικῆς ἐφοίτων πανταχόθεν οἱ περίοικοι, καμήλων εὖ τεθραμμένων ἑκατόμβας τοῖς ἐν τῷ τεμένει θεοῖς θύσοντες, ὁμοίως δὲ καὶ τῶν ὑδάτων τῶν ἐξ αὐτοῦ κομιοῦντες εἰς τὰς πατρίδας διὰ τὸ παραδίδοσθαι τοῦτο τὸ ποτὸν παρασκευάζειν τοῖς προσενεγκαμένοις τὴν ὑγίειαν.
2 διὰ δὴ ταύτας τὰς αἰτίας τῶν Μαρανιτῶν καταντησάντων εἰς τὴν πανήγυριν, οἱ Γαρινδανεῖς τοὺς μὲν ἀπολελειμμένους ἐν τῇ χώρᾳ κατασφάξαντες, τοὺς δ' ἐκ τῆς πανηγύρεως ἐπανιόντας ἐνεδρεύσαντες διέφθειραν, ἐρημώσαντες δὲ τὴν χώραν τῶν οἰκητόρων κατεκληρούχησαν πεδία καρποφόρα καὶ
3 νομὰς τοῖς κτήνεσι δαψιλεῖς ἐκτρέφοντα. αὕτη δ' ἡ παράλιος λιμένας μὲν ὀλίγους ἔχει, διείληπται δ' ὄρεσι πυκνοῖς καὶ μεγάλοις, ἐξ ὧν παντοίας ποικιλίας χρωμάτων ἔχουσα θαυμαστὴν παρέχεται θέαν τοῖς παραπλέουσι.

4 Παραπλεύσαντι δὲ ταύτην τὴν χώραν ἐκδέχεται κόλπος Λαιανίτης, περιοικούμενος πολλαῖς κώμαις Ἀράβων τῶν προσαγορευομένων Ναβαταίων. οὗτοι δὲ πολλὴν μὲν τῆς παραλίου νέμονται, οὐκ

[1] So Dindorf: Μινναῖοι

this country, as it is reported, both the Gerrhaeans and Minaeans convey from Upper Arabia, as it is called, both the frankincense and the other aromatic wares.

43. The coast which comes next was originally inhabited by the Maranitae, and then by the Garindanes who were their neighbours. The latter secured the country somewhat in this fashion: In the above-mentioned Palm-grove a festival was celebrated every four years, to which the neighbouring peoples thronged from all sides, both to sacrifice to the gods of the sacred precinct hecatombs of well-fed camels and also to carry back to their native lands some of the water of the place, since the tradition prevailed that this drink gave health to such as partook of it. When for these reasons, then, the Maranitae gathered to the festival, the Garindanes, putting to the sword those who had been left behind in the country, and lying in ambush for those who were returning from the festival, utterly destroyed the tribe, and after stripping the country of its inhabitants they divided among themselves the plains, which were fruitful and supplied abundant pasture for their herds and flocks. This coast has few harbours and is divided by many large mountains, by reason of which it shows every shade of colour and affords a marvellous spectacle to those who sail past it.

After one has sailed past this country the Laeanites Gulf[1] comes next, about which are many inhabited villages of Arabs who are known as Nabataeans. This tribe occupies a large part of the coast and not a

[1] Diodorus turns north into the modern Gulf of Akaba, the "Aelanites" Gulf of Strabo 16. 4. 18.

ὀλίγην δὲ καὶ τῆς εἰς μεσόγειον ἀνηκούσης χώρας, τόν τε λαὸν ἀμύθητον ἔχοντες καὶ θρεμμάτων ἀγέλας ἀπίστους τοῖς πλήθεσιν. οἳ τὸ μὲν παλαιὸν ἐξῆγον[1] δικαιοσύνῃ χρώμενοι καὶ ταῖς ἀπὸ τῶν θρεμμάτων τροφαῖς ἀρκούμενοι, ὕστερον δὲ τῶν ἀπὸ τῆς Ἀλεξανδρείας βασιλέων πλωτὸν τοῖς ἐμπόροις ποιησάντων τὸν πόρον τοῖς τε ναυαγοῦσιν ἐπετίθεντο καὶ λῃστρικὰ σκάφη κατασκευάζοντες ἐλῄστευον τοὺς πλέοντας, μιμούμενοι τὰς ἀγριότητας καὶ παρανομίας τῶν ἐν τῷ Πόντῳ Ταύρων· μετὰ δὲ ταῦτα ληφθέντες ὑπὸ τετρηρικῶν σκαφῶν πελάγιοι προσηκόντως ἐκολάσθησαν.

6 Μετὰ δὲ τούτους τοὺς τόπους ὑπάρχει χώρα πεδιὰς κατάρρυτος, ἐκτρέφουσα διὰ τὰς πάντῃ διαρρεούσας πηγὰς ἄγρωστιν καὶ μηδίκην, ἔτι δὲ λωτὸν ἀνδρομήκη. διὰ δὲ τὸ πλῆθος καὶ τὴν ἀρετὴν τῆς νομῆς οὐ μόνον κτηνῶν παντοδαπῶν ἀμύθητον ἐκτρέφει πλῆθος, ἀλλὰ καὶ καμήλους 7 ἀγρίας, ἔτι δ' ἐλάφους καὶ δορκάδας. πρὸς δὲ τὸ πλῆθος τῶν ἐντρεφομένων ζῴων φοιτῶσιν ἐκ τῆς ἐρήμου λεόντων καὶ λύκων καὶ παρδάλεων ἀγέλαι, πρὸς ἃς οἱ κτηνοτροφοῦντες ἀναγκάζονται καὶ μεθ' ἡμέραν καὶ νύκτωρ θηριομαχεῖν ὑπὲρ τῶν θρεμμάτων· οὕτω τὸ τῆς χώρας εὐτύχημα τοῖς κατοικοῦσιν ἀτυχίας αἴτιον γίνεται διὰ τὸ τὴν φύσιν ὡς ἐπίπαν τοῖς ἀνθρώποις μετὰ τῶν ἀγαθῶν διδόναι τὰ βλάπτοντα.

44. Παραπλεύσαντι δὲ τὰ πεδία ταῦτα κόλπος ἐκδέχεται παράδοξον ἔχων τὴν φύσιν. συννεύει μὲν γὰρ εἰς τὸν μυχὸν τῆς χώρας, τῷ μήκει δ' ἐπὶ σταδίους πεντακοσίους παρεκτείνεται, περι-

[1] διῆγον Cobet; Vogel suggests διεξῆγον.

little of the country which stretches inland, and it has a people numerous beyond telling and flocks and herds in multitude beyond belief. Now in ancient times these men observed justice and were content with the food which they received from their flocks, but later, after the kings in Alexandria had made the ways of the sea navigable for their merchants, these Arabs not only attacked the shipwrecked, but fitting out pirate ships preyed upon the voyagers, imitating in their practices the savage and lawless ways of the Tauri of the Pontus[1]; some time afterward, however, they were caught on the high seas by some quadriremes and punished as they deserved.

Beyond these regions there is a level and well-watered stretch of land which produces, by reason of springs which flow through its whole extent, dog's-tooth grass, lucerne, and lotus as tall as a man. And because of the abundance and excellent quality of the pasturage, not only does it support every manner of flocks and herds in multitude beyond telling, but also wild camels, deer, and gazelles. And against the multitude of animals which are nourished in that place there gather in from the desert bands of lions and wolves and leopards, against which the herdsmen must perforce battle both day and night to protect their charges; and in this way the land's good fortune becomes a cause of misfortune for its inhabitants, seeing that it is generally Nature's way to dispense to men along with good things what is hurtful as well.

44. Next after these plains as one skirts the coast comes a gulf of extraordinary nature. It runs, namely, to a point deep into the land, extends in length a distance of some five hundred stades, and

[1] The Black Sea.

κλειόμενος δὲ κρημνοῖς θαυμασίοις τὸ μέγεθος σκολιὸν καὶ δυσέξιτον ἔχει τὸ στόμα· ἀλιτενοῦς γὰρ πέτρας τὸν εἴσπλουν διαλαμβανούσης οὔτ' εἰσπλεῦσαι δυνατόν ἐστιν εἰς τὸν κόλπον οὔτ' 2 ἐκπλεῦσαι. κατὰ δὲ τὰς τοῦ ῥοῦ προσπτώσεις καὶ τὰς τῶν ἀνέμων μεταβολὰς ὁ κλύδων προσπίπτων τῇ ῥαχίᾳ καχλάζει καὶ τραχύνεται πάντῃ περὶ τὴν παρήκουσαν πέτραν. οἱ δὲ τὴν κατὰ τὸν κόλπον χώραν νεμόμενοι, Βανιζομενεῖς ὀνομαζόμενοι, τὰς τροφὰς ἔχουσι κυνηγοῦντες καὶ σαρκοφαγοῦντες τὰ χερσαῖα ζῷα. ἱερὸν δ' ἁγιώτατον ἵδρυται, τιμώμενον ὑπὸ πάντων Ἀράβων περιττότερον.

3 Ἑξῆς δὲ τῇ προειρημένῃ παραλίᾳ νῆσοι τρεῖς ἐπίκεινται, λιμένας ποιοῦσαι πλείους. καὶ τούτων τὴν μὲν πρώτην ἱστοροῦσιν ὑπάρχειν ἱερὰν Ἴσιδος, ἔρημον οὖσαν, παλαιῶν δ' οἰκιῶν ἔχειν λιθίνας ὑποστάθμας καὶ στήλας γράμμασι βαρβαρικοῖς κεχαραγμένας· ὁμοίως δὲ καὶ τὰς ἄλλας ἐρήμους ὑπάρχειν· πάσας δ' ἐλαίαις καταπεφυτεῦσθαι 4 διαφόροις τῶν παρ' ἡμῖν. μετὰ δὲ τὰς νήσους ταύτας αἰγιαλὸς παρήκει κρημνώδης καὶ δυσπαράπλους ἐπὶ σταδίους ὡς χιλίους· οὔτε γὰρ λιμὴν οὔτε σάλος ἐπ' ἀγκύρας ὑπόκειται τοῖς ναυτίλοις, οὐ χηλὴ[1] δυναμένη τοῖς ἀπορουμένοις τῶν πλεόντων τὴν ἀναγκαίαν ὑπόδυσιν παρασχέσθαι. ὄρος δὲ ταύτῃ παράκειται κατὰ μὲν[2] κορυφὴν πέτρας ἀποτομάδας ἔχον καὶ τοῖς ὕψεσι καταπληκτικάς, ὑπὸ δὲ τὰς ῥίζας σπιλάδας ὀξείας καὶ πυκνὰς ἐνθαλάττους καὶ κατόπιν αὐτῶν φάραγγας ὑποβε-

---

[1] οὐ χηλὴ Hudson : οὐχ ὕλη.

shut in as it is by crags which are of wondrous size, its mouth is winding and hard to get out of; for a rock which extends into the sea obstructs its entrance and so it is impossible for a ship either to sail into or out of the gulf. Furthermore, at times when the current rushes in and there are frequent shiftings of the winds, the surf, beating upon the rocky beach, roars and rages all about the projecting rock. The inhabitants of the land about the gulf, who are known as Banizomenes, find their food by hunting the land animals and eating their meat. And a temple has been set up there, which is very holy and exceedingly revered by all Arabians.

Next there are three islands which lie off the coast just described and provide numerous harbours. The first of these, history relates, is sacred to Isis and is uninhabited, and on it are stone foundations of ancient dwellings and stelae which are inscribed with letters in a barbarian tongue; the other two islands are likewise uninhabited and all three are covered thick with olive trees which differ from those we have. Beyond these islands there extends for about a thousand stades a coast which is precipitous and difficult for ships to sail past; for there is neither harbour beneath the cliffs nor roadstead where sailors may anchor, and no natural breakwater which affords shelter in emergency for mariners in distress. And parallel to the coast here runs a mountain range at whose summit are rocks which are sheer and of a terrifying height, and at its base are sharp undersea ledges in many places and behind them are ravines which are eaten away underneath and turn this way

---

[2] τὴν after μὲν omitted DF, Vogel.

5 βρωμένας καὶ σκολιάς. συντετρημένων δ' αὐτῶν πρὸς ἀλλήλας, καὶ τῆς θαλάττης βάθος ἐχούσης, ὁ κλύδων ποτὲ μὲν εἰσπίπτων, ποτὲ δὲ παλισσυτῶν βρόμῳ μεγάλῳ παραπλήσιον ἦχον ἐξίησι. τοῦ δὲ κλύδωνος τὸ μὲν πρὸς μεγάλας πέτρας προσαραττόμενον εἰς ὕψος ἵσταται καὶ τὸν ἀφρὸν θαυμαστὸν τὸ πλῆθος κατασκευάζει, τὸ δὲ καταπινόμενον κοιλώμασι[1] σπασμὸν καταπληκτικὸν παρέχει, ὥστε τοὺς ἀκουσίως ἐγγίσαντας τοῖς τόποις διὰ τὸ δέος οἱονεὶ προαποθνήσκειν.

6 Ταύτην μὲν οὖν τὴν παράλιον ἔχουσιν Ἄραβες οἱ καλούμενοι Θαμουδηνοί· τὴν δ' ἑξῆς ἐπέχει κόλπος εὐμεγέθης, ἐπικειμένων αὐτῷ νήσων σποράδων, τὴν πρόσοψιν ἐχουσῶν ὁμοίαν ταῖς καλουμέναις Ἐχινάσι νήσοις. ἐκδέχονται δὲ ταύτην τὴν παράλιον ἀέριοι θῖνες ἄμμου κατά τε τὸ μῆκος καὶ 7 τὸ πλάτος, μέλανες τὴν χρόαν. μετὰ δὲ τούτους ὁρᾶται χερρόνησος καὶ λιμὴν κάλλιστος τῶν εἰς ἱστορίαν πεπτωκότων, ὀνομαζόμενος Χαρμούθας. ὑπὸ γὰρ χηλὴν ἐξαίσιον κεκλιμένην πρὸς ζέφυρον κόλπος ἐστὶν οὐ μόνον κατὰ τὴν ἰδέαν θαυμαστός, ἀλλὰ καὶ κατὰ τὴν εὐχρηστίαν πολὺ τοὺς ἄλλους ὑπερέχων· παρήκει γὰρ αὐτὸν ὄρος συνηρεφές, κυκλούμενον πανταχόθεν ἐπὶ σταδίους ἑκατόν, εἴσπλουν δ' ἔχει δίπλεθρον, ναυσὶ δισχιλίαις 8 ἄκλυστον λιμένα παρεχόμενος. χωρὶς δὲ τούτων εὔυδρός τ' ἐστὶ καθ' ὑπερβολήν, ποταμοῦ μείζονος εἰς αὐτὸν ἐμβάλλοντος, καὶ κατὰ μέσον ἔχει νῆσον εὔυδρον καὶ δυναμένην ἔχειν κηπεύματα. καθόλου δ' ἐμφερέστατός ἐστι τῷ κατὰ τὴν Καρχηδόνα

[1] So Wurm: κοίλωμα.

and that. And since these ravines are connected by passages with one another and the sea is deep, the surf, as it at one time rushes in and at another time retreats, gives forth a sound resembling a mighty crash of thunder. At one place the surf, as it breaks upon huge rocks, leaps on high and causes an astonishing mass of foam, at another it is swallowed up within the caverns and creates such a terrifying agitation of the waters that men who unwittingly draw near these places are so frightened that they die, as it were, a first death.

This coast, then, is inhabited by Arabs who are called Thamudeni; but the coast next to it is bounded by a very large gulf, off which lie scattered islands which are in appearance very much like the islands called the Echinades.[1] After this coast there come sand dunes, of infinite extent in both length and width and black in colour. Beyond them a neck of land is to be seen and a harbour, the fairest of any which have come to be included in history, called Charmuthas. For behind an extraordinary natural breakwater which slants towards the west there lies a gulf which not only is marvellous in its form but far surpasses all others in the advantages it offers; for a thickly wooded mountain stretches along it, enclosing it on all sides in a ring one hundred stades long; its entrance is two plethra wide, and it provides a harbour undisturbed by the waves sufficient for two thousand vessels. Furthermore, it is exceptionally well supplied with water, since a river, larger than ordinary, empties into it, and it contains in its centre an island which is abundantly watered and capable of supporting gardens. In general, it resembles most closely the

[1] Now called the Kurtzolares, off the Gulf of Corinth.

λιμένι, προσαγορευομένῳ δὲ Κώθωνι, περὶ οὗ τὰς κατὰ μέρος εὐχρηστίας ἐν τοῖς οἰκείοις χρόνοις πειρασόμεθα διελθεῖν. ἰχθύων δὲ πλῆθος ἐκ τῆς μεγάλης θαλάττης εἰς αὐτὸν ἀθροίζεται διά τε τὴν νηνεμίαν καὶ τὴν γλυκύτητα τῶν εἰς αὐτὸν ῥεόντων ὑδάτων.

45. Παραπλεύσαντι δὲ τοὺς τόπους τούτους ὄρη πέντε διεστηκότα ἀλλήλων εἰς ὕψος ἀνατείνει, συναγομένας ἔχοντα τὰς κορυφὰς εἰς πετρώδη μαστόν, παραπλήσιον φαντασίαν ἀποτελοῦντα ταῖς 2 κατ' Αἴγυπτον πυραμίσιν. ἑξῆς δ' ἐστὶ κόλπος κυκλοτερὴς μεγάλοις ἀκρωτηρίοις περιεχόμενος, οὗ κατὰ μέσην τὴν διάμετρον ἀνέστηκε λόφος τραπεζοειδής, ἐφ' οὗ τρεῖς ναοὶ θαυμαστοὶ τοῖς ὕψεσιν ᾠκοδόμηνται θεῶν, ἀγνοουμένων μὲν ὑπὸ τῶν Ἑλλήνων, τιμωμένων δ' ὑπὸ τῶν ἐγχωρίων 3 διαφερόντως. μετὰ δὲ ταῦτα αἰγιαλὸς παρήκει κάθυγρος, ναματιαίοις καὶ γλυκέσι ῥείθροις διειλημμένος·[1] καθ' ὃν ἐστιν ὄρος ὀνομαζόμενον μὲν Χαβῖνον, δρυμοῖς δὲ παντοδαποῖς πεπυκνωμένον. τὴν δὲ χέρσον τὴν ἐχομένην τῆς ὀρεινῆς νέμονται 4 τῶν Ἀράβων οἱ καλούμενοι Δέβαι. οὗτοι δὲ καμηλοτροφοῦντες πρὸς ἅπαντα χρῶνται τὰ μέγιστα τῶν κατὰ τὸν βίον τῇ τοῦ ζῴου τούτου χρείᾳ· πρὸς μὲν γὰρ τοὺς πολεμίους ἀπὸ τούτων μάχονται, τὰς δὲ κομιδὰς τῶν φορτίων ἐπὶ τούτων φοροῦντες[2] ῥᾳδίως ἅπαντα συντελοῦσι, τὸ δὲ γάλα πίνοντες ἀπὸ τούτων διατρέφονται, καὶ τὴν ὅλην χώραν περιπολοῦσιν ἐπὶ τῶν δρομάδων 5 καμήλων. κατὰ δὲ μέσην τὴν χώραν αὐτῶν

[1] So Wesseling: κατειλημμένος.
[2] φοροῦντες A, νωτοφοροῦντες other MSS., all editors.

harbour of Carthage, which is known as Cothon, of the advantages of which we shall endeavour to give a detailed discussion in connection with the appropriate time.[1] And a multitude of fish gather from the open sea into the harbour both because of the calm which prevails there and because of the sweetness of the waters which flow into it.

45. After these places, as a man skirts the coast, five mountains rise on high separated one from another, and their peaks taper into breast-shaped tips of stone which give them an appearance like that of the pyramids of Egypt. Then comes a circular gulf guarded on every side by great promontories, and midway on a line drawn across it rises a trapezium-shaped hill on which three temples, remarkable for their height, have been erected to gods, which indeed are unknown to the Greeks, but are accorded unusual honour by the natives. After this there is a stretch of dank coast, traversed at intervals by streams of sweet water from springs; on it there is a mountain which bears the name Chabinus and is heavily covered with thickets of every kind of tree. The land which adjoins the mountainous country is inhabited by the Arabs known as Debae. They are breeders of camels and make use of the services of this animal in connection with the most important needs of their life; for instance, they fight against their enemies from their backs, employ them for the conveyance of their wares and thus easily accomplish all their business, drink their milk and in this way get their food from them, and traverse their entire country riding upon their racing camels. And down the centre of their country runs a river which carries

---

[1] This description was probably in Book 32.

φέρεται ποταμὸς τοσοῦτο χρυσοῦ καταφέρων ψῆγμα φαινόμενον ὥστε κατὰ τὰς ἐκβολὰς τὴν ἰλὺν ἀποφέρεσθαι περιστίλβουσαν. οἱ δ' ἐγχώριοι τῆς μὲν ἐργασίας τῆς τοῦ χρυσοῦ παντελῶς εἰσιν ἄπειροι, φιλόξενοι δ' ὑπάρχουσιν, οὐ πρὸς πάντας τοὺς ἀφικνουμένους, ἀλλὰ πρὸς μόνους τοὺς ἀπὸ Βοιωτίας καὶ Πελοποννήσου διά τινα παλαιὰν ἀφ' Ἡρακλέους οἰκειότητα πρὸς τὸ ἔθνος, ἣν μυθικῶς ἑαυτοὺς παρειληφέναι παρὰ τῶν προγόνων ἱστοροῦσιν.

6 Ἡ δ' ἑξῆς χώρα κατοικεῖται μὲν ὑπὸ Ἀράβων Ἀλιλαίων καὶ Γασανδῶν, οὐκ ἔμπυρος οὖσα καθάπερ αἱ πλησίον, ἀλλὰ μαλακαῖς[1] καὶ δασείαις νεφέλαις πολλάκις κατεχομένη· ἐκ δὲ τούτων ὑετοὶ[2] γίνονται καὶ χειμῶνες εὔκαιροι καὶ ποιοῦντες τὴν θερινὴν ὥραν εὔκρατον. ἥ τε χώρα πάμφορός ἐστι καὶ διάφορος κατὰ τὴν ἀρετήν, οὐ μέντοι τυγχάνει τῆς ἐνδεχομένης ἐπιμελείας διὰ τὴν τῶν

7 λαῶν ἀπειρίαν. τὸν δὲ χρυσὸν εὑρίσκοντες ἐν τοῖς φυσικοῖς ὑπονόμοις τῆς γῆς συνάγουσι πολύν, οὐ τὸν ἐκ τοῦ ψήγματος συντηκόμενον, ἀλλὰ τὸν αὐτοφυῆ καὶ καλούμενον ἀπὸ τοῦ συμβεβηκότος ἄπυρον. κατὰ δὲ τὸ μέγεθος ἐλάχιστος μὲν εὑρίσκεται παραπλήσιος πυρῆνι, μέγιστος δὲ οὐ πολὺ λειπό-

8 μενος βασιλικοῦ καρύου. φοροῦσι δ' αὐτὸν περί τε τοὺς καρποὺς τῶν χειρῶν καὶ περὶ τοὺς τραχή-

[1] For μαλακαῖς Bezzel suggests μελαίναις; for δασείαις Capps suggests δροσεραῖς (Arist. Nubes 338).
[2] So Wesseling (cp. Agatharchides 96): νιφετοί.

BOOK III. 45. 5-8

down such an amount of what is gold dust to all appearance that the mud glitters all over as it is carried out at its mouth. The natives of the region are entirely without experience in the working of the gold, but they are hospitable to strangers, not, however, to everyone who arrives among them, but only to Boeotians and Peloponnesians, the reason for this being the ancient friendship shown by Heracles for the tribe, a friendship which, they relate, has come down to them in the form of a myth as a heritage from their ancestors.

The land which comes next is inhabited by Alilaei and Gasandi, Arab peoples, and is not fiery hot, like the neighbouring territories, but is often overspread by mild [1] and thick clouds, from which come heavy showers and timely storms that make the summer season temperate. The land produces everything and is exceptionally fertile, but it does not receive the cultivation of which it would admit because of the lack of experience of the folk. Gold they discover in underground galleries which have been formed by nature and gather in abundance—not that which has been fused into a mass out of gold-dust,[2] but the virgin gold, which is called, from its condition when found, "unfired" gold. And as for size the smallest nugget found is about as large as the stone of fruit,[3] and the largest not much smaller than a royal nut. This gold they wear about both their wrists and necks,

[1] The text may be corrupt; "dark and thick" and "mild and dewy" have been suggested (cp. critical note).

[2] *i.e.* fused into artificial nuggets.

[3] The word *puren* was used for the stone of any stone-fruit, such as olive, pomegranate, grape, and was, therefore, a very indefinite term of measurement; the "royal nut," mentioned below, however, was the Persian walnut.

λους, τετρημένον ἐναλλὰξ λίθοις διαφανέσι. καὶ τούτου μὲν τοῦ γένους ἐπιπολάζοντος παρ' αὐτοῖς, χαλκοῦ δὲ καὶ σιδήρου σπανίζοντος, ἐπ' ἴσης ἀλλάττονται ταῦτα τὰ φορτία πρὸς τοὺς ἐμπόρους.

46. Μετὰ δὲ τούτους ὑπάρχουσιν οἱ ὀνομαζόμενοι Κάρβαι, καὶ μετὰ τούτους Σαβαῖοι, πολυανθρωπότατοι τῶν Ἀραβικῶν ἐθνῶν ὄντες. νέμονται δὲ τὴν εὐδαίμονα λεγομένην Ἀραβίαν, φέρουσαν τὰ πλεῖστα τῶν παρ' ἡμῖν ἀγαθῶν καὶ θρεμμάτων παντοδαπῶν ἐκτρέφουσαν πλῆθος ἀμύθητον. εὐωδία τε[1] αὐτὴν πᾶσαν ἐπέχει φυσικὴ διὰ τὸ πάντα σχεδὸν τὰ ταῖς ὀσμαῖς πρωτεύοντα φύεσθαι 2 κατὰ τὴν χώραν ἀνέκλειπτα. κατὰ μὲν γὰρ τὴν παράλιον φύεται τὸ καλούμενον βάλσαμον καὶ κασία καὶ πόα τις ἄλλη ἰδιάζουσαν φύσιν ἔχουσα· αὕτη δὲ πρόσφατος μὲν οὖσα τοῖς ὄμμασι προσηνεστάτην παρέχεται τέρψιν, ἐγχρονισθεῖσα δὲ συντό3 μως γίνεται ἐξίτηλος. κατὰ δὲ τὴν μεσόγειον ὑπάρχουσι δρυμοὶ συνηρεφεῖς, καθ' οὓς ἐστι δένδρα μεγάλα λιβανωτοῦ καὶ σμύρνης, πρὸς δὲ τούτοις φοίνικος καὶ καλάμου καὶ κιναμώμου καὶ τῶν ἄλλων τῶν τούτοις ὁμοίαν ἐχόντων τὴν εὐωδίαν· οὐδὲ γὰρ ἐξαριθμήσασθαι δυνατὸν τὰς ἑκάστων ἰδιότητάς τε καὶ φύσεις διὰ τὸ πλῆθος καὶ τὴν ὑπερβολὴν τῆς ἐκ πάντων ἀθροιζομένης ὀσμῆς. 4 θεία γάρ τις φαίνεται καὶ λόγου κρείττων ἡ προσ-

---

[1] τε Bekker: τε γάρ.

BOOK III. 45. 8–46. 4

perforating it and alternating it with transparent stones. And since this precious metal abounds in their land, whereas there is a scarcity of copper and iron, they exchange it with merchants for equal parts of the latter wares.[1]

46. Beyond this people are the Carbae, as they are called, and beyond these the Sabaeans, who are the most numerous of the tribes of the Arabians. They inhabit that part of the country known as Arabia the Blest,[2] which produces most of the things which are held dear among us and nurtures flocks and herds of every kind in multitude beyond telling. And a natural sweet odour pervades the entire land because practically all the things which excel in fragrance grow there unceasingly. Along the coast, for instance, grow balsam, as it is called, and cassia and a certain other herb possessing a nature peculiar to itself; for when fresh it is most pleasing and delightful to the eye, but when kept for a time it suddenly fades to nothing. And throughout the interior of the land there are thick forests, in which are great trees which yield frankincense and myrrh, as well as palms and reeds, cinnamon trees and every other kind which possesses a sweet odour such as these have; for it is impossible to enumerate both the peculiar properties and natures of each one severally because of the great volume and the exceptional richness of the fragrance as it is gathered from each and all. For a divine thing and beyond the power of words to describe seems the fragrance which greets

---

[1] Here Diodorus departs radically from Agatharchides (96), who says that they exchange one part of gold for three of copper or two of iron; cp. Strabo 16. 4. 18.

[2] The *Arabia Felix* of the Romans.

πίπτουσα καὶ κινοῦσα τὰς ἑκάστων αἰσθήσεις εὐωδία. καὶ γὰρ τοὺς παραπλέοντας, καίπερ πολὺ τῆς χέρσου κεχωρισμένους, οὐκ ἀμοίρους ποιεῖ τῆς τοιαύτης ἀπολαύσεως· κατὰ γὰρ τὴν θερινὴν ὥραν, ὅταν ἄνεμος ἀπόγειος γένηται, συμβαίνει τὰς ἀπὸ τῶν σμυρνοφόρων δένδρων καὶ τῶν ἄλλων τῶν τοιούτων ἀποπνεομένας εὐωδίας διικνεῖσθαι πρὸς τὰ πλησίον μέρη τῆς θαλάττης· οὐ γὰρ ὥσπερ παρ' ἡμῖν ἀποκειμένην καὶ παλαιὰν ἔχει τὴν τῶν ἀρωμάτων φύσιν, ἀλλὰ τὴν ἀκμάζουσαν ἐν ἄνθει νεαρὰν δύναμιν καὶ διικνουμένην
5 πρὸς τὰ λεπτομερέστατα τῆς αἰσθήσεως. κομιζούσης γὰρ τῆς αὔρας τὴν ἀπόρροιαν τῶν εὐωδεστάτων, προσπίπτει τοῖς προσπλέουσι τὴν παράλιον προσηνὲς καὶ πολύ, πρὸς δὲ τούτοις ὑγιεινὸν καὶ παρηλλαγμένον ἐκ τῶν ἀρίστων μῖγμα, οὔτε[1] τετμημένου τοῦ καρποῦ καὶ τὴν ἰδίαν ἀκμὴν ἐκπεπνευκότος, οὔτε τὴν ἀπόθεσιν ἔχοντος ἐν ἑτερογενέσιν ἀγγείοις, ἀλλ' ἀπ' αὐτῆς τῆς νεαρωτάτης ὥρας καὶ τὸν βλαστὸν ἀκέραιον παρεχομένης τῆς θείας φύσεως, ὥστε τοὺς μεταλαμβάνοντας τῆς ἰδιότητος δοκεῖν ἀπολαύειν τῆς μυθολογουμένης ἀμβροσίας διὰ τὸ τὴν ὑπερβολὴν τῆς εὐωδίας μηδεμίαν ἑτέραν εὑρίσκειν οἰκείαν προσηγορίαν.

47. Οὐ μὴν ὁλόκληρον καὶ χωρὶς φθόνου τὴν εὐδαιμονίαν τοῖς ἀνθρώποις ἡ τύχη περιέθηκεν, ἀλλὰ τοῖς τηλικούτοις δωρήμασι παρέζευξε τὸ βλάπτον καὶ νουθετῆσον τοὺς διὰ τὴν συνέχειαν τῶν ἀγαθῶν εἰωθότας καταφρονεῖν τῶν θεῶν.

[1] γὰρ after οὔτε deleted by Dindorf.

the nostrils and stirs the senses of everyone. Indeed, even though those who sail along this coast may be far from the land, that does not deprive them of a portion of the enjoyment which this fragrance affords; for in the summer season, when the wind is blowing off shore, one finds that the sweet odours exhaled by the myrrh-bearing and other aromatic trees penetrate to the near-by parts of the sea; and the reason is that the essence of the sweet-smelling herbs is not, as with us, kept laid away until it has become old and stale, but its potency is in the full bloom of its strength and fresh, and penetrates to the most delicate parts of the sense of smell. And since the breeze carries the emanation of the most fragrant plants, to the voyagers who approach the coast there is wafted a blending of perfumes, delightful and potent, and healthful withal and exotic, composed as it is of the best of them, seeing that the product of the trees has not been minced into bits and so has exhaled its own special strength, nor yet lies stored away in vessels made of a different substance, but taken at the very prime of its freshness and while its divine nature keeps the shoot pure and undefiled. Consequently those who partake of the unique fragrance feel that they are enjoying the ambrosia of which the myths relate, being unable, because of the superlative sweetness of the perfume, to find any other name that would be fitting and worthy of it.

47. Nevertheless, fortune has not invested the inhabitants of this land with a felicity which is perfect and leaves no room for envy, but with such great gifts she has coupled what is harmful and may serve as a warning to such men as are wont to despise the gods because of the unbroken succession of their

DIODORUS OF SICILY

2 κατὰ γὰρ τοὺς εὐωδεστάτους δρυμοὺς ὄφεων ὑπάρχει πλῆθος, οἳ τὸ μὲν χρῶμα φοινικοῦν ἔχουσι, μῆκος δὲ σπιθαμῆς, δήγματα δὲ ποιοῦνται παντελῶς ἀνίατα· δάκνουσι δὲ προσπηδῶντες καὶ ἁλλόμενοι πρὸς ὕψος αἱμάττουσι τὸν χρῶτα.
3 ἴδιον δέ τι παρὰ τοῖς ἐγχωρίοις συμβαίνει περὶ τοὺς ἠσθενηκότας ὑπὸ μακρᾶς νόσου τὰ σώματα.[1] διαπνεομένου γὰρ τοῦ σώματος ὑπ' ἀκράτου καὶ τμητικῆς φύσεως, καὶ τῆς συγκρίσεως τῶν ὄγκων εἰς ἀραίωμα συναγομένης, ἔκλυσις ἐπακολουθεῖ δυσβοήθητος· διόπερ τοῖς τοιούτοις ἄσφαλτον παραθυμιῶσι καὶ τράγου πώγωνα, ταῖς ἐναντίαις φύσεσι καταμαχόμενοι τὴν ὑπερβολὴν τῆς εὐωδίας. τὸ γὰρ καλὸν ποσότητι μὲν καὶ τάξει μετρούμενον ὠφελεῖ καὶ τέρπει τοὺς ἀνθρώπους, ἀναλογίας δὲ καὶ καθήκοντος καιροῦ διαμαρτὸν ἀνόνητον ἔχει τὴν δωρεάν.

4 Τοῦ δ' ἔθνους τούτου μητρόπολίς ἐστιν ἣν καλοῦσι Σαβάς, ἐπ' ὄρους ᾠκισμένη. βασιλέας δ' ἐκ γένους ἔχει τοὺς διαδεχομένους, οἷς τὰ πλήθη τιμὰς ἀπονέμει μεμιγμένας ἀγαθοῖς καὶ κακοῖς. μακάριον μὲν γὰρ βίον ἔχειν δοκοῦσιν, ὅτι πᾶσιν ἐπιτάττοντες οὐδένα λόγον ὑπέχουσι τῶν πραττομένων· ἀτυχεῖς δὲ νομίζονται καθ' ὅσον οὐκ ἔξεστιν αὐτοῖς οὐδέποτε ἐξελθεῖν ἐκ τῶν βασιλείων, εἰ δὲ μή, γίνονται λιθόλευστοι ὑπὸ τῶν ὄχλων
5 κατά τινα χρησμὸν ἀρχαῖον. τοῦτο δὲ τὸ ἔθνος

---

[1] τὰ σώματα deleted by Reiske.

---

[1] 7½ inches.
[2] Strabo (16. 4. 19) says this was done to overcome the

BOOK III. 47. 2-5

blessings. For in the most fragrant forests is a multitude of snakes, the colour of which is dark-red, their length a span,[1] and their bites altogether incurable; they bite by leaping upon their victim, and as they spring on high they leave a stain of blood upon his skin. And there is also something peculiar to the natives which happens in the case of those whose bodies have become weakened by a protracted illness. For when the body has become permeated by an undiluted and pungent substance and the combination of foreign bodies settles in a porous area, an enfeebled condition ensues which is difficult to cure: consequently at the side of men afflicted in this way they burn asphalt and the beard of a goat,[2] combatting the excessively sweet odour by that from substances of the opposite nature. Indeed the good, when it is measured out in respect of quantity and order, is for human beings an aid and delight, but when it fails of due proportion and proper time the gift which it bestows is unprofitable.

The chief city of this tribe is called by them Sabae and is built upon a mountain. The kings of this city succeed to the throne by descent and the people accord to them honours mingled with good and ill. For though they have the appearance of leading a happy life, in that they impose commands upon all and are not accountable for their deeds, yet they are considered unfortunate, inasmuch as it is unlawful for them ever to leave the palace, and if they do so they are stoned to death, in accordance with a certain ancient oracle, by the common crowd. This tribe

drowsiness caused by the sweet odours; the disease appears to be mentioned by no other ancient writer, and presumably was caused by the continued inhaling of these powerful scents.

οὐ μόνον τῶν πλησιοχώρων Ἀράβων, ἀλλὰ καὶ τῶν ἄλλων ἀνθρώπων διαφέρει πλούτῳ καὶ ταῖς ἄλλαις ταῖς[1] κατὰ μέρος πολυτελείαις. ἐν γὰρ ταῖς τῶν φορτίων ἀλλαγαῖς καὶ πράσεσιν ὄγκοις ἐλαχίστοις πλείστην ἀποφέρονται τιμὴν ἁπάντων ἀνθρώπων τῶν ἀργυρικῆς ἀμείψεως ἕνεκα τὰς ἐμπορίας ποιουμένων. διόπερ ἐξ αἰῶνος ἀπορθήτων αὐτῶν γεγενημένων διὰ τὸν ἐκτοπισμόν, καὶ χρυσοῦ τε καὶ ἀργύρου πλήθους ἐπικεκλυκότος παρ' αὐτοῖς, καὶ μάλιστ' ἐν Σαβαῖς, ἐν ᾗ τὰ βασίλεια κεῖται, τορεύματα μὲν ἀργυρᾶ τε καὶ χρυσᾶ παντοδαπῶν ἐκπωμάτων ἔχουσι, κλίνας δὲ καὶ τρίποδας ἀργυρόποδας, καὶ τὴν ἄλλην κατασκευὴν ἄπιστον τῇ πολυτελείᾳ, κιόνων τε ἁδρῶν περίστυλα, τὰ μὲν ἐπίχρυσα, τὰ δ' ἀργυροειδεῖς τύπους ἐπὶ τῶν κιονοκράνων ἔχοντα. τὰς δ' ὀροφὰς καὶ θύρας χρυσαῖς φιάλαις λιθοκολλήτοις καὶ πυκναῖς διειληφότες ἅπασαν τὴν τῶν οἰκιῶν κατὰ μέρος οἰκοδομίαν πεποίηνται θαυμαστὴν ταῖς πολυτελείαις· τὰ μὲν γὰρ ἐξ ἀργύρου καὶ χρυσοῦ, τὰ δ' ἐξ ἐλέφαντος καὶ τῶν διαπρεπεστάτων λίθων, ἔτι δὲ τῶν ἄλλων τῶν τιμιωτάτων παρ' ἀνθρώποις, κατεσκευάκασιν. ἀλλὰ γὰρ οὗτοι μὲν ἐκ πολλῶν χρόνων τὴν εὐδαιμονίαν ἀσάλευτον ἔσχον διὰ τὸ παντελῶς ἀπεξενῶσθαι τῶν διὰ τὴν ἰδίαν πλεονεξίαν ἕρμαιον ἡγουμένων τὸν ἀλλότριον πλοῦτον. ἡ δὲ κατὰ τούτους θάλαττα λευκὴ φαίνεται τὴν χρόαν, ὥσθ' ἅμα θαυμάζειν τὸ παράδοξον καὶ τὴν αἰτίαν τοῦ συμβαίνοντος ἐπιζητεῖν. νῆσοι δ'

---

[1] ταῖς added by Dindorf.

BOOK III. 47. 5-9

surpasses not only the neighbouring Arabs but also all other men in wealth and in their several extravagancies besides. For in the exchange and sale of their wares they, of all men who carry on trade for the sake of the silver they receive in exchange, obtain the highest price in return for things of the smallest weight. Consequently, since they have never for ages suffered the ravages of war because of their secluded position, and since an abundance of both gold and silver abounds in the country, especially in Sabae, where the royal palace is situated, they have embossed goblets of every description, made of silver and gold, couches and tripods with silver feet, and every other furnishing of incredible costliness, and halls encircled by large columns, some of them gilded, and others having silver figures on the capitals. Their ceilings and doors they have partitioned by means of panels and coffers[1] made of gold, set with precious stones and placed close together, and have thus made the structure of their houses in every part marvellous for its costliness; for some parts they have constructed of silver and gold, others of ivory and the most showy precious stones or of whatever else men esteem most highly. For the fact is that these people have enjoyed their felicity unshaken since ages past because they have been entire strangers to those whose own covetousness leads them to feel that another man's wealth is their own godsend.[2] The sea in these parts looks to be white in colour, so that the beholder marvels at the surprising phenomenon and at the same time seeks for its cause. And there

---

[1] *i.e.* certain panels were deeply recessed.
[2] Literally "gift of Hermes," as the god of gain and good luck.

εὐδαίμονες πλησίον ὑπάρχουσιν, ἔχουσαι πόλεις ἀτειχίστους, ἐν αἷς τὰ βοσκήματα πάντα λευκὴν ἔχει τὴν χρόαν, καὶ τοῖς θήλεσιν αὐτῶν οὐκ ἐπιφύεται τὸ καθόλου κέρας. εἰς ταύτας δ' ἔμποροι πάντοθεν καταπλέουσι, μάλιστα δ' ἐκ[1] Ποτάνας, ἣν Ἀλέξανδρος ᾤκισε παρὰ τὸν Ἰνδὸν ποταμόν, ναύσταθμον ἔχειν βουλόμενος τῆς παρὰ τὸν ὠκεανὸν παραλίου.

Περὶ μὲν οὖν τῆς χώρας καὶ τῶν ἐν αὐτῇ κατοικούντων ἀρκεσθησόμεθα τοῖς εἰρημένοις.

48. Περὶ δὲ τῶν κατὰ τὸν οὐρανὸν ὁρωμένων παραδόξων ἐν τοῖς τόποις οὐ παραλειπτέον. θαυμασιώτατον μέν ἐστι τὸ περὶ τὴν ἄρκτον ἱστορούμενον καὶ πλείστην ἀπορίαν παρεχόμενον τοῖς πλοϊζομένοις· ἀπὸ γὰρ μηνὸς ὃν καλοῦσιν Ἀθηναῖοι Μαιμακτηριῶνα τῶν ἑπτὰ τῶν κατὰ τὴν ἄρκτον ἀστέρων οὐδένα φασὶν ὁρᾶσθαι μέχρι τῆς πρώτης φυλακῆς, τῷ δὲ Ποσειδεῶνι μέχρι δευτέρας, καὶ κατὰ τοὺς ἑξῆς ἐκ τοῦ κατ' ὀλίγον[2] πλοϊζομένοις[3] ἀθεωρήτους ὑπάρχειν.[4] τῶν δ' ἄλλων τοὺς ὀνομαζομένους πλανήτας τοὺς μὲν μείζονας τῶν παρ' ἡμῖν, ἑτέρους δὲ μηδὲ τὰς ὁμοίας ἀνατολὰς καὶ δύσεις ποιεῖσθαι· τὸν δ' ἥλιον οὐχ

[1] ἐκ Rhodomann: εἰς.
[2] κατ' ὀλίγον, κατὰ λόγον ("at the same rate") Agatharchides, 104.
[3] πλοϊζομένοις deleted by Bekker, Vogel.
[4] ἀθεωρήτους ὑπάρχειν after πλανήτας all MSS. but AD, Bekker, Dindorf.

---

[1] The adjective is that translated "Blest" in Arabia the Blest.
[2] The fifth month of the Attic year, approximately our November.
[3] The sixth month, approximately our December.

BOOK III. 47. 9–48. 2

are prosperous[1] islands near by, containing unwalled cities, all the herds of which are white in colour, while no female has any horn whatsoever. These islands are visited by sailors from every part and especially from Potana, the city which Alexander founded on the Indus river, when he wished to have a naval station on the shore of the ocean.

Now as regards Arabia the Blest and its inhabitants we shall be satisfied with what has been said.

48. But we must not omit to mention the strange phenomena which are seen in the heavens in these regions. The most marvellous is that which, according to accounts we have, has to do with the constellation of the Great Bear and occasions the greatest perplexity among navigators. What they relate is that, beginning with the month which the Athenians call Maemacterion,[2] not one of the seven stars of the Great Bear is seen until the first watch, in Poseideon[3] none until the second, and in the following months they gradually drop out of the sight of navigators.[4] As for the other heavenly bodies, the planets, as they are called, are, in the case of some, larger than they appear with us, and in the case of others their risings and settings are also not the same; and the sun does

[4] In the second century B.C., the period when Agatharchides, from whom Diodorus has taken this statement, wrote his work entitled *On the Red Sea*, at latitude 15 north, which is the probable region of this statement, on November 1st the sun set at approximately 5.45 p.m. and the first star (*alpha*) of the Great Bear rose at approximately 8.45 p.m. Its rising did, therefore, fall within the first watch of the night. However, the statement that on December 1st it did not rise until the second watch is false, since on that date it rose at approximately 6.40 p.m.; indeed the rising of the Great Bear, instead of receding month by month, as Diodorus states, in fact advances.

233

DIODORUS OF SICILY

ὥσπερ παρ' ἡμῖν βραχὺ πρὸ τῆς ἰδίας ἀνατολῆς προαποστέλλειν τὸ φῶς, ἀλλ' ἔτι νυκτὸς οὔσης σκοταίου παραδόξως ἄφνω φανέντα ἐκλάμπειν. 3 διὸ καὶ μηδέποθ' ἡμέραν μὲν ἐν ἐκείνοις τοῖς τόποις γίνεσθαι πρὶν ὁραθῆναι τὸν ἥλιον, ἐκ μέσου δὲ τοῦ πελάγους φασὶν ἀναφαινόμενον αὐτὸν ὁρᾶσθαι μὲν ἄνθρακι παραπλήσιον τῷ πυρωδεστάτῳ, σπινθῆρας δ' ἀφ' ἑαυτοῦ μεγάλους ἀπορρίπτειν, καὶ τῷ τύπῳ μὴ κωνοειδῆ[1] φαίνεσθαι, καθάπερ ἡμεῖς δοξάζομεν, ἀλλὰ κίονι τὸν τύπον ἔχειν ἐμφερῆ, μικρὸν ἐμβριθεστέραν ἔχοντι τὴν ἀπὸ τῆς κεφαλῆς ἐπιφάνειαν, πρὸς δὲ τούτοις μήτ' αὐγὴν ποιεῖν μήτ' ἀκτῖνας βάλλειν ἄχρι πρώτης ὥρας, φαινομένου πυρὸς ἀλαμποῦς ἐν σκότει· δευτέρας δ' ἀρχομένης ἀσπιδοειδῆ γίνεσθαι καὶ τὸ φῶς βάλλειν ἀπότομον καὶ πυρῶδες καθ' ὑπερβολήν. 4 κατὰ δὲ τὴν δύσιν ἐναντία γίνεσθαι συμπτώματα περὶ αὐτόν· δοκεῖν γὰρ τοῖς ὁρῶσι καιναῖς ἀκτῖσι φωτίζειν τὸν κόσμον οὐκ ἔλαττον[2] ὡρῶν δυοῖν, ὡς δ' Ἀγαθαρχίδης ὁ Κνίδιος ἀνέγραψε, τριῶν. τοῦτον δὲ τὸν καιρὸν ἥδιστον τοῖς ἐγχωρίοις φαίνεσθαι, ταπεινουμένου τοῦ καύματος διὰ τὴν δύσιν τοῦ ἡλίου.

5 Τῶν δ' ἀνέμων ζέφυροι μὲν καὶ λίβες, ἔτι δ' ἀργέσται καὶ εὖροι, πνέουσι καθάπερ καὶ παρὰ τοῖς ἄλλοις· νότοι δὲ κατὰ μὲν Αἰθιοπίαν οὔτε πνέουσιν

[1] δισκοειδῆ Agatharchides, 105.
[2] So Rhodomann: ἐλαττόνων.

---

[1] The cause for this statement is the phenomenon of twilight, which is dependent upon atmospheric as well as astronomical conditions. Its duration varies with the depth, clarity, and density of the atmosphere, the latitude and elevation of the

BOOK III. 48. 2-5

not, as with us, send forth its light shortly in advance of its actual rising, but while the darkness of night still continues, it suddenly and contrary to all expectation appears and sends forth its light.[1] Because of this there is no daylight in those regions before the sun has become visible, and when out of the midst of the sea, as they say, it comes into view, it resembles a fiery red ball of charcoal which discharges huge sparks, and its shape does not look like a cone,[2] as is the impression we have of it, but it has the shape of a column which has the appearance of being slightly thicker at the top; and furthermore it does not shine or send out rays before the first hour, appearing as a fire that gives forth no light in the darkness; but at the beginning of the second hour it takes on the form of a round shield and sends forth a light which is exceptionally bright and fiery. But at its setting the opposite manifestations take place with respect to it; for it seems to observers to be lighting up the whole universe with a strange kind of ray [3] for not less than two or, as Agatharchides of Cnidus has recorded, for three hours. And in the opinion of the natives this is the most pleasant period, when the heat is steadily lessening because of the setting of the sun.

As regards the winds, the west, the south-west, also the north-west and the east blow as in the other parts of the world; but in Ethiopia the south winds

place of observation, and the time of year. The Greek navigator found less twilight as he travelled south from Greece towards the equator, at which point, in fact, it has its minimum duration.

[2] Agatharchides (105) says " discus-shaped."

[3] Agatharchides (105) says that this takes place after the sun has already set.

οὔτε γνωρίζονται τὸ σύνολον, κατὰ δὲ τὴν Τρωγοδυτικὴν καὶ τὴν Ἀραβίαν θερμοὶ γίνονται καθ' ὑπερβολήν, ὥστε καὶ τὰς ὕλας ἐκπυροῦν καὶ τῶν καταφευγόντων εἰς τὰς ἐν ταῖς καλύβαις σκιὰς ἐκλύειν τὰ σώματα. ὁ δὲ βορέας δικαίως ἂν ἄριστος νομίζοιτο, διικνούμενος εἰς πάντα τόπον τῆς οἰκουμένης καὶ διαμένων ψυχρός.

49. Τούτων δ' ἡμῖν διευκρινημένων οἰκεῖον ἂν εἴη διελθεῖν περὶ τῶν Λιβύων τῶν πλησίον Αἰγύπτου κατοικούντων καὶ τῆς ὁμόρου χώρας. τὰ γὰρ περὶ Κυρήνην καὶ τὰς Σύρτεις, ἔτι δὲ τὴν μεσόγειον τῆς κατὰ τοὺς τόπους τούτους χέρσου, κατοικεῖ τέτταρα γένη Λιβύων· ὧν οἱ μὲν ὀνομαζόμενοι Νασαμῶνες νέμονται τὰ νεύοντα μέρη πρὸς νότον, οἱ δ' Αὐσχῖσαι τὰ πρὸς τὴν δύσιν, οἱ δὲ Μαρμαρίδαι κατοικοῦσι τὴν μεταξὺ ταινίαν Αἰγύπτου καὶ Κυρήνης, μετέχοντες καὶ τῆς παραλίου, οἱ δὲ Μάκαι πολυανθρωπίᾳ τῶν ὁμοεθνῶν προέχοντες νέμονται τοὺς τόπους τοὺς περὶ τὴν 2 Σύρτιν. τῶν δὲ προειρημένων Λιβύων γεωργοὶ μέν εἰσιν οἷς ὑπάρχει χώρα δυναμένη καρπὸν φέρειν δαψιλῆ, νομάδες δ' ὅσοι τῶν κτηνῶν τὴν ἐπιμέλειαν ποιούμενοι τὰς τροφὰς ἔχουσιν ἀπὸ τούτων· ἀμφότερα δὲ τὰ γένη ταῦτα βασιλέας ἔχει καὶ βίον οὐ παντελῶς ἄγριον οὐδ' ἀνθρωπίνης ἡμερότητος ἐξηλλαγμένον. τὸ δὲ τρίτον γένος οὔτε βασιλέως ὑπακοῦον οὔτε τοῦ δικαίου λόγον οὐδ' ἔννοιαν ἔχον ἀεὶ λῃστεύει, ἀπροσδοκήτως δὲ τὰς ἐμβολὰς ἐκ τῆς ἐρήμου ποιούμενον ἁρπάζει τὰ παρατυχόντα, καὶ ταχέως ἀνακάμπτει πρὸς τὸν

---

[1] *i.e.* to the plan of Diodorus' history.

neither blow nor are known at all, although in the Trogodyte country and Arabia they are so exceptionally hot that they set the forests on fire and cause the bodies of those who take refuge in the shade of their huts to collapse through weakness. The north wind, however, may justly be considered the most favourable of all, since it reaches into every region of the inhabited earth and is ever cool.

49. But now that we have examined these matters, it will be appropriate [1] to discuss the Libyans who dwell near Egypt and the country which borders upon them. The parts about Cyrenê and the Syrtes as well as the interior of the mainland in these regions are inhabited by four tribes of Libyans; of these the Nasamones, as they are called, dwell in the parts to the south, the Auschisae in those to the west, the Marmaridae occupy the narrow strip between Egypt and Cyrene and come down to the coast, and the Macae, who are more numerous than their fellow Libyans, dwell in the regions about the Syrtis.[2] Now of the Libyans whom we have just mentioned those are farmers who possess land which is able to produce abundant crops, while those are nomads who get their sustenance from the flocks and herds which they maintain; and both of these groups have kings and lead a life which is not entirely savage or different from that of civilized men. The third group, however, obeying no king and taking no account or even thought of justice, makes robbery its constant practice, and attacking unexpectedly from out of the desert it seizes whatever it has happened upon and quickly withdraws to the place from which it had set

[2] The Greater Syrtis.

3 αὐτὸν τόπον. πάντες δ' οἱ Λίβυες οὗτοι θηριώδη βίον ἔχουσιν, ὑπαίθριοι διαμένοντες καὶ τὸ τῶν ἐπιτηδευμάτων ἄγριον ἐζηλωκότες· οὔτε γὰρ ἡμέρου διαίτης οὔτ' ἐσθῆτος μετέχουσιν, ἀλλὰ δοραῖς αἰγῶν σκεπάζουσι τὰ σώματα. τοῖς δὲ δυνάσταις αὐτῶν πόλεις μὲν τὸ σύνολον οὐχ ὑπάρχουσι, πύργοι δὲ πλησίον τῶν ὑδάτων, εἰς οὓς ἀποτίθενται τὰ πλεονάζοντα τῆς ὠφελείας. τοὺς δ' ὑποτεταγμένους λαοὺς κατ' ἐνιαυτὸν ἐξορκίζουσι πειθαρχήσειν· καὶ τῶν μὲν ὑπακουσάντων ὡς συμμάχων φροντίζουσι, τῶν δὲ μὴ προσεχόντων θάνατον καταγνόντες ὡς λῃσταῖς πολε-
4 μοῦσιν. ὁ δ' ὁπλισμὸς αὐτῶν ἐστιν οἰκεῖος τῆς τε χώρας καὶ τῶν ἐπιτηδευμάτων· κοῦφοι γὰρ ὄντες τοῖς σώμασι καὶ χώραν οἰκοῦντες κατὰ τὸ πλεῖστον πεδιάδα, πρὸς τοὺς κινδύνους ὁρμῶσι λόγχας ἔχοντες τρεῖς καὶ λίθους ἐν ἄγγεσι σκυτίνοις· ξίφος δ' οὐ φοροῦσιν οὐδὲ κράνος οὐδ' ὅπλον οὐδὲν ἕτερον, στοχαζόμενοι τοῦ προτερεῖν ταῖς εὐκινησίαις ἐν τοῖς
5 διωγμοῖς καὶ πάλιν ἐν ταῖς ἀποχωρήσεσι. διόπερ εὔθετοι πρὸς δρόμον εἰσὶ καὶ λιθοβολίαν, διαπεπονηκότες τῇ μελέτῃ καὶ τῇ συνηθείᾳ τὰ τῆς φύσεως προτερήματα. καθόλου δὲ πρὸς τοὺς ἀλλοφύλους οὔτε τὸ δίκαιον οὔτε τὴν πίστιν κατ' οὐδένα τρόπον διατηροῦσιν.

50. Τῆς δὲ χώρας ἡ μὲν ὅμορος τῇ Κυρήνῃ γεώδης ἐστὶ καὶ πολλοὺς φέρουσα καρπούς· οὐ μόνον γὰρ ὑπάρχει σιτοφόρος, ἀλλὰ καὶ πολλὴν ἄμπελον, ἔτι δ' ἐλαίαν ἔχει καὶ τὴν ἀγρίαν ὕλην καὶ ποταμοὺς εὐχρηστίαν παρεχομένους· ἡ δ' ὑπὲρ τὸ νότιον μέρος ὑπερτείνουσα, καθ' ἣν τὸ νίτρον φύεσθαι συμβέβηκεν, ἄσπορος οὖσα καὶ σπανί-

out. All the Libyans of this third group lead a life like that of the wild beasts, spending their days under the open sky and practising the savage in their mode of life; for they have nothing to do with civilized food or clothing, but cover their bodies with the skins of goats. Their leaders have no cities whatsoever, but only towers near the sources of water, and into these they bring and store away the excess of their booty. Of the peoples who are their subjects they annually exact an oath of obedience to their authority, and to any who have submitted to them they extend their protection as being allies, and such as take no heed of them they first condemn to death and then make war upon them as robbers. Their weapons are appropriate to both the country and their mode of life; for since they are light of body and inhabit a country which is for the most part a level plain, they face the dangers which beset them armed with three spears and stones in leather bags; and they carry neither sword nor helmet nor any other armour, since their aim is to excel in agility both in pursuit and again in withdrawal. Consequently they are expert in running and hurling stones, having brought to full development by practice and habit the advantages accorded them by nature. And, speaking generally, they observe neither justice nor good faith in any respect in dealing with peoples of alien race.

50. That part of the country which lies near the city of Cyrenê has a deep soil and bears products of many kinds; for not only does it produce wheat, but it also possesses large vineyards and olive orchards and native forests, and rivers which are of great utility; but the area which extends beyond its southern border where nitre is found, being unculti-

ζουσα ναματιαίων ὑδάτων, τὴν πρόσοψιν ἔχει πελάγει παρεμφερῆ· οὐδεμίαν δὲ παρεχομένη ποικιλίαν κατὰ τὴν ἰδέαν ἐρήμῳ γῇ περιέχεται, τῆς ὑπερκειμένης ἐρήμου δυσέξιτον ἐχούσης τὸ
2 πέρας. διόπερ οὐδ᾽ ὄρνεον ἰδεῖν ἔστιν, οὐ τετράπουν ἐν αὐτῇ ζῷον πλὴν δορκάδος καὶ βοός, οὐ μὴν οὔτε φυτὸν οὔτ᾽ ἄλλο τῶν δυναμένων ψυχαγωγῆσαι τὴν ὅρασιν, ὡς ἂν τῆς εἰς μεσόγειον ἀνηκούσης γῆς ἐχούσης ἐπὶ τὸ μῆκος ἀθρόους θῖνας. ἐφ᾽ ὅσον δὲ σπανίζει τῶν πρὸς ἥμερον βίον ἀνηκόντων, ἐπὶ τοσοῦτο πλήθει παντοίων ταῖς ἰδέαις καὶ τοῖς μεγέθεσιν ὄφεων, μάλιστα δὲ τῶν τοιούτων οὓς προσαγορεύουσι κεράστας, οἳ τὰ μὲν δήγματα θανατηφόρα ποιοῦνται, τὴν δὲ χρόαν ἄμμῳ παρα-
3 πλησίαν ἔχουσι· διόπερ ἐξωμοιωμένων αὐτῶν κατὰ τὴν πρόσοψιν τοῖς ὑποκειμένοις ἐδάφεσιν ὀλίγοι μὲν ἐπιγινώσκουσιν, οἱ πολλοὶ δ᾽ ἀγνοοῦντες πατοῦσι καὶ κινδύνοις περιπίπτουσιν ἀπροσδοκήτοις. λέγεται δὲ τούτους τὸ παλαιὸν ἐπελθόντας ποτὲ πολλὴν τῆς Αἰγύπτου ποιῆσαι τὴν ὑποκειμένην χώραν ἀοίκητον.
4 Γίνεται δέ τι θαυμάσιον περί τε ταύτην[1] τὴν χέρσον καὶ τὴν ἐπέκεινα τῆς Σύρτεως Λιβύην. περὶ γάρ τινας καιροὺς καὶ μάλιστα κατὰ τὰς νηνεμίας συστάσεις ὁρῶνται κατὰ τὸν ἀέρα παντοίων ζῴων ἰδέας ἐμφαίνουσαι· τούτων δ᾽ αἱ μὲν ἠρεμοῦσιν, αἱ δὲ κίνησιν λαμβάνουσι, καὶ ποτὲ μὲν

[1] τὴν χώραν καὶ after ταύτην deleted by Reiske.

[1] Literally, " horned serpents," or asps.
[2] Cp. Aristophanes, *The Clouds*, 346: " Didst thou never espy a cloud in the sky which a centaur or leopard might be,

vated and lacking springs of water, is in appearance like a sea; and in addition to its showing no variety of landscape it is surrounded by desert land, the desert which lies beyond ending in a region from which egress is difficult. Consequently not even a bird is to be seen there nor any four-footed animal except the gazelle and the ox, nor indeed any plant or anything that delights the eye, since the land which stretches into the interior contains nearly continuous dunes throughout its length. And greatly as it is lacking in the things which pertain to civilized life, to the same degree does it abound in snakes of every manner of appearance and size, and especially in those which men call *cerastes*,[1] the stings of which are mortal and their colour is like sand; and since for this reason they look like the ground on which they lie, few men discern them and the greater number tread on them unwittingly and meet with unexpected perils. Moreover, the account runs that in ancient times these snakes once invaded a large part of that section of Egypt which lies below this desert and rendered it uninhabitable.

And both in this arid land and in Libya which lies beyond the Syrtis there takes place a marvellous thing. For at certain times, and especially when there is no wind, shapes are seen gathering in the sky which assume the forms of animals of every kind [2]; and some of these remain fixed, but others begin to move,

or a wolf or a cow?" (tr. by Rogers in the *L.C.L.*); and Lucretius 4. 139–42: "For often giants' countenances appear to fly over and to draw their shadow afar, sometimes great mountains and rocks torn from the mountains to go before and to pass by the sun, after them some monster pulling and dragging other clouds" (tr. by Rouse in the *L.C.L.*).

ὑποφεύγουσι, ποτὲ δὲ διώκουσι, πᾶσαι δὲ τὸ μέγεθος ἄπλατον ἔχουσαι θαυμαστὴν κατάπληξιν καὶ ταραχὴν παρασκευάζουσι τοῖς ἀπείροις. αἱ γὰρ ἐπιδιώκουσαι τοὺς ἀνθρώπους ἐπειδὰν καταλάβωσι, περιχέονται τοῖς σώμασι ψυχραὶ καὶ παλμώδεις, ὥστε τοὺς μὲν ξένους ἀσυνήθεις ὄντας διὰ τὸ δέος ἐκπεπλῆχθαι, τοὺς δ' ἐγχωρίους πολλάκις συγκεκυρηκότας τοῖς τοιούτοις καταφρονεῖν τοῦ συμβαίνοντος.

51. Παραδόξου δ' εἶναι δοκοῦντος τοῦ πράγματος καὶ μύθῳ πεπλασμένῳ παραπλησίου, πειρῶνταί τινες τῶν φυσικῶν αἰτίας ἀποδιδόναι τοῦ γινομένου 2 τοιαύτας. ἀνέμους φασὶ κατὰ τὴν χώραν τοὺς μὲν τὸ σύνολον μὴ πνεῖν, τοὺς δὲ παντελῶς εἶναι βληχροὺς καὶ κωφούς· ὑπάρχειν δὲ καὶ περὶ τὸν ἀέρα πολλάκις ἠρεμίαν καὶ θαυμαστὴν ἀκινησίαν διὰ τὸ μήτε νάπας μήτε συσκίους αὐλῶνας παρακεῖσθαι πλησίον μήτε λόφων ὑπάρχειν ἀναστήματα· ποταμῶν τε μεγάλων σπανίζειν τοὺς τόπους, καὶ καθόλου τὴν σύνεγγυς χώραν ἅπασαν ἄκαρπον οὖσαν μηδεμίαν ἔχειν ἀναθυμίασιν· ἐξ ὧν ἁπάντων εἰωθέναι γεννᾶσθαί τινας 3 ἀρχὰς καὶ συστάσεις πνευμάτων. διόπερ συμπνιγοῦς περιστάσεως τὴν χέρσον ἐπεχούσης, ὅπερ ὁρῶμεν ἐπὶ τῶν νεφῶν ἐνίοτε συμβαῖνον ἐν ταῖς νοτίαις ἡμέραις, τυπουμένων ἰδεῶν παντοδαπῶν, τοῦτο γίνεσθαι καὶ περὶ τὴν Λιβύην, πολλαχῶς μορφουμένου τοῦ συμπίπτοντος ἀέρος· ὃν ταῖς μὲν ἀσθενέσι καὶ βληχραῖς αὔραις ὀχεῖσθαι μετεωριζόμενον καὶ παλμοὺς ποιοῦντα καὶ συγκρούοντα συστήμασιν ἑτέροις ὁμοίοις, νηνεμίας δ' ἐπιλαμ-

sometimes retreating before a man and at other times pursuing him, and in every case, since they are of monstrous size, they strike such as have never experienced them with wondrous dismay and terror. For when the shapes which are pursuing overtake the persons they envelop their bodies, causing a chilling and shivering sensation, so that strangers who are unfamiliar with them are overcome with fear, although the natives, who have often met with such things, pay no attention to the phenomenon.

51. Now incredible though this effect may seem and like a fanciful tale, yet certain physical philosophers attempt to set forth the causes of it somewhat as follows: The winds, they say, either blow in this land not at all or else are altogether sluggish and without vigour; and often there prevails in the air a calm and wondrous lack of movement, because of the fact that neither wooded vales nor thickly-shaded glens lie near it nor are there any elevations that make hills; furthermore, these regions lack large rivers and, in general, the whole territory round about, being barren of plants, gives forth no vapour. Yet it is all these things which are wont, they explain, to generate beginnings, as it were, and gatherings of air-currents. Consequently, when so stifling an atmosphere extends over the arid land the phenomenon which we observe taking place now and then with respect to the clouds on humid days, when every kind of shape is formed, occurs likewise in Libya, they tell us, the air as it condenses assuming manifold shapes. Now this air is driven along by the weak and sluggish breezes, rising aloft and making quivering motions and impinging upon other bodies of similar character, but when a calm succeeds, it then descends

βανούσης καθίστασθαι πρὸς τὴν γῆν, βαρὺν ὄντα καὶ τετυπωμένον ὡς ἔτυχεν· ἔπειτα μηδενὸς ὄντος τοῦ συγχέοντος προσπελάζειν τοῖς αὐτομάτως
4 περιτυγχάνουσι τῶν ζῴων. τὰς δ' ἐφ' ἑκάτερα κινήσεις αὐτῶν φασι προαίρεσιν μὲν μηδεμίαν ἐμφαίνειν· ἐν ἀψύχῳ γὰρ ἀδύνατον ὑπάρχειν φυγὴν ἑκούσιον ἢ δίωξιν· τὰ μέντοι ζῷα λεληθότως αἴτια τῆς μεταρσίας κινήσεως γίνεσθαι· προσιόντων μὲν γὰρ αὐτῶν τὸν ὑποκείμενον ἀέρα μετὰ βίας ἀναστέλλειν, καὶ διὰ τοῦθ' ὑποχωρεῖν τὸ συνεστηκὸς εἴδωλον καὶ ποιεῖν τὴν ἔμφασιν ὑποφεύγοντος· τοῖς δ' ἀναχωροῦσι κατὰ τοὐναντίον ἐπακολουθεῖν, ἀντεστραμμένης τῆς αἰτίας, ὡς ἂν τοῦ κενοῦ καὶ τῆς ἀραιώσεως ἐπισπωμένης.
5 διόπερ ἐοικέναι διώκοντι τοὺς ὑποχωροῦντας· ἕλκεσθαι γὰρ αὐτὸ καὶ προπίπτειν εἰς τὸ πρόσθεν ἄθρουν ὑπὸ τῆς πάλιν ῥύμης· τοὺς δ' ὑποφεύγοντας, ὅταν ἐπιστραφῶσιν ἢ μένωσιν, εὐλόγως ὑπὸ τοῦ συνακολουθοῦντος εἰδώλου ψαύεσθαι τοῖς ὄγκοις· τοῦτο δὲ κατὰ τὴν πρὸς τὸ στερέμνιον πρόσπτωσιν περιθρύβεσθαι, καὶ πανταχόθεν προσχεόμενον καταψύχειν τὰ σώματα τῶν περιτυγχανόντων.

52. Τούτων δ' ἡμῖν διευκρινημένων οἰκεῖον ἂν εἴη τοῖς προειρημένοις τόποις διελθεῖν τὰ περὶ τὰς Ἀμαζόνας ἱστορούμενα τὰς γενομένας τὸ παλαιὸν κατὰ τὴν Λιβύην. οἱ πολλοὶ μὲν γὰρ ὑπειλήφασι

---

[1] i.e. either pursuing or retreatiug before men; cp. chap. 50. 4 and below.

towards the earth by reason of its weight and in the shape which it may chance to have assumed, whereupon, there being nothing to dissipate it, the air clings to such living creatures as accidentally come to be in the way. As for the movements which these shapes make in both directions,[1] these, they say, indicate no volition on their part, since it is impossible that voluntary flight or pursuit should reside in a soulless thing. And yet the living creatures are, unknown to themselves, responsible for this movement through the air; for, if they advance, they push up by their violent motion the air which lies beneath them, and this is the reason why the image which has formed retreats before them and gives the impression of fleeing; whereas if the living creatures withdraw, they follow in the opposite direction, the cause having been reversed, since that which is empty and rarefied draws the shapes towards itself. Consequently it has the appearance of pursuing men who withdraw before it, for the image is drawn to the empty space and rushes forward in a mass under the influence of the backward motion of the living creature; and as for those who flee, it is quite reasonable that, whether they turn about or stand still, their bodies should feel the light touch of the image which follows them; and this is broken in pieces as it strikes upon the solid object, and as it pours itself out in all directions it chills the bodies of all with whom it comes in contact.

52. But now that we have examined these matters it will be fitting, in connection with the regions we have mentioned, to discuss the account which history records of the Amazons who were in Libya in ancient times. For the majority of mankind believe that

τὰς περὶ τὸν Θερμώδοντα ποταμὸν ἐν τῷ Πόντῳ
λεγομένας κατῳκηκέναι μόνας ὑπάρξαι· τὸ δ'
ἀληθὲς οὐχ οὕτως ἔχει, διὰ τὸ πολὺ προτερεῖν
τοῖς χρόνοις τὰς κατὰ Λιβύην καὶ πράξεις ἀξιολό-
2 γους ἐπιτελέσασθαι. οὐκ ἀγνοοῦμεν δὲ διότι
πολλοῖς τῶν ἀναγινωσκόντων ἀνήκοος φανεῖται
καὶ ξένη παντελῶς ἡ περὶ τούτων ἱστορία· ἠφανισμένου γὰρ ὁλοσχερῶς τοῦ γένους τῶν Ἀμαζονίδων
τούτων πολλαῖς γενεαῖς πρότερον τῶν Τρωικῶν,
τῶν δὲ περὶ τὸν Θερμώδοντα ποταμὸν γυναικῶν[1]
ἠκμακυιῶν μικρὸν πρὸ τούτων τῶν χρόνων, οὐκ
ἀλόγως αἱ μεταγενέστεραι καὶ μᾶλλον γνωριζό-
μεναι τὴν δόξαν κεκληρονομήκασι τὴν τῶν παλαιῶν
καὶ παντελῶς ἀγνοουμένων διὰ τὸν χρόνον ὑπὸ
3 τῶν πλείστων. οὐ μὴν ἀλλ' ἡμεῖς εὑρίσκοντες
πολλοὺς μὲν τῶν ἀρχαίων ποιητῶν τε καὶ συγγραφέων, οὐκ ὀλίγους δὲ καὶ τῶν μεταγενεστέρων
μνήμην πεποιημένους αὐτῶν, ἀναγράφειν τὰς
πράξεις πειρασόμεθα ἐν κεφαλαίοις ἀκολούθως
Διονυσίῳ τῷ συντεταγμένῳ τὰ περὶ τοὺς Ἀργοναύτας καὶ τὸν Διόνυσον καὶ ἕτερα πολλὰ τῶν ἐν
τοῖς παλαιοτάτοις χρόνοις πραχθέντων.
4 Γέγονε μὲν οὖν πλείω γένη γυναικῶν κατὰ τὴν
Λιβύην μάχιμα καὶ τεθαυμασμένα μεγάλως ἐπ' ἀν-
δρείᾳ· τό τε γὰρ τῶν Γοργόνων ἔθνος, ἐφ' ὃ λέγεται
τὸν Περσέα στρατεῦσαι, παρειλήφαμεν ἀλκῇ δια-

[1] γυναικῶν omitted by E, Bekker, Dindorf, Vogel, retained by Jacoby.

---

[1] Cp. Book 2. 44–6.
[2] This Dionysius, nicknamed Skytobrachion, "of the leathern arm," lived in Alexandria in the middle of the second century B.C. and composed a mythical romance from which

the only Amazons were those who are reported to have dwelt in the neighbourhood of the Thermodon river on the Pontus[1]; but the truth is otherwise, since the Amazons of Libya were much earlier in point of time and accomplished notable deeds. Now we are not unaware that to many who read this account the history of this people will appear to be a thing unheard of and entirely strange; for since the race of these Amazons disappeared entirely many generations before the Trojan War, whereas the women about the Thermodon river were in their full vigour a little before that time, it is not without reason that the later people, who were also better known, should have inherited the fame of the earlier, who are entirely unknown to most men because of the lapse of time. For our part, however, since we find that many early poets and historians, and not a few of the later ones as well, have made mention of them, we shall endeavour to recount their deeds in summary, following the account of Dionysius,[2] who composed a narrative about the Argonauts and Dionysus, and also about many other things which took place in the most ancient times.

Now there have been in Libya a number of races of women who were warlike and greatly admired for their manly vigour; for instance, tradition tells us of the race of the Gorgons, against whom, as the account is given, Perseus made war, a race dis-

Diodorus drew the following account of the Amazons and his description of the Atlantians (cc. 56, 57, 60, 61), of the Dionysus born in Libya (cc. 66. 4–73. 8), and of the Argonauts (Book 4. 40–55). The following account is an excellent example of the syncretism and rationalization of the old Greek myths.

φέρον· τὸ γὰρ τὸν Διὸς μὲν υἱόν, τῶν δὲ καθ᾽ ἑαυτὸν Ἑλλήνων ἄριστον, τελέσαι μέγιστον ἆθλον τὴν ἐπὶ ταύτας στρατείαν τεκμήριον ἄν τις λάβοι τῆς περὶ τὰς προειρημένας γυναῖκας ὑπεροχῆς τε καὶ δυνάμεως· ἥ τε τῶν νῦν μελλουσῶν ἱστορεῖσθαι ἀνδρεία παράδοξον ἔχει τὴν ὑπεροχὴν πρὸς τὰς καθ᾽ ἡμᾶς φύσεις τῶν γυναικῶν συγκρινομένη.

53. Φασὶ γὰρ ὑπάρξαι τῆς Λιβύης ἐν τοῖς πρὸς ἑσπέραν μέρεσιν ἐπὶ τοῖς πέρασι τῆς οἰκουμένης ἔθνος γυναικοκρατούμενον καὶ βίον ἐζηλωκὸς οὐχ ὅμοιον τῷ παρ᾽ ἡμῖν. ταῖς μὲν γὰρ γυναιξὶν ἔθος εἶναι διαπονεῖν τὰ κατὰ πόλεμον, καὶ χρόνους ὡρισμένους ὀφείλειν στρατεύεσθαι, διατηρουμένης τῆς παρθενίας· διελθόντων δὲ τῶν ἐτῶν τῶν τῆς στρατείας προσιέναι μὲν τοῖς ἀνδράσι παιδοποιίας ἕνεκα, τὰς δ᾽ ἀρχὰς καὶ τὰ κοινὰ διοικεῖν ταύτας

2 ἅπαντα. τοὺς δ᾽ ἄνδρας ὁμοίως ταῖς παρ᾽ ἡμῖν γαμεταῖς τὸν κατοικίδιον ἔχειν βίον, ὑπηρετοῦντας τοῖς ὑπὸ τῶν συνοικουσῶν προσταττομένοις· μὴ μετέχειν δ᾽ αὐτοὺς μήτε στρατείας μήτ᾽ ἀρχῆς μήτ᾽ ἄλλης τινὸς ἐν τοῖς κοινοῖς παρρησίας, ἐξ ἧς ἔμελλον φρονηματισθέντες ἐπιθήσεσθαι ταῖς

3 γυναιξί. κατὰ δὲ τὰς γενέσεις τῶν τέκνων τὰ μὲν βρέφη παραδίδοσθαι τοῖς ἀνδράσι, καὶ τούτους διατρέφειν αὐτὰ γάλακτι καὶ ἄλλοις τισὶν ἑψήμασιν οἰκείως ταῖς τῶν νηπίων ἡλικίαις· εἰ δὲ τύχοι θῆλυ γεννηθέν, ἐπικάεσθαι αὐτοῦ τοὺς μαστούς,

---

[1] i.e. Perseus. [2] Literally, "freedom of speech."

tinguished for its valour; for the fact that it was the son of Zeus,[1] the mightiest Greek of his day, who accomplished the campaign against these women, and that this was his greatest Labour may be taken by any man as proof of both the pre-eminence and the power of the women we have mentioned. Furthermore, the manly prowess of those of whom we are now about to write presupposes an amazing pre-eminence when compared with the nature of the women of our day.

53. We are told, namely, that there was once in the western parts of Libya, on the bounds of the inhabited world, a race which was ruled by women and followed a manner of life unlike that which prevails among us. For it was the custom among them that the women should practise the arts of war and be required to serve in the army for a fixed period, during which time they maintained their virginity; then, when the years of their service in the field had expired, they went in to the men for the procreation of children, but they kept in their hands the administration of the magistracies and of all the affairs of the state. The men, however, like our married women, spent their days about the house, carrying out the orders which were given them by their wives; and they took no part in military campaigns or in office or in the exercise of free citizenship[2] in the affairs of the community by virtue of which they might become presumptuous and rise up against the women. When their children were born the babies were turned over to the men, who brought them up on milk and such cooked foods as were appropriate to the age of the infants; and if it happened that a girl was born, its breasts were

ἵνα μὴ μετεωρίζωνται κατὰ τοὺς τῆς ἀκμῆς χρόνους· ἐμπόδιον γὰρ οὐ τὸ τυχὸν εἶναι δοκεῖν[1] πρὸς τὰς στρατείας τοὺς ἐξέχοντας τοῦ σώματος μαστούς· διὸ καὶ τούτων αὐτὰς ἀπεστερημένας ὑπὸ τῶν Ἑλλήνων Ἀμαζόνας προσαγορεύεσθαι.

4 Μυθολογοῦσι δ' αὐτὰς ᾠκηκέναι νῆσον τὴν ἀπὸ μὲν τοῦ πρὸς δυσμὰς ὑπάρχειν αὐτὴν Ἑσπέραν προσαγορευθεῖσαν, κειμένην δ' ἐν τῇ Τριτωνίδι λίμνῃ. ταύτην δὲ πλησίον ὑπάρχειν τοῦ περιέχοντος τὴν γῆν ὠκεανοῦ, προσαγορεῦσθαι δ' ἀπό τινος ἐμβάλλοντος εἰς αὐτὴν ποταμοῦ Τρίτωνος· κεῖσθαι δὲ τὴν λίμνην ταύτην πλησίον Αἰθιοπίας καὶ τοῦ παρὰ τὸν ὠκεανὸν ὄρους, ὃ μέγιστον μὲν ὑπάρχειν τῶν ἐν τοῖς τόποις καὶ προσπεπτωκὸς[2] εἰς τὸν ὠκεανόν, ὀνομάζεσθαι δ' ὑπὸ τῶν Ἑλλήνων 5 Ἄτλαντα. τὴν δὲ προειρημένην νῆσον ὑπάρχειν μὲν εὐμεγέθη καὶ πλήρη καρπίμων δένδρων παντοδαπῶν, ἀφ' ὧν πορίζεσθαι τὰς τροφὰς τοὺς ἐγχωρίους. ἔχειν δ' αὐτὴν καὶ κτηνῶν πλῆθος, αἰγῶν καὶ προβάτων, ἐξ ὧν γάλα καὶ κρέα πρὸς διατροφὴν ὑπάρχειν τοῖς κεκτημένοις· σίτῳ δὲ τὸ σύνολον μὴ χρῆσθαι τὸ ἔθνος διὰ τὸ μήπω τοῦ καρποῦ τούτου τὴν χρείαν εὑρεθῆναι παρ' αὐτοῖς.

6 Τὰς δ' οὖν Ἀμαζόνας ἀλκῇ διαφερούσας καὶ πρὸς πόλεμον ὡρμημένας τὸ μὲν πρῶτον τὰς ἐν τῇ νήσῳ πόλεις καταστρέφεσθαι πλὴν τῆς ὀνομαζομένης Μήνης, ἱερᾶς δ' εἶναι νομιζομένης, ἣν κατοικεῖσθαι μὲν ὑπ' Αἰθιόπων Ἰχθυοφάγων, ἔχειν δὲ πυρὸς ἐκφυσήματα μεγάλα καὶ λίθων πολυτελῶν πλῆθος τῶν ὀνομαζομένων παρ' Ἑλ-

---

[1] δοκεῖν Dindorf: δοκεῖ.

seared that they might not develop at the time of maturity; for they thought that the breasts, as they stood out from the body, were no small hindrance in warfare; and in fact it is because they have been deprived of their breasts that they are called by the Greeks Amazons.[1]

As mythology relates, their home was on an island which, because it was in the west, was called Hespera, and it lay in the marsh Tritonis. This marsh was near the ocean which surrounds the earth and received its name from a certain river Triton which emptied into it; and this marsh was also near Ethiopia and that mountain by the shore of the ocean·which is the highest of those in the vicinity and impinges upon the ocean and is called by the Greeks Atlas. The island mentioned above was of great size and full of fruit-bearing trees of every kind, from which the natives secured their food. It contained also a multitude of flocks and herds, namely, of goats and sheep, from which the possessors received milk and meat for their sustenance; but grain the nation used not at all because the use of this fruit of the earth had not yet been discovered among them.

The Amazons, then, the account continues, being a race superior in valour and eager for war, first of all subdued all the cities on the island except the one called Menê, which was considered to be sacred and was inhabited by Ethiopian Ichthyophagi, and was also subject to great eruptions of fire and possessed a multitude of the precious stones which the Greeks

---

[1] Cp. p. 33, note 1.

[2] προσπεπτωκὸς AB, Jacoby, προπεπτωκὸς other MSS., Dindorf, Bekker, Vogel.

λησιν ἀνθράκων καὶ σαρδίων καὶ σμαράγδων· μετὰ δὲ ταῦτα πολλοὺς τῶν πλησιοχώρων Λιβύων καὶ νομάδων καταπολεμῆσαι, καὶ κτίσαι πόλιν μεγάλην ἐντὸς τῆς Τριτωνίδος λίμνης, ἣν ἀπὸ τοῦ σχήματος ὀνομάσαι Χερρόνησον.

54. Ἐκ δὲ ταύτης ὁρμωμένας ἐγχειρῆσαι μεγάλαις ἐπιβολαῖς, ὁρμῆς αὐταῖς ἐμπεσούσης ἐπελθεῖν πολλὰ μέρη τῆς οἰκουμένης. ἐπὶ πρώτους δ' αὐτὰς στρατεῦσαι λέγεται τοὺς Ἀτλαντίους, ἄνδρας, ἡμερωτάτους τῶν ἐν τοῖς τόποις ἐκείνοις καὶ χώραν νεμομένους εὐδαίμονα καὶ πόλεις μεγάλας· παρ' οἷς δὴ μυθολογεῖσθαί φασι τὴν τῶν θεῶν γένεσιν ὑπάρξαι πρὸς τοῖς κατὰ τὸν ὠκεανὸν τόποις, συμφώνως τοῖς παρ' Ἕλλησι μυθολόγοις, περὶ ὧν τὰ κατὰ μέρος μικρὸν ὕστερον διέξιμεν.

2 Τῶν οὖν Ἀμαζόνων λέγεται βασιλεύουσαν Μύριναν συστήσασθαι στρατόπεδον πεζῶν μὲν τρισμυρίων, ἱππέων δὲ τρισχιλίων, ζηλουμένης παρ' αὐταῖς περιττότερον ἐν τοῖς πολέμοις τῆς ἀπὸ τῶν 3 ἱππέων χρείας. ὅπλοις δὲ χρῆσθαι σκεπαστηρίοις ὄφεων μεγάλων δοραῖς, ἐχούσης τῆς Λιβύης ταῦτα τὰ ζῷα τοῖς μεγέθεσιν ἄπιστα, ἀμυντηρίοις δὲ ξίφεσι καὶ λόγχαις,[1] ἔτι δὲ τόξοις, οἷς μὴ μόνον ἐξ ἐναντίας βάλλειν, ἀλλὰ καὶ κατὰ τὰς φυγὰς

τοῖς ξίφεσι καὶ ταῖς λόγχαις all MSS. but A.

---

[1] The *anthrax* was a precious stone of dark red colour, such as the carbuncle, ruby, and garnet; the *sardion* included our cornelian and sardine; the *smaragdos* was any green stone.

call *anthrax*, *sardion*, and *smaragdos* [1]; and after this they subdued many of the neighbouring Libyans and nomad tribes, and founded within the marsh Tritonis a great city which they named Cherronesus [2] after its shape.

54. Setting out from the city of Cherronesus, the account continues, the Amazons embarked upon great ventures, a longing having come over them to invade many parts of the inhabited world. The first people against whom they advanced, according to the tale, was the Atlantians, the most civilized men among the inhabitants of those regions, who dwelt in a prosperous country and possessed great cities; it was among them, we are told, that mythology places the birth of the gods, in the regions which lie along the shore of the ocean, in this respect agreeing with those among the Greeks who relate legends, and about this [3] we shall speak in detail a little later.

Now the queen of the Amazons, Myrina, collected, it is said, an army of thirty thousand foot-soldiers and three thousand cavalry, since they favoured to an unusual degree the use of cavalry in their wars.[4] For protective devices they used the skins of large snakes, since Libya contains such animals of incredible size, and for offensive weapons, swords and lances; they also used bows and arrows, with which they struck not only when facing the enemy but also when in flight, by shooting backwards at their

---

[2] *i.e.* "Peninsula"; presumably the city lay on a ridge of land running out into the marsh.

[3] *i.e.* the birth of the gods; cp. chap. 56 below.

[4] A strange statement, in connection with so small a number of cavalry. Perhaps the numbers should be transposed.

τοὺς ἐπιδιώκοντας εἰς τοὐπίσω τοξεύειν εὐστόχως. 4 ἐμβαλούσας δ' αὐτὰς εἰς τὴν τῶν Ἀτλαντίων χώραν τοὺς μὲν τὴν Κέρνην καλουμένην οἰκοῦντας παρατάξει νικῆσαι, καὶ συνεισπεσούσας τοῖς φεύγουσιν ἐντὸς τῶν τειχῶν κυριεῦσαι τῆς πόλεως· βουλομένας δὲ τῷ φόβῳ καταπλήξασθαι τοὺς περιοίκους ὠμῶς προσενεχθῆναι τοῖς ἁλοῦσι, καὶ τοὺς μὲν ἄνδρας ἡβηδὸν ἀποσφάξαι, τέκνα δὲ καὶ γυναῖκας ἐξανδραποδισαμένας κατασκάψαι τὴν 5 πόλιν. τῆς δὲ περὶ τοὺς Κερναίους συμφορᾶς διαδοθείσης εἰς τοὺς ὁμοεθνεῖς, λέγεται τοὺς μὲν Ἀτλαντίους καταπλαγέντας δι' ὁμολογίας παραδοῦναι τὰς πόλεις καὶ πᾶν τὸ προσταχθὲν ποιήσειν ἐπαγγείλασθαι, τὴν δὲ βασίλισσαν Μύριναν ἐπιεικῶς αὐτοῖς προσενεχθεῖσαν φιλίαν τε συνθέσθαι καὶ πόλιν ἀντὶ τῆς κατασκαφείσης ὁμώνυμον ἑαυτῆς κτίσαι· κατοικίσαι δ' εἰς αὐτὴν τούς τε αἰχμαλώτους καὶ τῶν ἐγχωρίων τὸν βουλόμενον. 6 μετὰ δὲ ταῦτα τῶν Ἀτλαντίων δῶρά τε μεγαλοπρεπῆ δόντων αὐτῇ καὶ τιμὰς ἀξιολόγους κοινῇ ψηφισαμένων, ἀποδέξασθαί τε τὴν φιλανθρωπίαν αὐτῶν καὶ προσεπαγγείλασθαι τὸ ἔθνος 7 εὐεργετήσειν. τῶν δ' ἐγχωρίων πεπολεμημένων πολλάκις ὑπὸ τῶν ὀνομαζομένων Γοργόνων, οὐσῶν πλησιοχώρων, καὶ τὸ σύνολον ἔφεδρον ἐχόντων[1] τοῦτο τὸ ἔθνος, φασὶν ἀξιωθεῖσαν τὴν Μύριναν ὑπὸ τῶν Ἀτλαντίων ἐμβαλεῖν εἰς τὴν χώραν τῶν προειρημένων. ἀντιταξαμένων δὲ τῶν Γοργόνων γενέσθαι καρτερὰν μάχην, καὶ τὰς Ἀμαζόνας ἐπὶ τοῦ προτερήματος γενομένας ἀνελεῖν μὲν τῶν ἀντιταχθεισῶν παμπληθεῖς, ζωγρῆσαι δ' οὐκ

[1] So Eichstädt: ἐχουσῶν.

pursuers with good effect. Upon entering the land of the Atlantians they defeated in a pitched battle the inhabitants of the city of Cernê, as it is called, and making their way inside the walls along with the fleeing enemy, they got the city into their hands; and desiring to strike terror into the neighbouring peoples they treated the captives savagely, put to the sword the men from the youth upward, led into slavery the children and women, and razed the city. But when the terrible fate of the inhabitants of Cernê became known among their fellow tribesmen, it is related that the Atlantians, struck with terror, surrendered their cities on terms of capitulation and announced that they would do whatever should be commanded them, and that the queen Myrina, bearing herself honourably towards the Atlantians, both established friendship with them and founded a city to bear her name in place of the city which had been razed; and in it she settled both the captives and any native who so desired. Whereupon the Atlantians presented her with magnificent presents and by public decree voted to her notable honours, and she in return accepted their courtesy and in addition promised that she would show kindness to their nation. And since the natives were often being warred upon by the Gorgons, as they were named, a folk which resided upon their borders, and in general had that people lying in wait to injure them, Myrina, they say, was asked by the Atlantians to invade the land of the afore-mentioned Gorgons. But when the Gorgons drew up their forces to resist them a mighty battle took place in which the Amazons, gaining the upper hand, slew great numbers of their opponents and took no fewer than

ἐλάττους τρισχιλίων· τῶν δ' ἄλλων εἴς τινα δρυμώδη τόπον συμφυγουσῶν ἐπιβαλέσθαι μὲν τὴν Μύριναν ἐμπρῆσαι τὴν ὕλην, σπεύδουσαν ἄρδην ἀνελεῖν τὸ ἔθνος, οὐ δυνηθεῖσαν δὲ κρατῆσαι τῆς ἐπιβολῆς ἐπανελθεῖν ἐπὶ τοὺς ὅρους τῆς χώρας·

55. Τῶν δ' Ἀμαζόνων νυκτὸς τὰ περὶ τὰς φυλακὰς ῥᾳθυμουσῶν διὰ τὴν εὐημερίαν, ἐπιθεμένας τὰς αἰχμαλωτίδας, σπασαμένας τὰ ξίφη τῶν δοκουσῶν κεκρατηκέναι πολλὰς ἀνελεῖν· τέλος δὲ τοῦ πλήθους αὐτὰς πανταχόθεν περιχυθέντος εὐγε-
2 νῶς μαχομένας ἁπάσας κατακοπῆναι. τὴν δὲ Μύριναν θάψασαν τὰς ἀναιρεθείσας τῶν συστρατευουσῶν ἐν τρισὶ πυραῖς χωμάτων μεγάλων ἐπιστῆσαι τάφους τρεῖς, οὓς μέχρι τοῦ νῦν Ἀμα-
3 ζόνων σωροὺς ὀνομάζεσθαι. τὰς δὲ Γοργόνας ἐν τοῖς ὕστερον χρόνοις αὐξηθείσας πάλιν ὑπὸ Περσέως τοῦ Διὸς καταπολεμηθῆναι, καθ' ὃν καιρὸν ἐβασίλευεν αὐτῶν Μέδουσα· τὸ δὲ τελευταῖον ὑφ' Ἡρακλέους ἄρδην ἀναιρεθῆναι ταύτας τε καὶ τὸ τῶν Ἀμαζόνων ἔθνος, καθ' ὃν καιρὸν τοὺς πρὸς ἑσπέραν τόπους ἐπελθὼν ἔθετο τὰς ἐπὶ τῆς Λιβύης στήλας, δεινὸν ἡγούμενος, εἰ προελόμενος τὸ γένος κοινῇ τῶν ἀνθρώπων εὐεργετεῖν περιόψεταί τινα τῶν ἐθνῶν γυναικοκρατούμενα. λέγεται δὲ καὶ τὴν Τριτωνίδα λίμνην σεισμῶν γενομένων ἀφανισθῆναι, ῥαγέντων αὐτῆς τῶν πρὸς τὸν ὠκεανὸν μερῶν κεκλιμένων.

4 Τὴν δὲ Μύρινάν φασι τῆς τε Λιβύης τὴν πλείστην ἐπελθεῖν, καὶ παραβαλοῦσαν εἰς Αἴγυπτον πρὸς

three thousand prisoners; and since the rest had fled for refuge into a certain wooded region, Myrina undertook to set fire to the timber, being eager to destroy the race utterly, but when she found that she was unable to succeed in her attempt she retired to the borders of her country.

55. Now as the Amazons, they go on to say, relaxed their watch during the night because of their success, the captive women, falling upon them and drawing the swords of those who thought they were conquerors, slew many of them; in the end, however, the multitude poured in about them from every side and the prisoners fighting bravely were butchered one and all. Myrina accorded a funeral to her fallen comrades on three pyres and raised up three great heaps of earth as tombs, which are called to this day " Amazon Mounds." But the Gorgons, grown strong again in later days, were subdued a second time by Perseus, the son of Zeus, when Medusa was queen over them; and in the end both they and the race of the Amazons were entirely destroyed by Heracles, when he visited the regions to the west and set up his pillars [1] in Libya, since he felt that it would ill accord with his resolve to be the benefactor of the whole race of mankind if he should suffer any nations to be under the rule of women. The story is also told that the marsh Tritonis disappeared from sight in the course of an earthquake, when those parts of it which lay towards the ocean were torn asunder.

As for Myrina, the account continues, she visited the larger part of Libya, and passing over into

[1] Cp. Book 4. 18.

μὲν Ὧρον τὸν Ἴσιδος βασιλεύοντα τότε τῆς Αἰγύπτου φιλίαν συνθέσθαι, πρὸς δ' Ἄραβας διαπολεμήσασαν καὶ πολλοὺς αὐτῶν ἀνελοῦσαν, τὴν μὲν Συρίαν καταστρέψασθαι, τῶν δὲ Κιλίκων ἀπαντησάντων αὐτῇ μετὰ δώρων καὶ τὸ κελευόμενον ποιήσειν ὁμολογούντων, ἐλευθέρους ἀφεῖναι τοὺς ἑκουσίως προσχωρήσαντας, οὓς ἀπὸ ταύτης τῆς αἰτίας μέχρι τοῦ νῦν Ἐλευθεροκίλικας καλεῖ-
5 σθαι. καταπολεμῆσαι δ' αὐτὴν καὶ τὰ περὶ τὸν Ταῦρον ἔθνη, διάφορα ταῖς ἀλκαῖς ὄντα, καὶ διὰ Φρυγίας τῆς μεγάλης ἐπὶ θάλατταν καταβῆναι· ἑξῆς δὲ τὴν παραθαλάττιον χώραν προσαγαγομένην ὅρους θέσθαι τῆς στρατείας
6 τὸν Κάϊκον ποταμόν. τῆς δὲ δορικτήτου χώρας ἐκλεξαμένην τοὺς εὐθέτους τόπους εἰς πόλεων κτίσεις οἰκοδομῆσαι πλείους πόλεις, καὶ τούτων ὁμώνυμον μίαν ἑαυτῇ κτίσαι, τὰς δ' ἄλλας ἀπὸ τῶν τὰς ἡγεμονίας τὰς μεγίστας ἐχουσῶν, Κύμην, Πιτάναν, Πριήνην.

7 Ταύτας μὲν οὖν οἰκίσαι παρὰ θάλατταν, ἄλλας δὲ πλείους ἐν τοῖς πρὸς μεσόγειον ἀνήκουσι τόποις. κατασχεῖν δ' αὐτὴν καὶ τῶν νήσων τινάς, καὶ μάλιστα τὴν Λέσβον, ἐν ᾗ κτίσαι πόλιν Μυτιλήνην ὁμώνυμον τῇ μετεχούσῃ τῆς στρατείας ἀδελφῇ.
8 ἔπειτα καὶ τῶν ἄλλων νήσων τινὰς καταστρεφομένην χειμασθῆναι, καὶ ποιησαμένην τῇ μητρὶ τῶν θεῶν εὐχὰς ὑπὲρ τῆς σωτηρίας προσενεχθῆναι νήσῳ τινὶ τῶν ἐρήμων· ταύτην δὲ κατά τινα ἐν

---

[1] The Mediterranean.
[2] This river flows past Pergamum and empties into the Aegean Sea.

BOOK III. 55. 4-8

Egypt she struck a treaty of friendship with Horus, the son of Isis, who was king of Egypt at that time, and then, after making war to the end upon the Arabians and slaying many of them, she subdued Syria; but when the Cilicians came out with presents to meet her and agreed to obey her commands, she left those free who yielded to her of their free will and for this reason these are called to this day the "Free Cilicians." She also conquered in war the races in the region of the Taurus, peoples of outstanding courage, and descended through Greater Phrygia to the sea[1]; then she won over the land lying along the coast and fixed the bounds of her campaign at the Caïcus River.[2] And selecting in the territory which she had won by arms sites well suited for the founding of cities, she built a considerable number of them and founded one[3] which bore her own name, but the others she named after the women who held the most important commands, such as Cymê, Pitana, and Prienê.

These, then, are the cities she settled along the sea, but others, and a larger number, she planted in the regions stretching towards the interior. She seized also some of the islands, and Lesbos in particular, on which she founded the city of Mitylenê, which was named after her sister who took part in the campaign. After that, while subduing some of the rest of the islands, she was caught in a storm, and after she had offered up prayers for her safety to the Mother of the Gods,[4] she was carried to one of the uninhabited islands; this island, in obedience

[3] The city of Myrina in Mysia; cp. Strabo 13. 3. 6.
[4] Cybelê.

τοῖς ὀνείροις φαντασίαν καθιερῶσαι τῇ προειρημένῃ θεῷ καὶ βωμοὺς ἱδρύσασθαι καὶ θυσίας μεγαλοπρεπεῖς ἐπιτελέσαι· ὀνομάσαι δ' αὐτὴν Σαμοθρᾴκην, ὅπερ εἶναι μεθερμηνευόμενον εἰς τὴν Ἑλληνικὴν διάλεκτον ἱερὰν νῆσον· ἔνιοι δὲ τῶν ἱστορικῶν λέγουσι τὸ πρὸ τοῦ Σάμον αὐτὴν καλουμένην ὑπὸ τῶν κατοικούντων ἐν αὐτῇ ποτε 9 Θρᾳκῶν Σαμοθρᾴκην ὀνομασθῆναι. οὐ μὴν ἀλλὰ τῶν Ἀμαζόνων ἐπανελθουσῶν εἰς τὴν ἤπειρον μυθολογοῦσι τὴν μητέρα τῶν θεῶν εὐαρεστηθεῖσαν τῇ νήσῳ ἄλλους τέ τινας ἐν αὐτῇ κατοικίσαι καὶ τοὺς ἑαυτῆς υἱοὺς τοὺς ὀνομαζομένους Κορύβαντας· ἐξ οὗ δ' εἰσὶ πατρὸς ἐν ἀπορρήτῳ κατὰ τὴν τελετὴν παραδίδοσθαι· καταδεῖξαι δὲ καὶ τὰ νῦν ἐν αὐτῇ συντελούμενα μυστήρια καὶ τὸ τέμενος ἄσυλον νομοθετῆσαι.

10 Περὶ δὲ τούτους τοὺς χρόνους Μόψον τὸν Θρᾷκα, φυγάδα γενόμενον ὑπὸ Λυκούργου τοῦ βασιλέως τῶν Θρᾳκῶν, ἐμβαλεῖν εἰς τὴν χώραν τῶν Ἀμαζόνων μετὰ στρατιᾶς τῆς συνεκπεσούσης αὐτῷ· συστρατεῦσαι δὲ καὶ Σίπυλον τῷ Μόψῳ τὸν Σκύθην, πεφυγαδευμένον ὁμοίως ἐκ τῆς ὁμόρου 11 τῇ Θρᾴκῃ Σκυθίας. γενομένης δὲ παρατάξεως, καὶ τῶν περὶ τὸν Σίπυλον καὶ Μόψον προτερησάντων, τήν τε βασίλισσαν τῶν Ἀμαζόνων Μύριναν ἀναιρεθῆναι καὶ τῶν ἄλλων τὰς πλείους. τοῦ δὲ χρόνου προβαίνοντος, καὶ κατὰ τὰς μάχας ἀεὶ τῶν Θρᾳκῶν ἐπικρατούντων, τὸ τελευταῖον τὰς περιλειφθείσας τῶν Ἀμαζόνων ἀνακάμψαι πάλιν εἰς Λιβύην. καὶ τὴν μὲν στρατείαν τῶν ἀπὸ Λιβύης Ἀμαζόνων μυθολογοῦσι τοιοῦτο λαβεῖν τὸ πέρας.

BOOK III. 55. 8–11

to a vision which she beheld in her dreams, she made sacred to this goddess, and set up altars there and offered magnificent sacrifices. She also gave it the name of Samothrace, which means, when translated into Greek, "sacred island," although some historians say that it was formerly called Samos and was then given the name of Samothrace by Thracians who at one time dwelt on it. However, after the Amazons had returned to the continent, the myth relates, the Mother of the Gods, well pleased with the island, settled in it certain other people, and also her own sons, who are known by the name of Corybantes—who their father was is handed down in their rites as a matter not to be divulged; and she established the mysteries which are now celebrated on the island and ordained by law that the sacred area should enjoy the right of sanctuary.

In these times, they go on to say, Mopsus the Thracian, who had been exiled by Lycurgus, the king of the Thracians, invaded the land of the Amazons with an army composed of fellow-exiles, and with Mopsus on the campaign was also Sipylus the Scythian, who had likewise been exiled from that part of Scythia which borders upon Thrace. There was a pitched battle, Sipylus and Mopsus gained the upper hand, and Myrina, the queen of the Amazons, and the larger part of the rest of her army were slain. In the course of the years, as the Thracians continued to be victorious in their battles, the surviving Amazons finally withdrew again into Libya. And such was the end, as the myth relates, of the campaign which the Amazons of Libya made.

DIODORUS OF SICILY

56. Ἡμεῖς δ' ἐπειδὴ περὶ τῶν Ἀτλαντίων ἐμνήσθημεν, οὐκ ἀνοίκειον ἡγούμεθα διελθεῖν τὰ μυθολογούμενα παρ' αὐτοῖς περὶ τῆς τῶν θεῶν γενέσεως, διὰ τὸ μὴ πολὺ διαλλάττειν αὐτὰ τῶν μυθολογου-
2 μένων παρ' Ἕλλησιν. οἱ τοίνυν Ἀτλάντιοι τοὺς παρὰ τὸν ὠκεανὸν τόπους κατοικοῦντες καὶ χώραν εὐδαίμονα νεμόμενοι πολὺ[1] μὲν εὐσεβείᾳ καὶ φιλανθρωπίᾳ τῇ πρὸς τοὺς ξένους δοκοῦσι διαφέρειν τῶν πλησιοχώρων, τὴν δὲ γένεσιν τῶν θεῶν παρ' αὐτοῖς γενέσθαι φασί. συμφωνεῖν δὲ τοῖς λεγομένοις ὑπ' αὐτῶν καὶ τὸν ἐπιφανέστατον τῶν παρ' Ἕλλησι ποιητῶν ἐν οἷς παρεισάγει τὴν Ἥραν λέγουσαν

εἶμι γὰρ ὀψομένη πολυφόρβου πείρατα γαίης,
Ὠκεανόν τε θεῶν γένεσιν καὶ μητέρα Τηθύν.

3 Μυθολογοῦσι δὲ πρῶτον παρ' αὐτοῖς Οὐρανὸν βασιλεῦσαι καὶ τοὺς ἀνθρώπους σποράδην οἰκοῦντας συναγαγεῖν εἰς πόλεως περίβολον, καὶ τῆς μὲν ἀνομίας καὶ τοῦ θηριώδους βίου παῦσαι τοὺς ὑπακούοντας, εὑρόντα τὰς τῶν ἡμέρων καρπῶν χρείας καὶ παραθέσεις καὶ τῶν ἄλλων τῶν χρησίμων οὐκ ὀλίγα· κατακτήσασθαι δ' αὐτὸν καὶ τῆς οἰκουμένης τὴν πλείστην, καὶ μάλιστα τοὺς πρὸς
4 τὴν ἑσπέραν καὶ τὴν ἄρκτον τόπους. τῶν δὲ ἄστρων γενόμενον ἐπιμελῆ παρατηρητὴν πολλὰ προλέγειν τῶν κατὰ τὸν κόσμον μελλόντων γίνεσθαι· εἰσηγήσασθαι δὲ τοῖς ὄχλοις τὸν μὲν ἐνιαυτὸν ἀπὸ τῆς τοῦ ἡλίου κινήσεως, τοὺς δὲ μῆνας ἀπὸ τῆς[2]

---

[1] πολὺ Dindorf, Bekker, πολλῷ Vogel, πολλῇ MSS.
[2] τῆς added by Oldfather.

BOOK III. 56. 1-4

56. But since we have made mention of the Atlantians, we believe that it will not be inappropriate in this place to recount what their myths relate about the genesis of the gods, in view of the fact that it does not differ greatly from the myths of the Greeks. Now the Atlantians, dwelling as they do in the regions on the edge of the ocean and inhabiting a fertile territory, are reputed far to excel their neighbours in reverence towards the gods and the humanity they showed in their dealings with strangers, and the gods, they say, were born among them. And their account, they maintain, is in agreement with that of the most renowned of the Greek poets [1] when he represents Hera as saying:

> For I go to see the ends of the bountiful earth,
> Oceanus source of the gods and Tethys divine
> Their mother.

This is the account given in their myth: Their first king was Uranus, and he gathered the human beings, who dwelt in scattered habitations, within the shelter of a walled city and caused his subjects to cease from their lawless ways and their bestial manner of living, discovering for them the uses of cultivated fruits, how to store them up, and not a few other things which are of benefit to man; and he also subdued the larger part of the inhabited earth, in particular the regions to the west and the north. And since he was a careful observer of the stars he foretold many things which would take place throughout the world; and for the common people he introduced the year on the basis of the movement of the sun and the months on that of the

[1] Homer; the lines are from the *Iliad* 14. 200-1.

τῆς σελήνης, καὶ τὰς κατ' ἔτος ἕκαστον ὥρας
5 διδάξαι. διὸ καὶ τοὺς πολλούς, ἀγνοοῦντας μὲν
τὴν τῶν ἄστρων αἰώνιον τάξιν, θαυμάζοντας δὲ
τὰ γινόμενα κατὰ τὰς προρρήσεις, ὑπολαβεῖν τὸν
τούτων εἰσηγητὴν θείας μετέχειν φύσεως, μετὰ δὲ
τὴν ἐξ ἀνθρώπων αὐτοῦ μετάστασιν διά τε τὰς
εὐεργεσίας καὶ τὴν τῶν ἄστρων ἐπίγνωσιν ἀθανάτους τιμὰς ἀπονεῖμαι· μεταγαγεῖν δ' αὐτοῦ τὴν
προσηγορίαν ἐπὶ τὸν κόσμον, ἅμα μὲν τῷ δοκεῖν
οἰκείως ἐσχηκέναι πρὸς τὰς τῶν ἄστρων ἐπιτολάς
τε καὶ δύσεις καὶ τἆλλα τὰ γινόμενα περὶ τὸν
κόσμον, ἅμα δὲ τῷ μεγέθει τῶν τιμῶν ὑπερβάλλειν
τὰς εὐεργεσίας, καὶ πρὸς τὸν αἰῶνα βασιλέα τῶν
ὅλων αὐτὸν ἀναγορεύσαντας.

57. Οὐρανοῦ δὲ μυθολογοῦσι γενέσθαι παῖδας ἐκ
πλειόνων γυναικῶν πέντε πρὸς τοῖς τετταράκοντα,
καὶ τούτων ὀκτωκαίδεκα λέγουσιν ὑπάρχειν ἐκ
Τιταίας ὄνομα μὲν ἴδιον ἔχοντας ἑκάστου, κοινῇ
δὲ πάντας ἀπὸ τῆς μητρὸς ὀνομαζομένους Τιτᾶνας.
2 τὴν δὲ Τιταίαν, σώφρονα οὖσαν καὶ πολλῶν
ἀγαθῶν αἰτίαν γενομένην τοῖς λαοῖς, ἀποθεωθῆ-
ναι μετὰ τὴν τελευτὴν ὑπὸ τῶν εὖ παθόντων
Γῆν μετονομασθεῖσαν. γενέσθαι δ' αὐτῷ καὶ
θυγατέρας, ὧν εἶναι δύο τὰς πρεσβυτάτας πολὺ
τῶν ἄλλων ἐπιφανεστάτας, τήν τε καλουμένην
Βασίλειαν καὶ Ῥέαν τὴν ὑπ' ἐνίων Πανδώραν
3 ὀνομασθεῖσαν. τούτων δὲ τὴν μὲν Βασίλειαν,
πρεσβυτάτην οὖσαν καὶ σωφροσύνῃ τε καὶ συνέσει
πολὺ τῶν ἄλλων διαφέρουσαν, ἐκθρέψαι πάντας
τοὺς ἀδελφοὺς κοινῇ μητρὸς εὔνοιαν παρεχομέ-

moon, and instructed them in the seasons which recur year after year. Consequently the masses of the people, being ignorant of the eternal arrangement of the stars and marvelling at the events which were taking place as he had predicted, conceived that the man who taught such things partook of the nature of the gods, and after he had passed from among men they accorded to him immortal honours, both because of his benefactions and because of his knowledge of the stars; and then they transferred his name to the firmament of heaven, both because they thought that he had been so intimately acquainted with the risings and the settings of the stars and with whatever else took place in the firmament, and because they would surpass his benefactions by the magnitude of the honours which they would show him, in that for all subsequent time they proclaimed him to be the king of the universe.

57. To Uranus, the myth continues, were born forty-five sons from a number of wives, and, of these, eighteen, it is said, were by Titaea, each of them bearing a distinct name, but all of them as a group were called, after their mother, Titans. Titaea, because she was prudent and had brought about many good deeds for the peoples, was deified after her death by those whom she had helped and her name was changed to Gê. To Uranus were also born daughters, the two eldest of whom were by far the most renowned above the others and were called Basileia and Rhea, whom some also named Pandora. Of these daughters Basileia, who was the eldest and far excelled the others in both prudence and understanding, reared all her brothers, showing them collectively a mother's kindness; consequently she was

νην· διὸ καὶ μεγάλην μητέρα προσαγορευθῆναι· μετὰ δὲ τὴν τοῦ πατρὸς ἐξ ἀνθρώπων εἰς θεοὺς μετάστασιν, συγχωρούντων τῶν ὄχλων καὶ τῶν ἀδελφῶν, διαδέξασθαι τὴν βασιλείαν παρθένον οὖσαν ἔτι[1] καὶ διὰ τὴν ὑπερβολὴν τῆς σωφροσύνης οὐδενὶ συνοικῆσαι βουληθεῖσαν. ὕστερον δὲ βουλομένην διαδόχους τῆς βασιλείας ἀπολιπεῖν υἱούς, Ὑπερίονι συνοικῆσαι τῶν ἀδελφῶν ἑνί, πρὸς ὃν 4 οἰκειότατα διέκειτο. γενομένων δ' αὐτῇ δύο τέκνων, Ἡλίου καὶ Σελήνης, καὶ θαυμαζομένων ἐπί τε τῷ κάλλει καὶ τῇ σωφροσύνῃ, φασὶ τοὺς ἀδελφοὺς ταύτῃ μὲν ἐπ' εὐτεκνίᾳ φθονοῦντας, τὸν δ' Ὑπερίονα φοβηθέντας μήποτε τὴν βασιλείαν εἰς αὑτὸν περισπάσῃ, πρᾶξιν ἐπιτελέσασθαι παντε- 5 λῶς ἀνόσιον. συνωμοσίαν γὰρ ποιησαμένους τὸν μὲν Ὑπερίονα κατασφάξαι, τὸν δ' Ἥλιον ὄντα παῖδα τὴν ἡλικίαν ἐμβαλόντας εἰς τὸν Ἠριδανὸν ποταμὸν ἀποπνῖξαι· καταφανοῦς δὲ γενομένης τῆς ἀτυχίας, τὴν μὲν Σελήνην φιλάδελφον οὖσαν καθ' ὑπερβολὴν ἀπὸ τοῦ τέγους ἑαυτὴν ῥῖψαι, τὴν δὲ μητέρα ζητοῦσαν τὸ σῶμα παρὰ τὸν ποταμὸν σύγκοπον γενέσθαι, καὶ κατενεχθεῖσαν εἰς ὕπνον ἰδεῖν ὄψιν, καθ' ἣν ἔδοξεν ἐπιστάντα τὸν Ἥλιον παρακαλεῖν αὐτὴν μὴ θρηνεῖν τὸν τῶν τέκνων θάνατον· τοὺς μὲν γὰρ Τιτᾶνας τεύξεσθαι τῆς προσηκούσης τιμωρίας, ἑαυτὸν δὲ καὶ τὴν ἀδελφήν εἰς ἀθανάτους φύσεις μετασχηματισθήσεσθαι θείᾳ τινὶ προνοίᾳ· ὀνομασθήσεσθαι γὰρ ὑπὸ τῶν ἀνθρώπων ἥλιον μὲν τὸ πρότερον ἐν οὐρανῷ πῦρ ἱερὸν καλούμενον,

[1] ἔτι Bekker: ἔτι δέ.

---

[1] The "sun" and the "moon" respectively.

given the appellation of "Great Mother;" and after her father had been translated from among men into the circle of the gods, with the approval of the masses and of her brothers she succeeded to the royal dignity, though she was still a maiden and because of her exceedingly great chastity had been unwilling to unite in marriage with any man. But later, because of her desire to leave sons who should succeed to the throne, she united in marriage with Hyperion, one of her brothers, for whom she had the greatest affection. And when there were born to her two children, Helius and Selenê,[1] who were greatly admired for both their beauty and their chastity, the brothers of Basileia, they say, being envious of her because of her happy issue of children and fearing that Hyperion would divert the royal power to himself, committed an utterly impious deed; for entering into a conspiracy among themselves they put Hyperion to the sword, and casting Helius, who was still in years a child, into the Eridanus[2] river, drowned him. When this crime came to light, Selenê, who loved her brother very greatly, threw herself down from the roof, but as for his mother, while seeking his body along the river, her strength left her and falling into a swoon she beheld a vision in which she thought that Helius stood over her and urged her not to mourn the death of her children; for, he said, the Titans would meet the punishment which they deserve, while he and his sister would be transformed, by some divine providence, into immortal natures, since that which had formerly been called the "holy fire" in the heavens would be called by men Helius ("the sun") and that

[2] The Po.

6 σελήνην δὲ τὴν μήνην προσαγορευομένην. διεγερθεῖσαν δὲ καὶ τοῖς ὄχλοις τόν τε ὄνειρον καὶ τὰ περὶ αὐτὴν ἀτυχήματα διελθοῦσαν ἀξιῶσαι τοῖς μὲν τετελευτηκόσιν ἀπονεῖμαι τιμὰς ἰσοθέους, τοῦ δ' αὐτῆς σώματος μηκέτι μηδένα θιγεῖν. 7 μετὰ δὲ ταῦτα ἐμμανῆ γενομένην καὶ τῶν τῆς θυγατρὸς παιγνίων τὰ δυνάμενα ψόφον ἐπιτελεῖν ἁρπάσασαν πλανᾶσθαι κατὰ τὴν χώραν, λελυμένην[1] μὲν τὰς τρίχας, τῷ δὲ διὰ τῶν τυμπάνων καὶ κυμβάλων ψόφῳ ἐνθεάζουσαν, ὥστε καταπλήτ- 8 τεσθαι τοὺς ὁρῶντας. πάντων δὲ τὸ περὶ αὐτὴν πάθος ἐλεούντων, καί τινων ἀντεχομένων τοῦ σώματος, ἐπιγενέσθαι πλῆθος ὄμβρου καὶ συνεχεῖς κεραυνῶν πτώσεις· ἐνταῦθα δὲ τὴν μὲν Βασίλειαν ἀφανῆ γενέσθαι, τοὺς δ' ὄχλους θαυμάσαντας τὴν περιπέτειαν τὸν μὲν Ἥλιον καὶ τὴν Σελήνην τῇ προσηγορίᾳ καὶ ταῖς τιμαῖς μεταγαγεῖν ἐπὶ τὰ κατ' οὐρανὸν ἄστρα, τὴν δὲ μητέρα τούτων θεόν τε νομίσαι καὶ βωμοὺς ἱδρύσασθαι, καὶ ταῖς διὰ τῶν τυμπάνων καὶ κυμβάλων ἐνεργείαις καὶ τοῖς ἄλλοις ἅπασιν ἀπομιμουμένους τὰ περὶ αὐτὴν συμβάντα θυσίας καὶ τὰς ἄλλας τιμὰς ἀπονεῖμαι.

58. Παραδέδοται δὲ τῆς θεοῦ ταύτης καὶ κατὰ τὴν Φρυγίαν γένεσις. οἱ γὰρ ἐγχώριοι μυθολογοῦσι τὸ παλαιὸν γενέσθαι βασιλέα Φρυγίας καὶ

[1] So Eusebius (*Praep. Ev.* 2. 2. 39): καταλελυμένην.

BOOK III. 57. 5–58. 1

addressed as "menê" would be called Selenê ("the moon"). When she was aroused from the swoon she recounted to the common crowd both the dream and the misfortunes which had befallen her, asking that they render to the dead honours like those accorded to the gods and asserting that no man should thereafter touch her body. And after this she became frenzied, and seizing such of her daughter's playthings as could make a noise, she began to wander over the land, with her hair hanging free, inspired by the noise of the kettledrums and cymbals, so that those who saw her were struck with astonishment. And all men were filled with pity at her misfortune and some were clinging to her body,[1] when there came a mighty storm and continuous crashes of thunder and lightning; and in the midst of this Basileia passed from sight, whereupon the crowds of people, amazed at this reversal of fortune, transferred the names and the honours of Helius and Selenê to the stars of the sky, and as for their mother, they considered her to be a goddess and erected altars to her, and imitating the incidents of her life by the pounding of the kettledrums and the clash of the cymbals they rendered unto her in this way sacrifices and all other honours.

58. However, an account is handed down also that this goddess[2] was born in Phrygia. For the natives of that country have the following myth: In ancient times Meïon became king of Phrygia and Lydia;

---

[1] Cp. the scene in Sophocles, *Oedipus at Colonus*, 1620–1, immediately before Oedipus passes from earth in the storm:

  So clinging to each other sobbed and wept
  Father and daughters both.
    (tr. by Storr in the *L.C.L.*)

[2] *i.e.* the Magna Mater.

Λυδίας Μήονα· γήμαντα δὲ Δινδύμην γεννῆσαι μὲν παιδίον θῆλυ, τρέφειν δ' αὐτὸ μὴ βουλόμενον εἰς ὄρος ἐκθεῖναι τὸ προσαγορευόμενον Κύβελον. ἐνταῦθα τῷ παιδίῳ κατά τινα θείαν πρόνοιαν τάς τε παρδάλεις καί τινα τῶν ἄλλων τῶν ἀλκῇ διαφερόντων θηρίων παρέχεσθαι τὴν θηλὴν καὶ

2 διατρέφειν, γύναια δέ τινα περὶ τὸν τόπον ποιμαίνοντα κατιδεῖν τὸ γινόμενον, καὶ θαυμάσαντα τὴν περιπέτειαν ἀνελέσθαι τὸ βρέφος, καὶ προσαγορεῦσαι Κυβέλην ἀπὸ τοῦ τόπου. αὐξομένην δὲ τὴν παῖδα τῷ τε κάλλει καὶ σωφροσύνῃ διενεγκεῖν, ἔτι δὲ συνέσει γενέσθαι θαυμαστήν· τήν τε γὰρ πολυκάλαμον σύριγγα πρώτην ἐπινοῆσαι καὶ πρὸς τὰς παιδιὰς καὶ χορείας εὑρεῖν κύμβαλα καὶ τύμπανα, πρὸς δὲ τούτοις καθαρμοὺς τῶν νοσούντων κτηνῶν τε καὶ νηπίων παίδων εἰσηγήσασθαι·

3 διὸ καὶ τῶν βρεφῶν ταῖς ἐπῳδαῖς σῳζομένων καὶ τῶν πλείστων ὑπ' αὐτῆς ἐναγκαλιζομένων, διὰ τὴν εἰς ταῦτα σπουδὴν καὶ φιλοστοργίαν ὑπὸ πάντων αὐτὴν ὀρείαν μητέρα προσαγορευθῆναι. συναστρέφεσθαι δ' αὐτῇ καὶ φιλίαν ἔχειν ἐπὶ πλέον φασὶ Μαρσύαν τὸν Φρύγα, θαυμαζόμενον ἐπὶ συνέσει καὶ σωφροσύνῃ· καὶ τῆς μὲν συνέσεως τεκμήριον λαμβάνουσι τὸ μιμήσασθαι τοὺς φθόγγους τῆς πολυκαλάμου σύριγγος καὶ μετενεγκεῖν ἐπὶ τοὺς αὐλοὺς τὴν ὅλην ἁρμονίαν, τῆς δὲ σωφροσύνης σημεῖον εἶναί φασι τὸ μέχρι τῆς τελευτῆς ἀπείρατον γενέσθαι τῶν ἀφροδισίων.

4 Τὴν οὖν Κυβέλην εἰς ἀκμὴν ἡλικίας ἐλθοῦσαν ἀγαπῆσαι τῶν ἐγχωρίων τινὰ νεανίσκον τὸν

BOOK III. 58. 1–4

and marrying Dindymê he begat an infant daughter, but being unwilling to rear her he exposed her on the mountain which was called Cybelus. There, in accordance with some divine providence, both the leopards and some of the other especially ferocious wild beasts offered their nipples to the child and so gave it nourishment, and some women who were tending the flocks in that place witnessed the happening, and being astonished at the strange event took up the babe and called her Cybelê after the name of the place. The child, as she grew up, excelled in both beauty and virtue and also came to be admired for her intelligence; for she was the first to devise the pipe of many reeds and to invent cymbals and kettledrums with which to accompany the games and the dance, and in addition she taught how to heal the sicknesses of both flocks and little children by means of rites of purification; in consequence, since the babes were saved from death by her spells and were generally taken up in her arms, her devotion to them and affection for them led all the people to speak of her as the " mother of the mountain." The man who associated with her and loved her more than anyone else, they say, was Marsyas the Phrygian, who was admired for his intelligence and chastity; and a proof of his intelligence they find in the fact that he imitated the sounds made by the pipe of many reeds and carried all its notes over into the flute,[1] and as an indication of his chastity they cite his abstinence from sexual pleasures until the day of his death.

Now Cybelê, the myth records, having arrived at full womanhood, came to love a certain native youth

[1] *i.e.* into a single pipe.

προσαγορευόμενον μὲν Ἄττιν, ὕστερον δ' ἐπικληθέντα Πάπαν· συνελθοῦσαν δ' εἰς ὁμιλίαν αὐτῷ λάθρᾳ καὶ γενομένην ἔγκυον ἐπιγνωσθῆναι κατὰ τοῦτον τὸν καιρὸν ὑπὸ τῶν γονέων. 59. διόπερ ἀναχθείσης αὐτῆς εἰς τὰ βασίλεια, καὶ τοῦ πατρὸς τὸ μὲν πρῶτον ὡς παρθένον προσδεξαμένου, μετὰ δὲ ταῦτα γνόντος τὴν φθοράν, καὶ τάς τε τροφοὺς καὶ τὸν Ἄττιν ἀνελόντος καὶ τὰ σώματα ἐκρίψαντος ἄταφα, φασὶ τὴν Κυβέλην διὰ τὴν πρὸς τὸ μειράκιον φιλοστοργίαν καὶ τὴν ἐπὶ ταῖς τροφοῖς λύπην ἐμμανῆ γενομένην εἰς τὴν χώραν ἐκπηδῆσαι. καὶ ταύτην μὲν ὀλολύζουσαν καὶ τυμπανίζουσαν μόνην ἐπιέναι πᾶσαν χώραν, λελυμένην τὰς τρίχας, τὸν δὲ Μαρσύαν ἐλεοῦντα τὸ πάθος ἑκουσίως αὐτῇ συνακολουθεῖν καὶ συμπλανᾶσθαι διὰ τὴν προϋπάρ-
2 χουσαν φιλίαν. παραγενομένους δ' αὐτοὺς πρὸς Διόνυσον εἰς τὴν Νῦσαν καταλαβεῖν τὸν Ἀπόλλω τυγχάνοντα μεγάλης ἀποδοχῆς διὰ τὴν κιθάραν, ἣν Ἑρμῆν εὑρεῖν φασιν, Ἀπόλλωνα δὲ πρῶτον αὐτῇ κατὰ τρόπον χρῆσθαι· ἐρίζοντος δὲ τοῦ Μαρσύου πρὸς τὸν Ἀπόλλω περὶ τῆς τέχνης, καὶ τῶν Νυσαίων ἀποδειχθέντων δικαστῶν, τὸν μὲν Ἀπόλλωνα πρῶτον κιθαρίσαι ψιλήν, τὸν δὲ Μαρσύαν ἐπιβαλόντα τοῖς αὐλοῖς καταπλῆξαι τὰς ἀκοὰς τῷ ξενίζοντι, καὶ διὰ τὴν εὐμέλειαν[1] δόξαι πολὺ
3 προέχειν τοῦ προηγωνισμένου. συντεθειμένων δ' αὐτῶν παρ' ἄλληλα τοῖς δικασταῖς ἐπιδείκνυσθαι

[1] Reiske suggests ἐμμέλειαν ("harmony").

who was known as Attis, but at a later time received the appellation Papas[1]; with him she consorted secretly and became with child, and at about the same time her parents recognized her as their child. 59. Consequently she was brought up into the palace, and her father welcomed her at the outset under the impression that she was a virgin, but later, when he learned of her seduction, he put to death her nurses and Attis as well and cast their bodies forth to lie unburied; whereupon Cybelê, they say, because of her love for the youth and grief over the nurses, became frenzied and rushed out of the palace into the countryside. And crying aloud and beating upon a kettledrum she visited every country alone, with hair hanging free, and Marsyas, out of pity for her plight, voluntarily followed her and accompanied her in her wanderings because of the love which he had formerly borne her. When they came to Dionysus in the city of Nysa they found there Apollo, who was being accorded high favour because of the lyre, which, they say, Hermes invented, though Apollo was the first to play it fittingly; and when Marsyas strove with Apollo in a contest of skill and the Nysaeans had been appointed judges, the first time Apollo played upon the lyre without accompanying it with his voice, while Marsyas, striking up upon his pipes, amazed the ears of his hearers by their strange music and in their opinion far excelled, by reason of his melody, the first contestant. But since they had agreed to take turn about in displaying their skill to the judges,

---

[1] "Papa" or "father." Attis-Papas was the supreme god of the Phrygians, occupying the position held by Zeus in the Greek world.

τὴν τέχνην, τὸν μὲν Ἀπόλλωνά φασιν ἐπιβαλεῖν τὸ δεύτερον ἁρμόττουσαν τῷ μέλει τῆς κιθάρας ᾠδήν, καθ' ἣν ὑπερβαλέσθαι τὴν προϋπάρξασαν τῶν αὐλῶν ἀποδοχήν· τὸν δὲ πρότερον ἀγανακτήσαντα διδάσκειν τοὺς ἀκροατὰς ὅτι παρὰ πᾶν τὸ δίκαιον αὐτὸς ἐλαττοῦται· δεῖν γὰρ γίνεσθαι τέχνης σύγκρισιν, οὐ φωνῆς, καθ' ἣν προσήκει τὴν ἁρμονίαν καὶ τὸ μέλος ἐξετάζεσθαι τῆς κιθάρας καὶ τῶν αὐλῶν· καὶ πρὸς τούτοις ἄδικον εἶναι δύο τέχνας ἅμα πρὸς μίαν συγκρίνεσθαι. τὸν δὲ Ἀπόλλω μυθολογοῦσιν εἰπεῖν ὡς οὐδὲν αὐτὸν
4 πλεονεκτοίη· καὶ γὰρ τὸν Μαρσύαν τὸ παραπλήσιον αὐτῷ ποιεῖν, εἰς τοὺς αὐλοὺς ἐμφυσῶντα· δεῖν οὖν ἢ τὴν ἐξουσίαν ταύτην ἴσην ἀμφοτέροις δίδοσθαι τῆς κράσεως,[1] ἢ μηδέτερον τῷ στόματι διαγωνιζόμενον διὰ μόνων τῶν χειρῶν ἐνδείκνυ-
5 σθαι τὴν ἰδίαν τέχνην. ἐπικρινάντων δὲ τῶν ἀκροατῶν τὸν Ἀπόλλω δικαιότερα λέγειν, συγκριθῆναι πάλιν τὰς τέχνας, καὶ τὸν μὲν Μαρσύαν λειφθῆναι, τὸν δ' Ἀπόλλω διὰ τὴν ἔριν πικρότερον χρησάμενον ἐκδεῖραι ζῶντα τὸν ἡττηθέντα. ταχὺ δὲ μεταμεληθέντα καὶ βαρέως ἐπὶ τοῖς ὑπ' αὐτοῦ πραχθεῖσιν ἐνέγκαντα τῆς κιθάρας ἐκρῆξαι τὰς χορδὰς καὶ τὴν εὑρημένην ἁρμονίαν ἀφανίσαι.
6 ταύτης δ' ὕστερον Μούσας μὲν ἀνευρεῖν τὴν μέσην, Λίνον δὲ τὴν λίχανον, Ὀρφέα δὲ καὶ

---

[1] κράσεως Eichstädt: κρίσεως.

Apollo, they say, added, this second time, his voice in harmony with the music of the lyre, whereby he gained greater approval than that which had formerly been accorded to the pipes. Marsyas, however, was enraged and tried to prove to the hearers that he was losing the contest in defiance of every principle of justice; for, he argued, it should be a comparison of skill and not of voice, and only by such a test was it possible to judge between the harmony and music of the lyre and of the pipes; and furthermore, it was unjust that two skills should be compared in combination against but one. Apollo, however, as the myth relates, replied that he was in no sense taking any unfair advantage of the other; in fact, when Marsyas blew into his pipes he was doing almost the same thing as himself [1]; consequently the rule should be made either that they should both be accorded this equal privilege of combining their skills, or that neither of them should use his mouth in the contest but should display his special skill by the use only of his hands. When the hearers decided that Apollo presented the more just argument, their skills were again compared; Marsyas was defeated, and Apollo, who had become somewhat embittered by the quarrel, flayed the defeated man alive. But quickly repenting and being distressed at what he had done, he broke the strings of the lyre and destroyed the harmony of sounds which he had discovered. This harmony of the strings, however, was rediscovered, when the Muses added later the middle string, Linus the string struck with the forefinger, and Orpheus and Thamyras the lowest

[1] *i.e.* they were both using their breath; Marsyas to make the pipes sound, Apollo to produce vocal notes.

DIODORUS OF SICILY

Θαμύραν ὑπάτην καὶ παρυπάτην. τὸν δ' Ἀπόλλω φασὶν εἰς τὸ ἄντρον τοῦ Διονύσου τήν τε κιθάραν καὶ τοὺς αὐλοὺς ἀναθέντα, καὶ τῆς Κυβέλης ἐρασθέντα, συμπλανηθῆναι ταύτῃ μέχρι τῶν Ὑπερβορέων. 7 Κατὰ δὲ τὴν Φρυγίαν ἐμπεσούσης νόσου τοῖς ἀνθρώποις καὶ τῆς γῆς ἀκάρπου γενομένης, ἐπερωτησάντων τῶν ἀτυχούντων τὸν θεὸν[1] περὶ τῆς τῶν κακῶν ἀπαλλαγῆς προστάξαι φασὶν αὐτοῖς θάψαι τὸ Ἄττιδος σῶμα καὶ τιμᾶν τὴν Κυβέλην ὡς θεόν. διόπερ τοὺς Φρύγας ἠφανισμένου τοῦ σώματος διὰ τὸν χρόνον εἴδωλον κατασκευάσαι τοῦ μειρακίου, πρὸς ᾧ θρηνοῦντας ταῖς οἰκείαις τιμαῖς τοῦ πάθους ἐξιλάσκεσθαι τὴν τοῦ παρανομηθέντος μῆνιν· ὅπερ μέχρι τοῦ καθ' 8 ἡμᾶς βίου ποιοῦντας αὐτοὺς διατελεῖν. τῆς δὲ Κυβέλης τὸ παλαιὸν βωμοὺς ἱδρυσαμένους θυσίας ἐπιτελεῖν κατ' ἔτος· ὕστερον δ' ἐν Πισινοῦντι τῆς Φρυγίας κατασκευάσαι νεὼν πολυτελῆ καὶ τιμὰς καὶ θυσίας καταδεῖξαι μεγαλοπρεπεστάτας, Μίδου[2] τοῦ βασιλέως εἰς ταῦτα συμφιλοκαλήσαντος· τῷ δ' ἀγάλματι τῆς θεοῦ παραστῆσαι παρδάλεις καὶ λέοντας διὰ τὸ δοκεῖν ὑπὸ τούτων πρῶτον τραφῆναι.

Περὶ μὲν οὖν μητρὸς θεῶν τοιαῦτα μυθολογεῖται παρά τε τοῖς Φρυξὶ καὶ τοῖς Ἀτλαντίοις τοῖς παρὰ τὸν ὠκεανὸν οἰκοῦσιν.

---

[1] So Dindorf: τὸν θεὸν ἀτυχούντων D, ἀτυχούντων omitted in Vulgate.
[2] Μίδου Wesseling: Μήδου.

---

[1] Hermes had discovered the three-stringed lyre (cp. Book 1. 16. 1), and Apollo had presumably added four more strings.

string and the one next to it.[1] And Apollo, they say, laid away both the lyre and the pipes as a votive offering in the cave of Dionysus, and becoming enamoured of Cybelê joined in her wanderings as far as the land of the Hyperboreans.

But, the myth goes on to say, a pestilence fell upon human beings throughout Phrygia and the land ceased to bear fruit, and when the unfortunate people inquired of the god how they might rid themselves of their ills he commanded them, it is said, to bury the body of Attis and to honour Cybelê as a goddess. Consequently the Phrygians, since the body had disappeared in the course of time, made an image of the youth, before which they sang dirges and by means of honours in keeping with his suffering propitiated the wrath of him who had been wronged; and these rites they continue to perform down to our own lifetime. As for Cybelê, in ancient times they erected altars and performed sacrifices to her yearly; and later they built for her a costly temple in Pisinus of Phrygia, and established honours and sacrifices of the greatest magnificence, Midas their king taking part in all these works out of his devotion to beauty; and beside the statue of the goddess they set up panthers and lions, since it was the common opinion that she had first been nursed by these animals.

Such, then, are the myths which are told about the Mother of the Gods both among the Phrygians and by the Atlantians who dwell on the coast of the ocean.

---

[1] It is these additional four strings which then had to be rediscovered.

DIODORUS OF SICILY

60. Μετὰ δὲ τὴν Ὑπερίονος τελευτὴν μυθολογοῦσι τοὺς υἱοὺς τοῦ Οὐρανοῦ διελέσθαι τὴν βασιλείαν, ὧν ὑπάρχειν ἐπιφανεστάτους Ἄτλαντα καὶ Κρόνον. τούτων δὲ τὸν μὲν Ἄτλαντα λαχεῖν τοὺς παρὰ τὸν ὠκεανὸν τόπους, καὶ τούς τε λαοὺς Ἀτλαντίους ὀνομάσαι καὶ τὸ μέγιστον τῶν κατὰ τὴν χώραν ὀρῶν ὁμοίως Ἄτλαντα προσαγορεῦσαι. 2 φασὶ δ' αὐτὸν τὰ περὶ τὴν ἀστρολογίαν ἐξακριβῶσαι καὶ τὸν σφαιρικὸν λόγον εἰς ἀνθρώπους πρῶτον ἐξενεγκεῖν· ἀφ' ἧς αἰτίας δόξαι τὸν σύμπαντα κόσμον ἐπὶ τῶν Ἄτλαντος ὤμων ὀχεῖσθαι, τοῦ μύθου τὴν τῆς σφαίρας εὕρεσιν καὶ καταγραφὴν αἰνιττομένου. γενέσθαι δ' αὐτῷ πλείους υἱούς, ὧν ἕνα διενεγκεῖν εὐσεβείᾳ καὶ τῇ πρὸς τοὺς ἀρχομένους δικαιοσύνῃ καὶ φιλανθρωπίᾳ, τὸν 3 προσαγορευόμενον Ἕσπερον. τοῦτον δ' ἐπὶ τὴν κορυφὴν τοῦ Ἄτλαντος ὄρους ἀναβαίνοντα καὶ τὰς τῶν ἄστρων παρατηρήσεις ποιούμενον ἐξαίφνης ὑπὸ πνευμάτων συναρπαγέντα μεγάλων ἄφαντον γενέσθαι· διὰ δὲ τὴν ἀρετὴν αὐτοῦ τὸ πάθος τὰ πλήθη ἐλεήσαντα τιμὰς ἀθανάτους ἀπονεῖμαι καὶ τὸν ἐπιφανέστατον τῶν κατὰ τὸν οὐρανὸν ἀστέρων ὁμωνύμως ἐκείνῳ προσαγορεῦσαι.

4 Ὑπάρξαι δ' Ἄτλαντι καὶ θυγατέρας ἑπτά, τὰς κοινῶς μὲν ἀπὸ τοῦ πατρὸς καλουμένας Ἀτλαντί-

---

[1] The account is resumed which was dropped at the end of chap. 57.

[2] This phrase must be interpreted in the light of the context and of the statement in Book 4. 27. 5, that Atlas "discovered the spherical nature of the stars." Ancient writers in many places refer to Atlas as the discoverer of astronomy; and since Diodorus is referring to the first

BOOK III. 60. 1-4

60. After the death of Hyperion,[1] the myth relates, the kingdom was divided among the sons of Uranus, the most renowned of whom were Atlas and Cronus. Of these sons Atlas received as his part the regions on the coast of the ocean, and he not only gave the name of Atlantians to his peoples but likewise called the greatest mountain in the land Atlas. They also say that he perfected the science of astrology and was the first to publish to mankind the doctrine of the sphere [2]; and it was for this reason that the idea was held that the entire heavens were supported upon the shoulders of Atlas, the myth darkly hinting in this way at his discovery and description of the sphere. There were born to him a number of sons, one of whom was distinguished above the others for his piety, justice to his subjects, and love of mankind, his name being Hesperus. This king, having once climbed to the peak of Mount Atlas, was suddenly snatched away by mighty winds while he was making his observations of the stars, and never was seen again; and because of the virtuous life he had lived and their pity for his sad fate the multitudes accorded to him immortal honours and called the brightest [3] of the stars of heaven after him.

Atlas, the myth goes on to relate, also had seven daughters, who as a group were called Atlantides

beginnings of astronomical thinking among the Greeks, we have in these references to the "doctrine of the sphere" and the "spherical nature of the stars" a memory of the Pythagorean *quadrivium*, in which "'sphaeric' means astronomy, being the geometry of the sphere considered solely with reference to the problem of accounting for the motions of the heavenly bodies" (T. L. Heath, *Greek Mathematics*, 1. p. 11).

[3] Hesperus.

δας, ἰδίᾳ δ' ἑκάστην ὀνομαζομένην Μαῖαν, Ἠλέκτραν, Ταϋγέτην, Στερόπην, Μερόπην, Ἀλκυόνην καὶ τελευταίαν Κελαινώ. ταύτας δὲ μιγείσας τοῖς ἐπιφανεστάτοις ἥρωσι καὶ θεοῖς ἀρχηγοὺς καταστῆναι τοῦ πλείστου[1] γένους τῶν ἀνθρώπων, τεκούσας τοὺς δι' ἀρετὴν θεοὺς καὶ ἥρωας ὀνομασθέντας, οἷον τὴν πρεσβυτάτην Μαῖαν Διὶ μιγεῖσαν Ἑρμῆν τεκνῶσαι, πολλῶν εὑρετὴν γενόμενον τοῖς ἀνθρώποις· παραπλησίως δὲ καὶ τὰς ἄλλας Ἀτλαντίδας γεννῆσαι παῖδας ἐπιφανεῖς, ὧν τοὺς μὲν ἐθνῶν, τοὺς δὲ πόλεων γενέσθαι κτίστας. 5 διόπερ οὐ μόνον παρ' ἐνίοις τῶν βαρβάρων, ἀλλὰ καὶ παρὰ τοῖς Ἕλλησι τοὺς πλείστους τῶν ἀρχαιοτάτων ἡρώων εἰς ταύτας ἀναφέρειν τὸ γένος. ὑπάρξαι δ' αὐτὰς καὶ σώφρονας διαφερόντως, καὶ μετὰ τὴν τελευτὴν τυχεῖν ἀθανάτου τιμῆς παρ' ἀνθρώποις καὶ[2] καθιδρυθείσας ἐν τῷ κόσμῳ καὶ τῇ τῶν Πλειάδων προσηγορίᾳ περιληφθείσας. ἐκλήθησαν δὲ αἱ[3] Ἀτλαντίδες καὶ νύμφαι διὰ τὸ τοὺς ἐγχωρίους κοινῇ τὰς γυναῖκας νύμφας προσαγορεύειν.

61. Κρόνον δὲ μυθολογοῦσιν, ἀδελφὸν μὲν Ἄτλαντος ὄντα, διαφέροντα δ' ἀσεβείᾳ καὶ πλεονεξίᾳ, γῆμαι τὴν ἀδελφὴν Ῥέαν, ἐξ ἧς γεννῆσαι Δία τὸν Ὀλύμπιον ὕστερον ἐπικληθέντα. γεγονέναι δὲ καὶ ἕτερον Δία, τὸν ἀδελφὸν μὲν Οὐρανοῦ, τῆς δὲ

[1] πλείστου omitted by DF, Vogel.
[2] καί after ἀνθρώποις deleted by Dindorf, Bekker, Vogel.
[3] αἱ added by Reiske.

BOOK III. 60. 4–61. 1

after their father, but their individual names were Maea, Electra, Taÿgetê, Steropê, Meropê, Halcyonê, and the last Celaeno. These daughters lay with the most renowned heroes and gods and thus became the first ancestors of the larger part of the race of human beings, giving birth to those who, because of their high achievements, came to be called gods and heroes; Maea the eldest, for instance, lay with Zeus and bore Hermes, who was the discoverer of many things for the use of mankind; similarly the other Atlantides also gave birth to renowned children, who became the founders in some instances of nations and in other cases of cities. Consequently, not only among certain barbarians but among the Greeks as well, the great majority of the most ancient heroes trace their descent back to the Atlantides. These daughters were also distinguished for their chastity and after their death attained to immortal honour among men, by whom they were both enthroned in the heavens and endowed with the appellation of Pleiades.[1] The Atlantides were also called "nymphs" because the natives of that land addressed their women by the common appellation of "nymph."[2]

61. Cronus, the brother of Atlas, the myth continues, who was a man notorious for his impiety and greed, married his sister Rhea, by whom he begat that Zeus who was later called "the Olympian." But there had been also another Zeus, the brother of Uranus

[1] It has been conjectured that the name is derived from the verb "to sail" (*Pleō*), since this constellation rose at the beginning of the sailing season.
[2] *i.e.* in addressing their women they did not distinguish between the married and unmarried, as most Greeks did.

Κρήτης βασιλεύσαντα, τῇ δόξῃ πολὺ λειπόμενον
2 τοῦ μεταγενεστέρου. τοῦτον μὲν οὖν βασιλεῦσαι
τοῦ σύμπαντος κόσμου, τὸν δὲ προγενέστερον,
δυναστεύοντα τῆς προειρημένης νήσου, δέκα παῖδας
γεννῆσαι τοὺς ὀνομασθέντας Κουρῆτας· προσαγορεῦσαι δὲ καὶ τὴν νῆσον ἀπὸ τῆς γυναικὸς Ἰδαίαν,
ἐν ᾗ καὶ τελευτήσαντα ταφῆναι, δεικνυμένου τοῦ
τὴν ταφὴν δεξαμένου τόπου μέχρι τῶν καθ᾽
3 ἡμᾶς χρόνων. οὐ μὴν οἵ γε Κρῆτες ὁμολογού-
μενα τούτοις μυθολογοῦσι,[1] περὶ ὧν ἡμεῖς ἐν
τοῖς περὶ Κρήτης τὰ κατὰ μέρος ἀναγράψομεν·
δυναστεῦσαι δέ φασι τὸν Κρόνον κατὰ Σικελίαν καὶ
Λιβύην, ἔτι δὲ τὴν Ἰταλίαν, καὶ τὸ σύνολον ἐν τοῖς
πρὸς ἑσπέραν τόποις συστήσασθαι τὴν βασιλείαν·
παρὰ πᾶσι δὲ φρουραῖς διακατέχειν τὰς ἀκροπό-
λεις καὶ τοὺς ὀχυροὺς τῶν τόπων·[2] ἀφ᾽ οὗ δὴ
μέχρι τοῦ νῦν χρόνου κατά τε τὴν Σικελίαν καὶ
τὰ πρὸς ἑσπέραν νεύοντα μέρη πολλοὺς τῶν ὑψηλῶν
τόπων ἀπ᾽ ἐκείνου Κρόνια προσαγορεύεσθαι.

4 Κρόνου δὲ γενόμενον υἱὸν Δία τὸν ἐναντίον τῷ
πατρὶ βίον ζηλῶσαι, καὶ παρεχόμενον ἑαυτὸν
πᾶσιν ἐπιεικῆ καὶ φιλάνθρωπον ὑπὸ τοῦ πλήθους
πατέρα προσαγορευθῆναι. διαδέξασθαι δ᾽ αὐτόν
φασι τὴν βασιλείαν οἱ μὲν ἑκουσίως τοῦ πατρὸς
παραχωρήσαντος, οἱ δ᾽ ὑπὸ τῶν ὄχλων αἱρε-
θέντα διὰ τὸ μῖσος τὸ πρὸς τὸν πατέρα· ἐπιστρα-
τεύσαντος δ᾽ ἐπ᾽ αὐτὸν τοῦ Κρόνου μετὰ τῶν
Τιτάνων κρατῆσαι τῇ μάχῃ τὸν Δία, καὶ κύριον
γενόμενον τῶν ὅλων ἐπελθεῖν ἅπασαν τὴν οἰκουμένην, εὐεργετοῦντα τὸ γένος τῶν ἀνθρώπων.

[1] μυθολογοῦσι ABD, ἱστοροῦσι II, Jacoby.
[2] τούτων after τόπων deleted by Dindorf.

and a king of Crete, who, however, was far less famous than the Zeus who was born at a later time.[1] Now the latter was king over the entire world, whereas the earlier Zeus, who was lord of the abovementioned island, begat ten sons who were given the name of Curetes; and the island he named after his wife Idaea, and on it he died and was buried, and the place which received his grave is pointed out to our day. The Cretans, however, have a myth which does not agree with the story given above, and we shall give a detailed account of it when we speak of Crete.[2] Cronus, they say, was lord of Sicily and Libya, and Italy as well, and, in a word, established his kingdom over the regions to the west; and everywhere he occupied with garrisons the commanding hills and the strongholds of the regions, this being the reason why both throughout Sicily and the parts which incline towards the west many of the lofty places are called to this day after him "Cronia."

Zeus, however, the son of Cronus, emulated a manner of life the opposite of that led by his father, and since he showed himself honourable and friendly to all, the masses addressed him as "father." As for his succession to the kingly power, some say that his father yielded it to him of his own accord, but others state that he was chosen as king by the masses because of the hatred they bore towards his father, and that when Cronus made war against him with the aid of the Titans, Zeus overcame him in battle, and on gaining supreme power visited all the inhabited world, conferring benefactions upon the

---

[1] *i.e.* "the Olympian."   [2] In Book 5. 64 ff.

5 διενεγκεῖν δ' αὐτὸν καὶ σώματος ῥώμῃ καὶ ταῖς ἄλλαις ἁπάσαις ἀρεταῖς, καὶ διὰ τοῦτο ταχὺ κύριον γενέσθαι τοῦ σύμπαντος κόσμου. καθόλου δ' αὐτὸν τὴν ἅπασαν σπουδὴν ἔχειν εἰς κόλασιν μὲν τῶν ἀσεβῶν καὶ πονηρῶν, εὐεργεσίαν δὲ 6 τῶν ὄχλων. ἀνθ' ὧν μετὰ τὴν ἐξ ἀνθρώπων μετάστασιν ὀνομασθῆναι μὲν Ζῆνα διὰ τὸ δοκεῖν τοῦ καλῶς ζῆν αἴτιον γενέσθαι τοῖς ἀνθρώποις, καθιδρυθῆναι δ' ἐν τῷ κόσμῳ τῇ τῶν εὖ παθόντων τιμῇ, πάντων προθύμως ἀναγορευόντων θεὸν καὶ κύριον εἰς τὸν αἰῶνα τοῦ σύμπαντος κόσμου.

Τῶν μὲν οὖν παρὰ τοῖς Ἀτλαντίοις θεολογουμένων τὰ κεφάλαια ταῦτ' ἐστίν.

62. Ἡμεῖς δ' ἐπεὶ προειρήκαμεν ἐν τοῖς Αἰγυπτιακοῖς περὶ τῆς τοῦ Διονύσου γενέσεως καὶ τῶν ὑπ' αὐτοῦ πραχθέντων ἀκολούθως ταῖς ἐγχωρίοις ἱστορίαις, οἰκεῖον εἶναι διαλαμβάνομεν προσθεῖναι τὰ μυθολογούμενα περὶ τοῦ θεοῦ τούτου παρὰ τοῖς 2 Ἕλλησι. τῶν δὲ παλαιῶν μυθογράφων καὶ ποιητῶν περὶ Διονύσου γεγραφότων ἀλλήλοις ἀσύμφωνα καὶ πολλοὺς καὶ τερατώδεις λόγους καταβεβλημένων, δυσχερές ἐστιν ὑπὲρ τῆς γενέσεως τοῦ θεοῦ τούτου καὶ τῶν πράξεων καθαρῶς εἰπεῖν. οἱ μὲν γὰρ ἕνα Διόνυσον, οἱ δὲ τρεῖς γεγονέναι παραδεδώκασιν, εἰσὶ δ' οἱ γένεσιν μὲν τούτου ἀνθρωπόμορφον μὴ γεγονέναι τὸ παράπαν ἀποφαινόμενοι, τὴν δὲ

---

[1] This is another form of the name "Zeus," and also the infinitive of the verb "live."

BOOK III. 61. 5-62. 2

race of men. He was pre-eminent also in bodily strength and in all the other qualities of virtue and for this reason quickly became master of the entire world. And in general he showed all zeal to punish impious and wicked men and to show kindness to the masses. In return for all this, after he had passed from among men he was given the name of Zên,[1] because he was the cause of right " living " among men, and those who had received his favours showed him honour by enthroning him in the heavens, all men eagerly acclaiming him as god and lord for ever of the whole universe.

These, then, are in summary the facts regarding the teachings of the Atlantians about the gods.

62. But since we have previously made mention, in connection with our discussion of Egypt, of the birth of Dionysus and of his deeds as they are preserved in the local histories of that country,[2] we are of the opinion that it is appropriate in this place to add the myths about this god which are current among the Greeks. But since the early composers of myths and the early poets who have written about Dionysus do not agree with one another and have committed to writing many monstrous tales, it is a difficult undertaking to give a clear account of the birth and deeds of this god. For some have handed down the story that there was but one Dionysus, others that there were three,[3] and there are those who state that there was never any birth of him in human form whatsoever, and think that

[2] Cp. Book 1. 23.
[3] Cicero (*On the Nature of the Gods*, 3. 58) said there had been five.

τοῦ οἴνου δόσιν Διόνυσον εἶναι νομίζοντες. διόπερ ἡμεῖς τῶν παρ' ἑκάστοις λεγομένων τὰ κεφάλαια πειρασόμεθα συντόμως ἐπιδραμεῖν.

Οἱ τοίνυν φυσιολογοῦντες περὶ τοῦ θεοῦ τούτου καὶ τὸν ἀπὸ τῆς ἀμπέλου καρπὸν Διόνυσον ὀνομάζοντές φασι τὴν γῆν αὐτομάτως μετὰ τῶν ἄλλων φυτῶν ἐνεγκεῖν τὴν ἄμπελον, ἀλλ' οὐκ ἐξ ἀρχῆς 4 ὑπό τινος εὑρετοῦ φυτευθῆναι. τεκμήριον δ' εἶναι τούτου τὸ μέχρι τοῦ νῦν ἐν πολλοῖς τόποις ἀγρίας ἀμπέλους φύεσθαι, καὶ καρποφορεῖν αὐτὰς παραπλησίως ταῖς ὑπὸ τῆς ἀνθρωπίνης ἐμπειρίας χει- 5 ρουργουμέναις. διμήτορα δὲ τὸν Διόνυσον ὑπὸ τῶν παλαιῶν ὠνομάσθαι, μιᾶς μὲν καὶ πρώτης γενέσεως ἀριθμουμένης ὅταν τὸ φυτὸν εἰς τὴν γῆν τεθὲν λαμβάνῃ τὴν αὔξησιν, δευτέρας δ' ὅταν βρίθῃ καὶ τοὺς βότρυς πεπαίνῃ, ὥστε τὴν μὲν ἐκ γῆς, τὴν δ' ἐκ τῆς ἀμπέλου γένεσιν τοῦ θεοῦ νομίζεσθαι.

6 παραδεδωκότων δὲ τῶν μυθογράφων καὶ τρίτην γένεσιν, καθ' ἣν φασι τὸν θεὸν ἐκ Διὸς καὶ Δήμητρος τεκνωθέντα διασπασθῆναι μὲν ὑπὸ τῶν γηγενῶν καὶ καθεψηθῆναι, πάλιν δ' ὑπὸ τῆς Δήμητρος τῶν μελῶν συναρμοσθέντων ἐξ ἀρχῆς νέον γεννηθῆναι, εἰς φυσικάς τινας αἰτίας μετάγουσι τοὺς 7 τοιούτους λόγους. Διὸς μὲν γὰρ καὶ Δήμητρος αὐτὸν λέγεσθαι διὰ τὸ τὴν ἄμπελον ἔκ τε γῆς καὶ ὄμβρων λαμβάνουσαν τὴν αὔξησιν καρποφορεῖν τὸν ἐκ τοῦ βότρυος ἀποθλιβόμενον οἶνον· τὸ δ' ὑπὸ τῶν γηγενῶν νέον ὄντα διασπασθῆναι δηλοῦν τὴν ὑπὸ

---

[1] "Twice-born."
[2] *i.e.* the Titans, or "sons of earth."

the word Dionysus means only " the gift of wine " (*oinou dosis*). For this reason we shall endeavour to run over briefly only the main facts as they are given by each writer.

Those authors, then, who use the phenomena of nature to explain this god and call the fruit of the vine " Dionysus " speak like this: The earth brought forth of itself the vine at the same time with the other plants and it was not originally planted by some man who discovered it. And they allege as proof of this the fact that to this day vines grow wild in many regions and bear fruit quite similar to that of plants which are tended by the experienced hand of man. Furthermore, the early men have given Dionysus the name of " Dimetor,"[1] reckoning it as a single and first birth when the plant is set in the ground and begins to grow, and as a second birth when it becomes laden with fruit and ripens its clusters, the god, therefore, being considered as having been born once from the earth and again from the vine. And though the writers of myths have handed down the account of a third birth as well, at which, as they say, the Sons of Gaia[2] tore to pieces the god, who was a son of Zeus and Demeter, and boiled him, but his members were brought together again by Demeter and he experienced a new birth as if for the first time, such accounts as this they trace back to certain causes found in nature. For he is considered to be the son of Zeus and Demeter, they hold, by reason of the fact that the vine gets its growth both from the earth and from rains and so bears as its fruit the wine which is pressed out from the clusters of grapes; and the statement that he was torn to pieces, while yet a youth, by the

DIODORUS OF SICILY

τῶν γεωργῶν συγκομιδὴν τῶν καρπῶν,[1] τὴν δὲ καθέψησιν τῶν μελῶν μεμυθοποιῆσθαι διὰ τὸ τοὺς πλείστους ἕψειν τὸν οἶνον καὶ μίσγοντας εὐωδεστέραν αὐτοῦ καὶ βελτίονα τὴν φύσιν κατασκευάζειν· τὸ δὲ τὰ[2] ὑπὸ τῶν γηγενῶν λυμανθέντα τῶν μελῶν ἁρμοσθέντα πάλιν ἐπὶ τὴν προγεγενημένην φύσιν ἀποκαθίστασθαι παρεμφαίνειν ὅτι πάλιν ἡ γῆ τὴν τρυγηθεῖσαν ἄμπελον καὶ τμηθεῖσαν ταῖς κατ' ἔτος ὥραις εἰς τὴν προϋπάρξασαν ἐν τῷ καρποφορεῖν ἀκμὴν ἀποκαθίστησι. καθόλου γὰρ ὑπὸ τῶν ἀρχαίων ποιητῶν καὶ μυθογράφων τὴν Δήμητραν γῆν

8 μητέρα προσαγορεύεσθαι. σύμφωνα δὲ τούτοις εἶναι τά τε δηλούμενα διὰ τῶν Ὀρφικῶν ποιημάτων καὶ τὰ παρεισαγόμενα κατὰ τὰς τελετάς, περὶ ὧν οὐ θέμις τοῖς ἀμυήτοις ἱστορεῖν τὰ κατὰ μέρος.

9 Ὁμοίως δὲ καὶ τὴν ἐκ Σεμέλης γένεσιν εἰς φυσικὰς ἀρχὰς ἀνάγουσιν, ἀποφαινόμενοι Θυώνην ὑπὸ τῶν ἀρχαίων τὴν γῆν ὠνομάσθαι, καὶ τεθεῖσθαι τὴν προσηγορίαν[3] Σεμέλην μὲν ἀπὸ τοῦ σεμνὴν εἶναι τῆς θεοῦ ταύτης τὴν ἐπιμέλειαν καὶ τιμήν, Θυώνην δ' ἀπὸ τῶν θυομένων αὐτῇ θυσιῶν καὶ

10 θυηλῶν. δὶς δ' αὐτοῦ τὴν γένεσιν ἐκ Διὸς παραδεδόσθαι διὰ τὸ δοκεῖν μετὰ τῶν ἄλλων ἐν τῷ κατὰ τὸν Δευκαλίωνα κατακλυσμῷ φθαρῆναι καὶ τούτους

---

[1] διὰ τὸ τοὺς ἀνθρώπους τὴν γῆν Δήμητραν νομίζειν after καρπῶν deleted by Reiske.
[2] τὸ δὲ τὰ Dindorf: τὰ δ'.
[3] καὶ after προσηγορίαν deleted by Eichstädt.

---

[1] An epithet of the Giants, who were the sons of Gaia ("Earth").
[2] Literally, the "workers of the earth." Here the MSS.

"earth-born"[1] signifies the harvesting of the fruit by the labourers,[2] and the boiling of his members has been worked into a myth by reason of the fact that most men boil the wine and then mix it, thereby improving its natural aroma and quality. Again, the account of his members, which the "earth-born" treated with despite, being brought together again and restored to their former natural state, shows forth that the vine, which has been stripped of its fruit and pruned at the yearly seasons, is restored by the earth to the high level of fruitfulness which it had before. For, in general, the ancient poets and writers of myths spoke of Demeter as Gê Meter (Earth Mother). And with these stories the teachings agree which are set forth in the Orphic poems and are introduced into their rites, but it is not lawful to recount them in detail to the uninitiated.

In the same manner the account that Dionysus was born of Semelê they trace back to natural beginnings, offering the explanation that Thuonê[3] was the name which the ancients gave to the earth, and that this goddess received the appellation Semelê because the worship and honour paid to her was dignified (*semnê*), and she was called *Thuonê* because of the sacrifices (*thusiai*) and burnt offerings (*thuelai*) which were offered (*thuomenai*) to her. Furthermore, the tradition that Dionysus was born twice of Zeus arises from the belief that these fruits also perished in common with all other plants in the flood at the time of Deucalion, and that when they

interpolate the explanation "because men consider the earth to be Demeter"; cp. Book 1. 12. 4.

[3] Thyonê was the name which was given Semelê after she was received into the circle of the gods (cp. Book 4. 25. 4).

τοὺς καρπούς, καὶ μετὰ τὴν ἐπομβρίαν πάλιν
ἀναφύντων ὡσπερεὶ δευτέραν ἐπιφάνειαν ταύτην
ὑπάρξαι τοῦ θεοῦ παρ' ἀνθρώποις, καθ' ἣν ἐκ τοῦ
Διὸς μηροῦ γενέσθαι πάλιν τὸν θεὸν[1] μεμυθοποιῆσθαι. οἱ μὲν οὖν τὴν χρείαν καὶ δύναμιν τοῦ κατὰ
τὸν οἶνον εὑρήματος ἀποφαινόμενοι Διόνυσον
ὑπάρχειν τοιαῦτα περὶ αὐτοῦ μυθολογοῦσι.

63. Τῶν δὲ μυθογράφων οἱ σωματοειδῆ τὸν θεὸν
παρεισάγοντες τὴν μὲν εὕρεσιν τῆς ἀμπέλου καὶ
φυτείαν καὶ πᾶσαν τὴν περὶ τὸν οἶνον πραγματείαν
συμφώνως αὐτῷ προσάπτουσι, περὶ δὲ τοῦ πλείους
2 γεγονέναι Διονύσους ἀμφισβητοῦσιν. ἔνιοι μὲν
γὰρ ἕνα καὶ τὸν αὐτὸν ἀποφαίνονται γενέσθαι τόν
τε καταδείξαντα τὰ κατὰ τὰς οἰνοποιίας καὶ
συγκομιδὰς τῶν ξυλίνων καλουμένων καρπῶν καὶ
τὸν στρατευσάμενον ἐπὶ πᾶσαν τὴν οἰκουμένην,
ἔτι δὲ τὸν τὰ μυστήρια καὶ τελετὰς καὶ βακχείας
εἰσηγησάμενον· ἔνιοι δέ, καθάπερ προεῖπον, τρεῖς
ὑποστησάμενοι γεγονέναι κατὰ διεστηκότας χρόνους, ἑκάστῳ προσάπτουσιν ἰδίας πράξεις.

3 Καί φασι τὸν μὲν ἀρχαιότατον Ἰνδὸν γεγονέναι,
καὶ τῆς χώρας αὐτομάτως διὰ τὴν εὐκρασίαν
φερούσης πολλὴν ἄμπελον πρῶτον τοῦτον ἀποθλῖψαι
βότρυας καὶ τὴν χρείαν τῆς περὶ τὸν οἶνον φύσεως

---

[1] τοῦτον after θεὸν omitted CD, Vogel.

---

[1] Cp. Book 2. 38. 4, and chap. 62 below. The story of the birth of Dionysus from the thigh of Zeus is partly etymological, *Dio-* from *Dios*, the genitive form of the nominative *Zeus*.

[2] The "mythographi" appeared in Greek literature

BOOK III. 62. 10–63. 3

sprang up again after the Deluge it was as if there had been a second epiphany of the god among men, and so the myth was created that the god had been born again from the thigh of Zeus.[1] However this may be, those who explain the name Dionysus as signifying the use and importance of the discovery of wine recount such a myth regarding him.

63. Those mythographers,[2] however, who represent the god as having a human form ascribe to him, with one accord, the discovery and cultivation of the vine and all the operations of the making of wine, although they disagree on whether there was a single Dionysus or several. Some, for instance, who assert that he who taught how to make wine and to gather " the fruits of the trees,"[3] as they are called, he who led an army over all the inhabited world, and he who introduced the mysteries and rites and Bacchic revelries were one and the same person; but there are others, as I have said, who conceive that there were three persons, at separate periods, and to each of these they ascribe deeds which were peculiarly his own.

This, then, is their account: The most ancient Dionysus was an Indian, and since his country, because of the excellent climate, produced the vine in abundance without cultivation, he was the first to press out the clusters of grapes and to devise the use of wine as a natural product, likewise to give the

towards the close of the fourth century B.C. By that time the myths tended to drop out of sober historical writing and to become the subject of separate treatises, the writers of such works being called by the Greeks "mythographi."

[3] This was a vernacular term used to include wine, fruit, olive-oil, etc., as opposed to cereals ("dry fruit").

DIODORUS OF SICILY

ἐπινοῆσαι, ὁμοίως δὲ καὶ[1] τῶν σύκων καὶ τῶν ἄλλων ἀκροδρύων τὴν καθήκουσαν ἐπιμέλειαν ποιήσασθαι, καὶ καθόλου τὰ πρὸς τὴν συγκομιδὴν καὶ παράθεσιν[2] τούτων τῶν καρπῶν ἐπινοῆσαι.[3] τὸν αὐτὸν δὲ καὶ καταπώγωνα λέγουσι γενέσθαι διὰ τὸ τοῖς Ἰνδοῖς νόμιμον εἶναι μέχρι τῆς τελευτῆς ἐπιμελῶς ὑποτρέφειν τοὺς πώγωνας.
4 τὸν δ' οὖν Διόνυσον ἐπελθόντα μετὰ στρατοπέδου πᾶσαν τὴν οἰκουμένην διδάξαι τήν τε φυτείαν τῆς ἀμπέλου καὶ τὴν ἐν ταῖς ληνοῖς ἀπόθλιψιν τῶν βοτρύων· ἀφ' οὗ Ληναῖον αὐτὸν ὀνομασθῆναι. ὁμοίως δὲ καὶ τῶν ἄλλων εὑρημάτων μεταδόντα πᾶσι τυχεῖν αὐτὸν μετὰ τὴν ἐξ ἀνθρώπων μετάστασιν ἀθανάτου τιμῆς παρὰ τοῖς εὖ παθοῦσιν.
5 δείκνυσθαι δὲ παρ' Ἰνδοῖς μέχρι τοῦ νῦν τόν τε τόπον ἐν ᾧ συνέβη γενέσθαι τὸν θεὸν καὶ προσηγορίας πόλεων ἀπ'[4] αὐτοῦ κατὰ τὴν τῶν ἐγχωρίων διάλεκτον· καὶ πολλὰ ἕτερα διαμένειν ἀξιόλογα τεκμήρια τῆς παρ' Ἰνδοῖς γενέσεως, περὶ ὧν μακρὸν ἂν εἴη γράφειν.

64. Δεύτερον δὲ μυθολογοῦσι γενέσθαι Διόνυσον ἐκ Διὸς καὶ Φερσεφόνης, ὡς δέ τινες, ἐκ Δήμητρος. τοῦτον δὲ παρεισάγουσι πρῶτον βοῦς ὑπ' ἄροτρον ζεῦξαι, τὸ πρὸ τοῦ ταῖς χερσὶ τῶν ἀνθρώπων τὴν γῆν κατεργαζομένων. πολλὰ δὲ καὶ ἄλλα φιλοτέχνως ἐπινοῆσαι τῶν πρὸς τὴν γεωργίαν χρησίμων, δι' ὧν ἀπολυθῆναι τοὺς ὄχλους τῆς πολλῆς κακοπαθείας·
2 ἀνθ' ὧν τοὺς εὖ παθόντας ἀπονεῖμαι τιμὰς

[1] τὴν after καὶ deleted by Dindorf.
[2] καὶ παράθεσιν added by Dindorf (cp. 2. 38. 5; 3. 56. 3).
[3] Here the MSS. add διὸ καὶ ληναῖον ὀνομασθῆναι, which editors omit as an interpolation; cp. § 4 below.

proper care to the figs and other fruits which grow upon trees, and, speaking generally, to devise whatever pertains to the harvesting and storing of these fruits. The same Dionysus is, furthermore, said to have worn a long beard, the reason for the report being that it is the custom among the Indians to give great care, until their death, to the raising of a beard. Now this Dionysus visited with an army all the inhabited world and gave instruction both as to the culture of the vine and the crushing of the clusters in the wine-vats (*lenoi*), which is the reason why the god was named Lenaeus. Likewise, he allowed all people to share in his other discoveries, and when he passed from among men he received immortal honour at the hands of those who had received his benefactions. Furthermore, there are pointed out among the Indians even to this day the place where it came to pass that the god was born, as well as cities which bear his name in the language of the natives;[1] and many other notable testimonials to his birth among the Indians still survive, but it would be a long task to write of them.

64. The second Dionysus, the writers of myths relate, was born to Zeus by Persephonê, though some say it was Demeter. He is represented by them as the first man to have yoked oxen to the plough, human beings before that time having prepared the ground by hand. Many other things also, which are useful for agriculture, were skilfully devised by him, whereby the masses were relieved of their great distress; and in return for this those whom he had

---

[1] Cp. Book 1. 19. 7.

[4] ἀπ' Dindorf: ὑπ'.

ἰσοθέους αὐτῷ καὶ θυσίας, προθύμως ἁπάντων ἀνθρώπων διὰ τὸ μέγεθος τῆς εὐεργεσίας ἀπονειμάντων τὴν ἀθανασίαν. παράσημον δ' αὐτῷ ποιῆσαι κέρατα τοὺς κατασκευάζοντας τὰς γραφὰς ἢ τοὺς ἀνδριάντας, ἅμα μὲν δηλοῦντας ἑτέραν Διονύσου φύσιν, ἅμα δὲ ἀπὸ τῆς περὶ τὸ ἄροτρον εὑρέσεως ἐμφαίνοντας τὸ μέγεθος τῆς ἐπινοηθείσης τοῖς γεωργοῖς εὐχρηστίας.

3 Τρίτον δὲ γενέσθαι Διόνυσόν φασιν ἐν Θήβαις ταῖς Βοιωτίαις ἐκ Διὸς καὶ Σεμέλης τῆς Κάδμου. μυθολογοῦσι γὰρ ἐρασθέντα Δία μιγῆναι πλεονάκις αὐτῇ διὰ τὸ κάλλος, τὴν δ' Ἥραν ζηλοτυποῦσαν καὶ βουλομένην τιμωρίᾳ περιβαλεῖν τὴν ἄνθρωπον, ὁμοιωθῆναι μέν τινι τῶν ἀποδοχῆς τυγχανουσῶν παρ' αὐτῇ γυναικῶν, παρακρούσασθαι 4 δὲ τὴν Σεμέλην· εἰπεῖν γὰρ πρὸς αὐτὴν ὅτι καθῆκον ἦν τὸν Δία μετὰ τῆς αὐτῆς ἐπιφανείας τε καὶ τιμῆς ποιεῖσθαι τὴν ὁμιλίαν ᾗπερ χρᾶται κατὰ τὴν πρὸς τὴν Ἥραν συμπεριφοράν. διὸ καὶ τὸν μὲν Δία, τῆς Σεμέλης ἀξιούσης τυγχάνειν τῶν ἴσων Ἥρᾳ τιμῶν, παραγενέσθαι μετὰ βροντῶν καὶ κεραυνῶν, τὴν δὲ Σεμέλην οὐχ ὑπομείνασαν τὸ μέγεθος τῆς περιστάσεως τελευτῆσαι καὶ τὸ βρέφος 5 ἐκτρῶσαι πρὸ τοῦ καθήκοντος χρόνου. καὶ τοῦτο μὲν τὸν Δία ταχέως εἰς τὸν ἑαυτοῦ μηρὸν ἐγκρύψαι· μετὰ δὲ ταῦτα τοῦ κατὰ φύσιν τῆς γενέσεως χρόνου τὴν τελείαν αὔξησιν ποιήσαντος ἀπενεγ- 6 κεῖν τὸ βρέφος εἰς Νῦσαν τῆς Ἀραβίας. ἐνταῦθα δ' ὑπὸ νυμφῶν τραφέντα τὸν παῖδα προσαγορευθῆναι μὲν ἀπὸ τοῦ πατρὸς καὶ τοῦ τόπου Διόνυσον,

benefited accorded to him honours and sacrifices like those offered to the gods, since all men were eager, because of the magnitude of his service to them, to accord to him immortality. And as a special symbol and token the painters and sculptors represented him with horns, at the same time making manifest thereby the other nature of Dionysus and also showing forth the magnitude of the service which he had devised for the farmers by his invention of the plough.

The third Dionysus, they say, was born in Boeotian Thebes of Zeus and Semelê, the daughter of Cadmus.[1] The myth runs as follows: Zeus had become enamoured of Semelê and often, lured by her beauty, had consorted with her, but Hera, being jealous and anxious to punish the girl, assumed the form of one of the women who was an intimate of Semelê's and led her on to her ruin; for she suggested to her that it was fitting that Zeus should lie with her while having the same majesty and honour in his outward appearance as when he took Hera to his arms. Consequently Zeus, at the request of Semelê that she be shown the same honours as Hera, appeared to her accompanied by thunder and lightning, but Semelê, unable to endure the majesty of his grandeur, died and brought forth the babe before the appointed time. This babe Zeus quickly took and hid in his thigh, and afterwards, when the period which nature prescribed for the child's birth had completed its growth, he brought it to Nysa in Arabia. There the boy was reared by nymphs and was given the name Dionysus after his father (*Dios*) and after the place (*Nysa*); and since he grew to be

[1] Cp. the other account of this Semelê in Book 1. 23. 4 f.

DIODORUS OF SICILY

γενόμενον δὲ τῷ κάλλει διάφορον τὸ μὲν πρῶτον ἐν χορείαις καὶ γυναικῶν θιάσοις καὶ παντοδαπῇ τρυφῇ καὶ παιδιᾷ διατελεῖν· μετὰ δὲ ταῦτα στρατόπεδον ἐκ τῶν γυναικῶν συναγαγόντα καὶ θύρσοις καθοπλίσαντα στρατείαν ἐπὶ πᾶσαν ποιή-
7 σασθαι τὴν οἰκουμένην. καταδεῖξαι δὲ καὶ τὰ περὶ τὰς τελετὰς καὶ μεταδοῦναι τῶν μυστηρίων τοῖς εὐσεβέσι τῶν ἀνθρώπων καὶ δίκαιον βίον ἀσκοῦσι, πρὸς δὲ τούτοις πανταχοῦ πανηγύρεις ἄγειν καὶ μουσικοὺς ἀγῶνας συντελεῖν, καὶ τὸ σύνολον συλλύοντα τὰ[1] νείκη τῶν ἐθνῶν καὶ πόλεων ἀντὶ τῶν στάσεων καὶ τῶν πολέμων ὁμόνοιαν καὶ πολλὴν εἰρήνην κατασκευάζειν.

65. διαβοηθείσης δὲ κατὰ πάντα τόπον τῆς τοῦ θεοῦ παρουσίας, καὶ διότι πᾶσιν ἐπιεικῶς προσφερόμενος πολλὰ συμβάλλεται πρὸς τὴν ἐξημέρωσιν τοῦ κοινοῦ βίου, πανδημεὶ συναντᾶν αὐτῷ καὶ
2 προσδέχεσθαι μετὰ πολλῆς χαρᾶς. ὀλίγων δ' ὄντων τῶν δι' ὑπερηφανίαν καὶ ἀσέβειαν καταφρονούντων καὶ φασκόντων τὰς μὲν βάκχας δι' ἀκρασίαν αὐτὸν περιάγεσθαι, τὰς δὲ τελετὰς καὶ τὰ μυστήρια φθορᾶς ἕνεκα τῶν ἀλλοτρίων γυναικῶν καταδεικνύειν, κολάζεσθαι τοὺς τοιούτους ὑπ'
3 αὐτοῦ παραχρῆμα. ἐνίοτε γὰρ τῇ τῆς θείας φύσεως ὑπεροχῇ χρώμενον τιμωρεῖσθαι τοὺς ἀσεβεῖς, ποτὲ μὲν αὐτοῖς ἐμβάλλοντα μανίαν, ποτὲ δὲ ταῖς τῶν γυναικῶν χερσὶ ζῶντας διαμελίζοντα· ἐνίοτε δὲ καὶ διὰ τῆς στρατηγικῆς ἐπινοίας

[1] τὰ Bekker: τά τε.

---

[1] Wands wreathed in ivy and vine-leaves with a pine-cone at the top.

of unusual beauty he at first spent his time at dances and with bands of women and in every kind of luxury and amusement, and after that, forming the women into an army and arming them with thyrsi,[1] he made a campaign over all the inhabited world. He also instructed all men who were pious and cultivated a life of justice in the knowledge of his rites and initiated them into his mysteries, and, furthermore, in every place he held great festive assemblages and celebrated musical contests;[2] and, in a word, he composed the quarrels between the nations and cities and created concord and deep peace where there had existed civil strifes and wars.

65. Now since the presence of the god, the myth goes on to say, became noised abroad in every region, and the report spread that he was treating all men honourably and contributing greatly to the refinement of man's social life, the whole populace everywhere thronged to meet him and welcomed him with great joy. There were a few, however, who, out of disdain and impiety, looked down upon him and kept saying that he was leading the Bacchantes about with him because of his incontinence and was introducing the rites and the mysteries that he might thereby seduce the wives of other men, but such persons were punished by him right speedily. For in some cases he made use of the superior power which attended his divine nature and punished the impious, either striking them with madness or causing them while still living to be torn limb from limb by the hands of the women; in other cases he destroyed such as opposed him by a military device which took

---

[2] *e.g.* the "Dionysia."

παραδόξως ἀναιρεῖν τοὺς ἐναντιοπραγοῦντας. ἀναδιδόναι γὰρ ταῖς βάκχαις ἀντὶ τῶν θύρσων λόγχας τῷ κιττῷ κεκαλυμμένας τὴν ἀκμὴν τοῦ σιδήρου· διὸ καὶ τῶν βασιλέων διὰ τὴν ἄγνοιαν καταφρονούντων ὡς ἂν γυναικῶν, καὶ διὰ τοῦτ' ἀπαρασκεύων ὄντων, 4 ἀνελπίστως ἐπιτιθέμενον κατακοντίζειν. τῶν δὲ κολασθέντων ὑπ' αὐτοῦ φασιν ἐπιφανεστάτους εἶναι Πενθέα μὲν παρὰ τοῖς Ἕλλησι, Μύρρανον δὲ τὸν βασιλέα παρ' Ἰνδοῖς, Λυκοῦργον δὲ παρὰ τοῖς Θρᾳξί. μυθολογοῦσι γὰρ τὸν Διόνυσον ἐκ τῆς Ἀσίας μέλλοντα τὴν δύναμιν διαβιβάζειν εἰς τὴν Εὐρώπην, συνθέσθαι φιλίαν πρὸς Λυκοῦργον τὸν Θρᾴκης βασιλέα τῆς ἐφ' Ἑλλησπόντῳ· διαβιβάσαντος δὲ αὐτοῦ πρώτας τὰς βάκχας ὡς εἰς φιλίαν χώραν, τὸν μὲν Λυκοῦργον παραγγεῖλαι τοῖς στρατιώταις νυκτὸς ἐπιθέσθαι καὶ τόν τε Διόνυσον καὶ τὰς μαινάδας πάσας ἀνελεῖν, τὸν δὲ Διόνυσον παρά τινος τῶν ἐγχωρίων, ὃς ἐκαλεῖτο Χάροψ, μαθόντα τὴν ἐπιβουλὴν καταπλαγῆναι διὰ τὸ τὴν δύναμιν ἐν τῷ πέραν εἶναι, παντελῶς δ' ὀλίγους 5 αὐτῷ τῶν φίλων συνδιαβεβηκέναι. διόπερ λάθρᾳ τούτου διαπλεύσαντος πρὸς τὸ σφέτερον στρατόπεδον, τὸν μὲν Λυκοῦργόν φασιν ἐπιθέμενον ταῖς μαινάσιν ἐν τῷ καλουμένῳ Νυσίῳ πάσας ἀποκτεῖναι, τὸν δὲ Διόνυσον περαιώσαντα τὰς δυνάμεις μάχῃ κρατῆσαι τῶν Θρᾳκῶν, καὶ τὸν Λυκοῦργον ζωγρήσαντα τυφλῶσαί τε καὶ πᾶσαν αἰκίαν 6 εἰσενεγκάμενον ἀνασταυρῶσαι. μετὰ δὲ ταῦτα τῷ μὲν Χάροπι χάριν ἀποδιδόντα τῆς εὐεργεσίας παραδοῦναι τὴν τῶν Θρᾳκῶν βασιλείαν καὶ διδάξαι τὰ κατὰ τὰς τελετὰς ὄργια· Χάροπος δ' υἱὸν γενό-

them by surprise. For he distributed to the women, instead of the thyrsi, lances whose tips of iron were covered with ivy leaves; consequently, when the kings in their ignorance disdained them because they were women and for this reason were unprepared, he attacked them when they did not expect it and slew them with the spears. Among those who were punished by him, the most renowned, they say, were Pentheus among the Greeks, Myrrhanus the king of the Indians, and Lycurgus among the Thracians. For the myth relates that when Dionysus was on the point of leading his force over from Asia into Europe, he concluded a treaty of friendship with Lycurgus, who was king of that part of Thrace which lies upon the Hellespont. Now when he had led the first of the Bacchantes over into a friendly land, as he thought, Lycurgus issued orders to his soldiers to fall upon them by night and to slay both Dionysus and all the Maenads, and Dionysus, learning of the plot from a man of the country who was called Charops, was struck with dismay, because his army was on the other side of the Hellespont and only a mere handful of his friends had crossed over with him. Consequently he sailed across secretly to his army, and then Lycurgus, they say, falling upon the Maenads in the city known as Nysium, slew them all, but Dionysus, bringing his forces over, conquered the Thracians in a battle, and taking Lycurgus alive put out his eyes and inflicted upon him every kind of outrage, and then crucified him. Thereupon, out of gratitude to Charops for the aid the man had rendered him, Dionysus made over to him the kingdom of the Thracians and instructed him in the secret rites connected with the initiations; and Oeagrus,

μενον Οἴαγρον παραλαβεῖν τήν τε βασιλείαν καὶ τὰς ἐν τοῖς μυστηρίοις παραδεδομένας τελετάς, ἃς ὕστερον Ὀρφέα τὸν Οἰάγρου μαθόντα παρὰ τοῦ πατρός, καὶ φύσει καὶ παιδείᾳ τῶν ἁπάντων διενεγκόντα, πολλὰ μεταθεῖναι τῶν ἐν τοῖς ὀργίοις· διὸ καὶ τὰς ὑπὸ τοῦ Διονύσου γενομένας τελετὰς Ὀρφικὰς προσαγορευθῆναι.

7 Τῶν δὲ ποιητῶν τινες, ὧν ἐστι καὶ Ἀντίμαχος, ἀποφαίνονται τὸν Λυκοῦργον οὐ Θρᾴκης, ἀλλὰ τῆς Ἀραβίας γεγονέναι βασιλέα, καὶ τῷ τε Διονύσῳ καὶ ταῖς βάκχαις τὴν ἐπίθεσιν ἐν τῇ κατὰ τὴν Ἀραβίαν Νύσῃ πεποιῆσθαι. τὸν δ᾽ οὖν Διόνυσόν φασι κολάσαντα μὲν τοὺς ἀσεβεῖς, ἐπιεικῶς δὲ προσενεχθέντα τοῖς ἄλλοις ἀνθρώποις, ἐκ τῆς Ἰνδικῆς ἐπ᾽ ἐλέφαντος τὴν εἰς Θήβας ἐπ-
8 άνοδον ποιήσασθαι. τριετοῦς δὲ διαγεγενημένου τοῦ σύμπαντος χρόνου, φασὶ τοὺς Ἕλληνας ἀπὸ ταύτης τῆς αἰτίας ἄγειν τὰς τριετηρίδας. μυθολογοῦσι δ᾽ αὐτὸν καὶ λαφύρων ἠθροικότα πλῆθος ὡς ἂν ἀπὸ τηλικαύτης στρατείας, πρῶτον τῶν ἁπάντων καταγαγεῖν θρίαμβον εἰς τὴν πατρίδα.

66. Αὗται μὲν οὖν αἱ γενέσεις συμφωνοῦνται μάλιστα παρὰ τοῖς παλαιοῖς· ἀμφισβητοῦσι δὲ καὶ πόλεις οὐκ ὀλίγαι Ἑλληνίδες τῆς τούτου τεκνώσεως· καὶ γὰρ Ἠλεῖοι καὶ Νάξιοι, πρὸς δὲ τούτοις οἱ τὰς Ἐλευθερὰς οἰκοῦντες καὶ Τήιοι καὶ πλείους
2 ἕτεροι παρ᾽ ἑαυτοῖς ἀποφαίνονται τεκνωθῆναι. καὶ Τήιοι μὲν τεκμήριον φέρουσι τῆς παρ᾽ αὐτοῖς γενέσεως τοῦ θεοῦ τὸ μέχρι τοῦ νῦν τεταγμένοις χρόνοις

the son of Charops, then took over both the kingdom and the initiatory rites which were handed down in the mysteries, the rites which afterwards Orpheus, the son of Oeagrus, who was the superior of all men in natural gifts and education, learned from his father; Orpheus also made many changes in the practices and for that reason the rites which had been established by Dionysus were also called "Orphic."

But some of the poets, one of whom is Antimachus,[1] state that Lycurgus was king, not of Thrace, but of Arabia, and that the attack upon Dionysus and the Bacchantes was made at the Nysa which is in Arabia. However this may be, Dionysus, they say, punished the impious but treated all other men honourably, and then made his return journey from India to Thebes upon an elephant. The entire time consumed in the journey was three years, and it is for this reason, they say, that the Greeks hold his festival every other year. The myth also relates that he gathered a great mass of booty, such as would result from such a campaign, and that he was the first of all men to make his return to his native country in a triumph.

66. Now these accounts of the birth of Dionysus are generally agreed upon by the ancient writers; but rival claims are raised by not a few Greek cities to having been the place of his birth. The peoples of Elis and Naxos, for instance, and the inhabitants of Eleutherae and Teos and several other peoples, state that he was born in their cities. The Teans advance as proof that the god was born among them the fact that, even to this day, at fixed times in their

[1] Antimachus of Colophon lived in the latter part of the fifth century B.C. in the period of the Peloponnesian War.

ἐν τῇ πόλει πηγὴν αὐτομάτως ἐκ τῆς γῆς οἴνου ῥεῖν εὐωδίᾳ διαφέροντος· τῶν δ' ἄλλων οἱ μὲν ἱερὰν Διονύσου δεικνύουσι τὴν χώραν, οἱ δὲ ναοὺς καὶ τεμένη διαφερόντως ἐκ παλαιῶν χρόνων αὐτῷ καθι-
3 δρυμένα. καθόλου δ' ἐν πολλοῖς τόποις τῆς οἰκουμένης ἀπολελοιπότος τοῦ θεοῦ σημεῖα τῆς ἰδίας εὐεργεσίας ἅμα καὶ παρουσίας, οὐδὲν παράδοξον ἑκάστους νομίζειν οἰκειότητά τινα γεγονέναι τῷ Διονύσῳ πρὸς τὴν ἑαυτῶν πόλιν τε καὶ χώραν. μαρτυρεῖ δὲ τοῖς ὑφ' ἡμῶν λεγομένοις καὶ ὁ ποιητὴς ἐν τοῖς ὕμνοις, λέγων περὶ τῶν ἀμφισβητούντων τῆς τούτου γενέσεως καὶ ἅμα τεκνωθῆναι παρεισάγων αὐτὸν ἐν τῇ κατὰ τὴν Ἀραβίαν Νύσῃ,

οἱ μὲν γὰρ Δρακάνῳ σ', οἱ δ' Ἰκάρῳ ἠνεμοέσσῃ
φάσ',[1] οἱ δ' ἐν Νάξῳ, δῖον γένος, εἰραφιῶτα,
οἱ δέ σ' ἐπ' Ἀλφειῷ ποταμῷ βαθυδινήεντι
κυσαμένην Σεμέλην τεκέειν Διὶ τερπικεραύνῳ,
ἄλλοι δ' ἐν Θήβῃσιν, ἄναξ, σε λέγουσι γενέσθαι,
ψευδόμενοι· σὲ δ' ἔτικτε πατὴρ ἀνδρῶν τε θεῶν τε
πολλὸν ἀπ' ἀνθρώπων κρύπτων λευκώλενον Ἥρην.
ἔστι δέ τις Νύσῃ, ὕπατον ὄρος, ἀνθέον ὕλῃ,
τηλοῦ Φοινίκης, σχεδὸν Αἰγύπτοιο ῥοάων.

[1] φασ' Rhodomann : φασίν.

---

[1] Archaeological evidence that a miraculous flow of wine was caused by the priests of a temple (of Dionysus?) of the fifth century B.C. in Corinth is presented by Campbell Bonner, "A Dionysiac Miracle at Corinth," *Am. Journal of Archaeology*, 33 (1929), 368–75.

[2] *Homeric Hymns*, 1. 1–9.

BOOK III. 66. 2–3

city a fountain of wine,[1] of unusually sweet fragrance, flows of its own accord from the earth; and as for the peoples of the other cities, they in some cases point out a plot of land which is sacred to Dionysus, in other cases shrines and sacred precincts which have been consecrated to him from ancient times. But, speaking generally, since the god has left behind him in many places over the inhabited world evidences of his personal favour and presence, it is not surprising that in each case the people should think that Dionysus had had a peculiar relationship to both their city and country. And testimony to our opinion is also offered by the poet in his Hymns,[2] when he speaks of those who lay claim to the birthplace of Dionysus and, in that connection, represents him as being born in the Nysa which is in Arabia:

> Some Dracanum, wind-swept Icarus some,
> Some Naxos, Zeus-born one, or Alpheius' stream
> Deep-eddied, call the spot where Semelê
> Bore thee, Eiraphiotes,[3] unto Zeus
> Who takes delight in thunder; others still
> Would place thy birth, O Lord, in Thebes. 'Tis false;
> The sire of men and gods brought thee to light,
> Unknown to white-armed Hera, far from men.
> There is a certain Nysa, mountain high,
> With forests thick, in Phoenicê afar,
> Close to Aegyptus' streams.

[3] Of the seven explanations offered in antiquity for the origin of this name for Dionysus the most probable is that which derives it from the Greek word *eriphos* ("kid"), on the basis of the myth that Zeus changed the infant Dionysus into a kid which Hermes took to Nysa and turned over to the Nymphs.

4 Οὐκ ἀγνοῶ δ' ὅτι καὶ τῶν τὴν Λιβύην νεμομένων οἱ παρὰ τὸν ὠκεανὸν οἰκοῦντες ἀμφισβητοῦσι τῆς τοῦ θεοῦ γενέσεως, καὶ τὴν Νῦσαν καὶ τἄλλα τὰ περὶ αὐτοῦ μυθολογούμενα παρ' ἑαυτοῖς δεικνύουσι γεγενημένα, καὶ πολλὰ τεκμήρια τούτων μέχρι τοῦ καθ' ἡμᾶς βίου διαμένειν κατὰ τὴν χώραν φασί· πρὸς δὲ τούτοις ὅτι πολλοὶ τῶν παλαιῶν παρ' Ἕλλησι μυθογράφων καὶ ποιητῶν συμφωνούμενα τούτοις ἱστοροῦσι καὶ τῶν μεταγενεστέρων συγ- 5 γραφέων οὐκ ὀλίγοι. διόπερ, ἵνα μηδὲν παραλίπωμεν τῶν ἱστορημένων περὶ Διονύσου, διέξιμεν ἐν κεφαλαίοις τὰ παρὰ τοῖς Λίβυσι λεγόμενα καὶ τῶν Ἑλληνικῶν συγγραφέων ὅσοι τούτοις σύμφωνα γεγράφασι καὶ Διονυσίῳ τῷ συνταξαμένῳ τὰς 6 παλαιὰς μυθοποιίας. οὗτος γὰρ τά τε περὶ τὸν Διόνυσον καὶ τὰς Ἀμαζόνας, ἔτι δὲ τοὺς Ἀργοναύτας καὶ τὰ κατὰ τὸν Ἰλιακὸν πόλεμον πραχθέντα καὶ πόλλ' ἕτερα συντέτακται, παρατιθεὶς τὰ ποιήματα τῶν ἀρχαίων, τῶν τε μυθολόγων καὶ τῶν ποιητῶν.

67. Φησὶ τοίνυν παρ' Ἕλλησι πρῶτον εὑρετὴν γενέσθαι Λίνον ῥυθμῶν καὶ μέλους, ἔτι δὲ Κάδμου κομίσαντος ἐκ Φοινίκης τὰ καλούμενα γράμματα πρῶτον εἰς τὴν Ἑλληνικὴν μεταθεῖναι διάλεκτον, καὶ τὰς προσηγορίας ἑκάστῳ τάξαι καὶ τοὺς χαρακτῆρας διατυπῶσαι. κοινῇ μὲν οὖν τὰ γράμματα Φοινίκεια κληθῆναι διὰ τὸ παρὰ τοὺς Ἕλληνας ἐκ Φοινίκων μετενεχθῆναι, ἰδίᾳ δὲ τῶν Πελασγῶν πρώτων χρησαμένων τοῖς μετατεθεῖσι χαρακτῆρσι

BOOK III. 66. 4-67. 1

I am not unaware that also those inhabitants of Libya who dwell on the shore of the ocean lay claim to the birthplace of the god, and point out that Nysa and all the stories which the myths record are found among themselves, and many witnesses to this statement, they say, remain in the land down to our own lifetime; and I also know that many of the ancient Greek writers of myths and poets, and not a few of the later historians as well, agree with this in their accounts. Consequently, in order not to omit anything which history records about Dionysus, we shall present in summary what is told by the Libyans and those Greek historians whose writings are in accord with these and with that Dionysius[1] who composed an account out of the ancient fabulous tales. For this writer has composed an account of Dionysus and the Amazons, as well as of the Argonauts and the events connected with the Trojan War and many other matters, in which he cites the versions of the ancient writers, both the composers of myths and the poets.

67. This, then, is the account of Dionysius: Among the Greeks Linus was the first to discover the different rhythms and song, and when Cadmus brought from Phoenicia the letters, as they are called, Linus was again the first to transfer them into the Greek language, to give a name to each character, and to fix its shape. Now the letters, as a group, are called "Phoenician" because they were brought to the Greeks from the Phoenicians, but as single letters the Pelasgians were the first to make use of the transferred characters and so they were called

[1] Cp. p. 246, n. 2.

DIODORUS OF SICILY

2 Πελασγικὰ προσαγορευθῆναι. τὸν δὲ Λίνον ἐπὶ ποιητικῇ καὶ μελῳδίᾳ θαυμασθέντα μαθητὰς σχεῖν πολλούς, ἐπιφανεστάτους δὲ τρεῖς, Ἡρακλέα, Θαμύραν,[1] Ὀρφέα. τούτων δὲ τὸν μὲν Ἡρακλέα κιθαρίζειν μανθάνοντα διὰ τὴν τῆς ψυχῆς βραδυτῆτα μὴ δύνασθαι δέξασθαι τὴν μάθησιν, ἔπειθ᾽ ὑπὸ τοῦ Λίνου πληγαῖς ἐπιτιμηθέντα διοργισθῆναι καὶ τῇ κιθάρᾳ τὸν διδάσκαλον πατάξαντα ἀποκτεῖναι. 3 Θαμύραν δὲ φύσει διαφόρῳ κεχορηγημένον ἐκπονῆσαι τὰ περὶ τὴν μουσικήν, καὶ κατὰ τὴν ἐν τῷ μελῳδεῖν ὑπεροχὴν φάσκειν ἑαυτὸν τῶν Μουσῶν ἐμμελέστερον ᾄδειν. διὸ καὶ τὰς θεὰς αὐτῷ χολωθείσας τήν τε μουσικὴν ἀφελέσθαι καὶ πηρῶσαι τὸν ἄνδρα, καθάπερ καὶ τὸν Ὅμηρον τούτοις προσμαρτυρεῖν λέγοντα

ἔνθα τε Μοῦσαι
ἀντόμεναι Θάμυριν τὸν Θρήικα παῦσαν ἀοιδῆς,

καὶ ἔτι

αἱ δὲ χολωσάμεναι πηρὸν θέσαν, αὐτὰρ ἀοιδὴν
θεσπεσίην ἀφέλοντο καὶ ἐκλέλαθον κιθαριστύν.

4 περὶ δὲ Ὀρφέως τοῦ τρίτου μαθητοῦ τὰ[2] κατὰ μέρος ἀναγράψομεν, ὅταν τὰς πράξεις αὐτοῦ διεξίωμεν.

[1] Θάμυριν CF.   [2] τὰ added by Dindorf.

---

[1] As our knowledge of the history of the development of the Greek letters has increased in recent years and as early Phoenician and Semitic inscriptions have come to light, all the evidence confirms the Greek tradition that their alphabet was derived from the Phoenician. The question now is, How early did the Phoenician letters appear on the Greek mainland? The "palace" of Cadmus, if Cadmus is an historical figure, has been discovered in Thebes, and may be roughly dated around 1400–1200 B.C.; and "letters" were

"Pelasgic."[1] Linus also, who was admired because of his poetry and singing, had many pupils and three of greatest renown, Heracles, Thamyras, and Orpheus. Of these three Heracles, who was learning to play the lyre, was unable to appreciate what was taught him because of his sluggishness of soul, and once when he had been punished with rods by Linus he became violently angry and killed his teacher with a blow of the lyre. Thamyras, however, who possessed unusual natural ability, perfected the art of music and claimed that in the excellence of song his voice was more beautiful than the voices of the Muses. Whereupon the goddesses, angered at him, took from him his gift of music and maimed the man, even as Homer also bears witness when he writes[2]:

> There met the Muses Thamyris of Thrace
> And made an end of his song;

and again:

> But him, enraged, they maimed, and from him took
> The gift of song divine and made him quite
> Forget his harping.

About Orpheus, the third pupil, we shall give a detailed account when we come to treat of his deeds.[3]

---

found in it, but they were not of Semitic origin. See Rhys Carpenter, "Letters of Cadmus," *Am. Journ. of Philology*, 56 (1935), 5–13. The present evidence appears to indicate that the Greeks took over the Phoenician letters around 800 B.C. Arguments for this view, an excellent brief discussion of the more recent literature, and two Tables showing the forms of Semitic letters between the thirteenth and eighth centuries B.C. and of the earliest Greek letters, are given by John Day, in *The Classical Weekly*, 28 (1934), 65–9 (Dec. 10), 73–80 (Dec. 17).

[2] *Iliad* 2. 594–5, and 599–600 below.   [3] Cp. Book 4. 25.

Τὸν δ' οὖν Λίνον φασὶ τοῖς Πελασγικοῖς γράμμασι συνταξάμενον τὰς τοῦ πρώτου Διονύσου πράξεις καὶ τὰς ἄλλας μυθολογίας ἀπολιπεῖν ἐν τοῖς ὑπομνήμασιν. ὁμοίως δὲ τούτοις χρήσασθαι τοῖς Πελασγικοῖς γράμμασι τὸν Ὀρφέα καὶ Προναπίδην τὸν Ὁμήρου διδάσκαλον, εὐφυῆ γεγονότα μελοποιόν· πρὸς δὲ τούτοις Θυμοίτην τὸν Θυμοίτου τοῦ Λαομέδοντος, κατὰ τὴν ἡλικίαν γεγονότα τὴν Ὀρφέως, ὅν[1] πλανηθῆναι κατὰ πολλοὺς τόπους τῆς οἰκουμένης, καὶ παραβαλεῖν τῆς Λιβύης εἰς τὴν πρὸς ἑσπέραν χώραν[2] ἕως ὠκεανοῦ· θεάσασθαι δὲ καὶ τὴν Νῦσαν, ἐν ᾗ μυθολογοῦσιν οἱ ἐγχώριοι ἀρχαῖοι[3] τραφῆναι τὸν Διόνυσον, καὶ τὰς κατὰ μέρος τοῦ θεοῦ τούτου πράξεις μαθόντα παρὰ τῶν Νυσαέων συντάξασθαι τὴν Φρυγίαν ὀνομαζομένην ποίησιν, ἀρχαϊκοῖς[4] τῇ τε διαλέκτῳ καὶ τοῖς γράμμασι χρησάμενον.

68. Φησὶ δ' οὖν Ἄμμωνα βασιλεύοντα τοῦ μέρους τῆς Λιβύης Οὐρανοῦ γῆμαι θυγατέρα τὴν προσαγορευομένην Ῥέαν, ἀδελφὴν οὖσαν Κρόνου τε καὶ τῶν ἄλλων Τιτάνων. ἐπιόντα δὲ τὴν βασιλείαν εὑρεῖν πλησίον τῶν Κεραυνίων καλουμένων ὀρῶν παρθένον τῷ κάλλει διαφέρουσαν Ἀμάλθειαν 2 ὄνομα. ἐρασθέντα δ' αὐτῆς καὶ πλησιάσαντα γεννῆσαι παῖδα τῷ τε κάλλει καὶ τῇ ῥώμῃ θαυμαστόν, καὶ τὴν μὲν Ἀμάλθειαν ἀποδεῖξαι κυρίαν τοῦ σύνεγγυς τόπου παντός, ὄντος τῷ σχήματι παραπλησίου κέρατι βοός, ἀφ' ἧς αἰτίας Ἑσπέρου

[1] ὅν added by Jacoby.
[2] τῆς οἰκουμένης after χώραν deleted by Rhodomann.
[3] ἀρχαῖοι deleted by Jacoby.
[4] ἀρχαϊκοῖς Dindorf: ἀρχαικῶς.

BOOK III. 67. 4–68. 2

Now Linus, they say, composed an account in the Pelasgic letters of the deeds of the first Dionysus and of the other mythical legends and left them among his memoirs. And in the same manner use was made of these Pelasgic letters by Orpheus and Pronapides who was the teacher of Homer and a gifted writer of songs; and also by Thymoetes, the son of Thymoetes, the son of Laomedon, who lived at the same time as Orpheus, wandered over many regions of the inhabited world, and penetrated to the western part of Libya as far as the ocean. He also visited Nysa, where the ancient natives of the city relate the myth that Dionysus was reared there, and, after he had learned from the Nysaeans of the deeds of this god one and all, he composed the " Phrygian poem," as it is called, wherein he made use of the archaic manner both of speech and of letters.

68. Dionysius, then,[1] continues his account as follows: Ammon, the king of that part of Libya, married a daughter of Uranus who was called Rhea and was a sister of Cronus and the other Titans. And once when Ammon was going about his kingdom, near the Ceraunian Mountains, as they are called, he came upon a maiden of unusual beauty whose name was Amaltheia. And becoming enamoured of her he lay with the maiden and begat a son of marvellous beauty as well as bodily vigour, and Amaltheia herself he appointed mistress of all the region round about, which was shaped like the horn of a bull and for this reason was known as

---

[1] The narrative of Dionysius is apparently resumed from the end of chapter 61.

κέρας προσαγορευθῆναι· διὰ δὲ τὴν ἀρετὴν τῆς χώρας εἶναι πλήρη παντοδαπῆς ἀμπέλου καὶ τῶν ἄλλων δένδρων τῶν ἡμέρους φερόντων καρπούς.

3 τῆς δὲ προειρημένης γυναικὸς τὴν δυναστείαν παραλαβούσης, ἀπὸ ταύτης τὴν χώραν Ἀμαλθείας κέρας ὀνομασθῆναι· διὸ καὶ τοὺς μεταγενεστέρους ἀνθρώπους διὰ τὴν προειρημένην αἰτίαν τὴν κρατίστην γῆν καὶ παντοδαποῖς καρποῖς πλήθουσαν ὡσαύτως Ἀμαλθείας κέρας προσαγορεύειν.

4 Τὸν δ' οὖν Ἄμμωνα φοβούμενον τὴν τῆς Ῥέας ζηλοτυπίαν κρύψαι τὸ γεγονός, καὶ τὸν παῖδα λάθρα μετενεγκεῖν εἴς τινα πόλιν Νῦσαν, μακρὰν 5 ἀπ' ἐκείνων τῶν τόπων ἀπηρτημένην. κεῖσθαι δὲ ταύτην ἔν τινι νήσῳ περιεχομένῃ μὲν ὑπὸ τοῦ Τρίτωνος ποταμοῦ, περικρήμνῳ δὲ καὶ καθ' ἕνα τόπον ἐχούσῃ στενὰς εἰσβολάς, ἃς ὠνομάσθαι πύλας Νυσίας. εἶναι δ' ἐν αὐτῇ χώραν εὐδαίμονα λειμῶσί τε μαλακοῖς διειλημμένην καὶ πηγαίοις[1] ὕδασιν ἀρδευομένην δαψιλέσι, δένδρα τε καρποφόρα παντοῖα καὶ πολλὴν ἄμπελον αὐτοφυῆ 6 καὶ ταύτης τὴν πλείστην ἀναδενδράδα. ὑπάρχειν δὲ καὶ πάντα τὸν[2] τόπον εὔπνουν, ἔτι δὲ καθ' ὑπερβολὴν ὑγιεινόν· καὶ διὰ τοῦτο τοὺς ἐν αὐτῷ κατοικοῦντας μακροβιωτάτους ὑπάρχειν τῶν πλησιοχώρων. εἶναι δὲ τῆς νήσου τὴν μὲν πρώτην εἰσβολὴν αὐλωνοειδῆ, σύσκιον ὑψηλοῖς καὶ πυκνοῖς δένδρεσιν, ὥστε τὸν ἥλιον μὴ παντάπασι διαλάμπειν διὰ τὴν συνάγκειαν, αὐγὴν δὲ μόνην ὁρᾶσθαι φωτός.

69. Πάντῃ δὲ κατὰ τὰς παρόδους προχεῖσθαι

[1] πηγαίοις Dindorf: κηπίοις D, κηπείοις C, κηπείαις F.
[2] τὸν added by Dindorf.

BOOK III. 68. 2–69. 1

Hesperoukeras [1]; and the region, because of the excellent quality of the land, abounds in every variety of the vine and all other trees which bear cultivated fruits. When the woman whom we have just mentioned took over the supreme power the country was named after her Amaltheias Keras [2]; consequently the men of later times, for the reason which we have just given, likewise call any especially fertile bit of ground which abounds in fruits of every kind " Amaltheia's Horn."

Now Ammon, fearing the jealousy of Rhea, concealed the affair and brought the boy secretly to a certain city called Nysa, which was at a great distance from those parts. This city lies on a certain island which is surrounded by the river Triton and is precipitous on all sides save at one place where there is a narrow pass which bears the name " Nysaean Gates." The land of the island is rich, is traversed at intervals by pleasant meadows and watered by abundant streams from springs, and possesses every kind of fruit-bearing tree and the wild vine in abundance, which for the most part grows up trees. The whole region, moreover, has a fresh and pure air and is furthermore exceedingly healthful; and for this reason its inhabitants are the longest lived of any in those parts. The entrance into the island is like a glen at its beginning, being thickly shaded by lofty trees growing close together, so that the sun never shines at all through the close-set branches but only the radiance of its light may be seen.

69. Everywhere along the lanes, the account con-

---

[1] " Horn of Hesperus."
[2] " Horn of Amaltheia."

πηγὰς ὑδάτων τῇ γλυκύτητι διαφόρων, ὥστε τὸν τόπον εἶναι τοῖς βουλομένοις ἐνδιατρῖψαι προσηνέστατον. ἑξῆς δ' ὑπάρχειν ἄντρον τῷ μὲν σχήματι κυκλοτερές, τῷ δὲ μεγέθει καὶ τῷ κάλλει θαυμαστόν. ὑπερκεῖσθαι γὰρ αὐτοῦ πανταχῇ κρημνὸν πρὸς ὕψος ἐξαίσιον, πέτρας ἔχοντα τοῖς χρώμασι διαφόρους· ἐναλλὰξ γὰρ ἀποστίλβειν τὰς μὲν θαλαττίᾳ πορφύρᾳ τὴν χρόαν ἐχούσας παραπλήσιον, τὰς δὲ κυανῷ, τινὰς δ' ἄλλαις φύσεσι περιλαμπομέναις, ὥστε μηδὲν εἶναι χρῶμα τῶν ἑωραμένων
2 παρ' ἀνθρώποις περὶ τὸν τόπον ἀθεώρητον. πρὸ δὲ τῆς εἰσόδου πεφυκέναι δένδρα θαυμαστά, τὰ μὲν κάρπιμα, τὰ δὲ ἀειθαλῆ, πρὸς αὐτὴν μόνον τὴν ἀπὸ τῆς θέας τέρψιν ὑπὸ τῆς φύσεως δεδημιουργημένα· ἐν δὲ τούτοις ἐννεοττεύειν ὄρνεα παντοδαπὰ ταῖς φύσεσιν, ἃ τὴν χρόαν ἔχειν ἐπιτερπῆ καὶ τὴν μελῳδίαν προσηνεστάτην. διὸ καὶ πάντα τὸν τόπον ὑπάρχειν μὴ μόνον θεοπρεπῆ κατὰ τὴν πρόσοψιν, ἀλλὰ καὶ κατὰ τὸν ἦχον, ὡς ἂν τῆς αὐτοδιδάκτου γλυκυφωνίας νικώσης τὴν ἐναρμόνιον τῆς τέχνης μελῳδίαν.
3 διελθόντι δὲ τὴν εἴσοδον θεωρεῖσθαι μὲν ἄντρον ἀναπεπταμένον καὶ τῇ κατὰ τὸν ἥλιον αὐγῇ περιλαμπόμενον, ἄνθη δὲ παντοδαπὰ πεφυκότα, καὶ μάλιστα τήν τε κασίαν καὶ τἆλλα τὰ δυνάμενα δι' ἐνιαυτῶν διαφυλάττειν τὴν εὐωδίαν· ὁρᾶσθαι δὲ καὶ νυμφῶν εὐνὰς ἐν αὐτῷ πλείους ἐξ ἀνθῶν παντοδαπῶν, οὐ χειροποιήτους, ἀλλ' ὑπ' αὐτῆς
4 τῆς φύσεως ἀνειμένας θεοπρεπῶς. κατὰ πάντα δὲ τὸν τῆς περιφερείας κύκλον οὔτ' ἄνθος οὔτε φύλλον πεπτωκὸς ὁρᾶσθαι. διὸ καὶ τοῖς θεωμένοις οὐ μόνον ἐπιτερπῆ φαίνεσθαι τὴν πρόσοψιν, ἀλλὰ καὶ τὴν εὐωδίαν προσηνεστάτην.

tinues, springs of water gush forth of exceeding sweetness, making the place most pleasant to those who desire to tarry there. Further in there is a cave, circular in shape and of marvellous size and beauty. For above and all about it rises a crag of immense height, formed of rocks of different colours; for the rocks lie in bands and send forth a bright gleam, some like that purple which comes from the sea,[1] some bluish and others like every other kind of brilliant hue, the result being that there is not a colour to be seen among men which is not visible in that place. Before the entrance grow marvellous trees, some fruit-bearing, others evergreen, and all of them fashioned by nature for no other end than to delight the eye; and in them nest every kind of bird of pleasing colour and most charming song. Consequently the whole place is meet for a god, not merely in its aspect but in its sound as well, since the sweet tones which nature teaches are always superior to the song which is devised by art. When one has passed the entrance the cave is seen to widen out and to be lighted all about by the rays of the sun, and all kinds of flowering plants grow there, especially the cassia and every other kind which has the power to preserve its fragrance throughout the year; and in it are also to be seen several couches of nymphs, formed of every manner of flower, made not by hand but by the light touch of Nature herself, in manner meet for a god. Moreover, throughout the whole place round about not a flower or leaf is to be seen which has fallen. Consequently those who gaze upon this spot find not only its aspect delightful but also its fragrance most pleasant.

[1] *i.e.* the purple derived from the mollusc *Murex brandaris*.

DIODORUS OF SICILY

70. Εἰς τοῦτο οὖν τὸ ἄντρον τὸν Ἄμμωνα παραγενόμενον παραθέσθαι τὸν παῖδα καὶ παραδοῦναι τρέφειν Νύσῃ, μιᾷ τῶν Ἀρισταίου θυγατέρων· ἐπιστάτην δ' αὐτοῦ τάξαι τὸν Ἀρισταῖον, ἄνδρα συνέσει καὶ σωφροσύνῃ καὶ πάσῃ παιδείᾳ διαφέροντα.
2 πρὸς δὲ τὰς ἀπὸ τῆς μητρυιᾶς Ῥέας ἐπιβουλὰς φύλακα τοῦ παιδὸς καταστῆσαι τὴν Ἀθηνᾶν, μικρὸν πρὸ τούτων τῶν χρόνων γηγενῆ φανεῖσαν ἐπὶ τοῦ Τρίτωνος ποταμοῦ, δι' ὃν Τριτωνίδα προσηγορεῦ-
3 σθαι. μυθολογοῦσι δὲ τὴν θεὸν ταύτην ἑλομένην τὸν πάντα χρόνον τὴν παρθενίαν σωφροσύνῃ τε διενεγκεῖν καὶ τὰς πλείστας τῶν τεχνῶν ἐξευρεῖν, ἀγχίνουν οὖσαν καθ' ὑπερβολήν· ζηλῶσαι δὲ καὶ τὰ κατὰ τὸν πόλεμον, ἀλκῇ δὲ καὶ ῥώμῃ διαφέρουσαν ἄλλα τε πολλὰ πρᾶξαι μνήμης ἄξια καὶ τὴν Αἰγίδα προσαγορευομένην ἀνελεῖν, θηρίον τι καταπληκτι-
4 κὸν καὶ παντελῶς δυσκαταγώνιστον. γηγενὲς γὰρ ὑπάρχον καὶ φυσικῶς ἐκ τοῦ στόματος ἄπλατον ἐκβάλλον φλόγα τὸ μὲν πρῶτον φανῆναι περὶ τὴν Φρυγίαν, καὶ κατακαῦσαι τὴν χώραν, ἣν μέχρι τοῦ νῦν κατακεκαυμένην Φρυγίαν ὀνομάζεσθαι· ἔπειτ' ἐπελθεῖν τὰ περὶ τὸν Ταῦρον ὄρη συνεχῶς, καὶ κατακαῦσαι τοὺς ἑξῆς δρυμοὺς μέχρι τῆς Ἰνδικῆς. μετὰ δὲ ταῦτα πάλιν ἐπὶ θάλατταν τὴν ἐπάνοδον ποιησάμενον περὶ μὲν τὴν Φοινίκην ἐμπρῆσαι τοὺς κατὰ τὸν Λίβανον δρυμούς, καὶ δι' Αἰγύπτου πορευθὲν ἐπὶ τῆς Λιβύης διελθεῖν τοὺς περὶ τὴν ἑσπέραν τόπους, καὶ τὸ τελευταῖον εἰς

---

[1] Cp. Book 1. 12. 8 for the explanation of the name "Tritogeneia" for Athena.

BOOK III. 70. 1-4

70. Now to this cave, the account runs, Ammon came and brought the child and gave him into the care of Nysa, one of the daughters of Aristaeus; and he appointed Aristaeus to be the guardian of the child, he being a man who excelled in understanding, and in self-control, and in all learning. The duty of protecting the boy against the plottings of his stepmother Rhea he assigned to Athena, who a short while before had been born of the earth and had been found beside the river Triton, from which she had been called Tritonis.[1] And according to the myth this goddess, choosing to spend all her days in maidenhood, excelled in virtue and invented most of the crafts, since she was exceedingly ready of wit; she cultivated also the arts of war, and since she excelled in courage and in bodily strength she performed many other deeds worthy of memory and slew the Aegis, as it was called, a certain frightful monster which was a difficult antagonist to overcome. For it was sprung from the earth and in accordance with its nature breathed forth terrible flames of fire from its mouth, and its first appearance it made about Phrygia and burned up the land, which to this day is called " Burned Phrygia ";[2] and after that it ravaged unceasingly the lands about the Taurus mountains and burned up the forests extending from that region as far as India. Thereupon, returning again towards the sea round about Phoenicia, it sent up in flames the forests on Mt. Lebanon, and making its way through Egypt it passed over Libya to the regions of the west and at the end of its wanderings

[2] Strabo (12. 8. 18-19) says that this area of Phrygia was occupied by Lydians and Mysians, and that the cause of the name was the frequent earthquakes.

τοὺς περὶ τὰ Κεραύνια δρυμοὺς ἐγκατασκῆψαι. 5 ἐπιφλεγομένης δὲ τῆς χώρας πάντῃ, καὶ τῶν ἀνθρώπων τῶν μὲν ἀπολλυμένων, τῶν δὲ διὰ τὸν φόβον ἐκλειπόντων τὰς πατρίδας καὶ μακρὰν ἐκτοπιζομένων, τὴν Ἀθηνᾶν φασι τὰ μὲν συνέσει τὰ δ' ἀλκῇ καὶ ῥώμῃ περιγενομένην ἀνελεῖν τὸ θηρίον, καὶ τὴν δορὰν αὐτοῦ περιαψαμένην φορεῖν τῷ στήθει, ἅμα μὲν σκέπης ἕνεκα καὶ τῆς φυλακῆς τοῦ σώματος πρὸς τοὺς ὕστερον κινδύνους, ἅμα δ' ἀρετῆς ὑπόμνημα καὶ δικαίας δόξης. 6 τὴν δὲ μητέρα τοῦ θηρίου Γῆν ὀργισθεῖσαν ἀνεῖναι τοὺς ὀνομαζομένους Γίγαντας ἀντιπάλους τοῖς θεοῖς, οὓς ὕστερον ὑπὸ Διὸς ἀναιρεθῆναι, συναγωνιζομένης Ἀθηνᾶς καὶ Διονύσου μετὰ τῶν ἄλλων θεῶν.

7 Οὐ μὴν ἀλλὰ τὸν Διόνυσον ἐν τῇ Νύσῃ τρεφόμενον καὶ μετέχοντα τῶν καλλίστων ἐπιτηδευμάτων μὴ μόνον γενέσθαι τῷ κάλλει καὶ τῇ ῥώμῃ διάφορον, ἀλλὰ καὶ φιλότεχνον καὶ πρὸς πᾶν τὸ χρήσι- 8 μον εὑρετικόν. ἐπινοῆσαι γὰρ αὐτὸν ἔτι παῖδα τὴν ἡλικίαν ὄντα τοῦ μὲν οἴνου τὴν φύσιν τε καὶ χρείαν, ἀποθλίψαντα βότρυς τῆς αὐτοφυοῦς ἀμπέλου, τῶν δ' ὡραίων τὰ δυνάμενα[1] ξηραίνεσθαι καὶ πρὸς ἀποθησαυρισμὸν ὄντα χρήσιμα, μετὰ δὲ ταῦτα καὶ τὰς ἑκάστων κατὰ τρόπον φυτείας εὑρεῖν, καὶ βουληθῆναι τῷ γένει τῶν ἀνθρώπων μεταδοῦναι τῶν ἰδίων εὑρημάτων, ἐλπίσαντα διὰ τὸ μέγεθος τῆς εὐεργεσίας ἀθανάτων τεύξεσθαι τιμῶν.

71. Τῆς δὲ περὶ αὐτὸν ἀρετῆς τε καὶ δόξης διαδιδομένης, λέγεται τὴν Ῥέαν ὀργισθεῖσαν Ἄμμωνι

[1] μὲν after δυνάμενα D, Vogel, Jacoby, omitted Vulgate, Bekker, Dindorf.

fell upon the forests about Ceraunia. And since the country round about was going up in flames and the inhabitants in some cases were being destroyed and in others were leaving their native countries in their terror and removing to distant regions, Athena, they say, overcoming the monster partly through her intelligence and partly through her courage and bodily strength, slew it, and covering her breast with its hide bore this about with her, both as a covering and protection for her body against later dangers, and as a memorial of her valour and of her well-merited fame. Gê (Earth), however, the mother of the monster, was enraged and sent up the Giants, as they are called, to fight against the gods; but they were destroyed at a later time by Zeus, Athena and Dionysus and the rest of the gods taking part in the conflict on the side of Zeus.

Dionysus, however, being reared according to the account in Nysa and instructed in the best pursuits, became not only conspicuous for his beauty and bodily strength, but skilful also in the arts and quick to make every useful invention. For while still a boy he discovered both the nature and use of wine, in that he pressed out the clusters of grapes of the vine while it still grew wild, and such ripe fruits as could be dried and stored away to advantage, and how each one of them should be planted and cared for was likewise a discovery of his; also it was his desire to share the discoveries which he had made with the race of men, in the hope that by reason of the magnitude of his benefactions he would be accorded immortal honours.

71. When the valour and fame of Dionysus became spread abroad, Rhea, it is said, angered at Ammon,

φιλοτιμηθῆναι λαβεῖν ὑποχείριον τὸν Διόνυσον· οὐ δυναμένην δὲ κρατῆσαι τῆς ἐπιβολῆς τὸν μὲν Ἄμμωνα καταλιπεῖν, ἀπαλλαγεῖσαν δὲ πρὸς τοὺς ἀδελφοὺς Τιτᾶνας συνοικῆσαι Κρόνῳ τῷ ἀδελφῷ. 2 τοῦτον δ' ὑπὸ τῆς Ῥέας πεισθέντα στρατεῦσαι μετὰ τῶν Τιτάνων ἐπ' Ἄμμωνα, καὶ γενομένης παρατάξεως τὸν μὲν Κρόνον ἐπὶ τοῦ προτερήματος ὑπάρξαι, τὸν δ' Ἄμμωνα σιτοδείᾳ πιεζόμενον φυγεῖν εἰς Κρήτην, καὶ γήμαντα τῶν τότε βασιλευόντων Κουρήτων ἑνὸς θυγατέρα Κρήτην δυναστεῦσαί τε τῶν τόπων καὶ τὸ πρὸ τοῦ τὴν νῆσον Ἰδαίαν καλουμένην ἀπὸ τῆς γυναικὸς ὀνομάσαι Κρήτην. 3 τὸν δὲ Κρόνον μυθολογοῦσι κρατήσαντα τῶν Ἀμμωνίων τόπων τούτων μὲν ἄρχειν πικρῶς, ἐπὶ δὲ τὴν Νῦσαν καὶ τὸν Διόνυσον στρατεῦσαι μετὰ πολλῆς δυνάμεως. τὸν δὲ Διόνυσον πυθόμενον τά τε τοῦ πατρὸς ἐλαττώματα καὶ τὴν τῶν Τιτάνων ἐπ' αὐτὸν συνδρομήν, ἀθροῖσαι στρατιώτας ἐκ τῆς Νύσης, ὧν εἶναι συντρόφους διακοσίους, διαφόρους τῇ τε ἀλκῇ καὶ τῇ πρὸς αὐτὸν εὐνοίᾳ· προσλαβέσθαι δὲ καὶ τῶν πλησιοχώρων τούς τε Λίβυας καὶ τὰς Ἀμαζόνας, περὶ ὧν προειρήκαμεν ὅτι δοκοῦσιν ἀλκῇ διενεγκεῖν, καὶ πρῶτον μὲν στρατείαν ὑπερόριον στείλασθαι, πολλὴν δὲ τῆς 4 οἰκουμένης τοῖς ὅπλοις καταστρέψασθαι. μάλιστα δ' αὐτάς φασι παρορμῆσαι πρὸς τὴν συμμαχίαν Ἀθηνᾶν διὰ τὸν ὅμοιον τῆς προαιρέσεως ζῆλον, ὡς ἂν τῶν Ἀμαζόνων ἀντεχομένων ἐπὶ πολὺ τῆς ἀνδρείας καὶ παρθενίας. διῃρημένης δὲ τῆς δυνά-

BOOK III. 71. 1-4

strongly desired to get Dionysus into her power; but being unable to carry out her design she forsook Ammon and, departing to her brothers, the Titans, married Cronus her brother. Cronus, then, upon the solicitation of Rhea, made war with the aid of the Titans upon Ammon, and in the pitched battle which followed Cronus gained the upper hand, whereas Ammon, who was hard pressed by lack of supplies, fled to Crete, and marrying there Cretê, the daughter of one of the Curetes who were the kings at that time, gained the sovereignty over those regions, and to the island, which before that time had been called Idaea, he gave the name Crete after his wife. As for Cronus, the myth relates, after his victory he ruled harshly over these regions which had formerly been Ammon's, and set out with a great force against Nysa and Dionysus. Now Dionysus, on learning both of the reverses suffered by his father and of the uprising of the Titans against himself, gathered soldiers from Nysa, two hundred of whom were foster-brothers of his and were distinguished for their courage and their loyalty to him; and to these he added from neighbouring peoples both the Libyans and the Amazons, regarding the latter of whom we have already observed that it is reputed that they were distinguished for their courage and first of all campaigned beyond the borders of their country and subdued with arms a large part of the inhabited world. These women, they say, were urged on to the alliance especially by Athena, because their zeal for their ideal of life was like her own, seeing that the Amazons clung tenaciously to manly courage and virginity. The force was divided into two parts,

μεως, καὶ τῶν μὲν ἀνδρῶν στρατηγοῦντος Διονύσου, τῶν δὲ γυναικῶν τὴν ἡγεμονίαν ἐχούσης Ἀθηνᾶς, προσπεσόντας μετὰ τῆς στρατιᾶς τοῖς Τιτᾶσι συνάψαι μάχην. γενομένης δὲ παρατάξεως ἰσχυρᾶς, καὶ πολλῶν παρ' ἀμφοτέροις πεσόντων, τρωθῆναι μὲν τὸν Κρόνον, ἐπικρατῆσαι δὲ τὸν Διόνυσον ἀριστεύ-
5 σαντα κατὰ τὴν μάχην. μετὰ δὲ ταῦτα τοὺς μὲν Τιτᾶνας φυγεῖν εἰς τοὺς κατακτηθέντας ὑπὸ τῶν περὶ τὸν Ἄμμωνα τόπους, τὸν δὲ Διόνυσον ἀθροίσαντα πλῆθος αἰχμαλώτων ἐπανελθεῖν εἰς τὴν Νῦσαν. ἐνταῦθα δὲ τὴν δύναμιν περιστήσαντα καθωπλισμένην τοῖς ἁλοῦσι κατηγορίαν ποιήσασθαι τῶν Τιτάνων, καὶ πᾶσαν ὑπόνοιαν καταλιπεῖν ὡς μέλλοντα κατακόπτειν τοὺς αἰχμαλώτους. ἀπολύσαντος δ' αὐτοὺς τῶν ἐγκλημάτων καὶ τὴν ἐξουσίαν δόντος εἴτε συστρατεύειν εἴτε ἀπιέναι βούλοιντο, πάντας ἑλέσθαι συστρατεύειν· διὰ δὲ τὸ παράδοξον τῆς σωτηρίας προσκυνεῖν αὐτοὺς
6 ὡς θεόν. τὸν δὲ Διόνυσον παράγοντα καθ' ἕνα τῶν αἰχμαλώτων καὶ διδόντα σπονδὴν οἴνου πάντας ἐξορκῶσαι συστρατεύσειν[1] ἀδόλως καὶ μέχρι τελευτῆς βεβαίως διαγωνιεῖσθαι· διὸ καὶ τούτων πρώτων ὑποσπόνδων ὀνομασθέντων τοὺς μεταγενεστέρους ἀπομιμουμένους τὰ τότε πραχθέντα τὰς ἐν τοῖς πολέμοις διαλύσεις σπονδὰς προσαγορεύειν.

72. Τοῦ δ' οὖν Διονύσου μέλλοντος στρατεύειν ἐπὶ τὸν Κρόνον καὶ τῆς δυνάμεως ἐκ τῆς Νύσης ἐξιούσης, μυθολογοῦσιν Ἀρισταῖον τὸν ἐπιστάτην αὐτοῦ θυσίαν τε παραστῆσαι καὶ πρῶτον ἀνθρώπων ὡς θεῷ θῦσαι. συστρατεῦσαι δέ φασι καὶ

[1] So Wesseling: συστρατεύειν.

the men having Dionysus as their general and the women being under the command of Athena, and coming with their army upon the Titans they joined battle. The struggle having proved sharp and many having fallen on both sides, Cronus finally was wounded and victory lay with Dionysus, who had distinguished himself in the battle. Thereupon the Titans fled to the regions which had once been possessed by Ammon, and Dionysus gathered up a multitude of captives and returned to Nysa. Here, drawing up his force in arms about the prisoners, he brought a formal accusation against the Titans and gave them every reason to suspect that he was going to execute the captives. But when he got them free from the charges and allowed them to make their choice either to join him in his campaign or to go scot free, they all chose to join him, and because their lives had been spared contrary to their expectation they venerated him like a god. Dionysus, then, taking the captives singly and giving them a libation (*spondê*) of wine, required of all of them an oath that they would join in the campaign without treachery and fight manfully until death; consequently, these captives being the first to be designated as "freed under a truce" (*hypospondoi*), men of later times, imitating the ceremony which had been performed at that time, speak of the truces in wars as *spondai*.

72. Now when Dionysus was on the point of setting out against Cronus and his force was already passing out of Nysa, his guardian Aristaeus, the myth relates, offered a sacrifice and so was the first man to sacrifice to him as to a god. And companions of his on the campaign, they say, were also the most nobly born

τῶν Νυσαίων τοὺς εὐγενεστάτους, οὓς ὀνομάζεσθαι Σειληνούς.[1] πρῶτον γὰρ τῶν ἁπάντων βασιλεῦσαί φασι τῆς Νύσης [2] Σειληνόν, οὗ [3] τὸ γένος ὅθεν ἦν ὑπὸ πάντων ἀγνοεῖσθαι διὰ τὴν ἀρχαιότητα. ἔχοντος δ' αὐτοῦ κατὰ τὴν ὀσφῦν οὐράν, διατελέσαι καὶ τοὺς ἐκγόνους τὸ παράσημον τοῦτο φοροῦντας διὰ τὴν τῆς φύσεως κοινωνίαν.

Τὸν δ' οὖν Διόνυσον ἀναζεύξαντα μετὰ τῆς δυνάμεως, καὶ διελθόντα πολλὴν μὲν ἄνυδρον χώραν, οὐκ ὀλίγην δ' ἔρημον καὶ θηριώδη, καταστρατοπεδεῦσαι περὶ πόλιν Λιβυκὴν τὴν ὀνομαζομένην Ζάβιρναν. πρὸς δὲ ταύτῃ γηγενὲς ὑπάρχον θηρίον καὶ πολλοὺς ἀναλίσκον τῶν ἐγχωρίων, τὴν ὀνομαζομένην Κάμπην, ἀνελεῖν καὶ μεγάλης τυχεῖν δόξης ἐπ' ἀνδρείᾳ παρὰ τοῖς ἐγχωρίοις. ποιῆσαι δ' αὐτὸν καὶ χῶμα παμμέγεθες ἐπὶ τῷ φονευθέντι θηρίῳ, βουλόμενον ἀθάνατον ἀπολιπεῖν ὑπόμνημα τῆς ἰδίας ἀρετῆς, τὸ καὶ διαμεῖναν μέχρι τῶν νεωτέρων χρόνων. ἔπειτα τὸν μὲν Διόνυσον προάγειν πρὸς τοὺς Τιτᾶνας, εὐτάκτως ποιούμενον τὰς ὁδοιπορίας καὶ πᾶσι τοῖς ἐγχωρίοις φιλανθρώπως προσφερόμενον καὶ τὸ σύνολον ἑαυτὸν ἀποφαινόμενον στρατεύειν ἐπὶ κολάσει μὲν τῶν ἀσεβῶν, εὐεργεσίᾳ δὲ τοῦ κοινοῦ γένους τῶν ἀνθρώπων. τοὺς δὲ Λίβυας θαυμάζοντας τὴν εὐταξίαν καὶ τὸ τῆς ψυχῆς μεγαλοπρεπές, τροφάς τε παρέχεσθαι τοῖς ἀνθρώποις δαψιλεῖς καὶ συστρατεύειν προθυμότατα.

Συνεγγιζούσης δὲ τῆς δυνάμεως τῇ πόλει τῶν Ἀμμωνίων, τὸν Κρόνον πρὸ τοῦ τείχους παρα-

[1] Σιλήνους D, Σιλίνους C, Σιληνοὺς other MSS.; all editors but Jacoby emend to Σειληνούς (cp. 4. 4. 3).

BOOK III. 72. 1-5

of the Nysaeans, those, namely, who bear the name
Seileni. For the first man of all, they say, to be king
of Nysa was Seilenus, but his ancestry was unknown
to all men because of its antiquity. This man had a
tail at the lower part of his back and his descendants
also regularly carried this distinguishing mark because of their participation in his nature.

Dionysus, then, set out with his army, and after
passing through a great extent of waterless land, no
small portion of which was desert and infested with
wild beasts, he encamped beside a city of Libya
named Zabirna. Near this city an earth-born monster
called Campê, which was destroying many of the
natives, was slain by him, whereby he won great
fame among the natives for valour. Over the
monster which he had killed he also erected an
enormous mound, wishing to leave behind him an
immortal memorial of his personal bravery, and this
mound remained until comparatively recent times.
Then Dionysus advanced against the Titans, maintaining strict discipline on his journeyings, treating
all the inhabitants kindly, and, in a word, making it
clear that his campaign was for the purpose of punish-
ing the impious and of conferring benefits upon the
entire human race. The Libyans, admiring his
strict discipline and high-mindedness, provided his
followers with supplies in abundance and joined in
the campaign with the greatest eagerness.

As the army approached the city of the Ammon-
ians, Cronus, who had been defeated in a pitched

---

[2] τῆς Νύσης omitted D, Dindorf, Vogel.
[3] οὐ Vulgate, all editors; οὗτος D, Jacoby.

τάξει λειφθέντα τὴν μὲν πόλιν νυκτὸς ἐμπρῆσαι, σπεύδοντα εἰς τέλος καταφθεῖραι[1] τοῦ Διονύσου τὰ πατρῷα βασίλεια, αὐτὸν δ' ἀναλαβόντα τὴν γυναῖκα Ῥέαν καί τινας τῶν συνηγωνισμένων φίλων λαθεῖν ἐκ τῆς πόλεως διαδράντα. οὐ μὴν τόν γε Διόνυσον ὁμοίαν ἔχειν τούτῳ προαίρεσιν· λαβόντα γὰρ τόν τε Κρόνον καὶ τὴν Ῥέαν αἰχμαλώτους οὐ μόνον ἀφεῖναι τῶν ἐγκλημάτων διὰ τὴν συγγένειαν, ἀλλὰ καὶ παρακαλέσαι τὸν λοιπὸν χρόνον γονέων ἔχειν πρὸς αὐτὸν εὔνοιάν τε καὶ τάξιν καὶ συζῆν τιμω-
6 μένους ὑπ' αὐτοῦ μάλιστα πάντων. τὴν μὲν οὖν Ῥέαν διατελέσαι πάντα τὸν βίον ὡς υἱὸν ἀγαπῶσαν, τὸν δὲ Κρόνον ὕπουλον ἔχειν τὴν εὔνοιαν. γενέσθαι δ' αὐτοῖς περὶ τούτους τοὺς χρόνους υἱόν, ὃν προσαγορευθῆναι Δία, τιμηθῆναι δὲ μεγάλως ὑπὸ τοῦ Διονύσου, καὶ δι' ἀρετὴν ἐν τοῖς ὕστερον χρόνοις γενέσθαι πάντων βασιλέα.

73. Τῶν δὲ Λιβύων εἰρηκότων αὐτῷ πρὸ τῆς μάχης ὅτι καθ' ὃν καιρὸν ἐξέπεσεν ἐκ τῆς βασιλείας Ἄμμων, τοῖς ἐγχωρίοις προειρηκὼς εἴη τεταγμένοις χρόνοις ἥξειν υἱὸν αὐτοῦ Διόνυσον, καὶ τήν τε πατρῴαν ἀνακτήσεσθαι βασιλείαν καὶ πάσης τῆς οἰκουμένης κυριεύσαντα θεὸν νομισθήσεσθαι, ὑπολαβὼν ἀληθῆ γεγονέναι μάντιν τό τε χρηστήριον ἱδρύσατο τοῦ πατρὸς καὶ τὴν πόλιν ἀνοικοδομήσας[2] τιμὰς ὥρισεν ὡς θεῷ καὶ τοὺς ἐπιμελησομένους τοῦ μαντείου κατέστησε. παραδεδόσθαι δὲ τὸν Ἄμμωνα ἔχειν κριοῦ κεφαλὴν τετυπωμένην, παράσημον

[1] καταφθεῖραι Vulg., διαφθεῖραι D, Jacoby.
[2] So Dindorf: οἰκοδομήσας MSS., Bekker, Vogel.

battle before the walls, set fire to the city in the night, intending to destroy utterly the ancestral palace of Dionysus, and himself taking with him his wife Rhea and some of his friends who had aided him in the struggle, he stole unobserved out of the city. Dionysus, however, showed no such a temper as this; for though he took both Cronus and Rhea captive, not only did he waive the charges against them because of his kinship to them, but he entreated them for the future to maintain both the good-will and the position of parents towards him and to live in a common home with him, held in honour above all others. Rhea, accordingly, loved him like a son for all the rest of her life, but the good-will of Cronus was a pretence. And about this time there was born to both of these a son who was called Zeus, and he was honoured greatly by Dionysus and at a later time, because of his high achievements, was made king over all.

73. Since the Libyans had said to Dionysus before the battle that, at the time when Ammon had been driven from the kingdom, he had prophesied to the inhabitants that at an appointed time his son Dionysus would come, and that he would recover his father's kingdom and, after becoming master of all the inhabited world, would be looked upon as a god, Dionysus, believing him to have been a true prophet, established there the oracle of his father,[1] rebuilt the city and ordained honours to him as to a god, and appointed men to have charge of the oracle. Tradition also has recorded that the head of Ammon was shaped like that of a ram, since as his device he

[1] The great oracle of Ammon; cp. Book 17. 49 ff. for the famous visit of Alexander to this shrine.

ἐσχηκότος αὐτοῦ τὸ[1] κράνος κατὰ τὰς στρατείας. 2 εἰσὶ δ' οἱ μυθολογοῦντες αὐτῷ πρὸς ἀλήθειαν γενέσθαι καθ' ἑκάτερον μέρος τῶν κροτάφων κεράτια· διὸ καὶ τὸν Διόνυσον, υἱὸν αὐτοῦ γεγονότα, τὴν ὁμοίαν ἔχειν πρόσοψιν, καὶ τοῖς ἐπιγινομένοις τῶν ἀνθρώπων παραδεδόσθαι τὸν θεὸν τοῦτον γεγονότα κερατίαν.

3 Μετὰ δ' οὖν τὴν τῆς πόλεως οἰκοδομίαν καὶ τὴν περὶ τὸ χρηστήριον κατάστασιν πρῶτόν φασι τὸν Διόνυσον χρήσασθαι τῷ θεῷ περὶ τῆς στρατείας, καὶ λαβεῖν παρὰ τοῦ πατρὸς χρησμὸν ὅτι τοὺς ἀνθρώπους εὐεργετῶν τεύξεται τῆς ἀθανασίας. 4 διὸ καὶ μετεωρισθέντα τῇ ψυχῇ τὸ μὲν πρῶτον ἐπὶ τὴν Αἴγυπτον στρατεῦσαι, καὶ τῆς χώρας καταστῆσαι βασιλέα Δία τὸν Κρόνου καὶ Ῥέας, παῖδα τὴν ἡλικίαν ὄντα. παρακαταστῆσαι δ' αὐτῷ καὶ ἐπιστάτην Ὄλυμπον, ἀφ' οὗ τὸν Δία παιδευθέντα καὶ πρωτεύσαντα κατ' ἀρετὴν Ὀλύμπιον προσαγορευθῆναι. 5 τὸν δ' οὖν Διόνυσον λέγεται διδάξαι τοὺς Αἰγυπτίους τήν τε τῆς ἀμπέλου φυτείαν καὶ τὴν χρῆσιν καὶ τὴν παράθεσιν τοῦ τε οἴνου καὶ τῶν ἀκροδρύων καὶ τῶν ἄλλων καρπῶν. πάντῃ δὲ διαδιδομένης περὶ αὐτοῦ φήμης ἀγαθῆς μηδένα καθάπερ πρὸς πολέμιον ἀντιτάττεσθαι, πάντας δὲ προθύμως ὑπακούοντας ἐπαίνοις καὶ θυσίαις ὡς θεὸν 6 τιμᾶν. τῷ δ' αὐτῷ τρόπῳ φασὶν ἐπελθεῖν τὴν οἰκουμένην, ἐξημεροῦντα μὲν τὴν χώραν ταῖς φυτείαις, εὐεργετοῦντα δὲ τοὺς λαοὺς μεγάλαις καὶ τιμίαις[2] χάρισι πρὸς τὸν αἰῶνα. διὸ καὶ πάντας

---

[1] For τὸ Capps suggests τοιοῦτο.
[2] καὶ τιμίαις suggested by Vogel for τιμαῖς καί, MSS.; δωρεαῖς for τιμαῖς Rhodomann.

had worn a helmet of that form in his campaigns. But there are some writers of myths who recount that in very truth there were little horns on both sides of his temples and that therefore Dionysus also, being Ammon's son, had the same aspect as his father and so the tradition has been handed down to succeeding generations of mankind that this god had horns.

However this may be, after Dionysus had built the city and established the oracle he first of all, they say, inquired of the god with regard to his expedition, and he received from his father the reply that, if he showed himself a benefactor of mankind, he would receive the reward of immortality. Consequently, elated in spirit at this prophecy, he first of all directed his campaign against Egypt and as king of the country he set up Zeus, the son of Cronus and Rhea, though he was still but a boy in years. And at his side as his guardian he placed Olympus, by whom Zeus had been instructed and after whom he came to be called "Olympian," when he had attained pre-eminence in high achievements. As for Dionysus, he taught the Egyptians, it is said, both the cultivation of the vine and how to use and to store both wine and the fruits which are gathered from trees, as well as all others. And since a good report of him was spread abroad everywhere, no man opposed him as if he were an enemy, but all rendered him eager obedience and honoured him like a god with panegyrics and sacrifices. In like manner as in Egypt, they say, he visited the inhabited world, bringing the land under cultivation by means of the plantings which he made and conferring benefactions upon the people for all time by bestowing upon them great and valuable gifts. For this reason it comes

τοὺς ἀνθρώπους ἐν ταῖς πρὸς τοὺς ἄλλους θεοὺς τιμαῖς οὐχ ὁμοίαν ἔχοντας προαίρεσιν ἀλλήλοις σχεδὸν ἐπὶ μόνου τοῦ Διονύσου συμφωνουμένην ἀποδεικνύειν μαρτυρίαν τῆς ἀθανασίας· οὐδένα γὰρ οὔθ᾽ Ἑλλήνων οὔτε βαρβάρων ἄμοιρον εἶναι τῆς τούτου δωρεᾶς καὶ χάριτος, ἀλλὰ καὶ τοὺς ἀπηγριωμένην ἔχοντας χώραν ἢ πρὸς φυτείαν ἀμπέλου παντελῶς ἀπηλλοτριωμένην μαθεῖν τὸ κατασκευαζόμενον ἐκ τῶν κριθῶν πόμα βραχὺ λειπόμενον τῆς περὶ τὸν οἶνον εὐωδίας.

7 Τὸν δ᾽ οὖν Διόνυσόν φασι τὴν κατάβασιν ἐκ τῆς Ἰνδικῆς ἐπὶ τὴν θάλατταν ποιησάμενον καταλαβεῖν ἅπαντας τοὺς Τιτᾶνας ἠθροικότας δυνάμεις καὶ διαβεβηκότας εἰς Κρήτην ἐπ᾽ Ἄμμωνα. προσβεβοηθηκότος δὲ καὶ τοῦ Διὸς ἐκ τῆς Αἰγύπτου τοῖς περὶ τὸν Ἄμμωνα, καὶ πολέμου μεγάλου συνεστῶτος ἐν τῇ νήσῳ, ταχέως καὶ τοὺς περὶ τὸν Διόνυσον καὶ τὴν Ἀθηνᾶν καί τινας τῶν ἄλλων 8 θεῶν νομισθέντων συνδραμεῖν εἰς Κρήτην. γενομένης δὲ παρατάξεως μεγάλης ἐπικρατῆσαι τοὺς περὶ τὸν Διόνυσον καὶ πάντας ἀνελεῖν τοὺς Τιτᾶνας. μετὰ δὲ ταῦτα Ἄμμωνος καὶ Διονύσου μεταστάντων ἐκ τῆς ἀνθρωπίνης φύσεως εἰς τὴν ἀθανασίαν, τὸν Δία φασὶ βασιλεῦσαι τοῦ σύμπαντος κόσμου, κεκολασμένων τῶν Τιτάνων, καὶ μηδενὸς ὄντος τοῦ τολμήσοντος δι᾽ ἀσέβειαν ἀμφισβητῆσαι τῆς ἀρχῆς.

74. Τὸν μὲν οὖν πρῶτον Διόνυσον ἐξ Ἄμμωνος καὶ Ἀμαλθείας γενόμενον τοιαύτας οἱ Λίβυες ἱστοροῦσιν ἐπιτελέσασθαι πράξεις· τὸν δὲ δεύτερόν φασιν ἐξ Ἰοῦς τῆς Ἰνάχου Διὶ γενόμενον

---

[1] Cp. Book 1. 20. 4.

BOOK III. 73. 6–74. 1

about that, although not all men are of one belief with one another concerning the honours which they accord to the other gods, in the case of Dionysus alone we may almost say that they are in complete agreement in testifying to his immortality; for there is no man among Greeks or barbarians who does not share in the gift and favour which this god dispenses, nay, even those who possess a country which has become a wilderness or altogether unsuited to the cultivation of the vine learned from him how to prepare from barley a drink which is little inferior to wine in aroma.[1]

Now Dionysus, they say, as he was marching out of India to the sea,[2] learned that all the Titans had assembled their united forces together and had crossed over to Crete to attack Ammon. Already Zeus had passed over from Egypt to the aid of Ammon and a great war had arisen on the island, and forthwith Dionysus and Athena and certain others who had been considered to be gods rushed over in a body to Crete. In a great battle which followed Dionysus was victorious and slew all the Titans. And when after this Ammon and Dionysus exchanged their mortal nature for immortality, Zeus, they say, became king of the entire world, since the Titans had been punished and there was no one whose impiety would make him bold enough to dispute with him for the supreme power.

74. As for the first Dionysus, the son of Ammon and Amaltheia, these, then, are the deeds he accomplished as the Libyans recount the history of them; the second Dionysus, as men say, who was born to Zeus by Io, the daughter of Inachus, became

[2] The Mediterranean.

329

DIODORUS OF SICILY

βασιλεῦσαι μὲν τῆς Αἰγύπτου, καταδεῖξαι δὲ τὰς τελετάς· τελευταῖον δὲ τὸν ἐκ Διὸς καὶ Σεμέλης τεκνωθέντα παρὰ τοῖς Ἕλλησι ζηλωτὴν γενέσθαι 2 τῶν προτέρων. τὰς δ' ἀμφοτέρων προαιρέσεις μιμησάμενον στρατεῦσαι μὲν ἐπὶ πᾶσαν τὴν οἰκουμένην, στήλας δ' οὐκ ὀλίγας ἀπολιπεῖν τῶν ὅρων τῆς στρατείας· καὶ τὴν μὲν χώραν ἐξημεροῦν ταῖς φυτείαις, στρατιώτιδας δ' ἐπιλέξασθαι γυναῖκας, καθάπερ καὶ ὁ παλαιὸς τὰς Ἀμαζόνας. ἐνεργῆσαι δ' ἐπὶ πλέον καὶ τὰ περὶ τοὺς ὀργιασμούς, καὶ τελετὰς ἃς μὲν μεταθεῖναι πρὸς τὸ 3 κρεῖττον, ἃς δ' ἐπινοῆσαι. διὰ δὲ τὸ πλῆθος τοῦ χρόνου τῶν προτέρων εὑρετῶν ἀγνοηθέντων ὑπὸ τῶν πολλῶν, τοῦτον κληρονομῆσαι τὴν τῶν προγενεστέρων προαίρεσίν τε καὶ δόξαν. οὐκ ἐπὶ τούτου δὲ μόνου συμβῆναι τὸ προειρημένον, ἀλλὰ καὶ 4 μετὰ ταῦτ' ἐφ' Ἡρακλέους. δυοῖν γὰρ ὄντων τῶν προγενεστέρων τῶν τὴν αὐτὴν ἐσχηκότων προσηγορίαν, τὸν μὲν ἀρχαιότατον Ἡρακλέα μυθολογεῖσθαι γεγονέναι παρ' Αἰγυπτίοις, καὶ πολλὴν τῆς οἰκουμένης τοῖς ὅπλοις καταστρεψάμενον θέσθαι τὴν ἐπὶ τῆς Λιβύης στήλην, τὸν δὲ δεύτερον ἐκ Κρήτης ἕνα τῶν Ἰδαίων ὄντα Δακτύλων καὶ γενόμενον γόητα καὶ στρατηγικὸν συστήσασθαι τὸν Ὀλυμπικὸν ἀγῶνα· τὸν δὲ τελευταῖον μικρὸν πρὸ τῶν Τρωικῶν ἐξ Ἀλκμήνης καὶ Διὸς τεκνωθέντα πολλὴν ἐπελθεῖν τῆς οἰκουμένης, ὑπηρετοῦντα 5 τοῖς Εὐρυσθέως προστάγμασιν. ἐπιτυχόντα δὲ πᾶσι τοῖς ἄθλοις θέσθαι μὲν καὶ στήλην τὴν ἐπὶ τῆς

BOOK III. 74. 1-5

king of Egypt and appointed the initiatory rites of that land; and the third and last was sprung from Zeus and Semelê and became, among the Greeks, the rival of the first two. Imitating the principles of both the others he led an army over all the inhabited world and left behind him not a few pillars to mark the bounds of his campaign; the land he also brought under cultivation by means of the plantings which he made, and he selected women to be his soldiers, as the ancient Dionysus had done in the case of the Amazons. He went beyond the others in developing the orgiastic practices, and as regards the rites of initiation, he improved some of them, and others he introduced for the first time. But since in the long passage of time the former discoverers had become unknown to the majority of men, this last Dionysus fell heir to both the plan of life and the fame of his predecessors of the same name. And this Dionysus is not the only one to whom has happened that which we have related, but in later times Heracles likewise experienced the same fortune. For there had been two persons of an earlier period who had borne the same name, the most ancient Heracles who, according to the myths, had been born in Egypt, had subdued with arms a large part of the inhabited world, and had set up the pillar which is in Libya, and the second, who was one of the Idaean Dactyls of Crete and a wizard with some knowledge of generalship, was the founder of the Olympic Games; but the third and last, who was born of Alcmenê and Zeus a short time before the Trojan War, visited a large part of the inhabited world while he was serving Eurystheus and carrying out his commands. And after he had successfully completed all the Labours

Εὐρώπης, διὰ δὲ τὴν ὁμωνυμίαν καὶ τὴν τῆς προαιρέσεως ὁμοιότητα χρόνων ἐπιγενομένων τελευτήσαντα κληρονομῆσαι τὰς τῶν ἀρχαιοτέρων πράξεις, ὡς ἑνὸς Ἡρακλέους γεγονότος ἐν παντὶ τῷ πρότερον αἰῶνι.

6 Ὑπὲρ δὲ τοῦ πλείους Διονύσους γεγονέναι σὺν ἄλλαις ἀποδείξεσι πειρῶνται φέρειν τὴν ἐκ τῆς Τιτανομαχίας· συμφωνουμένου γὰρ παρὰ πᾶσιν ὅτι Διόνυσος τῷ Διὶ συνηγωνίσατο τὸν πρὸς τοὺς Τιτᾶνας πόλεμον, οὐδαμῶς πρέπειν φασὶ τὴν τῶν Τιτάνων γενεὰν τιθέναι κατὰ τοὺς τῆς Σεμέλης χρόνους οὐδὲ Κάδμον τὸν Ἀγήνορος ἀποφαίνεσθαι πρεσβύτερον εἶναι τῶν Ὀλυμπίων θεῶν.

Οἱ μὲν οὖν Λίβυες περὶ Διονύσου τοιαῦτα μυθολογοῦσιν· ἡμεῖς δὲ τὴν ἐν ἀρχῇ πρόθεσιν τετελεκότες αὐτοῦ περιγράψομεν[1] τὴν τρίτην βίβλον.

---

[1] So Wesseling : παραγράψωμεν.

he also set up the pillar which is in Europe, but because he bore the same name as the other two and pursued the same plan of life as did they, in the course of time and upon his death he inherited the exploits of the more ancient persons of the name, as if there had been in all the previous ages but one Heracles.

To support the view that there were several of the name Dionysus the effort is made to cite, along with the other proofs, the battle waged against the Titans. For since all men agree that Dionysus fought on the side of Zeus in his war against the Titans, it will not do at all, they argue, to date the generation of the Titans in the time when Semelê lived or to declare that Cadmus, the son of Agenor, was older than the gods of Olympus.

Such, then, is the myth which the Libyans recount concerning Dionysus; but for our part, now that we have brought to an end the plan[1] which we announced at the beginning, we shall close the Third Book at this point.

[1] Cp. chap. 1. 3.

BOOK IV

Τάδε ἔνεστιν ἐν τῇ τετάρτῃ τῶν Διοδώρου βίβλων

Προοίμιον περὶ τῶν μυθολογουμένων παρὰ τοῖς ἱστοριογράφοις.

Περὶ Διονύσου καὶ Πριάπου καὶ Ἑρμαφροδίτου καὶ Μουσῶν.

Περὶ Ἡρακλέους καὶ τῶν δώδεκα ἄθλων καὶ τῶν ἄλλων τῶν πραχθέντων ὑπ' αὐτοῦ μέχρι τῆς ἀποθεώσεως.

Περὶ τῶν Ἀργοναυτῶν καὶ Μηδείας καὶ τῶν Πελίου θυγατέρων.

Περὶ τῶν ἀπογόνων τοῦ Ἡρακλέους.

Περὶ Θησέως καὶ τῶν ἄθλων αὐτοῦ.

Περὶ τῶν ἑπτὰ ἐπὶ Θήβας.

Περὶ τῶν ἐπιγόνων τῶν ἑπτὰ ἐπὶ Θήβας.

Περὶ Νηλέως καὶ τῶν ἀπογόνων αὐτοῦ.

Περὶ Λαπιθῶν καὶ Κενταύρων.

Περὶ Ἀσκληπιοῦ καὶ τῶν ἀπογόνων αὐτοῦ.

Περὶ τῶν Ἀσωποῦ θυγατέρων καὶ τῶν Αἰακῷ γενομένων υἱῶν.

Περὶ Πέλοπος καὶ Ταντάλου καὶ Οἰνομάου καὶ Νιόβης.

Περὶ Δαρδάνου καὶ τῶν ἀπογόνων αὐτοῦ μέχρι Πριάμου.

Περὶ Δαιδάλου καὶ Μινωταύρου καὶ τῆς Μίνω στρατείας ἐπὶ Κώκαλον τὸν βασιλέα.

Περὶ Ἀρισταίου καὶ Δάφνιδος καὶ Ἔρυκος, ἔτι δὲ Ὠρίωνος.

---

[1] *i.e.* immediate descendants.

CONTENTS OF THE FOURTH BOOK OF DIODORUS

Introduction on the myths recounted by the historians (chap. 1).

On Dionysus, Priapus, Hermaphroditus, and the Muses (chaps. 2–7).

On Heracles and the twelve Labours, and the other deeds of his up to the time of his deification (chaps. 8–39).

On the Argonauts and Medea and the daughters of Pelias (chaps. 40–56).

On the descendants of Heracles (chaps. 57–58).

On Theseus and his labours (chaps. 59–63).

On The Seven against Thebes (chaps. 64–65).

On the Epigoni[1] of The Seven against Thebes (chaps. 66–67).

On Neleus and his descendants (chap. 68).

On the Lapiths and Centaurs (chaps. 69–70).

On Asclepius and his descendants (chap. 71).

On the daughters of Asopus and the sons born to Aeacus (chap. 72).

On Pelops, Tantalus, Oenomaus, and Niobê (chaps. 73–74).

On Dardanus and his descendants as far as Priam (chap. 75).

On Daedalus, the Minotaur, and the campaign cf Minos against the king Cocalus (chaps. 76–80).

On Aristaeus, Daphnis, Eryx, and Orion (chaps. 81–85).

ΒΙΒΛΟΣ ΤΕΤΑΡΤΗ

1. Οὐκ ἀγνοῶ μὲν ὅτι τοῖς τὰς παλαιὰς μυθολογίας συνταττομένοις συμβαίνει κατὰ τὴν γραφὴν ἐν πολλοῖς ἐλαττοῦσθαι. ἡ μὲν γὰρ τῶν ἀναγραφομένων ἀρχαιότης δυσεύρετος οὖσα πολλὴν ἀπορίαν παρέχεται τοῖς γράφουσιν, ἡ δὲ τῶν χρόνων ἀπαγγελία τὸν ἀκριβέστατον ἔλεγχον οὐ προσδεχομένη καταφρονεῖν ποιεῖ τῆς ἱστορίας τοὺς ἀναγινώσκοντας· πρὸς δὲ τούτοις ἡ ποικιλία καὶ τὸ πλῆθος τῶν γενεαλογουμένων ἡρώων τε καὶ ἡμιθέων καὶ τῶν ἄλλων ἀνδρῶν δυσέφικτον ἔχει τὴν ἀπαγγελίαν· τὸ δὲ μέγιστον καὶ πάντων ἀτοπώτατον, ὅτι συμβαίνει τοὺς ἀναγεγραφότας τὰς ἀρχαιοτάτας πράξεις τε καὶ μυθολογίας ἀσυμφώνους εἶναι πρὸς 2 ἀλλήλους. διόπερ τῶν μεταγενεστέρων ἱστοριογράφων οἱ πρωτεύοντες τῇ δόξῃ τῆς μὲν ἀρχαίας μυθολογίας ἀπέστησαν διὰ τὴν δυσχέρειαν, τὰς δὲ νεωτέρας πράξεις ἀναγράφειν ἐπεχείρησαν. 3 Ἔφορος μὲν γὰρ ὁ Κυμαῖος, Ἰσοκράτους ὢν μαθητής, ὑποστησάμενος γράφειν τὰς κοινὰς πράξεις, τὰς μὲν παλαιὰς μυθολογίας ὑπερέβη, τὰ δ' ἀπὸ τῆς Ἡρακλειδῶν καθόδου πραχθέντα συνταξάμενος ταύτην ἀρχὴν ἐποιήσατο τῆς ἱστο-

BOOK IV

1. I AM not unaware of the fact that those who compile the narratives of ancient mythology labour under many disadvantages in their composition. For, in the first place, the antiquity of the events they have to record, since it makes record difficult, is a cause of much perplexity to those who would compose an account of them; and again, inasmuch as any pronouncement they may make of the dates of events does not admit of the strictest kind of proof or disproof, a feeling of contempt for the narration is aroused in the mind of those who read it; furthermore, the variety and the multitude of the heroes, demi-gods, and men in general whose genealogies must be set down make their recital a difficult thing to achieve; but the greatest and most disconcerting obstacle of all consists in the fact that those who have recorded the deeds and myths of the earliest times are in disagreement among themselves. For these reasons the writers of greatest reputation among the later historians have stood aloof from the narration of the ancient mythology because of its difficulty, and have undertaken to record only the more recent events. Ephorus of Cymê, for instance, a pupil of Isocrates, when he undertook to write his universal history, passed over the tales of the old mythology and commenced his history with a narration of the events which took place after the Return of the Heracleidae. Like-

ρίας. ὁμοίως δὲ τούτῳ Καλλισθένης καὶ Θεόπομπος, κατὰ τὴν αὐτὴν ἡλικίαν γεγονότες,
4 ἀπέστησαν τῶν παλαιῶν μύθων. ἡμεῖς δὲ τὴν ἐναντίαν τούτοις κρίσιν ἔχοντες, καὶ τὸν ἐκ τῆς ἀναγραφῆς πόνον ὑποστάντες, τὴν πᾶσαν ἐπιμέλειαν ἐποιησάμεθα τῆς ἀρχαιολογίας. μέγισται γὰρ καὶ πλεῖσται συνετελέσθησαν πράξεις ὑπὸ τῶν ἡρώων τε καὶ ἡμιθέων καὶ πολλῶν ἄλλων ἀνδρῶν ἀγαθῶν· ὧν διὰ τὰς κοινὰς εὐεργεσίας οἱ μεταγενέστεροι τοὺς μὲν ἰσοθέοις, τοὺς δ' ἡρωικαῖς θυσίαις ἐτίμησαν, πάντας δ' ὁ τῆς ἱστορίας λόγος τοῖς καθήκουσιν ἐπαίνοις εἰς τὸν αἰῶνα καθύμνησεν.

5 Ἐν μὲν οὖν ταῖς πρὸ ταύτης βίβλοις τρισὶν ἀνεγράψαμεν τὰς παρὰ τοῖς ἄλλοις ἔθνεσι μυθολογουμένας πράξεις καὶ τὰ περὶ θεῶν παρ' αὐτοῖς ἱστορούμενα, πρὸς δὲ τούτοις τὰς τοποθεσίας τῆς παρ' ἑκάστοις χώρας καὶ τὰ φυόμενα παρ' αὐτοῖς θηρία καὶ τἄλλα ζῷα καὶ καθόλου πάντα τὰ μνήμης ἄξια καὶ παραδοξολογούμενα διεξιόντες, ἐν ταύτῃ δὲ τὰ παρὰ τοῖς Ἕλλησιν ἱστορούμενα κατὰ τοὺς ἀρχαίους χρόνους περὶ τῶν ἐπιφανεστάτων ἡρώων τε καὶ ἡμιθέων καὶ καθόλου τῶν κατὰ πόλεμον ἀξιόλογόν τι κατειργασμένων, ὁμοίως δὲ καὶ τῶν ἐν εἰρήνῃ τι χρήσιμον πρὸς τὸν κοινὸν
6 βίον εὑρόντων ἢ νομοθετησάντων. ποιησόμεθα δὲ τὴν ἀρχὴν ἀπὸ Διονύσου διὰ τὸ καὶ παλαιὸν εἶναι σφόδρα τοῦτον καὶ μεγίστας εὐεργεσίας κατατεθεῖσθαι τῷ γένει τῶν ἀνθρώπων.

BOOK IV. 1. 3-6

wise Callisthenes and Theopompus, who were contemporaries of Ephorus, held aloof from the old myths. We, however, holding the opposite opinion to theirs, have shouldered the labour which such a record involves and have expended all the care within our power upon the ancient legends. For very great and most numerous deeds have been performed by the heroes and demi-gods and by many good men likewise, who, because of the benefits they conferred which have been shared by all men, have been honoured by succeeding generations with sacrifices which in some cases are like those offered to the gods, in other cases like such as are paid to heroes, and of one and all the appropriate praises have been sung by the voice of history for all time.

Now in the three preceding Books we have recorded the deeds of mythological times which are found among other nations and what their histories relate about the gods, also the topography of the land in every case and the wild beasts and other animals which are found among them, and, speaking generally, we have described everything which was worthy of mention and was marvellous to relate; and in the present Book we shall set forth what the Greeks in their histories of the ancient periods tell about their most renowned heroes and demi-gods and, in general, about all who have performed any notable exploit in war, and likewise about such also as in time of peace have made some useful discovery or enacted some good law contributing to man's social life. And we shall begin with Dionysus because he not only belongs to a very ancient time but also conferred very great benefactions upon the race of men.

DIODORUS OF SICILY

Εἴρηται μὲν οὖν ἡμῖν ἐν ταῖς προειρημέναις βίβλοις ὅτι τινὲς τῶν βαρβάρων ἀντιποιοῦνται τῆς γενέσεως τοῦ θεοῦ τούτου. Αἰγύπτιοι μὲν γὰρ τὸν παρ' αὑτοῖς θεὸν Ὄσιριν ὀνομαζόμενόν φασιν εἶναι τὸν παρ' Ἕλλησι Διόνυσον καλούμενον. 7 τοῦτον δὲ μυθολογοῦσιν ἐπελθεῖν ἅπασαν τὴν οἰκουμένην, εὑρετὴν γενόμενον τοῦ οἴνου, καὶ τὴν φυτείαν διδάξαι τῆς ἀμπέλου τοὺς ἀνθρώπους, καὶ διὰ ταύτην τὴν εὐεργεσίαν τυχεῖν συμφωνουμένης ἀθανασίας. ὁμοίως δὲ τοὺς Ἰνδοὺς τὸν θεὸν τοῦτον παρ' ἑαυτοῖς ἀποφαίνεσθαι γεγονέναι, καὶ τὰ περὶ τὴν φυτείαν τῆς ἀμπέλου φιλοτεχνήσαντα μεταδοῦναι τῆς τοῦ οἴνου χρήσεως τοῖς κατὰ τὴν οἰκουμένην ἀνθρώποις. ἡμεῖς δὲ τὰ κατὰ μέρος περὶ τούτων εἰρηκότες νῦν τὰ παρὰ τοῖς Ἕλλησι λεγόμενα περὶ τοῦ θεοῦ τούτου διέξιμεν.

2. Κάδμον μὲν γάρ φασι τὸν Ἀγήνορος ἐκ Φοινίκης ὑπὸ τοῦ βασιλέως ἀποσταλῆναι πρὸς ζήτησιν τῆς Εὐρώπης, ἐντολὰς λαβόντα ἢ τὴν παρθένον ἀγαγεῖν[1] ἢ μὴ ἀνακάμπτειν εἰς τὴν Φοινίκην. ἐπελθόντα δὲ πολλὴν χώραν, καὶ μὴ δυνάμενον ἀνευρεῖν, ἀπογνῶναι τὴν εἰς οἶκον ἀνακομιδήν· καταντήσαντα δ' εἰς τὴν Βοιωτίαν κατὰ τὸν παραδεδομένον χρησμὸν κτίσαι τὰς Θήβας. ἐνταῦθα δὲ κατοικήσαντα γῆμαι μὲν Ἁρμονίαν τὴν Ἀφροδίτης, γεννῆσαι δ' ἐξ αὐτῆς Σεμέλην καὶ Ἰνὼ καὶ Αὐτονόην καὶ Ἀγαύην, ἔτι δὲ 2 Πολύδωρον. τῇ δὲ Σεμέλῃ διὰ τὸ κάλλος Δία μιγέντα καὶ μεθ' ἡσυχίας ποιούμενον τὰς ὁμιλίας

[1] Vogel suggests ἀνάγειν.

BOOK IV. 1. 6–2. 2

We have stated in the previous Books that certain barbarian peoples claim for themselves the birthplace of this god. The Egyptians, for example, say that the god who among them bears the name Osiris is the one whom the Greeks call Dionysus.[1] And this god, as their myths relate, visited all the inhabited world, was the discoverer of wine, taught mankind how to cultivate the vine, and because of this benefaction of his received the gift of immortality with the approval of all. But the Indians likewise declare that this god was born among them, and that after he had ingeniously discovered how to cultivate the vine he shared the benefit which wine imparts with human beings throughout the inhabited world.[2] But for our part, since we have spoken of these matters in detail, we shall at this point recount what the Greeks have to say about this god.

2. The Greek account of Dionysus runs like this: Cadmus, the son of Agenor, was sent forth from Phoenicia by the king to seek out Europê, under orders either to bring him the maiden or never to come back to Phoenicia. After Cadmus had traversed a wide territory without being able to find her, he despaired of ever returning to his home; and when he had arrived in Boeotia, in obedience to the oracle which he had received he founded the city of Thebes. Here he made his home and marrying Harmonia, the daughter of Aphroditê, he begat by her Semelê, Ino, Autonoê, Agavê, and Polydorus. Semelê was loved by Zeus because of her beauty, but since he had his intercourse with her secretly and without speech she thought that the

[1] Cp. Book 1. 15. 6 ff., and Vol. 1. p. 71 and note.
[2] Cp. Book 1. 19. 7 f.

δόξαι καταφρονεῖν αὐτῆς· διόπερ ὑπ' αὐτῆς παρακληθῆναι τὰς ἐπιπλοκὰς ὁμοίας ποιεῖσθαι ταῖς πρὸς τὴν Ἥραν συμπεριφοραῖς. τὸν μὲν οὖν Δία παραγενόμενον θεοπρεπῶς μετὰ βροντῶν καὶ ἀστραπῶν ἐπιφανῶς ποιεῖσθαι τὴν συνουσίαν· τὴν δὲ Σεμέλην ἔγκυον οὖσαν καὶ τὸ μέγεθος τῆς περιστάσεως οὐκ ἐνέγκασαν τὸ μὲν βρέφος ἐκτρῶσαι, ὑπὸ δὲ τοῦ πυρὸς αὐτὴν τελευτῆσαι. ἔπειτα τὸ παιδίον ἀναλαβόντα τὸν Δία παραδοῦναι τῷ Ἑρμῇ, καὶ προστάξαι τοῦτο μὲν ἀποκομίσαι πρὸς τὸ ἄντρον τὸ ἐν τῇ Νύσῃ, κείμενον μεταξὺ Φοινίκης καὶ Νείλου, ταῖς δὲ νύμφαις παραδοῦναι τρέφειν καὶ μετὰ πολλῆς σπουδῆς ἐπιμέλειαν αὐτοῦ ποιεῖσθαι τὴν ἀρίστην. διὸ καὶ τραφέντα τὸν Διόνυσον ἐν τῇ Νύσῃ τυχεῖν τῆς προσηγορίας ταύτης ἀπὸ Διὸς καὶ Νύσης. καὶ τὸν Ὅμηρον δὲ τούτοις μαρτυρῆσαι ἐν τοῖς ὕμνοις ἐν οἷς λέγει

ἔστι δέ τις Νύση, ὕπατον ὄρος, ἀνθέον ὕλῃ,
τηλοῦ Φοινίκης, σχεδὸν Αἰγύπτοιο ῥοάων.

Τραφέντα δ' αὐτὸν ὑπὸ τῶν νυμφῶν ἐν τῇ Νύσῃ φασὶν εὑρετήν τε τοῦ οἴνου γενέσθαι καὶ τὴν φυτείαν διδάξαι τῆς ἀμπέλου τοὺς ἀνθρώπους. ἐπιόντα δὲ σχεδὸν ὅλην τὴν οἰκουμένην πολλὴν χώραν ἐξημερῶσαι, καὶ διὰ τοῦτο τυχεῖν παρὰ πᾶσι μεγίστων τιμῶν. εὑρεῖν δ' αὐτὸν καὶ τὸ ἐκ τῆς κριθῆς κατασκευαζόμενον πόμα, τὸ προσαγορευόμενον μὲν ὑπ' ἐνίων ζῦθος, οὐ πολὺ δὲ λειπόμενον τῆς περὶ τὸν οἶνον εὐωδίας. τοῦτο δὲ διδά-

---

[1] Cp. Book 3. 69.

god despised her; consequently she made the request of him that he come to her embraces in the same manner as in his approaches to Hera. Accordingly, Zeus visited her in a way befitting a god, accompanied by thundering and lightning, revealing himself to her as he embraced her; but Semelê, who was pregnant and unable to endure the majesty of the divine presence, brought forth the babe untimely and was herself slain by the fire. Thereupon Zeus, taking up the child, handed it over to the care of Hermes, and ordered him to take it to the cave in Nysa,[1] which lay between Phoenicia and the Nile, where he should deliver it to the nymphs that they should rear it and with great solicitude bestow upon it the best of care. Consequently, since Dionysus was reared in Nysa, he received the name he bears from Zeus and Nysa.[2] And Homer bears witness to this in his Hymns,[3] when he says:

There is a certain Nysa, mountain high,
With forests thick, in Phoenicê afar,
Close to Aegyptus' streams.

After he had received his rearing by the nymphs in Nysa, they say, he made the discovery of wine and taught mankind how to cultivate the vine. And as he visited the inhabited world almost in its entirety, he brought much land under cultivation and in return for this received most high honours at the hands of all men. He also discovered the drink made out of barley and called by some *zythos*, the bouquet of which is not much inferior to that of wine. The preparation of this drink he taught to

[2] *i.e. Dio-* (from *Dios*, the genitive form of the nominative *Zeus*) and *-nysus* (*Nysa*); cp. Book 1. 15. 6.
[3] *Homeric Hymns* 1. 8–9.

DIODORUS OF SICILY

ξαι τοὺς χώραν ἔχοντας μὴ δυναμένην ἐπιδέ-
6 χεσθαι τὴν τῆς ἀμπέλου φυτείαν. περιάγεσθαι δ'
αὐτὸν καὶ στρατόπεδον οὐ μόνον ἀνδρῶν, ἀλλὰ
καὶ γυναικῶν, καὶ τοὺς ἀδίκους καὶ ἀσεβεῖς τῶν
ἀνθρώπων κολάζειν. καὶ κατὰ μὲν τὴν Βοιωτίαν
ἀποδιδόντα τῇ πατρίδι χάριτας ἐλευθερῶσαι πάσας
τὰς πόλεις, καὶ κτίσαι πόλιν ἐπώνυμον τῆς
αὐτονομίας, ἣν Ἐλευθερὰς προσαγορεῦσαι.

3. Στρατεύσαντα δ' εἰς τὴν Ἰνδικὴν τριετεῖ
χρόνῳ τὴν ἐπάνοδον εἰς τὴν Βοιωτίαν ποιήσασθαι,
κομίζοντα μὲν λαφύρων ἀξιόλογον πλῆθος, καταγαγεῖν δὲ πρῶτον τῶν ἁπάντων θρίαμβον ἐπ'
2 ἐλέφαντος Ἰνδικοῦ. καὶ τοὺς μὲν Βοιωτοὺς καὶ
τοὺς ἄλλους Ἕλληνας καὶ Θρᾷκας ἀπομνημονεύον-
τας τῆς κατὰ τὴν Ἰνδικὴν στρατείας καταδεῖξαι
τὰς τριετηρίδας θυσίας Διονύσῳ, καὶ τὸν θεὸν
νομίζειν κατὰ τὸν χρόνον τοῦτον ποιεῖσθαι τὰς
3 παρὰ τοῖς ἀνθρώποις ἐπιφανείας. διὸ καὶ παρὰ
πολλαῖς τῶν Ἑλληνίδων πόλεων διὰ τριῶν ἐτῶν
βακχεῖά τε γυναικῶν ἀθροίζεσθαι, καὶ ταῖς
παρθένοις νόμιμον εἶναι θυρσοφορεῖν καὶ συνεν-
θουσιάζειν εὐαζούσαις καὶ τιμώσαις τὸν θεόν·
τὰς δὲ γυναῖκας κατὰ συστήματα θυσιάζειν τῷ
θεῷ καὶ βακχεύειν καὶ καθόλου τὴν παρουσίαν
ὑμνεῖν τοῦ Διονύσου, μιμουμένας τὰς ἱστορου-
μένας τὸ παλαιὸν παρεδρεύειν τῷ θεῷ μαινάδας.

---

[1] *i.e.* " City of Freedom."
[2] *i.e.* after one year had intervened.
[3] Literally, "every three years," since the Greeks in reckoning from an event included the year in which it took place.
[4] Scholars have wondered why Dionysus, who was originally

those peoples whose country was unsuited to the cultivation of the vine. He also led about with himself an army composed not only of men but of women as well, and punished such men as were unjust and impious. In Boeotia, out of gratitude to the land of his birth, he freed all the cities and founded a city whose name signified independence, which he called Eleutherae.[1]

3. Then he made a campaign into India, whence he returned to Boeotia in the third year,[2] bringing with him a notable quantity of booty, and he was the first man ever to celebrate a triumph seated on an Indian elephant. And the Boeotians and other Greeks and the Thracians, in memory of the campaign in India, have established sacrifices every other year[3] to Dionysus, and believe that at that time the god reveals himself to human beings. Consequently in many Greek cities every other year[4] Bacchic bands of women gather, and it is lawful for the maidens to carry the thyrsus and to join in the frenzied revelry, crying out "Euai!" and honouring the god; while the matrons, forming in groups, offer sacrifices to the god and celebrate his mysteries and, in general, extol with hymns the presence of Dionysus, in this manner acting the part of the Maenads[5] who, as history records, were of old the companions of the god. He also punished

---

a vegetation god, should have had his special festival only every other year. L. R. Farnell (*The Cults of the Greek States*, 5. 181) suggests that the Thracians, from whom the worship of Dionysus came to the Greeks, "may have shifted their corn-land every other year," and so stood in special need of the vegetation god for the new soil only after this interval.

[5] Cp. Book 3. 65. 4.

4 κολάσαι δ' αὐτὸν πολλοὺς μὲν καὶ ἄλλους κατὰ πᾶσαν τὴν οἰκουμένην τοὺς δοκοῦντας ἀσεβεῖν, ἐπιφανεστάτους δὲ Πενθέα καὶ Λυκοῦργον. τῆς δὲ κατὰ τὸν οἶνον εὑρέσεως καὶ δωρεᾶς κεχαρισμένης τοῖς ἀνθρώποις καθ' ὑπερβολὴν διά τε τὴν ἡδονὴν τὴν ἐκ τοῦ ποτοῦ καὶ διὰ τὸ τοῖς σώμασιν εὐτονωτέρους γίνεσθαι τοὺς τὸν οἶνον πίνοντας, φασὶν ἐπὶ τῶν δείπνων,[1] ὅταν ἄκρατος οἶνος ἐπιδιδῶται, προσεπιλέγειν ἀγαθοῦ δαίμονος· ὅταν δὲ μετὰ τὸ δεῖπνον διδῶται κεκραμένος ὕδατι, Διὸς σωτῆρος ἐπιφωνεῖν. τὸν γὰρ οἶνον ἄκρατον μὲν πινόμενον μανιώδεις διαθέσεις ἀποτελεῖν, τοῦ δ' ἀπὸ Διὸς ὄμβρου μιγέντος τὴν μὲν τέρψιν καὶ τὴν ἡδονὴν μένειν, τὸ δὲ τῆς μανίας καὶ
5 παραλύσεως βλάπτον διορθοῦσθαι. καθόλου δὲ μυθολογοῦσι τῶν θεῶν μεγίστης ἀποδοχῆς τυγχάνειν παρ' ἀνθρώποις τοὺς ταῖς εὐεργεσίαις ὑπερβαλομένους κατὰ τὴν εὕρεσιν τῶν ἀγαθῶν Διόνυσόν τε καὶ Δήμητραν, τὸν μὲν τοῦ προσηνεστάτου ποτοῦ γενόμενον εὑρετήν, τὴν δὲ τῆς ξηρᾶς τροφῆς τὴν κρατίστην παραδοῦσαν τῷ γένει τῶν ἀνθρώπων.

4. Μυθολογοῦσι δέ τινες καὶ ἕτερον Διόνυσον γεγονέναι πολὺ τοῖς χρόνοις προτεροῦντα τούτου. φασὶ γὰρ ἐκ Διὸς καὶ Φερσεφόνης Διόνυσον γενέσθαι τὸν ὑπό τινων Σαβάζιον ὀνομαζόμενον, οὗ τήν τε γένεσιν καὶ τὰς θυσίας καὶ τιμὰς νυκτε-

[1] τῶν δείπνων F, Bekker, Dindorf, τὸ δεῖπνον D, Vogel.

[1] The Attic custom, as given by the scholiasts on Aristophanes, *Knights*, 85; *Peace*, 300, was slightly different: The toast to the "Good Deity" was given in unmixed wine

here and there throughout all the inhabited world many men who were thought to be impious, the most renowned among the number being Pentheus and Lycurgus. And since the discovery of wine and the gift of it to human beings were the source of such great satisfaction to them, both because of the pleasure which derives from the drinking of it and because of the greater vigour which comes to the bodies of those who partake of it, it is the custom, they say, when unmixed wine is served during a meal to greet it with the words, "To the Good Deity!" but when the cup is passed around after the meal diluted with water, to cry out, "To Zeus Saviour!"[1] For the drinking of unmixed wine results in a state of madness, but when it is mixed with the rain from Zeus the delight and pleasure continue, but the ill effect of madness and stupor is avoided. And, in general, the myths relate that the gods who receive the greatest approval at the hands of human beings are those who excelled in their benefactions by reason of their discovery of good things, namely, Dionysus and Demeter, the former because he was the discoverer of the most pleasing drink, the latter because she gave to the race of men the most excellent [2] of the dry foods.

4. Some writers of myths, however, relate that there was a second Dionysus who was much earlier in time than the one we have just mentioned. For according to them there was born of Zeus and Persephonê a Dionysus who is called by some Sabazius and whose birth and sacrifices and honours are

after the dinner was over and the table removed, that to "Zeus Saviour" just before the guests went home.
[2] Wheat.

ρινὰς καὶ κρυφίους παρεισάγουσι διὰ τὴν αἰσχύνην
2 τὴν ἐκ τῆς συνουσίας ἐπακολουθοῦσαν. λέγουσι
δ' αὐτὸν ἀγχινοίᾳ διενεγκεῖν, καὶ πρῶτον ἐπιχειρῆσαι
βοῦς ζευγνύειν καὶ διὰ τούτων τὸν
σπόρον τῶν καρπῶν ἐπιτελεῖν· ἀφ' οὗ δὴ καὶ
κερατίαν αὐτὸν παρεισάγουσι.

Καὶ τὸν μὲν ἐκ Σεμέλης γενόμενον ἐν τοῖς
νεωτέροις χρόνοις φασὶ τῷ σώματι γενέσθαι τρυφερὸν
καὶ παντελῶς ἁπαλόν, εὐπρεπείᾳ δὲ πολὺ
τῶν ἄλλων διενεγκεῖν καὶ πρὸς τὰς ἀφροδισιακὰς
ἡδονὰς εὐκατάφορον γεγονέναι, κατὰ δὲ τὰς
στρατείας γυναικῶν πλῆθος περιάγεσθαι καθωπλισ-
3 μένων λόγχαις τεθυρσωμέναις. φασὶ δὲ καὶ τὰς
Μούσας αὐτῷ συναποδημεῖν, παρθένους οὔσας
καὶ πεπαιδευμένας διαφερόντως· ταύτας δὲ διά
τε τῆς μελῳδίας καὶ τῶν ὀρχήσεων, ἔτι δὲ τῶν
ἄλλων τῶν ἐν παιδείᾳ καλῶν ψυχαγωγεῖν τὸν
θεόν. φασὶ δὲ καὶ παιδαγωγὸν καὶ τροφέα
συνέπεσθαι κατὰ τὰς στρατείας αὐτῷ Σειληνόν,
εἰσηγητὴν καὶ διδάσκαλον γινόμενον τῶν καλλίστων
ἐπιτηδευμάτων, καὶ μεγάλα συμβάλλεσθαι
4 τῷ Διονύσῳ πρὸς ἀρετήν τε καὶ δόξαν. καὶ κατὰ
μὲν τὰς ἐν τοῖς πολέμοις μάχας ὅπλοις αὐτὸν
πολεμικοῖς κεκοσμῆσθαι καὶ δοραῖς παρδάλεων,
κατὰ δὲ τὰς ἐν εἰρήνῃ πανηγύρεις καὶ ἑορτὰς
ἐσθῆσιν ἀνθειναῖς καὶ κατὰ τὴν μαλακότητα τρυφεραῖς
χρῆσθαι. πρὸς δὲ τὰς ἐκ τοῦ πλεονάζοντος
οἴνου κεφαλαλγίας τοῖς πίνουσι γινομένας
διαδεδέσθαι λέγουσιν αὐτὸν μίτρᾳ[1] τὴν

---

[1] μίτρᾳ Wesseling, following Eusebius: μίτρῃ.

BOOK IV. 4. 1-4

celebrated at night and in secret, because of the disgrace resulting from the intercourse of the sexes. They state also that he excelled in sagacity and was the first to attempt the yoking of oxen and by their aid to effect the sowing of the seed, this being the reason why they also represent him as wearing a horn.

But the Dionysus who was born of Semelê in more recent times, they say, was a man who was effeminate in body and altogether delicate; in beauty, however, he far excelled all other men and was addicted to indulgence in the delights of love, and on his campaigns he led about with himself a multitude of women who were armed with lances which were shaped like thyrsi.[1] They say also that when he went abroad he was accompanied by the Muses, who were maidens that had received an unusually excellent education, and that by their songs and dancing and other talents in which they had been instructed these maidens delighted the heart of the god. They also add that he was accompanied on his campaigns by a personal attendant and caretaker, Seilenus, who was his adviser and instructor in the most excellent pursuits and contributed greatly to the high achievements and fame of Dionysus. And in the battles which took place during his wars he arrayed himself in arms suitable for war and in the skins of panthers, but in assemblages and at festive gatherings in time of peace he wore garments which were bright-coloured and luxurious in their effeminacy. Furthermore, in order to ward off the headaches which every man gets from drinking too much wine he bound about his head, they report,

[1] Cp. p. 296, n. 1.

κεφαλήν, ἀφ' ἧς αἰτίας καὶ μιτρηφόρον ὀνομάζεσθαι· ἀπὸ δὲ ταύτης τῆς μίτρας ὕστερον παρὰ τοῖς βασιλεῦσι καταδειχθῆναι τὸ διάδημά φασι. 5 διμήτορα δ' αὐτὸν προσαγορευθῆναι λέγουσι διὰ τὸ πατρὸς μὲν ἑνὸς ὑπάρξαι τοὺς δύο Διονύσους, μητέρων δὲ δυοῖν. κεκληρονομηκέναι δὲ τὸν νεώτερον καὶ τὰς τοῦ προγενεστέρου πράξεις· διόπερ τοὺς μεταγενεστέρους ἀνθρώπους, ἀγνοοῦντας μὲν τἀληθές, πλανηθέντας δὲ διὰ τὴν ὁμωνυμίαν, ἕνα γεγονέναι νομίσαι Διόνυσον.

6 Τὸν δὲ νάρθηκα προσάπτουσιν αὐτῷ διά τινας τοιαύτας αἰτίας. κατὰ τὴν ἐξ ἀρχῆς εὕρεσιν τοῦ οἴνου μήπω τῆς τοῦ ὕδατος κράσεως εὑρημένης ἄκρατον πίνειν τὸν οἶνον· κατὰ δὲ τὰς τῶν φίλων συναναστροφὰς καὶ εὐωχίας τοὺς συνεορτάζοντας δαψιλῆ τὸν ἄκρατον ἐμφορησαμένους μανιώδεις γίνεσθαι, καὶ ταῖς βακτηρίαις ξυλίναις 7 χρωμένους ταύταις ἀλλήλους τύπτειν. διὸ καὶ τινῶν μὲν τραυματιζομένων, τινῶν δὲ καὶ τελευτώντων ἐκ τῶν καιρίων τραυμάτων, προσκόψαντα τὸν Διόνυσον ταῖς τοιαύταις περιστάσεσι τὸ μὲν ἀποστῆσαι τοῦ πίνειν δαψιλῆ τὸν ἄκρατον ἀποδοκιμάσαι διὰ τὴν ἡδονὴν τοῦ ποτοῦ, καταδεῖξαι δὲ νάρθηξι χρῆσθαι καὶ μὴ ξυλίναις βακτηρίαις.

5. Ἐπωνυμίας δ' αὐτῷ τοὺς ἀνθρώπους πολλὰς προσάψαι, τὰς ἀφορμὰς ἀπὸ τῶν περὶ αὐτὸν ἐπιτηδευμάτων λαβόντας. Βάκχειον μὲν γὰρ ἀπὸ

---

[1] "Wearer of a *mitra*."

a band (*mitra*), which was the reason for his receiving the name Mitrephorus [1]; and it was this head-band, they say, that in later times led to the introduction of the diadem for kings. He was also called Dimetor,[2] they relate, because the two Dionysi were born of one father, but of two mothers. The younger one also inherited the deeds of the older, and so the men of later times, being unaware of the truth and being deceived because of the identity of their names, thought there had been but one Dionysus.

The *narthex* [3] is also associated with Dionysus for the following reason. When wine was first discovered, the mixing of water with it had not as yet been devised and the wine was drunk unmixed; but when friends gathered together and enjoyed good cheer, the revellers, filling themselves to abundance with the unmixed wine, became like madmen and used their wooden staves to strike one another. Consequently, since some of them were wounded and some died of wounds inflicted in vital spots, Dionysus was offended at such happenings, and though he did not decide that they should refrain from drinking the unmixed wine in abundance, because the drink gave such pleasure, he ordered them hereafter to carry a *narthex* and not a wooden staff.

5. Many epithets, so we are informed, have been given him by men, who have found the occasions from which they arose in the practices and customs which have become associated with him. So, for instance, he has been called Baccheius from the

[2] " Of two mothers "; but see Book 2. 62. 5 for a different explanation of the name.
[3] *i.e.* the reed which formed the staff of the thyrsus.

τῶν συνεπομένων βακχῶν ὀνομάσαι, Ληναῖον δὲ ἀπὸ τοῦ πατῆσαι τὰς σταφυλὰς ἐν ληνῷ, Βρόμιον δ' ἀπὸ τοῦ κατὰ τὴν γένεσιν αὐτοῦ γενομένου βρόμου· ὁμοίως δὲ καὶ πυριγενῆ διὰ τὴν ὁμοίαν 2 αἰτίαν ὠνομάσθαι. Θρίαμβον δ' αὐτὸν ὀνομασθῆναί φασιν ἀπὸ τοῦ πρῶτον τῶν μνημονευομένων καταγαγεῖν ἀπὸ τῆς στρατείας θρίαμβον εἰς τὴν πατρίδα, τὴν ἐξ Ἰνδῶν ποιησάμενον ἐπάνοδον μετὰ πολλῶν λαφύρων. παραπλησίως δὲ καὶ τὰς λοιπὰς προσηγορίας ἐπιθετικὰς αὐτῷ γεγενῆσθαι, περὶ ὧν μακρὸν ἂν εἴη λέγειν καὶ τῆς ὑποκειμένης ἱστορίας ἀνοίκειον.

Δίμορφον δ' αὐτὸν δοκεῖν ὑπάρχειν διὰ τὸ δύο Διονύσους γεγονέναι, τὸν μὲν παλαιὸν καταπώγωνα διὰ τὸ τοὺς ἀρχαίους πάντας πωγωνοτροφεῖν, τὸν δὲ νεώτερον ὡραῖον καὶ τρυφερὸν καὶ νέον, 3 καθότι προείρηται. ἔνιοι δὲ λέγουσιν ὅτι τῶν μεθυόντων διττὰς διαθέσεις ἐχόντων, καὶ τῶν μὲν ἱλαρῶν, τῶν δὲ ὀργίλων γινομένων, δίμορφον ὠνομάσθαι τὸν θεόν. καὶ Σατύρους δέ φασιν αὐτὸν περιάγεσθαι, καὶ τούτους ἐν ταῖς ὀρχήσεσι καὶ ταῖς τραγῳδίαις τέρψιν καὶ πολλὴν ἡδονὴν 4 παρέχεσθαι τῷ θεῷ. καθόλου δὲ τὰς μὲν Μούσας τοῖς ἐκ τῆς παιδείας ἀγαθοῖς ὠφελούσας τε καὶ τερπούσας, τοὺς δὲ Σατύρους τοῖς πρὸς γέλωτα συνεργοῦσιν ἐπιτηδεύμασι χρωμένους, παρασκευάζειν τῷ Διονύσῳ τὸν εὐδαίμονα καὶ κεχαρισμένον βίον. καθόλου δὲ τοῦτον τῶν θυμελικῶν

---

[1] Chap. 4. 2. But in Book 3. 63. 3 the long beard is explained as due to the fact that the first Dionysus was an Indian.

BOOK IV. 5. 1-4

Bacchic bands of women who accompanied him, Lenaeus from the custom of treading the clusters of grapes in a wine-tub (*lenos*), and Bromius from the thunder (*bromos*) which attended his birth; likewise for a similar reason he has been called Pyrigenes ("Born-of-Fire"). Thriambus is a name that has been given him, they say, because he was the first of those of whom we have a record to have celebrated a triumph (*thriambos*) upon entering his native land after his campaign, this having been done when he returned from India with great booty. It is on a similar basis that the other appellations or epithets have been given to him, but we feel that it would be a long task to tell of them and inappropriate to the history which we are writing.

He was thought to have two forms, men say, because there were two Dionysi, the ancient one having a long beard, because all men in early times wore long beards, the younger one being youthful and effeminate and young, as we have mentioned before.[1] Certain writers say, however, that it was because men who become drunk get into two states, being either joyous or sullen, that the god has been called "two-formed." Satyrs also, it is reported, were carried about by him in his company and afforded the god great delight and pleasure in connection with their dancings and their goat-songs.[2] And, in general, the Muses who bestowed benefits and delights through the advantages which their education gave them, and the Satyrs by the use of the devices which contribute to mirth, made the life of Dionysus happy and agreeable. There is general agreement also, they say, that he was the

[2] The Greek word usually translated "tragedies."

ἀγώνων φασὶν εὑρετὴν γενέσθαι, καὶ θέατρα καταδεῖξαι, καὶ μουσικῶν ἀκροαμάτων σύστημα ποιήσασθαι· πρὸς δὲ τούτοις ἀλειτουργήτους ποιῆσαι καὶ[1] τοὺς ἐν ταῖς στρατείαις μεταχειριζομένους τι τῆς μουσικῆς ἐπιστήμης· ἀφ᾽ ὧν τοὺς μεταγενεστέρους μουσικὰς συνόδους συστήσασθαι τῶν περὶ τὸν Διόνυσον τεχνιτῶν, καὶ ἀτελεῖς ποιῆσαι τοὺς τὰ τοιαῦτα ἐπιτηδεύοντας.

Καὶ περὶ μὲν Διονύσου καὶ τῶν περὶ αὐτοῦ μυθολογουμένων ἀρκεσθησόμεθα τοῖς ῥηθεῖσι στοχαζόμενοι τῆς συμμετρίας.

6. Περὶ δὲ Πριάπου καὶ τῶν μυθολογουμένων περὶ αὐτοῦ νῦν διέξιμεν, οἰκεῖον ὁρῶντες τὸν περὶ τούτου λόγον ταῖς Διονυσιακαῖς ἱστορίαις. μυθολογοῦσιν οὖν οἱ παλαιοὶ τὸν Πρίαπον υἱὸν μὲν εἶναι Διονύσου καὶ Ἀφροδίτης, πιθανῶς τὴν γένεσιν ταύτην ἐξηγούμενοι· τοὺς γὰρ οἰνωθέντας φυσικῶς 2 ἐντετάσθαι πρὸς τὰς ἀφροδισιακὰς ἡδονάς. τινὲς δέ φασι τὸ αἰδοῖον τῶν ἀνθρώπων τοὺς παλαιοὺς μυθωδῶς ὀνομάζειν βουλομένους Πρίαπον προσαγορεῦσαι. ἔνιοι δὲ λέγουσι τὸ γεννητικὸν μόριον, αἴτιον ὑπάρχον τῆς γενέσεως τῶν ἀνθρώπων καὶ διαμονῆς εἰς ἅπαντα τὸν αἰῶνα, τυχεῖν τῆς

[1] καὶ deleted by Bekker.

---

[1] The *thymele* was the altar of Dionysus which stood in the centre of the orchestra of the theatre, and so the adjective "thymelic" came to signify the action of the chorus as opposed to that of the actors. "Thymelic" contests included non-dramatic performances, such as the singing of songs, dancing, jugglery, and the like.
[2] From the fourth century B.C. onward for at least eight centuries these "Artists of Dionysus" were members of

BOOK IV. 5. 4–6. 2

inventor of thymelic[1] contests, and that he introduced places where the spectators could witness the shows and organized musical concerts; furthermore, he freed from any forced contribution to the state those who had cultivated any sort of musical skill during his campaigns, and it is for these reasons that later generations have formed musical associations of the artists of Dionysus[2] and have relieved of taxes the followers of this profession.

As for Dionysus and the myths which are related about him we shall rest content with what has been said, since we are aiming at due proportion in our account.

6. We shall at this point discuss Priapus and the myths related about him, realizing that an account of him is appropriate in connection with the history of Dionysus. Now the ancients record in their myths that Priapus was the son of Dionysus and Aphroditê and they present a plausible argument for this lineage; for men when under the influence of wine find the members of their bodies tense and inclined to the pleasures of love. But certain writers say that when the ancients wished to speak in their myths of the sexual organ of males they called it Priapus. Some, however, relate that the generative member, since it is the cause of the reproduction of human beings and of their continued existence through all

---

powerful guilds which bore that title together with the name of the city in which their headquarters were situated. These guilds made contracts with cities in their territories for furnishing theatrical exhibitions of every description and their members in many cases enjoyed freedom from military service and similar privileges, as well as the exemption from taxation mentioned below.

3 ἀθανάτου τιμῆς. οἱ δ' Αἰγύπτιοι περὶ τοῦ Πριάπου μυθολογοῦντές φασι τὸ παλαιὸν τοὺς Τιτᾶνας ἐπιβουλεύσαντας Ὀσίριδι τοῦτον μὲν ἀνελεῖν, τὸ δὲ σῶμα αὐτοῦ διελόντας εἰς ἴσας μερίδας ἑαυτοῖς καὶ λαβόντας ἀπενεγκεῖν ἐκ τῆς οἰκείας λαθραίως, μόνον δὲ τὸ αἰδοῖον εἰς τὸν ποταμὸν ῥῖψαι διὰ τὸ μηδένα βούλεσθαι τοῦτο ἀνελέσθαι. τὴν δὲ Ἶσιν τὸν φόνον τοῦ ἀνδρὸς ἀναζητοῦσαν, καὶ τοὺς μὲν Τιτᾶνας ἀνελοῦσαν, τὰ δὲ τοῦ σώματος μέρη περιπλάσασαν εἰς ἀνθρώπου τύπον, ταῦτα μὲν δοῦναι θάψαι τοῖς ἱερεῦσι καὶ τιμᾶν προστάξαι ὡς θεὸν τὸν Ὄσιριν, τὸ δὲ αἰδοῖον μόνον οὐ δυναμένην ἀνευρεῖν καταδεῖξαι τιμᾶν ὡς θεὸν καὶ ἀναθεῖναι κατὰ τὸ ἱερὸν ἐντεταμένον. περὶ μὲν οὖν τῆς γενέσεως τοῦ Πριάπου καὶ τῆς τιμῆς τοιαῦτα μυθολογεῖται παρὰ τοῖς παλαιοῖς τῶν Αἰγυπτίων.

4 Τοῦτον δὲ τὸν θεὸν τινὲς μὲν Ἰθύφαλλον ὀνομάζουσι, τινὲς δὲ Τύχωνα. τὰς δὲ τιμὰς οὐ μόνον κατὰ πόλιν ἀπονέμουσιν αὐτῷ ἐν τοῖς ἱεροῖς,[1] ἀλλὰ καὶ κατὰ τὰς ἀγροικίας ὀπωροφύλακα τῶν ἀμπελώνων ἀποδεικνύντες καὶ τῶν κήπων, ἔτι δὲ πρὸς τοὺς βασκαίνοντάς τι τῶν καλῶν τοῦτον κολαστὴν παρεισάγοντες. ἔν τε ταῖς τελεταῖς οὐ μόνον ταῖς Διονυσιακαῖς, ἀλλὰ καὶ ταῖς ἄλλαις σχεδὸν ἁπάσαις οὗτος ὁ θεὸς τυγχάνει τινὸς τιμῆς, μετὰ γέλωτος καὶ παιδιᾶς παρεισαγόμενος ἐν ταῖς θυσίαις.

[1] ἐν τοῖς ἱεροῖς deleted by Vogel.

[1] Cp. Book 1. 21-2, where the murderer of Osiris is Typhon not the Titans.

time, became the object of immortal honour. But the Egyptians in their myths about Priapus say that in ancient times the Titans formed a conspiracy against Osiris and slew him, and then, taking his body and dividing it into equal parts among themselves, they slipped them secretly out of the house, but this organ alone they threw into the river, since no one of them was willing to take it with him.[1] But Isis tracked down the murder of her husband, and after slaying the Titans and fashioning the several pieces of his body into the shape of a human figure,[2] she gave them to the priests with orders that they pay Osiris the honours of a god, but since the only member she was unable to recover was the organ of sex she commanded them to pay to it the honours of a god and to set it up in their temples in an erect position.[3] Now this is the myth about the birth of Priapus and the honour paid to him, as it is given by the ancient Egyptians.

This god is also called by some Ithyphallus, by others Tychon. Honours are accorded him not only in the city, in the temples, but also throughout the countryside, where men set up his statue to watch over their vineyards and gardens, and introduce him as one who punishes any who cast a spell over some fair thing which they possess. And in the sacred rites, not only of Dionysus but of practically all other gods as well, this god receives honour to some extent, being introduced in the sacrifices to the accompaniment of laughter and sport.

[2] According to the account in Book 1. 21. 5 Isis used spices and wax to build each piece up to the size of a human body.

[3] Diodorus is equating Priapus with the Egyptian god Min, a deity of fertility, whose statues were ithyphallic.

5 Παραπλησίως δὲ τῷ Πριάπῳ τινὲς μυθολογοῦσι γεγενῆσθαι τὸν ὀνομαζόμενον Ἑρμαφρόδιτον, ὃν ἐξ Ἑρμοῦ καὶ Ἀφροδίτης γεννηθέντα τυχεῖν τῆς ἐξ ἀμφοτέρων τῶν γονέων συντεθείσης προσηγορίας. τοῦτον δ' οἱ μέν φασιν εἶναι θεὸν καὶ κατά τινας χρόνους φαίνεσθαι παρ' ἀνθρώποις, καὶ γεννᾶσθαι τὴν τοῦ σώματος φύσιν ἔχοντα μεμιγμένην ἐξ ἀνδρὸς καὶ γυναικός· καὶ τὴν μὲν εὐπρέπειαν καὶ μαλακότητα τοῦ σώματος ἔχειν γυναικὶ παρεμφερῆ, τὸ δ' ἀρρενωπὸν καὶ δραστικὸν ἀνδρὸς ἔχειν·[1] ἔνιοι δὲ τὰ τοιαῦτα γένη ταῖς φύσεσιν ἀποφαίνονται τέρατα ὑπάρχειν, καὶ γεννώμενα σπανίως προσημαντικὰ γίνεσθαι ποτὲ μὲν κακῶν ποτὲ δ' ἀγαθῶν. καὶ περὶ μὲν τῶν τοιούτων ἅλις ἡμῖν ἐχέτω.

7. Περὶ δὲ τῶν Μουσῶν, ἐπειδήπερ ἐμνήσθημεν ἐν ταῖς τοῦ Διονύσου πράξεσιν, οἰκεῖον ἂν εἴη διελθεῖν ἐν κεφαλαίοις. ταύτας γὰρ οἱ πλεῖστοι τῶν μυθογράφων καὶ μάλιστα δεδοκιμασμένοι φασὶ θυγατέρας εἶναι Διὸς καὶ Μνημοσύνης· ὀλίγοι δὲ τῶν ποιητῶν, ἐν οἷς ἐστι καὶ Ἀλκμάν,
2 θυγατέρας ἀποφαίνονται Οὐρανοῦ καὶ Γῆς. ὁμοίως δὲ καὶ κατὰ τὸν ἀριθμὸν διαφωνοῦσιν· οἱ μὲν γὰρ τρεῖς λέγουσιν, οἱ δ' ἐννέα, καὶ κεκράτηκεν ὁ τῶν ἐννέα ἀριθμὸς ὑπὸ τῶν ἐπιφανεστάτων ἀνδρῶν βεβαιούμενος, λέγω δὲ Ὁμήρου τε καὶ Ἡσιόδου καὶ τῶν ἄλλων τῶν τοιούτων. Ὅμηρος μὲν γὰρ λέγει

Μοῦσαι δ' ἐννέα πᾶσαι ἀμειβόμεναι ὀπὶ καλῇ·

[1] τὰ δὲ φυσικὰ μόρια συγγεννᾶσθαι τούτῳ καὶ γυναικὸς καὶ ἀνδρός ("and he is born with the physical organs both of a woman and of a man") after ἔχειν BD.

BOOK IV. 6. 5–7. 2

A birth like that of Priapus is ascribed by some writers of myths to Hermaphroditus, as he has been called, who was born of Hermes and Aphroditê and received a name which is a combination of those of both his parents. Some say that this Hermaphroditus is a god and appears at certain times among men, and that he is born with a physical body which is a combination of that of a man and that of a woman, in that he has a body which is beautiful and delicate like that of a woman, but has the masculine quality and vigour of a man. But there are some who declare that such creatures of two sexes are monstrosities, and coming rarely into the world as they do they have the quality of presaging the future, sometimes for evil and sometimes for good. But let this be enough for us on such matters.

7. As for the Muses, since we have referred to them in connection with the deeds of Dionysus, it may be appropriate to give the facts about them in summary. For the majority of the writers of myths and those who enjoy the greatest reputation say that they were daughters of Zeus and Mnemosynê; but a few poets, among whose number is Alcman, state that they were daughters of Uranus and Gê. Writers similarly disagree also concerning the number of the Muses; for some say that they are three, and others that they are nine, but the number nine has prevailed since it rests upon the authority of the most distinguished men, such as Homer and Hesiod and others like them. Homer,[1] for instance, writes:

The Muses, nine in all, replying each
To each with voices sweet;

[1] *Odyssey* 24. 60.

DIODORUS OF SICILY

Ἡσίοδος δὲ καὶ τὰ ὀνόματα αὐτῶν ἀποφαίνεται λέγων

Κλειώ τ' Εὐτέρπη τε Θάλειά τε Μελπομένη τε
Τερψιχόρη τ' Ἐρατώ τε Πολύμνιά τ' Οὐρανίη τε
Καλλιόπη θ', ἣ σφεων προφερεστάτη ἐστὶν
ἁπασέων.

3 Τούτων δ' ἑκάστῃ προσάπτουσι τὰς οἰκείας διαθέσεις τῶν περὶ μουσικὴν ἐπιτηδευμάτων, οἷον ποιητικήν, μελῳδίαν, ὀρχήσεις καὶ χορείας, ἀστρολογίαν τε καὶ τὰ λοιπὰ τῶν ἐπιτηδευμάτων. παρθένους δ' αὐτὰς οἱ πλεῖστοι[1] μυθολογοῦσι διὰ τὸ τὰς κατὰ τὴν παιδείαν ἀρετὰς ἀφθόρους δοκεῖν 4 εἶναι. Μούσας δ' αὐτὰς ὠνομάσθαι ἀπὸ τοῦ μυεῖν τοὺς ἀνθρώπους, τοῦτο δ' ἐστὶν ἀπὸ τοῦ διδάσκειν τὰ καλὰ καὶ συμφέροντα καὶ ὑπὸ τῶν ἀπαιδεύτων ἀγνοούμενα. ἑκάστῃ δὲ προσηγορίᾳ τὸν οἰκεῖον λόγον ἀπονέμοντές φασιν ὠνομάσθαι τὴν μὲν Κλειὼ διὰ τὸ τὸν ἐκ τῆς ποιήσεως τῶν ἐγκωμιαζομένων ἔπαινον μέγα κλέος περιποιεῖν τοῖς ἐπαινουμένοις, Εὐτέρπην δ' ἀπὸ τοῦ τέρπειν τοὺς ἀκροωμένους τοῖς ἀπὸ τῆς παιδείας ἀγαθοῖς, Θάλειαν δ' ἀπὸ τοῦ θάλλειν ἐπὶ πολλοὺς χρόνους τοὺς διὰ τῶν ποιημάτων ἐγκωμιαζομένους, Μελπομένην δ' ἀπὸ τῆς μελῳδίας, δι' ἧς τοὺς ἀκούοντας ψυχαγωγεῖσθαι, Τερψιχόρην δ' ἀπὸ τοῦ τέρπειν τοὺς ἀκροατὰς τοῖς ἐκ παιδείας περιγινομένοις

[1] γεγονέναι after πλεῖστοι omitted by D.

BOOK IV. 7. 2-4

and Hesiod [1] even gives their names when he writes:

Cleio, Euterpê, and Thaleia, Melpomenê,
Terpsichorê and Erato, and Polymnia, Urania,
Calliopê too, of them all the most comely.

To each of the Muses men assign her special aptitude for one of the branches of the liberal arts, such as poetry, song, pantomimic dancing, the round dance with music, the study of the stars, and the other liberal arts. They are also believed to be virgins, as most writers of myths say, because men consider that the high attainment which is reached through education is pure and uncontaminated. Men have given the Muses their name from the word *muein*, which signifies the teaching of those things which are noble and expedient and are not known by the uneducated.[2] For the name of each Muse, they say, men have found a reason appropriate to her: Cleio is so named because the praise which poets sing in their encomia bestows great glory (*kleos*) upon those who are praised; Euterpê, because she gives to those who hear her sing delight (*terpein*) in the blessings which education bestows; Thaleia, because men whose praises have been sung in poems flourish (*thallein*) through long periods of time; Melpomenê, from the chanting (*melodia*) by which she charms the souls of her listeners; Terpsichorê, because she delights (*terpein*) her disciples with the good things which come from education;

[1] *Theogony* 77-9.
[2] But *muein* means "to close" the eyes or mouth; Plato, *Cratylus* 406 A, derives the word from μῶσθαι, which he explains as meaning "searching and philosophy." There is no agreement among modern scholars on the etymology of the word "Muse."

ἀγαθοῖς, Ἐρατὼ δ' ἀπὸ τοῦ τοὺς παιδευθέντας ποθεινοὺς καὶ ἐπεράστους ἀποτελεῖν, Πολύμνιαν δ' ἀπὸ τοῦ διὰ πολλῆς ὑμνήσεως ἐπιφανεῖς κατασκευάζειν τοὺς διὰ τῶν ποιημάτων ἀπαθανατιζομένους τῇ δόξῃ, Οὐρανίαν δ' ἀπὸ τοῦ τοὺς παιδευθέντας ὑπ' αὐτῆς ἐξαίρεσθαι πρὸς οὐρανόν· τῇ γὰρ δόξῃ καὶ τοῖς φρονήμασι μετεωρίζεσθαι τὰς ψυχὰς εἰς ὕψος οὐράνιον· Καλλιόπην δ' ἀπὸ τοῦ καλὴν ὄπα προΐεσθαι, τοῦτο δ' ἐστὶ τῇ εὐεπείᾳ διάφορον οὖσαν ἀποδοχῆς τυγχάνειν ὑπὸ τῶν ἀκουόντων.

Τούτων δ' ἡμῖν ἀρκούντως εἰρημένων μεταβιβάσομεν τὸν λόγον ἐπὶ τὰς Ἡρακλέους πράξεις.

8. Οὐκ ἀγνοῶ δ' ὅτι πολλὰ δύσχρηστα συμβαίνει τοῖς ἱστοροῦσι τὰς παλαιὰς μυθολογίας, καὶ μάλιστα τὰς περὶ Ἡρακλέους. τῷ μὲν γὰρ μεγέθει τῶν κατεργασθέντων ὁμολογουμένως οὗτος παραδέδοται πάντας τοὺς ἐξ αἰῶνος ὑπεράραι τῇ μνήμῃ παραδοθέντας· δυσέφικτον οὖν ἐστι τὸ κατὰ τὴν ἀξίαν ἕκαστον τῶν πραχθέντων ἀπαγγεῖλαι καὶ τὸν λόγον ἐξισῶσαι τοῖς τηλικούτοις ἔργοις, οἷς 2 διὰ τὸ μέγεθος ἔπαθλον ἦν ἡ ἀθανασία. διὰ δὲ τὴν παλαιότητα καὶ τὸ παράδοξον τῶν ἱστορουμένων παρὰ πολλοῖς ἀπιστουμένων τῶν μύθων, ἀναγκαῖον ἢ παραλιπόντας τὰ μέγιστα τῶν πραχθέντων καθαιρεῖν τι τῆς τοῦ θεοῦ δόξης ἢ

---

[1] "The lovely one."

[2] The following account of Heracles is generally considered to have been drawn from a *Praise of Heracles* by Matris of Thebes, who is otherwise unknown and appears to have omitted nothing that would redound to the glory of the greatest Greek hero.

Erato,[1] because she makes those who are instructed by her men who are desired and worthy to be loved; Polymnia, because by her great (*polle*) praises (*humnēsis*) she brings distinction to writers whose works have won for them immortal fame; Urania, because men who have been instructed of her she raises aloft to heaven (*ouranos*), for it is a fact that imagination and the power of thought lift men's souls to heavenly heights; Calliopê, because of her beautiful (*kalē*) voice (*ops*), that is, by reason of the exceeding beauty of her language she wins the approbation of her auditors.

But since we have spoken sufficiently on these matters we shall turn our discussion to the deeds of Heracles.[2]

8. I am not unaware that many difficulties beset those who undertake to give an account of the ancient myths, and especially is this true with respect to the myths about Heracles. For as regards the magnitude of the deeds which he accomplished it is generally agreed that Heracles has been handed down as one who surpassed all men of whom memory from the beginning of time has brought down an account; consequently it is a difficult attainment to report each one of his deeds in a worthy manner and to present a record which shall be on a level with labours so great, the magnitude of which won for him the prize of immortality. Furthermore, since in the eyes of many men the very early age and astonishing nature of the facts which are related make the myths incredible, a writer is under the necessity either of omitting the greatest deeds and so detracting somewhat from the fame of the god, or of recounting them all and in so doing making

πάντα διεξιόντας τὴν ἱστορίαν ποιεῖν ἀπιστουμένην.
3 ἔνιοι γὰρ τῶν ἀναγινωσκόντων οὐ δικαίᾳ χρώμενοι κρίσει τἀκριβὲς ἐπιζητοῦσιν ἐν ταῖς ἀρχαίαις μυθολογίαις ἐπ᾿ ἴσης τοῖς πραττομένοις ἐν τοῖς καθ᾿ ἡμᾶς χρόνοις, καὶ τὰ διστοζόμενα τῶν ἔργων διὰ τὸ μέγεθος ἐκ τοῦ καθ᾿ αὑτοὺς βίου τεκμαιρόμενοι, τὴν Ἡρακλέους δύναμιν ἐκ τῆς ἀσθενείας τῶν νῦν ἀνθρώπων θεωροῦσιν, ὥστε διὰ τὴν ὑπερβολὴν τοῦ μεγέθους τῶν ἔργων ἀπιστεῖ-
4 σθαι τὴν γραφήν. καθόλου μὲν γὰρ ἐν ταῖς μυθολογουμέναις ἱστορίαις οὐκ ἐκ παντὸς τρόπου πικρῶς τὴν ἀλήθειαν ἐξεταστέον. καὶ γὰρ ἐν τοῖς θεάτροις, πεπεισμένοι μήτε Κενταύρους διφυεῖς ἐξ ἑτερογενῶν σωμάτων ὑπάρξαι μήτε Γηρυόνην τρισώματον, ὅμως προσδεχόμεθα τὰς τοιαύτας μυθολογίας, καὶ ταῖς ἐπισημασίαις συναύξομεν τὴν τοῦ θεοῦ
5 τιμήν. καὶ γὰρ ἄτοπον Ἡρακλέα μὲν ἔτι κατ᾿ ἀνθρώπους ὄντα τοῖς ἰδίοις πόνοις ἐξημερῶσαι τὴν οἰκουμένην, τοὺς δ᾿ ἀνθρώπους ἐπιλαθομένους τῆς κοινῆς εὐεργεσίας συκοφαντεῖν τὸν ἐπὶ τοῖς καλλίστοις ἔργοις ἔπαινον,[1] καὶ τοὺς μὲν προγόνους διὰ τὴν ὑπερβολὴν τῆς ἀρετῆς ὁμολογουμένην αὐτῷ συγχωρῆσαι τὴν ἀθανασίαν, ἡμᾶς δὲ πρὸς τὸν θεὸν μηδὲ τὴν πατροπαράδοτον εὐσέβειαν διαφυλάττειν. ἀλλὰ γὰρ τῶν τοιούτων λόγων ἀφέμενοι διέξιμεν αὐτοῦ τὰς πράξεις ἀπ᾿ ἀρχῆς ἀκολούθως τοῖς παλαιοτάτοις τῶν ποιητῶν τε καὶ μυθολόγων.

[1] ἔπαινον D, ὑπεροχὴν Vulgate.

the history of them incredible. For some readers set up an unfair standard and require in the accounts of the ancient myths the same exactness as in the events of our own time, and using their own life as a standard they pass judgment on those deeds the magnitude of which throw them open to doubt, and estimate the might of Heracles by the weakness of the men of our day, with the result that the exceeding magnitude of his deeds makes the account of them incredible. For, speaking generally, when the histories of myths are concerned, a man should by no means scrutinize the truth with so sharp an eye. In the theatres, for instance, though we are persuaded there have existed no Centaurs who are composed of two different kinds of bodies nor any Geryones with three bodies, we yet look with favour upon such products of the myths as these, and by our applause we enhance the honour of the god. And strange it would be indeed that Heracles, while yet among mortal men, should by his own labours have brought under cultivation the inhabited world, and that human beings should nevertheless forget the benefactions which he rendered them generally and slander the commendation he receives for the noblest deeds, and strange that our ancestors should have unanimously accorded immortality to him because of his exceedingly great attainments, and that we should nevertheless fail to cherish and maintain for the god the pious devotion which has been handed down to us from our fathers. However, we shall leave such considerations and relate his deeds from the beginning, basing our account on those of the most ancient poets and writers of myths.

9. Τῆς Ἀκρισίου τοίνυν Δανάης καὶ Διός φασι γενέσθαι Περσέα· τούτῳ δὲ μιγεῖσαν τὴν Κηφέως Ἀνδρομέδαν Ἠλεκτρύωνα γεννῆσαι, ἔπειτα τούτῳ τὴν Πέλοπος Εὐρυδίκην συνοικήσασαν Ἀλκμήνην τεκνῶσαι, καὶ ταύτῃ Δία μιγέντα δι' ἀπάτης Ἡρα-
2 κλέα γεννῆσαι. τὴν μὲν οὖν ὅλην τοῦ γένους ῥίζαν ἀπ' ἀμφοτέρων τῶν γονέων εἰς τὸν μέγιστον τῶν θεῶν ἀναφέρειν λέγεται τὸν εἰρημένον τρόπον. τὴν δὲ γεγενημένην περὶ αὐτὸν ἀρετὴν οὐκ ἐν ταῖς πράξεσι θεωρηθῆναι μόνον, ἀλλὰ καὶ πρὸ τῆς γενέσεως γινώσκεσθαι. τὸν γὰρ Δία μισγόμενον Ἀλκμήνῃ τριπλασίαν τὴν νύκτα ποιῆσαι, καὶ τῷ πλήθει τοῦ πρὸς τὴν παιδοποιίαν ἀναλωθέντος χρόνου προσημῆναι τὴν ὑπερβολὴν τῆς τοῦ γεννη-
3 θησομένου ῥώμης. καθόλου δὲ τὴν ὁμιλίαν ταύτην οὐκ ἐρωτικῆς ἐπιθυμίας ἕνεκα ποιήσασθαι, καθάπερ ἐπὶ τῶν ἄλλων γυναικῶν, ἀλλὰ τὸ πλέον τῆς παιδοποιίας χάριν. διὸ καὶ βουλόμενον τὴν ἐπιπλοκὴν νόμιμον ποιήσασθαι βιάσασθαι μὲν μὴ βουληθῆναι, πεῖσαι δ' οὐδαμῶς ἐλπίζειν διὰ τὴν σωφροσύνην· τὴν ἀπάτην οὖν προκρίναντα διὰ ταύτης παρακρούσασθαι τὴν Ἀλκμήνην, Ἀμφιτρύωνι κατὰ πᾶν ὁμοιωθέντα.

4 Διελθόντος δὲ τοῦ κατὰ φύσιν χρόνου ταῖς ἐγκύοις, τὸν μὲν Δία πρὸς τὴν Ἡρακλέους γένεσιν ἐνεχθέντα τῇ διανοίᾳ προειπεῖν παρόντων ἁπάντων τῶν θεῶν ὅτι τὸν κατ' ἐκείνην τὴν ἡμέραν Περσειδῶν γεννώμενον ποιήσει βασιλέα, τὴν δ' Ἥραν ζηλοτυποῦσαν καὶ συνεργὸν ἔχουσαν Εἰλείθυιαν τὴν

---

[1] i.e. to Zeus.

BOOK IV. 9. 1-4

9. This, then, is the story as it has been given us: Perseus was the son of Danaê, the daughter of Acrisius, and Zeus. Now Andromeda, the daughter of Cepheus, lay with him and bore Electryon, and then Eurydicê, the daughter of Pelops, married him and gave birth to Alcmenê, who in turn was wooed by Zeus, who deceived her, and bore Heracles. Consequently the sources of his descent, in their entirety, lead back, as is claimed, through both his parents to the greatest of the gods,[1] in the manner we have shown. The prowess which was found in him was not only to be seen in his deeds, but was also recognized even before his birth. For when Zeus lay with Alcmenê he made the night three times its normal length and by the magnitude of the time expended on the procreation he presaged the exceptional might of the child which would be begotten. And, in general, he did not effect this union from the desire of love, as he did in the case of other women, but rather only for the sake of procreation. Consequently, desiring to give legality to his embraces, he did not choose to offer violence to Alcmenê, and yet he could not hope to persuade her because of her chastity; and so, deciding to use deception, he deceived Alcmenê by assuming in every respect the shape of Amphitryon.

When the natural time of pregnancy had passed, Zeus, whose mind was fixed upon the birth of Heracles, announced in advance in the presence of all the gods that it was his intention to make the child who should be born that day king over the descendants of Perseus; whereupon Hera, who was filled with jealousy, using as her helper Eileithyia[2] her daughter,

[2] The goddess who assisted in travail.

θυγατέρα, τῆς μὲν Ἀλκμήνης παρακατασχεῖν τὰς ὠδῖνας, τὸν δ' Εὐρυσθέα πρὸ τοῦ καθήκοντος χρόνου πρὸς τὸ φῶς ἀγαγεῖν. τὸν δὲ Δία καταστρατηγηθέντα βουληθῆναι τήν τε ὑπόσχεσιν βεβαιῶσαι καὶ τῆς Ἡρακλέους ἐπιφανείας προνοηθῆναι· διό φασιν αὐτὸν τὴν μὲν Ἥραν πεῖσαι συγχωρῆσαι βασιλέα μὲν ὑπάρξαι κατὰ τὴν ἰδίαν ὑπόσχεσιν Εὐρυσθέα, τὸν δ' Ἡρακλέα τεταγμένον ὑπὸ τὸν Εὐρυσθέα τελέσαι δώδεκα ἄθλους οὓς ἂν ὁ Εὐρυσθεὺς προστάξῃ, καὶ τοῦτο πράξαντα 6 τυχεῖν τῆς ἀθανασίας. Ἀλκμήνη δὲ τεκοῦσα καὶ φοβηθεῖσα τὴν τῆς Ἥρας ζηλοτυπίαν, ἐξέθηκε τὸ βρέφος εἰς τὸν τόπον ὃς νῦν ἀπ' ἐκείνου καλεῖται πεδίον Ἡράκλειον. καθ' ὃν δὴ χρόνον Ἀθηνᾶ μετὰ τῆς Ἥρας προσιοῦσα,[1] καὶ θαυμάσασα τοῦ παιδίου τὴν φύσιν, συνέπεισε τὴν Ἥραν ὑποσχεῖν τὴν θηλήν. τοῦ δὲ παιδὸς ὑπὲρ τὴν ἡλικίαν βιαιότερον ἐπισπασαμένου τὴν θηλήν, ἡ μὲν Ἥρα διαλγήσασα τὸ βρέφος ἔρριψεν, Ἀθηνᾶ δὲ κομίσασα αὐτὸ πρὸς τὴν μητέρα τρέφειν παρεκελεύσατο. 7 θαυμάσαι δ' ἄν τις εἰκότως τὸ τῆς περιπετείας παράδοξον· ἡ μὲν γὰρ στέργειν ὀφείλουσα μήτηρ τὸ ἴδιον τέκνον ἀπώλλυεν, ἡ δὲ μητρυιᾶς ἔχουσα μῖσος δι' ἄγνοιαν ἔσωζε τὸ τῇ φύσει πολέμιον.

10. Μετὰ δὲ ταῦτα ἡ μὲν Ἥρα δύο δράκοντας ἀπέστειλε τοὺς ἀναλώσοντας τὸ βρέφος, ὁ δὲ παῖς οὐ καταπλαγεὶς ἑκατέρᾳ τῶν χειρῶν τὸν αὐχένα σφίγξας ἀπέπνιξε τοὺς δράκοντας. διόπερ

[1] προσιοῦσα ABD, προιοῦσα Π, παριοῦσα Bekker.

checked the birth-pains of Alcmenê and brought Eurystheus [1] forth to the light before his full time. Zeus, however, though he had been outgeneralled, wished both to fulfill his promise and to take thought for the future fame of Heracles; consequently, they say, he persuaded Hera to agree that Eurystheus should be king as he had promised, but that Heracles should serve Eurystheus and perform twelve Labours, these to be whatever Eurystheus should prescribe, and that after he had done so he should receive the gift of immortality. After Alcmenê had brought forth the babe, fearful of Hera's jealousy she exposed it at a place which to this time is called after him the Field of Heracles. Now at this very time Athena, approaching the spot in the company of Hera and being amazed at the natural vigour of the child, persuaded Hera to offer it the breast. But when the boy tugged upon her breast with greater violence than would be expected at his age, Hera was unable to endure the pain and cast the babe from her, whereupon Athena took it to its mother and urged her to rear it. And anyone may well be surprised at the unexpected turn of the affair; for the mother whose duty it was to love her own offspring was trying to destroy it, while she who cherished towards it a stepmother's hatred, in ignorance saved the life of one who was her natural enemy.

10. After this Hera sent two serpents to destroy the babe, but the boy, instead of being terrified, gripped the neck of a serpent in each hand and strangled them both. Consequently the inhabitants

[1] Descendant of Perseus by another line and later king of Argos.

DIODORUS OF SICILY

Ἀργεῖοι πυθόμενοι τὸ γεγονὸς Ἡρακλέα προσηγόρευσαν, ὅτι δι' Ἥραν ἔσχε κλέος, Ἀλκαῖον πρότερον καλούμενον. τοῖς μὲν οὖν ἄλλοις οἱ γονεῖς τοὔνομα περιτιθέασι, τούτῳ δὲ μόνῳ ἡ ἀρετὴ τὴν προσηγορίαν ἔθετο.

2 Μετὰ δὲ ταῦτα ὁ μὲν Ἀμφιτρύων φυγαδευθεὶς ἐκ Τίρυνθος μετῴκησεν εἰς Θήβας· ὁ δ' Ἡρακλῆς τραφεὶς καὶ παιδευθεὶς καὶ μάλιστ' ἐν τοῖς γυμνασίοις διαπονηθεὶς ἐγένετο ῥώμῃ τε σώματος πολὺ προέχων τῶν ἄλλων ἁπάντων καὶ ψυχῆς λαμπρότητι περιβόητος, ὅς γε τὴν ἡλικίαν ἔφηβος ὢν πρῶτον μὲν ἠλευθέρωσε τὰς Θήβας, ἀποδιδοὺς ὡς πατρίδι 3 τὰς προσηκούσας χάριτας. ὑποτεταγμένων γὰρ τῶν Θηβαίων Ἐργίνῳ τῷ βασιλεῖ τῶν Μινυῶν, καὶ κατ' ἐνιαυτὸν ὡρισμένους φόρους τελούντων,[1] οὐ καταπλαγεὶς τὴν τῶν δεδουλωμένων ὑπεροχὴν ἐτόλμησε πρᾶξιν ἐπιτελέσαι περιβόητον· τοὺς γὰρ παραγενομένους τῶν Μινυῶν ἐπὶ τὴν ἀπαίτησιν τῶν δασμῶν καὶ μεθ' ὕβρεως εἰσπραττομένους 4 ἀκρωτηριάσας ἐξέβαλεν ἐκ τῆς πόλεως. Ἐργίνου δ' ἐξαιτοῦντος τὸν αἴτιον, Κρέων βασιλεύων τῶν Θηβαίων, καταπλαγεὶς τὸ βάρος τῆς ἐξουσίας, ἕτοιμος ἦν ἐκδιδόναι τὸν αἴτιον τῶν ἐγκλημάτων. ὁ δ' Ἡρακλῆς πείσας τοὺς ἡλικιώτας ἐλευθεροῦν τὴν πατρίδα, κατέσπασεν ἐκ τῶν ναῶν τὰς προση-

[1] μεθ' ὕβρεως after τελούντων deleted by Bekker.

---

[1] Cp. Book 1. 24. 4. But Heracles won his fame, not through Hera, but through his own achievements; and so many philologists derive the first part of his name, not from *Hera*, but from ἦρα (" service ").

[2] Literally, an "ephebus," in Athens at the age of eighteen.

BOOK IV. 10. 1–4

of Argos, on learning of what had taken place, gave him the name Heracles because he had gained glory (*kleos*) by the aid of Hera,[1] although he had formerly been called Alcaeus. Other children are given their names by their parents, this one alone gained his name by his valour.

After this time Amphitryon was banished from Tiryns and changed his residence to Thebes; and Heracles, in his rearing and education and especially in the thorough instruction which he received in physical exercises, came to be the first by far in bodily strength among all the rest and famed for his nobility of spirit. Indeed, while he was still a youth[2] in age he first of all restored the freedom of Thebes, returning in this way to the city, as though it were the place of his birth, the gratitude which he owed it. For though the Thebans had been made subject to Erginus, the king of the Minyans, and were paying him a fixed yearly tribute, Heracles was not dismayed at the superior power of these overlords but had the courage to accomplish a deed of fame. Indeed, when the agents of the Minyans appeared to require the tribute and were insolent in their exactions, Heracles mutilated[3] them and then expelled them from the city. Erginus then demanded that the guilty party be handed over to him, and Creon, the king of the Thebans, dismayed at the great power of Erginus, was prepared to deliver the man who was responsible for the crime complained of. Heracles, however, persuading the young men of his age to strike for the freedom of their fatherland, took out of the temples the suits of armour which had been affixed to their walls,

---

[3] *i.e.* cut off their hands and their feet.

DIODORUS OF SICILY

λωμένας πανοπλίας, ἃς οἱ πρόγονοι σκῦλα τοῖς θεοῖς ἦσαν ἀνατεθεικότες· οὐ γὰρ ἦν εὑρεῖν κατὰ τὴν πόλιν ἰδιωτικὸν ὅπλον διὰ τὸ τοὺς Μινύας παρωπλικέναι τὴν πόλιν, ἵνα μηδεμίαν λαμβάνωσιν οἱ κατὰ τὰς Θήβας ἀποστάσεως ἔννοιαν. ὁ δ᾽ Ἡρακλῆς πυθόμενος Ἐργῖνον τὸν βασιλέα τῶν Μινυῶν προσάγειν τῇ πόλει μετὰ στρατιωτῶν, ἀπαντήσας αὐτῷ κατά τινα στενοχωρίαν, καὶ τὸ μέγεθος τῆς τῶν πολεμίων δυνάμεως ἄχρηστον ποιήσας, αὐτόν τε τὸν Ἐργῖνον ἀνεῖλε καὶ τοὺς μετ᾽ αὐτοῦ σχεδὸν ἅπαντας ἀπέκτεινεν. ἄφνω δὲ προσπεσὼν τῇ πόλει τῶν Ὀρχομενίων καὶ παρεισπεσὼν ἐντὸς τῶν πυλῶν τά τε βασίλεια τῶν Μινυῶν ἐνέπρησε καὶ τὴν πόλιν κατέσκαψε.

6 Περιβοήτου δὲ τῆς πράξεως γενομένης καθ᾽ ὅλην τὴν Ἑλλάδα καὶ πάντων θαυμαζόντων τὸ παράδοξον, ὁ μὲν βασιλεὺς Κρέων θαυμάσας τὴν ἀρετὴν τοῦ νεανίσκου τήν τε θυγατέρα Μεγάραν συνῴκισεν αὐτῷ καὶ καθάπερ υἱῷ γνησίῳ τὰ κατὰ τὴν πόλιν ἐπέτρεψεν, Εὐρυσθεὺς δ᾽ ὁ τὴν βασιλείαν ἔχων τῆς Ἀργείας ὑποπτεύσας τὴν Ἡρακλέους αὔξησιν μετεπέμπετό τε αὐτὸν καὶ προσέταττε 7 τελεῖν ἄθλους. οὐχ ὑπακούοντος δὲ τοῦ Ἡρακλέους, Ζεὺς μὲν ἀπέστειλε διακελευόμενος ὑπουργεῖν Εὐρυσθεῖ, Ἡρακλῆς δὲ παρελθὼν εἰς Δελφοὺς καὶ περὶ τούτων ἐπερωτήσας τὸν θεόν, ἔλαβε χρησμὸν τὸν δηλοῦντα διότι τοῖς θεοῖς δέδοκται δώδεκα ἄθλους τελέσαι προστάττοντος Εὐρυσθέως, καὶ τοῦτο πράξαντα τεύξεσθαι τῆς ἀθανασίας.

BOOK IV. 10. 4-7

dedicated to the gods by their forefathers as spoil from their wars; for there was not to be found in the city any arms in the hands of a private citizen, the Minyans having stripped the city of its arms in order that the inhabitants of Thebes might not entertain any thought of revolting from them. And when Heracles learned that Erginus, the king of the Minyans, was advancing with troops against the city he went out to meet him in a certain narrow place, whereby he rendered the multitude of the hostile force of no avail, killed Erginus himself, and slew practically all the men who had accompanied him. Then appearing unawares before the city of the Orchomenians and slipping in at their gates he both burned the palace of the Minyans and razed the city to the ground.

After this deed had been noised about throughout the whole of Greece and all men were filled with wonder at the unexpected happening, Creon the king, admiring the high achievement of the young man, united his daughter Megara in marriage to him and entrusted him with the affairs of the city as though he were his lawful son; but Eurystheus, who was ruler of Argolis, viewing with suspicion the growing power of Heracles, summoned him to his side and commanded him to perform Labours. And when Heracles ignored the summons Zeus despatched word to him to enter the service of Eurystheus; whereupon Heracles journeyed to Delphi, and on inquiring of the god regarding the matter he received a reply which stated that the gods had decided that he should perform twelve Labours at the command of Eurystheus and that upon their conclusion he should receive the gift of immortality.

11. Τούτων δὲ πραχθέντων[1] ὁ μὲν Ἡρακλῆς ἐνέπεσεν εἰς ἀθυμίαν οὐ τὴν τυχοῦσαν· τό τε γὰρ τῷ ταπεινοτέρῳ δουλεύειν οὐδαμῶς ἄξιον ἔκρινε τῆς ἰδίας ἀρετῆς, τό τε τῷ Διὶ καὶ πατρὶ μὴ πείθεσθαι καὶ ἀσύμφορον ἐφαίνετο καὶ ἀδύνατον. εἰς πολλὴν οὖν ἀμηχανίαν ἐμπίπτοντος αὐτοῦ, Ἥρα μὲν ἔπεμψεν[2] αὐτῷ λύτταν· ὁ δὲ τῇ ψυχῇ δυσφορῶν εἰς μανίαν ἐνέπεσε. τοῦ πάθους δ' αὐξομένου τῶν φρενῶν ἐκτὸς γενόμενος τὸν μὲν Ἰόλαον ἐπεβάλετο κτείνειν, ἐκείνου δὲ φυγόντος καὶ τῶν παίδων τῶν ἐκ Μεγάρας πλησίον διατριβόντων, τούτους ὡς
2 πολεμίους κατετόξευσε. μόγις δὲ τῆς μανίας ἀπολυθείς, καὶ ἐπιγνοὺς τὴν ἰδίαν ἄγνοιαν, περιαλγὴς ἦν ἐπὶ τῷ μεγέθει τῆς συμφορᾶς. πάντων δ' αὐτῷ συλλυπουμένων καὶ συμπενθούντων, ἐπὶ πολὺν χρόνον κατὰ τὴν οἰκίαν ἡσύχαζεν, ἐκκλίνων τὰς τῶν ἀνθρώπων ὁμιλίας τε καὶ ἀπαντήσεις· τέλος δὲ τοῦ χρόνου τὸ πάθος πραΰναντος κρίνας ὑπομένειν τοὺς κινδύνους παρεγένετο πρὸς Εὐρυσθέα.
3 Καὶ πρῶτον μὲν ἔλαβεν ἆθλον ἀποκτεῖναι τὸν ἐν Νεμέᾳ λέοντα. οὗτος δὲ μεγέθει μὲν ὑπερφυὴς ἦν, ἄτρωτος δὲ ὢν σιδήρῳ καὶ χαλκῷ καὶ λίθῳ τῆς κατὰ χεῖρα βιαζομένης προσεδεῖτο ἀνάγκης. διέτριβε δὲ μάλιστα μεταξὺ Μυκηνῶν καὶ Νεμέας περὶ ὄρος τὸ καλούμενον ἀπὸ τοῦ συμβεβηκότος Τρητόν· εἶχε γὰρ περὶ τὴν ῥίζαν διώρυχα διηνεκῆ,
4 καθ' ἣν εἰώθει φωλεύειν τὸ θηρίον. ὁ δ' Ἡρακλῆς

[1] προσταχθέντων Wesseling.
[2] ἐπέπεμψεν Reiske.

---

[1] "Perforated."

11. At such a turn of affairs Heracles fell into despondency of no ordinary kind; for he felt that servitude to an inferior was a thing which his high achievements did not deserve, and yet he saw that it would be hurtful to himself and impossible not to obey Zeus, who was his father as well. While he was thus greatly at a loss, Hera sent upon him a frenzy, and in his vexation of soul he fell into a madness. As the affliction grew on him he lost his mind and tried to slay Iolaüs, and when Iolaüs made his escape but his own children by Megara were near by, he shot his bow and killed them under the impression that they were enemies of his. When he finally recovered from his madness and recognized the mistake he had made through a misapprehension, he was plunged in grief over the magnitude of the calamity. And while all extended him sympathy and joined in his grief, for a long while he stayed inactive at home, avoiding any association or meeting with men; at last, however, time assuaged his grief, and making up his mind to undergo the dangers he made his appearance at the court of Eurystheus.

The first Labour which he undertook was the slaying of the lion in Nemea. This was a beast of enormous size, which could not be wounded by iron or bronze or stone and required the compulsion of the human hand for his subduing. It passed the larger part of its time between Mycenae and Nemea, in the neighbourhood of a mountain which was called Tretus[1] from a peculiarity which it possessed; for it had a cleft at its base which extended clean through it and in which the beast was accustomed to lurk. Heracles came to the region

καταντήσας ἐπὶ τὸν τόπον προσέβαλεν αὐτῷ, καὶ τοῦ θηρίου συμφυγόντος εἰς τὴν διώρυχα συνακολουθῶν αὐτῷ καὶ τὸ ἕτερον τῶν στομίων ἐμφράξας συνεπλάκη, καὶ τὸν αὐχένα σφίγξας τοῖς βραχίοσιν ἀπέπνιξε. τὴν δὲ δορὰν αὐτοῦ περιθέμενος, καὶ διὰ τὸ μέγεθος ἅπαν τὸ ἴδιον σῶμα περιλαβών, εἶχε σκεπαστήριον τῶν μετὰ ταῦτα κινδύνων.

5 Δεύτερον δ' ἔλαβεν ἆθλον ἀποκτεῖναι τὴν Λερναίαν ὕδραν, ἧς ἐξ ἑνὸς σώματος ἑκατὸν αὐχένες ἔχοντες κεφαλὰς ὄφεων διετετύποντο.[1] τούτων δ' εἰ μία διαφθαρείη, διπλασίας ὁ τμηθεὶς ἀνίει τόπος· δι' ἣν αἰτίαν ἀήττητος ὑπάρχειν διείληπτο, καὶ κατὰ λόγον· τὸ γὰρ χειρωθὲν αὐτῆς μέρος 6 διπλάσιον ἀπεδίδου βοήθημα. πρὸς δὲ τὴν δυστραπέλειαν ταύτην ἐπινοήσας τι φιλοτέχνημα προσέταξεν Ἰολάῳ λαμπάδι καομένῃ τὸ ἀποτμηθὲν μέρος ἐπικάειν, ἵνα τὴν ῥύσιν ἐπίσχῃ τοῦ αἵματος. οὕτως οὖν χειρωσάμενος τὸ ζῷον εἰς τὴν χολὴν ἀπέβαπτε τὰς ἀκίδας, ἵνα τὸ βληθὲν βέλος ἔχῃ τὴν ἐκ τῆς ἀκίδος πληγὴν ἀνίατον.

12. Τρίτον δὲ πρόσταγμα ἔλαβεν ἐνεγκεῖν τὸν Ἐρυμάνθιον κάπρον ζῶντα, ὃς διέτριβεν[2] ἐν τῇ Λαμπείᾳ τῆς Ἀρκαδίας. ἐδόκει δὲ τὸ πρόσταγμα τοῦτο πολλὴν ἔχειν δυσχέρειαν· ἔδει γὰρ τὸν ἀγωνιζόμενον τοιούτῳ θηρίῳ τοσαύτην ἔχειν περιουσίαν ὥστε ἐπ' αὐτῆς τῆς μάχης ἀκριβῶς στοχάσασθαι τοῦ καιροῦ. ἔτι μὲν γὰρ ἰσχύοντα ἀφεὶς αὐτὸν ἀπὸ

---
[1] So Dindorf: διετυποῦντο.
[2] So Dindorf: διέτριβε μέν.

---
[1] Cp. Strabo 8. 3. 10.

BOOK IV. 11. 4–12. 1

and attacked the lion, and when the beast retreated into the cleft, after closing up the other opening he followed in after it and grappled with it, and winding his arms about its neck choked it to death. The skin of the lion he put about himself, and since he could cover his whole body with it because of its great size, he had in it a protection against the perils which were to follow.

The second Labour which he undertook was the slaying of the Lernaean hydra, springing from whose single body were fashioned a hundred necks, each bearing the head of a serpent. And when one head was cut off, the place where it was severed put forth two others; for this reason it was considered to be invincible, and with good reason, since the part of it which was subdued sent forth a two-fold assistance in its place. Against a thing so difficult to manage as this Heracles devised an ingenious scheme and commanded Iolaüs to sear with a burning brand the part which had been severed, in order to check the flow of the blood. So when he had subdued the animal by this means he dipped the heads of his arrows in the venom, in order that when the missile should be shot the wound which the point made might be incurable.

12. The third Command which he received was the bringing back alive of the Erymanthian boar which lived on Mount Lampeia [1] in Arcadia. This Command was thought to be exceedingly difficult, since it required of the man who fought such a beast that he possess such a superiority over it as to catch precisely the proper moment in the very heat of the encounter. For should he let it loose while it still retained its strength he would be in

τῶν ὀδόντων ἂν ἐκινδύνευσε, πλέον [1] δὲ τοῦ δέοντος καταπολεμήσας ἀπέκτεινεν, ὥστε τὸν ἆθλον ὑπάρ-
2 χειν ἀσυντέλεστον. ὅμως δὲ κατὰ τὴν μάχην ταμιευσάμενος ἀκριβῶς τὴν συμμετρίαν ἀπήνεγκε τὸν κάπρον ζῶντα πρὸς Εὐρυσθέα· ὃν ἰδὼν ὁ βασιλεὺς ἐπὶ τῶν ὤμων φέροντα, καὶ φοβηθείς, ἔκρυψεν ἑαυτὸν εἰς χαλκοῦν πίθον.

3 Ἅμα δὲ τούτοις πραττομένοις Ἡρακλῆς κατηγωνίσατο τοὺς ὀνομαζομένους Κενταύρους διὰ τοιαύτας αἰτίας. Φόλος ἦν Κένταυρος, ἀφ' οὗ συνέβη τὸ πλησίον ὄρος Φολόην ὀνομασθῆναι· οὗτος ξενίοις δεχόμενος Ἡρακλέα τὸν κατακεχωσμένον οἴνου πίθον ἀνέῳξε. τοῦτον γὰρ μυθολογοῦσι τὸ παλαιὸν Διόνυσον παρατεθεῖσθαί τινι Κενταύρῳ, καὶ προστάξαι τότε ἀνοῖξαι ὅταν Ἡρακλῆς παραγένηται. διόπερ ὕστερον τέτταρσι γενεαῖς ἐπιξενωθέντος αὐτοῦ μνησθῆναι τὸν Φόλον τῆς
4 Διονύσου παραγγελίας. ἀνοιχθέντος οὖν τοῦ πίθου, καὶ τῆς εὐωδίας διὰ τὴν παλαιότητα καὶ δύναμιν τοῦ οἴνου προσπεσούσης τοῖς πλησίον οἰκοῦσι Κενταύροις, συνέβη διοιστρηθῆναι τούτους· διὸ καὶ προσπεσόντες ἀθρόοι τῇ οἰκήσει τοῦ Φόλου
5 καταπληκτικῶς ὥρμησαν πρὸς ἁρπαγήν. ὁ μὲν οὖν Φόλος φοβηθεὶς ἔκρυψεν ἑαυτόν, ὁ δ' Ἡρακλῆς παραδόξως συνεπλάκη τοῖς βιαζομένοις· ἔδει γὰρ διαγωνίζεσθαι πρὸς τοὺς ἀπὸ μὲν μητρὸς ὄντας θεούς, τὸ δὲ τάχος ἔχοντας ἵππων, ῥώμῃ δὲ δισωμάτους θῆρας, ἐμπειρίαν δὲ καὶ σύνε-

[1] So Dindorf: πλείω.

danger from its tushes, and should he attack it more violently than was proper, then he would have killed it and so the Labour would remain unfulfilled. However, when it came to the struggle he kept so careful an eye on the proper balance that he brought back the boar alive to Eurystheus; and when the king saw him carrying the boar on his shoulders, he was terrified and hid himself in a bronze vessel.

About the time that Heracles was performing these Labours, there was a struggle between him and the Centaurs, as they are called, the reason being as follows. Pholus was a Centaur, from whom the neighbouring mountain came to be called Pholoê, and receiving Heracles with the courtesies due to a guest he opened for him a jar of wine which had been buried in the earth. This jar, the writers of myths relate, had of old been left with a certain Centaur by Dionysus, who had given him orders only to open it when Heracles should come to that place. And so, four generations after that time, when Heracles was being entertained as a guest, Pholus recalled the orders of Dionysus. Now when the jar had been opened and the sweet odour of the wine, because of its great age and strength, came to the Centaurs dwelling near there, it came to pass that they were driven mad; consequently they rushed in a body to the dwelling of Pholus and set about plundering him of the wine in a terrifying manner. At this Pholus hid himself in fear, but Heracles, to their surprise, grappled with those who were employing such violence. He had indeed to struggle with beings who were gods on their mother's side, who possessed the swiftness of horses, who had the strength of two bodies, and enjoyed in addition

σιν ἔχοντας ἀνδρῶν. τῶν δὲ Κενταύρων οἱ μὲν πεύκας αὐτορρίζους ἔχοντες ἐπῆσαν, οἱ δὲ πέτρας μεγάλας, τινὲς δὲ λαμπάδας ἡμμένας, ἕτεροι δὲ 6 βουφόνους πελέκεις. ὁ δ' ἀκαταπλήκτως ὑποστὰς ἀξίαν τῶν προκατειργασμένων συνεστήσατο μάχην. συνηγωνίζετο δ' αὐτοῖς ἡ μήτηρ Νεφέλη πολὺν ὄμβρον ἐκχέουσα, δι' οὗ τοὺς μὲν τετρασκελεῖς οὐκ ἔβλαπτε, τῷ δὲ δυσὶν ἠρεισμένῳ σκέλεσι τὴν βάσιν ὀλισθηρὰν κατεσκεύαζεν. ἀλλ' ὅμως τοὺς τοιούτοις προτερήμασι πλεονεκτοῦντας Ἡρακλῆς παραδόξως κατηγωνίσατο, καὶ τοὺς μὲν πλείστους ἀπέ7 κτεινε, τοὺς δ' ὑπολειφθέντας φυγεῖν ἠνάγκασε. τῶν δ' ἀναιρεθέντων Κενταύρων ὑπῆρχον ἐπιφανέστατοι Δάφνις καὶ Ἀργεῖος καὶ Ἀμφίων, ἔτι δὲ Ἱπποτίων καὶ Ὄρειος καὶ Ἰσοπλῆς καὶ Μελαγχαίτης, πρὸς δὲ τούτοις Θηρεὺς καὶ Δούπων καὶ Φρίξος. τῶν δὲ διαφυγόντων τὸν κίνδυνον ὕστερον ἕκαστος τιμωρίας ἠξιώθη· Ὅμαδος μὲν γὰρ ἐν Ἀρκαδίᾳ τὴν Εὐρυσθέως ἀδελφὴν Ἀλκυόνην βιαζόμενος ἀνῃρέθη. ἐφ' ᾧ συνέβη θαυμασθῆναι τὸν Ἡρακλέα διαφερόντως· τὸν μὲν γὰρ ἐχθρὸν κατ' ἰδίαν ἐμίσησε, τὴν δ' ὑβριζομένην ἐλεῶν ἐπιεικείᾳ διαφέρειν ὑπελάμβανεν.

8 Ἴδιον δέ τι συνέβη καὶ περὶ τὸν Ἡρακλέους φίλον τὸν ὀνομαζόμενον Φόλον. οὗτος γὰρ διὰ τὴν συγγένειαν θάπτων τοὺς πεπτωκότας Κενταύρους, καὶ βέλος ἔκ τινος ἐξαιρῶν, ὑπὸ τῆς ἀκίδος ἐπλήγη, καὶ τὸ τραῦμα ἔχων ἀνίατον ἐτελεύτησεν.

---

[1] The word means a "cloud."
[2] i.e. Eurystheus.

the experience and wisdom of men. The Centaurs advanced upon him, some with pine trees which they had plucked up together with the roots, others with great rocks, some with burning firebrands, and still others with axes such as are used to slaughter oxen. But he withstood them without sign of fear and maintained a battle which was worthy of his former exploits. The Centaurs were aided in their struggle by their mother Nephelê,[1] who sent down a heavy rain, by which she gave no trouble to those which had four legs, but for him who was supported upon two made the footing slippery. Despite all this Heracles maintained an astonishing struggle with those who enjoyed such advantages as these, slew the larger part of them, and forced the survivors to flee. Of the Centaurs which were killed the most renowned were Daphnis, Argeius, Amphion, also Hippotion, Oreius, Isoples, Melanchaetes, and Thereus, Doupon, and Phrixus. As for those who escaped the peril by flight, every one of them later received a fitting punishment: Homadus, for instance, was killed in Arcadia when he was attempting to violate Alcyonê, the sister of Eurystheus. And for this feat it came to pass that Heracles was marvelled at exceedingly; for though he had private grounds for hating his enemy,[2] yet because he pitied her who was being outraged, he determined to be superior to others in humanity.

A peculiar thing also happened in the case of him who was called Pholus, the friend of Heracles. While he was burying the fallen Centaurs, since they were his kindred, and was extracting an arrow from one of them, he was wounded by the barb, and since the wound could not be healed he came to his death.

ὃν Ἡρακλῆς μεγαλοπρεπῶς θάψας ὑπὸ τὸ ὄρος ἔθηκεν, ὃ στήλης ἐνδόξου γέγονε κρεῖττον· Φολόη γὰρ ὀνομαζόμενον διὰ τῆς ἐπωνυμίας μηνύει τὸν ταφέντα καὶ οὐ δι' ἐπιγραφῆς. ὁμοίως δὲ καὶ Χείρωνα τὸν ἐπὶ τῇ ἰατρικῇ θαυμαζόμενον ἀκουσίως τόξου βολῇ διέφθειρε. καὶ περὶ μὲν τῶν Κενταύρων ἱκανῶς ἡμῖν εἰρήσθω.

13. Μετὰ δὲ ταῦτ' ἔλαβε πρόσταγμα τὴν χρυσόκερων μὲν οὖσαν ἔλαφον, τάχει δὲ διαφέρουσαν, ἀγαγεῖν. τοῦτον δὲ τὸν ἆθλον συντελῶν τὴν ἐπίνοιαν ἔσχεν οὐκ ἀχρηστοτέραν τῆς κατὰ τὸ σῶμα ῥώμης. οἱ μὲν γάρ φασιν αὐτὴν ἄρκυσιν ἑλεῖν, οἱ δὲ διὰ τῆς στιβείας χειρώσασθαι καθεύδουσαν, τινὲς δὲ συνεχεῖ διωγμῷ καταπονῆσαι· πλὴν ἄνευ βίας καὶ κινδύνων διὰ τῆς κατὰ τὴν ψυχὴν ἀγχινοίας τὸν ἆθλον τοῦτον κατειργάσατο.

2 Ὁ δ' Ἡρακλῆς πρόσταγμα λαβὼν τὰς ἐκ τῆς Στυμφαλίδος λίμνης ὄρνιθας ἐξελάσαι, τέχνῃ καὶ ἐπινοίᾳ ῥᾳδίως συνετέλεσε τὸν ἆθλον. ἐπεπόλασε γάρ, ὡς ἔοικεν, ὀρνίθων πλῆθος ἀμύθητον, καὶ τοὺς ἐν τῇ πλησίον χώρᾳ καρποὺς ἐλυμαίνετο. βίᾳ μὲν οὖν ἀδύνατον ἦν χειρώσασθαι τὰ ζῷα διὰ τὴν ὑπερβολὴν τοῦ πλήθους, φιλοτέχνου δ' ἐπινοίας ἡ πρᾶξις προσεδεῖτο. διόπερ κατασκευάσας χαλκῆν πλαταγήν, καὶ διὰ ταύτης ἐξαίσιον κατασκευάζων ψόφον, ἐξεφόβει τὰ ζῷα, καὶ πέρας τῇ συνεχείᾳ

Heracles gave him a magnificent funeral and buried him at the foot of the mountain, which serves better than a gravestone to preserve his glory; for Pholoê makes known the identity of the buried man by bearing his name and no inscription is needed. Likewise Heracles unwittingly by a shot from his bow killed the Centaur Cheiron, who was admired for his knowledge of healing. But as for the Centaurs let what we have said suffice.

13. The next Command which Heracles received was the bringing back of the hart which had golden horns and excelled in swiftness of foot. In the performance of this Labour his sagacity stood him in not less stead than his strength of body. For some say that he captured it by the use of nets, others that he tracked it down and mastered it while it was asleep, and some that he wore it out by running it down. One thing is certain, that he accomplished this Labour by his sagacity of mind, without the use of force and without running any perils.

Heracles then received a Command to drive the birds out of the Stymphalian Lake, and he easily accomplished the Labour by means of a device of art and by ingenuity. The lake abounded, it would appear, with a multitude of birds without telling, which destroyed the fruits of the country roundabout. Now it was not possible to master the animals by force because of the exceptional multitude of them, and so the deed called for ingenuity in cleverly discovering some device. Consequently he fashioned a bronze rattle whereby he made a terrible noise and frightened the animals away, and furthermore, by maintaining a continual din, he

DIODORUS OF SICILY

τοῦ κρότου ῥᾳδίως ἐκπολιορκήσας καθαρὰν ἐποίησε τὴν λίμνην.

3 Τελέσας δὲ καὶ τοῦτον τὸν ἆθλον ἔλαβε παρ' Εὐρυσθέως πρόσταγμα τὴν αὐλὴν τὴν Αὐγέου καθᾶραι μηδενὸς βοηθοῦντος· αὕτη δ' ἐκ πολλῶν χρόνων ἠθροισμένην κόπρον εἶχεν ἄπλατον, ἣν ὕβρεως ἕνεκεν Εὐρυσθεὺς προσέταξε καθᾶραι. ὁ δ' Ἡρακλῆς τὸ μὲν τοῖς ὤμοις ἐξενεγκεῖν ταύτην ἀπεδοκίμασεν, ἐκκλίνων τὴν ἐκ τῆς ὕβρεως αἰσχύνην· ἐπαγαγὼν δὲ τὸν Ἀλφειὸν καλούμενον ποταμὸν ἐπὶ τὴν αὐλήν, καὶ διὰ τοῦ ῥεύματος ἐκκαθάρας αὐτήν, χωρὶς ὕβρεως συνετέλεσε τὸν ἆθλον ἐν ἡμέρᾳ μιᾷ. διὸ καὶ θαυμάσαι τις ἂν τὴν ἐπίνοιαν· τὸ γὰρ ὑπερήφανον τοῦ προστάγματος χωρὶς αἰσχύνης ἐπετέλεσεν, οὐδὲν ὑπομείνας ἀνάξιον τῆς ἀθανασίας.

4 Μετὰ δὲ ταῦτα λαβὼν ἆθλον τὸν ἐκ Κρήτης ταῦρον ἀγαγεῖν, οὗ Πασιφάην ἐρασθῆναί φασι, πλεύσας εἰς τὴν νῆσον, καὶ Μίνω τὸν βασιλέα συνεργὸν λαβών, ἤγαγεν αὐτὸν εἰς Πελοπόννησον, τὸ τηλικοῦτον πέλαγος ἐπ' αὐτῷ ναυστοληθείς.

14. Τελέσας δὲ τοῦτον τὸν ἆθλον τὸν Ὀλυμπικὸν ἀγῶνα συνεστήσατο, κάλλιστον τῶν τόπων πρὸς τηλικαύτην πανήγυριν προκρίνας τὸ παρὰ τὸν Ἀλφειὸν ποταμὸν πεδίον, ἐν ᾧ τὸν ἀγῶνα τοῦτον τῷ Διὶ τῷ πατρίῳ καθιέρωσε. στεφανίτην δ' αὐτὸν

---

[1] Usually known as the Minotaur, "bull of Minos"; cp. chap. 77.

easily forced them to abandon their siege of the place and cleansed the lake of them.

Upon the performance of this Labour he received a Command from Eurystheus to cleanse the stables of Augeas, and to do this without the assistance of any other man. These stables contained an enormous mass of dung which had accumulated over a great period, and it was a spirit of insult which induced Eurystheus to lay upon him the command to clean out this dung. Heracles declined as unworthy of him to carry this out upon his shoulders, in order to avoid the disgrace which would follow upon the insulting command; and so, turning the course of the Alpheius river, as it is called, into the stables and cleansing them by means of the stream, he accomplished the Labour in a single day, and without suffering any insult. Surely, then, we may well marvel at the ingenuity of Heracles; for he accomplished the ignoble task involved in the Command without incurring any disgrace or submitting to something which would render him unworthy of immortality.

The next Labour which Heracles undertook was to bring back from Crete the bull [1] of which, they say, Pasiphaê had been enamoured, and sailing to the island he secured the aid of Minos the king and brought it back to Peloponnesus, having voyaged upon its back over so wide an expanse of sea.

14. After the performance of this Labour Heracles established the Olympic Games, having selected for so great a festival the most beautiful of places, which was the plain lying along the banks of the Alpheius river, where he dedicated these Games to Zeus the Father. And he stipulated that the prize

387

ἐποίησεν, ὅτι καὶ αὐτὸς εὐηργέτησε τὸ γένος τῶν
2 ἀνθρώπων οὐδένα λαβὼν μισθόν. τὰ δ' ἀθλήματα
πάντα αὐτὸς ἀδηρίτως ἐνίκησε, μηδενὸς τολμήσαν-
τος αὐτῷ συγκριθῆναι διὰ τὴν ὑπερβολὴν τῆς
ἀρετῆς, καίπερ τῶν ἀθλημάτων ἐναντίων ἀλλήλοις
ὄντων· τὸν γὰρ πύκτην ἢ παγκρατιαστὴν τοῦ
σταδιέως δύσκολον περιγενέσθαι, καὶ πάλιν τὸν
ἐν τοῖς κούφοις ἀθλήμασι πρωτεύοντα[1] τοὺς ἐν
τοῖς βαρέσιν ὑπερέχοντας δυσχερὲς καταπονῆσαι.[2]
διόπερ εἰκότως ἐγένετο τιμιώτατος ἁπάντων τῶν
ἀγώνων οὗτος, τὴν ἀρχὴν ἀπ' ἀγαθοῦ λαβών.
3 Οὐκ ἄξιον δὲ παραλιπεῖν οὐδὲ τὰς ὑπὸ τῶν
θεῶν αὐτῷ δοθείσας δωρεὰς διὰ τὴν ἀρετήν. ἀπὸ
γὰρ τῶν πολέμων τραπέντος αὐτοῦ πρὸς ἀνέσεις τε
καὶ πανηγύρεις, ἔτι δ' ἑορτὰς καὶ ἀγῶνας, ἐτίμησαν
αὐτὸν δωρεαῖς οἰκείαις ἕκαστος τῶν θεῶν, Ἀθηνᾶ
μὲν πέπλῳ, Ἥφαιστος δὲ ῥοπάλῳ καὶ θώρακι·
καὶ πρὸς ἀλλήλους ἐφιλοτιμήθησαν οἱ προειρημένοι
θεοὶ κατὰ τὰς τέχνας, τῆς μὲν πρὸς εἰρηνικὴν
ἀπόλαυσιν καὶ τέρψιν, τοῦ δὲ πρὸς τὴν τῶν πολε-
μικῶν κινδύνων ἀσφάλειαν. τῶν δ' ἄλλων Ποσει-
δῶν μὲν ἵππους ἐδωρήσατο, Ἑρμῆς δὲ ξίφος,
Ἀπόλλων δὲ τόξον τε ἔδωκε καὶ τοξεύειν ἐδίδαξε,
Δημήτηρ δὲ πρὸς τὸν καθαρμὸν τοῦ Κενταύρων
φόνου τὰ μικρὰ μυστήρια συνεστήσατο, τὸν
Ἡρακλέα τιμῶσα.

[1] καταγωνίσασθαι after πρωτεύοντα deleted by all editors but Vogel.
[2] καταπονῆσαι Π, all editors, κατανοῆσαι ABD, Vogel.

[1] The contest in boxing and wrestling.
[2] The famous foot-race, 606¾ feet long.

in them should be only a crown, since he himself had conferred benefits upon the race of men without receiving any monetary reward. All the contests were won by him without opposition by anyone else, since no one was bold enough to contend with him because of his exceeding prowess. And yet the contests are very different one from another, since it is hard for a boxer or one who enters for the "Pankration"[1] to defeat a man who runs the "stadion,"[2] and equally difficult for the man who wins first place in the light contests to wear down those who excel in the heavy. Consequently it was fitting that of all Games the Olympic should be the one most honoured, since they were instituted by a noble man.

It would also not be right to overlook the gifts which were bestowed upon Heracles by the gods because of his high achievements. For instance, when he returned from the wars to devote himself to both relaxations and festivals, as well as to feasts and contests, each one of the gods honoured him with appropriate gifts; Athena with a robe, Hephaestus with a war-club and coat of mail, these two gods vying with one another in accordance with the arts they practised, the one with an eye to the enjoyment and delight afforded in times of peace, the other looking to his safety amid the perils of war. As for the other gods, Poseidon presented him with horses, Hermes with a sword, Apollo gave him a bow and arrows and taught him their use, and Demeter instituted the Lesser Mysteries[3] in honour of Heracles, that she might purify him of the guilt he had incurred in the slaughter of the Centaurs.

[3] These were celebrated at Agrae, south-east of the Acropolis, on the Ilissus, the "Greater Mysteries" at Eleusis.

4 Ἴδιον δέ τι συνέβη καὶ κατὰ τὴν γένεσιν τοῦ θεοῦ τούτου συντελεσθῆναι. Ζεὺς γὰρ πρώτῃ μὲν ἐμίγη γυναικὶ θνητῇ Νιόβῃ τῇ Φορωνέως, ἐσχάτῃ δ' Ἀλκμήνῃ· ταύτην δ' ἀπὸ Νιόβης ἑκκαιδεκάτην οἱ μυθογράφοι γενεαλογοῦσιν· ὥστε τοῦ[1] γεννᾶν ἀνθρώπους ἐκ μὲν τῶν ταύτης προγόνων ἤρξατο, εἰς αὐτὴν δὲ ταύτην κατέληξεν· ἐν ταύτῃ γὰρ τὰς πρὸς θνητὴν ὁμιλίας κατέλυσε, καὶ κατὰ τοὺς ὕστερον χρόνους οὐδένα τούτων γεννήσειν ἄξιον ἐλπίζων οὐκ ἐβουλήθη τοῖς κρείττοσιν ἐπεισάγειν τὰ χείρω.

15. Μετὰ δὲ ταῦτα τῶν περὶ τὴν Παλλήνην γιγάντων ἑλομένων[2] τὸν πρὸς τοὺς ἀθανάτους πόλεμον, Ἡρακλῆς τοῖς θεοῖς συναγωνισάμενος καὶ πολλοὺς ἀνελὼν τῶν γηγενῶν ἀποδοχῆς ἔτυχε τῆς μεγίστης. Ζεὺς γὰρ τοὺς μὲν συναγωνισαμένους τῶν θεῶν μόνους ὠνόμασεν Ὀλυμπίους, ἵνα τῇ ταύτης τιμῇ ὁ ἀγαθὸς κοσμηθεὶς ἐπωνυμίᾳ διαφέρῃ τοῦ χείρονος· ἠξίωσε δὲ ταύτης τῆς προσηγορίας τῶν ἐκ θνητῶν γυναικῶν γενομένων Διόνυσον καὶ Ἡρακλέα, οὐ μόνον ὅτι πατρὸς ἦσαν Διός, ἀλλὰ διότι καὶ τὴν προαίρεσιν ὁμοίαν ἔσχον, εὐεργετήσαντες μεγάλα τὸν βίον τῶν ἀνθρώπων.

2 Ζεὺς δέ, Προμηθέως παραδόντος τὸ πῦρ τοῖς ἀνθρώποις, δεσμοῖς κατελάβετο καὶ παρέστησεν ἀετὸν τὸν ἐσθίοντα τὸ ἧπαρ αὐτοῦ. Ἡρακλῆς δ' ὁρῶν τῆς τιμωρίας αὐτὸν τυγχάνοντα διὰ τὴν τῶν ἀνθρώπων εὐεργεσίαν, τὸν μὲν ἀετὸν κατετόξευσε,

---
[1] ὥστε τοῦ Dindorf: εἰς δὲ τό.
[2] Dindorf conjectures ἀνελομένων.

BOOK IV. 14. 4–15. 2

A peculiar thing also came to pass in connection with the birth of this god. The first mortal woman, for instance, with whom Zeus lay was Niobê, the daughter of Phoroneus, and the last was Alcmenê, who, as the writers of myths state in their genealogies, was the sixteenth lineal descendant from Niobê. It appears, then, that Zeus began to beget human beings with the ancestors of this Alcmenê and ceased with her; that is, he stopped with her his intercourse with mortal women, since he had no hope that he would beget in after times one who would be worthy of his former children and was unwilling to have the better followed by the worse.

15. After this, when the Giants about Pallenê chose to begin the war against the immortals, Heracles fought on the side of the gods, and slaying many of the Sons of Earth he received the highest approbation. For Zeus gave the name of "Olympian" only to those gods who had fought by his side, in order that the courageous, by being adorned by so honourable a title, might be distinguished by this designation from the coward; and of those who were born of mortal women he considered only Dionysus and Heracles worthy of this name, not only because they had Zeus for their father, but also because they had avowed the same plan of life as he and conferred great benefits upon the life of men.

And Zeus, when Prometheus had taken fire and given it to men, put him in chains and set an eagle at his side which devoured his liver. But when Heracles saw him suffering such punishment because of the benefit which he had conferred upon men, he killed the eagle with an arrow, and then persuad-

τὸν δὲ Δία πείσας λῆξαι τῆς ὀργῆς ἔσωσε τὸν κοινὸν εὐεργέτην.

3 Μετὰ δὲ ταῦτα ἔλαβεν ἆθλον ἀγαγεῖν τὰς Διομήδους τοῦ Θρᾳκὸς ἵππους. αὗται δὲ χαλκᾶς μὲν φάτνας εἶχον διὰ τὴν ἀγριότητα, ἁλύσεσι δὲ σιδηραῖς διὰ τὴν ἰσχὺν ἐδεσμεύοντο, τροφὴν δ' ἐλάμβανον οὐ τὴν ἐκ γῆς φυομένην, ἀλλὰ τὰ τῶν ξένων μέλη διαιρούμεναι τροφὴν εἶχον τὴν συμφορὰν τῶν ἀκληρούντων. ταύτας ὁ Ἡρακλῆς βουλόμενος χειρώσασθαι τὸν κύριον Διομήδην παρέβαλε, καὶ ταῖς τοῦ παρανομεῖν διδάξαντος σαρξὶν ἐκπληρώσας τὴν ἔνδειαν τῶν ζῴων εὐπειθεῖς 4 ἔσχεν. Εὐρυσθεὺς δ' ἀχθεισῶν πρὸς αὐτὸν τῶν ἵππων ταύτας μὲν ἱερὰς ἐποίησεν Ἥρας, ὧν τὴν ἐπιγονὴν συνέβη διαμεῖναι μέχρι τῆς Ἀλεξάνδρου τοῦ Μακεδόνος βασιλείας.

Τοῦτον δὲ τὸν ἆθλον ἐπιτελέσας μετ' Ἰάσονος συνεξέπλευσε συστρατεύσων ἐπὶ τὸ χρυσόμαλλον δέρος εἰς Κόλχους. ἀλλὰ περὶ μὲν τούτων ἐν τῇ τῶν Ἀργοναυτῶν στρατείᾳ τὰ κατὰ μέρος διέξιμεν.

16. Ἡρακλῆς δὲ λαβὼν πρόσταγμα τὸν Ἱππολύτης τῆς Ἀμαζόνος ἐνεγκεῖν ζωστῆρα, τὴν ἐπὶ τὰς Ἀμαζόνας στρατείαν ἐποιήσατο. πλεύσας οὖν εἰς τὸν Εὔξεινον ὑπ'[1] ἐκείνου κληθέντα Πόντον, καὶ καταπλεύσας ἐπὶ τὰς ἐκβολὰς τοῦ Θερμώδοντος ποταμοῦ, πλησίον Θεμισκύρας πόλεως κατεστρατοπέδευσεν, ἐν ᾗ τὰ βασίλεια τῶν Ἀμαζόνων ὑπῆρχε. 2 καὶ τὸ μὲν πρῶτον ᾔτει παρ' αὐτῶν τὸν προστεταγ-

[1] ὑπ' suggested by Vogel: ἀπ'.

[1] In chaps. 41-56.

BOOK IV. 15. 2–16. 2

ing Zeus to cease from his anger he rescued him who had been the benefactor of all.

The next Labour which Heracles undertook was the bringing back of the horses of Diomedes, the Thracian. The feeding-troughs of these horses were of brass because the steeds were so savage, and they were fastened by iron chains because of their strength, and the food they ate was not the natural produce of the soil but they tore apart the limbs of strangers and so got their food from the ill lot of hapless men. Heracles, in order to control them, threw to them their master Diomedes, and when he had satisfied the hunger of the animals by means of the flesh of the man who had taught them to violate human law in this fashion, he had them under his control. And when the horses were brought to Eurystheus he consecrated them to Hera, and in fact their breed continued down to the reign of Alexander of Macedon.

When this Labour was finished Heracles sailed forth with Jason as a member of the expedition to the Colchi to get the golden fleece. But we shall give a detailed account of these matters in connection with the expedition of the Argonauts.[1]

16. Heracles then received a Command to bring back the girdle of Hippolytê the Amazon and so made the expedition against the Amazons. Accordingly he sailed into the Pontus, which was named by him Euxeinus,[2] and continuing to the mouth of the Thermodon River he encamped near the city of Themiscyra, in which was situated the palace of the Amazons. And first of all he demanded of them the girdle which he had been commanded

i.e. " hospitable to strangers."

μένον ζωστῆρα· ὡς δ' οὐχ ὑπήκουον, συνῆψε μάχην αὐταῖς. τὸ μὲν οὖν ἄλλο πλῆθος αὐτῶν ἀντετάχθη τοῖς πολλοῖς, αἱ δὲ τιμιώταται κατ' αὐτὸν ταχθεῖσαι τὸν Ἡρακλέα μάχην καρτερὰν συνεστήσαντο. πρώτη μὲν γὰρ αὐτῷ συνάψασα μάχην Ἄελλα,[1] διὰ τὸ τάχος ταύτης τετευχυῖα τῆς προσηγορίας, ὀξύτερον εὗρεν αὐτῆς τὸν ἀντιταχθέντα. δευτέρα δὲ Φιλιππὶς εὐθὺς ἐκ τῆς πρώτης συστάσεως καιρίῳ πληγῇ περιπεσοῦσα διεφθάρη. μετὰ δὲ ταῦτα Προθόη συνῆψε μάχην, ἣν ἐκ προκλήσεως ἔφασαν ἑπτάκις νενικηκέναι τὸν ἀντιταξάμενον. πεσούσης δὲ καὶ ταύτης, τετάρτην ἐχειρώσατο τὴν ὀνομαζομένην Ἐρίβοιαν. αὕτη δὲ διὰ τὴν ἐν τοῖς πολεμικοῖς ἀγῶσιν ἀνδραγαθίαν καυχωμένη μηδενὸς χρείαν ἔχειν βοηθοῦ, ψευδῆ τὴν ἐπαγγελίαν ἔσχε κρείττονι περιπεσοῦσα. μετὰ δὲ ταύτας Κελαινὼ καὶ Εὐρυβία καὶ Φοίβη, τῆς Ἀρτέμιδος οὖσαι συγκυνηγοὶ καὶ διὰ παντὸς εὐστόχως ἀκοντίζουσαι, τὸν ἕνα στόχον οὐκ ἔτρωσαν, ἀλλ' ἑαυταῖς συνασπίζουσαι τότε πᾶσαι κατεκόπησαν. μετὰ δὲ ταύτας Δηιάνειραν καὶ Ἀστερίαν καὶ Μάρπην, ἔτι δὲ Τέκμησσαν καὶ Ἀλκίππην ἐχειρώσατο. αὕτη δ' ὁμόσασα παρθένος διαμενεῖν τὸν μὲν ὅρκον ἐφύλαξε,[2] τὸ δὲ ζῆν οὐ διετήρησεν.[3] ἡ δὲ τὴν στρατηγίαν ἔχουσα τῶν Ἀμαζόνων Μελανίππη καὶ θαυμαζομένη μάλιστα δι' ἀνδρείαν ἀπέβαλε τὴν ἡγεμονίαν. Ἡρακλῆς δὲ τὰς ἐπιφανεστάτας τῶν Ἀμαζονίδων ἀνελὼν καὶ τὸ λοιπὸν πλῆθος φυγεῖν

---

[1] καὶ after Ἄελλα deleted by Vogel.
[2] ἐφύλαξε D, Vogel, διετήρησε CF, Dindorf, Bekker.
[3] διετήρησεν D, Vogel, διεφύλαξεν CF, Dindorf, Bekker.

[1] i.e. "Whirlwind."

to get; but when they would pay no heed to him, he joined battle with them. Now the general mass of the Amazons were arrayed against the main body of the followers of Heracles, but the most honoured of the women were drawn up opposite Heracles himself and put up a stubborn battle. The first, for instance, to join battle with him was Aella,[1] who had been given this name because of her swiftness, but she found her opponent more agile than herself. The second, Philippis, encountering a mortal blow at the very first conflict, was slain. Then he joined battle with Prothoê, who, they said, had been victorious seven times over the opponents whom she had challenged to battle. When she fell, the fourth whom he overcame was known as Eriboea. She had boasted that because of the manly bravery which she displayed in contests of war she had no need of anyone to help her, but she found her claim was false when she encountered her better. The next, Celaeno, Eurybia, and Phoebê, who were companions of Artemis in the hunt and whose spears found their mark invariably, did not even graze the single target, but in that fight they were one and all cut down as they stood shoulder to shoulder with each other. After them Deïaneira, Asteria and Marpê, and Tecmessa and Alcippê were overcome. The last-named had taken a vow to remain a maiden, and the vow she kept, but her life she could not preserve. The commander of the Amazons, Melanippê, who was also greatly admired for her manly courage, now lost her supremacy. And Heracles, after thus killing the most renowned of the Amazons and forcing the remaining multitude to turn in flight, cut down the

συναναγκάσας, κατέκοψε τὰς πλείστας, ὥστε παντελῶς τὸ ἔθνος αὐτῶν συντριβῆναι. τῶν δ' αἰχμαλωτίδων Ἀντιόπην μὲν ἐδωρήσατο Θησεῖ, Μελανίππην δ' ἀπελύτρωσεν ἀντιλαβὼν τὸν ζωστῆρα.

17. Εὐρυσθέως δὲ προστάξαντος ἆθλον δέκατον τὰς Γηρυόνου βοῦς ἀγαγεῖν, ἃς νέμεσθαι συνέβαινε τῆς Ἰβηρίας ἐν τοῖς πρὸς τὸν ὠκεανὸν κεκλιμένοις μέρεσιν, Ἡρακλῆς θεωρῶν τὸν πόνον τοῦτον μεγάλης προσδεόμενον παρασκευῆς καὶ κακοπαθείας, συνεστήσατο στόλον ἀξιόλογον καὶ πλῆθος στρατιωτῶν ἀξιόχρεων ἐπὶ ταύτην τὴν στρατείαν.
2 διεβεβόητο γὰρ κατὰ πᾶσαν τὴν οἰκουμένην ὅτι Χρυσάωρ ὁ λαβὼν ἀπὸ τοῦ πλούτου τὴν προσηγορίαν βασιλεύει μὲν ἁπάσης Ἰβηρίας, τρεῖς δ' ἔχει συναγωνιστὰς υἱούς, διαφέροντας ταῖς τε ῥώμαις τῶν σωμάτων καὶ ταῖς ἐν τοῖς πολεμικοῖς ἀγῶσιν ἀνδραγαθίαις, πρὸς δὲ τούτοις ὅτι τῶν υἱῶν ἕκαστος μεγάλας ἔχει δυνάμεις συνεστώσας ἐξ ἐθνῶν μαχίμων· ὧν δὴ χάριν ὁ μὲν Εὐρυσθεὺς νομίζων δυσέφικτον εἶναι τὴν ἐπὶ τούτους στρατείαν,
3 προσετετάχει τὸν προειρημένον ἆθλον. ὁ δ' Ἡρακλῆς ἀκολούθως ταῖς προκατειργασμέναις πράξεσι τεθαρρηκότως ὑπέστη τοὺς κινδύνους. καὶ τὰς μὲν δυνάμεις ἤθροισεν εἰς Κρήτην, κεκρικὼς ἐκ ταύτης ποιεῖσθαι τὴν ὁρμήν· σφόδρα γὰρ εὐφυῶς ἡ νῆσος αὕτη κεῖται πρὸς τὰς ἐφ' ὅλην τὴν οἰκουμένην στρατείας. πρὸ δὲ τῆς ἀναγωγῆς τιμηθεὶς ὑπὸ τῶν ἐγχωρίων μεγαλοπρεπῶς, καὶ βουλόμενος τοῖς Κρησὶ χαρίσασθαι, καθαρὰν ἐποίησε τὴν νῆσον τῶν θηρίων. διόπερ ἐν τοῖς ὕστερον

---

[1] "He of the Golden Sword."

greater number of them, so that the race of them was utterly exterminated. As for the captives, he gave Antiopê as a gift to Theseus and set Melanippê free, accepting her girdle as her ransom.

17. Eurystheus then enjoined upon him as a tenth Labour the bringing back of the cattle of Geryones, which pastured in the parts of Iberia which slope towards the ocean. And Heracles, realizing that this task called for preparation on a large scale and involved great hardships, gathered a notable armament and a multitude of soldiers such as would be adequate for this expedition. For it had been noised abroad throughout all the inhabited world that Chrysaor,[1] who received this appellation because of his wealth, was king over the whole of Iberia, and that he had three sons to fight at his side, who excelled in both strength of body and the deeds of courage which they displayed in contests of war; it was known, furthermore, that each of these sons had at his disposal great forces which were recruited from warlike tribes. It was because of these reports that Eurystheus, thinking any expedition against these men would be too difficult to succeed, had assigned to Heracles the Labour just described. But Heracles met the perils with the same bold spirit which he had displayed in the deeds which he had performed up to this time. His forces he gathered and brought to Crete, having decided to make his departure from that place; for this island is especially well situated for expeditions against any part of the inhabited world. Before his departure he was magnificently honoured by the natives, and wishing to show his gratitude to the Cretans he cleansed the island of the wild beasts which infested it. And this

χρόνοις οὐδὲν ἔτι τῶν ἀγρίων ζώων ὑπῆρχεν ἐν τῇ νήσῳ, οἷον ἄρκτων, λύκων, ὄφεων ἢ τῶν ἄλλων τῶν τοιούτων. ταῦτα δ' ἔπραξεν ἀποσεμνύνων τὴν νῆσον, ἐν ᾗ μυθολογοῦσι καὶ γενέσθαι καὶ τραφῆναι τὸν Δία.

4 Ποιησάμενος οὖν τὸν ἐκ ταύτης πλοῦν κατῆρεν εἰς τὴν Λιβύην, καὶ πρῶτον μὲν Ἀνταῖον τὸν ῥώμῃ σώματος καὶ παλαίστρας ἐμπειρίᾳ διαβεβοημένον καὶ τοὺς ὑπ' αὐτοῦ καταπαλαισθέντας ξένους ἀποκτείνοντα[1] προκαλεσάμενος εἰς μάχην καὶ συμπλακεὶς διέφθειρεν. ἀκολούθως δὲ τούτοις τὴν μὲν Λιβύην πλήθουσαν ἀγρίων ζῴων, πολλὰ τῶν κατὰ τὴν ἔρημον χώραν χειρωσάμενος, ἐξημέρωσεν, ὥστε καὶ γεωργίαις καὶ ταῖς ἄλλαις φυτείαις ταῖς τοὺς καρποὺς παρασκευαζούσαις πληρωθῆναι πολλὴν μὲν ἀμπελόφυτον χώραν, πολλὴν δ' ἐλαιοφόρον· καθόλου δὲ τὴν Λιβύην διὰ τὸ πλῆθος τῶν κατὰ τὴν χώραν θηρίων ἀοίκητον πρότερον οὖσαν ἐξημερώσας ἐποίησε μηδεμιᾶς 5 χώρας εὐδαιμονίᾳ λείπεσθαι. ὁμοίως δὲ καὶ τοὺς παρανομοῦντας ἀνθρώπους ἢ δυνάστας ὑπερηφάνους ἀποκτείνας τὰς πόλεις ἐποίησεν εὐδαίμονας. μυθολογοῦσι δ' αὐτὸν διὰ τοῦτο μισῆσαι καὶ πολεμῆσαι τὸ γένος τῶν ἀγρίων θηρίων καὶ παρανόμων ἀνδρῶν, ὅτι παιδὶ μὲν ὄντι νηπίῳ συνέβη τοὺς ὄφεις ἐπιβούλους αὐτῷ γενέσθαι, ἀνδρωθέντι δὲ πεσεῖν ὑπ' ἐξουσίαν ὑπερηφάνου καὶ ἀδίκου μονάρχου τοῦ τοὺς ἄθλους προστάττοντος.

18. Μετὰ δὲ τὸν Ἀνταίου θάνατον παρελθὼν εἰς

[1] So Bekker: ἀποκτείναντα MSS., Dindorf, Vogel.

[1] Cp. Book 1. 21. 4.

is the reason why in later times not a single wild animal, such as a bear, or wolf, or serpent, or any similar beast, was to be found on the island. This deed he accomplished for the glory of the island, which, the myths relate, was both the birthplace and the early home of Zeus.

Setting sail, then, from Crete, Heracles put in at Libya, and first of all he challenged to a fight Antaeus,[1] whose fame was noised abroad because of his strength of body and his skill in wrestling, and because he was wont to put to death all strangers whom he had defeated in wrestling, and grappling with him Heracles slew the giant. Following up this great deed he subdued Libya, which was full of wild animals, and large parts of the adjoining desert, and brought it all under cultivation, so that the whole land was filled with ploughed fields and such plantings in general as bear fruit, much of it being devoted to vineyards and much to olive orchards; and, speaking generally, Libya, which before that time had been uninhabitable because of the multitude of the wild beasts which infested the whole land, was brought under cultivation by him and made inferior to no other country in point of prosperity. He likewise punished with death such men as defied the law or arrogant rulers and gave prosperity to the cities. And the myths relate that he hated every kind of wild beast and lawless men and warred upon them because of the fact that it had been his lot that while yet an infant the serpents made an attempt on his life, and that when he came to man's estate he became subject to the power of an arrogant and unjust despot who laid upon him these Labours.

18. After Heracles had slain Antaeus he passed into

DIODORUS OF SICILY

Αἴγυπτον ἀνεῖλε Βούσιριν τὸν βασιλέα ξενοκτονοῦντα τοὺς παρεπιδημοῦντας. διεξιὼν δὲ τὴν ἄνυδρον τῆς Λιβύης, καὶ περιτυχὼν χώρᾳ καταρρύτῳ καὶ καρποφόρῳ, πόλιν ἔκτισε θαυμαστὴν τῷ μεγέθει, τὴν ὀνομαζομένην Ἑκατόμπυλον, ᾗ ἔθετο τὴν προσηγορίαν ἀπὸ τοῦ πλήθους τῶν κατ' αὐτὴν πυλῶν. διαμεμένηκε δὲ ἡ ταύτης τῆς πόλεως εὐδαιμονία μέχρι τῶν νεωτέρων καιρῶν, ἐν οἷς[1] Καρχηδόνιοι δυνάμεσιν ἀξιολόγοις καὶ στρατηγοῖς ἀγαθοῖς στρατεύσαντες ἐπ' αὐτὴν κύριοι κατέ-
2 στησαν. ὁ δ' Ἡρακλῆς πολλὴν τῆς Λιβύης ἐπελθὼν παρῆλθεν ἐπὶ τὸν πρὸς Γαδείροις ὠκεανόν, καὶ στήλας ἔθετο καθ' ἑκατέραν τῶν ἠπείρων. συμπαραπλέοντος δὲ τοῦ στόλου διαβὰς εἰς τὴν Ἰβηρίαν, καὶ καταλαβὼν τοὺς Χρυσάορος υἱοὺς τρισὶ δυνάμεσι μεγάλαις κατεστρατοπεδευκότας ἐκ διαστήματος, πάντας τοὺς ἡγεμόνας ἐκ προκλήσεως ἀνελὼν καὶ τὴν Ἰβηρίαν χειρωσάμενος ἀπήλασε τὰς διωνομασμένας τῶν βοῶν ἀγέλας.
3 διεξιὼν δὲ τὴν τῶν Ἰβήρων χώραν, καὶ τιμηθεὶς ὑπό τινος τῶν ἐγχωρίων βασιλέως, ἀνδρὸς εὐσεβείᾳ καὶ δικαιοσύνῃ διαφέροντος, κατέλιπε μέρος τῶν βοῶν ἐν δωρεαῖς τῷ βασιλεῖ. ὁ δὲ λαβὼν ἁπάσας καθιέρωσεν Ἡρακλεῖ, καὶ κατ' ἐνιαυτὸν ἐκ τούτων ἔθυεν αὐτῷ τὸν καλλιστεύοντα τῶν ταύρων· τὰς δὲ βοῦς τηρουμένας συνέβη ἱερὰς διαμεῖναι κατὰ τὴν Ἰβηρίαν μέχρι τῶν καθ' ἡμᾶς καιρῶν.
4 Ἡμεῖς δ' ἐπεὶ περὶ τῶν Ἡρακλέους στηλῶν ἐμνήσθημεν, οἰκεῖον εἶναι νομίζομεν περὶ αὐτῶν

---
[1] οἷς Hertlein : οἷς καί.

[1] Cp. Book 1. 88. 5.

BOOK IV. 18. 1-4

Egypt and put to death Busiris,[1] the king of the land, who made it his practice to kill the strangers who visited that country. Then he made his way through the waterless part of Libya, and coming upon a land which was well watered and fruitful he founded a city of marvellous size, which was called Hecatompylon,[2] giving it this name because of the multitude of its gates. And the prosperity of this city continued until comparatively recent times, when the Carthaginians made an expedition against it with notable forces under the command of able generals and made themselves its masters. And after Heracles had visited a large part of Libya he arrived at the ocean near Gadeira,[3] where he set up pillars on each of the two continents. His fleet accompanied him along the coast and on it he crossed over into Iberia. And finding there the sons of Chrysaor encamped at some distance from one another with three great armies, he challenged each of the leaders to single combat and slew them all, and then after subduing Iberia he drove off the celebrated herds of cattle. He then traversed the country of the Iberians, and since he had received honours at the hands of a certain king of the natives, a man who excelled in piety and justice, he left with the king a portion of the cattle as a present. The king accepted them, but dedicated them all to Heracles and made it his practice each year to sacrifice to Heracles the fairest bull of the herd; and it came to pass that the kine are still maintained in Iberia and continue to be sacred to Heracles down to our own time.

But since we have mentioned the pillars of Heracles, we deem it to be appropriate to set forth the facts con-

[2] "Of a Hundred Gates." [3] Cadiz.

διελθεῖν. Ἡρακλῆς γὰρ παραβαλὼν εἰς τὰς ἄκρας τῶν ἠπείρων τὰς παρὰ τὸν ὠκεανὸν κειμένας τῆς τε Λιβύης καὶ τῆς Εὐρώπης ἔγνω τῆς στρατείας θέσθαι στήλας ταύτας. βουλόμενος δ' ἀείμνηστον ἔργον ἐπ' αὐτῷ συντελέσαι, φασὶ τὰς ἄκρας
5 ἀμφοτέρας ἐπὶ πολὺ προχῶσαι· διὸ καὶ πρότερον διεστηκυίας ἀπ' ἀλλήλων πολὺ διάστημα, συναγαγεῖν τὸν πόρον εἰς στενόν, ὅπως ἁλιτενοῦς καὶ στενοῦ γενομένου κωλύηται τὰ μεγάλα κήτη διεκπίπτειν ἐκ τοῦ ὠκεανοῦ πρὸς τὴν ἐντὸς θάλατταν, ἅμα δὲ καὶ διὰ τὸ μέγεθος τῶν ἔργων μένῃ ἀείμνηστος ἡ δόξα τοῦ κατασκευάσαντος· ὡς δέ τινές φασι, τοὐναντίον τῶν ἠπείρων ἀμφοτέρων συνεζευγμένων διασκάψαι ταύτας, καὶ τὸν πόρον ἀνοίξαντα ποιῆσαι τὸν ὠκεανὸν μίσγεσθαι τῇ καθ' ἡμᾶς θαλάττῃ. ἀλλὰ περὶ μὲν τούτων ἐξέσται σκοπεῖν ὡς ἂν ἕκαστος ἑαυτοῦ πείθῃ.

6 Τὸ παραπλήσιον δὲ τούτοις ἔπραξε πρότερον κατὰ τὴν Ἑλλάδα. περὶ μὲν γὰρ τὰ καλούμενα Τέμπη τῆς πεδιάδος χώρας ἐπὶ πολὺν τόπον λιμναζούσης διέσκαψε τὸν συνεχῆ τόπον, καὶ κατὰ τῆς διώρυχος δεξάμενος ἅπαν τὸ κατὰ τὴν λίμνην ὕδωρ ἐποίησε τὰ πεδία φανῆναι τὰ κατὰ τὴν
7 Θετταλίαν παρὰ τὸν Πηνειὸν ποταμόν· ἐν δὲ τῇ Βοιωτίᾳ τοὐναντίον ἐμφράξας τὸ περὶ τὸν Μινύειον Ὀρχομενὸν ῥεῖθρον ἐποίησε λιμνάζειν τὴν χώραν καὶ φθαρῆναι τὰ κατ' αὐτὴν ἅπαντα. ἀλλὰ τὰ μὲν κατὰ τὴν Θετταλίαν ἔπραξεν εὐερ-

---

[1] The Straits of Gibraltar are twelve miles wide and for eight miles the average depth is 250 fathoms.
[2] The reference is to Lake Copaïs.

cerning them. When Heracles arrived at the farthest points of the continents of Libya and Europe which lie upon the ocean, he decided to set up these pillars to commemorate his campaign. And since he wished to leave upon the ocean a monument which would be had in everlasting remembrance, he built out both the promontories, they say, to a great distance; consequently, whereas before that time a great space had stood between them, he now narrowed the passage, in order that by making it shallow and narrow[1] he might prevent the great sea-monsters from passing out of the ocean into the inner sea, and that at the same time the fame of their builder might be held in everlasting remembrance by reason of the magnitude of the structures. Some authorities, however, say just the opposite, namely, that the two continents were originally joined and that he cut a passage between them, and that by opening the passage he brought it about that the ocean was mingled with our sea. On this question, however, it will be possible for every man to think as he may please.

A thing very much like this he had already done in Greece. For instance, in the region which is called Tempê, where the country is like a plain and was largely covered with marshes, he cut a channel through the territory which bordered on it, and carrying off through this ditch all the water of the marsh he caused the plains to appear which are now in Thessaly along the Peneius river. But in Boeotia he did just the opposite and damming the stream which flowed near the Minyan city of Orchomenus he turned the country into a lake[2] and caused the ruin of that whole region. But what he did in Thessaly was to

γετῶν τοὺς Ἕλληνας, τὰ δὲ κατὰ τὴν Βοιωτίαν τιμωρίαν λαμβάνων παρὰ τῶν τὴν Μινυάδα κατοικούντων διὰ τὴν τῶν Θηβαίων καταδούλωσιν.

19. Ὁ δ' Ἡρακλῆς τῶν μὲν Ἰβήρων παρέδωκε τὴν βασιλείαν τοῖς ἀρίστοις τῶν ἐγχωρίων, αὐτὸς δ' ἀναλαβὼν τὴν δύναμιν καὶ καταντήσας εἰς τὴν Κελτικὴν καὶ πᾶσαν ἐπελθὼν κατέλυσε μὲν τὰς συνήθεις παρανομίας καὶ ξενοκτονίας, πολλοῦ δὲ πλήθους ἀνθρώπων ἐξ ἅπαντος ἔθνους ἑκουσίως συστρατεύοντος ἔκτισε πόλιν εὐμεγέθη τὴν ὀνο-
2 μασθεῖσαν ἀπὸ τῆς κατὰ τὴν στρατείαν ἄλης Ἀλησίαν. πολλοὺς δὲ καὶ τῶν ἐγχωρίων ἀνέμιξεν εἰς τὴν πόλιν· ὧν ἐπικρατησάντων τῷ πλήθει πάντας τοὺς ἐνοικοῦντας ἐκβαρβαρωθῆναι συνέβη. οἱ δὲ Κελτοὶ μέχρι τῶνδε τῶν καιρῶν τιμῶσι ταύτην τὴν πόλιν, ὡς ἁπάσης τῆς Κελτικῆς οὖσαν ἑστίαν καὶ μητρόπολιν. διέμεινε δ' αὕτη πάντα τὸν ἀφ' Ἡρακλέους χρόνον ἐλευθέρα καὶ ἀπόρθητος μέχρι τοῦ καθ' ἡμᾶς χρόνου· τὸ δὲ τελευταῖον ὑπὸ Γαΐου Καίσαρος τοῦ διὰ τὸ μέγεθος τῶν πράξεων θεοῦ προσαγορευθέντος ἐκ βίας ἁλοῦσα συνηναγκάσθη μετὰ πάντων τῶν ἄλλων Κελτῶν
3 ὑποταγῆναι Ῥωμαίοις. ὁ δ' Ἡρακλῆς τὴν ἐκ τῆς Κελτικῆς πορείαν ἐπὶ τὴν Ἰταλίαν ποιούμενος, καὶ διεξιὼν τὴν ὀρεινὴν τὴν κατὰ τὰς Ἄλπεις, ὡδοποίησε τὴν τραχύτητα τῆς ὁδοῦ καὶ τὸ δύσβατον, ὥστε δύνασθαι στρατοπέδοις καὶ ταῖς τῶν
4 ὑποζυγίων ἀποσκευαῖς βάσιμον εἶναι. τῶν δὲ τὴν ὀρεινὴν ταύτην κατοικούντων βαρβάρων εἰωθότων τὰ διεξιόντα τῶν στρατοπέδων περικόπτειν

confer a benefit upon the Greeks, whereas in Boeotia he was exacting punishment from those who dwelt in Minyan territory, because they had enslaved the Thebans.

19. Heracles, then, delivered over the kingdom of the Iberians to the noblest men among the natives and, on his part, took his army and passing into Celtica and traversing the length and breadth of it he put an end to the lawlessness and murdering of strangers to which the people had become addicted; and since a great multitude of men from every tribe flocked to his army of their own accord, he founded a great city which was named Alesia after the "wandering" (*alê*) on his campaign. But he also mingled among the citizens of the city many natives, and since these surpassed the others in multitude, it came to pass that the inhabitants as a whole were barbarized. The Celts up to the present time hold this city in honour, looking upon it as the hearth and mother-city of all Celtica. And for the entire period from the days of Heracles this city remained free and was never sacked until our own time; but at last Gaius Caesar, who has been pronounced a god because of the magnitude of his deeds, took it by storm and made it and the other Celts subjects of the Romans.[1] Heracles then made his way from Celtica to Italy, and as he traversed the mountain pass through the Alps he made a highway out of the route, which was rough and almost impassable, with the result that it can now be crossed by armies and baggage-trains. The barbarians who inhabited this mountain region had been accustomed to butcher and to plunder such

[1] In 52 B.C.; the account of the siege and capture of Alesia is in Caesar, *The Gallic War*, 7. 68 ff.

καὶ λῃστεύειν ἐν ταῖς δυσχωρίαις, χειρωσάμενος ἅπαντας καὶ τοὺς ἡγεμόνας τῆς παρανομίας ἀνελὼν ἐποίησεν ἀσφαλῆ τοῖς μεταγενεστέροις τὴν ὁδοιπορίαν. διελθὼν δὲ τὰς Ἄλπεις καὶ τῆς νῦν καλουμένης Γαλατίας τὴν πεδιάδα διεξιὼν ἐποιήσατο τὴν πορείαν διὰ τῆς Λιγυστικῆς.

20. Οἱ δὲ ταύτην τὴν χώραν οἰκοῦντες Λίγυες νέμονται γῆν τραχεῖαν καὶ παντελῶς λυπράν· τῶν δ' ἐγχωρίων ταῖς ἐργασίαις καὶ ταῖς τῆς κακοπαθείας ὑπερβολαῖς φέρει καρποὺς πρὸς βίαν ὀλίγους. διὸ καὶ τοῖς ὄγκοις εἰσὶ συνεσταλμένοι καὶ διὰ τὴν συνεχῆ γυμνασίαν εὔτονοι· τῆς γὰρ κατὰ τὴν τρυφὴν ῥᾳστώνης πολὺ κεχωρισμένοι ἐλαφροὶ μὲν ταῖς εὐκινησίαις εἰσίν, ἐν δὲ τοῖς 2 πολεμικοῖς ἀγῶσι ταῖς ἀλκαῖς διάφοροι. καθόλου δὲ τῶν πλησιοχώρων τὸ πονεῖν συνεχῶς ἠσκηκότων, καὶ τῆς χώρας πολλῆς ἐργασίας προσδεομένης, εἰθίκασι τὰς γυναῖκας τῶν κακοπαθειῶν τῶν ἐν ταῖς ἐργασίαις κοινωνοὺς ποιεῖσθαι. μισθοῦ δὲ παρ' ἀλλήλοις ἐργαζομένων τῶν τε ἀνδρῶν καὶ τῶν γυναικῶν, ἴδιόν τι καὶ παράδοξον καθ' 3 ἡμᾶς συνέβη περὶ μίαν γυναῖκα γενέσθαι. ἔγκυος γὰρ οὖσα καὶ μετὰ τῶν ἀνδρῶν ἐργαζομένη μισθοῦ, μεταξὺ συνεχομένη ταῖς ὠδῖσιν ἀπῆλθεν εἴς τινας θάμνους ἀθορύβως· ἐν οἷς τεκοῦσα, καὶ τὸ παιδίον φύλλοις ἐνειλήσασα, τοῦτο μὲν[1] ἀπέκρυψεν, αὐτὴ δὲ συμμίξασα τοῖς ἐργαζομένοις τὴν αὐτὴν ἐκείνοις ὑπέμεινε κακοπάθειαν, οὐδὲν δηλώσασα περὶ τοῦ συμβεβηκότος. τοῦ βρέφους δὲ κλαυθμυ-

[1] εἴς τινας θάμνους after μὲν deleted by Bekker.

[1] Cisalpine Gaul.

armies as passed through when they came to the difficult portions of the way, but he subdued them all, slew those that were the leaders in lawlessness of this kind, and made the journey safe for succeeding generations. And after crossing the Alps he passed through the level plain of what is now called Galatia [1] and made his way through Liguria.

20. The Ligurians who dwell in this land possess a soil which is stony and altogether wretched, and, in return for the labours and exceedingly great hardships of the natives, produces only scanty crops which are wrung from it. Consequently the inhabitants are of small bulk and are kept vigorous by their constant exercise; for since they are far removed from the care-free life which accompanies luxury, they are light in their movements and excel in vigour when it comes to contests of war. In general, the inhabitants of the region round about are inured to continuous work, and since the land requires much labour for its cultivation, the Ligurians have become accustomed to require the women to share in the hardships which the cultivation involves. And since both the men and the women work side by side for hire, it came to pass that a strange and surprising thing took place in our day in connection with a certain woman. She was with child, and while working for hire in company with the men she was seized by the labour-pains in the midst of her work and quietly withdrew into a thicket; here she gave birth to the child, and then, after covering it with leaves, she hid the babe there and herself rejoined the labourers, continuing to endure the same hardship as that in which they were engaged and giving no hint of what had happened. And when the babe wailed and the occurrence be-

ριζομένου, καὶ τῆς πράξεως φανερᾶς γενομένης, ὁ μὲν ἐφεστηκὼς οὐδαμῶς ἠδύνατο πεῖσαι παύσασθαι τῶν ἔργων· ἡ δ' οὐ πρότερον ἀπέστη τῆς κακοπαθείας, ἕως ὁ μισθωσάμενος ἐλεήσας καὶ τὸν μισθὸν ἀποδοὺς ἀπέλυσε τῶν ἔργων.

21. Ἡρακλῆς δὲ διελθὼν τήν τε τῶν Λιγύων καὶ τὴν τῶν Τυρρηνῶν χώραν, καταντήσας πρὸς τὸν Τίβεριν ποταμὸν κατεστρατοπέδευσεν οὗ νῦν ἡ Ῥώμη ἐστίν. ἀλλ' αὕτη μὲν πολλαῖς γενεαῖς ὕστερον ὑπὸ Ῥωμύλου τοῦ Ἄρεος ἐκτίσθη, τότε δέ τινες τῶν ἐγχωρίων κατῴκουν ἐν τῷ νῦν καλουμένῳ Παλατίῳ, μικρὰν παντελῶς πόλιν 2 οἰκοῦντες. ἐν ταύτῃ δὲ τῶν ἐπιφανῶν ὄντες ἀνδρῶν Κάκιος καὶ Πινάριος ἐδέξαντο τὸν Ἡρακλέα ξενίοις ἀξιολόγοις καὶ δωρεαῖς κεχαρισμέναις ἐτίμησαν· καὶ τούτων τῶν ἀνδρῶν ὑπομνήματα μέχρι τῶνδε τῶν καιρῶν διαμένει κατὰ τὴν Ῥώμην. τῶν γὰρ νῦν εὐγενῶν ἀνδρῶν τὸ τῶν Πιναρίων ὀνομαζομένων[1] γένος διαμένει παρὰ τοῖς Ῥωμαίοις, ὡς ὑπάρχον ἀρχαιότατον, τοῦ δὲ Κακίου ἐν τῷ Παλατίῳ κατάβασίς ἐστιν ἔχουσα λιθίνην κλίμακα τὴν ὀνομαζομένην ἀπ' ἐκείνου Κακίαν, οὖσαν πλησίον τῆς τότε γενομένης οἰκίας 3 τοῦ Κακίου. ὁ δ' οὖν Ἡρακλῆς ἀποδεξάμενος τὴν εὔνοιαν τῶν τὸ Παλάτιον οἰκούντων, προεῖπεν αὐτοῖς ὅτι μετὰ τὴν ἑαυτοῦ μετάστασιν εἰς θεοὺς τοῖς εὐξαμένοις ἐκδεκατεύσειν Ἡρακλεῖ τὴν οὐσίαν συμβήσεται τὸν βίον εὐδαιμονέστερον ἔχειν.[2] ὃ καὶ συνέβη κατὰ τοὺς ὕστερον χρόνους διαμεῖναι

---

[1] So Hertlein: ὀνομαζόμενον.
[2] ἔχειν Hertlein: ἕξειν.

came known, the overseer could in no wise persuade her to stop her work; and indeed she did not desist from the hardship until her employer took pity upon her, paid her the wages due her, and set her free from work.[1]

21. After Heracles had passed through the lands of the Ligurians and of the Tyrrhenians [2] he came to the river Tiber and pitched his camp at the site where Rome now stands. But this city was founded many generations afterwards by Romulus, the son of Ares, and at this time certain people of the vicinity had their homes on the Palatine Hill, as it is now called, and formed an altogether inconsiderable city. Here some of the notable men, among them Cacius and Pinarius, welcomed Heracles with marked acts of hospitality and honoured him with pleasing gifts; and memorials of these men abide in Rome to the present day. For, of the nobles of our time, the *gens* which bears the name Pinarii still exists among the Romans, being regarded as very ancient, and as for Cacius, there is a passage on the Palatine which leads downward, furnished with a stairway of stone, and is called after him the "Steps of Cacius," [3] and it lies near the original house of Cacius. Now Heracles received with favour the good-will shown him by the dwellers on the Palatine and foretold to them that, after he had passed into the circle of the gods, it would come to pass that whatever men should make a vow to dedicate to Heracles a tithe of their goods would lead a more happy and prosperous life. And in fact this custom did arise in later times and has

[1] A similar story of women of Liguria is told by Strabo (3.4.17), on the authority of Posidonius.
[2] Etruscans.   [3] The *scalae Caci*.

DIODORUS OF SICILY

4 μέχρι τῶν καθ' ἡμᾶς χρόνων· πολλοὺς γὰρ τῶν Ῥωμαίων οὐ μόνον τῶν συμμέτρους οὐσίας κεκτημένων, ἀλλὰ καὶ τῶν μεγαλοπλούτων τινὰς εὐξαμένους ἐκδεκατεύσειν Ἡρακλεῖ, καὶ μετὰ ταῦτα γενομένους εὐδαίμονας, ἐκδεκατεῦσαι τὰς οὐσίας οὔσας ταλάντων τετρακισχιλίων. Λεύκολλος γὰρ ὁ τῶν καθ' αὑτὸν Ῥωμαίων σχεδόν τι πλουσιώτατος ὢν διατιμησάμενος τὴν ἰδίαν οὐσίαν κατέθυσε τῷ θεῷ πᾶσαν τὴν δεκάτην, εὐωχίας ποιῶν συνεχεῖς καὶ πολυδαπάνους. κατεσκεύασαν δὲ καὶ Ῥωμαῖοι τούτῳ τῷ θεῷ παρὰ τὸν Τίβεριν ἱερὸν ἀξιόλογον, ἐν ᾧ νομίζουσι συντελεῖν τὰς ἐκ τῆς δεκάτης θυσίας.

5 Ὁ δ' οὖν Ἡρακλῆς ἀπὸ τοῦ Τιβέρεως ἀναζεύξας, καὶ διεξιὼν τὴν παράλιον τῆς νῦν Ἰταλίας ὀνομαζομένης, κατήντησεν εἰς τὸ Κυμαῖον πεδίον, ἐν ᾧ μυθολογοῦσιν ἄνδρας γενέσθαι ταῖς τε ῥώμαις προέχοντας καὶ ἐπὶ παρανομίᾳ διωνομασμένους, οὓς ὀνομάζεσθαι γίγαντας. ὠνομάσθαι δὲ καὶ τὸ πεδίον τοῦτο Φλεγραῖον ἀπὸ τοῦ λόφου τοῦ τὸ παλαιὸν ἐκφυσῶντος ἄπλατον πῦρ παραπλησίως τῇ κατὰ τὴν Σικελίαν Αἴτνῃ· καλεῖται δὲ νῦν ὁ λόφος[1] Οὐεσούιος,[2] ἔχων πολλὰ σημεῖα τοῦ

6 κεκαῦσθαι κατὰ τοὺς ἀρχαίους χρόνους. τοὺς δ' οὖν γίγαντας πυθομένους τὴν Ἡρακλέους παρουσίαν ἀθροισθῆναι πάντας καὶ παρατάξασθαι τῷ προειρημένῳ. θαυμαστῆς δὲ γενομένης μάχης κατά τε τὴν ῥώμην καὶ τὴν ἀλκὴν τῶν γιγάντων, φασὶ τὸν Ἡρακλέα, συμμαχούντων αὐτῷ τῶν θεῶν, κρατῆσαι τῇ μάχῃ, καὶ τοὺς πλείστους ἀνελόντα τὴν χώραν

[1] λόφος Dindorf : τόπος.
[2] Οὐεσούιος (cp. Strabo 5. 4. 8), Οὐεσουούιος Bekker, Dindorf, Vogel, οὐεσούσιος MSS.

persisted to our own day; for many Romans, and not only those of moderate fortunes but some even of great wealth, who have taken a vow to dedicate a tenth to Heracles and have thereafter become happy and prosperous, have presented him with a tenth of their possessions, which came to four thousand talents. Lucullus, for instance, who was perhaps the wealthiest Roman of his day, had his estate appraised and then offered a full tenth of it to the god, thus providing continuous feastings and expensive ones withal. Furthermore, the Romans have built to this god a notable temple on the bank of the Tiber, with the purpose of performing in it the sacrifices from the proceeds of the tithe.

Heracles then moved on from the Tiber, and as he passed down the coast of what now bears the name of Italy he came to the Cumaean Plain. Here, the myths relate, there were men of outstanding strength the fame of whom had gone abroad for lawlessness and they were called Giants. This plain was called Phlegraean ("fiery") from the mountain which of old spouted forth a huge fire as Aetna did in Sicily; at this time, however, the mountain is called Vesuvius and shows many signs of the fire which once raged in those ancient times. Now the Giants, according to the account, on learning that Heracles was at hand, gathered in full force and drew themselves up in battle-order against him. The struggle which took place was a wonderful one, in view of both the strength and the courage of the Giants, but Heracles, they say, with the help of the gods who fought on his side, gained the upper hand in the battle, slew most of the Giants, and brought the land under cultivation.

7 ἐξημερῶσαι. μυθολογοῦνται δ' οἱ γίγαντες γηγενεῖς γεγονέναι διὰ τὴν ὑπερβολὴν τοῦ κατὰ τὸ σῶμα μεγέθους. καὶ περὶ μὲν τῶν ἐν Φλέγρᾳ φονευθέντων γιγάντων τοιαῦτα μυθολογοῦσί τινες, οἷς καὶ Τίμαιος ὁ συγγραφεὺς ἠκολούθησεν.

22. Ὁ δ' Ἡρακλῆς ἐκ τοῦ Φλεγραίου πεδίου κατελθὼν ἐπὶ τὴν θάλατταν κατεσκεύασεν ἔργα περὶ τὴν Ἄορνον ὀνομαζομένην λίμνην, ἱερὰν δὲ Φερσεφόνης νομιζομένην.[1] κεῖται μὲν οὖν ἡ λίμνη μεταξὺ Μισηνοῦ καὶ Δικαιαρχείων, πλησίον τῶν θερμῶν ὑδάτων, ἔχει δὲ τὴν μὲν περίμετρον ὡς πέντε σταδίων, τὸ δὲ βάθος ἄπιστον· ἔχουσα γὰρ ὕδωρ καθαρώτατον φαίνεται τῇ χρόᾳ κυανοῦν διὰ τὴν
2 ὑπερβολὴν τοῦ βάθους. μυθολογοῦσι δὲ τὸ μὲν παλαιὸν γεγενῆσθαι νεκυομαντεῖον πρὸς αὐτῇ, ὃ τοῖς ὕστερον χρόνοις καταλελύσθαι φασίν. ἀναπεπταμένης δὲ τῆς λίμνης εἰς τὴν θάλατταν, τὸν Ἡρακλέα λέγεται τὸν μὲν ἔκρουν ἐγχῶσαι, τὴν δ' ὁδὸν τὴν νῦν οὖσαν παρὰ θάλατταν κατασκευάσαι, τὴν ἀπ' ἐκείνου καλουμένην Ἡρακλείαν.

3 Ταῦτα μὲν οὖν ἔπραξε περὶ ἐκείνους τοὺς τόπους. ἐντεῦθεν δ' ἀναζεύξας κατήντησε τῆς Ποσειδωνιατῶν χώρας πρός τινα πέτραν, πρὸς ᾗ μυθολογοῦσιν ἴδιόν τι γενέσθαι καὶ παράδοξον. τῶν γὰρ ἐγχωρίων τινὰ κυνηγὸν ἐν τοῖς κατὰ τὴν

[1] So Stephanus: ὀνομαζομένην.

---

[1] Timaeus of Tauromenium in Sicily was born about 350 B.C. and is reputed to have lived to the age of ninety-six. His greatest work was a history of Sicily and the West from the earliest times to 264 B.C.

BOOK IV. 21. 6–22. 3

The myths record that the Giants were sons of the earth because of the exceedingly great size of their bodies. With regard, then, to the Giants who were slain in Phlegra, this is the account of certain writers of myths, who have been followed by the historian Timaeus [1] also.

22. From the Phlegraean Plain Heracles went down to the sea, where he constructed works about the lake which bears the name Lake of Avernus and is held sacred to Persephonê. Now this lake lies between Misenum and Dicaearcheia [2] near the hot waters,[3] and is about five stades in circumference and of incredible depth; for its water is very pure and nas to the eye a dark blue colour because of its very great depth. And the myths record that in ancient times there had been on its shores an oracle of the dead which, they say, was destroyed in later days. Lake Avernus once had an opening into the sea, but Heracles is said to have filled up the outlet and constructed the road which runs at this time along the sea and is called after him the "Way of Heracles."

These, then, are the deeds of Heracles in the regions mentioned above. And moving on from there he came to a certain rock in the country of the people of Poseidonia,[4] where the myths relate that a peculiar and marvellous thing once took place. There was, that is, among the natives of the region a certain

[2] The Roman Puteoli.
[3] The hot springs of Baiae, the famous summer resort of the Romans, which, according to Strabo (5. 45), "were suited both to the taste of the fastidious and to the cure of disease" (tr. of Jones in the *L.C.L.*).
[4] The Roman Paestum, modern Pesto.

θήραν ἀνδραγαθήμασι διωνομασμένον ἐν μὲν τοῖς ἔμπροσθεν χρόνοις εἰωθέναι τῶν ληφθέντων θηρίων τὰς κεφαλὰς καὶ τοὺς πόδας ἀνατιθέναι τῇ Ἀρτέμιδι καὶ προσηλοῦν τοῖς δένδρεσι, τότε δ' οὖν ὑπερφυῆ κάπρον χειρωσάμενον, ὡς[1] τῆς θεοῦ καταφρονήσαντα, εἰπεῖν ὅτι τὴν κεφαλὴν τοῦ θηρίου ἑαυτῷ ἀνατίθησι, καὶ τοῖς λόγοις ἀκολούθως ἔκ τινος δένδρου κρεμάσαι ταύτην, αὐτὸν δέ, καυματώδους περιστάσεως οὔσης, κατὰ μεσημβρίαν εἰς ὕπνον τραπῆναι· καθ' ὃν δὴ χρόνον τοῦ δεσμοῦ λυθέντος αὐτομάτως πεσεῖν τὴν κεφαλὴν ἐπὶ τὸν κοιμώμενον 4 καὶ διαφθεῖραι. ἀλλὰ γὰρ οὐκ ἄν τις θαυμάσειε τὸ γεγονός, ὅτι τῆς θεᾶς ταύτης πολλαὶ περιστάσεις μνημονεύονται περιέχουσαι τὴν κατὰ τῶν ἀσεβῶν τιμωρίαν. τῷ δ' Ἡρακλεῖ διὰ τὴν εὐσέβειαν 5 τοὐναντίον συνέβη γενέσθαι. καταντήσαντος γὰρ αὐτοῦ πρὸς τὰ μεθόρια τῆς Ῥηγίνης καὶ Λοκρίδος, καὶ διὰ τὸν ἐκ τῆς ὁδοιπορίας κόπον ἀναπαυομένου, φασὶν ὑπὸ τῶν τεττίγων αὐτὸν ἐνοχλούμενον εὔξασθαι τοῖς θεοῖς ἀφανεῖς γενέσθαι τοὺς ἐνοχλοῦντας αὐτόν· καὶ διὰ τοῦτο, τῶν θεῶν βεβαιωσάντων τὴν εὐχήν, μὴ μόνον κατὰ τὸ παρὸν ἀφανεῖς γενέσθαι τούτους, ἀλλὰ καὶ κατὰ τὸν ὕστερον χρόνον ἅπαντα μηδένα τέττιγα φαίνεσθαι κατὰ τὴν χώραν.
6 Ὁ δ' Ἡρακλῆς καταντήσας ἐπὶ τὸν πορθμὸν κατὰ τὸ στενώτατον τῆς θαλάττης τὰς μὲν βοῦς ἐπεραίωσεν εἰς τὴν Σικελίαν, αὐτὸς δὲ ταύρου κέρως λαβόμενος διενήξατο τὸν πόρον, ὄντος τοῦ διαστήματος σταδίων τριῶν καὶ δέκα, ὡς Τίμαιός φησι.

[1] ὡς Capps: καί.

hunter, the fame of whom had gone abroad because of his brave exploits in hunting. On former occasions it had been his practice to dedicate to Artemis the heads and feet of the animals he secured and to nail them to the trees, but once, when he had overpowered a huge wild boar, he said, as though in contempt of the goddess, "The head of the beast I dedicate to myself," and bearing out his words he hung the head on a tree, and then, the atmosphere being very warm, at midday he fell asleep. And while he was thus asleep the thong broke, and the head fell down of itself upon the sleeper and killed him. And in truth there is no reason why anyone should marvel at this happening, for many actual occurrences are recorded which illustrate the vengeance this goddess takes upon the impious. But in the case of Heracles his piety was such that the opposite happened to him. For when he had arrived at the border between Rheginê and Locris[1] and lay down to rest after his wearying journey, they say that he was disturbed by the crickets and that he prayed to the gods that the creatures which were disturbing him might disappear; whereupon the gods granted his petition, and not only did his prayer cause the insects to disappear for the moment, but in all later times as well not a cricket has ever been seen in the land.

When Heracles arrived at the strait[2] where the sea is narrowest, he had the cattle taken over into Sicily, but as for himself, he took hold of the horn of a bull and swam across the passage, the distance between the shores being thirteen stades, as Timaeus says.

[1] In the toe of Italy.   [2] The Strait of Messina.

DIODORUS OF SICILY

23. Μετὰ δὲ ταῦτα βουλόμενος ἐγκυκλωθῆναι πᾶσαν Σικελίαν, ἐποιεῖτο τὴν πορείαν ἀπὸ τῆς Πελωριάδος ἐπὶ τὸν Ἔρυκα. διεξιόντος δ' αὐτοῦ τὴν παράλιον τῆς νήσου, μυθολογοῦσι τὰς Νύμφας ἀνεῖναι θερμὰ λουτρὰ πρὸς τὴν ἀνάπαυσιν τῆς κατὰ τὴν ὁδοιπορίαν αὐτῷ γενομένης κακοπαθείας. τούτων δ' ὄντων διττῶν, τὰ μὲν Ἱμεραῖα, τὰ δ' Ἐγεσταῖα προσαγορεύεται, τὴν ὀνομασίαν ἔχοντα ταύτην ἀπὸ 2 τῶν τόπων. τοῦ δ' Ἡρακλέους πλησιάσαντος τοῖς κατὰ τὸν Ἔρυκα τόποις, προεκαλέσατο αὐτὸν Ἔρυξ εἰς πάλην, υἱὸς[1] ὢν Ἀφροδίτης καὶ Βούτα τοῦ τότε βασιλεύοντος τῶν τόπων. γενομένης δὲ τῆς φιλοτιμίας μετὰ προστίμου, καὶ τοῦ μὲν Ἔρυκος διδόντος τὴν χώραν, τοῦ δ' Ἡρακλέους τὰς βοῦς, τὸ μὲν πρῶτον ἀγανακτεῖν τὸν Ἔρυκα, διότι πολὺ λείπονται τῆς ἀξίας αἱ βόες, συγκρινομένης τῆς χώρας πρὸς αὐτάς· πρὸς ταῦτα δὲ τοῦ Ἡρακλέους ἀποφαινομένου διότι, ταύτας ἂν ἀποβάλῃ, στερήσεται τῆς ἀθανασίας, εὐδοκήσας ὁ Ἔρυξ τῇ συνθήκῃ καὶ παλαίσας ἐλείφθη καὶ τὴν 3 χώραν ἀπέβαλεν. ὁ δ' Ἡρακλῆς τὴν μὲν χώραν παρέθετο τοῖς ἐγχωρίοις, συγχωρήσας αὐτοῖς λαμβάνειν τοὺς καρπούς, μέχρι ἄν τις τῶν ἐκγόνων αὐτοῦ παραγενόμενος ἀπαιτήσῃ· ὅπερ καὶ συνέβη γενέσθαι. πολλαῖς γὰρ ὕστερον γενεαῖς Δωριεὺς ὁ Λακεδαιμόνιος καταντήσας εἰς τὴν Σικελίαν καὶ

[1] μὲν after υἱὸς deleted by Bekker.

---

[1] *i.e.* from the eastern extremity of the north coast to the western.
[2] Cp. Aristophanes, *The Clouds*, 1051: "Where, pray, did you ever see Baths of Heracles (Ἡράκλεια λουτρά) that

BOOK IV. 23. 1-3

23. Upon his arrival in Sicily Heracles desired to make the circuit of the entire island and so set out from Pelorias in the direction of Eryx.[1] While passing along the coast of the island, the myths relate, the Nymphs caused warm baths[2] to gush forth so that he might refresh himself after the toil sustained in his journeying. There are two of these, called respectively Himeraea and Egestaea, each of them having its name from the place where the baths are. As Heracles approached the region of Eryx,[3] he was challenged to a wrestling match by Eryx, who was the son of Aphroditê and Butas, who was then king of that country. The contest of the rivals carried with it a penalty, whereby Eryx was to surrender his land and Heracles the cattle. Now at first Eryx was displeased at such terms, maintaining that the cattle were of far less value as compared with the land; but when Heracles in answer to his arguments showed that if he lost the cattle he would likewise lose his immortality, Eryx agreed to the terms, and wrestling with him was defeated and lost his land. Heracles turned the land over to the natives of the region, agreeing with them that they should gather the fruits of it until one of his descendants should appear among them and demand it back; and this actually came to pass. For in fact many generations later Dorieus[4] the Lacedaemonian

were cold ? " All naturally hot springs were commonly called "Heracleia" by the Greeks.

[3] *i.e.* Mount Eryx, at the north-west corner of Sicily, now Mt. San Giuliano.

[4] The chequered career of Dorieus, of the royal line of Sparta and so a Heraclid, is given in some detail in Herodotus 5. 41-8.

τὴν χώραν ἀπολαβὼν ἔκτισε πόλιν Ἡράκλειαν. ταχὺ δ' αὐτῆς αὐξομένης, οἱ Καρχηδόνιοι φθονήσαντες ἅμα καὶ φοβηθέντες μήποτε πλέον ἰσχύσασα τῆς Καρχηδόνος ἀφέληται τῶν Φοινίκων τὴν ἡγεμονίαν, στρατεύσαντες ἐπ' αὐτὴν μεγάλαις δυνάμεσι καὶ κατὰ κράτος ἑλόντες κατέσκαψαν. ἀλλὰ περὶ μὲν τούτων τὰ κατὰ μέρος ἐν τοῖς οἰκείοις χρόνοις ἀναγράψομεν.

4 Τότε δ' ὁ Ἡρακλῆς ἐγκυκλούμενος τὴν Σικελίαν, καταντήσας εἰς τὴν νῦν οὖσαν τῶν Συρακοσίων πόλιν καὶ πυθόμενος τὰ μυθολογούμενα κατὰ τὴν τῆς Κόρης ἁρπαγήν, ἔθυσέ τε ταῖς θεαῖς μεγαλοπρεπῶς καὶ εἰς τὴν Κυάνην τὸν καλλιστεύοντα τῶν ταύρων καθαγίσας κατέδειξε θύειν τοὺς ἐγχωρίους κατ' ἐνιαυτὸν τῇ Κόρῃ καὶ πρὸς τῇ Κυάνῃ λαμ-
5 πρῶς ἄγειν πανήγυρίν τε καὶ θυσίαν. αὐτὸς δὲ μετὰ τῶν βοῶν διὰ τῆς μεσογείου διεξιών, καὶ τῶν ἐγχωρίων Σικανῶν μεγάλαις δυνάμεσιν ἀντιταξαμένων, ἐνίκησεν ἐπιφανεῖ παρατάξει καὶ πολλοὺς ἀπέκτεινεν, ἐν οἷς μυθολογοῦσί τινες καὶ στρατηγοὺς ἐπιφανεῖς γεγενῆσθαι τοὺς μέχρι τοῦ νῦν ἡρωικῆς τιμῆς τυγχάνοντας, Λεύκασπιν καὶ Πεδιακράτην καὶ Βουφόναν καὶ Γλυχάταν, ἔτι δὲ Βυταίαν καὶ Κρυτίδαν.

24. Μετὰ δὲ ταῦτα διελθὼν τὸ Λεοντῖνον πεδίον, τὸ μὲν κάλλος τῆς χώρας ἐθαύμασε, πρὸς δὲ τοὺς τιμῶντας αὐτὸν οἰκείως διατιθέμενος ἀπέλιπε παρ'

[1] No account of this is in the extant portions of Diodorus. This Heracleia in the region about Mt. Eryx is not to be

BOOK IV. 23. 3-24. 1

came to Sicily, and taking back the land founded the city of Heracleia. Since the city grew rapidly, the Carthaginians, being jealous of it and also afraid that it would grow stronger than Carthage and take from the Phoenicians their sovereignty, came up against it with a great army, took it by storm, and razed it to the ground. But this affair we shall discuss in detail in connection with the period in which it falls.[1]

While Heracles was making the circuit of Sicily at this time he came to the city which is now Syracuse, and on learning what the myth relates about the Rape of Corê he offered sacrifices to the goddesses [2] on a magnificent scale, and after dedicating to her the fairest bull of his herd and casting it in the spring Cyanê [3] he commanded the natives to sacrifice each year to Corê and to conduct at Cyanê a festive gathering and a sacrifice in splendid fashion. He then passed with his cattle through the interior of the island, and when the native Sicani opposed him in great force, he overcame them in a notable battle and slew many of their number, among whom, certain writers of myths relate, were also some distinguished generals who receive the honours accorded to heroes even to this day, such as Leucaspis, Pediacrates,[4] Buphonas, Glychatas, Bytaeas, and Crytidas.

24. After this Heracles, as he passed through the plain of Leontini, marvelled at the beauty of the land, and to show his affection for the men who

confused with the well-known Heracleia Minoa in the territory of Agrigentum. The date of its destruction is not known.

[2] Corê ("The Maiden," *i.e.* Persephonê) and Demeter.

[3] Cp. Book 5. 4 for an account of the connection of this spring with the myth of Corê.

[4] Called Pediocrates by Xenagoras, *Frg.* 21 (Jacoby).

αὐτοῖς ἀθάνατα μνημεῖα τῆς ἑαυτοῦ παρουσίας. ἴδιον δέ τι συνέβη γενέσθαι περὶ τὴν πόλιν τῶν Ἀγυριναίων. ἐν ταύτῃ γὰρ τιμηθεὶς ἐπ' ἴσης τοῖς Ὀλυμπίοις θεοῖς πανηγύρεσι καὶ θυσίαις λαμπραῖς, καίπερ κατὰ τοὺς ἔμπροσθεν χρόνους οὐδεμίαν θυσίαν προσδεχόμενος, τότε πρώτως συνευδόκησε, τοῦ δαιμονίου τὴν ἀθανασίαν αὐτῷ προσημαίνοντος.
2 ὁδοῦ γὰρ οὔσης οὐκ ἄπωθεν τῆς πόλεως πετρώδους, αἱ βόες τὰ ἴχνη καθάπερ ἐπὶ κηροῦ τινος ἀπετυποῦντο. ὁμοίως δὲ καὶ αὐτῷ τῷ Ἡρακλεῖ τούτου συμβαίνοντος, καὶ τοῦ ἄθλου δεκάτου τελουμένου, νομίσας ἤδη τι λαμβάνειν τῆς ἀθανασίας, προσεδέχετο τὰς τελουμένας ὑπὸ τῶν ἐγχω-
3 ρίων κατ' ἐνιαυτὸν θυσίας. διόπερ τοῖς εὐδοκουμένοις[1] τὰς χάριτας ἀποδιδούς, πρὸ μὲν τῆς πόλεως κατεσκεύασε λίμνην, ἔχουσαν τὸν περίβολον σταδίων τεττάρων, ἣν ἐπώνυμον αὑτῷ καλεῖσθαι προσέταξεν· ὡσαύτως δὲ καὶ τῶν βοῶν τοῖς ἀποτυπωθεῖσιν ἴχνεσι τὴν ἐφ' ἑαυτοῦ προσηγορίαν ἐπιθείς, τέμενος κατεσκεύασεν ἥρωι Γηρυόνῃ, ὃ μέχρι τοῦ νῦν τιμᾶται παρὰ τοῖς ἐγχωρίοις.
4 Ἰολάου τε τοῦ ἀδελφιδοῦ συστρατεύοντος τέμενος ἀξιόλογον ἐποίησε, καὶ τιμὰς καὶ θυσίας κατέδειξεν αὐτῷ γίνεσθαι κατ' ἐνιαυτὸν τὰς μέχρι τοῦ νῦν τηρουμένας· πάντες γὰρ οἱ κατὰ ταύτην τὴν πόλιν οἰκοῦντες ἐκ γενετῆς τὰς κόμας[2] Ἰολάῳ τρέφουσι, μέχρι ἂν ὅτου θυσίαις μεγαλο-

[1] So Dindorf: εὐδοκιμουμένοις.
[2] ἱερὰς after κόμας omitted D, Vogel; retained by Bekker, Dindorf.

---

[1] The native city of Diodorus.

420

honoured him he left behind him there imperishable memorials of his presence. And it came to pass that a peculiar thing took place near the city of Agyrium.[1] Here he was honoured on equal terms with the Olympian gods by festivals and splendid sacrifices, and though before this time he had accepted no sacrifice, he then gave his consent for the first time, since the deity was giving intimations to him of his coming immortality. For instance, there was a road not far from the city which was all of rock, and yet the cattle left their tracks in it as if in a waxy substance. Since, then, this same thing happened in the case of Heracles as well[2] and his tenth Labour was likewise coming to an end, he considered that he was already to a degree participating in immortality and so accepted the annual sacrifices which were offered him by the people of the city. Consequently, as a mark of his gratitude to the people who had found favour with him, he built before the city a lake, four stades in circumference, which he ordained should be called by his name; and he likewise gave his name to the moulds of the tracks which the cattle had left in the rock and dedicated to the hero Geryones a sacred precinct which is honoured to this day by the people of that region. To Iolaüs, his nephew, who was his companion on the expedition, he likewise dedicated a notable sacred precinct, and ordained that annual honours and sacrifices should be offered to him, as is done even to this day; for all the inhabitants of this city let the hair of their heads grow from their birth in honour of Iolaüs, until they have obtained good omens in costly sacri-

[2] *i.e.* Heracles also left his footprints in the rock.

πρεπέσι καλλιερήσαντες τὸν θεὸν ἵλεων κατα-
5 σκευάσωσι. τοσαύτη δ' ἐστὶν ἁγνεία καὶ σεμνότης
περὶ τὸ τέμενος ὥστε τοὺς μὴ τελοῦντας τὰς εἰθισ-
μένας θυσίας παῖδας ἀφώνους γίνεσθαι καὶ τοῖς
τετελευτηκόσιν ὁμοίους. ἀλλ' οὗτοι μέν, ὅταν
εὔξηταί τις ἀποδώσειν τὴν θυσίαν καὶ ἐνέχυρον τῆς
θυσίας ἀναδείξῃ τῷ θεῷ, παραχρῆμα ἀποκαθίστα-
σθαί φασι τοὺς τῇ προειρημένῃ νόσῳ κατεχο-
6 μένους. οἱ δ' οὖν ἐγχώριοι τούτοις ἀκολούθως
τὴν μὲν πύλην, πρὸς ᾗ τὰς ἀπαντήσεις καὶ θυσίας
τῷ θεῷ παρέστησαν, Ἡράκλειαν προσηγόρευσαν,
ἀγῶνα δὲ γυμνικὸν καὶ ἱππικὸν καθ' ἕκαστον
ἔτος μετὰ πάσης προθυμίας ποιοῦσι. πανδήμου
δὲ τῆς ἀποδοχῆς ἐλευθέρων τε καὶ δούλων γινομένης,
κατέδειξαν καὶ τοὺς οἰκέτας ἰδίᾳ τιμῶντας τὸν
θεὸν θιάσους τε συνάγειν καὶ συνιόντας εὐωχίας τε
καὶ θυσίας τῷ θεῷ συντελεῖν.
7 Ὁ δ' Ἡρακλῆς μετὰ τῶν βοῶν περαιωθεὶς εἰς
τὴν Ἰταλίαν προῆγε διὰ τῆς παραλίας, καὶ Λακίνιον
μὲν κλέπτοντα τῶν βοῶν ἀνεῖλε, Κρότωνα δὲ
ἀκουσίως ἀποκτείνας ἔθαψε μεγαλοπρεπῶς καὶ
τάφον αὐτοῦ κατεσκεύασε· προεῖπε δὲ καὶ τοῖς
ἐγχωρίοις ὅτι καὶ κατὰ τοὺς ὕστερον χρόνους ἔσται
πόλις ἐπίσημος ὁμώνυμος τῷ τετελευτηκότι.

25. Αὐτὸς δ' ἐγκυκλωθεὶς τὸν Ἀδρίαν καὶ πεζῇ
περιελθὼν τὸν προειρημένον κόλπον κατήντησεν εἰς
τὴν Ἤπειρον, ἐξ ἧς πορευθεὶς εἰς τὴν Πελοπόννησον, καὶ τετελεκὼς τὸν δέκατον ἆθλον, ἔλαβε
πρόσταγμα παρ' Εὐρυσθέως τὸν ἐξ ᾅδου Κέρβερον
πρὸς τὸ φῶς ἀγαγεῖν. πρὸς δὲ τοῦτον τὸν ἆθλον

fices and have rendered the god propitious. And such a holiness and majesty pervade the sacred precinct that the boys who fail to perform the customary rites lose their power of speech and become like dead men. But so soon as anyone of them who is suffering from this malady takes a vow that he will pay the sacrifice and vouchsafes to the god a pledge to that effect, at once, they say, he is restored to health. Now the inhabitants, in pursuance of these rites, call the gate, at which they come into the presence of the god and offer him these sacrifices, "The Heracleian," and every year with the utmost zeal they hold games which include gymnastic contests and horse-races. And since the whole populace, both free men and slaves, unite in approbation of the god, they have commanded their servants, as they do honour to him apart from the rest, to gather in bands and when they come together to hold banquets and perform sacrifices to the god.

Heracles then crossed over into Italy with the cattle and proceeded along the coast; there he slew Lacinius as he was attempting to steal some of the cattle, and to Croton, whom he killed by accident, he accorded a magnificent funeral and erected for him a tomb; and he foretold to the natives of the place that also in after times a famous city would arise which should bear the name of the man who had died.

25. But when Heracles had made the circuit of the Adriatic, and had journeyed around the gulf on foot, he came to Epirus, whence he made his way to Peloponnesus. And now that he had performed the tenth Labour he received a Command from Eurystheus to bring Cerberus up from Hades to the light of day. And assuming that it would be to

ὑπολαβὼν συνοίσειν αὐτῷ, παρῆλθεν εἰς τὰς Ἀθήνας καὶ μετέσχε τῶν ἐν Ἐλευσῖνι μυστηρίων, Μουσαίου τοῦ Ὀρφέως υἱοῦ τότε προεστηκότος τῆς τελετῆς.

2 Ἐπεὶ δ' Ὀρφέως ἐμνήσθημεν, οὐκ ἀνοίκειόν ἐστι παρεκβάντας βραχέα περὶ αὐτοῦ διελθεῖν. οὗτος γὰρ ἦν υἱὸς μὲν Οἰάγρου, Θρᾷξ δὲ τὸ γένος, παιδείᾳ δὲ καὶ μελῳδίᾳ καὶ ποιήσει πολὺ προέχων τῶν μνημονευομένων· καὶ γὰρ ποίημα συνετάξατο θαυμαζόμενον καὶ τῇ[1] κατὰ τὴν ᾠδὴν εὐμελείᾳ διαφέρον. ἐπὶ τοσοῦτο δὲ προέβη τῇ δόξῃ ὥστε δοκεῖν τῇ μελῳδίᾳ θέλγειν τά τε θηρία 3 καὶ τὰ δένδρα. περὶ δὲ παιδείαν ἀσχοληθεὶς καὶ τὰ περὶ τῆς θεολογίας μυθολογούμενα μαθών, ἀπεδήμησε μὲν εἰς Αἴγυπτον, κἀκεῖ πολλὰ προσεπιμαθὼν μέγιστος ἐγένετο τῶν Ἑλλήνων ἔν τε ταῖς θεολογίαις καὶ ταῖς τελεταῖς καὶ ποιήμασι καὶ 4 μελῳδίαις. συνεστρατεύσατο δὲ καὶ τοῖς Ἀργοναύταις, καὶ διὰ τὸν ἔρωτα τὸν πρὸς τὴν γυναῖκα καταβῆναι μὲν εἰς ᾅδου παραδόξως ἐτόλμησε, τὴν δὲ Φερσεφόνην διὰ τῆς εὐμελείας ψυχαγωγήσας ἔπεισε συνεργῆσαι ταῖς ἐπιθυμίαις καὶ συγχωρῆσαι τὴν γυναῖκα αὐτοῦ τετελευτηκυῖαν ἀναγαγεῖν ἐξ ᾅδου παραπλησίως τῷ Διονύσῳ· καὶ γὰρ ἐκεῖνον μυθολογοῦσιν ἀναγαγεῖν τὴν μητέρα Σεμέλην ἐξ ᾅδου, καὶ μεταδόντα τῆς ἀθανασίας Θυώνην μετονομάσαι.

Ἡμεῖς δ' ἐπεὶ περὶ Ὀρφέως διεληλύθαμεν, μεταβησόμεθα πάλιν ἐπὶ τὸν Ἡρακλέα.

26. Οὗτος γὰρ κατὰ τοὺς παραδεδομένους μύθους καταβὰς εἰς τοὺς καθ' ᾅδου τόπους, καὶ προσδε-

[1] τῇ added by Dindorf.

his advantage for the accomplishment of this Labour, he went to Athens and took part in the Eleusinian Mysteries, Musaeus, the son of Orpheus, being at that time in charge of the initiatory rites.

Since we have mentioned Orpheus it will not be inappropriate for us in passing to speak briefly about him. He was the son of Oeagrus, a Thracian by birth, and in culture and song-music and poesy he far surpassed all men of whom we have a record; for he composed a poem which was an object of wonder and excelled in its melody when it was sung. And his fame grew to such a degree that men believed that with his music he held a spell over both the wild beasts and the trees. And after he had devoted his entire time to his education and had learned whatever the myths had to say about the gods, he journeyed to Egypt, where he further increased his knowledge and so became the greatest man among the Greeks both for his knowledge of the gods and for their rites, as well as for his poems and songs. He also took part in the expedition of the Argonauts, and because of the love he held for his wife he dared the amazing deed of descending into Hades, where he entranced Persephonê by his melodious song and persuaded her to assist him in his desires and to allow him to bring up his dead wife from Hades, in this exploit resembling Dionysus; for the myths relate that Dionysus brought up his mother Semelê from Hades, and that, sharing with her his own immortality, he changed her name to Thyonê.

But now that we have discussed Orpheus, we shall return to Heracles.

26. Heracles, then, according to the myths which have come down to us, descended into the realm of

DIODORUS OF SICILY

χθεὶς ὑπὸ τῆς Φερσεφόνης ὡς ἂν ἀδελφός, Θησέα μὲν ἀνήγαγεν ἐκ δεσμῶν μετὰ Πειρίθου, χαρισαμένης τῆς Κόρης, τὸν δὲ κύνα παραλαβὼν δεδεμένον παραδόξως ἀπήγαγε καὶ φανερὸν κατέστησεν ἀνθρώποις.

2 Τελευταῖον δ' ἆθλον λαβὼν ἐνεγκεῖν τὰ τῶν Ἑσπερίδων χρυσᾶ μῆλα, πάλιν ἔπλευσεν εἰς τὴν Λιβύην. περὶ δὲ τῶν μήλων τούτων διαπεφωνήκασιν οἱ μυθογράφοι, καί τινες μέν φασιν ἔν τισι κήποις τῶν Ἑσπερίδων ὑπάρξαι κατὰ τὴν Λιβύην μῆλα χρυσᾶ, τηρούμενα συνεχῶς ὑπό τινος δράκοντος φοβερωτάτου, τινὲς δὲ λέγουσι ποίμνας προβάτων κάλλει διαφερούσας κεκτῆσθαι τὰς Ἑσπερίδας, χρυσᾶ δὲ μῆλα ἀπὸ τοῦ κάλλους ὠνομάσθαι ποιητικῶς, ὥσπερ καὶ τὴν Ἀφροδίτην

3 χρυσῆν καλεῖσθαι διὰ τὴν εὐπρέπειαν. ἔνιοι δὲ λέγουσιν[1] τὰ πρόβατα τὴν χρόαν ἰδιάζουσαν ἔχοντα καὶ παρόμοιον χρυσῷ τετευχέναι ταύτης τῆς προσηγορίας, Δράκοντα δὲ τῶν ποιμνῶν ἐπιμελητὴν καθεσταμένον, καὶ ῥώμῃ σώματος καὶ ἀλκῇ διαφέροντα, τηρεῖν τὰ πρόβατα καὶ τοὺς λῃστεύειν αὐτὰ τολμῶντας ἀποκτείνειν. ἀλλὰ περὶ μὲν τούτων ἐξέσται διαλαμβάνειν ὡς ἂν ἕκαστος ἑαυτὸν πείθῃ.

4 ὁ δ' Ἡρακλῆς τὸν φύλακα τῶν μήλων ἀνελών, καὶ ταῦτα ἀποκομίσας πρὸς Εὐρυσθέα, καὶ τοὺς ἄθλους ἀποτετελεκώς, προσεδέχετο τῆς ἀθανασίας τεύξεσθαι, καθάπερ ὁ Ἀπόλλων ἔχρησεν.

[1] ὅτι after λέγουσιν deleted by Dindorf, Bekker, retained by Vogel.

BOOK IV. 26. 1-4

Hades, and being welcomed like a brother by Persephonê brought Theseus and Peirithoüs back to the upper world after freeing them from their bonds. This he accomplished by the favour of Persephonê, and receiving the dog Cerberus in chains he carried him away to the amazement of all and exhibited him to men.

The last Labour which Heracles undertook was the bringing back of the golden apples of the Hesperides, and so he again sailed to Libya. With regard to these apples there is disagreement among the writers of myths, and some say that there were golden apples in certain gardens of the Hesperides in Libya, where they were guarded without ceasing by a most formidable dragon, whereas others assert that the Hesperides possessed flocks of sheep which excelled in beauty and were therefore called for their beauty, as the poets might do, " golden apples," [1] just as Aphroditê is called " golden " because of her loveliness. There are some, however, who say that it was because the sheep had a peculiar colour like gold that they got this designation, and that Dracon (" dragon ") was the name of the shepherd of the sheep, a man who excelled in strength of body and courage, who guarded the sheep and slew any who might dare try to carry them off. But with regard to such matters it will be every man's privilege to form such opinions as accord with his own belief. At any rate Heracles slew the guardian of the apples, and after he had duly brought them to Eurystheus and had in this wise finished his Labours he waited to receive the gift of immortality, even as Apollo had prophesied to him.

[1] The word μῆλον means both " sheep " and " apple."

27. Ἡμῖν δ' οὐ παραλειπτέον τὰ περὶ Ἄτλαντος μυθολογούμενα καὶ τὰ περὶ τοῦ γένους τῶν Ἑσπερίδων. κατὰ γὰρ τὴν Ἑσπερῖτιν ὀνομαζομένην χώραν φασὶν ἀδελφοὺς δύο γενέσθαι δόξῃ διωνομασμένους, Ἕσπερον καὶ Ἄτλαντα. τούτους δὲ κεκτῆσθαι πρόβατα τῷ μὲν κάλλει διάφορα, τῇ δὲ χρόᾳ ξανθὰ καὶ χρυσοειδῆ· ἀφ' ἧς αἰτίας τοὺς ποιητὰς τὰ πρόβατα μῆλα καλοῦντας ὀνομά-
2 σαι χρυσᾶ μῆλα. τὸν μὲν οὖν Ἕσπερον θυγατέρα γεννήσαντα τὴν ὀνομαζομένην Ἑσπερίδα συνοικίσαι τἀδελφῷ, ἀφ' ἧς τὴν χώραν Ἑσπερῖτιν ὀνομασθῆναι· τὸν δ' Ἄτλαντα ἐκ ταύτης ἑπτὰ γεννῆσαι θυγατέρας, ἃς ἀπὸ μὲν τοῦ πατρὸς Ἀτλαντίδας, ἀπὸ δὲ τῆς μητρὸς Ἑσπερίδας ὀνομασθῆναι. τούτων δὲ τῶν Ἀτλαντίδων κάλλει καὶ σωφροσύνῃ διαφερουσῶν, λέγουσι Βούσιριν τὸν βασιλέα τῶν Αἰγυπτίων ἐπιθυμῆσαι τῶν παρθένων ἐγκρατῆ γενέσθαι· διὸ καὶ λῃστὰς[1] κατὰ θάλατταν ἀποστείλαντα διακελεύσασθαι τὰς κόρας ἁρπάσαι καὶ διακομίσαι πρὸς ἑαυτόν.
3 Κατὰ δὲ τοῦτον τὸν καιρὸν τὸν Ἡρακλέα τελοῦντα τὸν ὕστατον ἆθλον Ἀνταῖον μὲν ἀνελεῖν ἐν τῇ Λιβύῃ τὸν συναναγκάζοντα τοὺς ξένους διαπαλαίειν, Βούσιριν δὲ κατὰ τὴν Αἴγυπτον τῷ Διὶ[2] σφαγιάζοντα τοὺς παρεπιδημοῦντας ξένους τῆς προσηκούσης τιμωρίας καταξιῶσαι. μετὰ δὲ ταῦτα ἀνὰ τὸν Νεῖλον πλεύσαντα εἰς τὴν Αἰθιοπίαν τὸν βασιλεύοντα τῶν Αἰθιόπων Ἠμαθίωνα κατάρχοντα μάχης ἀποκτεῖναι, τὸ δ' ὕστατον
4 ἐπανελθεῖν πάλιν ἐπὶ τὸν ἆθλον. τοὺς δὲ λῃστὰς

[1] ἐπ' αὐτὰς after λῃστὰς omitted D, Dindorf, Vogel, retained by Bekker.

BOOK IV. 27. 1-4

27. But we must not fail to mention what the myths relate about Atlas and about the race of the Hesperides. The account runs like this: In the country known as Hesperitis there were two brothers whose fame was known abroad, Hesperus and Atlas. These brothers possessed flocks of sheep which excelled in beauty and were in colour of a golden yellow, this being the reason why the poets, in speaking of these sheep as *mela*, called them golden *mela*. Now Hesperus begat a daughter named Hesperis, whom he gave in marriage to his brother and after whom the land was given the name Hesperitis; and Atlas begat by her seven daughters, who were named after their father Atlantides, and after their mother, Hesperides. And since these Atlantides excelled in beauty and chastity, Busiris the king of the Egyptians, the account says, was seized with the desire to get the maidens into his power; and consequently he dispatched pirates by sea with orders to seize the girls and deliver them into his hands.

About this time Heracles, while engaged in the performance of his last Labour, slew in Libya Antaeus, who was compelling all strangers to wrestle with him, and upon Busiris in Egypt, who was sacrificing to Zeus the strangers who visited his country, he inflicted the punishment which he deserved. After this Heracles sailed up the Nile into Ethiopia, where he slew Emathion, the king of the Ethiopians, who made battle with him unprovoked, and then returned to the completion of his last Labour. Meanwhile the

---

² καλλιερεῖν after Διί deleted by Dindorf.

ἐν κήπῳ τινὶ παιζούσας τὰς κόρας συναρπάσαι, καὶ ταχὺ φυγόντας εἰς τὰς ναῦς ἀποπλεῖν. τούτοις δ' ἐπί τινος ἀκτῆς δειπνοποιουμένοις ἐπιστάντα τὸν Ἡρακλέα, καὶ παρὰ τῶν παρθένων μαθόντα τὸ συμβεβηκός, τοὺς μὲν λῃστὰς ἅπαντας ἀποκτεῖναι, τὰς δὲ κόρας ἀποκομίσαι πρὸς Ἄτλαντα τὸν πατέρα· ἀνθ' ὧν τὸν Ἄτλαντα χάριν τῆς εὐεργεσίας ἀποδιδόντα μὴ μόνον δοῦναι τὰ πρὸς τὸν ἆθλον καθήκοντα προθύμως, ἀλλὰ καὶ τὰ κατὰ τὴν 5 ἀστρολογίαν ἀφθόνως διδάξαι. περιττότερον γὰρ αὐτὸν τὰ κατὰ τὴν ἀστρολογίαν ἐκπεπονηκότα καὶ τὴν τῶν ἄστρων σφαῖραν φιλοτέχνως εὑρόντα[1] ἔχειν ὑπόληψιν ὡς τὸν κόσμον ὅλον ἐπὶ τῶν ὤμων φοροῦντα. παραπλησίως δὲ καὶ τοῦ Ἡρακλέους ἐξενέγκαντος εἰς τοὺς Ἕλληνας τὸν σφαιρικὸν λόγον, δόξης μεγάλης τυχεῖν, ὡς διαδεδεγμένον τὸν Ἀτλαντικὸν κόσμον, αἰνιττομένων τῶν ἀνθρώπων τὸ γεγονός.

28. Τοῦ δ' Ἡρακλέους περὶ ταῦτ' ὄντος φασὶ τὰς ὑπολειφθείσας Ἀμαζόνας περὶ τὸν Θερμώδοντα ποταμὸν ἀθροισθείσας πανδημεὶ σπεῦσαι τοὺς Ἕλληνας ἀμύνασθαι περὶ ὧν Ἡρακλῆς στρατεύσας διειργάσατο. διαφορώτατα δὲ τοὺς Ἀθηναίους ἐφιλοτιμοῦντο Κολάσαι[2] διὰ τὸ τὸν Θησέα καταδεδουλῶσθαι τὴν ἡγεμόνα τῶν Ἀμαζόνων Ἀντιόπην, 2 ὡς δ' ἔνιοι γράφουσιν, Ἱππολύτην. συστρατευσάντων δὲ τῶν Σκυθῶν ταῖς Ἀμαζόσι συνέβη δύναμιν

[1] εὑρόντα Dindorf: ἔχοντα.
[2] κολάσαι added by Kallenberg to govern Ἀθηναίους.

BOOK IV. 27. 4–28. 2

pirates had seized the girls while they were playing in a certain garden and carried them off, and fleeing swiftly to their ships had sailed away with them. Heracles came upon the pirates as they were taking their meal on a certain strand, and learning from the maidens what had taken place he slew the pirates to a man and brought the girls back to Atlas their father; and in return Atlas was so grateful to Heracles for his kindly deed that he not only gladly gave him such assistance as his Labour called for, but he also instructed him quite freely in the knowledge of astrology. For Atlas had worked out the science of astrology to a degree surpassing others and had ingeniously discovered the spherical nature of the stars,[1] and for that reason was generally believed to be bearing the entire firmament upon his shoulders. Similarly in the case of Heracles, when he had brought to the Greeks the doctrine of the sphere, he gained great fame, as if he had taken over the burden of the firmament which Atlas had borne, since men intimated in this enigmatic way what had actually taken place.

28. While Heracles was busied with the matters just described, the Amazons, they say, of whom there were some still left in the region of the Thermodon river, gathered in a body and set out to get revenge upon the Greeks for what Heracles had done in his campaign against them. They were especially eager to punish the Athenians because Theseus had made a slave of Antiopê, the leader of the Amazons, or, as others write, of Hippolytê. The Scythians had joined forces with the Amazons, and so it came

---

[1] Or the phrase may mean "the spherical arrangement of the stars"; but cp. p. 278, n. 2.

ἀξιόλογον ἀθροισθῆναι, μεθ' ἧς αἱ προηγούμεναι τῶν Ἀμαζονίδων περαιωθεῖσαι τὸν Κιμμέριον Βόσπορον προῆγον διὰ τῆς Θρᾴκης. τέλος δὲ πολλὴν τῆς Εὐρώπης ἐπελθοῦσαι κατήντησαν εἰς τὴν Ἀττικήν, καὶ κατεστρατοπέδευσαν ὅπου νῦν ἐστι τὸ καλούμενον ἀπ' ἐκείνων Ἀμαζονεῖον.

3 Θησεὺς δὲ πυθόμενος τὴν τῶν Ἀμαζόνων ἔφοδον ἐβοήθει ταῖς πολιτικαῖς δυνάμεσιν, ἔχων μεθ' ἑαυτοῦ τὴν Ἀμαζονίδα Ἀντιόπην, ἐξ ἧς ἦν πεπαιδοποιημένος υἱὸν Ἱππόλυτον. συνάψας δὲ μάχην ταῖς Ἀμαζόσι, καὶ τῶν Ἀθηναίων ὑπερεχόντων ταῖς ἀνδραγαθίαις, ἐνίκησαν οἱ περὶ τὸν Θησέα, καὶ τῶν ἀντιταχθεισῶν Ἀμαζονίδων ἃς μὲν κατέκοψαν, ἃς δ' ἐκ τῆς Ἀττικῆς ἐξέβαλον.

4 συνέβη δὲ καὶ τὴν Ἀντιόπην συναγωνισαμένην τἀνδρὶ Θησεῖ, καὶ κατὰ τὴν μάχην ἀριστεύουσαν, ἡρωικῶς καταστρέψαι τὸν βίον. αἱ δ' ὑπολειφθεῖσαι τῶν Ἀμαζόνων ἀπογνοῦσαι τὴν πατρῴαν γῆν, ἐπανῆλθον μετὰ τῶν Σκυθῶν εἰς τὴν Σκυθίαν καὶ μετ' ἐκείνων κατῴκησαν.

Ἡμεῖς δ' ἀρκούντως περὶ τούτων διεληλυθότες ἐπάνιμεν πάλιν ἐπὶ τὰς Ἡρακλέους πράξεις.

29. Τετελεκότος γὰρ αὐτοῦ τοὺς ἄθλους, καὶ τοῦ θεοῦ χρήσαντος συμφέρειν πρὸ τῆς εἰς θεοὺς μεταλλαγῆς ἀποικίαν εἰς Σαρδὼ πέμψαι καὶ τοὺς ἐκ τῶν Θεσπιάδων αὐτῷ γενομένους υἱοὺς ἡγεμόνας ποιῆσαι ταύτης, ἔκρινε τὸν ἀδελφιδοῦν Ἰόλαον ἐκπέμψαι μετὰ τῶν παίδων διὰ τὸ παντελῶς νέους

---

[1] The Strait of Kertch, which connects the Sea of Azof with the Black Sea.

[2] This spot was probably on the slopes of the Areopagus. Cp. Aeschylus, *Eumenides*, 685 ff.: "And this hill of Ares,

about that a notable army had been assembled, with which the leaders of the Amazons crossed the Cimmerian Bosporus [1] and advanced through Thrace. Finally they traversed a large part of Europe and came to Attica, where they pitched their camp in what is at present called after them "the Amazoneum." [2] When Theseus learned of the oncoming of the Amazons he came to the aid of the forces of his citizens, bringing with him the Amazon Antiopê, by whom he already had a son Hippolytus. Theseus joined battle with the Amazons, and since the Athenians surpassed them in bravery, he gained the victory, and of the Amazons who opposed him, some he slew at the time and the rest he drove out of Attica. And it came to pass that Antiopê, who was fighting at the side of her husband Theseus, distinguished herself in the battle and died fighting heroically. The Amazons who survived renounced their ancestral soil, and returned with the Scythians into Scythia and made their homes among that people.

But we have spoken enough about the Amazons, and shall return to the deeds of Heracles.

29. After Heracles had performed his Labours, the god revealed to him that it would be well if, before he passed into the company of the gods, he should despatch a colony to Sardinia and make the sons who had been born to him by the daughters of Thespius the leaders of the settlement, and so he decided to send his nephew Iolaüs with the boys, since

whereon the Amazons had their seat and pitched their tents, what time they came, embattled, in resentment against Theseus, and in those days built up this new citadel with lofty towers to rival his, and sacrificed to Ares . . ." (tr. of Smyth in the *L.C.L.*).

DIODORUS OF SICILY

2 εἶναι. ἀναγκαῖον δ' ἡμῖν φαίνεται προδιελθεῖν περὶ τῆς γενέσεως τῶν παίδων, ἵνα τὸν περὶ τῆς ἀποικίας λόγον καθαρώτερον ἐκθέσθαι δυνηθῶμεν.

Θέσπιος ἦν ἀνὴρ τὸ γένος ἐπιφανὴς ἐκ τῶν Ἀθηνῶν, υἱὸς Ἐρεχθέως, βασιλεύων δὲ τῆς ὁμωνύμου χώρας ἐγέννησεν ἐκ πλειόνων γυναικῶν
3 θυγατέρας πεντήκοντα. Ἡρακλέους δ' ἔτι παιδὸς ὄντος τὴν ἡλικίαν, καὶ ῥώμῃ σώματος ὑπερφυοῦς ὄντος, ἐφιλοτιμήθη τὰς θυγατέρας ἐκ τούτου τεκνοποιήσασθαι. διὸ καλέσας αὐτὸν ἐπί τινα θυσίαν καὶ λαμπρῶς ἑστιάσας, ἀπέστειλε κατὰ μίαν τῶν θυγατέρων· αἷς ἁπάσαις μιγεὶς καὶ ποιήσας ἐγκύους ἐγένετο πατὴρ υἱῶν πεντήκοντα. ὧν λαβόντων τὴν κοινὴν προσηγορίαν ἀπὸ τῶν Θεσπιάδων, καὶ γενομένων ἐνηλίκων, ἔκρινεν ἐκπέμπειν τούτους εἰς τὴν ἀποικίαν τὴν εἰς
4 Σαρδόνα κατὰ τὸν χρησμόν. ἡγουμένου δὲ τοῦ στόλου παντὸς Ἰολάου, καὶ συνεστρατευμένου σχεδὸν ἁπάσας τὰς στρατείας, ἐπέτρεψεν αὐτῷ τὰ περὶ τοὺς Θεσπιάδας καὶ τὴν ἀποικίαν. τῶν δὲ πεντήκοντα παίδων δύο μὲν κατέμειναν ἐν ταῖς Θήβαις, ὧν τοὺς ἀπογόνους φασὶ μέχρι τοῦ νῦν τιμᾶσθαι, ἑπτὰ δ' ἐν Θεσπιαῖς, οὓς ὀνομάζουσι δημούχους, ὧν καὶ τοὺς ἀπογόνους ἡγήσασθαί

---

[1] The territory of the city of Thespiae in Boeotia.

[2] This was done, according to some ancient writers, on fifty successive nights; according to others, on seven nights when seven daughters lay with Heracles each night, one refusing and being sentenced by him to lifelong maidenhood.

BOOK IV. 29. 1-4

they were still quite young. Now it seems to us indispensable that we should speak first of the birth of the boys, in order that we may be able to set forth more clearly what is to be said about the colony.

Thespius was by birth a distinguished man of Athens and son of Erechtheus, and he was king of the land which bears his name [1] and begot by his wives, of whom he had a great number, fifty daughters. And when Heracles was still a boy, but already of extraordinary strength of body, the king strongly desired that his daughters should bear children by him. Consequently he invited Heracles to a sacrifice, and after entertaining him in brilliant fashion he sent his daughters one by one in to him; and Heracles lay with them all,[2] brought them all with child, and so became the father of fifty sons. These sons all took the same name after the daughters of Thespius,[3] and when they had arrived at manhood Heracles decided to send them to Sardinia to found a colony, as the oracle had commanded. And since the expedition was under the general command of Iolaüs, who had accompanied Heracles on practically all of his campaigns, the latter entrusted him with the care of the Thespiadae and the planting of the colony. Of the fifty boys, two continued to dwell in Thebes, their descendants, they say, being honoured even to the present day, and seven in Thespiae, where they are called *demouchi*,[4] and where their

But some writers (*e.g.* Pausanias, 9. 27. 7, Gregorius Nazianzenus, *Orat.* IV, *Contra Julianum* I (Migne, *S. Gr.* 35. 661)) state that this deed was accomplished by Heracles in one night and counted as his thirteenth Labour.

[3] *i.e.* each took the name Thespiades, "son of Thespius."

[4] The word means "protector of the people."

DIODORUS OF SICILY

φασι τῆς πόλεως μέχρι τῶν νεωτέρων καιρῶν. τοὺς δὲ λοιποὺς ἅπαντας Ἰόλαος ἀναλαβὼν καὶ πολλοὺς ἄλλους τοὺς βουλομένους κοινωνεῖν τῆς ἀποικίας, ἔπλευσεν εἰς τὴν Σαρδόνα. κρατήσας δὲ μάχῃ τῶν ἐγχωρίων, κατεκληρούχησε τὸ κάλλιστον τῆς νήσου, καὶ μάλιστα τὴν πεδιάδα χώραν, ἣν μέχρι τοῦ νῦν καλεῖσθαι Ἰολάειον. ἐξημερώσας δὲ τὴν χώραν καὶ καταφυτεύσας δένδρεσι καρπίμοις κατεσκεύασε περιμάχητον· ἐπὶ τοσοῦτο γὰρ ἡ νῆσος διωνομάσθη τῇ τῶν καρπῶν ἀφθονίᾳ ὥστε Καρχηδονίους ὕστερον αὐξηθέντας ἐπιθυμῆσαι τῆς νήσου, καὶ πολλοὺς ἀγῶνας καὶ κινδύνους ὑπὲρ αὐτῆς ἀναδέξασθαι. ἀλλὰ περὶ μὲν τούτων ἐν τοῖς οἰκείοις χρόνοις ἀναγράψομεν.

30. Τότε δ' ὁ Ἰόλαος καταστήσας τὰ περὶ τὴν ἀποικίαν, καὶ τὸν Δαίδαλον ἐκ τῆς Σικελίας μεταπεμψάμενος, κατεσκεύασεν ἔργα πολλὰ καὶ μεγάλα μέχρι τῶν νῦν καιρῶν διαμένοντα καὶ ἀπὸ τοῦ κατασκευάσαντος Δαιδάλεια καλούμενα. ᾠκοδόμησε δὲ καὶ γυμνάσια μεγάλα τε καὶ πολυτελῆ, καὶ δικαστήρια κατέστησε καὶ τἆλλα τὰ πρὸς τὴν εὐδαιμονίαν συντείνοντα. ὠνόμασε δὲ καὶ τοὺς λαοὺς Ἰολαεῖς,[1] ἀφ' ἑαυτοῦ θέμενος τὴν προσηγορίαν, συγχωρησάντων τῶν Θεσπιαδῶν, καὶ δόντων αὐτῷ τοῦτο τὸ γέρας καθαπερεί τινι πατρί. διὰ γὰρ τὴν πρὸς αὐτοὺς σπουδὴν ἐπὶ τοσοῦτ' εὐνοίας προήχθησαν ὥστ' ἐπώνυμον αὐτῷ περιθεῖναι τὴν τοῦ γονέως προσηγορίαν· διόπερ ἐν τοῖς ὕστερον χρόνοις

---

[1] Ἰολαεῖς (cp. Strabo 5. 2. 7), Ἰολάους MSS, Ἰολαείους Wesseling and editors.

descendants, they say, were the chief men of the city until recent times. All the other Thespiadae and many more who wished to join in the founding of the colony Iolaüs took with him and sailed away to Sardinia. Here he overcame the natives in battle and divided the fairest part of the island into allotments, especially the land which was a level plain and is called to this day Iolaeium. When he had brought the land under cultivation and planted it with fruit-bearing trees he made of the island an object of contention; for instance, it gained such fame for the abundance of its fruits that at a later time the Carthaginians, when they had grown powerful, desired the island and faced many struggles and perils for possession of it. But we shall write of these matters in connection with the period to which they belong.[1]

30. At the time we are considering, Iolaüs established the colony, and summoning Daedalus from Sicily he built through him many great works which stand to this day and are called " Daedaleia " after their builder. He also had large and expensive gymnasia constructed and established courts of justice and the other institutions which contribute to the prosperity of a state. Furthermore, Iolaüs named the folk of the colony Iolaeis, calling them after himself, the Thespiadae consenting to this and granting to him this honour as to a father. In fact his regard for them led them to entertain such a kindly feeling towards him that they bestowed upon him as a title the appellation usually given to the progenitor of a people; consequently those who in later times

---

[1] This is not found in the extant portions of Diodorus.

οἱ τὰς θυσίας τελοῦντες τούτῳ τῷ θεῷ προσαγορεύουσιν αὐτὸν Ἰόλαον πατέρα, καθάπερ οἱ Πέρσαι τὸν Κῦρον.

3 Μετὰ δὲ ταῦτα ὁ μὲν Ἰόλαος ἐπανιὼν εἰς τὴν Ἑλλάδα, καὶ προσπλεύσας τῇ Σικελίᾳ, οὐκ ὀλίγον χρόνον διέτριψεν ἐν τῇ νήσῳ. καθ' ὃν δὴ χρόνον καί τινες τῶν συναποδημούντων αὐτῷ διὰ τὸ κάλλος τῆς χώρας κατέμειναν ἐν τῇ Σικελίᾳ, καὶ τοῖς Σικανοῖς καταμιγέντες ἐν ταύτῃ κατῴκησαν, τιμώμενοι διαφερόντως ὑπὸ τῶν ἐγχωρίων. ὁ δ' Ἰόλαος μεγάλης ἀποδοχῆς τυγχάνων καὶ πολλοὺς εὐεργετῶν ἐν πολλαῖς τῶν πόλεων ἐτι-
4 μήθη τεμένεσι καὶ τιμαῖς ἡρωικαῖς. ἴδιον δέ τι καὶ παράδοξον συνέβη γενέσθαι κατὰ τὴν ἀποικίαν ταύτην· ὁ μὲν γὰρ θεὸς ἔχρησεν αὐτοῖς ὅτι πάντες οἱ τῆς ἀποικίας ταύτης μετασχόντες καὶ οἱ τούτων ἔκγονοι διατελέσουσιν ἅπαντα τὸν αἰῶνα διαμένοντες ἐλεύθεροι, τὸ δ' ἀποτέλεσμα τούτων ἀκολούθως τῷ χρησμῷ διέμεινε μέχρι τῶν καθ' ἡμᾶς καιρῶν.
5 οἱ μὲν γὰρ λαοὶ διὰ τὸ πλῆθος τοῦ χρόνου, πλειόνων τῶν βαρβάρων ὄντων τῶν μετεσχηκότων τῆς ἀποικίας, ἐξεβαρβαρώθησαν, καὶ μεταστάντες εἰς τὴν ὀρεινὴν ἐν ταῖς δυσχωρίαις κατῴκησαν, ἐθίσαντες δ' ἑαυτοὺς τρέφεσθαι γάλακτι καὶ κρέασι καὶ πολλὰς ἀγέλας κτηνῶν τρέφοντες οὐκ ἐπεδέοντο σίτου· κατασκευάσαντες δ' οἰκήσεις ἑαυτοῖς καταγείους καὶ τὴν τοῦ βίου διεξαγωγὴν ἐν τοῖς ὀρύγμασι ποιούμενοι τοὺς ἐκ τῶν πολέμων
6 κινδύνους ἐξέφυγον. διὸ καὶ πρότερον μὲν Καρχηδόνιοι, μετὰ δὲ ταῦτα Ῥωμαῖοι πολλάκις πολεμήσαντες τούτοις τῆς προθέσεως διήμαρτον.

offer sacrifices to this god address him as "Father Iolaüs," as the Persians do when they address Cyrus.

After this Iolaüs, on his return to Greece, sailed over to Sicily and spent a considerable time on that island. And at this time several of those who were visiting the island in his company remained in Sicily because of the beauty of the land, and uniting with the Sicani they settled in the island, being especially honoured by the natives. Iolaüs also received a great welcome, and since he conferred benefits upon many men he was honoured in many of the cities with sacred precincts and with such distinctions as are accorded to heroes. And a peculiar and astonishing thing came to pass in connection with this colony in Sardinia. For the god [1] had told them in an oracle that all who joined in this colony and their descendants should continually remain free men for evermore, and the event in their case has continued to be in harmony with the oracle even to our own times. For the people of the colony in the long course of time came to be barbarized, since the barbarians who took part in the colony about them outnumbered them, and so they removed into the mountainous part of the island and made their home in the rough and barren regions and there, accustoming themselves to live on milk and meat and raising large flocks and herds, they had no need of grain. They also built themselves underground dwellings, and by spending their lives in such dug-out homes they avoided the perils which wars entail. As a consequence both the Carthaginians in former days and the Romans later, despite the many wars which they waged with this people, did not attain their design.[2]

[1] Apollo in Delphi.   [2] Cp. Book 5. 15.

Καὶ περὶ μὲν Ἰολάου καὶ Θεσπιαδῶν, ἔτι δὲ τῆς ἀποικίας τῆς εἰς Σαρδόνα γενομένης ἀρκεσθησόμεθα τοῖς ῥηθεῖσι, περὶ δ' Ἡρακλέους τὰ συνεχῆ τοῖς προειρημένοις προσθήσομεν.

31. Τελέσας γὰρ τοὺς ἄθλους τὴν μὲν ἑαυτοῦ γυναῖκα Μεγάραν συνῴκισεν Ἰολάῳ, διὰ τὴν περὶ τὰ τέκνα συμφορὰν ὑποπτευσάμενος τὴν ἐξ ἐκείνης παιδοποιίαν, ἑτέραν ‹δ›' ἐζήτει πρὸς τέκνων γένεσιν ἀνύποπτον. διόπερ ἐμνήστευσεν Ἰόλην 2 τὴν Εὐρύτου τοῦ δυναστεύσαντος Οἰχαλίας. ὁ δ' Εὔρυτος διὰ τὴν ἐκ τῆς Μεγάρας γενομένην ἀτυχίαν εὐλαβηθείς, ἀπεκρίθη βουλεύσεσθαι περὶ τοῦ γάμου. ὁ δ' ἀποτυχὼν τῆς μνηστείας διὰ τὴν 3 ἀτιμίαν ἐξήλασε τὰς ἵππους τοῦ Εὐρύτου. Ἰφίτου δὲ τοῦ Εὐρύτου τὸ γεγονὸς ὑποπτεύσαντος καὶ παραγενομένου κατὰ ζήτησιν τῶν ἵππων εἰς Τίρυνθα, τοῦτον μὲν ἀναβιβάσας ὁ Ἡρακλῆς[1] ἐπί τινα πύργον ὑψηλὸν ἐκέλευσεν ἀφορᾶν μή που νέμονται τυγχάνουσιν· οὐ δυναμένου δὲ κατανοῆσαι τοῦ Ἰφίτου, φήσας αὐτὸν ψευδῶς κατῃτιᾶσθαι τὴν κλοπὴν κατεκρήμνισεν ἀπὸ τοῦ πύργου.

4 Διὰ δὲ τὸν τούτου θάνατον Ἡρακλῆς νοσήσας παρῆλθεν εἰς Πύλον πρὸς Νηλέα, καὶ παρεκάλεσεν αὐτὸν καθᾶραι τὸν φόνον. ὁ μὲν οὖν Νηλεὺς βουλευσάμενος μετὰ τῶν υἱῶν ἔλαβε πάντας πλὴν Νέστορος τοῦ νεωτάτου συγκαταινοῦντας μὴ προσ-

[1] ὁ Ἡρακλῆς omitted by DF, Vogel.

As regards Iolaüs, then, and the Thespiadae and the colony which was sent to Sardinia, we shall rest satisfied with what has been said, and we shall continue the story of Heracles from the point at which our account left off.

31. After Heracles had completed his Labours he gave his own wife Megara in marriage to Iolaüs, being apprehensive of begetting any children by her because of the calamity which had befallen their other offspring, and sought another wife by whom he might have children without apprehension.[1] Consequently he wooed Iolê, the daughter of Eurytus who was ruler of Oechalia. But Eurytus was hesitant because of the ill fortune which had come in the case of Megara and replied that he would deliberate concerning the marriage. Since Heracles had met with a refusal to his suit, because of the dishonour which had been shown him he now drove off the mares of Eurytus. But Iphitus, the son of Eurytus, harboured suspicions of what had been done and came to Tiryns in search of the horses, whereupon Heracles, taking him up on a lofty tower of the castle, asked him to see whether they were by chance grazing anywhere; and when Iphitus was unable to discover them, he claimed that Iphitus had falsely accused him of the theft and threw him down headlong from the tower.

Because of his murder of Iphitus Heracles was attacked by a disease, and coming to Neleus at Pylus he besought him to purify him of the blood-guilt. Thereupon Neleus took counsel with his sons and found that all of them, with the exception of Nestor who was the youngest, agreed in advising him that he

[1] Cp. chap. 11.

5 δέξασθαι τὸν καθαρμόν· ὁ δ' Ἡρακλῆς τότε μὲν παρελθὼν πρὸς Δηίφοβον τὸν Ἱππολύτου καὶ πείσας αὐτὸν ἐκαθάρθη, οὐ δυνάμενος δ' ἀπολυθῆναι τῆς νόσου ἐπηρώτησε τὸν Ἀπόλλω περὶ τῆς θεραπείας. τούτου δὲ χρήσαντος ὅτι ῥᾷον οὕτως ἀπολυθήσεται τῆς νόσου, εἰ πραθεὶς δικαίως τὴν ἑαυτοῦ τιμὴν ἀποδοίη τοῖς Ἰφίτου παισίν, ἀναγκαζόμενος πείθεσθαι[1] τῷ χρησμῷ μετά τινων φίλων ἔπλευσεν εἰς τὴν Ἀσίαν. ἐκεῖ δ' ὑπομείνας ἑκουσίως ὑπό τινος τῶν φίλων ἐπράθη, καὶ παρθένου δοῦλος ἐγένετο Ὀμφάλης τῆς Ἰαρδάνου, βασιλευούσης τῶν τότε Μαιόνων, νῦν δὲ Λυδῶν ὀνομαζομένων.
6 καὶ τὴν μὲν τιμὴν ὁ ἀποδόμενος τὸν Ἡρακλέα τοῖς Ἰφίτου παισὶν ἀπέδωκε κατὰ τὸν χρησμόν, ὁ δ' Ἡρακλῆς ὑγιασθεὶς καὶ δουλεύων τῇ Ὀμφάλῃ
7 τοὺς κατὰ τὴν χώραν λῃστεύοντας ἐκόλασε. τοὺς μὲν γὰρ ὀνομαζομένους Κέρκωπας, λῃστεύοντας καὶ πολλὰ κακὰ διεργαζομένους, οὓς μὲν ἀπέκτεινεν, οὓς δὲ ζωγρήσας δεδεμένους παρέδωκε τῇ Ὀμφάλῃ· Συλέα δὲ τοὺς παριόντας ξένους συναρπάζοντα καὶ τοὺς ἀμπελῶνας σκάπτειν ἀναγκάζοντα τῷ σκαφείῳ πατάξας ἀπέκτεινεν· Ἰτώνων δὲ λεηλατούντων πολλὴν τῆς ὑπὸ Ὀμφάλῃ χώρας, τήν τε λείαν ἀφείλετο καὶ τὴν πόλιν, ἐξ ἧς ἐποιοῦντο τὴν ὁρμήν, ἐκπορθήσας ἐξηνδραποδίσατο
8 καὶ κατέσκαψεν. ἡ δ' Ὀμφάλη ἀποδεχομένη τὴν ἀνδρείαν τὴν Ἡρακλέους, καὶ πυθομένη τίς ἐστι καὶ τίνων, ἐθαύμασε τὴν ἀρετήν, ἐλεύθερον δ'

[1] ὑπὸ τῆς νόσου after πείθεσθαι deleted by Dindorf, Vogel, retained by Bekker.

should not undertake the rite of purification.
Heracles then went to Deïphobus, the son of Hippolytus, and prevailing upon him was given the rite of purification, but being still unable to rid himself of the disease he inquired of Apollo how to heal it. Apollo gave him the answer that he would easily rid himself of the disease if he should be sold as a slave and honourably pay over the purchase price of himself to the sons of Iphitus, and so, being now under constraint to obey the oracle, he sailed over to Asia in company with some of his friends. There he willingly submitted to be sold by one of his friends and became the slave of Omphalê, the daughter of Iardanus, who was still unmarried and was queen of the people who were called at that time Maeonians, but now Lydians. The man who had sold Heracles paid over the purchase price to the sons of Iphitus, as the oracle had commanded, and Heracles, healed now of the disease and serving Omphalê as her slave, began to mete out punishment upon the robbers who infested the land. As for the Cercopes, for instance, as they are called, who were robbing and committing many evil acts, some of them he put to death and others he took captive and delivered in chains to Omphalê. Syleus, who was seizing any strangers who passed by and forcing them to hoe his vineyards, he slew by a blow with his own hoe; and from the Itoni, who had been plundering a large part of the land of Omphalê, he took away their booty, and the city which they had made the base of their raids he sacked, and enslaving its inhabitants razed it to the ground. Omphalê was pleased with the courage Heracles displayed, and on learning who he was and who had been his parents she marvelled at his valour, set him

ἀφεῖσα καὶ συνοικήσασα αὐτῷ Λάμον ἐγέννησε. προϋπῆρχε δὲ τῷ Ἡρακλεῖ κατὰ τὸν τῆς δουλείας καιρὸν ἐκ δούλης υἱὸς Κλεόδαιος.

32. Μετὰ δὲ ταῦτα ἐπανελθὼν εἰς Πελοπόννησον ἐστράτευσεν εἰς Ἴλιον, ἐγκαλῶν Λαομέδοντι τῷ βασιλεῖ. οὗτος γὰρ Ἡρακλέους στρατεύοντος μετὰ Ἰάσονος ἐπὶ τὸ χρυσόμαλλον δέρος, καὶ τὸ κῆτος ἀνελόντος, ἀπεστέρησε τῶν ὡμολογημένων ἵππων, περὶ ὧν ἐν τοῖς Ἀργοναύταις τὰ κατὰ 2 μέρος μικρὸν ὕστερον διέξιμεν. καὶ τότε μὲν διὰ τὴν μετ᾽ Ἰάσονος στρατείαν ἀσχοληθείς, ὕστερον δὲ λαβὼν καιρὸν ἐπὶ τὴν Τροίαν ἐστράτευσεν, ὡς μέν τινές φασι, ναυσὶ μακραῖς ὀκτωκαίδεκα, ὡς δὲ Ὅμηρος γέγραφεν, ἓξ ταῖς ἁπάσαις, ἐν οἷς παρεισάγει τὸν υἱὸν αὐτοῦ Τληπόλεμον λέγοντα

ἀλλ᾽ οἷόν τινά φασι βίην Ἡρακληείην
εἶναι, ἐμὸν πατέρα θρασυμέμνονα, θυμολέοντα,
ὅς ποτε δεῦρ᾽ ἐλθὼν ἕνεχ᾽ ἵππων Λαομέδοντος
ἐξ οἴης σὺν νηυσὶ καὶ ἀνδράσι παυροτέροισιν
Ἰλίου ἐξαλάπαξε πόλιν, χήρωσε δ᾽ ἀγυιάς.

3 Ὁ δ᾽ οὖν Ἡρακλῆς καταπλεύσας εἰς τὴν Τρῳάδα αὐτὸς μὲν μετὰ τῶν ἀρίστων προῆγεν ἐπὶ τὴν πόλιν, ἐπὶ δὲ τῶν νεῶν ἀπέλιπεν ἡγεμόνα τὸν Ἀμφιαράου υἱὸν Οἰκλέα. Λαομέδων δ᾽ ἀπροσδοκήτου τῆς παρουσίας τῶν πολεμίων γενομένης δύναμιν ἀξιόλογον συναγαγεῖν ἐξεκλείσθη διὰ τὴν ὀξύτητα τῶν καιρῶν, ἀθροίσας δ᾽ ὅσους ἐδύνατο,

---

[1] This story is told below in chap. 42.
[2] Iliad 5. 638–42.

BOOK IV. 31. 8–32. 3

free, and marrying him bore him Lamus. Already before this, while he was yet a slave, there had been born to Heracles by a slave a son Cleodaeus.

32. After this Heracles, returning to Peloponnesus, made war against Ilium, since he had a ground of complaint against its king, Laomedon. For when Heracles was on the expedition with Jason to get the golden fleece and had slain the sea-monster, Laomedon had withheld from him the mares which he had agreed to give him and of which we shall give a detailed account a little later in connection with the Argonauts.[1] At that time Heracles had not had the leisure, since he was engaged upon the expedition of Jason, but later he found an opportunity and made war upon Troy with eighteen ships of war, as some say, but, as Homer writes, with six in all, when he introduces Heracles' son Tlepolemus as saying [2]:

> Aye, what a man, they say, was Heracles
> In might, my father he, steadfast, with heart
> Of lion, who once came here to carry off
> The mares of King Laomedon, with but
> Six ships and scantier men, yet sacked he then
> The city of proud Ilium, and made
> Her streets bereft.

When Heracles, then, had landed on the coast of the Troad, he advanced in person with his select troops against the city and left in command of the ships Oecles, the son of Amphiaraus. And since the presence of the enemy had not been expected, it proved impossible for Laomedon, on account of the exigencies of the moment, to collect a passable army, but gathering as many soldiers as he could he advanced

μετὰ τούτων ἦλθεν ἐπὶ τὰς ναῦς, ἐλπίζων, εἰ ταύτας ἐμπρήσειε, τέλος ἐπιθήσειν τῷ πολέμῳ. τοῦ δὲ Οἰκλέους ἀπαντήσαντος, ὁ μὲν στρατηγὸς Οἰκλῆς ἔπεσεν, οἱ δὲ λοιποὶ συνδιωχθέντες εἰς τὰς ναῦς ἔφθασαν ἀναπλεύσαντες ἀπὸ τῆς γῆς.
4 Λαομέδων δ' ἐπανελθὼν καὶ πρὸς τῇ πόλει τοῖς μεθ' Ἡρακλέους συμβαλὼν αὐτός τε ἔπεσε καὶ τῶν συναγωνιζομένων οἱ πλείους· Ἡρακλῆς δὲ τὴν πόλιν ἑλὼν κατὰ κράτος καὶ πολλοὺς ἐν χειρῶν νόμῳ κατασφάξας, Πριάμῳ τὴν βασιλείαν ἀπ-
5 έδωκε τῶν Ἰλιαδῶν διὰ τὴν δικαιοσύνην· οὗτος γὰρ μόνος τῶν υἱῶν τοῦ Λαομέδοντος ἐναντιούμενος τῷ πατρὶ τὰς ἵππους ἀποδοῦναι συνεβούλευσεν τῷ Ἡρακλεῖ κατὰ τὰς ἐπαγγελίας. ὁ δ' Ἡρακλῆς ἐστεφάνωσε Τελαμῶνα ἀριστείοις, δοὺς αὐτῷ τὴν Λαομέδοντος θυγατέρα Ἡσιόνην· οὗτος γὰρ κατὰ τὴν πολιορκίαν πρῶτος βιασάμενος εἰσέπεσεν εἰς τὴν πόλιν, Ἡρακλέους προσβαλόντος κατὰ τὸ καρτερώτατον μέρος τοῦ τείχους τῆς ἀκροπόλεως.

33. Μετὰ δὲ ταῦτα Ἡρακλῆς μὲν ἐπανελθὼν εἰς Πελοπόννησον ἐστράτευσεν ἐπ' Αὐγέαν διὰ τὴν ἀποστέρησιν τοῦ μισθοῦ· γενομένης δὲ μάχης πρὸς τοὺς Ἠλείους, τότε μὲν ἄπρακτος ἐπανῆλθεν εἰς Ὤλενον πρὸς Δεξαμενόν· τῆς δὲ τούτου θυγατρὸς Ἱππολύτης συνοικιζομένης Ἀζᾶνι, συνδειπνῶν Ἡρακλῆς καὶ θεασάμενος ἐν τοῖς γάμοις ὑβρίζοντα τὸν Κένταυρον Εὐρυτίωνα καὶ τὴν Ἱππολύ-
2 την βιαζόμενον, ἀπέκτεινεν. εἰς Τίρυνθα δὲ Ἡρακλέους ἐπανελθόντος, Εὐρυσθεὺς αἰτιασά-

---

[1] Augeas had agreed to give Heracles one-tenth of his herds in payment for the cleansing of his stables.

with them against the ships, in the hope that if he could burn them he could bring an end to the war. Oecles came out to meet him, but when he, the general, fell, the rest succeeded in making good their flight to the ships and in putting out to sea from the land. Laomedon then withdrew and joining combat with the troops of Heracles near the city he was slain himself and most of the soldiers with him. Heracles then took the city by storm and after slaughtering many of its inhabitants in the action he gave the kingdom of the Iliadae to Priam because of his sense of justice; for Priam was the only one of the sons of Laomedon who had opposed his father and had counselled him to give the mares back to Heracles, as he had promised to do. And Heracles crowned Telamon with the meed of valour by bestowing upon him Hesionê the daughter of Laomedon, for in the siege he had been the first to force his way into the city, while Heracles was assaulting the strongest section of the wall of the acropolis.

33. After this Heracles returned to Peloponnesus and set out against Augeas, since the latter had defrauded him of his reward.[1] It came to a battle between him and the Eleans, but on this occasion he had no success and so returned to Olenus[2] to Dexamenus. The latter's daughter Hippolytê was being joined in marriage to Azan, and when Heracles, as he sat at the wedding feast, observed the Centaur Eurytion acting in an insulting manner towards Hippolytê and endeavouring to do violence to her, he slew him. When Heracles returned to Tiryns, Eurystheus charged him with plotting to seize the

---

[2] A city of Achaea.

μενος αὐτὸν ἐπιβουλεύειν τῇ βασιλείᾳ προσέταξεν ἀπελθεῖν ἐκ Τίρυνθος αὐτόν τε καὶ τὴν Ἀλκμήνην καὶ Ἰφικλέα καὶ Ἰόλαον. διόπερ ἀναγκασθεὶς ἔφυγε μετὰ τούτων καὶ κατῴκησε 3 τῆς Ἀρκαδίας ἐν Φενεῷ. ἐντεῦθεν δὲ ὁρμώμενος, καὶ πυθόμενος ἐξ Ἤλιδος πομπὴν ἀποστέλλεσθαι Ποσειδῶνι εἰς Ἰσθμόν, καὶ ταύτης ἀφηγεῖσθαι Εὔρυτον τὸν Αὐγέου, προσπεσὼν ἄφνω τὸν Εὔρυτον ἀπέκτεινε περὶ Κλεωνάς, ἔνθα νῦν 4 ἐστιν ἱερὸν Ἡρακλέους. μετὰ δὲ ταῦτα στρατεύσας ἐπὶ τὴν Ἦλιν τόν τε βασιλέα ἐφόνευσεν Αὐγέαν, καὶ τὴν πόλιν ἑλὼν κατὰ κράτος Φυλέα τὸν Αὐγέου μετεπέμψατο, καὶ τούτῳ τὴν βασιλείαν παρέδωκεν· ἦν γὰρ ὑπὸ τοῦ πατρὸς πεφυγαδευμένος καθ' ὃν καιρὸν δικαστὴς γενόμενος τῷ πατρὶ πρὸς Ἡρακλέα περὶ τοῦ μισθοῦ τὸ νίκημα ἀπέδωκεν Ἡρακλεῖ.

5 Μετὰ δὲ ταῦτα Ἱπποκόων μὲν ἐφυγάδευσεν ἐκ τῆς Σπάρτης τὸν ἀδελφὸν Τυνδάρεων, Οἰωνὸν δὲ τὸν Λικυμνίου φίλον ὄντα Ἡρακλέους οἱ υἱοὶ τοῦ Ἱπποκόωντος εἴκοσι τὸν ἀριθμὸν ὄντες ἀπέκτειναν· ἐφ' οἷς ἀγανακτήσας Ἡρακλῆς ἐστράτευσεν ἐπ' αὐτούς· μεγάλῃ δὲ μάχῃ νικήσας παμπληθεῖς ἀπέκτεινε. τὴν δὲ Σπάρτην ἑλὼν κατὰ κράτος, κατήγαγεν ἐπὶ τὴν βασιλείαν Τυνδάρεων τὸν πατέρα τῶν Διοσκόρων, καὶ τὴν βασιλείαν ὡς δορίκτητον Τυνδάρεῳ παρέθετο, προστάξας 6 τοῖς ἀφ' ἑαυτοῦ γενομένοις φυλάττειν. ἔπεσον δ' ἐν τῇ μάχῃ τῶν μὲν μεθ' Ἡρακλέους ὀλίγοι παντελῶς, ἐν οἷς ἦσαν ἐπιφανεῖς ἄνδρες Ἴφικλος καὶ Κηφεὺς καὶ Κηφέως υἱοὶ τὸν ἀριθμὸν ὄντες ἑπτακαίδεκα· τρεῖς γὰρ ἀπὸ τῶν[1] εἴκοσι μόνον

kingdom and commanded that he and Alcmenê and Iphicles and Iolaüs should depart from Tiryns. Consequently he was forced to go into exile along with these just mentioned and made his dwelling in Pheneus in Arcadia. This city he took for his headquarters, and learning once that a sacred procession had been sent forth from Elis to the Isthmus in honour of Poseidon and that Eurytus, the son of Augeas, was at the head of it, he fell unexpectedly upon Eurytus and killed him near Cleonae, where a temple of Heracles still stands. After this he made war upon Elis and slew Augeas its king, and taking the city by storm he recalled Phyleus, the son of Augeas, and gave the kingdom into his hands; for the son had been exiled by his father at the time when he had served as arbitrator between his father and Heracles in the matter of the reward and had given the decision to Heracles.

After this Hippocoön exiled from Sparta his brother Tyndareüs, and the sons of Hippocoön, twenty in number, put to death Oeonus who was the son of Licymnius and a friend of Heracles; whereupon Heracles was angered and set out against them, and being victorious in a great battle he made a slaughter of every man of them. Then, taking Sparta by storm he restored Tyndareüs, who was the father of the Dioscori, to his kingdom and bestowed upon him the kingdom on the ground that it was his by right of war, commanding him to keep it safe for Heracles' own descendants. There fell in the battle but a very few of the comrades of Heracles, though among them were famous men, such as Iphiclus and Cepheus and seventeen sons of Cepheus, since only three of his

---

[1] τῶν deleted by Kallenberg.

διεσώθησαν· τῶν δ' ἐναντίων αὐτός τε ὁ Ἱπποκόων καὶ μετ' αὐτοῦ δέκα μὲν υἱοί, τῶν δ' ἄλλων
7 Σπαρτιατῶν παμπληθεῖς. ἀπὸ δὲ ταύτης τῆς στρατείας ἐπανιὼν εἰς τὴν Ἀρκαδίαν, καὶ καταλύσας παρὰ Ἀλέῳ τῷ βασιλεῖ, τῇ θυγατρὶ τούτου λάθρᾳ μιγεὶς Αὔγῃ καὶ ταύτην ποιήσας ἔγκυον εἰς
8 Στύμφαλον ἐπανῆλθεν. Ἀλέως δ' ἀγνοῶν τὸ πεπραγμένον, ὡς ὁ τῆς γαστρὸς ὄγκος ἐμήνυσε τὴν φθοράν, ἐζήτει τὸν φθείραντα. τῆς δ' Αὔγης ἀποφαινομένης ὅτι βιάσαιτο αὐτὴν Ἡρακλῆς, ἀπιστήσας τοῖς ὑπὸ ταύτης λεγομένοις ταύτην μὲν παρέδωκε Ναυπλίῳ φίλῳ καθεστῶτι, καὶ προσέταξε
9 καταποντίσαι. Αὔγη δ' ἀπαγομένη εἰς Ναυπλίαν, καὶ γενομένη κατὰ τὸ Παρθένιον ὄρος, ὑπὸ τῶν ὠδίνων καταβαρουμένη παρῆλθεν εἰς τὴν πλησίον ὕλην ὡς ἐπί τινα χρείαν ἀναγκαίαν· τεκοῦσα δὲ παιδίον ἄρρεν ἀπέλιπε τὸ βρέφος εἴς τινας θάμνους κρύψασα. μετὰ δὲ ταῦτα Αὔγη μὲν ἀπηλλάγη πρὸς τὸν Ναύπλιον, καὶ καταντήσασα τῆς Ἀργείας εἰς τὸν ἐν Ναυπλίᾳ λιμένα παραδόξου σωτηρίας
10 ἔτυχεν· ὁ γὰρ Ναύπλιος καταποντίσαι μὲν αὐτὴν κατὰ τὰς ἐντολὰς οὐκ ἔκρινε, ξένοις δέ τισι Καρσὶν ἀναγομένοις εἰς τὴν Ἀσίαν δωρήσασθαι· οὗτοι δ' ἀπαγαγόντες εἰς τὴν Ἀσίαν ἀπέδοντο τὴν Αὔγην τῷ βασιλεῖ τῆς Μυσίας Τεύθραντι.
11 τὸ δ' ἀπολειφθὲν ἐν τῷ Παρθενίῳ βρέφος ὑπὸ τῆς Αὔγης βουκόλοι τινὲς Κορύθου τοῦ βασιλέως εὑρόντες ὑπό τινος ἐλάφου τῷ μαστῷ τρεφόμενον, ἐδωρήσαντο τῷ δεσπότῃ. ὁ δὲ Κόρυθος παραλαβὼν τὸ παιδίον ἀσμένως ὡς ἴδιον υἱὸν ἔτρεφε, προσαγορεύσας Τήλεφον ἀπὸ τῆς τρεφούσης ἐλάφου. Τήλεφος δ' ἀνδρωθεὶς καὶ τὴν μητέρα

twenty sons came out alive; whereas of the opponents Hippocoön himself fell, and ten sons along with him, and vast numbers of the rest of the Spartans. From this campaign Heracles returned into Arcadia, and as he stopped at the home of Aleos the king he lay secretly with his daughter Augê, brought her with child, and went back to Stymphalus. Aleos was ignorant of what had taken place, but when the bulk of the child in the womb betrayed the violation of his daughter he inquired who had violated her. And when Augê disclosed that it was Heracles who had done violence to her, he would not believe what she had said, but gave her into the hands of Nauplius his friend with orders to drown her in the sea. But as Augê was being led off to Nauplia and was near Mount Parthenium, she felt herself overcome by the birth-pains and withdrew into a near-by thicket as if to perform a certain necessary act; here she gave birth to a male child, and hiding the babe in some bushes she left it there. After doing this Augê went back to Nauplius, and when she had arrived at the harbour of Nauplia in Argolis she was saved from death in an unexpected manner. Nauplius, that is, decided not to drown her, as he had been ordered, but to make a gift of her to some Carians who were setting out for Asia; and these men took Augê to Asia and gave her to Teuthras the king of Mysia. As for the babe that had been left on Parthenium by Augê, certain herdsmen belonging to Corythus the king came upon it as it was getting its food from the teat of a hind and brought it as a gift to their master. Corythus received the child gladly, raised him as if he were his own son, and named him Telephus after the hind (*elaphos*) which had suckled it. After Telephus had

μαθεῖν σπεύδων, παρῆλθεν εἰς Δελφούς, καὶ χρησμὸν ἔλαβε πλεῖν εἰς τὴν Μυσίαν πρὸς Τεύθραντα τὸν βασιλέα. ἀνευρὼν δὲ τὴν μητέρα, καὶ γνωσθεὶς τίνος ἦν πατρός, ἀποδοχῆς ἐτύγχανε τῆς μεγίστης. ὁ δὲ Τεύθρας ἄπαις ὢν ἀρρένων παίδων[1] τὴν θυγατέρα Ἀργιόπην συνῴκισε τῷ Τηλέφῳ, καὶ διάδοχον ἀπέδειξε τῆς βασιλείας.

34. Ἡρακλῆς δὲ μετὰ τὴν ἐν Φενεῷ κατοίκησιν ἔτει πέμπτῳ, δυσφορῶν ἐπὶ τῷ τετελευτηκέναι Οἰωνὸν τὸν Λικυμνίου καὶ Ἴφικλον τὸν ἀδελφόν, ἀπῆλθεν ἑκουσίως ἐξ Ἀρκαδίας καὶ πάσης Πελοποννήσου. συναπελθόντων δ' αὐτῷ πολλῶν ἐκ τῆς Ἀρκαδίας, ἀπῆλθε τῆς Αἰτωλίας εἰς Καλυδῶνα κἀκεῖ κατῴκησεν. οὐκ ὄντων δ' αὐτῷ παίδων γνησίων οὐδὲ γαμετῆς γυναικός, ἔγημε Δηιάνειραν τὴν Οἰνέως, τετελευτηκότος ἤδη Μελεάγρου. οὐκ ἀνοίκειον δ' εἶναι νομίζομεν βραχὺ παρεκβάντας ἡμᾶς ἀπαγγεῖλαι τὴν περὶ τὸν Μελέαγρον περιπέτειαν.

2 Οἰνεὺς γάρ, γενομένης εὐκαρπίας αὐτῷ τοῦ σίτου, τοῖς μὲν ἄλλοις θεοῖς ἐτέλεσε θυσίας, μόνης δὲ τῆς Ἀρτέμιδος ὠλιγώρησεν· δι' ἣν αἰτίαν ἡ θεὸς αὐτῷ μηνίσασα τὸν διαβεβοημένον Καλυδώνιον ὗν ἀνῆκεν, ὑπερφυῆ τὸ μέγεθος. 3 οὗτος δὲ τὴν σύνεγγυς χώραν καταφθείρων τὰς κτήσεις ἐλυμαίνετο· διόπερ Μελέαγρος ὁ Οἰνέως, τὴν μὲν ἡλικίαν μάλιστα ἀκμάζων, ῥώμῃ δὲ καὶ ἀνδρείᾳ διαφέρων, παρέλαβε πολλοὺς τῶν ἀρίστων ἐπὶ τὴν τούτου κυνηγίαν. πρώτου δὲ Μελεάγρου τὸ θηρίον ἀκοντίσαντος, ὁμολογούμενον αὐτῷ τὸ

[1] παίδων added by Wesseling.

BOOK IV. 33. 11-34. 3

come to manhood, being seized with the desire to learn who his mother was, he went to Delphi and received the reply to sail to Mysia to Teuthras the king. Here he discovered his mother, and when it was known who his father was he received the heartiest welcome. And since Teuthras had no male children he joined his daughter Argiopê in marriage to Telephus and named him his successor to the kingdom.

34. In the fifth year after Heracles had changed his residence to Pheneus, being grieved over the death of Oeonus, the son of Licymnius, and of Iphiclus his brother, he removed of his free will from Arcadia and all Peloponnesus. There withdrew with him a great many people of Arcadia and he went to Calydon in Aetolia and made his home there. And since he had neither legitimate children nor a lawful wife, he married Deïaneira, the daughter of Oeneus, Meleager being now dead. In this connection it would not, in our opinion, be inappropriate for us to digress briefly and to speak of the reversal of fortune which befel Meleager.

The facts are these: Once when Oeneus had an excellent crop of grain, he offered sacrifices to the other gods, but neglected Artemis alone; and angered at him for this the goddess sent forth against him the famous Calydonian boar, a creature of enormous size. This animal harried the neighbouring land and damaged the farms; whereupon Meleager, the son of Oeneus, being then in the bloom of youth and excelling in strength and in courage, took along with himself many of the bravest men and set out to hunt the beast. Meleager was the first to plunge his javelin into it and by general

πρωτεῖον συνεχωρήθη· τοῦτο δ' ἦν ἡ δορὰ τοῦ
4 ζώου. μετεχούσης δὲ τῆς κυνηγίας Ἀταλάντης
τῆς Σχοινέως, ἐρασθεὶς αὐτῆς ὁ Μελέαγρος παρ-
εχώρησε τῆς δορᾶς καὶ τοῦ κατὰ τὴν ἀριστείαν
ἐπαίνου. ἐπὶ δὲ τοῖς πραχθεῖσιν οἱ Θεστίου
παῖδες συγκυνηγοῦντες ἠγανάκτησαν, ὅτι ξένην
γυναῖκα προετίμησεν αὐτῶν, παραπέμψας τὴν
οἰκειότητα. διόπερ ἀκυροῦντες τοῦ Μελεάγρου
τὴν δωρεὰν ἐνήδρευσαν Ἀταλάντῃ, καὶ κατὰ τὴν
εἰς Ἀρκαδίαν ἐπάνοδον ἐπιθέμενοι τὴν δορὰν
5 ἀφείλοντο. Μελέαγρος δὲ διά τε τὸν πρὸς τὴν
Ἀταλάντην ἔρωτα καὶ διὰ τὴν ἀτιμίαν παροξυνθείς,
ἐβοήθησε τῇ Ἀταλάντῃ. καὶ τὸ μὲν πρῶτον
παρεκάλει τοὺς ἡρπακότας ἀποδοῦναι τῇ γυναικὶ
τὸ δοθὲν ἀριστεῖον· ὡς δ' οὐ προσεῖχον, ἀπέκτεινεν αὐτούς, ὄντας τῆς Ἀλθαίας ἀδελφούς.
διόπερ ἡ μὲν Ἀλθαία γενομένη περιαλγὴς ἐπὶ τῇ
τῶν ὁμαίμων ἀναιρέσει ἀρὰς ἔθετο, καθ' ἃς ἠξίωσεν
ἀποθανεῖν Μελέαγρον· καὶ τοὺς ἀθανάτους ὑπακού-
σαντας ἐπενεγκεῖν αὐτῷ τὴν τοῦ βίου καταστροφήν.
6 Ἔνιοι δὲ μυθολογοῦσιν ὅτι κατὰ τὴν Μελεάγρου
γένεσιν τῇ Ἀλθαίᾳ τὰς Μοίρας καθ' ὕπνον ἐπιστά-
σας εἰπεῖν ὅτι τότε τελευτήσει Μελέαγρος ὁ υἱὸς
αὐτῆς, ὅταν ὁ δαλὸς κατακαυθῇ. διόπερ τεκοῦσαν,
καὶ νομίσασαν ἐν τῇ τοῦ δαλοῦ φυλακῇ τὴν σωτηρίαν
τοῦ τέκνου κεῖσθαι, τὸν δαλὸν ἐπιμελῶς τηρεῖν.

---

[1] The mother of Meleager.

agreement was accorded the reward of valour, which consisted of the skin of the animal. But Atalantê, the daughter of Schoeneus, participated in the hunt, and since Meleager was enamoured of her, he relinquished in her favour the skin and the praise for the greatest bravery. The sons of Thestius, however, who had also joined in the hunt, were angered at what he had done, since he had honoured a stranger woman above them and set kinship aside. Consequently, setting at naught the award which Meleager had made, they lay in wait for Atalantê, and falling upon her as she returned to Arcadia took from her the skin. Meleager, however, was deeply incensed both because of the love which he bore Atalantê and because of the dishonour shown her, and espoused the cause of Atalantê. And first of all he urged the robbers to return to the woman the meed of valour which he had given her; and when they paid no heed to him he slew them, although they were brothers of Althaea.[1] Consequently Althaea, overcome with anguish at the slaying of the men of her own blood, uttered a curse in which she demanded the death of Meleager; and the immortals, so the account runs, gave heed to her and made an end of his life.

But certain writers of myths give the following account:—At the time of the birth of Meleager the Fates stood over Althaea in her sleep and said to her that her son Meleager would die at the moment when the brand in the fire had been consumed. Consequently, when she had given birth, she believed that the safety of her child depended upon the preservation of the brand and so she guarded the brand with every care. Afterward, however, being

7 ὕστερον δ' ἐπὶ τῷ φόνῳ τῶν ἀδελφῶν παροξυνθεῖσαν κατακαῦσαι τὸν δαλὸν καὶ τῷ Μελεάγρῳ τῆς τελευτῆς αἰτίαν καταστῆναι· ἀεὶ δὲ μᾶλλον ἐπὶ τοῖς πεπραγμένοις λυπουμένην τὸ τέλος ἀγχόνῃ τὸν βίον καταστρέψαι.

35. Ἅμα δὲ τούτοις πραττομένοις Ἱππόνουν ἐν Ὠλένῳ πρὸς τὴν θυγατέρα Περίβοιαν, φάσκουσαν αὑτὴν ἐξ Ἄρεος ὑπάρχειν ἔγκυον, διενεχθέντα πέμψαι ταύτην εἰς Αἰτωλίαν πρὸς Οἰνέα καὶ παρακελεύσασθαι ταύτην ἀφανίσαι τὴν ταχίστην.
2 ὁ δ' Οἰνεὺς ἀπολωλεκὼς προσφάτως υἱὸν καὶ γυναῖκα, τὸ μὲν ἀποκτεῖναι τὴν Περίβοιαν ἀπέγνω, γήμας δ' αὐτὴν ἐγέννησεν υἱὸν Τυδέα. τὰ μὲν οὖν περὶ Μελέαγρον καὶ Ἀλθαίαν, ἔτι δ' Οἰνέα τοιαύτης ἔτυχε διεξόδου.

3 Ἡρακλῆς δὲ τοῖς Καλυδωνίοις βουλόμενος χαρίσασθαι τὸν Ἀχελῷον ποταμὸν ἀπέστρεψε, καὶ ῥύσιν ἄλλην κατασκευάσας ἀπέλαβε χώραν πολλὴν καὶ πάμφορον, ἀρδευομένην ὑπὸ τοῦ 4 προειρημένου ῥείθρου. διὸ καὶ τῶν ποιητῶν τινας μυθοποιῆσαι τὸ πραχθέν· παρεισήγαγον γὰρ τὸν Ἡρακλέα πρὸς τὸν Ἀχελῷον συνάψαι μάχην, ὠμοιωμένου τοῦ ποταμοῦ ταύρῳ, κατὰ δὲ τὴν συμπλοκὴν θάτερον τῶν κεράτων κλάσαντα δωρήσασθαι τοῖς Αἰτωλοῖς, ὃ προσαγορεῦσαι κέρας Ἀμαλθείας. ἐν ᾧ πλάττουσι πλῆθος ὑπάρχειν πάσης ὀπωρινῆς ὥρας, βοτρύων τε καὶ μήλων καὶ τῶν ἄλλων τῶν τοιούτων, αἰνιττομένων τῶν ποιητῶν κέρας μὲν τοῦ Ἀχελῴου τὸ διὰ τῆς διώρυχος φερόμενον ῥεῖθρον, τὰ δὲ μῆλα καὶ τὰς ῥόας καὶ τοὺς βότρυς δηλοῦν τὴν καρποφόρον χώραν τὴν ὑπὸ τοῦ ποταμοῦ ἀρδευομένην καὶ τὸ πλῆθος

deeply incensed at the murder of her brothers, she burned the brand and so made herself the cause of the death of Meleager; but as time went on she grieved more and more over what she had done and finally made an end of her life by hanging.

35. At the time that these things were taking place, the myth continues, Hipponoüs in Olenus, angered at his daughter Periboea because she claimed that she was with child by Ares, sent her away into Aetolia to Oeneus with orders for him to do away with her at the first opportunity. Oeneus, however, who had recently lost his son and wife, was unwilling to slay Periboea, but married her instead and begat a son Tydeus. Such, then, is the way the story runs of Meleager and Althaea and Oeneus.

But Heracles, desiring to do a service to the Calydonians, diverted the river Acheloüs, and making another bed for it he recovered a large amount of fruitfull and which was now irrigated by this stream. Consequently certain poets, as we are told, have made this deed into a myth; for they have introduced Heracles as joining battle with Acheloüs, the river assuming the form of a bull, and as breaking off in the struggle one of his horns, which he gave to the Aetolians. This they call the "Horn of Amaltheia," and represent it as filled with a great quantity of every kind of autumn fruit, such as grapes and apples and the like, the poets signifying in this obscure manner by the horn of Acheloüs the stream which ran through the canal, and by the apples and pomegranates and grapes the fruitful land which was watered by the river and the multi-

DIODORUS OF SICILY

τῶν καρποφορούντων φυτῶν· Ἀμαλθείας δ' εἶναι κέρας οἱονεί τινος ἀμαλακιστίας, δι' ἧς τὴν εὐτονίαν τοῦ κατασκευάσαντος δηλοῦσθαι.

36. Ἡρακλῆς δὲ τοῖς Καλυδωνίοις συστρατεύσας ἐπὶ Θεσπρωτοὺς πόλιν τε Ἐφύραν κατὰ κράτος εἷλε καὶ Φυλέα τὸν βασιλέα τῶν Θεσπρωτῶν ἀπέκτεινε. λαβὼν δὲ αἰχμάλωτον τὴν θυγατέρα τοῦ Φυλέως 2 ἐπεμίγη ταύτῃ καὶ ἐτέκνωσε Τληπόλεμον. μετὰ δὲ τὸν Δηιανείρας γάμον τρισὶν ὕστερον ἔτεσι δειπνῶν παρ' Οἰνεῖ, διακονοῦντος Εὐρυνόμου τοῦ Ἀρχιτέλους υἱοῦ, παιδὸς τὴν ἡλικίαν, ἁμαρτάνοντος δ' ἐν τῷ διακονεῖν, πατάξας κονδύλῳ, καὶ βαρυτέρας τῆς πληγῆς γενομένης, ἀπέκτεινεν ἀκουσίως 3 τὸν παῖδα. περιαλγὴς δὲ γενόμενος ἐπὶ τῷ πάθει πάλιν ἐκ τῆς Καλυδῶνος ἑκουσίως ἔφυγε μετὰ τῆς γυναικὸς Δηιανείρας καὶ Ὕλλου τοῦ ἐκ ταύτης, παιδὸς ὄντος τὴν ἡλικίαν. ἐπεὶ δὲ πορευόμενος ἦλθε πρὸς τὸν Εὔηνον ποταμόν, κατέλαβε Νέσσον τὸν Κένταυρον μισθοῦ διαβιβάζοντα τὸν ποταμόν. 4 οὗτος δὲ πρώτην διαβιβάσας τὴν Δηιάνειραν, καὶ διὰ τὸ κάλλος ἐρασθείς, ἐπεχείρησε βιάσασθαι ταύτην. ἐπιβοωμένης δ' αὐτῆς τὸν ἄνδρα, ὁ μὲν Ἡρακλῆς ἐτόξευσε τὸν Κένταυρον, ὁ δὲ Νέσσος μεταξὺ μισγόμενος, καὶ διὰ τὴν ὀξύτητα τῆς πληγῆς εὐθὺς ἀποθνήσκων, ἔφησε τῇ Δηιανείρᾳ δώσειν φίλτρον, ὅπως μηδεμιᾷ τῶν ἄλλων γυναικῶν

---

[1] *i.e.* the idea of Heracles' strength is suggested both by the name Amaltheia, the first part of which is the same as that of *amalakistia* ("hardness") and by the hard thing a horn is—

tude of its fruit-bearing plants. Moreover, they say that the phrase " Amaltheia's Horn " is used as of a quality incapable of being softened (*a-malakistia*), whereby is indicated the tense vigour of the man who built the work.[1]

36. Heracles took the field with the Calydonians against the Thesprotians, captured the city of Ephyra by storm, and slew Phyleus the king of the Thesprotians. And taking prisoner the daughter of Phyleus he lay with her and begat Tlepolemus. Three years after his marriage to Deïaneira Heracles was dining in the home of Oeneus and Eurynomus, the son of Architeles, who was still a lad in years, was serving him, and when the boy made some slip in the service Heracles gave him a blow with his fist, and striking him too hard he unintentionally killed the lad. Overcome with grief at this misfortune he went again into voluntary exile from Calydonia along with his wife Deïaneira and Hyllus, his son by her, who was still a boy in years. And when in his journeying he arrived at the Euenus river he found there the Centaur Nessus who was conveying travellers across the river for a fee. Nessus carried Deïaneira across first, and becoming enamoured of her because of her beauty he tried to assault her. But when she called to her husband for help Heracles shot the Centaur with an arrow, and Nessus, struck even while he was having intercourse with her and because of the sharpness of the blow being at once on the point of death, told Deïaneira that he would give her a love-charm to the end that Heracles should never desire to approach any other

a most fanciful conception. For another explanation of the origin of the phrase " Amaltheia's Horn " cp. Book 3. 68.

5 Ἡρακλῆς θελήσῃ πλησιάσαι. παρεκελεύσατο οὖν λαβοῦσαν τὸν ἐξ αὑτοῦ πεσόντα γόνον, καὶ τούτῳ προσμίξασαν ἔλαιον καὶ τὸ ἀπὸ τῆς ἀκίδος ἀποστάζον αἷμα, χρῖσαι τὸν χιτῶνα τοῦ Ἡρακλέους. οὗτος μὲν οὖν ταύτην τὴν ὑποθήκην δοὺς τῇ Δηιανείρᾳ παραχρῆμα ἐξέπνευσεν. ἡ δὲ κατὰ τὴν γενομένην ὑπὸ τοῦ Νέσσου παραγγελίαν εἰς ἄγγος ἀναλαβοῦσα τὸν γόνον, καὶ τὴν ἀκίδα βάψασα, λάθρᾳ τοῦ Ἡρακλέους ἐφύλαττεν. ὁ δὲ διαβὰς τὸν ποταμὸν κατήντησε πρὸς Κήυκα τὸν τῆς Τραχῖνος βασιλέα, καὶ μετὰ τούτου κατῴκησεν, ἔχων τοὺς ἀεὶ συστρατεύοντας τῶν Ἀρκάδων.

37. Μετὰ δὲ ταῦτα Φύλαντος τοῦ Δρυόπων βασιλέως δόξαντος εἰς τὸ ἐν Δελφοῖς ἱερὸν παρανενομηκέναι, στρατεύσας μετὰ Μηλιέων τόν τε βασιλέα τῶν Δρυόπων ἀνεῖλε καὶ τοὺς ἄλλους ἐκ τῆς χώρας ἐξαναστήσας Μηλιεῦσι παρέδωκε τὴν χώραν· τὴν δὲ Φύλαντος θυγατέρα λαβὼν αἰχμάλωτον καὶ μιγεὶς αὐτῇ υἱὸν Ἀντίοχον ἐγέννησεν. ἐτέκνωσε δὲ καὶ ἐκ τῆς Δηιανείρας νεωτέρους τοῦ Ὕλλου 2 υἱοὺς δύο, Γληνέα καὶ Ὀδίτην. τῶν δ᾽ ἐκπεσόντων Δρυόπων οἱ μὲν εἰς τὴν Εὔβοιαν καταντήσαντες ἔκτισαν πόλιν Κάρυστον, οἱ δ᾽ εἰς Κύπρον τὴν νῆσον πλεύσαντες καὶ τοῖς ἐγχωρίοις ἀναμιχθέντες ἐνταῦθα κατῴκησαν, οἱ δὲ λοιποὶ τῶν Δρυόπων καταφυγόντες ἐπὶ τὸν Εὐρυσθέα βοηθείας ἔτυχον διὰ τὴν ἔχθραν τὴν πρὸς Ἡρακλέα·

---

[1] This differs slightly from the account in Sophocles, *Women of Trachis*, 572 ff., where Nessus enjoins upon Deïaneira: "If thou gatheredst with thy hands the blood clotted round my wound, at the place where the Hydra, Lerna's monstrous growth, hath tinged the arrow with black

BOOK IV. 36. 4-37. 2

woman. He urged her, accordingly, to take the seed which had fallen from him and, mixing it with olive oil and the blood which was dripping from the barb of the arrow, to anoint with this the shirt of Heracles.[1] This counsel, then, Nessus gave Deïaneira and at once breathed his last. And she put the seed, as Nessus had enjoined upon her, into a jar and dipped in it the barb of the arrow and kept it all unknown to Heracles. And he, after crossing the river, came to Ceÿx, the king of Trachis, and made his dwelling with him, having with him the Arcadians who always accompanied him on his campaigns.

37. After this, when Phylas, the king of the Dryopes, had in the eyes of men committed an act of impiety against the temple of Delphi, Heracles took the field against him in company with the inhabitants of Melis, slew the king of the Dryopes, drove the rest of them out of the land, and gave it to the people of Melis; and the daughter of Phylas he took captive and lying with her begat a son Antiochus. By Deïaneira he became the father of two sons, younger than Hyllus, Gleneus and Hodites. Of the Dryopes who had been driven from their land some passed over into Euboea and founded there the city Carystus, others sailed to the island of Cyprus, where they mixed with the natives of the island and made their home, while the rest of the Dryopes took refuge with Eurystheus and won his aid because of the enmity which he bore to Heracles;

gall—this shall be to thee a charm for the soul of Heracles, so that he shall never look upon any woman to love her more than thee" (tr. of Jebb). And the incident takes place while Heracles is taking Deïaneira home as his bride.

τούτου γὰρ αὐτοῖς συνεργοῦντος τρεῖς πόλεις ᾤκισαν ἐν Πελοποννήσῳ, Ἀσίνην καὶ Ἑρμιόνην, ἔτι δ' Ἠιόνα.

3 Μετὰ δὲ τὴν Δρυόπων ἀνάστασιν, πολέμου συνεστῶτος τοῖς Δωριεῦσι τοῖς τὴν Ἑστιαιῶτιν καλουμένην οἰκοῦσιν, ὧν ἐβασίλευεν Αἰγίμιος, καὶ τοῖς Λαπίθαις τοῖς περὶ τὸν Ὄλυμπον ἱδρυμένοις, ὧν ἐδυνάστευε Κόρωνος ὁ Καινέως, ὑπερεχόντων δὲ τῶν Λαπιθῶν πολὺ ταῖς δυνάμεσιν, οἱ Δωριεῖς κατέφυγον ἐπὶ τὸν Ἡρακλέα, καὶ σύμμαχον αὐτὸν ἐκάλεσαν ἐπὶ τρίτῳ μέρει τῆς Δωρίδος χώρας καὶ τῆς βασιλείας· πείσαντες δὲ κοινῇ τὴν ἐπὶ τοὺς Λαπίθας στρατείαν ἐποιήσαντο. ὁ δ' Ἡρακλῆς ἔχων ἀεὶ τοὺς μεθ' ἑαυτοῦ στρατεύσαντας Ἀρκάδας, καὶ μετὰ τούτων χειρωσάμενος τοὺς Λαπίθας, αὐτόν τε τὸν βασιλέα Κόρωνον ἀνεῖλε καὶ τῶν ἄλλων τοὺς πλείστους κατακόψας ἠνάγκασεν ἐκχωρῆσαι τῆς ἀμφισβητησίμου χώρας.

4 τούτων δὲ πραχθέντων, Αἰγιμίῳ μὲν τὸ ἐπιβάλλον τῆς χώρας τρίτον μέρος παρέθετο καὶ παρεκελεύσατο φυλάττειν τοῖς ἀπ' αὐτοῦ· ἐπανιὼν δ' εἰς Τραχῖνα, καὶ προκληθεὶς ὑπὸ Κύκνου τοῦ Ἄρεος, τοῦτον μὲν ἀπέκτεινεν, ἐκ δὲ τῆς Ἰτώνου πορευόμενος καὶ διὰ τῆς Πελασγιώτιδος γῆς βαδίζων Ὀρμενίῳ τῷ βασιλεῖ συνέμιξεν, οὗ τὴν θυγατέρα ἐμνήστευεν Ἀστυδάμειαν· οὐ προσέχοντος δ' αὐτοῦ διὰ τὸ ἔχειν αὐτὸν γαμετὴν Δηιάνειραν τὴν Οἰνέως, στρατεύσας ἐπ' αὐτὸν τήν τε πόλιν εἷλε καὶ τὸν ἀπειθοῦντα βασιλέα ἀπέκτεινε, τὴν δ' Ἀστυδάμειαν αἰχμάλωτον λαβών, καὶ μιγεὶς
5 αὐτῇ, Κτήσιππον υἱὸν ἐγέννησε. ταῦτα δὲ δια-

and with the aid of Eurystheus they founded three cities in Peloponnesus, Asinê, Hermionê, and Eïon.

After the removal of the Dryopes from their land a war arose between the Dorieis who inhabit the land called Hestiaeotis, whose king was Aegimius, and the Lapithae dwelling about Mount Olympus, whose king was Coronus, the son of Caeneus. And since the Lapithae greatly excelled in the number of their forces, the Dorieis turned to Heracles for aid and implored him to join with them, promising him a third part of the land of Doris and of the kingship, and when they had won him over they made common cause in the campaign against the Lapithae. Heracles had with him the Arcadians who accompanied him on his campaigns, and mastering the Lapithae with their aid he slew king Coronus himself, and massacring most of the rest he compelled them to withdraw from the land which was in dispute. After accomplishing these deeds he entrusted to Aegimius the third part of the land, which was his share, with orders that he keep it in trust in favour of Heracles' descendants. He now returned to Trachis, and upon being challenged to combat by Cycnus, the son of Ares, he slew the man; and as he was leaving the territory of Itonus and was making his way through Pelasgiotis he fell in with Ormenius the king and asked of him the hand of his daughter Astydameia. When Ormenius refused him because he already had for lawful wife Deïaneira, the daughter of Oeneus, Heracles took the field against him, captured his city, and slew the king who would not obey him, and taking captive Astydameia he lay with her and begat a son Ctesippus. After finishing this exploit he set out to

πραξάμενος ἐστράτευσεν εἰς τὴν Οἰχαλίαν ἐπὶ τοὺς Εὐρύτου παῖδας, ὅτι τὴν Ἰόλην μνηστεύσας ἀπέτυχε· συναγωνιζομένων δ' αὐτῷ τῶν Ἀρκάδων, τήν τε πόλιν εἷλε καὶ τοὺς Εὐρύτου παῖδας ἀπέκτεινε, Τοξέα καὶ Μολίονα καὶ Κλυτίον.[1] λαβὼν δὲ καὶ τὴν Ἰόλην αἰχμάλωτον ἀπῆλθε τῆς Εὐβοίας ἐπὶ τὸ ἀκρωτήριον τὸ καλούμενον Κηναῖον.

38. Ἐνταῦθα δὲ θυσίαν ἐπιτελῶν ἀπέστειλε Λίχαν τὸν ὑπηρέτην εἰς Τραχῖνα πρὸς τὴν γυναῖκα Δηιάνειραν· τούτῳ δὲ προστεταγμένον ἦν αἰτῆσαι χιτῶνα καὶ ἱμάτιον, οἷς εἰώθει χρῆσθαι πρὸς τὰς θυσίας. ἡ δὲ Δηιάνειρα πυθομένη τοῦ Λίχα τὴν πρὸς Ἰόλην φιλοστοργίαν καὶ βουλομένη πλέον ἑαυτὴν ἀγαπᾶσθαι, τὸν χιτῶνα ἔχρισε τῷ παρὰ τοῦ Κενταύρου δεδομένῳ πρὸς ἀπώλειαν φίλτρῳ. 2 ὁ μὲν οὖν Λίχας ἀγνοῶν περὶ τούτων ἀπήνεγκε τὴν ἐσθῆτα πρὸς τὴν θυσίαν· ὁ δ' Ἡρακλῆς ἐνδὺς τὸν κεχριμένον χιτῶνα, καὶ κατ' ὀλίγον τῆς τοῦ σηπτικοῦ φαρμάκου δυνάμεως ἐνεργούσης, περιέπεσε συμφορᾷ τῇ μεγίστῃ. τῆς γὰρ ἀκίδος τὸν ἐκ τῆς ἐχίδνης ἰὸν ἀνειληφυίας, καὶ διὰ τοῦτο τοῦ χιτῶνος διὰ τὴν θερμασίαν τὴν σάρκα τοῦ σώματος λυμαινομένου, περιαλγὴς γενόμενος ὁ Ἡρακλῆς τὸν μὲν διακονήσαντα Λίχαν ἀπέκτεινε, τὸ δὲ στρατόπεδον ἀπολύσας ἐπανῆλθεν εἰς τὴν Τραχῖνα. 3 Ἀεὶ δὲ μᾶλλον τῇ νόσῳ βαρυνόμενος αὐτὸς μὲν ἀπέστειλεν εἰς Δελφοὺς Λικύμνιον καὶ Ἰόλαον ἐπερωτήσοντας τὸν Ἀπόλλωνα τί χρὴ περὶ τῆς νόσου πράττειν, Δηιάνειρα δὲ τὸ μέγεθος τῆς Ἡρακλέους συμφορᾶς καταπεπληγμένη, καὶ συν-

---

[1] So Burmann: Τύτιον Π, Αἰγύπτιον D.

BOOK IV. 37. 5–38. 3

Oechalia to take the field against the sons of Eurytus because he had been refused in his suit for the hand of Iolê. The Arcadians again fought on his side and he captured the city and slew the sons of Eurytus, who were Toxeus, Molion, and Clytius. And taking Iolê captive he departed from Euboea to the promontory which is called Cenaeum.

38. At Cenaeon Heracles, wishing to perform a sacrifice, dispatched his attendant Lichas to Deïaneira his wife, commanding him to ask her for the shirt and robe which he customarily wore in the celebration of sacrifices. But when Deïaneira learned from Lichas of the love which Heracles had for Iolê, she wished him to have a greater affection for herself and so anointed the shirt with the love-charm which had been given her by the Centaur, whose intention was to bring about the death of Heracles. Lichas, then, in ignorance of these matters, brought back the garments for the sacrifice; and Heracles put on the shirt which had been anointed, and as the strength of the toxic drug began slowly to work he met with the most terrible calamity. For the arrow's barb had carried the poison of the adder,[1] and when the shirt for this reason, as it became heated, attacked the flesh of the body, Heracles was seized with such anguish that he slew Lichas, who had been his servant, and then, disbanding his army, returned to Trachis.

As Heracles continued to suffer more and more from his malady he dispatched Licymnius and Iolaüs to Delphi to inquire of Apollo what he must do to heal the malady, but Deïaneira was so stricken by the magnitude of Heracles' misfortune that, being

[1] *i.e.* of the Lernaean Hydra; cp. chap. 11. 5.

εἰδυῖα ἑαυτῇ τὴν ἁμαρτίαν, ἀγχόνῃ τὸν βίον κατέστρεψεν. ὁ δὲ θεὸς ἔχρησε κομισθῆναι τὸν Ἡρακλέα μετὰ τῆς πολεμικῆς διασκευῆς εἰς τὴν Οἴτην, κατασκευάσαι δὲ πλησίον αὐτοῦ πυρὰν εὐμεγέθη·
4 περὶ δὲ τῶν λοιπῶν ἔφησε Διὶ μελήσειν. τῶν δὲ περὶ τὸν Ἰόλαον ποιησάντων τὰ προστεταγμένα καὶ ἐκ διαστήματος ἀποθεωρούντων τὸ ἀποβησόμενον, ὁ μὲν Ἡρακλῆς ἀπογνοὺς τὰ καθ' ἑαυτόν, καὶ παρελθὼν εἰς τὴν πυράν, παρεκάλει τὸν ἀεὶ προσιόντα ὑφάψαι τὴν πυράν. οὐδενὸς δὲ τολμῶντος ὑπακοῦσαι μόνος Φιλοκτήτης ἐπείσθη· λαβὼν δὲ τῆς ὑπουργίας χάριν τὴν τῶν τόξων δωρεὰν ἧψε τὴν πυράν. εὐθὺς δὲ καὶ κεραυνῶν ἐκ τοῦ περιέχοντος πεσόντων, ἡ πυρὰ πᾶσα κατεφλέχθη.
5 μετὰ δὲ ταῦτα οἱ μὲν περὶ τὸν Ἰόλαον ἐλθόντες ἐπὶ τὴν ὀστολογίαν, καὶ μηδὲν ὅλως ὀστοῦν εὑρόντες, ὑπέλαβον τὸν Ἡρακλέα τοῖς χρησμοῖς ἀκολούθως ἐξ ἀνθρώπων εἰς θεοὺς μεθεστάσθαι.

39. Διόπερ ὡς ἥρωι ποιήσαντες ἁγισμοὺς καὶ χώματα κατασκευάσαντες ἀπηλλάγησαν εἰς Τραχῖνα. μετὰ δὲ τούτους Μενοίτιος ὁ Ἄκτορος υἱός, φίλος ὢν Ἡρακλεῖ, κάπρον καὶ ταῦρον καὶ κριὸν θύσας ὡς ἥρωι κατέδειξε κατ' ἐνιαυτὸν ἐν Ὀποῦντι θύειν καὶ τιμᾶν ὡς ἥρωα τὸν Ἡρακλέα. τὸ παραπλήσιον δὲ καὶ τῶν Θηβαίων ποιησάντων, Ἀθηναῖοι πρῶτοι τῶν ἄλλων ὡς θεὸν ἐτίμησαν θυσίαις τὸν Ἡρακλέα, καὶ τοῖς ἄλλοις ἀνθρώποις παράδειγμα τὴν ἑαυτῶν εἰς τὸν θεὸν εὐσέβειαν ἀποδείξαντες προετρέψαντο τὸ μὲν πρῶτον ἅπαντας

conscious of her error, she ended her life by hanging herself. The god gave the reply that Heracles should be taken, and with him his armour and weapons of war, unto Oetê and that they should build a huge pyre near him; what remained to be done, he said, would rest with Zeus. Now when Iolaüs had carried out these orders and had withdrawn to a distance to see what would take place, Heracles, having abandoned hope for himself, ascended the pyre and asked each one who came up to him to put torch to the pyre. And when no one had the courage to obey him Philoctetes alone was prevailed upon; and he, having received in return for his compliance the gift of the bow and arrows of Heracles, lighted the pyre. And immediately lightning also fell from the heavens and the pyre was wholly consumed. After this, when the companions of Iolaüs came to gather up the bones of Heracles and found not a single bone anywhere, they assumed that, in accordance with the words of the oracle, he had passed from among men into the company of the gods.

39. These men, therefore, performed the offerings to the dead as to a hero, and after throwing up a great mound of earth returned to Trachis. Following their example Menoetius, the son of Actor and a friend of Heracles, sacrificed a boar and a bull and a ram to him as to a hero and commanded that each year in Opus Heracles should receive the sacrifices and honours of a hero. Much the same thing was likewise done by the Thebans, but the Athenians were the first of all other men to honour Heracles with sacrifices like as to a god, and by holding up as an example for all other men to follow their own

Ἕλληνας, μετὰ δὲ ταῦτα καὶ τοὺς κατὰ τὴν οἰκουμένην ἀνθρώπους ἅπαντας ὡς θεὸν τιμᾶν τὸν Ἡρακλέα.

2 Προσθετέον δ' ἡμῖν τοῖς εἰρημένοις ὅτι μετὰ τὴν ἀποθέωσιν αὐτοῦ Ζεὺς Ἥραν μὲν ἔπεισεν υἱοποιήσασθαι τὸν Ἡρακλέα καὶ τὸ λοιπὸν εἰς τὸν ἅπαντα χρόνον μητρὸς εὔνοιαν παρέχεσθαι, τὴν δὲ τέκνωσιν γενέσθαι φασὶ τοιαύτην· τὴν Ἥραν ἀναβᾶσαν ἐπὶ κλίνην καὶ τὸν Ἡρακλέα προσλαβομένην πρὸς τὸ σῶμα διὰ τῶν ἐνδυμάτων ἀφεῖναι πρὸς τὴν γῆν, μιμουμένην τὴν ἀληθινὴν γένεσιν· ὅπερ μέχρι τοῦ νῦν ποιεῖν τοὺς βαρβάρους 3 ὅταν θετὸν υἱὸν ποιεῖσθαι βούλωνται. τὴν δ' Ἥραν μετὰ τὴν τέκνωσιν μυθολογοῦσι συνοικίσαι τὴν Ἥβην τῷ Ἡρακλεῖ, περὶ ἧς καὶ τὸν ποιητὴν τεθεικέναι κατὰ τὴν Νεκυίαν

εἴδωλον, αὐτὸς δὲ μετ' ἀθανάτοισι θεοῖσι
τέρπεται ἐν θαλίαις καὶ ἔχει καλλίσφυρον Ἥβην.

4 τὸν δ' οὖν Ἡρακλέα λέγουσι καταλεγόμενον ὑπὸ τοῦ Διὸς εἰς τοὺς δώδεκα θεοὺς μὴ προσδέξασθαι τὴν τιμὴν ταύτην· ἀδύνατον γὰρ ἦν τοῦτον καταλεχθῆναι μὴ πρότερον ἑνὸς τῶν δώδεκα θεῶν ἐκβληθέντος· ἄτοπον οὖν εἶναι προσδέξασθαι τιμὴν ἑτέρῳ θεῷ φέρουσαν ἀτιμίαν.

Περὶ μὲν οὖν Ἡρακλέους εἰ καὶ πεπλεονάκαμεν, ἀλλ' οὖν οὐδὲν τῶν μυθολογουμένων περὶ αὐτοῦ παραλελοίπαμεν.

40. Περὶ δὲ τῶν Ἀργοναυτῶν, ἐπειδὴ τούτοις

reverence for the god they induced the Greeks first of all, and after them all men throughout the inhabited world, to honour Heracles as a god.

We should add to what has been said about Heracles, that after his apotheosis Zeus persuaded Hera to adopt him as her son and henceforth for all time to cherish him with a mother's love, and this adoption, they say, took place in the following manner. Hera lay upon a bed, and drawing Heracles close to her body then let him fall through her garments to the ground, imitating in this way the actual birth; and this ceremony is observed to this day by the barbarians whenever they wish to adopt a son. Hera, the myths relate, after she had adopted Heracles in this fashion, joined him in marriage to Hebê, regarding whom the poet speaks in the "Necyïa"[1]:

> I saw the shade of Heracles, but for
> Himself he takes delight of feasts among
> Th' immortal gods and for his wife he hath
> The shapely-ankled Hebê.

They report of Heracles further that Zeus enrolled him among the twelve gods but that he would not accept this honour; for it was impossible for him thus to be enrolled unless one of the twelve gods were first cast out; hence in his eyes it would be monstrous for him to accept an honour which involved depriving another god of his honour.

Now on the subject of Heracles if we have dwelt over-long, we have at least omitted nothing from the myths which are related concerning him.

40. As for the Argonauts, since Heracles joined

[1] *Odyssey* 11. 602-3.

DIODORUS OF SICILY

Ἡρακλῆς συνεστράτευσεν, οἰκεῖον ἂν εἴη διελθεῖν περὶ αὐτῶν.

Ἰάσονα γενέσθαι λέγουσιν υἱὸν μὲν Αἴσονος, ἀδελφιδοῦν δὲ Πελίου τοῦ Θετταλῶν βασιλέως, ῥώμῃ δὲ σώματος καὶ ψυχῆς λαμπρότητι διενέγκαντα τῶν ἡλικιωτῶν ἐπιθυμῆσαί τι πρᾶξαι 2 μνήμης ἄξιον. ὁρῶντα δὲ τῶν[1] πρὸ αὑτοῦ Περσέα καί τινας ἄλλους διὰ τὰς ὑπερορίους στρατείας καὶ τὸ παράβολον τῶν ἄθλων δόξης ἀειμνήστου τετευχότας, ζηλῶσαι τὰς προαιρέσεις αὐτῶν. διὸ καὶ τὴν ἐπιβολὴν ἀνακοινωσάμενον τῷ βασιλεῖ ταχέως λαβεῖν αὐτὸν συγκάταινον, οὐχ οὕτω τοῦ Πελίου σπεύδοντος προαγαγεῖν εἰς ἐπιφάνειαν τὸν νεανίσκον ὡς ἐλπίζοντος ἐν 3 ταῖς παραβόλοις στρατείαις διαφθαρήσεσθαι· αὐτὸν μὲν γὰρ ἐκ φύσεως ἐστερῆσθαι παίδων ἀρρένων, τὸν δ' ἀδελφὸν εὐλαβεῖσθαι μήποτε συνεργὸν ἔχων τὸν υἱὸν ἐπίθηται τῇ βασιλείᾳ. κρύπτοντα δὲ τὴν ὑποψίαν ταύτην, καὶ τὰ πρὸς τὴν στρατείαν χρήσιμα χορηγήσειν ἐπαγγειλάμενον, παρακαλεῖν ἆθλον τελέσαι στειλάμενον τὸν πλοῦν εἰς Κόλχους ἐπὶ τὸ διαβεβοημένον τοῦ κριοῦ δέρος χρυσόμαλλον.
4 τὸν δὲ Πόντον κατ' ἐκείνους τοὺς χρόνους περιοικούμενον ὑπὸ ἐθνῶν βαρβάρων καὶ παντελῶς ἀγρίων Ἄξενον προσαγορεύεσθαι, ξενοκτονούντων 5 τῶν ἐγχωρίων τοὺς καταπλέοντας. Ἰάσονα δὲ δόξης ὀρεγόμενον καὶ τὸν ἆθλον δυσέφικτον μέν, οὐ κατὰ πᾶν δ' ἀδύνατον κρίνοντα, καὶ διὰ

---

[1] τῶν Dindorf: τόν.

---

[1] "Hostile to strangers;" cp. p. 393, n. 2.

them in their campaign, it may be appropriate to speak of them in this connection.

This is the account which is given:—Jason was the son of Aeson and the nephew through his father of Pelias, the king of the Thessalians, and excelling as he did above those of his years in strength of body and nobility of spirit he was eager to accomplish a deed worthy of memory. And since he observed that of the men of former times Perseus and certain others had gained glory which was held in everlasting remembrance from the campaigns which they had waged in foreign lands and the hazard attending the labours they had performed, he was eager to follow the examples they had set. As a consequence he revealed his undertaking to the king and quickly received his approval. It was not so much that Pelias was eager to bring distinction to the youth as that he hoped that in the hazardous expeditions he would lose his life; for he himself had been deprived by nature of any male children and was fearful that his brother, with his son to aid him, would make an attempt upon the kingdom. Hiding, however, this suspicion and promising to supply everything which would be needed for the expedition, he urged Jason to undertake an exploit by sailing to Colchis after the renowned golden-fleeced skin of the ram. The Pontus at that time was inhabited on all its shores by nations which were barbarous and altogether fierce and was called " Axenos,"[1] since the natives were in the habit of slaying the strangers who landed on its shores. Jason, who was eager for glory, recognizing that the labour was difficult of accomplishment and yet not altogether impossible, and concluding that for this

τοῦτο μᾶλλον αὐτὸν ἐπιφανέστερον ἔσεσθαι διαλαμβάνοντα, παρασκευάσασθαι τὰ πρὸς τὴν ἐπιβολήν.

41. Καὶ πρῶτον μὲν περὶ τὸ Πήλιον ναυπηγήσασθαι σκάφος, πολὺ τῷ μεγέθει καὶ τῇ λοιπῇ κατασκευῇ τὴν τότε συνήθειαν ὑπερβάλλον, διὰ τὸ σχεδίαις πλεῖν τοὺς τότε ἀνθρώπους καὶ μικροῖς παντελῶς ἀκατίοις. διὸ καὶ τῶν ἰδόντων αὐτὸ τότε καταπληττομένων, καὶ τῆς φήμης διαδοθείσης κατὰ τὴν Ἑλλάδα περί τε τοῦ ἄθλου[1] καὶ τῆς κατὰ τὴν ναυπηγίαν ἐπιβολῆς, οὐκ ὀλίγους τῶν ἐν ὑπεροχαῖς νεανίσκων ἐπιθυμῆσαι μετασχεῖν τῆς στρατείας. 2 Ἰάσονα δὲ καθελκύσαντα τὸ σκάφος καὶ κοσμήσαντα πᾶσι τοῖς ἀνήκουσι πρὸς ἔκπληξιν λαμπρῶς, ἐκλέξαι τῶν ὀρεγομένων τῆς αὐτῆς προαιρέσεως τοὺς ἐπιφανεστάτους ἀριστεῖς, ὥστε σὺν αὐτῷ τοὺς ἅπαντας εἶναι πεντήκοντα καὶ τέτταρας. τούτων δ' ὑπάρχειν ἐνδοξοτάτους Κάστορα καὶ Πολυδείκην, ἔτι δ' Ἡρακλέα καὶ Τελαμῶνα, πρὸς δὲ τούτοις Ὀρφέα καὶ τὴν Σχοινέως Ἀταλάντην, ἔτι δὲ τοὺς Θεσπίου παῖδας καὶ αὐτὸν τὸν 3 στελλόμενον τὸν πλοῦν ἐπὶ τὴν Κολχίδα. τὴν δὲ ναῦν Ἀργὼ προσαγορευθῆναι κατὰ μέν τινας τῶν μυθογράφων ἀπὸ τοῦ τὸ σκάφος ἀρχιτεκτονήσαντος Ἄργου καὶ συμπλεύσαντος ἕνεκα τοῦ θεραπεύειν ἀεὶ τὰ πονοῦντα μέρη τῆς νεώς, ὡς δ' ἔνιοι λέγουσιν ἀπὸ τῆς περὶ τὸ τάχος ὑπερβολῆς, ὡς ἂν τῶν ἀρχαίων ἀργὸν τὸ ταχὺ προσαγορευόντων. τοὺς δ' οὖν ἀριστεῖς συνελθόντας ἑλέσθαι σφῶν αὐτῶν στρατηγὸν Ἡρακλέα, προκρίναντας κατ' ἀνδρείαν.

[1] So Dindorf: πρός τε τὸ ἆθλον.

BOOK IV. 40. 5-41. 3

very reason the greater renown would attach to himself, made ready everything needed for the undertaking.

41. First of all, in the vicinity of Mount Pelion he built a ship which far surpassed in its size and in its equipment in general any vessel known in those days, since the men of that time put to sea on rafts or in very small boats. Consequently those who saw the ship at the time were greatly astonished, and when the report was noised about throughout Greece both of the exploit and of the enterprise of building the ship, no small number of the youths of prominence were eager to take part in the expedition. Jason, then, after he had launched the ship and fitted it out in brilliant fashion with everything which would astonish the mind, picked out the most renowned chieftains from those who were eager to share his plan, with the result that the whole number of those in his company amounted to fifty-four. Of these the most famous were Castor and Polydeuces, Heracles and Telamon, Orpheus and Atalantê the daughter of Schoeneus, and the sons of Thespius, and the leader himself who was setting out on the voyage to Colchis. The vessel was called Argo after Argus, as some writers of myths record, who was the master-builder of the ship and went along on the voyage in order to repair the parts of the vessel as they were strained from time to time, but, as some say, after its exceeding great swiftness, since the ancients called what is swift *argos*. Now after the chieftains had gathered together they chose Heracles to be their general, preferring him because of his courage.

DIODORUS OF SICILY

42. Ἔπειτ' ἐκ τῆς Ἰωλκοῦ τὸν ἔκπλουν ποιησαμένους, καὶ παραλλάξαντας τόν τε Ἄθω καὶ Σαμοθρᾴκην, χειμῶνι περιπεσεῖν, καὶ προσενεχθῆναι τῆς Τρῳάδος πρὸς Σίγειον. ἐνταῦθα δ' αὐτῶν τὴν ἀπόβασιν ποιησαμένων, εὑρεθῆναί φασι παρθένον δεδεμένην παρὰ τὸν αἰγιαλὸν διὰ τοιαύτας αἰτίας.
2 λέγεται τὸν Ποσειδῶνα διὰ τὴν μυθολογουμένην τῶν Τρωικῶν τειχῶν κατασκευὴν μηνίσαντα Λαομέδοντι τῷ βασιλεῖ κῆτος ἀνεῖναι ἐκ τοῦ πελάγους πρὸς τὴν χώραν· ὑπὸ δὲ τούτου τούς τε παρὰ τὸν αἰγιαλὸν διατρίβοντας καὶ τοὺς γεωργοῦντας τὴν παραθαλάττιον παραδόξως συναρπάζεσθαι· πρὸς δὲ τούτοις λοιμὸν ἐμπεσεῖν εἰς τὰ πλήθη καὶ καρπῶν παντελῆ φθοράν, ὥστε πάντας ἐκπλήτ-
3 τεσθαι τὸ μέγεθος τῆς περιστάσεως. διὸ καὶ συντρεχόντων τῶν ὄχλων εἰς ἐκκλησίαν καὶ ζητούντων ἀπαλλαγὴν τῶν ἀτυχημάτων, λέγεται τὸν βασιλέα πέμψαι πρὸς τὸν Ἀπόλλω τοὺς ἐπερωτήσοντας περὶ τῶν συμβεβηκότων. ἐκπεσόντος οὖν χρησμοῦ μῆνιν ὑπάρχειν Ποσειδῶνος, καὶ τότε ταύτην λήξειν ὅταν οἱ Τρῶες τὸ λαχὸν τῶν τέκνων ἑκουσίως παραδῶσι βορὰν τῷ κήτει, φασὶν ἁπάντων εἰς τὸν κλῆρον ἐμβαινόντων ἐπανελθεῖν εἰς Ἡσιόνην τὴν τοῦ βασιλέως θυγα-
4 τέρα. διόπερ τὸν Λαομέδοντα συναναγκασθέντα παραδοῦναι τὴν παρθένον καὶ δεσμοῖς καταλα-
5 βόμενον ἀπολιπεῖν παρὰ τὸν αἰγιαλόν. ἐνταῦθα

BOOK IV. 42. 1-5

42. After they had sailed from Iolcus, the account continues, and had gone past Athos and Samothrace, they encountered a storm and were carried to Sigeium in the Troad. When they disembarked there, it is said, they discovered a maiden bound in chains upon the shore, the reason for it being as follows. Poseidon, as the story runs, became angry with Laomedon the king of Troy in connection with the building of its walls,[1] according to the mythical story, and sent forth from the sea a monster to ravage the land. By this monster those who made their living by the seashore and the farmers who tilled the land contiguous to the sea were being surprised and carried off. Furthermore, a pestilence fell upon the people and a total destruction of their crops, so that all the inhabitants were at their wits' end because of the magnitude of what had befallen them. Consequently the common crowd gathered together into an assembly and sought for a deliverance from their misfortunes, and the king, it is said, dispatched a mission to Apollo to inquire of the god regarding what had befallen them. When the oracle, then, became known, which told that the cause was the anger of Poseidon and that only then would it cease when the Trojans should of their free will select by lot one of their children and deliver him to the monster for his food, although all the children submitted to the lot, it fell upon the king's daughter Hesionê. Consequently Laomedon was constrained by necessity to deliver the maiden and to leave her, bound in chains, upon the shore. Here

[1] Poseidon and Apollo had been compelled by Zeus to labour for Laomedon for hire, but when they had built the walls of Troy Laomedon refused to pay them.

δὲ τὸν μὲν Ἡρακλέα μετὰ τῶν Ἀργοναυτῶν τὴν
ἀπόβασιν ποιησάμενον, καὶ μαθόντα παρὰ τῆς
κόρης τὴν περιπέτειαν, ἀναρρῆξαι μὲν τοὺς περὶ
τὸ σῶμα δεσμούς, ἀναβάντα δ' εἰς τὴν πόλιν
ἐπαγγείλασθαι τῷ βασιλεῖ διαφθερεῖν τὸ κῆτος.
6 τοῦ δὲ Λαομέδοντος ἀποδεξαμένου τὸν λόγον
καὶ δωρεὰν δώσειν ἐπαγγειλαμένου τὰς ἀνικήτους
ἵππους, φασὶ τὸ μὲν κῆτος ὑφ' Ἡρακλέους ἀναιρεθῆναι, τῇ δ' Ἡσιόνῃ δοθῆναι τὴν ἐξουσίαν εἴτε
βούλοιτο μετὰ τοῦ σώσαντος ἀπελθεῖν εἴτε μετὰ
τῶν γονέων καταμένειν ἐν τῇ πατρίδι. τὴν μὲν
οὖν κόρην ἑλέσθαι τὸν μετὰ τοῦ ξένου βίον, οὐ
μόνον τὴν εὐεργεσίαν τῆς συγγενείας προκρίνασαν,
ἀλλὰ καὶ φοβουμένην μὴ πάλιν φανέντος κήτους
πρὸς τὴν ὁμοίαν ὑπὸ τῶν πολιτῶν ἐκτεθῇ τιμωρίαν.
7 τὸν δ' Ἡρακλέα δώροις καὶ τοῖς προσήκουσι
ξενίοις λαμπρῶς τιμηθέντα τὴν Ἡσιόνην καὶ τὰς
ἵππους παραθέσθαι τῷ Λαομέδοντι, συνταξάμενον μετὰ τὴν ἐκ Κόλχων ἐπάνοδον ἀπολήψεσθαι,
αὐτὸν δ' ἀναχθῆναι μετὰ τῶν Ἀργοναυτῶν κατὰ
σπουδὴν ἐπὶ τὸν προκείμενον ἆθλον.

43. Ἐπιγενομένου δὲ μεγάλου χειμῶνος, καὶ τῶν
ἀριστέων ἀπογινωσκόντων τὴν σωτηρίαν, φασὶν
Ὀρφέα, τῆς τελετῆς μόνον τῶν συμπλεόντων μετ-
εσχηκότα, ποιήσασθαι τοῖς Σαμόθραξι τὰς ὑπὲρ τῆς
2 σωτηρίας εὐχάς. εὐθὺς δὲ τοῦ πνεύματος ἐνδόν-
τος, καὶ δυοῖν ἀστέρων ἐπὶ τὰς τῶν Διοσκόρων
κεφαλὰς ἐπιπεσόντων, ἅπαντας μὲν ἐκπλαγῆναι
τὸ παράδοξον, ὑπολαβεῖν δὲ θεῶν προνοίᾳ τῶν κιν-

---

[1] i.e. the Cabeiri.   [2] i.e. Castor and Polydeuces.

Heracles, when he had disembarked with the Argonauts and learned from the girl of her sudden change of fortune, rent asunder the chains which were about her body and going up to the city made an offer to the king to slay the monster. When Laomedon accepted the proposal and promised to give him as his reward his invincible mares, Heracles, they say, did slay the monster and Hesionê was given the choice either to leave her home with her saviour or to remain in her native land with her parents. The girl, then, chose to spend her life with the stranger, not merely because she preferred the benefaction she had received to the ties of kinship, but also because she feared that a monster might again appear and she be exposed by the citizens to the same fate as that from which she had just escaped. As for Heracles, after he had been splendidly honoured with gifts and the appropriate tokens of hospitality, he left Hesionê and the mares in keeping with Laomedon, having arranged that after he had returned from Colchis, he should receive them again; he then set sail with all haste in the company of the Argonauts to accomplish the labour which lay before them.

43. But there came on a great storm and the chieftains had given up hope of being saved, when Orpheus, they say, who was the only one on shipboard who had ever been initiated in the mysteries of the deities of Samothrace,[1] offered to these deities the prayers for their salvation. And immediately the wind died down and two stars fell over the heads of the Dioscori,[2] and the whole company was amazed at the marvel which had taken place and concluded that they had been rescued from their perils by an

δύνων ἑαυτοὺς ἀπηλλάχθαι. διὸ καὶ τοῖς ἐπιγινομένοις παραδοσίμου γεγενημένης τῆς περιπετείας, ἀεὶ τοὺς χειμαζομένους τῶν πλεόντων εὐχὰς μὲν τίθεσθαι τοῖς Σαμόθραξι, τὰς δὲ τῶν ἀστέρων παρουσίας ἀναπέμπειν εἰς τὴν τῶν Διοσκόρων ἐπιφάνειαν.

3 Οὐ μὴν ἀλλὰ τότε λήξαντος τοῦ χειμῶνος ἀποβῆναι μὲν τοὺς ἀριστεῖς τῆς Θρᾴκης εἰς τὴν ὑπὸ Φινέως βασιλευομένην χώραν, περιπεσεῖν δὲ δυσὶ νεανίσκοις ἐπὶ τιμωρίᾳ διωρυγμένοις καὶ μάστιξι πληγὰς συνεχεῖς λαμβάνουσι· τούτους δ' ὑπάρχειν Φινέως υἱοὺς καὶ Κλεοπάτρας, ἥν φασιν ἐξ Ὠρειθυίας τῆς Ἐρεχθέως γεννηθῆναι καὶ Βορέου, διὰ δὲ[1] μητρυιᾶς τόλμαν καὶ διαβολὰς ψευδεῖς τυγχάνοντας ὑπὸ τοῦ πατρὸς ἀδίκως τῆς 4 προειρημένης τιμωρίας. τὸν γὰρ Φινέα γεγαμηκότα Ἰδαίαν τὴν Δαρδάνου τοῦ Σκυθῶν βασιλέως θυγατέρα, καὶ διὰ τὸν πρὸς αὐτὴν ἔρωτα πάντα χαριζόμενον, πιστεῦσαι διότι τῇ μητρυιᾷ βίαν ἐφ' ὕβρει προσήγαγον οἱ πρόγονοι, βουλόμενοι τῇ 5 μητρὶ χαρίζεσθαι. τῶν δὲ περὶ τὸν Ἡρακλέα παραδόξως ἐπιφανέντων, φασὶ τοὺς μὲν ἐν ταῖς ἀνάγκαις ὄντας ἐπικαλέσασθαι καθάπερ θεοὺς τοὺς ἀριστεῖς, καὶ τὰς αἰτίας δηλώσαντας τῆς τοῦ

---

[1] δὲ deleted by Vogel, retained by Bekker, Dindorf, Jacoby.

---

[1] The Gemini, the appearance of which was believed to have a quieting influence on the sea; thus Horace (*Odes*, l. 3. 2) prays to "Helen's brethren, stars of light," safely

BOOK IV. 43. 2–5

act of Providence of the gods. For this reason, the story of this reversal of fortune for the Argonauts has been handed down to succeeding generations, and sailors when caught in storms always direct their prayers to the deities of Samothrace and attribute the appearance of the two stars [1] to the epiphany of the Dioscori.

At that time, however, the tale continues, when the storm had abated, the chieftains landed in Thrace on the country which was ruled over by Phineus. Here they came upon two youths who by way of punishment had been shut within a burial vault where they were being subjected to continual blows of the whip; these were sons of Phineus and Cleopatra, who men said was born of Oreithyïa, the daughter of Erechtheus, and Boreas, and had unjustly been subjected to such a punishment because of the unscrupulousness and lying accusations of their mother-in-law. For Phineus had married Idaea, the daughter of Dardanus the king of the Scythians, and yielding to her every desire out of his love for her he had believed her charge that his sons by an earlier marriage had insolently offered violence to their mother-in-law out of a desire to please their mother. And when Heracles and his friends unexpectedly appeared, the youths who were suffering these tortures, they say, made supplication to the chieftains as they would to gods, and setting forth the causes of their father's unlawful

to bring to Greece the ship which bears Vergil. Cp. Macaulay, *The Lays of Ancient Rome*:

> Safe comes the ship to haven,
>   Through billows and through gales,
> If once the Great Twin Brethren
>   Sit shining on the sails.

πατρὸς παρανομίας δεῖσθαι τῶν ἀτυχημάτων αὐτοὺς ἐξελέσθαι.

44. Τὸν δὲ Φινέα πικρῶς ἀπαντήσαντα τοῖς ξένοις παραγγεῖλαι μηδὲν τῶν καθ' ἑαυτὸν πολυπραγμονεῖν· μηδένα γὰρ πατέρα λαβεῖν παρ' υἱῶν ἑκουσίως τιμωρίαν, εἰ μὴ τῷ μεγέθει τῶν ἀδικημάτων ὑπέρθοιντο τὴν φυσικὴν τῶν γονέων εἰς 2 τέκνα φιλοστοργίαν. ἐνταῦθα συμπλέοντας τοῖς περὶ τὸν Ἡρακλέα τοὺς ἐπικαλουμένους μὲν Βορεάδας, ἀδελφοὺς δ' ὄντας Κλεοπάτρας, λέγεται διὰ τὴν συγγένειαν πρώτους ὁρμῆσαι πρὸς τὴν βοήθειαν, καὶ τοὺς μὲν περικειμένους τοῖς νεανίσκοις δεσμοὺς περιρρῆξαι, τοὺς δ' ἐναντιουμένους 3 τῶν βαρβάρων ἀποκτεῖναι. ὁρμήσαντος δὲ τοῦ Φινέως πρὸς μάχην, καὶ τοῦ πλήθους τῶν Θρακῶν συνδραμόντος, φασὶ τὸν Ἡρακλέα πάντων ἄριστα διαγωνισάμενον αὐτόν τε τὸν Φινέα καὶ τῶν ἄλλων οὐκ ὀλίγους ἀνελεῖν, τὸ δὲ τελευταῖον κρατήσαντα τῶν βασιλείων τὴν μὲν Κλεοπάτραν ἐκ[1] τῆς φυλακῆς προαγαγεῖν, τοῖς δὲ Φινείδαις ἀποκαταστῆσαι τὴν πατρῴαν ἀρχήν· βουλομένων δ' αὐτῶν τὴν μητρυιὰν μετ' αἰκίας ἀποκτεῖναι, πεῖσαι τῆς μὲν τιμωρίας ταύτης ἀποστῆναι, πρὸς δὲ τὸν πατέρα πέμψαντας εἰς τὴν Σκυθίαν ἐκεῖνον παρακαλέσαι τῶν εἰς αὐτοὺς ἀνομημάτων λαβεῖν 4 κόλασιν. οὗ γενηθέντος τὸν μὲν Σκύθην τῆς θυγατρὸς καταγνῶναι θάνατον, τοὺς δ' ἐκ τῆς Κλεοπάτρας υἱοὺς ἀπενέγκασθαι παρὰ τοῖς Θραξὶ δόξαν ἐπιεικείας.

Οὐκ ἀγνοῶ δὲ διότι τινὲς τῶν μυθογράφων τυφλωθῆναί φασι τοὺς Φινείδας ὑπὸ τοῦ πατρός, καὶ

[1] ἐκ Vulgate, Bekker, Jacoby, omitted D, Dindorf, Vogel.

conduct implored that they be delivered from their unfortunate lot.

44. Phineus, however, the account continues, met the strangers with bitter words and ordered them not to busy themselves with his affairs; for no father, he said, exacts punishment of his sons of his free will, unless they have overcome, by the magnitude of their crimes, the natural love which parents bear towards their children. Thereupon the young men, who were known as Boreadae[1] and were of the company which sailed with Heracles, since they were brothers of Cleopatra, and because of their kinship with the young men, were the first, it is said, to rush to their aid, and they tore apart the chains which encircled them and slew such barbarians as offered resistance. And when Phineus hastened to join battle with them and the Thracian multitude ran together, Heracles, they say, who performed the mightiest deeds of them all, slew Phineus himself and no small number of the rest, and finally capturing the royal palace led Cleopatra forth from out the prison, and restored to the sons of Phineus their ancestral rule. But when the sons wished to put their stepmother to death under torture, Heracles presuaded them to renounce such a vengeance, and so the sons, sending her to her father in Scythia, urged that she be punished for her wicked treatment of them. And this was done; the Scythian condemned his daughter to death, and the sons of Cleopatra gained in this way among the Thracians a reputation for equitable dealing.

I am not unaware that certain writers of myths say that the sons of Phineus were blinded by their

---

[1] "Sons of Boreas."

DIODORUS OF SICILY

τὸν Φινέα τῆς ὁμοίας τυχεῖν συμφορᾶς ὑπὸ Βορέου.
5 ὁμοίως δὲ καὶ τὸν Ἡρακλέα τινὲς παραδεδώκασι πρὸς ὑδρείαν ἐξελθόντα κατὰ τὴν Ἀσίαν ὑπὸ τῶν Ἀργοναυτῶν ἐπὶ τῆς χώρας ἀπολειφθῆναι. καθόλου δὲ τοὺς παλαιοὺς μύθους οὐχ ἁπλῆν οὐδὲ συμπεφωνημένην ἱστορίαν ἔχειν συμβέβηκε· διόπερ
6 οὐ χρὴ θαυμάζειν, ἐάν τινα τῶν ἀρχαιολογουμένων μὴ συμφώνως ἅπασι τοῖς ποιηταῖς καὶ συγγραφεῦσι συγκρίνωμεν.

Οὐ μὴν ἀλλὰ καὶ τοὺς Φινείδας λέγεται τὴν βασιλείαν παραδόντας τῇ μητρὶ Κλεοπάτρᾳ συστρα-
7 τεῦσαι τοῖς ἀριστεῦσιν. ἀναχθέντας δ' αὐτοὺς ἐκ τῆς Θρᾴκης καὶ κομισθέντας εἰς τὸν Πόντον προσχεῖν[1] τῇ Ταυρικῇ, τὴν ἀγριότητα τῶν ἐγχωρίων ἀγνοοῦντας· νόμιμον γὰρ εἶναι τοῖς τὴν χώραν ταύτην οἰκοῦσι βαρβάροις θύειν Ἀρτέμιδι Ταυροπόλῳ τοὺς καταπλέοντας ξένους· παρ' οἷς φασι τὴν Ἰφιγένειαν ἐν τοῖς ὕστερον χρόνοις ἱέρειαν τῆς εἰρημένης θεοῦ κατασταθεῖσαν θύειν τοὺς ἁλισκομένους.

45. Ἐπιζητούσης δὲ τῆς ἱστορίας τὰς τῆς ξενοκτονίας αἰτίας, ἀναγκαῖον βραχέα διελθεῖν, ἄλλως τε καὶ τῆς παρεκβάσεως οἰκείας ἐσομένης ταῖς τῶν Ἀργοναυτῶν πράξεσι. φασὶ γὰρ Ἡλίου δύο γενέσθαι παῖδας, Αἰήτην τε καὶ Πέρσην· τούτων δὲ τὸν μὲν Αἰήτην βασιλεῦσαι τῆς Κολχίδος, τὸν δ' ἕτερον τῆς Ταυρικῆς, ἀμφοτέρους δὲ διενεγκεῖν
2 ὠμότητι. καὶ Πέρσου μὲν Ἑκάτην γενέσθαι θυγατέρα, τόλμῃ καὶ παρανομίᾳ προέχουσαν τοῦ

---

[1] προσσχεῖν Eichstädt, προσχεῖν (προσέχειν D^a) MSS., editors.

father and that Phineus suffered the like fate at the hands of Boreas. Likewise certain writers have passed down the account that Heracles, when he went ashore once in Asia to get water, was left behind in the country by the Argonauts. But, as a general thing, we find that the ancient myths do not give us a simple and consistent story; consequently it should occasion no surprise if we find, when we put the ancient accounts together, that in some details they are not in agreement with those given by every poet and historian.

At any rate, according to these ancient accounts, the sons of Phineus turned over the kingdom to their mother Cleopatra and joined with the chieftains in the expedition. And after they had set sail from Thrace and had entered the Pontus, they put in at the Tauric Chersonese, being ignorant of the savage ways of the native people. For it is customary among the barbarians who inhabit this land to sacrifice to Artemis Tauropolus the strangers who put in there, and it is among them, they say, that at a later time Iphigeneia became a priestess of this goddess and sacrificed to her those who were taken captive.

45. Since it is the task of history to inquire into the reasons for this slaying of strangers, we must discuss these reasons briefly, especially since the digression on this subject will be appropriate in connection with the deeds of the Argonauts. We are told, that is, that Helius had two sons, Aeëtes and Perses, Aeëtes being king of Colchis and the other king of the Tauric Chersonese, and that both of them were exceedingly cruel. And Perses had a daughter Hecatê, who surpassed her father in bold-

πατρός· φιλοκύνηγον δ' οὖσαν ἐν ταῖς ἀποτυχίαις ἀνθρώπους ἀντὶ τῶν θηρίων κατατοξεύειν. φιλότεχνον δ' εἰς φαρμάκων θανασίμων συνθέσεις γενομένην τὸ καλούμενον ἀκόνιτον ἐξευρεῖν, καὶ τῆς ἑκάστου δυνάμεως πεῖραν λαμβάνειν μίσγουσαν ταῖς διδομέναις τοῖς ξένοις τροφαῖς. ἐμπειρίαν δὲ μεγάλην ἐν τούτοις ἔχουσαν πρῶτον μὲν τὸν πατέρα φαρμάκῳ διαφθεῖραι καὶ διαδέξασθαι τὴν βασιλείαν, ἔπειτ' Ἀρτέμιδος ἱερὸν ἱδρυσαμένην καὶ τοὺς καταπλέοντας ξένους θύεσθαι τῇ θεῷ καταδεί-
3 ξασαν ἐπ' ὠμότητι διονομασθῆναι. μετὰ δὲ ταῦτα συνοικήσασαν Αἰήτῃ γεννῆσαι δύο θυγατέρας, Κίρκην τε καὶ Μήδειαν, ἔτι δ' υἱὸν Αἰγιαλέα.

Καὶ τὴν μὲν Κίρκην εἰς φαρμάκων παντοδαπῶν ἐπίνοιαν ἐκτραπεῖσαν ἐξευρεῖν ῥιζῶν παντοίας φύσεις καὶ δυνάμεις ἀπιστουμένας· οὐκ ὀλίγα μὲν γὰρ ὑπὸ τῆς μητρὸς Ἑκάτης διδαχθῆναι, πολὺ δὲ πλείω διὰ τῆς ἰδίας ἐπιμελείας ἐξευροῦσαν μηδεμίαν ὑπερβολὴν ἀπολιπεῖν ἑτέρᾳ πρὸς ἐπίνοιαν
4 φαρμακείας. δοθῆναι δ' αὐτὴν εἰς γάμον τῷ βασιλεῖ τῶν Σαρματῶν, οὓς ἔνιοι Σκύθας προσαγορεύουσι. καὶ τὸ μὲν πρῶτον τὸν ἄνδρα φαρμάκοις ἀνελεῖν, μετὰ δὲ ταῦτα τὴν βασιλείαν διαδεξαμένην πολλὰ κατὰ τῶν ἀρχομένων ὠμὰ
5 πρᾶξαι καὶ βίαια. διόπερ ἐκπεσοῦσαν τῆς βασιλείας κατὰ μέν τινας τῶν μυθογράφων φυγεῖν ἐπὶ τὸν ὠκεανόν, καὶ νῆσον ἔρημον καταλαβομένην

---

[1] According to Ovid, *Metamorphoses*, 7. 408 ff., the plant which gave aconite came from the foam which dropped from the jaws of Cerberus when Heracles brought him out of Hades.

ness and lawlessness; she was also fond of hunting, and when she had no luck she would turn her arrows upon human beings instead of the beasts. Being likewise ingenious in the mixing of deadly poisons she discovered the drug called aconite[1] and tried out the strength of each poison by mixing it in the food given to the strangers. And since she possessed great experience in such matters she first of all poisoned her father and so succeeded to the throne, and then, founding a temple of Artemis and commanding that strangers who landed there should be sacrificed to the goddess, she became known far and wide for her cruelty. After this she married Aeëtes and bore two daughters, Circê and Medea, and a son Aegialeus.

Although Circê also, it is said, devoted herself to the devising of all kinds of drugs and discovered roots of all manner of natures and potencies such as are difficult to credit, yet, notwithstanding that she was taught by her mother Hecatê about not a few drugs, she discovered by her own study a far greater number, so that she left to the other woman no superiority whatever in the matter of devising uses of drugs. She was given in marriage to the king of the Sarmatians, whom some call Scythians, and first she poisoned her husband and after that, succeeding to the throne, she committed many cruel and violent acts against her subjects. For this reason she was deposed from her throne and, according to some writers of myths, fled to the ocean, where she seized a desert island, and there established herself with

[1] For this reason the plant was reputed to grow near Heraclea on the Black Sea where the entrance to Hades was pointed out.

ἐνταῦθα μετὰ τῶν συμφυγουσῶν γυναικῶν καθιδρυθῆναι, κατὰ δέ τινας τῶν ἱστορικῶν ἐκλιποῦσαν τὸν Πόντον κατοικῆσαι τῆς Ἰταλίας ἀκρωτήριον τὸ μέχρι τοῦ νῦν ἀπ' ἐκείνης Κίρκαιον[1] ὀνομαζόμενον.

46. Τὴν δὲ Μήδειαν ἱστοροῦσι μαθεῖν παρά τε τῆς μητρὸς καὶ τῆς ἀδελφῆς ἁπάσας τὰς τῶν φαρμάκων δυνάμεις, προαιρέσει δ' ἐναντιωτάτῃ χρῆσθαι· διατελεῖν γὰρ τοὺς καταπλέοντας τῶν ξένων ἐξαιρουμένην ἐκ τῶν κινδύνων, καὶ ποτὲ μὲν παρὰ τοῦ πατρὸς αἰτεῖσθαι δεήσει καὶ χάριτι τὴν τῶν μελλόντων ἀπόλλυσθαι σωτηρίαν, ποτὲ δ' αὐτὴν ἐκ τῆς φυλακῆς ἀφιεῖσαν προνοεῖσθαι τῆς τῶν ἀτυχούντων ἀσφαλείας· τὸν γὰρ Αἰήτην τὰ μὲν διὰ τὴν ἰδίαν ὠμότητα, τὰ δ' ὑπὸ τῆς γυναικὸς Ἑκάτης πεισθέντα, προσδέξασθαι τὸ τῆς ξενοκτονίας 2 νόμιμον. ἀντιπραττούσης δὲ τῆς Μηδείας ἀεὶ μᾶλλον τῇ προαιρέσει τῶν γονέων, φασὶ τὸν Αἰήτην ὑποπτεύσαντα τὴν ἐκ τῆς θυγατρὸς ἐπιβουλὴν εἰς ἐλευθέραν αὐτὴν ἀποθέσθαι φυλακήν· τὴν δὲ Μήδειαν διαδρᾶσαν καταφυγεῖν εἴς τι 3 τέμενος Ἡλίου κείμενον παρὰ θάλατταν. καθ' ὃν δὴ χρόνον τοὺς Ἀργοναύτας ἀπὸ τῆς Ταυρικῆς κομισθέντας νυκτὸς καταπλεῦσαι τῆς Κολχίδος εἰς τὸ προειρημένον τέμενος. ἔνθα δὴ περιτυχόντας τῇ Μηδείᾳ πλανωμένῃ παρὰ τὸν αἰγιαλόν, καὶ μαθόντας παρ' αὐτῆς τὸ τῆς ξενοκτονίας νόμιμον, ἀποδέξασθαι μὲν τὴν ἡμερότητα τῆς παρθένου, δηλώσαντας δ' αὐτῇ τὴν ἑαυτῶν ἐπι-

[1] Κίρκειον Π, Jacoby.

---

[1] In early times the southern boundary of Latium.

the women who had fled with her, though according to some historians she left the Pontus and settled in Italy on a promontory which to this day bears after her the name Circaeum.[1]

46. Concerning Medea this story is related:— From her mother and sister she learned all the powers which drugs possess, but her purpose in using them was exactly the opposite. For she made a practice of rescuing from their perils the strangers who came to their shores, sometimes demanding from her father by entreaty and coaxing that the lives be spared of those who were to die, and sometimes herself releasing them from prison and then devising plans for the safety of the unfortunate men. For Aeëtes, partly because of his own natural cruelty and partly because he was under the influence of his wife Hecatê, had given his approval to the custom of slaying strangers. But since Medea as time went on opposed the purpose of her parents more and more, Aeëtes, they say, suspecting his daughter of plotting against him consigned her to free custody[2]; Medea, however, made her escape and fled for refuge to a sacred precinct of Helius on the shore of the sea. This happened at the very time when the Argonauts arrived from the Tauric Chersonese and landed by night in Colchis at this precinct. There they came upon Medea, as she wandered along the shore, and learning from her of the custom of slaying strangers they praised the maiden for her kindly spirit, and then, revealing to her their own project, they learned in turn from

[2] The *libera custodia* of the Romans, which corresponded in general to our release on bail or on parole, a citizen frequently assuming responsibility for the person of the prisoner.

βολὴν πάλιν παρ' ἐκείνης μαθεῖν τὸν ὑπάρχοντα αὐτῇ κίνδυνον ἀπὸ[1] τοῦ πατρὸς διὰ τὴν πρὸς τοὺς 4 ξένους εὐσέβειαν. κοινοῦ δὲ τοῦ συμφέροντος φανέντος, τὴν μὲν Μήδειαν ἐπαγγείλασθαι συνεργήσειν αὐτοῖς μέχρι ἂν συντελέσωσι τὸν προκείμενον ἆθλον, τὸν δ' Ἰάσονα διὰ τῶν ὅρκων δοῦναι πίστεις ὅτι γήμας αὐτὴν ἕξει σύμβιον ἅπαντα 5 τὸν τοῦ ζῆν χρόνον. μετὰ δὲ ταῦτα τοὺς Ἀργοναύτας ἀπολιπόντας φυλακὰς τῆς νεώς, νυκτὸς ὁρμῆσαι μετὰ τῆς Μηδείας ἐπὶ τὸ χρυσόμαλλον δέρος· περὶ οὗ τὰ[2] κατὰ μέρος οἰκεῖον ἂν εἴη διελθεῖν, ἵνα μηδὲν τῶν ἀνηκόντων εἰς τὴν ὑποκειμένην ἱστορίαν ἀγνοῆται.

47. Φρίξον τὸν Ἀθάμαντος μυθολογοῦσι διὰ τὰς ἀπὸ τῆς μητρυιᾶς ἐπιβουλὰς ἀναλαβόντα τὴν ἀδελφὴν Ἕλλην φυγεῖν ἐκ τῆς Ἑλλάδος. περαιουμένων δ' αὐτῶν κατά τινα θεῶν πρόνοιαν ἐκ τῆς Εὐρώπης εἰς τὴν Ἀσίαν ἐπὶ κριοῦ χρυσομάλλου, τὴν μὲν παρθένον ἀποπεσεῖν εἰς τὴν θάλατταν, ἣν ἀπ' ἐκείνης Ἑλλήσποντον ὀνομασθῆναι, τὸν δὲ Φρίξον εἰς τὸν Πόντον πορευθέντα καταχθῆναι μὲν πρὸς τὴν Κολχίδα, κατὰ δέ τι λόγιον θύσαντα τὸν κριὸν ἀναθεῖναι τὸ δέρος εἰς τὸ τοῦ Ἄρεος 2 ἱερόν. μετὰ δὲ ταῦτα βασιλεύοντος τῆς Κολχίδος Αἰήτου χρησμὸν ἐκπεσεῖν ὅτι τότε καταστρέψει τὸν βίον ὅταν ξένοι καταπλεύσαντες τὸ χρυσόμαλλον δέρος ἀπενέγκωσι. διὰ δὴ ταύτας τὰς αἰτίας καὶ διὰ[3] τὴν ἰδίαν ὠμότητα καταδεῖξαι θύειν τοὺς ξένους, ἵνα διαδοθείσης τῆς φήμης εἰς

[1] ἀπὸ Wesseling : ὑπό.
[2] τὰ Hertlein : omitted D, τὸ Vulgate.
[3] διὰ omitted by D, Vogel.

her of the danger which threatened her from her father because of the reverence which she showed to strangers. Since they now recognized that it was to their mutual advantage, Medea promised to co-operate with them until they should perform the labour which lay before them, while Jason gave her his pledge under oath that he would marry her and keep her as his life's companion so long as he lived. After this the Argonauts left guards to watch the ship and set off by night with Medea to get the golden fleece, concerning which it may be proper for us to give a detailed account, in order that nothing which belongs to the history which we have undertaken may remain unknown.

47. Phrixus, the son of Athamas, the myths relate, because of his stepmother's plots against him, took his sister Hellê and fled with her from Greece. And while they were making the passage from Europe to Asia, as a kind of Providence of the gods directed, on the back of a ram, whose fleece was of gold, the maiden fell into the sea, which was named after her Hellespont,[1] but Phrixus continued on into the Pontus and was carried to Colchis, where, as some oracle had commanded, he sacrificed the ram and hung up its fleece as a dedicatory offering in the temple of Ares. After this, while Aeëtes was king of Colchis, an oracle became known, to the effect that he was to come to the end of his life whenever strangers should land there and carry off the golden fleece. For this reason and because of his own cruelty as well, Aeëtes ordained that strangers should be offered up in sacrifice, in order that, the report of

[1] *i.e.* Sea of Hellê.

ἅπαντα τόπον περὶ τῆς Κόλχων ἀγριότητος μηδεὶς τῶν ξένων ἐπιβῆναι τολμήσῃ τῆς χώρας. περιβαλεῖν δὲ καὶ τῷ τεμένει τεῖχος καὶ φύλακας πολλοὺς ἐπιστῆσαι τῶν ἐκ τῆς Ταυρικῆς· ἀφ' ὧν καὶ τερατώδεις παρὰ τοῖς Ἕλλησι πλασθῆ-
3 ναι μύθους. διαβεβοῆσθαι γὰρ ὅτι πυρίπνοοι ταῦροι περὶ τὸ τέμενος ὑπῆρχον, δράκων δ' ἄυπνος[1] ἐτήρει τὸ δέρος, ἀπὸ μὲν τῶν Ταύρων μετενεχθείσης τῆς ὁμωνυμίας ἐπὶ τὴν τῶν βοῶν ἰσχύν, ἀπὸ δὲ τῆς κατὰ τὴν ξενοκτονίαν ὠμότητος πυρπνεῖν[2] τοὺς ταύρους μυθολογηθέντος· παραπλησίως δὲ τοῦ τηροῦντος τὸ τέμενος Δράκοντος ὀνομαζομένου, μετενηνοχέναι τοὺς ποιητὰς ἐπὶ τὸ
4 τερατῶδες καὶ καταπληκτικὸν τοῦ ζῴου. τῆς ὁμοίας δὲ μυθολογίας ἔχεσθαι καὶ τὰ περὶ τοῦ Φρίξου λεγόμενα. διαπλεῦσαι γὰρ αὐτόν φασιν οἱ μὲν ἐπὶ νεὼς προτομὴν ἐπὶ τῆς πρώρας ἐχούσης κριοῦ, καὶ τὴν Ἕλλην δυσφοροῦσαν ἐπὶ τῇ ναυτίᾳ, καὶ διὰ τοῦτ' ἐπὶ τοῦ τοίχου τῆς νεὼς ἐκκύ-
5 πτουσαν, εἰς τὴν θάλατταν προπεσεῖν. ἔνιοι δέ φασι τὸν βασιλέα τῶν Σκυθῶν, ὄντα γαμβρὸν Αἰήτου, παρὰ τοῖς Κόλχοις ἐπιδημῆσαι καθ' ὃν καιρὸν ἁλῶναι συνέβη τὸν Φρίξον μετὰ τοῦ παιδαγωγοῦ, ἐρωτικῶς δὲ σχόντα τοῦ παιδὸς λαβεῖν αὐτὸν ἐν δωρεᾷ παρ' Αἰήτου, καὶ καθάπερ υἱὸν γνήσιον ἀγαπήσαντα καταλιπεῖν αὐτῷ τὴν βασιλείαν. τὸν δὲ παιδαγωγὸν ὀνομαζόμενον Κριὸν τυθῆναι τοῖς θεοῖς, καὶ τοῦ σώματος ἐκδα-

---

[1] ἄυπνος Vogel: αὐτοῖς.   [2] So Dindorf: πῦρ πνεῖν.

the cruelty of the Colchi having been spread abroad to every part of the world, no stranger should have the courage to set foot on the land. He also threw a wall about the precinct and stationed there many guardians, these being men of the Tauric Chersonese, and it is because of these guards that the Greeks invented monstrous myths. For instance, the report was spread abroad that there were fire-breathing bulls (*tauroi*) round about the precinct and that a sleepless dragon (*drakon*) guarded the fleece, the identity of the names having led to the transfer from the men who were Taurians to the cattle because of their strength and the cruelty shown in the murder of strangers having been made into the myth of the bulls breathing fire; and similarly the name of the guardian who watched over the sacred precinct, which was Dracon, has been transferred by the poets to the monstrous and fear-inspiring beast, the dragon. Also the account of Phrixus underwent a similar working into a myth. For, as some men say, he made his voyage upon a ship which bore the head of a ram upon its bow, and Hellê, being troubled with sea-sickness, while leaning far over the side of the boat for this reason, fell into the sea. Some say, however, that the king of the Scythians, who was a son-in-law of Aeëtes, was visiting among the Colchi at the very time when, as it happened, Phrixus and his attendant were taken captive, and conceiving a passion for the boy[1] he received him from Aeëtes as a gift, loved him like a son of his own loins, and left his kingdom to him. The attendant, however, whose name was Crius (ram), was sacrificed to the gods, and when his

[1] *i.e.* Phrixus.

ρέντος προσηλωθῆναι τῷ νεῷ[1] τὸ δέρμα κατά τι[2]
6 νόμιμον. μετὰ δὲ ταῦτα Αἰήτῃ γενομένου χρησμοῦ, καθ' ὃν ἐσημαίνετο τότε[3] τελευτήσειν αὐτὸν ὅταν ξένοι καταπλεύσαντες τὸ τοῦ Κριοῦ δέρος ἀπενέγκωσι, τὸν βασιλέα φασὶ τειχίσαι τὸ τέμενος καὶ φρουρὰν ἐγκαταστῆσαι, πρὸς δὲ τούτοις χρυσῶσαι τὸ δέρος, ἵνα διὰ τὴν ἐπιφάνειαν ὑπὸ τῶν στρατιωτῶν ἐπιμελεστάτης ἀξιωθῇ φυλακῆς. ταῦτα μὲν οὖν ἐξέσται τοὺς ἀναγινώσκοντας κρίνειν πρὸς τὰς ἰδίας ἑκάστου προαιρέσεις.

48. Τὴν δὲ Μήδειαν ἱστοροῦσι καθηγήσασθαι τοῖς Ἀργοναύταις[4] πρὸς τὸ τοῦ Ἄρεος τέμενος, ἀπέχον ἑβδομήκοντα σταδίους ἀπὸ τῆς πόλεως, ἣν καλεῖσθαι μὲν Σύβαριν, ἔχειν δὲ τὰ βασίλεια τῶν Κόλχων. προσελθοῦσαν δὲ ταῖς πύλαις κεκλειμέναις νυκτὸς τῇ Ταυρικῇ διαλέκτῳ προσ-
2 φωνῆσαι τοὺς φρουρούς.[5] τῶν δὲ στρατιωτῶν ἀνοιξάντων προθύμως ὡς ἂν βασιλέως θυγατρί, φασὶ τοὺς Ἀργοναύτας εἰσπεσόντας ἐσπασμένοις τοῖς ξίφεσι πολλοὺς μὲν φονεῦσαι τῶν βαρβάρων, τοὺς δ' ἄλλους διὰ τὸ παράδοξον καταπληξαμένους ἐκβαλεῖν ἐκ τοῦ τεμένους, καὶ τὸ δέρος ἀναλαβόντας
3 πρὸς τὴν ναῦν ἐπείγεσθαι κατὰ σπουδήν. παραπλησίως δὲ τούτοις καὶ τὴν Μήδειαν ἐν τῷ τεμένει τὸν μυθολογούμενον ἄυπνον δράκοντα περιεσπειραμένον τὸ δέρος τοῖς φαρμάκοις ἀποκτεῖναι, καὶ μετὰ Ἰάσονος τὴν ἐπὶ θάλατταν κατάβασιν ποιή-
4 σασθαι. τῶν δὲ διαφυγόντων Ταύρων ἀπαγγειλάντων τῷ βασιλεῖ τὴν γενομένην ἐπίθεσιν, φασὶ τὸν

[1] νεῷ Dindorf: θεῷ.
[2] τι II, Bekker, Dindorf, Vogel, τὸ ABD, Jacoby.
[3] τότε added by Dindorf, ἐσημαίνετο ὁ θεὸς Jacoby.

BOOK IV. 47. 5–48. 4

body had been flayed the skin was nailed up on the temple, in keeping with a certain custom. And when later an oracle was delivered to Aeëtes to the effect that he was to die whenever strangers would sail to his land and carry off the skin of Crius, the king, they say, built a wall about the precinct and stationed a guard over it; furthermore, he gilded the skin in order that by reason of its brilliant appearance the soldiers should consider it worthy of the most careful guarding. As for these matters, however, it rests with my readers to judge each in accordance with his own predilections.

48. Medea, we are told, led the way for the Argonauts to the sacred precinct of Ares, which was seventy stades distant from the city which was called Sybaris and contained the palace of the rulers of the Colchi. And approaching the gates, which were kept closed at night, she addressed the guards in the Tauric speech. And when the soldiers readily opened the gates to her as being the king's daughter, the Argonauts, they say, rushing in with drawn swords slew many of the barbarians and drove the rest, who were struck with terror by the unexpected happening, out of the precinct, and then, taking with them the fleece, made for the ship with all speed. Medea likewise, assisting the Argonauts, slew with poisons the dragon which, according to the myths, never slept as it lay coiled about the fleece in the precinct, and made her way with Jason down to the sea. The Tauri who had escaped by flight reported to the king the attack which had

---

[4] τοὺς 'Αργοναύτας Jacoby.
[5] So Hertlein, Vogel, τοῖς φρουροῖς D, Dindorf, Bekker, Jacoby.

Αἰήτην μετὰ τῶν περὶ αὐτὸν στρατιωτῶν διώξαντα τοὺς Ἕλληνας καταλαβεῖν πλησίον τῆς θαλάττης· ἐξ ἐφόδου δὲ συνάψαντα μάχην ἀνελεῖν ἕνα τῶν Ἀργοναυτῶν Ἴφιτον τὸν Εὐρυσθέως ἀδελφὸν τοῦ τοὺς ἄθλους Ἡρακλεῖ προστάξαντος, ἔπειτα τοῖς ἄλλοις τῷ πλήθει τῶν συναγωνιζομένων περιχυθέντα καὶ βιαιότερον ἐγκείμενον ὑπὸ Μελεάγρου
5 φονευθῆναι. ἔνθα δὴ πεσόντος τοῦ βασιλέως καὶ τῶν Ἑλλήνων ἐπαρθέντων, τραπῆναι πρὸς φυγὴν τοὺς Κόλχους, καὶ κατὰ τὸν διωγμὸν τοὺς πλείστους αὐτῶν ἀναιρεθῆναι. γενέσθαι δὲ καὶ τῶν ἀριστέων τραυματίαν Ἰάσονα καὶ Λαέρτην, ἔτι δ' Ἀταλάντην καὶ τοὺς Θεσπιάδας προσαγορευομένους. τούτους μὲν οὖν φασιν ὑπὸ τῆς Μηδείας ἐν ὀλίγαις ἡμέραις ῥίζαις καὶ βοτάναις[1] τισὶ θεραπευθῆναι, τοὺς δ' Ἀργοναύτας ἐπισιτισαμένους ἐκπλεῦσαι, καὶ μέσον ἤδη τὸ Ποντικὸν πέλαγος ἔχοντας περιπεσεῖν χειμῶνι παντελῶς ἐπικιν-
6 δύνῳ. τοῦ δ' Ὀρφέως, καθάπερ καὶ πρότερον, εὐχὰς ποιησαμένου τοῖς Σαμόθραξι, λῆξαι μὲν τοὺς ἀνέμους, φανῆναι δὲ πλησίον τῆς νεὼς τὸν προσαγορευόμενον θαλάττιον Γλαῦκον. τοῦτον δ' ἐπὶ δύο νύκτας καὶ δύο ἡμέρας συνεχῶς τῇ νηὶ συμπλεύσαντα προειπεῖν μὲν Ἡρακλεῖ περὶ τῶν ἄθλων καὶ τῆς ἀθανασίας, τοῖς δὲ Τυνδαρίδαις, ὅτι προσαγορευθήσονται μὲν Διόσκοροι, τιμῆς δ'
7 ἰσοθέου τεύξονται παρὰ πᾶσιν ἀνθρώποις. καθόλου δ' ἐξ ὀνόματος προσφωνήσαντα πάντας τοὺς Ἀργοναύτας εἰπεῖν ὡς διὰ τὰς Ὀρφέως εὐχὰς

[1] καὶ βοτάναις deleted by Dindorf.

been made upon them, and Aeëtes, they say, took with him the soldiers who guarded his person, set out in pursuit of the Greeks, and came upon them near the sea. Joining battle on the first contact with them, he slew one of the Argonauts, Iphitus, the brother of that Eurystheus who had laid the Labours upon Heracles, but soon, when he enveloped the rest of them with the multitude of his followers and pressed too hotly into the fray, he was slain by Meleager. The moment the king fell, the Greeks took courage, and the Colchi turned in flight and the larger part of them were slain in the pursuit. There were wounded among the chieftains Jason, Laërtes, Atalantê, and the sons of Thespius, as they are called. However they were all healed in a few days, they say, by Medea by means of roots and certain herbs, and the Argonauts, after securing provisions for themselves, set out to sea, and they had already reached the middle of the Pontic sea when they ran into a storm which put them in the greatest peril. But when Orpheus, as on the former occasion,[1] offered up prayers to the deities of Samothrace, the winds ceased and there appeared near the ship Glaucus the Sea-god, as he is called. The god accompanied the ship in its voyage without ceasing for two days and nights and foretold to Heracles his Labours and immortality, and to the Tyndaridae that they should be called Dioscori ("Sons of Zeus") and receive at the hands of all mankind honour like that offered to the gods. And, in general, he addressed all the Argonauts by name and told them that because of the prayers of Orpheus he had appeared in accordance with a Providence

[1] Cp. chap. 43. 1.

θεῶν προνοίᾳ φανεὶς αὐτοῖς σημαίνει τὰ μέλλοντα γενήσεσθαι· συμβουλεύειν οὖν αὐτοῖς, ὅταν τῆς γῆς ἅψωνται, τὰς εὐχὰς ἀποδοῦναι τοῖς θεοῖς, δι' οὓς τετεύχασι δὶς ἤδη τῆς σωτηρίας.

49. Ἔπειτα τὸν μὲν Γλαῦκον δῦναι πάλιν εἰς τὸ πέλαγος, τοὺς δ' Ἀργοναύτας κατὰ στόμα τοῦ Πόντου γενομένους προσπλεῦσαι τῇ γῇ, βασιλεύοντος τότε τῆς χώρας Βύζαντος, ἀφ' οὗ καὶ τὴν 2 πόλιν τῶν Βυζαντίων ὠνομάσθαι. ἐνταῦθα δὲ βωμοὺς ἱδρυσαμένους καὶ τοῖς θεοῖς τὰς εὐχὰς ἀποδόντας καθιερῶσαι τὸν τόπον τὸν ἔτι καὶ 3 νῦν τιμώμενον ὑπὸ τῶν παραπλεόντων. μετὰ δὲ ταῦτα ἀναχθέντας, καὶ διαπλεύσαντας τήν τε Προποντίδα καὶ τὸν Ἑλλήσποντον, προσενεχθῆναι τῇ Τρῳάδι. ἐνταῦθα δ' Ἡρακλέους πέμψαντος εἰς τὴν πόλιν Ἴφικλόν τε τὸν ἀδελφὸν καὶ Τελαμῶνα τάς[1] τε ἵππους καὶ τὴν Ἡσιόνην ἀπαιτήσοντας, λέγεται τὸν Λαομέδοντα τοὺς μὲν πρεσβευτὰς εἰς φυλακὴν ἀποθέσθαι, τοῖς δ' ἄλλοις Ἀργοναύταις δι' ἐνέδρας βουλεῦσαι[2] θάνατον· καὶ τοὺς μὲν ἄλλους υἱοὺς ἔχειν τῇ πράξει συνεργούς, Πρίαμον δὲ μόνον ἐναντιοπραγοῦντα· τοῦτον γὰρ ἀποφήνασθαι δεῖν τὰ πρὸς τοὺς ξένους δίκαια τηρεῖν, καὶ τήν τε ἀδελφὴν καὶ τὰς ὡμολογημένας ἵππους 4 ἀποδιδόναι. οὐδενὸς δ' αὐτῷ προσέχοντος, φασὶν εἰς τὴν φυλακὴν δύο ξίφη παρενέγκαντα λάθρᾳ δοῦναι τοῖς περὶ τὸν Τελαμῶνα, καὶ τὴν τοῦ πατρὸς προαίρεσιν ἐξηγησάμενον αἴτιον γενέσθαι τῆς

[1] τάς Eichstädt: τούς.   [2] βουλεύσασθαι DF, Jacoby.

[1] This was on the Asiatic side and was called by Polybius (4. 39. 6) the " Holy Place, where they say Jason on his voyage

of the gods and was showing forth to them what was
destined to take place; and he counselled them,
accordingly, that so soon as they touched land they
should pay their vows to the gods through the inter-
vention of whom they had twice already been
saved.

49. After this, the account continues, Glaucus
sank back beneath the deep, and the Argonauts,
arriving at the mouth of the Pontus, put in to the
land, the king of the country being at that time
Byzas, after whom the city of Byzantium was named.
There they set up altars, and when they had paid
their vows to the gods they sanctified the place,[1]
which is even to this day held in honour by the
sailors who pass by. After this they put out to sea,
and after sailing through the Propontis and Hellespont they landed at the Troad. Here, when Heracles
dispatched to the city his brother Iphiclus and
Telamon to demand back both the mares and Hesionê,
Laomedon, it is said, threw the ambassadors into
prison and planned to lay an ambush for the other
Argonauts and encompass their death. He had the
rest of his sons as willing aids in the deed, but Priam
alone opposed it; for he declared that Laomedon
should observe justice in his dealings with the
strangers and should deliver to them both his sister
and the mares which had been promised. But when
no one paid any heed to Priam, he brought two
swords to the prison, they say, and gave them
secretly to Telamon and his companions, and by
disclosing the plan of his father he became the cause

back from Colchis first sacrificed to the twelve gods " (tr.
of Paton in the *L.C.L.*).

DIODORUS OF SICILY

5 σωτηρίας αὐτοῖς. εὐθὺς γὰρ τοὺς περὶ τὸν Τελαμῶνα φονεῦσαι μὲν τῶν φυλάκων τοὺς ἀντεχομένους, φυγόντας δ' ἐπὶ θάλατταν ἀπαγγεῖλαι τὰ κατὰ μέρος τοῖς Ἀργοναύταις. διόπερ τούτους μὲν ἑτοίμους γενομένους πρὸς μάχην ἀπαντῆσαι τοῖς ἐκ τῆς πόλεως ἐκχεομένοις μετὰ τοῦ βασιλέως.
6 γενομένης δὲ μάχης ἰσχυρᾶς, καὶ τῶν ἀριστέων διὰ τὰς ἀρετὰς ἐπικρατούντων, μυθολογοῦσι τὸν Ἡρακλέα πάντων ἄριστα διαγωνίσασθαι· τόν τε γὰρ Λαομέδοντα φονεῦσαι, καὶ τῆς πόλεως ἐξ ἐφόδου κρατήσαντα κολάσαι μὲν τοὺς μετασχόντας τῷ βασιλεῖ τῆς ἐπιβουλῆς, Πριάμῳ δὲ διὰ τὴν δικαιοσύνην παραδοῦναι τὴν βασιλείαν, καὶ φιλίαν συνθέμενον ἐκπλεῦσαι μετὰ τῶν Ἀργοναυτῶν.
7 ἔνιοι δὲ τῶν ἀρχαίων ποιητῶν παραδεδώκασιν οὐ μετὰ τῶν Ἀργοναυτῶν, ἀλλ' ἰδίᾳ στρατεύσαντα τὸν Ἡρακλέα ναυσὶν ἓξ ἕνεκα τῶν ἵππων ἑλεῖν τὴν Τροίαν· προσμαρτυρεῖν δὲ τούτοις καὶ Ὅμηρον ἐν τοῖσδε τοῖς ἔπεσιν,

ἀλλ' οἷόν τινά φασι βίην Ἡρακληείην
εἶναι, ἐμὸν πατέρα θρασυμέμνονα, θυμολέοντα,
ὅς ποτε δεῦρ' ἐλθὼν ἕνεχ' ἵππων Λαομέδοντος
ἐξ οἴης σὺν νηυσὶ καὶ ἀνδράσι παυροτέροισιν
Ἰλίου ἐξαλάπαξε πόλιν, χήρωσε δ' ἀγυιάς.

8 τοὺς δ' Ἀργοναύτας φασὶν ἐκ τῆς Τρῳάδος ἀναχθέντας εἰς Σαμοθρᾴκην κομισθῆναι, καὶ τοῖς μεγάλοις θεοῖς τὰς εὐχὰς ἀποδόντας πάλιν ἀναθεῖναι τὰς φιάλας εἰς τὸ τέμενος τὰς ἔτι καὶ νῦν διαμενούσας.

---

[1] *Iliad* 5. 638–42; quoted before, chap. 32.

of their deliverance. For immediately Telamon and his companions slew such of the guards as offered resistance, and fleeing to the sea gave the Argonauts a full account of what had happened. Accordingly, these got ready for battle and went out to meet the forces which were pouring out of the city with the king. There was a sharp battle, but their courage gave the chieftains the upper hand, and Heracles, the myths report, performed the bravest feats of them all; for he slew Laomedon, and taking the city at the first assault he punished those who were parties with the king to the plot, but to Priam, because of the spirit of justice he had shown, he gave the kingship, entered into a league of friendship with him, and then sailed away in company with the Argonauts. But certain of the ancient poets have handed down the account that Heracles took Troy, not with the aid of the Argonauts, but on a campaign of his own with six ships, in order to get the mares; and Homer also adds his witness to this version in the following lines [1]:

> Aye, what a man, they say, was Heracles
> In might, my father he, steadfast, with heart
> Of lion, who once came here to carry off
> The mares of King Laomedon, with but
> Six ships and scantier men, yet sacked he then
> The city of proud Ilium, and made
> Her streets bereft.

But the Argonauts, they say, set forth from the Troad and arrived at Samothrace, where they again paid their vows to the great gods and dedicated in the sacred precinct the bowls which are preserved there even to this day.

50. Τῆς δὲ τῶν ἀριστέων ἀνακομιδῆς ἀγνοουμένης ἔτι κατὰ τὴν Θετταλίαν, φασὶ προσπεσεῖν φήμην ὅτι πάντες οἱ μετὰ Ἰάσονος στρατεύσαντες ἐν τοῖς κατὰ τὸν Πόντον τόποις ἀπολώλασι. διόπερ τὸν Πελίαν καιρὸν ἔχειν ὑπολαμβάνοντα τοὺς ἐφέδρους τῆς βασιλείας πάντας ἄρδην ἀνελεῖν, τὸν μὲν πατέρα τὸν Ἰάσονος ἀναγκάσαι πιεῖν αἷμα ταύρου, τὸν δ' ἀδελφὸν Πρόμαχον, παῖδα τὴν ἡλικίαν 2 ὄντα, φονεῦσαι. Ἀμφινόμην δὲ τὴν μητέρα μέλλουσαν ἀναιρεῖσθαί φασιν ἔπανδρον καὶ μνήμης ἀξίαν ἐπιτελέσασθαι πρᾶξιν· καταφυγοῦσαν γὰρ ἐπὶ τὴν ἑστίαν τοῦ βασιλέως καὶ καταρασαμένην παθεῖν αὐτὸν ἄξια τῶν ἀσεβημάτων, ξίφει πατάξασαν ἑαυτῆς τὸ στῆθος ἡρωικῶς καταστρέψαι τὸν 3 βίον. τὸν δὲ Πελίαν τούτῳ τῷ τρόπῳ πᾶσαν τὴν Ἰάσονος συγγένειαν ἄρδην ἀνελόντα ταχὺ τὴν προσήκουσαν τοῖς ἀσεβήμασι κομίσασθαι τιμωρίαν. τὸν γὰρ Ἰάσονα καταπλεύσαντα νυκτὸς τῆς Θετταλίας εἰς ὅρμον οὐ μακρὰν μὲν τῆς Ἰωλκοῦ κείμενον, ἀθεώρητον δὲ τοῖς ἐκ τῆς πόλεως, μαθεῖν παρά τινος τῶν κατὰ τὴν χώραν τὰ γενόμενα περὶ 4 τοὺς συγγενεῖς ἀτυχήματα. πάντων δὲ τῶν ἀριστέων ἑτοίμων ὄντων βοηθεῖν τῷ Ἰάσονι καὶ πάντα κίνδυνον ἀναδέχεσθαι, περὶ τῆς ἐπιθέσεως ἐμπεσεῖν αὐτοῖς ἀμφισβήτησιν· τοὺς μὲν γὰρ συμβουλεύειν παραχρῆμα βιασαμένους εἰς τὴν πόλιν ἀπροσδοκήτως ἐπιθέσθαι τῷ βασιλεῖ, τινὰς δ' ἀποφαίνεσθαι δεῖν στρατιώτας ἀπὸ τῆς ἰδίας πατρίδος ἕκαστον συλλέξαντα κοινὸν ἄρασθαι πόλεμον· ἀδύνατον γὰρ εἶναι πεντήκοντα καὶ

---

[1] Cp. chap. 40.

50. While the return of the chieftains was as yet not known in Thessaly, a rumour, they say, went the rounds there that all the companions of Jason in the expedition had perished in the region of the Pontus. Consequently Pelias, thinking that an occasion was now come to do away with all who were waiting for the throne,[1] forced the father of Jason to drink the blood of a bull,[2] and murdered his brother Promachus, who was still a mere lad in years. But Amphinomê, his mother, they say, when on the point of being slain, performed a manly deed and one worthy of mention; for fleeing to the hearth of the king she pronounced a curse against him, to the effect that he might suffer the fate which his impious deeds merited, and then, striking her own breast with a sword, she ended her life heroically. But as for Pelias, when he had utterly destroyed in this fashion all the relatives of Jason, he speedily received the punishment befitting his impious deeds. For Jason, who had sailed that night into a roadstead which lay not far from Iolcus and yet was not in sight of the dwellers in the city, learned from one of the country-folk of the misfortunes which had befallen his kinsmen. Now all the chieftains stood ready to lend Jason their aid and to face any peril on his behalf, but they fell into dispute over how they should make the attack; some, for instance, advised that they force their way at once into the city and fall upon the king while he was not expecting them, but certain others declared that each one of them should gather soldiers from his own birthplace and then raise a general war; since it was impossible,

[2] According to Aristotle, *Historia Animalium* (3. 19), the blood was supposed to coagulate and choke the drinker

τρισὶν ἀνδράσι περιγενέσθαι βασιλέως δύναμιν ἔχοντος καὶ πόλεις ἀξιολόγους. τοιαύτης δ' οὔσης ἐν αὐτοῖς ἀπορίας, λέγεται τὴν Μήδειαν ἐπαγγείλασθαι δι' ἑαυτῆς τόν τε Πελίαν ἀποκτενεῖν[1] δόλῳ καὶ τὰ βασίλεια παραδώσειν τοῖς ἀριστεῦσιν ἀκινδύνως. ἐνταῦθα πάντων θαυμασάντων τὸν λόγον καὶ τὸν τρόπον τῆς ἐπιβουλῆς μαθεῖν ζητούντων, εἰπεῖν ὅτι κομίζει μεθ' ἑαυτῆς πολλὰς καὶ παραδόξους δυνάμεις φαρμάκων εὑρημένας ὑπό τε τῆς μητρὸς Ἑκάτης καὶ τῆς ἀδελφῆς Κίρκης· καὶ ταύταις μὲν μηδέποτε χρῆσθαι πρότερον πρὸς ἀπώλειαν ἀνθρώπων, νυνὶ δὲ δι' αὐτῶν ἀμυνεῖσθαι ῥᾳδίως τοὺς ἀξίους τιμωρίας. προειποῦσαν δὲ τοῖς ἀριστεῦσι τὰ κατὰ μέρος τῆς ἐπιθέσεως, ἐκ τῶν βασιλείων αὐτοῖς ἐπαγγείλασθαι σημανεῖν[2] τῆς μὲν ἡμέρας καπνῷ, τῆς δὲ νυκτὸς πυρί, πρὸς τὴν ὑπερκειμένην τῆς θαλάττης σκοπήν.

51. Αὐτὴν δὲ κατασκευάσασαν Ἀρτέμιδος εἴδωλον κοῖλον, εἰς μὲν τοῦτο παντοδαπὰς φύσεις φαρμάκων κατακρύψαι, ἑαυτῆς δὲ τὰς μὲν τρίχας δυνάμεσί τισι χρίσασαν ποιῆσαι πολιάς, τὸ δὲ πρόσωπον καὶ τὸ σῶμα ῥυτίδων πλῆρες, ὥστε τοὺς ἰδόντας δοκεῖν εἶναί τινα παντελῶς πρεσβῦτιν· τὸ δὲ τελευταῖον ἀναλαβοῦσαν τὴν θεὸν διεσκευασμένην καταπληκτικῶς εἰς ὄχλων δεισιδαιμονίαν, εἰς τὴν πόλιν εἰσβαλεῖν ἅμ' ἡμέρᾳ. ἐνθεαζούσης δ' αὐτῆς, καὶ τοῦ πλήθους κατὰ τὰς ὁδοὺς συντρεχον-

[1] So Hertlein: ἀποκτεῖναι.

they maintained, for fifty-three men to overcome a
king who controlled an army and important cities.
While they were in this perplexity Medea, it is
said, promised to slay Pelias all alone by means of
cunning and to deliver to the chieftains the royal
palace without their running any risk. And when
they all expressed astonishment at her statement
and sought to learn what sort of a scheme she had
in mind, she said that she had brought with her
many drugs of marvellous potency which had been
discovered by her mother Hecatê and by her sister
Circê; and though before this time she had never
used them to destroy human beings, on this occasion
she would by means of them easily wreak vengeance
upon men who were deserving of punishment.
Then, after disclosing beforehand to the chieftains
the detailed plans of the attack she would make,
she promised them that she would give them a
signal from the palace during the day by means of
smoke, during the night by fire, in the direction of
the look-out which stood high above the sea.

51. Then Medea, the tale goes on, fashioning a
hollow image of Artemis secreted in it drugs of
diverse natures, and as for herself, she anointed her
hair with certain potent ointments and made it
grey, and filled her face and body so full of wrinkles
that all who looked upon her thought that she was
surely an old woman. And finally, taking with her
the statue of the goddess which had been so made
as to strike with terror the superstitious populace
and move it to fear of the gods, at daybreak she
entered the city. She acted like one inspired, and
as the multitude rushed together along the streets

---

[2] So Hertlein: σημαίνειν.

DIODORUS OF SICILY

τος, παραγγέλλειν πᾶσι δέχεσθαι τὴν θεὸν εὐσεβῶς· παρεῖναι γὰρ αὐτὴν ἐξ Ὑπερβορέων ἐπ' ἀγαθῷ
3 δαίμονι τῇ τε πόλει πάσῃ καὶ τῷ βασιλεῖ. πάντων δὲ προσκυνούντων καὶ τιμώντων τὴν θεὸν θυσίαις, καὶ τὸ σύνολον τῆς πόλεως ἁπάσης συνενθεαζούσης,[1] εἰσβαλεῖν τὴν Μήδειαν εἰς τὰ βασίλεια, καὶ τόν τε Πελίαν εἰς δεισιδαίμονα διάθεσιν ἐμβαλεῖν καὶ τὰς θυγατέρας αὐτοῦ διὰ τῆς τερατείας εἰς τοιαύτην κατάπληξιν ἀγαγεῖν ὥστε πιστεῦσαι διότι πάρεστιν ἡ θεὸς εὐδαίμονα ποιήσουσα τὸν οἶκον τοῦ βασι-
4 λέως. ἀπεφαίνετο γὰρ ἐπὶ δρακόντων ὀχουμένην τὴν Ἄρτεμιν δι' ἀέρος ὑπερπετασθῆναι πολλὰ μέρη τῆς οἰκουμένης, καὶ πρὸς καθίδρυσιν ἑαυτῆς καὶ τιμὰς αἰωνίους ἐκλελέχθαι τὸν εὐσεβέστατον ἁπάντων τῶν βασιλέων· προστεταχέναι δ' αὐτῇ καὶ τὸ γῆρας ἀφελοῦσαν[2] τὸ Πελίου διά τινων δυνάμεων νέον παντελῶς ποιῆσαι τὸ σῶμα καὶ πολλὰ ἕτερα πρὸς μακάριον καὶ θεοφιλῆ βίον δωρήσασθαι.

5 Ἐκπληττομένου δὲ τοῦ βασιλέως τὸ παράδοξον τῶν λόγων, ἐπαγγείλασθαι τὴν Μήδειαν παραχρῆμα ἐπὶ τοῦ σώματος ἑαυτῆς τὰς τούτων πίστεις παρέξεσθαι. εἰποῦσαν γὰρ μιᾷ τῶν Πελίου θυγατέρων καθαρὸν ἐνεγκεῖν ὕδωρ, καὶ τῆς παρθένου τὸ ῥηθὲν εὐθὺς ἐπὶ τέλος ἀγαγούσης, φασὶν εἰς οἰκίσκον τινὰ συγκλείσασαν ἑαυτὴν καὶ περινιψαμένην τὸ σῶμα πᾶν ἀποκλύσασθαι τὰς

[1] So Reiske: συνθεαζούσης Vulgate, omitted by D.
[2] So Stephanus: ἀφελόντα.

she summoned the whole people to receive the goddess with reverence, telling them that the goddess had come to them from the Hyperboreans to bring good luck to both the whole city and the king. And while all the inhabitants were rendering obeisance to the goddess and honouring her with sacrifices, and the whole city, in a word, was, along with Medea herself, acting like people inspired, she entered the palace, and there she threw Pelias into such a state of superstitious fear and, by her magic arts, so terrified his daughters that they believed that the goddess was actually there in person to bring prosperity to the house of the king. For she declared that Artemis, riding through the air upon a chariot drawn by dragons, had flown in the air over many parts of the inhabited earth and had chosen out the realm of the most pious king in all the world for the establishment of her own worship and for honours which should be for ever and ever; and that the goddess had commanded her not only to divest Pelias, by means of certain powers which she possessed, of his old age and make his body entirely young, but also to bestow upon him many other gifts, to the end that his life should be blessed and pleasing to the gods.

The king was filled with amazement at these astonishing proposals, but Medea, we are informed, promised him that then and there, in the case of her own body, she would furnish the proof of what she had said. Then she told one of the daughters of Pelias to bring pure water, and when the maiden at once carried out her request, she shut herself up, they say, in a small chamber and washing thoroughly her whole body she made it clean of the

τῶν φαρμάκων δυνάμεις. ἀποκατασταθεῖσαν δ' εἰς τὴν προϋπάρχουσαν διάθεσιν καὶ φανεῖσαν τῷ βασιλεῖ καταπλήξασθαι τοὺς ὁρῶντας, καὶ δόξαι τινὶ θεῶν προνοίᾳ μετηλλαχέναι τὸ γῆρας εἰς 6 παρθένου νεότητα καὶ κάλλος περίβλεπτον. ποιῆσαι δ' αὐτὴν καὶ διά τινων φαρμάκων εἴδωλα φαντασθῆναι τῶν δρακόντων, ἐφ' ὧν ἀποφαίνεσθαι τὴν θεὸν κομισθεῖσαν δι' ἀέρος ἐξ Ὑπερβορέων ἐπιξενωθῆναι τῷ Πελίᾳ. τῶν δ' ἐνεργημάτων ὑπὲρ τὴν ἀνθρωπίνην φύσιν φανέντων, καὶ τοῦ βασιλέως μεγάλης ἀποδοχῆς ἀξιοῦντος τὴν Μήδειαν καὶ τὸ σύνολον πιστεύσαντος ἀληθῆ λέγειν, φασὶν αὐτὴν κατὰ μόνας ἐντυχοῦσαν τῷ Πελίᾳ παρακαλέσαι ταῖς θυγατράσι διακελεύσασθαι συνεργεῖν καὶ πράττειν ἅπερ ἂν αὐταῖς προστάττῃ· προσήκειν γὰρ τῷ τοῦ βασιλέως σώματι μὴ δουλικαῖς χερσίν, ἀλλὰ ταῖς τῶν τέκνων θεραπευθέντα τυχεῖν τῆς 7 παρὰ θεῶν εὐεργεσίας. διόπερ τοῦ Πελίου ταῖς θυγατράσι διαρρήδην εἰπόντος πάντα πράττειν ὅσα ἂν ἡ Μήδεια προστάττῃ περὶ τὸ σῶμα τοῦ πατρός, τὰς μὲν παρθένους ἑτοίμους εἶναι[1] τὸ κελευόμενον ἐπιτελεῖν.

52. Τὴν δὲ Μήδειαν νυκτὸς ἐπιγενομένης καὶ τοῦ Πελίου πρὸς ὕπνον τραπέντος λέγειν ὡς ἀναγκαῖον ἐν λέβητι καθεψῆσαι τὸ σῶμα τοῦ Πελίου. προσάντως[2] δὲ τῶν παρθένων δεξαμένων τὸν λόγον, ἑτέραν αὐτὴν ἐπινοῆσαι πίστιν τῶν ὑπ' αὐτῆς λεγομένων· τρεφομένου γὰρ κριοῦ πολυετοῦς κατὰ τὴν οἰκίαν, ἐπαγγείλασθαι ταῖς κόραις τοῦτον πρότερον καθεψήσειν καὶ ποιήσειν ἀπ' ἀρχῆς

---

[1] εἶναι Dindorf: οὔσας MSS, Vogel.
[2] So Dindorf: προσηνῶς.

potent influences of the drugs. Being restored, then, to her former condition, and showing herself to the king, she amazed those who gazed upon her, and they thought that a kind of Providence of the gods had transformed her old age into a maiden's youth and striking beauty. Also, by means of certain drugs, Medea caused shapes of the dragons to appear, which she declared had brought the goddess through the air from the Hyperboreans to make her stay with Pelias. And since the deeds which Medea had performed appeared to be too great for mortal nature, and the king saw fit to regard her with great approval and, in a word, believed that she was telling the truth, she now, they say, in private conversation with Pelias urged him to order his daughters to co-operate with her and to do whatever she might command them; for it was fitting, she said, that the king's body should receive the favour which the gods were according to him through the hands, not of servants, but of his own children. Consequently Pelias gave explicit directions to his daughters to do everything that Medea might command them with respect to the body of their father, and the maidens were quite ready to carry out her orders.

52. Medea then, the story relates, when night had come and Pelias had fallen asleep, informed the daughters that it was required that the body of Pelias be boiled in a cauldron. But when the maidens received the proposal with hostility, she devised a second proof that what she said could be believed. For there was a ram full of years which was kept in their home, and she announced to the maidens that she would first boil it and thus make

2 ἄρνα. συγκαταθεμένων δ' αὐτῶν, μυθολογοῦσι τὴν Μήδειαν κατὰ μέλη διελοῦσαν τὸ σῶμα τοῦ κριοῦ καθεψῆσαι, καὶ διά τινων φαρμάκων παρακρουσαμένην ἐξελεῖν ἐκ τοῦ λέβητος ἀρνὸς εἴδωλον. ἐνταῦθα τῶν παρθένων καταπλαγεισῶν, καὶ πίστεις τῆς ἐπαγγελίας ἡγησαμένων ἐνδεχομένας ἔχειν, ὑπουργῆσαι τοῖς προστάγμασι. καὶ τὰς μὲν ἄλλας ἁπάσας τὸν πατέρα τυπτούσας ἀποκτεῖναι, μόνην δ' Ἄλκηστιν δι' εὐσεβείας ὑπερβολὴν ἀποσχέσθαι τοῦ γεννήσαντος.

3 Μετὰ δὲ ταῦτα τὴν Μήδειάν φασι τοῦ μὲν τὸ σῶμα κατακόπτειν ἢ καθέψειν ἀποστῆναι, προσποιησαμένην δὲ δεῖν πρότερον εὐχὰς ποιήσασθαι τῇ σελήνῃ, τὰς μὲν παρθένους ἀναβιβάσαι μετὰ λαμπάδων ἐπὶ τὸ μετεωρότατον τέγος τῶν βασιλείων, αὐτὴν δὲ τῇ Κολχίδι διαλέκτῳ κατευχήν τινα μακρὰν διερχομένην ἐγχρονίζειν, ἀναστροφὴν διδοῦσαν τοῖς μέλλουσι ποιεῖσθαι τὴν ἐπίθεσιν.

4 διὸ καὶ τοὺς Ἀργοναύτας ἀπὸ τῆς σκοπῆς καταμαθόντας τὸ πῦρ, καὶ νομίσαντας συντετελέσθαι τὴν ἀναίρεσιν τοῦ βασιλέως, ὁρμῆσαι δρόμῳ πρὸς τὴν πόλιν, παρεισελθόντας δ' ἐντὸς τοῦ τείχους ἐσπασμένοις τοῖς ξίφεσιν εἰς τὰ βασίλεια καταντῆσαι καὶ τοὺς ἐναντιουμένους τῶν φυλάκων ἀνελεῖν. τὰς δὲ τοῦ Πελίου θυγατέρας ἄρτι καταβεβηκυίας ἀπὸ τοῦ τέγους πρὸς τὴν καθέψησιν, καὶ παραδόξως ἐν τοῖς βασιλείοις ἰδούσας τόν τε Ἰάσονα καὶ τοὺς ἀριστεῖς, περιαλγεῖς ἐπὶ τῇ συμφορᾷ γενέσθαι· οὔτε γὰρ ἀμύνασθαι τὴν Μήδειαν εἶχον ἐξουσίαν οὔτε τὸ πραχθὲν αὐταῖς μύσος δι'
5 ἀπάτην διορθώσασθαι. διόπερ ταύτας μὲν ὁρμη-

it into a lamb again. When they agreed to this, we are told that Medea severed it apart limb by limb, boiled the ram's body, and then, working a deception by means of certain drugs, she drew out of the cauldron an image which looked like a lamb. Thereupon the maidens were astounded, and were so convinced that they had received all possible proofs that she could do what she was promising that they carried out her orders. All the rest of them beat their father to death, but Alcestis alone, because of her great piety, would not lay hands upon him who had begotten her.

After Pelias had been slain in this way, Medea, they say, took no part in cutting the body to pieces or in boiling it, but pretending that she must first offer prayers to the moon, she caused the maidens to ascend with lamps to the highest part of the roof of the palace, while she herself took much time repeating a long prayer in the Colchian speech, thus affording an interval to those who were to make the attack. Consequently the Argonauts, when from their look-out they made out the fire, believing that the slaying of the king had been accomplished, hastened to the city on the run, and passing inside the walls entered the palace with drawn swords and slew such guards as offered opposition. The daughters of Pelias, who had only at that moment descended from the roof to attend to the boiling of their father, when they saw to their surprise both Jason and the chieftains in the palace, were filled with dismay at what had befallen them; for it was not within their power to avenge themselves on Medea, nor could they by deceit make amends for the abominable act which they had done. Consequently the daughters, it is

σαι λέγεται στερίσκειν αὐτὰς τοῦ ζῆν, τὸν δ' Ἰάσονα κατελεήσαντα τὰ πάθη παρακατασχεῖν αὐτάς, καὶ θαρρεῖν παρακαλέσαντα δεικνύειν ὡς ἐκ κακίας μὲν οὐδὲν ἥμαρτον, ἀκουσίως δὲ δι' ἀπάτην ἠτύχησαν.

53. Καθόλου δὲ πᾶσι τοῖς συγγενέσιν ἐπαγγειλάμενον ἐπιεικῶς καὶ μεγαλοψύχως προσενεχθήσεσθαι, συναγαγεῖν εἰς ἐκκλησίαν τὰ πλήθη. ἀπολογησάμενον δὲ περὶ τῶν πεπραγμένων, καὶ διδάξαντα διότι τοὺς προαδικήσαντας ἠμύνατο, τιμωρίαν ἐλάττονα λαβὼν ὧν αὐτὸς πέπονθεν, Ἀκάστῳ μὲν τῷ Πελίου τὴν πατρῴαν βασιλείαν παραδοῦναι, τῶν δὲ τοῦ βασιλέως θυγατέρων 2 ἀξιῶσαι αὐτὸν[1] φροντίδα ποιήσασθαι. καὶ πέρας συντελέσαι τὴν ὑπόσχεσιν αὐτόν φασι μετά τινα χρόνον συνοικίσαντα πάσας τοῖς ἐπιφανεστάτοις. Ἄλκηστιν μὲν γὰρ τὴν πρεσβυτάτην ἐκδοῦναι πρὸς γάμον Ἀδμήτῳ τῷ Φέρητος Θετταλῷ, Ἀμφινόμην δὲ Ἀνδραίμονι Λεοντέως ἀδελφῷ, Εὐάδνην δὲ Κάνῃ τῷ Κεφάλου, Φωκέων τότε βασιλεύοντι. ταῦτα μὲν αὐτὸν ὕστερον πρᾶξαι, τότε δὲ μετὰ τῶν ἀριστέων εἰς Ἰσθμὸν τὸν ἐν Πελοποννήσῳ πλεύσαντα θυσίαν ἐπιτελέσαι τῷ Ποσειδῶνι καὶ καθιερῶσαι τὴν Ἀργὼ τῷ θεῷ. 3 ἀποδοχῆς δὲ μεγάλης τυγχάνοντα παρὰ τῷ βασιλεῖ τῶν Κορινθίων Κρέοντι μετασχεῖν τῆς πολιτείας καὶ τὸν λοιπὸν χρόνον ἐν τῇ Κορίνθῳ κατοικῆσαι.

[1] αὐτὸν D, Vogel, αὑτὸν II, Bekker, Dindorf.

related, were about to make an end of their lives, but Jason, taking pity upon their distress, restrained them, and exhorting them to be of good courage, showed them that it was not from evil design that they had done wrong but it was against their will and because of deception that they had suffered this misfortune.

53. Jason now, we are informed, promising all his kindred in general that he would conduct himself honourably and magnanimously, summoned the people to an assembly. And after defending himself for what he had done and explaining that he had only taken vengeance on men who had wronged him first, inflicting a less severe punishment on them than the evils he himself had suffered, he bestowed upon Acastus, the son of Pelias, the ancestral kingdom, and as for the daughters of the king, he said that he considered it right that he himself should assume the responsibility for them. And ultimately he fulfilled his promise, they say, by joining them all in marriage after a time to the most renowned men. Alcestis, for instance, the eldest he gave in marriage to Admetus of Thessaly, the son of Pheres, Amphinomê to Andraemon, the brother of Leonteus, Euadnê to Canes, who was the son of Cephalus and king at that time of the Phocians. These marriages he arranged at a later period; but at the time in question, sailing together with the chieftains to the Isthmus of Peloponnesus, he performed a sacrifice to Poseidon and also dedicated to the god the ship Argo. And since he received a great welcome at the court of Creon, the king of the Corinthians, he became a citizen of that city and spent the rest of his days in Corinth.

4 Μελλόντων δὲ τῶν Ἀργοναυτῶν εἰς τὰς πατρίδας διαχωρίζεσθαι, φασὶ τὸν Ἡρακλέα συμβουλεῦσαι τοῖς ἀριστεῦσι πρὸς τὰ παράδοξα τῆς τύχης ἀλλήλοις ὅρκους δοῦναι συμμαχήσειν, ἐάν τις βοηθείας προσδεηθῇ· ἐκλέξασθαι δὲ καὶ τῆς Ἑλλάδος τὸν ἐπιφανέστατον τόπον εἰς ἀγώνων θέσιν καὶ πανήγυριν κοινήν, καὶ καθιερῶσαι τὸν ἀγῶνα τῷ μεγίστῳ τῶν θεῶν Διὶ Ὀλυμπίῳ.
5 συνομοσάντων δὲ τῶν ἀριστέων περὶ τῆς συμμαχίας, καὶ τὴν διάταξιν τῶν ἀγώνων ἐπιτρεψάντων Ἡρακλεῖ, φασὶ τοῦτον[1] τόπον προκρῖναι πρὸς τὴν πανήγυριν τῆς τῶν Ἠλείων χώρας τὸν παρὰ τὸν Ἀλφειόν. διὸ καὶ τὴν παραποταμίαν καθιερώσαντα τῷ μεγίστῳ τῶν θεῶν, Ὀλυμπίαν ἀπ' ἐκείνου προσαγορεῦσαι. ὑποστησάμενον δ' ἱππικὸν ἀγῶνα καὶ γυμνικόν, τά τε περὶ τῶν ἄθλων διατάξαι καὶ θεωροὺς ἀποστεῖλαι τοὺς ταῖς πόλεσι
6 προεροῦντας τὴν θέαν τῶν ἀγώνων. διὰ δὲ τὴν παρὰ τοῖς Ἀργοναύταις γενομένην ἀποδοχὴν αὐτοῦ κατὰ τὴν στρατείαν οὐ μετρίως δοξασθέντος, προσγενέσθαι τὴν ἐκ τῆς Ὀλυμπικῆς πανηγύρεως δόξαν, ὥστε πάντων τῶν Ἑλλήνων ἐπιφανέστατον ὑπάρχειν καὶ παρὰ ταῖς πλείσταις πόλεσι γνωσθέντα πολλοὺς ἔχειν ἐπιθυμητὰς τῆς φιλίας, οὓς προθύμους εἶναι μετασχεῖν παντὸς
7 κινδύνου. ταχὺ δ' ἐπ' ἀνδρείᾳ καὶ στρατηγίᾳ θαυμασθέντα στρατόπεδόν τε κράτιστον συστήσασθαι καὶ πᾶσαν ἐπελθεῖν τὴν οἰκουμένην εὐερ-

---

[1] τὸν after τοῦτον deleted by Hertlein.

BOOK IV. 53. 4-7

When the Argonauts were on the point of separating and departing to their native lands, Heracles, they say, proposed to the chieftains that, in view of the unexpected turns fortune takes, they should exchange oaths among one another to fight at the side of anyone of their number who should call for aid; and that, furthermore, they should choose out the most excellent place in Greece, there to institute games and a festival for the whole race, and should dedicate the games to the greatest of the gods, Olympian Zeus. After the chieftains had taken their oath concerning the alliance and had entrusted Heracles with the management of the games, he, they say, picked the place for the festival on the bank of the Alpheius river in the land of the Eleans. Accordingly, this place beside the river he made sacred to the greatest of the gods and called it Olympia after his appellation. When he had instituted horse-races and gymnastic contests, he fixed the rules governing the events and then dispatched sacred commissioners to announce to the cities the spectacle of the games. And although Heracles had won no moderate degree of fame because of the high esteem in which he was held by the Argonauts throughout their expedition, to this was now added the glory of having founded the festival at Olympia, so that he was the most renowned man among all the Greeks and, known as he was in almost every state, there were many who sought his friendship and who were eager to share with him in every danger. And since he was an object of admiration because of his bravery and his skill as a general, he gathered a most powerful army and visited all the inhabited world, conferring

γετοῦντα τὸ γένος τῶν ἀνθρώπων· ἀνθ' ὧν τυχεῖν
αὐτὸν συμφωνουμένης ἀθανασίας. τοὺς δὲ ποιητὰς
διὰ τὴν συνήθη τερατολογίαν μυθολογῆσαι μόνον
τὸν Ἡρακλέα καὶ γυμνὸν ὅπλων τελέσαι τοὺς
τεθρυλημένους ἄθλους.

54. Ἀλλὰ περὶ μὲν τοῦ θεοῦ τούτου τὰ μυθολογούμενα πάντα διήλθομεν, νυνὶ δὲ προσθετέον ἡμῖν καὶ ὑπὲρ Ἰάσονος τὸν ὑπολειπόμενον λόγον. φασὶ γὰρ αὐτὸν ἐν Κορίνθῳ κατοικοῦντα καὶ συμβιώσαντα δεκαετῆ χρόνον Μηδείᾳ γεννῆσαι παῖδας ἐξ αὐτῆς, τοὺς μὲν πρεσβυτάτους δύο διδύμους Θετταλόν τε καὶ Ἀλκιμένην, τὸν δὲ τρίτον πολὺ
2 νεώτερον τούτων Τίσανδρον. τοῦτον μὲν οὖν τὸν χρόνον ἱστοροῦσιν ἀποδοχῆς ἀξιωθῆναι τὴν Μήδειαν ὑπὸ τοῦ ἀνδρὸς διὰ τὸ μὴ μόνον κάλλει διαφέρειν αὐτήν, ἀλλὰ καὶ σωφροσύνῃ καὶ ταῖς ἄλλαις ἀρεταῖς κεκοσμῆσθαι· μετὰ δὲ ταῦτα ἀεὶ μᾶλλον τοῦ χρόνου τὴν φυσικὴν εὐπρέπειαν ἀφαιρουμένου, λέγεται τὸν Ἰάσονα Γλαύκης ἐρασθέντα τῆς Κρέοντος θυγατρὸς μνηστεῦσαι τὴν παρθένον.
3 συγκαταθεμένου δὲ τοῦ πατρὸς καὶ τάξαντος ἡμέραν τοῖς γάμοις, τὸ μὲν πρῶτον ἐπιβαλέσθαι φασὶν αὐτὸν πείθειν τὴν Μήδειαν ἑκουσίως παραχωρῆσαι τῆς συμβιώσεως· βούλεσθαι γὰρ αὐτὴν[1] γαμεῖν οὐκ ἀποδοκιμάσαντα τὴν πρὸς αὐτὴν ὁμιλίαν, ἀλλὰ[2] τοῖς τέκνοις σπεύδοντα συγγενῆ τὸν τοῦ βασιλέως
4 οἶκον ποιῆσαι. ἀγανακτούσης δὲ τῆς γυναικὸς καὶ θεοὺς μαρτυρομένης τοὺς ἐπόπτας γενομένους τῶν ὅρκων, φασὶ τὸν Ἰάσονα καταφρονήσαντα τῶν

[1] αὐτὴν MSS, Bekker, ἀλλὴν Dindorf, αὐτὸν Vogel, deleted by Jacoby. [2] καὶ after ἀλλὰ deleted by Dindorf.

[1] i.e. Heracles.

his benefactions upon the race of men, and it was in return for these that with general approval he received the gift of immortality. But the poets, following their custom of giving a tale of wonder, have recounted the myth that Heracles, single-handed and without the aid of armed forces, performed the Labours which are on the lips of all.

54. But we have now recounted all the myths which are told about this god,[1] and at this time must add what remains to be said about Jason. The account runs like this:—Jason made his home in Corinth and living with Medea as his wife for ten years be begat children by her, the two oldest, Thessalus and Alcimenes, being twins, and the third, Tisandrus, being much younger than the other two. Now during this period, we are informed, Medea was highly approved by her husband, because she not only excelled in beauty but was adorned with modesty and every other virtue; but afterward, as time more and more diminished her natural comeliness, Jason, it is said, became enamoured of Glaucê, Creon's daughter, and sought the maiden's hand in marriage. After her father had given his consent and had set a day for the marriage, Jason, they say, at first tried to persuade Medea to withdraw from their wedlock of her free-will; for, he told her, he desired to marry the maiden, not because he felt his relations with Medea were beneath him, but because he was eager to establish a kinship between the king's house and his children.[2] But when his wife was angered and called upon the gods who had been the witnesses of their vows, they say that Jason, disdaining the vows, married the daughter

[2] The plea urged by Jason in Euripides, *Medea*, 551 ff.

DIODORUS OF SICILY

ὅρκων γῆμαι τὴν τοῦ βασιλέως θυγατέρα. τὴν δὲ
5 Μήδειαν ἐξελαυνομένην ἐκ τῆς πόλεως, καὶ
μίαν ἡμέραν παρὰ τοῦ Κρέοντος λαβοῦσαν εἰς τὴν
τῆς φυγῆς παρασκευήν, εἰς μὲν τὰ βασίλεια νυκτὸς
εἰσελθεῖν ἀλλοιώσασαν τοῖς φαρμάκοις τὴν αὑτῆς
ὄψιν, καὶ τὴν οἰκίαν ὑφάψαι, ῥίζιόν τι προσθεῖσαν,
εὑρημένον μὲν ὑπὸ Κίρκης τῆς ἀδελφῆς, δύναμιν
δ' ἔχον, ἐπὰν ἐξαφθῇ, δυσκατάσβεστον. ἄφνω δὲ
φλεγομένων τῶν βασιλείων, τὸν μὲν Ἰάσονα
ταχέως ἐκπηδῆσαι, τὴν δὲ Γλαύκην καὶ τὸν
Κρέοντα τοῦ πυρὸς περικαταλαβόντος διαφθαρῆναι.
6 τινὲς δὲ τῶν συγγραφέων φασὶ τοὺς μὲν υἱοὺς
τῆς Μηδείας δῶρα κομίσαι τῇ νύμφῃ φαρμάκοις
κεχριμένα, τὴν δὲ Γλαύκην δεξαμένην καὶ τῷ
σώματι περιθεμένην αὐτήν τε συμφορᾷ περιπεσεῖν
καὶ τὸν πατέρα βοηθοῦντα καὶ τοῦ σώματος ἁψά-
μενον τελευτῆσαι.

7 Τὴν δὲ Μήδειαν ἐπιτυχοῦσαν τοῖς πρώτοις ἐγχει-
ρήμασιν οὐκ ἀποστῆναι τῆς Ἰάσονος τιμωρίας.
ἐπὶ τοσοῦτο γὰρ προελθεῖν αὐτὴν ὀργῆς ἅμα καὶ
ζηλοτυπίας, ἔτι δ' ὠμότητος, ὥστ' ἐπεὶ διέφυγε
τὸν μετὰ τῆς νύμφης κίνδυνον, τῇ σφαγῇ τῶν
κοινῶν τέκνων ἐμβαλεῖν αὐτὸν εἰς τὰς μεγίστας
συμφοράς· πλὴν γὰρ ἑνὸς τοῦ διαφυγόντος τοὺς
ἄλλους υἱοὺς ἀποσφάξαι[1] καὶ μετὰ τῶν πιστοτάτων

---

[1] καὶ τὰ σώματα τούτων ἐν τῷ τῆς Ἥρας τεμένει θάψαι after ἀποσφάξαι deleted by Vogel, Jacoby.

---

[1] i.e. from the territory of Corinth.
[2] This is the manner of Glaucê's death in the *Medea* of Euripides. His version also differs from the account which follows, in that there are only two sons of Jason and Medea, and after slaying them Medea carries off their bodies so that

BOOK IV. 54. 4–7

of the king. Thereupon Medea was driven out of the city, and being allowed by Creon but one day to make the preparations for her exile,[1] she entered the palace by night, having altered her appearance by means of drugs, and set fire to the building by applying to it a little root which had been discovered by her sister Circê and had the property that when it was once kindled it was hard to put out. Now when the palace suddenly burst into flames, Jason quickly made his way out of it, but as for Glaucê and Creon, the fire hemmed them in on all sides and they were consumed by it. Certain historians, however, say that the sons of Medea brought to the bride gifts which had been anointed with poisons, and that when Glaucê took them and put them about her body both she herself met her end and her father, when he ran to help her and embraced her body, likewise perished.[2]

Although Medea had been successful in her first undertakings, yet she did not refrain, so we are told, from taking her revenge upon Jason. For she had come to such a state of rage and jealousy, yes, even of savageness, that, since he had escaped from the peril which threatened him at the same time as his bride, she determined, by the murder of the children of them both, to plunge him into the deepest misfortunes; for, except for the one son who made his escape from her, she slew the other sons and in company with her most faithful maids

Jason may not even give them formal burial, and that Jason does not commit suicide. The fountain of Glaucê has been found (cp. *Am. Journ. of Archaeology*, 4 (1900), 458–75; 14 (1910), 19–50), but not as yet the tomb of the children which was pointed out to Pausanias (2. 3. 6).

θεραπαινίδων ἔτι νυκτὸς μέσης φυγεῖν ἐκ τῆς Κορίνθου, καὶ διεκπεσεῖν εἰς Θήβας πρὸς Ἡρακλέα· τοῦτον γὰρ μεσίτην γεγονότα τῶν ὁμολογιῶν ἐν Κόλχοις ἐπηγγέλθαι βοηθήσειν αὐτῇ παρασπονδουμένῃ.

55. Ἐν τοσούτῳ δὲ τὸν μὲν Ἰάσονα στερηθέντα τέκνων καὶ γυναικὸς δόξαι πᾶσι δίκαια πεπονθέναι· διὸ καὶ μὴ δυνάμενον ἐνεγκεῖν τὸ μέγεθος τῆς συμφορᾶς ἐκ τοῦ ζῆν ἑαυτὸν μεταστῆσαι. τοὺς δὲ Κορινθίους ἐκπεπλῆχθαι μὲν τὴν δεινότητα τῆς περιπετείας, μάλιστα δ' ἀπορεῖν περὶ τῆς ταφῆς τῶν παίδων. διόπερ ἀποστειλάντων αὐτῶν Πυθώδε τοὺς ἐπερωτήσοντας τὸν θεὸν ὅπως χρηστέον ἐστὶ τοῖς σώμασι τῶν παίδων, προστάξαι τὴν Πυθίαν ἐν τῷ τεμένει τῆς Ἥρας αὐτοὺς 2 θάψαι καὶ τιμῶν ἡρωικῶν αὐτοὺς ἀξιοῦν. ποιησάντων δὲ τῶν Κορινθίων τὸ προσταχθέν, φασὶ Θετταλὸν μὲν τὸν διαφυγόντα τὸν ἀπὸ τῆς μητρὸς φόνον ἐν Κορίνθῳ τραφέντα μετὰ ταῦτα ἐπανελθεῖν εἰς Ἰωλκόν, οὖσαν Ἰάσονος πατρίδα· ἐν ᾗ καταλαβόντα προσφάτως Ἄκαστον τὸν Πελίου τετελευτηκότα παραλαβεῖν κατὰ γένος προσήκουσαν τὴν βασιλείαν, καὶ τοὺς ὑφ' ἑαυτὸν τεταγμένους 3 ἀφ' ἑαυτοῦ προσαγορεῦσαι Θετταλούς. οὐκ ἀγνοῶ δὲ διότι περὶ τῆς τῶν Θετταλῶν προσηγορίας οὐ ταύτην μόνην τὴν ἱστορίαν, ἀλλὰ καὶ διαφώνους

---

[1] i.e. that Jason would wed Medea and "keep her as his life's companion so long as he lived" (cp. chap. 46. 4).

fled in the dead of night from Corinth and made her way safely to Heracles in Thebes. Her reason for doing so was that Heracles had acted as a mediator in connection with the agreements [1] which had been entered into in the land of the Colchians and had promised to come to her aid if she should ever find them violated.

55. Meanwhile, they go on to say, in the opinion of everyone Jason, in losing children and wife, had suffered only what was just; consequently, being unable to endure the magnitude of the affliction, he put an end to his life.[2] The Corinthians were greatly distressed at such a terrible reversal of fortune and were especially perplexed about the burial of the children. Accordingly, they dispatched messengers to Pytho to inquire of the god what should be done with the bodies of the children, and the Pythian priestess commanded them to bury the children in the sacred precinct of Hera and to pay them the honours which are accorded to heroes. After the Corinthians had performed this command, Thessalus, they say, who had escaped being murdered by his mother, was reared as a youth in Corinth and then removed to Iolcus, which was the native land of Jason; and finding on his arrival that Acastus, the son of Pelias, had recently died, he took over the throne which belonged to him by inheritance and called the people who were subject to himself Thessalians after his own name. I am not unaware that this is not the only explanation given of the name the Thessalians bear, but the fact is that the other accounts which have been handed down to us

[2] According to Euripides (*Medea*, 1386), a beam of wood fell from the rotting Argo upon Jason and killed him.

ἑτέρας παραδεδόσθαι συμβέβηκε, περὶ ὧν ἐν οἰκειοτέροις μνησθησόμεθα καιροῖς.

4 Τὴν δ' οὖν Μήδειαν ἐν Θήβαις φασὶ καταλαβοῦσαν Ἡρακλέα μανικῷ πάθει συνεχόμενον καὶ τοὺς υἱοὺς ἀπεκταγκότα, φαρμάκοις αὐτὸν ἰάσασθαι. τοῦ δ' Εὐρυσθέως ἐπικειμένου τοῖς προστάγμασιν, ἀπογνοῦσαν τὴν κατὰ τὸ παρὸν ἐκ τούτου βοήθειαν καταφυγεῖν εἰς Ἀθήνας πρὸς Αἰγέα τὸν
5 Πανδίονος. ἐνταῦθα δ' οἱ μέν φασιν αὐτὴν Αἰγεῖ συνοικήσασαν γεννῆσαι Μῆδον τὸν ὕστερον Μηδίας βασιλεύσαντα, τινὲς δ' ἱστοροῦσιν ὑφ' Ἱππότου τοῦ Κρέοντος ἐξαιτουμένην τυχεῖν κρίσεως
6 καὶ τῶν ἐγκλημάτων ἀπολυθῆναι. μετὰ δὲ ταῦτα Θησέως ἐπανελθόντος ἐκ Τροιζῆνος εἰς τὰς Ἀθήνας, ἐγκληθεῖσαν ἐπὶ φαρμακείᾳ φυγεῖν ἐκ τῆς πόλεως· δόντος δ' Αἰγέως τοὺς παραπέμψοντας εἰς ἣν βούλοιτο χώραν, εἰς τὴν Φοινίκην
7 κομισθῆναι. ἐντεῦθεν δ' εἰς τοὺς ἄνω τόπους τῆς Ἀσίας ἀναβᾶσαν συνοικῆσαί τινι τῶν ἐπιφανῶν βασιλέων, ἐξ οὗ γεννῆσαι παῖδα Μῆδον· καὶ τὸν[1] παῖδα μετὰ τὴν τοῦ πατρὸς τελευτὴν διαδεξάμενον τὴν βασιλείαν θαυμασθῆναί τε κατὰ τὴν ἀνδρείαν καὶ τοὺς λαοὺς[2] ἀφ' ἑαυτοῦ Μήδους ὀνομάσαι.

56. Καθόλου δὲ διὰ τὴν τῶν τραγῳδῶν τερατείαν ποικίλη τις καὶ διάφορος ἱστορία περὶ Μηδείας ἐξενήνεκται, καί τινες χαρίζεσθαι βουλόμενοι τοῖς Ἀθηναίοις φασὶν αὐτὴν ἀναλαβοῦσαν τὸν

---

[1] τὸν Bekker: τὸν μέν.   [2] λαοὺς Rhodomann: ἄλλους.

[1] This is not in the extant portions of Diodorus.
[2] Cp. chap. 11.

are likewise at variance with one another, and concerning these we shall speak on a more appropriate occasion.[1]

Now as for Medea, they say, on finding upon her arrival in Thebes that Heracles was possessed of a frenzy of madness and had slain his sons,[2] she restored him to health by means of drugs. But since Eurystheus was pressing Heracles with his commands,[3] she despaired of receiving any aid from him at the moment and sought refuge in Athens with Aegeus, the son of Pandion. Here, as some say, she married Aegeus and gave birth to Medus, who was later king of Media, but certain writers give the account that, when her person was demanded by Hippotes, the son of Creon, she was granted a trial and cleared of the charges he raised against her. After this, when Theseus returned to Athens from Troezen, a charge of poisoning was brought against her and she was exiled from the city; but by the gift of Aegeus she received an escort to go with her to whatever country she might wish and she came to Phoenicia. From there she journeyed into the interior regions of Asia and married a certain king of renown, to whom she bore a son Medus; and the son, succeeding to the throne after the death of the father, was greatly admired for his courage and named the people Medes after himself.

56. Speaking generally, it is because of the desire of the tragic poets for the marvellous that so varied and inconsistent an account of Medea has been given out; and some indeed, in their desire to win favour with the Athenians, say that she took that

[3] *i.e.* with the Labours which Heracles had to perform for him.

ἐξ Αἰγέως Μῆδον εἰς Κόλχους διασωθῆναι· κατὰ δὲ τοῦτον τὸν χρόνον Αἰήτην ἐκ τῆς βασιλείας ὑπὸ τἀδελφοῦ Πέρσου βιαίως ἐκπεπτωκότα τὴν ἀρχὴν ἀνακτήσασθαι, Μήδου τοῦ Μηδείας ἀνελόντος τὸν Πέρσην· μετὰ δὲ ταῦτα δυνάμεως ἐγκρατῆ γενόμενον τὸν Μῆδον πολλὴν ἐπελθεῖν τῆς ὑπὲρ τὸν Πόντον Ἀσίας, καὶ κατασχεῖν τὴν ἀπ' ἐκείνου
2 Μηδίαν προσαγορευθεῖσαν. ἀλλὰ γὰρ τὸ πάσας τὰς ἀποφάσεις τῶν περὶ τῆς Μηδείας μυθολογησάντων ἀναγράφειν οὐκ ἀναγκαῖον ἅμα καὶ μακρὸν εἶναι κρίνοντες τὰ καταλειπόμενα τῆς περὶ τῶν Ἀργοναυτῶν ἱστορίας προσθήσομεν.

3 Οὐκ ὀλίγοι γὰρ τῶν τε ἀρχαίων συγγραφέων καὶ τῶν μεταγενεστέρων, ὧν ἐστι καὶ Τίμαιος, φασὶ τοὺς Ἀργοναύτας μετὰ τὴν τοῦ δέρους ἁρπαγὴν πυθομένους ὑπ' Αἰήτου προκατειλῆφθαι ναυσὶ τὸ στόμα τοῦ Πόντου, πρᾶξιν ἐπιτελέσασθαι παράδοξον καὶ μνήμης ἀξίαν. ἀναπλεύσαντας γὰρ αὐτοὺς διὰ τοῦ Τανάιδος ποταμοῦ ἐπὶ τὰς πηγάς, καὶ κατὰ τόπον τινὰ τὴν ναῦν διελκύσαντας, καθ' ἑτέρου πάλιν ποταμοῦ τὴν ῥύσιν ἔχοντος εἰς τὸν ὠκεανὸν καταπλεῦσαι πρὸς τὴν θάλατταν, ἀπὸ δὲ τῶν ἄρκτων ἐπὶ τὴν δύσιν κομισθῆναι τὴν γῆν ἔχοντας ἐξ εὐωνύμων, καὶ πλησίον γινομένους Γαδείρων εἰς τὴν καθ' ἡμᾶς θάλατταν εἰσπλεῦσαι.
4 ἀποδείξεις δὲ τούτων φέρουσι, δεικνύντες τοὺς παρὰ τὸν ὠκεανὸν κατοικοῦντας Κελτοὺς σεβομένους μάλιστα τῶν θεῶν τοὺς Διοσκόρους· παραδόσιμον γὰρ αὐτοὺς ἔχειν ἐκ παλαιῶν χρόνων τὴν τούτων τῶν θεῶν παρουσίαν ἐκ τοῦ ὠκεανοῦ

---

[1] Cp. p. 412, n. 1.   [2] The Don.

BOOK IV. 56. 1-4

Medus whom she bore to Aegeus and got off safe to Colchis; and at that time Aeëtes, who had been forcibly driven from the throne by his brother Perses, had regained his kingdom, Medus, Medea's son, having slain Perses; and that afterwards Medus, securing the command of an army, advanced over a large part of Asia which lies above the Pontus and secured possession of Media, which has been named after this Medus. But since in our judgment it is unnecessary and would be tedious to record all the assertions which the writers of myths have made about Medea, we shall add only those items which have been passed over concerning the history of the Argonauts.

Not a few both of the ancient historians and of the later ones as well, one of whom is Timaeus,[1] say that the Argonauts, after the seizure of the fleece, learning that the mouth of the Pontus had already been blockaded by the fleet of Aeëtes, performed an amazing exploit which is worthy of mention. They sailed, that is to say, up the Tanaïs river [2] as far as its sources, and at a certain place they hauled the ship overland, and following in turn another river which flows into the ocean they sailed down it to the sea; then they made their course from the north to the west,[3] keeping the land on the left, and when they had arrived near Gadeira (Cadiz) they sailed into our sea.[4] And the writers even offer proofs of these things, pointing out that the Celts who dwell along the ocean venerate the Dioscori above any of the gods, since they have a tradition handed down from ancient times that these gods appeared among

---

[3] *i.e.* south-west.   [4] The Mediterranean.

γεγενημένην. εἶναι δὲ καὶ τὴν παρὰ τὸν ὠκεανὸν χώραν οὐκ ὀλίγας ἔχουσαν προσηγορίας ἀπό τε τῶν 5 Ἀργοναυτῶν καὶ τῶν Διοσκόρων. παραπλησίως δὲ καὶ τὴν ἐντὸς Γαδείρων ἤπειρον ἔχειν ἐμφανῆ σημεῖα τῆς τούτων ἀνακομιδῆς. περὶ μὲν γὰρ τὴν Τυρρηνίαν καταπλεύσαντας αὐτοὺς εἰς νῆσον τὴν ὀνομαζομένην Αἰθάλειαν τὸν ἐν αὐτῇ λιμένα, κάλλιστον ὄντα τῶν ἐν ἐκείνοις τοῖς τόποις, Ἀργῷον ἀπὸ τῆς νεὼς προσαγορεῦσαι, καὶ μέχρι τῶνδε τῶν 6 χρόνων διαμένειν αὐτοῦ τὴν προσηγορίαν. παραπλησίως δὲ τοῖς εἰρημένοις κατὰ μὲν τὴν Τυρρηνίαν ἀπὸ σταδίων ὀκτακοσίων τῆς Ῥώμης ὀνομάσαι λιμένα Τελαμῶνα, κατὰ δὲ Φορμίας τῆς Ἰταλίας Αἰήτην τὸν νῦν Καιήτην προσαγορευόμενον. πρὸς δὲ τούτοις ὑπ' ἀνέμων αὐτοὺς ἐκριφέντας εἰς τὰς Σύρτεις, καὶ μαθόντας παρὰ Τρίτωνος τοῦ τότε βασιλεύοντος τῆς Λιβύης τὴν ἰδιότητα τῆς θαλάττης, καὶ τὸν κίνδυνον ἐκφυγόντας, δωρήσασθαι χαλκοῦν τρίποδα τὸν ἀρχαίοις μὲν κεχαραγμένον γράμμασι, μέχρι δὲ τῶν νεωτέρων χρόνων διαμείναντα παρὰ τοῖς Εὐεσπερίταις.

7 Οὐ παραλειπτέον δ' ἡμῖν ἀνεξέλεγκτον τὴν ἱστορίαν τῶν ἀποφηναμένων τοὺς Ἀργοναύτας ἀνὰ τὸν Ἴστρον πλεύσαντας μέχρι τῶν πηγῶν κατενεχθῆναι διὰ τῆς ἀντιπροσώπου ῥύσεως πρὸς τὸν 8 Ἀδριατικὸν κόλπον. τούτους γὰρ ὁ χρόνος ἤλεγξεν ὑπολαβόντας τὸν ἐν τῷ Πόντῳ πλείοσι στόμασιν ἐξερευγόμενον Ἴστρον καὶ τὸν εἰς τὸν Ἀδρίαν ἐκβάλλοντα τὴν ῥύσιν ἔχειν ἀπὸ τῶν αὐτῶν τόπων.

---
[1] Elba.
[2] The Roman Portus Argous, the harbour of the present capital of the island, Portoferraio.

BOOK IV. 56. 4-8

them coming from the ocean. Moreover, the country which skirts the ocean bears, they say, not a few names which are derived from the Argonauts and the Dioscori. And likewise the continent this side of Gadeira contains visible tokens of the return voyage of the Argonauts. So, for example, as they sailed about the Tyrrhenian Sea, when they put in at an island called Aethaleia[1] they named its harbour, which is the fairest of any in those regions, Argoön[2] after their ship, and such has remained its name to this day. In like manner to what we have just narrated a harbour in Etruria eight hundred stades from Rome was named by them Telamon, and also at Phormia[3] in Italy the harbour Aeëtes, which is now known as Caeëtes.[4] Furthermore, when they were driven by winds to the Syrtes and had learned from Triton, who was king of Libya at that time, of the peculiar nature of the sea there, upon escaping safe out of the peril they presented him with the bronze tripod which was inscribed with ancient characters and stood until rather recent times among the people of Euhesperis.[5]

We must not leave unrefuted the account of those who state that the Argonauts sailed up the Ister[6] river as far as its sources and then, by its arm which flows in the opposite direction, descended to the Adriatic Gulf. For time has refuted those who assumed that the Ister which empties by several mouths into the Pontus and the Ister which issues into the Adriatic flow from the same regions. As a

[3] Formiae. [4] Gaëta.
[5] The most western city, later called Berenicê, of the Pentapolis in Cyrenê.
[6] Danube.

Ῥωμαίων γὰρ καταπολεμησάντων τὸ τῶν Ἴστρων ἔθνος, εὑρέθη τὰς πηγὰς ἔχων ὁ ποταμὸς ἀπὸ τετταράκοντα σταδίων τῆς θαλάττης. ἀλλὰ γὰρ τοῖς συγγραφεῦσιν αἰτίαν τῆς πλάνης φασὶ γενέσθαι τὴν ὁμωνυμίαν τῶν ποταμῶν.

57. Ἡμῖν δ' ἀρκούντως ἐξειργασμένοις τὴν περὶ τῶν Ἀργοναυτῶν ἱστορίαν καὶ τὰ ὑφ' Ἡρακλέους πραχθέντα οἰκεῖον ἂν εἴη κατὰ τὴν γενομένην ἐπαγγελίαν ἀναγράψαι τὰς τῶν υἱῶν αὐτοῦ πράξεις.

2 Μετὰ τὴν Ἡρακλέους τοίνυν ἀποθέωσιν οἱ παῖδες αὐτοῦ κατῴκουν ἐν Τραχῖνι παρὰ Κήυκι τῷ βασιλεῖ. μετὰ δὲ ταῦτα Ὕλλου καί τινων ἑτέρων ἀνδρωθέντων, Εὐρυσθεὺς φοβηθεὶς μὴ πάντων ἐνηλίκων γενομένων ἐκπέσῃ τῆς ἐν Μυκήναις βασιλείας, ἔγνω τοὺς Ἡρακλείδας ἐξ ὅλης τῆς

3 Ἑλλάδος φυγαδεῦσαι. διὸ Κήυκι μὲν τῷ βασιλεῖ προηγόρευσε τούς τε Ἡρακλείδας καὶ τοὺς Λικυμνίου παῖδας ἐκβαλεῖν, ἔτι δὲ Ἰόλαον καὶ τὸ σύστημα τῶν Ἀρκάδων τῶν Ἡρακλεῖ συνεστρατευκότων, ἢ ταῦτα μὴ ποιοῦντα πόλεμον ἀνα-

4 δέξασθαι. οἱ δ' Ἡρακλεῖδαι καὶ οἱ μετ' αὐτῶν θεωροῦντες αὑτοὺς οὐκ ἀξιομάχους ὄντας Εὐρυσθεῖ πολεμεῖν, ἔγνωσαν ἑκουσίως φεύγειν ἐκ τῆς Τραχῖνος· ἐπιόντες δὲ τῶν ἄλλων πόλεων τὰς ἀξιολογωτάτας ἐδέοντο δέξασθαι σφᾶς αὐτοὺς συνοίκους. μηδεμιᾶς δὲ τολμώσης ὑποδέξασθαι, μόνοι τῶν ἄλλων Ἀθηναῖοι διὰ τὴν ἔμφυτον παρ' αὐτοῖς ἐπιείκειαν προσεδέξαντο τοὺς Ἡρακλείδας· κατῴ-

---

[1] Strabo (1. 3. 15) mentions the same erroneous belief, and in language which shows that he knew no river of that name in Istria.

matter of fact, when the Romans subdued the nation of the Istrians it was discovered that the latter river has its sources only forty stades from the sea. But the cause of the error on the part of the historians was, they say, the identity in name of the two rivers.[1]

57. Since we have sufficiently elaborated the history of the Argonauts and the deeds accomplished by Heracles, it may be appropriate also to record, in accordance with the promise we made, the deeds of his sons.

Now after the deification of Heracles his sons made their home in Trachis at the court of Ceÿx the king. But later, when Hyllus and some of the others had attained to manhood, Eurystheus, being afraid lest, after they had all come of age, he might be driven from his kingdom at Mycenae, decided to send the Heracleidae into exile from the whole of Greece. Consequently he served notice upon Ceÿx, the king, to banish both the Heracleidae and the sons of Licymnius,[2] and Iolaüs as well and the band of Arcadians who had served with Heracles on his campaigns, adding that, if he should fail to do these things, he must submit to war. But the Heracleidae and their friends, perceiving that they were of themselves not sufficient in number to carry on a war against Eurystheus, decided to leave Trachis of their own free will, and going about among the most important of the other cities they asked them to receive them as fellow-townsmen. When no other city had the courage to take them in, the Athenians alone of all, such being their inborn sense of justice, extended a welcome to the sons of Heracles, and

[2] A half-brother of Alcmenê and so an uncle of Heracles.

κισαν δὲ αὐτοὺς μετὰ τῶν συμφυγόντων εἰς Τρικόρυθον πόλιν, ἥτις ἐστὶ μία τῆς ὀνομαζομένης 5 τετραπόλεως. μετὰ δέ τινα χρόνον ἁπάντων τῶν Ἡρακλέους παίδων ἠνδρωμένων, καὶ φρονήματος ἐμφυομένου τοῖς νεανίσκοις διὰ τὴν ἀφ' Ἡρακλέους δόξαν, ὑφορώμενος αὐτῶν τὴν αὔξησιν Εὐρυσθεὺς ἐστράτευσεν ἐπ' αὐτοὺς μετὰ πολλῆς 6 δυνάμεως. οἱ δ' Ἡρακλεῖδαι, βοηθούντων αὐτοῖς τῶν Ἀθηναίων, προστησάμενοι τὸν Ἡρακλέους ἀδελφιδοῦν Ἰόλαον, καὶ τούτῳ τε καὶ Θησεῖ καὶ Ὕλλῳ τὴν στρατηγίαν παραδόντες, ἐνίκησαν παρατάξει τὸν Εὐρυσθέα. κατὰ δὲ τὴν μάχην πλεῖστοι μὲν τῶν μετ' Εὐρυσθέως κατεκόπησαν, αὐτὸς δ' ὁ Εὐρυσθεύς, τοῦ ἅρματος κατὰ τὴν φυγὴν συντριβέντος, ὑπὸ Ὕλλου τοῦ Ἡρακλέους ἀνῃρέθη· ὁμοίως δὲ καὶ οἱ υἱοὶ τοῦ Εὐρυσθέως πάντες κατὰ τὴν μάχην ἐτελεύτησαν.

58. Μετὰ δὲ ταῦτα οἱ μὲν Ἡρακλεῖδαι πάντες περιβοήτῳ μάχῃ νενικηκότες τὸν Εὐρυσθέα, καὶ διὰ τὴν εὐημερίαν συμμάχων εὐπορήσαντες, ἐστράτευσαν ἐπὶ τὴν Πελοπόννησον Ὕλλου στρατηγοῦν-2 τος. Ἀτρεὺς δὲ μετὰ τὴν Εὐρυσθέως τελευτὴν καταλαβόμενος τὴν ἐν Μυκήναις βασιλείαν, καὶ προσλαβόμενος συμμάχους Τεγεάτας καί τινας 3 ἄλλους, ἀπήντησε τοῖς Ἡρακλείδαις. κατὰ δὲ τὸν Ἰσθμὸν τῶν στρατοπέδων ἀθροισθέντων, Ὕλλος μὲν ὁ Ἡρακλέους εἰς μονομαχίαν προεκα-

---

[1] A union of four cities in Attica of which Marathon was the most important.

they settled them and their companions in the flight in the city of Tricorythus, which is one of the cities of what is called the Tetrapolis.[1] And after some time, when all the sons of Heracles had attained to manhood and a spirit of pride sprang up in the young men because of the glory of descent from Heracles, Eurystheus, viewing with suspicion their growing power, came up against them with a great army. But the Heracleidae, who had the aid of the Athenians, chose as their leader Iolaüs, the nephew of Heracles, and after entrusting to him and Theseus and Hyllus the direction of the war, they defeated Eurystheus in a pitched battle. In the course of the battle the larger part of the army of Eurystheus was slain and Eurystheus himself, when his chariot was wrecked in the flight, was killed by Hyllus, the son of Heracles; likewise the sons of Eurystheus perished in the battle to a man.[2]

58. After these events all the Heracleidae, now that they had conquered Eurystheus in a battle whose fame was noised abroad and were well supplied with allies because of their success, embarked upon a campaign against Peloponnesus with Hyllus as their commander. Atreus, after the death of Eurystheus, had taken over the kingship in Mycenae, and having added to his forces the Tegeatans and certain other peoples as allies, he went forth to meet the Heracleidae. When the two armies were assembled at the Isthmus, Hyllus, Heracles' son, challenged to single combat any one of the enemy

[2] Euripides' drama, *The Children of Heracles,* centres about the persecution of the children by Eurystheus and about the war with Argos which Athens undertakes in defence of the refugees.

λέσατο τῶν πολεμίων τὸν βουλόμενον, ὁμολογίας θέμενος τοιαύτας, εἰ μὲν Ὕλλος νικήσειε[1] τὸν ἀντιταχθέντα, παραλαβεῖν Ἡρακλείδας τὴν Εὐρυσθέως βασιλείαν, εἰ δ' Ὕλλος λειφθείη, μὴ κατιέναι τοὺς Ἡρακλείδας εἰς Πελοπόννησον ἐντὸς ἐτῶν 4 πεντήκοντα. καταβάντος δ' εἰς τὴν πρόκλησιν Ἐχέμου τοῦ βασιλέως τῶν Τεγεατῶν, καὶ τῆς μονομαχίας γενομένης, ὁ μὲν Ὕλλος ἀνῃρέθη, οἱ δ' Ἡρακλεῖδαι κατὰ τὰς ὁμολογίας ἀπέστησαν τῆς καθόδου καὶ τὴν εἰς Τρικόρυθον ἐπάνοδον ἐποιή5 σαντο. μετὰ δέ τινας χρόνους Λικύμνιος μὲν μετὰ τῶν παίδων καὶ Τληπολέμου τοῦ Ἡρακλέους, ἑκουσίως τῶν Ἀργείων αὐτοὺς προσδεξαμένων, ἐν Ἄργει κατῴκησαν· οἱ δ' ἄλλοι πάντες ἐν Τρικορύθῳ κατοικήσαντες,[2] ὡς[3] ὁ πεντηκονταετὴς χρόνος διῆλθε, κατῆλθον εἰς Πελοπόννησον· ὧν τὰς πράξεις ἀναγράψομεν, ὅταν εἰς ἐκείνους τοὺς χρόνους παραγενηθῶμεν.
6 Ἀλκμήνη δ' εἰς Θήβας καταντήσασα, καὶ μετὰ ταῦτ' ἀφάντος γενομένη, τιμῶν ἰσοθέων ἔτυχε παρὰ τοῖς Θηβαίοις. τοὺς δ' ἄλλους Ἡρακλείδας φασὶν ἐλθόντας παρ' Αἰγίμιον τὸν Δώρου τὴν πατρῴαν τῆς χώρας παρακαταθήκην ἀπαιτή7 σαντας μετὰ Δωριέων κατοικῆσαι. Τληπόλεμον δὲ τὸν Ἡρακλέους ἐν Ἄργει κατοικοῦντα λέγουσιν ἀνελεῖν Λικύμνιον τὸν Ἠλεκτρύωνος ἐρίσαντα περί τινων, διὰ δὲ τὸν φόνον τοῦτον ἐξ Ἄργους φυγόντα εἰς Ῥόδον μετοικῆσαι.[4] τὴν δὲ νῆσον ταύτην τότε

---

[1] νικήσειε Bekker, νικῆσαι Vogel, νικήσει MSS, Dindorf.
[2] κατῴκησαν ABD, deleted by Vogel.
[3] δὲ after ὡς omitted Vulgate.
[4] So Hertlein: κατοικῆσαι.

who would face him, on the agreement that, if Hyllus should conquer his opponent, the Heracleidae should receive the kingdom of Eurystheus, but that, if Hyllus were defeated, the Heracleidae would not return to Peloponnesus for a period of fifty years.[1] Echemus, the king of the Tegeatans, came out to meet the challenge, and in the single combat which followed Hyllus was slain and the Heracleidae gave up, as they had promised, their effort to return and made their way back to Tricorythus. Some time later Licymnius and his sons and Tlepolemus, the son of Heracles, made their home in Argos, the Argives admitting them to citizenship of their own accord; but all the rest who had made their homes in Tricorythus, when the fifty-year period had expired, returned to Peloponnesus. Their deeds we shall record when we have come to those times.[2]

Alcmenê returned to Thebes, and when some time later she vanished from sight she received divine honours at the hands of the Thebans. The rest of the Heracleidae, they say, came to Aegimius, the son of Dorus, and demanding back the land which their father had entrusted to him [3] made their home among the Dorians. But Tlepolemus, the son of Heracles, while he dwelt in Argos, slew Licymnius, the son of Electryon, we are told, in a quarrel over a certain matter, and being exiled from Argos because of this murder changed his residence to Rhodes. This island was inhabited at that time by Greeks

---

[1] Herodotus (9. 26) says "one hundred" years and the statement of Thucydides (1. 12) would suggest about the same number.
[2] This is not in the extant portions of Diodorus.
[3] Cp. chap. 37. 4.

κατῴκουν Ἕλληνες οἱ ὑπὸ Τριόπα τοῦ Φόρβαντος
8 κατοικισθέντες. τὸν δ' οὖν Τληπόλεμον κοινῇ
μετὰ τῶν ἐγχωρίων τριμερῆ ποιῆσαι τὴν Ῥόδον,
καὶ τρεῖς ἐν αὐτῇ καταστῆσαι πόλεις, Λίνδον,
Ἰήλυσον, Κάμειρον· βασιλεῦσαι δ' αὐτὸν πάντων
τῶν Ῥοδίων διὰ τὴν τοῦ πατρὸς Ἡρακλέους
δόξαν, καὶ κατὰ τοὺς ὕστερον χρόνους μετ'
Ἀγαμέμνονος ἐπὶ τὴν Τροίαν στρατεῦσαι.

who had been planted there by Triopas, the son of Phorbas. Accordingly, Tlepolemus, acting with the common consent of the natives, divided Rhodes into three parts and founded there three cities, Lindus, Ielysus (Ialysus), and Cameirus; and he became king over all the Rhodians, because of the fame of his father Heracles, and in later times took part with Agamemnon in the war against Troy.

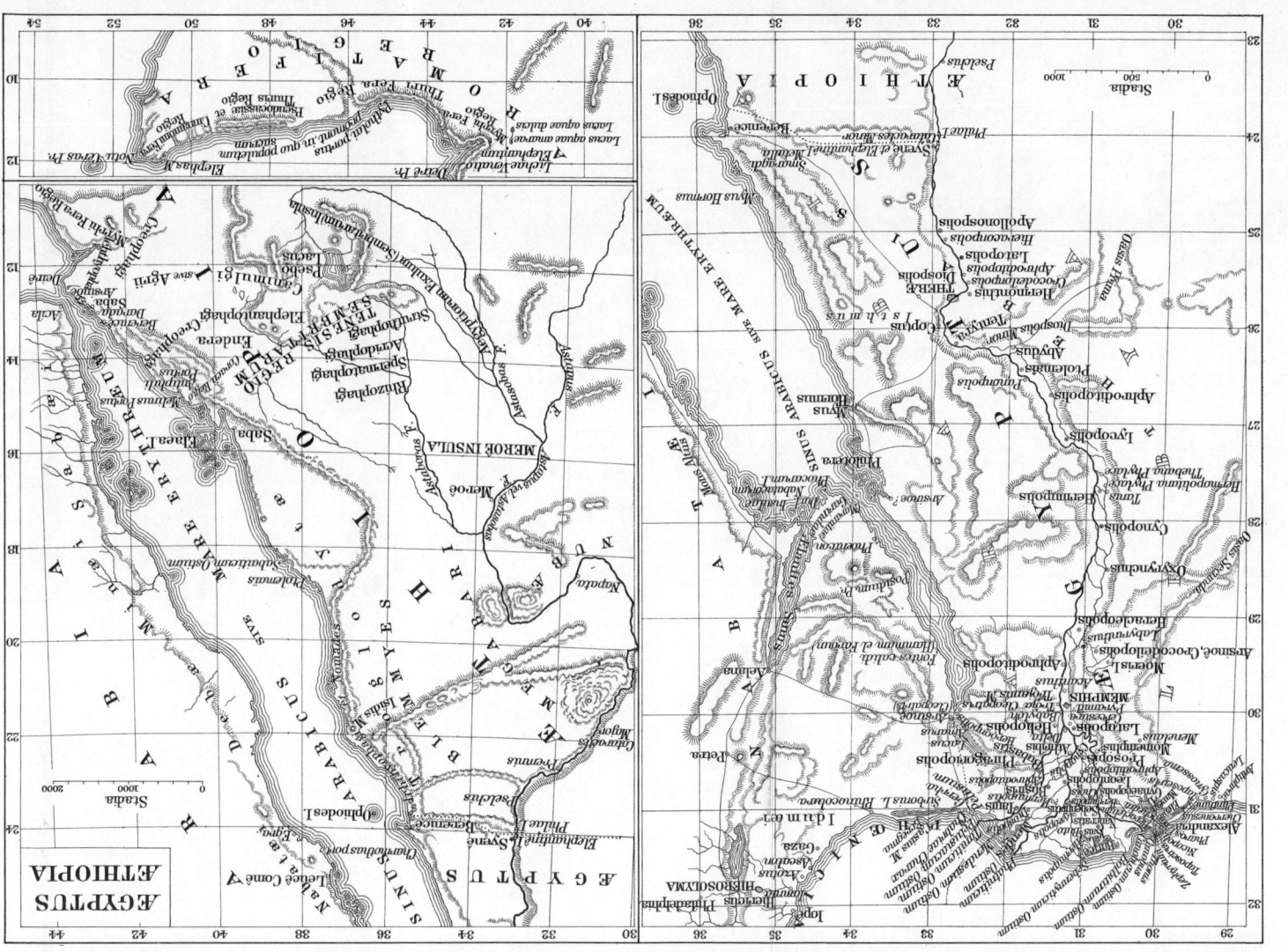

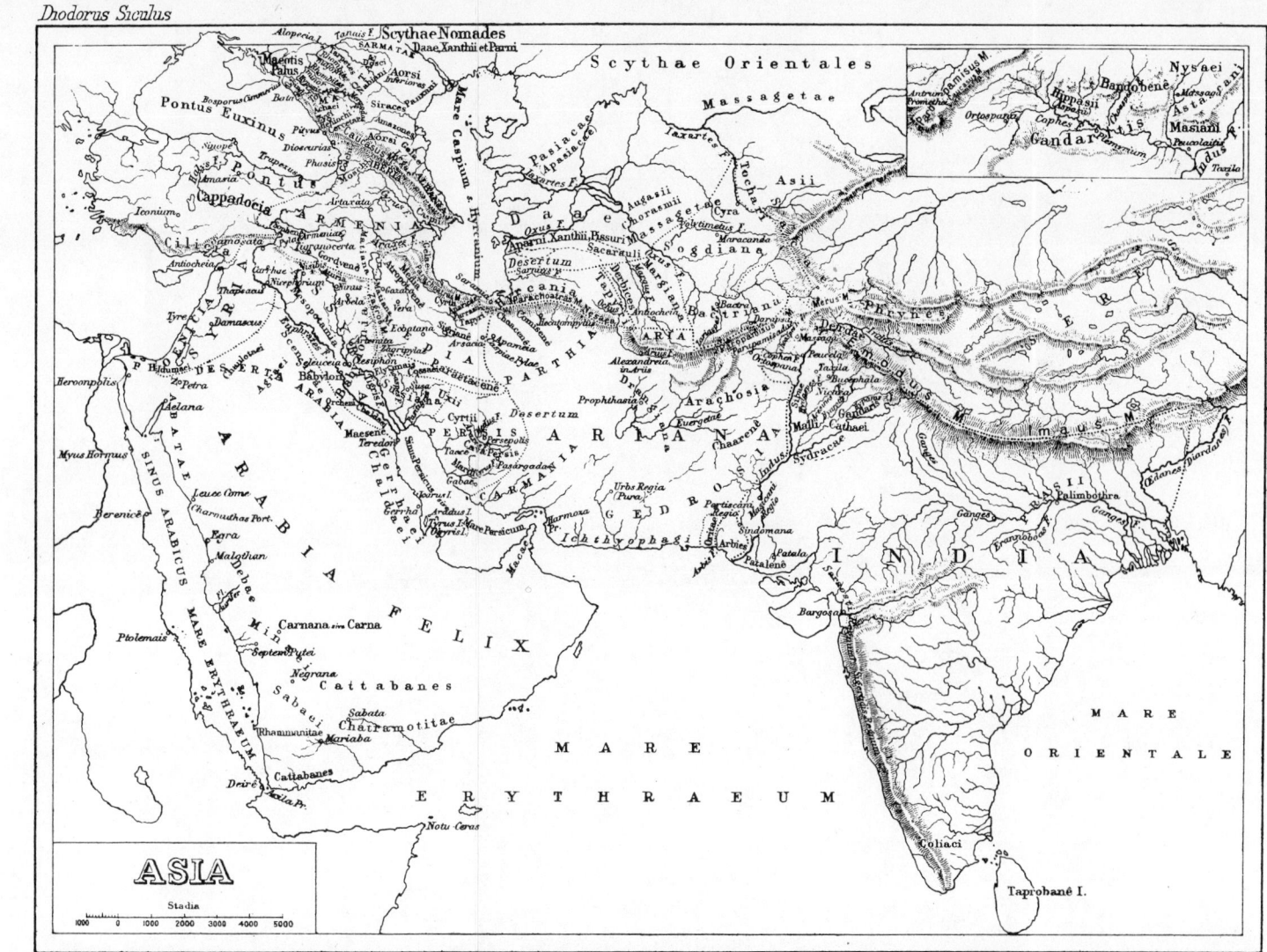

THEOPHRASTUS: ENQUIRY INTO PLANTS. Sir Arthur Hort, Bart. 2 Vols.
THEOPHRASTUS: DE CAUSIS PLANTARUM. G. K. K. Link and B. Einarson. 3 Vols. Vol. I.
THUCYDIDES. C. F. Smith. 4 Vols.
TRYPHIODORUS. Cf. OPPIAN.
XENOPHON: CYROPAEDIA. Walter Miller. 2 Vols.
XENOPHON: HELLENCIA. C. L. Brownson. 2 Vols.
XENOPHON: ANABASIS. C. L. Brownson.
XENOPHON: MEMORABILIA AND OECONOMICUS. E. C. Marchant. SYMPOSIUM AND APOLOGY. O. J. Todd.
XENOPHON: SCRIPTA MINORA. E. C. Marchant. CONSTITUTION OF THE ATHENIANS (Athenians.) G. W. Bowersock

PHILO. 10 Vols. Vols. I.–V. F. H. Colson and Rev. G. H. Whitaker. Vols. VI.–IX. F. H. Colson. Vol. X. F. H. Colson and the Rev. J. W. Earp.

PHILO: two supplementary Vols. (*Translation only.*) Ralph Marcus.

PHILOSTRATUS: THE LIFE OF APOLLONIUS OF TYANA. F. C. Conybeare. 2 Vols.

PHILOSTRATUS: IMAGINES; CALLISTRATUS: DESCRIPTIONS. A. Fairbanks.

PHILOSTRATUS and EUNAPIUS: LIVES OF THE SOPHISTS. Wilmer Cave Wright.

PINDAR. Sir J. E. Sandys.

PLATO: CHARMIDES, ALCIBIADES, HIPPARCHUS, THE LOVERS, THEAGES, MINOS and EPINOMIS. W. R. M. Lamb.

PLATO: CRATYLUS, PARMENIDES, GREATER HIPPIAS, LESSER HIPPIAS. H. N. Fowler.

PLATO: EUTHYPHRO, APOLOGY, CRITO, PHAEDO, PHAEDRUS, H. N. Fowler.

PLATO: LACHES, PROTAGORAS, MENO, EUTHYDEMUS. W. R. M. Lamb.

PLATO: LAWS. Rev. R. G. Bury. 2 Vols.

PLATO: LYSIS, SYMPOSIUM, GORGIAS. W. R. M. Lamb.

PLATO: Republic. Paul Shorey. 2 Vols.

PLATO: STATESMAN, PHILEBUS. H. N. Fowler; Ion. W. R. M. Lamb.

PLATO: THEAETETUS and SOPHIST. H. N. Fowler.

PLATO: TIMAEUS, CRITIAS, CLITOPHO, MENEXENUS, EPISTULAE. Rev. R. G. Bury.

PLOTINUS: A. H. Armstrong. Vols. I.–III.

PLUTARCH: MORALIA. 17 Vols. Vols. I.–V. F. C. Babbitt. Vol. VI. W. C. Helmbold. Vols. VII. and XIV. P. H. De Lacy and B. Einarson. Vol. VIII. P. A. Clement and H. B. Hoffleit. Vol. IX. E. L. Minar, Jr., F. H. Sandbach, W. C. Helmbold. Vol. X. H. N. Fowler. Vol. XI. L. Pearson and F. H. Sandbach. Vol. XII. H. Cherniss and W. C. Helmbold. Vol. XIII 1–2. H. Cherniss. Vol. XV. F. H. Sandbach.

PLUTARCH: THE PARALLEL LIVES. B. Perrin. 11 Vols.

POLYBIUS. W. R. Paton. 6 Vols.

PROCOPIUS: HISTORY OF THE WARS. H. B. Dewing. 7 Vols.

PTOLEMY: TETRABIBLOS. Cf. MANETHO.

QUINTUS SMYRNAEUS. A. S. Way. Verse trans.

SEXTUS EMPIRICUS. Rev. R. G. Bury. 4 Vols.

SOPHOCLES. F. Storr. 2 Vols. Verse trans.

STRABO: GEOGRAPHY. Horace L. Jones. 8 Vols.

THEOPHRASTUS: CHARACTERS. J. M. Edmonds. HERODES, etc. A. D. Knox.

GALEN: ON THE NATURAL FACULTIES. A. J. Brock.

THE GREEK ANTHOLOGY. W. R. Paton. 5 Vols.

GREEK ELEGY AND IAMBUS with the ANACREONTEA. J. M. Edmonds. 2 Vols.

THE GREEK BUCOLIC POETS (THEOCRITUS, BION, MOSCHUS). J. M. Edmonds.

GREEK MATHEMATICAL WORKS. Ivor Thomas. 2 Vols.

HERODES. Cf. THEOPHRASTUS: CHARACTERS.

HERODIAN. C. R. Whittaker. 2 Vols.

HERODOTUS. A. D. Godley. 4 Vols.

HESIOD AND THE HOMERIC HYMNS. H. G. Evelyn White.

HIPPOCRATES and the FRAGMENTS OF HERACLEITUS. W. H. S. Jones and E. T. Withington. 4 Vols.

HOMER: ILIAD. A. T. Murray. 2 Vols.

HOMER: ODYSSEY. A. T. Murray. 2 Vols.

ISAEUS. E. W. Forster.

ISOCRATES. George Norlin and LaRue Van Hook. 3 Vols.

[ST. JOHN DAMASCENE]: BARLAAM AND IOASAPH. Rev. G. R. Woodward, Harold Mattingly and D. M. Lang.

JOSEPHUS. 9 Vols. Vols. I.–IV. H. Thackeray. Vol. V. H. Thackeray and R. Marcus. Vols. VI.–VII. R. Marcus. Vol. VIII. R. Marcus and Allen Wikgren. Vol. IX. L. H. Feldman.

JULIAN. Wilmer Cave Wright. 3 Vols.

LIBANIUS. A. F. Norman. Vols. I.–II.

LUCIAN. 8 Vols. Vols. I.–V. A. M. Harmon. Vol. VI. K. Kilburn. Vols. VII.–VIII. M. D. Macleod.

LYCOPHRON. Cf. CALLIMACHUS.

LYRA GRAECA. J. M. Edmonds. 3 Vols.

LYSIAS. W. R. M. Lamb.

MANETHO. W. G. Waddell: PTOLEMY: TETRABIBLOS. F. E. Robbins.

MARCUS AURELIUS. C. R. Haines.

MENANDER. F. G. Allison.

MINOR ATTIC ORATORS (ANTIPHON, ANDOCIDES, LYCURGUS, DEMADES, DINARCHUS, HYPERIDES). K. J. Maidment and J. O. Burtt. 2 Vols.

MUSAEUS: HEOR AND LEANDER. Cf. CALLIMACHUS.

NONNOS: DIONYSIACA. W. H. D. Rouse. 3 Vols.

OPPIAN, COLLUTHUS, TRYPHIODORUS. A. W. Mair.

PAPYRI. NON-LITERARY SELECTIONS. A. S. Hunt and C. C. Edgar. 2 Vols. LITERARY SELECTIONS (Poetry). D. L. Page.

PARTHENIUS. Cf. DAPHNIS and CHLOE.

PAUSANIAS: DESCRIPTION OF GREECE. W. H. S. Jones. 4 Vols. and Companion Vol. arranged by R. E. Wycherley.

ARISTOTLE: PHYSICS. Rev. P. Wicksteed and F. M. Cornford. 2 Vols.
ARISTOTLE: POETICS and LONGINUS. W. Hamilton Fyfe; DEMETRIUS ON STYLE. W. Rhys Roberts.
ARISTOTLE: POLITICS. H. Rackham.
ARISTOTLE: PROBLEMS. W. S. Hett. 2 Vols.
ARISTOTLE: RHETORICA AD ALEXANDRUM (with PROBLEMS. Vol. II). H. Rackham.
ARRIAN: HISTORY OF ALEXANDER and INDICA. Rev. E. Iliffe Robson. 2 Vols. New version P. Brunt.
ATHENAEUS: DEIPNOSOPHISTAE. C. B. Gulick. 7 Vols.
BABRIUS AND PHAEDRUS (Latin). B. E. Perry.
ST. BASIL: LETTERS. R. J. Deferrair. 4 Vols.
CALLIMACHUS: FRAGMENTS. C. A. Trypanis. MUSAEUS: HERO AND LEANDER. T. Gelzer and C. Whitman.
CALLIMACHUS, Hymns and Epigrams, and LYCOPHRON. A. W. Mair; ARATUS. G. R. Mair.
CLEMENT OF ALEXANDRIA. Rev. G. W. Butterworth.
COLLUTHUS. Cf. OPPIAN.
DAPHNIS AND CHLOE. Thornley's Translation revised by J. M. Edmonds: and PARTHENIUS. S. Gaselee.
DEMOSTHENES I.: OLYNTHIACS, PHILIPPICS and MINOR ORATIONS. I.–XVII. AND XX. J. H. Vince.
DEMOSTHENES II.: DE CORONA and DE FALSA LEGATIONE. C. A. Vince and J. H. Vince.
DEMOSTHENES III.: MEIDIAS, ANDROTION, ARISTOCRATES, TIMOCRATES and ARISTOGEITON, I. and II. J. H. Vince.
DEMOSTHENES IV.–VI.: PRIVATE ORATIONS and IN NEAERAM. A. T. Murray.
DEMOSTHENES VII: FUNERAL SPEECH, EROTIC ESSAY, EXORDIA and LETTERS. N. W. and N. J. DeWitt.
DIO CASSIUS: ROMAN HISTORY. E. Cary. 9 Vols.
DIO CHRYSOSTOM. J. W. Cohoon and H. Lamar Crosby. 5 Vols.
DIODORUS SICULUS. 12 Vols. Vols. I.–VI. C. H. Oldfather. Vol. VII. C. L. Sherman. Vol. VIII. C. B. Welles. Vols. IX. and X. R. M. Geer. Vol. XI. F. Walton. Vol. XII. F. Walton. General Index. R. M. Geer.
DIOGENES LAERTIUS. R. D. Hicks. 2 Vols. New Introduction by H. S. Long.
DIONYSIUS OF HALICARNASSUS: ROMAN ANTIQUITIES. Spelman's translation revised by E. Cary. 7 Vols.
DIONYSIUS OF HALICARNASSUS: CRITICAL ESSAYS. S. Usher. 2 Vols.
EPICTETUS. W. A. Oldfather. 2 Vols.
EURIPIDES. A. S. Way. 4 Vols. Verse trans.
EUSEBIUS: ECCLESIASTICAL HISTORY. Kirsopp Lake and J. E. L. Oulton. 2 Vols.

Greek Authors

ACHILLES TATIUS. S. Gaselee.
AELIAN: ON THE NATURE OF ANIMALS. A. F. Scholfield. 3 Vols.
AENEAS TACTICUS, ASCLEPIODOTUS and ONASANDER. The Illinois Greek Club.
AESCHINES. C. D. Adams.
AESCHYLUS. H. Weir Smyth. 2 Vols.
ALCIPHRON, AELIAN, PHILOSTRATUS: LETTERS. A. R. Benner and F. H. Fobes.
ANDOCIDES, ANTIPHON, Cf. MINOR ATTIC ORATORS.
APOLLODORUS. Sir James G. Frazer. 2 Vols.
APOLLONIUS RHODIUS. R. C. Seaton.
THE APOSTOLIC FATHERS. Kirsopp Lake. 2 Vols.
APPIAN: ROMAN HISTORY. Horace White. 4 Vols.
ARATUS. Cf. CALLIMACHUS.
ARISTIDES: ORATIONS. C. A. Behr. Vol. I.
ARISTOPHANES. Benjamin Bickley Rogers. 3 Vols. Verse trans.
ARISTOTLE: ART OF RHETORIC. J. H. Freese.
ARISTOTLE: ATHENIAN CONSTITUTION, EUDEMIAN ETHICS, VICES AND VIRTUES. H. Rackham.
ARISTOTLE: GENERATION OF ANIMALS. A. L. Peck.
ARISTOTLE: HISTORIA ANIMALIUM. A. L. Peck. Vols I.–II.
ARISTOTLE: METAPHYSICS. H. Tredennick. 2 Vols.
ARISTOTLE: METEOROLOGICA. H. D. P. Lee.
ARISTOTLE: MINOR WORKS. W. S. Hett. On Colours, On Things Heard, On Physiognomies, On Plants, On Marvellous Things Heard, Mechanical Problems, On Indivisible Lines, On Situations and Names of Winds, On Melissus, Xenophanes, and Gorgias.
ARISTOTLE: NICOMACHEAN ETHICS. H. Rackham.
ARISTOTLE: OECONOMICA and MAGNA MORALIA. G. C. Armstrong; (with METAPHYSICS, Vol. II.).
ARISTOTLE: ON THE HEAVENS. W. K. C. Guthrie.
ARISTOTLE: ON THE SOUL. PARVA NATURALIA. ON BREATH. W. S. Hett.
ARISTOTLE: CATEGORIES, ON INTERPRETATION, PRIOR ANALYTICS. H. P. Cooke and H. Tredennick.
ARISTOTLE: POSTERIOR ANALYTICS, TOPICS. H. Tredennick and E. S. Forster.
ARISTOTLE: ON SOPHISTICAL REFUTATIONS.
On Coming to be and Passing Away, On the Cosmos. E. S. Forster and D. J. Furley.
ARISTOTLE: PARTS OF ANIMALS. A. L. Peck; MOTION AND PROGRESSION OF ANIMALS. E. S. Forster.

Ovid: Heroides and Amores. Grant Showerman. Revised by G. P. Goold
Ovid: Metamorphoses. F. J. Miller. 2 Vols. Vol. 1 revised by G. P. Goold.
Ovid: Tristia and Ex Ponto. A. L. Wheeler.
Persius. Cf. Juvenal.
Petronius. M. Heseltine; Seneca; Apocolocyntosis. W. H. D. Rouse.
Phaedrus and Babrius (Greek). B. E. Perry.
Plautus. Paul Nixon. 5 Vols.
Pliny: Letters, Panegyricus. Betty Radice. 2 Vols.
Pliny: Natural History. Vols. I.–V. and IX. H. Rackham. VI.–VIII. W. H. S. Jones. X. D. E. Eichholz. 10 Vols.
Propertius. H. E. Butler.
Prudentius. H. J. Thomson. 2 Vols.
Quintilian. H. E. Butler. 4 Vols.
Remains of Old Latin. E. H. Warmington. 4 Vols. Vol. I. (Ennius and Caecilius.) Vol. II. (Livius, Naevius, Pacuvius, Accius.) Vol. III. (Lucilius and Laws of XII Tables.) Vol. IV. (Archaic Inscriptions.)
Sallust. J. C. Rolfe.
Scriptores Historiae Augustae. D. Magie. 3 Vols.
Seneca, The Elder: Controversiae, Suasoriae. M. Winterbottom. 2 Vols.
Seneca: Apocolocyntosis. Cf. Petronius.
Seneca: Epistulae Morales. R. M. Gummere. 3 Vols.
Seneca: Moral Essays. J. W. Basore. 3 Vols.
Seneca: Tragedies. F. J. Miller. 2 Vols.
Seneca: Naturales Quaestiones. T. H. Corcoran. 2 Vols.
Sidonius: Poems and Letters. W. B. Anderson. 2 Vols.
Silius Italicus. J. D. Duff. 2 Vols.
Statius. J. H. Mozley. 2 Vols.
Suetonius. J. C. Rolfe. 2 Vols.
Tacitus: Dialogus. Sir Wm. Peterson. Agricola and Germania. Maurice Hutton. Revised by M. Winterbottom, R. M. Ogilvie, E. H. Warmington.
Tacitus: Histories and Annals. C. H. Moore and J. Jackson. 4 Vols.
Terence. John Sargeaunt. 2 Vols.
Tertullian: Apologia and De Spectaculis. T. R. Glover. Minucius Felix. G. H. Rendall.
Valerius Flaccus. J. H. Mozley.
Varro: De Lingua Latina. R. G. Kent. 2 Vols.
Velleius Paterculus and Res Gestae Divi Augusti. F. W. Shipley.
Virgil. H. R. Fairclough. 2 Vols.
Vitruvius: De Architectura. F. Granger. 2 Vols.

CICERO: DE SENECTUTE, DE AMICITIA, DE DIVINATIONE. W. A. Falconer.

CICERO: IN CATILINAM, PRO FLACCO, PRO MURENA, PRO SULLA. New version by C. Macdonald.

CICERO: LETTERS TO ATTICUS. E. O. Winstedt. 3 Vols.

CICERO: LETTERS TO HIS FRIENDS. W. Glynn Williams, M. Cary, M. Henderson. 4 Vols.

CICERO: PHILIPPICS. W. C. A. Ker.

CICERO: PRO ARCHIA POST REDITUM, DE DOMO, DE HARUSPICUM RESPONSIS, PRO PLANCIO. N. H. Watts.

CICERO: PRO CAECINA, PRO LEGE MANILIA, PRO CLUENTIO, PRO RABIRIO. H. Grose Hodge.

CICERO: PRO CAELIO, DE PROVINCIIS CONSULARIBUS, PRO BALBO. R. Gardner.

CICERO: PRO MILONE, IN PISONEM, PRO SCAURO, PRO FONTEIO, PRO RABIRIO POSTUMO, PRO MARCELLO, PRO LIGARIO, PRO REGE DEIOTARO. N. H. Watts.

CICERO: PRO QUINCTIO, PRO ROSCIO AMERINO, PRO ROSCIO COMOEDO, CONTRA RULLUM. J. H. Freese.

CICERO: PRO SESTIO, IN VATINIUM. R. Gardner.

CICERO: TUSCULAN DISPUTATIONS. J. E. King.

CICERO: VERRINE ORATIONS. L. H. G. Greenwood. 2 Vols.

CLAUDIAN. M. Platnauer. 2 Vols.

COLUMELLA: DE RE RUSTICA. DE ARBORIBUS. H. B. Ash, E. S. Forster and E. Heffner. 3 Vols.

CURTIUS, Q.: HISTORY OF ALEXANDER. J. C. Rolfe. 2 Vols.

FLORUS. E. S. Forster; and CORNELIUS NEPOS. J. C. Rolfe.

FRONTINUS: STRATAGEMS and AQUEDUCTS. C. E. Bennett and M. B. McElwain.

FRONTO: CORRESPONDENCE. C. R. Haines. 2 Vols.

GELLIUS, J. C. Rolfe. 3 Vols.

HORACE: ODES AND EPODES. C. E. Bennett.

HORACE: SATIRES, EPISTLES, ARS POETICA. H. R. Fairclough.

JEROME: SELECTED LETTERS. F. A. Wright.

JUVENAL and PERSIUS. G. G. Ramsay.

LIVY. B. O. Foster, F. G. Moore, Evan T. Sage, and A. C. Schlesinger and R. M. Geer (General Index). 14 Vols.

LUCAN. J. D. Duff.

LUCRETIUS. W. H. D. Rouse. Revised by M. F. Smith.

MANILIUS. G. P. Goold.

MARTIAL. W. C. A. Ker. 2 Vols.

MINOR LATIN POETS: from PUBLILIUS SYRUS TO RUTILIUS NAMATIANUS, including GRATTIUS, CALPURNIUS SICULUS, NEMESIANUS, AVIANUS, and others with "Aetna" and the "Phoenix." J. Wight Duff and Arnold M. Duff.

OVID: THE ART OF LOVE and OTHER POEMS. J. H. Mosley. Revised by G. P. Goold.

OVID: FASTI. Sir James G. Frazer.

THE LOEB CLASSICAL LIBRARY

VOLUMES ALREADY PUBLISHED

Latin Authors

AMMIANUS MARCELLINUS. Translated by J. C. Rolfe. 3 Vols.

APULEIUS: THE GOLDEN ASS (METAMORPHOSES). W. Adlington (1566). Revised by S. Gaselee.

ST. AUGUSTINE: CITY OF GOD. 7 Vols. Vol. I. G. E. McCracken. Vol. II. and VII. W. M. Green. Vol. III. D. Wiesen. Vol. IV. P. Levine. Vol. V. E. M. Sanford and W. M. Green. Vol. VI. W. C. Greene.

ST. AUGUSTINE, CONFESSIONS OF. W. Watts (1631). 2 Vols.

ST. AUGUSTINE, SELECT LETTERS. J. H. Baxter.

AUSONIUS. H. G. Evelyn White. 2 Vols.

BEDE. J. E. King. 2 Vols.

BOETHIUS: TRACTS and DE CONSOLATIONE PHILOSOPHIAE. REV. H. F. Stewart and E. K. Rand. Revised by S. J. Tester.

CAESER: ALEXANDRIAN, AFRICAN and SPANISH WARS. A. G. Way.

CAESER: CIVIL WARS. A. G. Peskett.

CAESER: GALLIC WAR. H. J. Edwards.

CATO: DE RE RUSTICA; VARRO: DE RE RUSTICA. H. B. Ash and W. D. Hooper.

CATULLUS. F. W. Cornish; TIBULLUS. J. B. Postgate; PERVIGILIUM VENERIS. J. W. Mackail.

CELSUS: DE MEDICINA. W. G. Spencer. 3 Vols.

CICERO: BRUTUS, and ORATOR. G. L. Hendrickson and H. M. Hubbell.

[CICERO]: AD HERENNIUM. H. Caplan.

CICERO: DE ORATORE, etc. 2 Vols. Vol. I. DE ORATORE, BOOKS I. and II. E. W. Sutton and H. Rackham. Vol. II. DE ORATORE, Book III. De Fato; Paradoxa Stoicorum; De Partitione Oratoria. H. Rackham.

CICERO: DE FINIBUS. H. Rackham.

CICERO: DE INVENTIONE, etc. H. M. Hubbell.

CICERO: DE NATURA DEORUM and ACADEMICA. H. Rackham.

CICERO: DE OFFICIIS. Walter Miller.

CICERO: DE REPUBLICA and DE LEGIBUS: SOMNIUM SCIPIONIS. Clinton W. Keyes.

*Printed in Great Britain by
Fletcher & Son Ltd,
Norwich*

INDEX

Polymnia, 363 f.
Pontus, 393, 471
Poseideion, 209
Poseideon, 233
Poseidon, 127, 209, 389, 475
Potana, 233
Priam, 447, 497
Priapus, 357 f.
Prienê, 259
Prometheus, 391 f.
Pronapides, 309
Ptolemaïs, 207
Ptolemy Euergetes, 133, 207
Ptolemy Philadelphus, 187 ff., 193
Pyrigenes, 355

Red Sea, 195–237 passim
Rhea, 265, 281, 309, 317 f., 325
Rhodes, 179, 531 f.
Rome, 409 f.
Romulus, 409

Sabae, 229, 231
Sabaeans, 225–33
Sabazius, 349 f.
Sacae, 3, 29
Samos, 261
Samothrace, 261
Sardinia, 433–41
Satyrs, 355
Sauromatae, 29
Scythes, 27
Scythia, 175 ff.
Scythians, 27 ff., 431 f.
Seileni, 323
Seilenus, 323, 351
Selenê, 267 f.
Semelê, 289, 295, 331, 343 f., 425
Semiramis, 93
Sicani, 439
Silla river, 13
Simi, 159 f.
Simmias, 133
Sipylus, 261
Soteria, Harbour of, 203
Sparta, 449
"Steps of Cacius," 409
Stymphalian Lake, 385
Sybaris, 493
Syleus, 443
Syracuse, 419
Syria, 59, 259

Tanaïs river, 27, 523 f.
Tauri, 215
Tauri, Promontories of the, 207
Tauric Chersonese, 483
Telamon, 447, 473, 497
Telephus, 451 f.
Tempê, 403
Teos, 301 f.
Terpsichorê, 363
Teuthras, 451 f.
Thaleia, 363
Thamudeni, 219
Thamyras, 275 f., 307
Thebes, 303, 373 f., 405
Themiscyra, 33, 393
Theopompus, 341
Thermodon, 31, 247, 393
Theseus, 427, 431 f.
Thespiadae, 435–41, 473
Thespius, 433 f.
Thesprotians, 459
Thessalians, 519 f.
Thessalus, 515, 519
Thestius, 455
Thymoetes, 309
Thyonê, 289, 425
Thriambus, 355
Timaeus, 415, 523
Tisandrus, 515 f.
Titaea, 265
Titans, 265 f., 287, 319 ff., 329, 359
Tlepolemus, 445, 459, 531 f.
Triopas, 531 f.
Triton river, 251, 311
Tritonis, 251, 257, 315
Trogodytes, 123, 171–203 passim
Tychon, 359
Tydeus, 457
Tyndareüs, 449
Tyrcaeus, 197

Urania, 363 f.
Uranus, 263 f., 309, 361

Vesuvius, 411

"Way of Heracles," 413

Zabirna, 323
Zeus, 27, 91, 107, 281–7, 295, 325–9, 349, 361, 369, 375, 387, 391, 469

539

INDEX

Lucullus, 411
Lycurgus, 261, 299 f., 349

Macae, 237
Macaria, 197
Maemacterion, 233
Maenads, 299, 347
Maeonians, 443
Maranitae, 213
Marmaridae, 237
Marsyas, 271 ff.
Massagetae, 29
Medea, 485–521 *passim*
Medes, 43, 521
Medus, 521 f.
Medusa, 257
Megabari, 173
Megara, 375 f., 441
Meïon, 269
Melanippê, 395 f.
Meleager, 453–7, 495
Melis, 461
Melpomenê, 363
Menê, 251
Menoetius, 467
Meroë, 101 f.
Meros, 15
Midas, 277
Minaeans, 211 f.
Minos, 387
Minotaur, 387
Minyans, 373 f.
Mitrephorus, 353
Mitylenê, 259
Mnemosynê, 361
Mopsus, 261
"Mother of the Mountain," 271
Musaeus, 425
Muses, 275, 351, 355, 361–5
Myrina, 253–61 *passim*
Myrrhanus, 299

Nabataeans, 41 f., 213 f.
Napae, 27
Napata, 103
Napes, 27
Nasamones, 237
Nauplius, 451
Naxos, 301
Neleus, 441 f.
Nephelê, 383
Nessus, 459 f.
Nestor, 441
Niobê, 391

Nysa, 295, 303, 305, 311 f., 315, 345
Nysaeans, 273 f.

Oeagrus, 299 f., 425
Oecles, 445 f.
Oeneus, 449, 453, 457
Oetê, 467
"Olympian,' 391
Olympic Games, 331, 387, 513
Olympus, 327
Omphalê, 443 f.
Ophiodes, 199 f.
Orchomenus, 403 f.
Ormenius, 463
Orpheus, 275, 301, 307, 309, 425, 473, 477, 495
Osiris, 93, 343, 359

Palatine Hill, 409
Pali, 27
Palibothra, 17 f., 83
Palus, 27
Pan, 107
Pandora, 265
Panormus, 197
Pappas, 273
Pasiphaê, 387
Peirithoüs, 427
Pelasgians, 305
Pelias, 471, 501–11
Pelops, 369
Peneius, 403
Penthesileia, 37
Pentheus, 299, 349
Periboea, 457
Persephonê, 293, 349, 413, 425 .
Perses, 483, 523
Perseus, 247 f., 257, 369
Petra, 43, 211 f.
Philoctetes, 467
Phineus, 477–83 *passim*
Phlegra, 413
Phlegraean Plain, 411
Phocaea, 211
Pholoê, 381, 385
Pholus, 381–5
Phrixus, 383, 489 f.
Phylas, 461
Phyleus, 449, 459
Pinarii, 409
Pinarius, 409
Pisinus, 277
Pleiades, 281
Polydeuces, 473

538

INDEX

Euadnê, 511
Euhesperis, 525
Eurydicê, 369
Eurystheus, 371-463 *passim*, 527 f.
Eurytus, 441, 449, 465
Euterpê, 363

" Field of Heracles," 371

Gadeira, 401, 523 f.
Gandaridae, 9 f.
Ganges, 9 f.
Garindanes, 213
Gasandi, 223
Gê, 317, 361
Gedrosia, 123
Gê Meter, 289
Gemini, 479
Gerrhaeans, 211 f.
Geryones, 367, 397, 421
Gibraltar, Straits of, 403
Glaucê, 515 f.
Glaucus, 495 f.
Gleneus, 461
Glychatas, 419
Gorgons, 247 f., 255 f.
" Great Mother," 265-77 *passim*
Greater Phrygia, 259

Halcyonê, 281
Hebê, 469
Hecataeus, 37 f.
Hecatê, 483 f.
Hecatompylon, 401
Helius, 267 f., 483
Hellê, 489
Hellespont, 489
Hephaestus, 389
Hera, 295, 369 f., 377, 393, 469
Heracleia, 419
Heracleidae, 339, 449, 527-33 *passim*
Heracles, 17 f., 35, 93, 107, 167, 223, 257, 307, 331 f., 365-513 *passim*
Hermaphroditus, 361
Hermes, 273, 281, 345, 361, 389
Hesiod, 361 f.
Hesionê, 447, 475 f.
Hespera, 251
Hesperides, 427 f.
Hesperis, 429
Hesperitis, 429
Hesperoukeras, 311
Hesperus, 279, 429
Himeraea, 417
Hippocoön, 449

Hippolytê, 35, 393 f., 431, 447
Hippolytus, 433, 443
Hipponoüs, 457
Hippotes, 521
Histiaeotis, 463
Homer, 91, 307 f., 345, 361, 445, 469, 499
Horus, 259
Hydaspes, 11
Hyllus, 459, 529 f.
Hypanis, 11
Hyperboreans, 37-41, 277

Iambulus, 65-83 *passim*
Icarus, 303
Ichthyophagi, 123-41 *passim*, 203, 207, 251
Idaea, 283, 319, 479 f.
Ilium, 445 f.
India, 3-27 *passim*, 347
Indus river, 3, 11, 233
Io, 329
Iolaeis, 437
Iolaeium, 437
Iolaüs, 377-467 *passim*, 52
Iolê, 441, 465
Iphicles, 449
Iphiclus, 449, 497
Iphigeneia, 483
Iphitus, 441, 495
Isis, 107, 217, 259, 359
" Islands of the Sun," 65-83
Isocrates, 339
Ister, 525 f.
Istrians, 527
Ithyphallus, 359
Itoni, 443

Jason, 471-519 *passim*

Lacinius, 423
Laeanites Gulf, 213
Lake Copaïs, 403
Lampeia, 379
Laomedon, 309, 445 f., 475 f., 497 f.
Lapithae, 463
Lenaeus, 293, 355
Leontini, 419 f.
Lesbos, 259
Leto, 39
Libya, 237-45, 399
Lichas, 465
Licymnius, 449, 465, 527, 531
Liguria, 407 f.
Linus, 275, 305 f., 309

537

INDEX

Banizomenes, 217
Basileia, 265-9
Boeotia, 403 f.
Boeotians, 223
Boreadae, 41, 481
Boreas, 479, 483
Bromius, 355
Buphonas, 419
"Burned Phrygia," 315
Busiris, 401, 429 f.
Butas, 417
Bytaeas, 419
Byzas, 497

Cabeiri, 479
Cacius, 409
Cadmus, 295, 305, 333, 343
Caeëtes, 525
Caesar, C. Julius, 197, 405
Calliope, 363
Callisthenes, 341
Cambyses, 93
Campê, 323
Carbae, 225
Carmania, 123
Carthage, 221
Carystus, 461
Castor, 473
Celaeno, 281, 395
Celts, 523 f.
Centaurs, 367, 381-5
Cepheus, 369, 449
Cerberus, 423-7
Cercopes, 443
Ceÿx, 461, 527
Chabinus, 221
Charmuthas, 219
Charops, 299
Cheiron, 385
Cherronesus, 253
"Children of the Sun," 69-81
Chrysaor, 397, 401
Cilicians, 259
Circaeum, 487
Circê, 485 f.
Cleio, 363
Cleopatra, 479 f.
Colobi, 173
Corê, 419
Corinthians, 519
Coronus, 463
Corybantes, 261
Cothon, 221
Creon, 373 f., 511, 515 f.
Crete, 397 f.

Crius, 491 f.
"Cronia," 283
Cronus, 281 f., 319 f., 323
Croton, 423
Curetes, 283, 319
Cyanê, 419
Cybelê, 259 f., 269-77
Cybelus, 271
Cymê, 259
Cyrenê, 237 f.
Cyrus, 31

Dactyls, 331
"Daedaleia," 437
Daedalus, 437
Dardanus, 479 f.
Dead Sea, 43 f.
Debae, 221
Deïaneira, 395, 453, 459 f., 465 f.
Deïphobus, 443
Delians, 39
Demeter, 127, 287 ff., 349, 389
Deucalion, 289
Dimetor, 287, 353
Dindyme, 271
Diodorus, 113 f., 341
Diomedes, 393
Dionysius, 247, 305
Dionysus, 13 ff., 93, 273, 285-333 passim, 343-57 passim, 381, 391, 425
Dioscori, 449, 477, 495, 523 f.
Dorieis, 463
Dorieus, 417 f.
Doris, 463
Dracanum, 303
Dracon, 427, 491
Dryopes, 461 f.

Echemus, 531
Echinades, 219
Egestaea, 417
Egypt, 93, 113-23 passim, 401, 425
Egyptians, 93 f.
Eileithyia, 369
Eiraphiotes, 303
Eleutherae, 301, 347
Emathion, 429
Ephorus, 339
Erato, 363 f.
Erechtheus, 435
Ergamenes, 101 f.
Erginus, 373 f.
Eryx, 417
Ethiopia, 93, 113-93 passim
Ethiopians, 67, 89-113 passim, 133

536

A PARTIAL INDEX OF PROPER NAMES[1]

ABARIS, 39 f.
Acastus, 511
Acheloüs, 457 f.
Achilles, 37
Admetus, 511
Aeëtes, 483–95 *passim*, 523
Aegeus, 521
Aegimius, 463, 531
Aegis, 315 f.
Aethaleis, 525
Aetna, 411
Agatharchides, 113, 133 f., 235
Agenor, 333, 343
Agyrium, 421 f.
Alcestis, 509 f.
Alcimenes, 515 f.
Alcman, 361
Alcmenê, 369 f., 391, 449, 531
Alcyonê, 383
Aleos, 451
Alesia, 405
Alexander of Macedon, 11, 233, 393
Alilaei, 223
Alpheius, 303, 387
Althaea, 455 f.
Amaltheia, 309 f.
"Amaltheia, Horn of," 311, 457 f.
Amazoneum, 433
Amazons, 31–7, 319, 245–61, 393–7, 431 f.
Ammon, 309–29 *passim*
Amphinomê, daughter of Pelias, 511
Amphinomê, mother of Jason, 501
Amphitryon, 369, 373
Andromeda, 369
Antaeus, 399, 429
Antimachus, 301
Antiopê, 397, 431 f.

Aphroditê, 357, 361, 417, 427
Aphroditê's Harbour, 199
Apollo, 39 f., 273 ff., 389
Arabia, 41–65 *passim*, 115–23, 237
Arabia Felix, 47–61, 123, 225–33
Arcadians, 463 f., 527
Arcturus, 5
Argives, 531
Argo, 473, 511
Argonauts, 469–515, 523–7
Argus, 473
Arimaspi, 29
Aristaeus, 315, 321
Ariston, 209
Arsinoê, 199
Artemidorus, 113
Artemis, 413 f., 453
Artemis Tauropolus, 35, 483
Assyrians, 29, 43
Astydameia, 463
Atalantê, 455, 473
Athena, 315 f., 329, 371, 389
Athenians, 39, 431 f., 467 f., 527 f.
Atlantians, 253 f., 263–9, 279–85
Atlantic Ocean, 195
Atlantides, 279 f., 429
Atlas, 279 f., 429 f.
Atreus, 529
Attis, 271 f., 277
Augê, 451
Augeas, 387, 447 f.
Auschisae, 237
Autariatae, 167
Azan, 447

Babylonia, 59 f., 145 f.
Bacchantes, 297 ff.
Baccheius, 353 f.

[1] A complete Index will appear in the last volume.

535